1 uno

Texas Edition

MCDOUGAL LITTELL

¡En español!

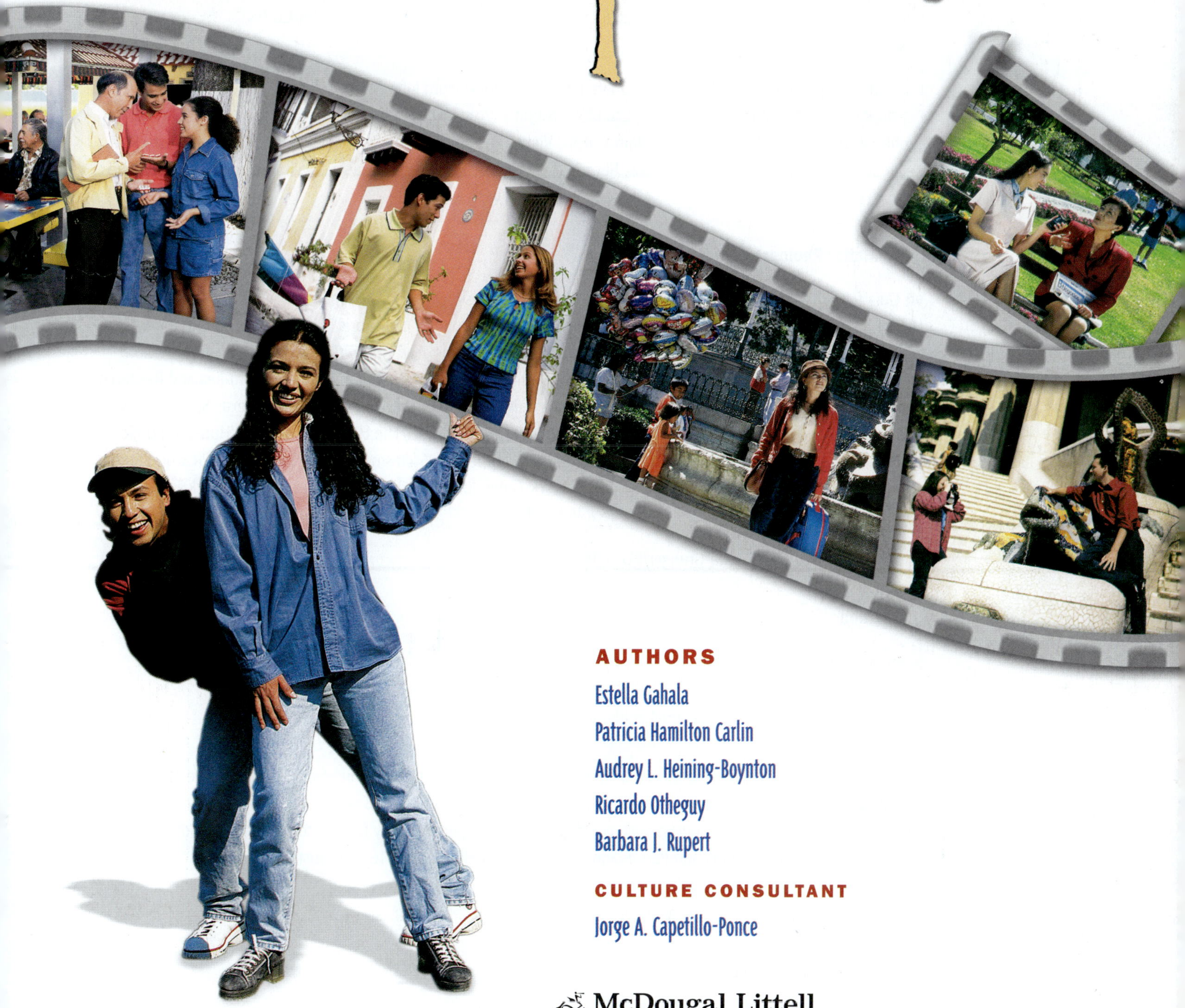

AUTHORS

Estella Gahala

Patricia Hamilton Carlin

Audrey L. Heining-Boynton

Ricardo Otheguy

Barbara J. Rupert

CULTURE CONSULTANT

Jorge A. Capetillo-Ponce

McDougal Littell

A DIVISION OF HOUGHTON MIFFLIN COMPANY

Evanston, Illinois • Boston • Dallas

Cover Photography

Foreground: Photo by Martha Granger/EDGE Productions.
Background: View of Pyramid of the Sun at Teotihuacán, Mexico City, Michael T. Sedam/Corbis (also appears on spine).

Back cover, top: Painted dog figure from Guatemala/Superstock; from left to right: El Morro Castle, San Juan, Puerto Rico, Bruce Adams/Corbis; Quito, Ecuador, Joseph F. Viesti/The Viesti Collection; Pyramid of the Sun at Teotihuacán, Mexico City, Michael T. Sedam/Corbis; View of Arenal Volcano from Tabacón Hot Springs, Costa Rica, Kevin Schafer; Aerial view of Las Ramblas, Barcelona, Spain, AGE Fotostock; Machu Picchu, Urubamba Valley, Peru, Robert Fried.

Front Matter Photography

vii Guía telefónica 1998, ICE Telecomunicaciones (tr); **ix** Courtesy *¡Qué Onda!* Magazine (br); **x** (tr), **xi** (tr) School Division, Houghton Mifflin Company; **xiii** David Sanger Photography (tr); **xv** Chris Brown/Unicorn Stock Photography & Dick Young/Unicorn Stock Photography (montage bc); **xvi** (tr), **xvii** (tr), **xxv** (tr), School Division, Houghton Mifflin Company; **xxviii** Bettmann/Corbis (tl, tr); The Center for Mexican-American Studies and Research, Our Lady of the Lake University, San Antonio (bl); Portrait of Lorenzo de Zavala, C.E. Proctor. Texas State Library and Archives Commission, Austin, Texas (br); **xxix** © 2003 Tom Colburn/The Houston Chronicle/Houston Public Library, Houston Metropolitan Research Center (tl); Austin American Statesman/Corbis Sygma (tc); Ricardo Santos (tr); Courtesy of Dr. Frank González (bl); The New York Times (br inset); Vincent Laforet/The New York Times (br); **xxxi** Patricia A. Eynon (tr); **xxxiii** Larry Busacca/Retna, Ltd. (cr)

All other photography Martha Granger/EDGE Productions

Illustration

xxxiv-xxxix Gary Antonetti/Ortelius Design.

ISBN: 0-618-43304-X 2 3 4 5 6 7 8 9 - VJM - 09 08 07 06 05

Internet: www.mcdougallittell.com

About the Authors

Estella Gahala holds a Ph.D. in Educational Administration and Curriculum from Northwestern University. A career teacher of Spanish and French, she has worked with a wide range of students at the secondary level. She has also served as foreign language department chair and district director of curriculum and instruction. Her workshops at national, regional, and state conferences as well as numerous published articles draw upon the current research in language learning, learning strategies, articulation of foreign language sequences, and implications of the national Standards for Foreign Language Learning upon curriculum, instruction, and assessment. She has coauthored twelve basal textbooks.

Patricia Hamilton Carlin completed her M.A. in Spanish at the University of California, Davis, where she also taught as a lecturer. Previously she had earned a Master of Secondary Education with specialization in foreign languages from the University of Arkansas and had taught Spanish and French at levels K–12. Her secondary programs in Arkansas received national recognition. A coauthor of the *¡DIME! UNO* and *¡DIME! DOS* secondary textbooks, Patricia currently teaches Spanish and foreign language/ESL methodology at the University of Central Arkansas, where she coordinates the second language teacher education program. In addition, Patricia is a frequent presenter at local, regional, and national foreign language conferences.

Audrey L. Heining-Boynton received her Ph.D. in Curriculum and Instruction from Michigan State University. She is a Professor of Education and Romance Languages at The University of North Carolina at Chapel Hill, where she is a second language teacher educator and Professor of Spanish. She has also taught Spanish, French, and ESL at the K–12 level. Dr. Heining-Boynton was elected President of the American Council on the Teaching of Foreign Languages (ACTFL), and was the president of the National Network for Early Language Learning. She has been awarded the ACTFL / NYSAFLT Anthony Papalia Award for Excellence in Teacher Education. Additionally, she has been involved with AATSP, Phi Delta Kappa, and state foreign language associations. She has presented both nationally and internationally, and has published over forty books, articles, and curricula.

Ricardo Otheguy received his Ph.D. in Linguistics from the City University of New York, where he is currently Professor of Linguistics at The Graduate Center. He has written extensively on topics related to Spanish grammar as well as on bilingual education and the Spanish of the United States. He is coauthor of *Tu mundo: Curso para hispanohablantes,* a Spanish high school textbook for Spanish speakers, and of *Prueba de ubicación para hispanohablantes,* a high school Spanish placement test.

Barbara J. Rupert has taught Level 1 through A.P. Spanish and has implemented a FLES program in her district. She completed her M.A. at Pacific Lutheran University. Barbara is the author of CD-ROM activities for the *¡Bravo!* series and has presented at local, regional, and national foreign language conferences. She is the past president of the Washington Association for Language Teaching and the president-elect of the Pacific Northwest Council for Languages. In 1996, Barbara received the Christa McAuliffe Award for Excellence in Education, and in 1999, she was selected Washington's "Spanish Teacher of the Year" by the Juan de Fuca Chapter of the AATSP. She is currently a school principal.

Culture Consultant

Jorge A. Capetillo-Ponce is currently Assistant Professor of Sociology at University of Massachusetts, Boston, where he teaches sociological theory and researches Latinos in the United States. He is also Researcher at the Mauricio Gastón Institute for Latino Community Development and Public Policy. His graduate studies include an M.A. and a Ph.D. in Sociology from the New School for Social Research in New York City, and an M.A. in Area Studies at El Colegio de México in Mexico City. He is the editor of the book *Images of Mexico in the U.S. News Media* and has published essays on a wide range of subjects such as media, art, politics, religion, international relations, and cultural theory. Dr. Capetillo's geographical areas of expertise are Latin America, the United States, and the Middle East. During the years 2000 and 2001 he was the Executive Director of the Mexican Cultural Institute of New York. He has also worked as an advisor to politicians and public figures, as a researcher and an editor, and as a university professor and television producer in Mexico, the United States, and Central America.

Consulting Authors

Dan Battisti
Dr. Teresa Carrera-Hanley
David Kleinbeck
Bill Lionetti
Patty Murguía Bohannan
Lorena Richins Layser

Contributing Writers

Ronni L. Gordon
Christa Harris
Debra Lowry
Sylvia Madrigal Velasco
Sandra Rosenstiel
David M. Stillman
Jill K. Welch

Senior Reviewers

O. Lynn Bolton
Dr. Jane Govoni
Ann Tollefson

Regional Language Reviewers

Dolores Acosta (Mexico)
Jaime M. Fatás Cabeza (Spain)
Grisel Lozano-Garcini (Puerto Rico)
Isabel Picado (Costa Rica)
Juan Pablo Rovayo (Ecuador)

Texas Consulting Author

Elías G. Rodríguez

Texas Program Consultant

Carl H. Johnson

Texas Teacher Panel

Jeanne Aréchiga
Northbrook High School
South Houston, TX

Hercilia Breton
Highlands High School
San Antonio, TX

Laura Cook
Evans Junior High School
Lubbock, TX

Terri Frésquez
Del Valle High School
El Paso, TX

Rose Jenkins
Clements High School
Sugarland, TX

Rudy Molina
McAllen Memorial High School
McAllen, TX

Fermín Pérez
McAllen High School
McAllen, TX

Rob Ramos
J.T. Hutchinson Junior High School
Lubbock, TX

Monserrat Rey
Hightower High School
Missouri City, TX

Sandra Rivera
Mary Carroll High School
Corpus Christi, TX

Dana Thacker
Scarborough High School
Houston, TX

Shannon Zerby
North Garland High School
Garland, TX

Teacher Panel

Linda Amour
Highland High School
Bakersfield, CA

Dena Bachman
Lafayette Senior High School
St. Joseph, MO

Sharon Barnes
J. C. Harmon High School
Kansas City, KS

Ben Barrientos
Calvin Simmons Junior High School
Oakland, CA

Paula Biggar
Sumner Academy of Arts & Science
Kansas City, KS

Gwen Cannell
Cajon High School
San Bernardino, CA

Edda Cárdenas
Blue Valley North High School
Leawood, KS

Joyce Chow
Crespi Junior High School
Richmond, CA

Mike Cooperider
Truman High School
Independence, MO

Judy Dozier
Shawnee Mission South High School
Shawnee Mission, KS

Maggie Elliott
Bell Junior High School
San Diego, CA

Dana Galloway-Grey
Ontario High School
Ontario, CA

Nieves Gerber
Chatsworth Senior High School
Chatsworth, CA

April Hansen
Livermore High School
Livermore, CA

Janet King
Long Beach Polytechnic High School
Long Beach, CA

Susanne Kissane
Shawnee Mission Northwest
High School
Shawnee Mission, KS

Ann López
Pala Middle School
San Jose, CA

Beatrice Marino
Palos Verdes Peninsula High School
Rolling Hills, CA

Anna Marxson
Laguna Creek High School
Elk Grove, CA

Barbara Mortanian
Tenaya Middle School
Fresno, CA

Vickie Musni
Pioneer High School
San Jose, CA

Teri Olsen
Alameda High School
Alameda, CA

Rodolfo Orihuela
C. K. McClatchy High School
Sacramento, CA

Terrie Rynard
Olathe South High School
Olathe, KS

Beth Slinkard
Lee's Summit High School
Lee's Summit, MO

Rosa Stein
Park Hill High School
Kansas City, MO

Marianne Villalobos
Modesto High School
Modesto, CA

Teacher Reviewers

Linda Amour
Highland High School
Bakersfield, CA

Susan Arbuckle
Mahomet-Seymour High School
Mahomet, IL

Dawne Ashton
Sequoia High School
Redwood City, CA

Sheila Bayles
Rogers High School
Rogers, AR

Warren Bender
Duluth East High School
Duluth, MN

Gail Block
Daly City, CA

Amy Brewer
Stonewall Jackson Middle School
Mechanicsville, VA

William Brill
Hollidaysburg Area Junior High School
Hollidaysburg, PA

Adrienne Chamberlain-Parris
Mariner High School
Everett, WA

Norma Coto
Bishop Moore High School
Orlando, FL

Roberto del Valle
Shorecrest High School
Shoreline, WA

Art Edwards
Canyon High School
Santa Clarita, CA

Rubén D. Elías
Roosevelt High School
Fresno, CA

José Esparza
Curie Metropolitan High School
Chicago, IL

Lorraine A. Estrada
Cabarrus County Schools
Concord, NC

Vincent Fazzolari
East Boston High School
East Boston, MA

Teacher Reviewers (cont.)

Alberto Ferreiro
Harrisburg High School
Harrisburg, PA

Judith C. Floyd
Henry Foss High School
Tacoma, WA

Valarie L. Forster
Jefferson Davis High School
Montgomery, AL

Michael Garber
Boston Latin Academy
Boston, MA

Becky Hay de García
James Madison Memorial High School
Madison, WI

Lucy H. García
Pueblo East High School
Pueblo, CO

Marco García
Lincoln Park High School
Chicago, IL

Raquel R. González
Odessa High School
Odessa, TX

Linda Grau
Shorecrest Preparatory School
St. Petersburg, FL

Myriam Gutiérrez
John O'Bryant School
Roxbury, MA

Deborah Hagen
Ionia High School
Ionia, MI

Sandra Hammond
St. Petersburg High School
St. Petersburg, FL

Bill Heller
Perry Junior/Senior High School
Perry, NY

Joan Heller
Lake Braddock Secondary School
Burke, VA

Paula Hirsch
Windward School
Los Angeles, CA

Ann Hively
Orangevale, CA

Robert Hughes
Martha Brown Middle School
Fairport, NY

Janet King
Long Beach Polytechnic High School
Long Beach, CA

Jody Klopp
Oklahoma State Department of Education
Edmond, OK

Richard Ladd
Ipswich High School
Ipswich, MA

Carol Leach
Francis Scott Key High School
Union Bridge, MD

Maria Leinenweber
Crescenta Valley High School
La Crescenta, CA

Sandra Martín
Palisades Charter High School
Pacific Palisades, CA

Laura McCormick
East Seneca Senior High School
West Seneca, NY

Karen McDowell
Aptos, CA

Sue McKee
Tustin, CA

Rafaela McLeod
Southeast Raleigh High School
Raleigh, NC

Kathleen L. Michaels
Palm Harbor University High School
Palm Harbor, FL

Vickie A. Mike
Horseheads High School
Horseheads, NY

Robert Miller
Woodcreek High School
Roseville, CA

Barbara Mortanian
Tenaya Middle School
Fresno, CA

Patty Murray
Cretin-Derham Hall High School
St. Paul, MN

Linda Nanos
West Roxbury High School
West Roxbury, MA

Terri Nies
Mannford High School
Mannford, OK

María Emma Nunn
John Tyler High School
Tyler, TX

Leslie Ogden
Nordhoff High School
Ojai, CA

Teri Olsen
Alameda High School
Alameda, CA

Lewis Olvera
Hiram Johnson West Campus High School
Sacramento, CA

Judith Pasco
Sequim High School
Sequim, WA

Anne-Marie Quihuis
Paradise Valley High School
Phoenix, AZ

Rita Risco
Palm Harbor University High School
Palm Harbor, FL

James J. Rudy, Jr.
Glen Este High School
Cincinnati, OH

Kathleen Solórzano
Homestead High School
Mequon, WI

Margery Sotomayor
Ferndale, CA

Carol Sparks
Foothill Middle School
Walnut Creek, CA

Sarah Spiesman
Whitmer High School
Toledo, OH

M. Mercedes Stephenson
Hazelwood Central High School
Florissant, MO

Carol Thorp
East Mecklenburg High School
Charlotte, NC

Elizabeth Torosian
Doherty Middle School
Andover, MA

Pamela Urdal Silva
East Lake High School
Tarpon Springs, FL

Dana Valverde
Arroyo Grande High School
Arroyo Grande, CA

Wendy Villanueva
Lakeville High School
Lakeville, MN

Helen Webb
Arkadelphia High School
Arkadelphia, AR

Jena Williams
Jonesboro High School
Jonesboro, AR

Janet Wohlers
Weston Middle School
Weston, MA

Urban Panel

Rebecca Carr
William G. Enloe High School
Raleigh, NC

Rita Dooley
Lincoln Park High School
Chicago, IL

Norha Franco
East Side High School
Newark, NJ

Kathryn Gardner
Riverside University High School
Milwaukee, WI

Eula Glenn
Remtec Center
Detroit, MI

Frank González
Mast Academy
Miami, FL

Jeana Harper
Detroit Fine Arts High School
Detroit, MI

Guillermina Jauregui
Los Angeles Senior High School
Los Angeles, CA

Lula Lewis
Hyde Park Career Academy High School
Chicago, IL

Florence Meyers
Overbrook High School
Philadelphia, PA

Vivian Selenikas
Long Island City High School
Long Island City, NY

Sadia White
Spingarn Stay Senior High School
Washington, DC

Block Scheduling Panel

Barbara Baker
Wichita Northwest High School
Wichita, KS

Patty Banker
Lexington High School
Lexington, NC

Beverly Blackburn
Reynoldsburg Senior High School
Reynoldsburg, OH

Henry Foust
Northwood High School
Pittsboro, NC

Gloria Hawks
A. L. Brown High School
Kannapolis, NC

Lois Hillman
North Kitsap High School
Poulsbo, WA

Nick Patterson
Central High School
Davenport, IA

Sharyn Petkus
Grafton Memorial High School
Grafton, MA

Cynthia Prieto
Mount Vernon High School
Alexandria, VA

Julie Sanchez
Western High School
Fort Lauderdale, FL

Marilyn Settlemyer
Freedom High School
Morganton, NC

Student Review Board

Andrea Avila
Fannin Middle School
Amarillo, TX

Maya Beynishes
Edward R. Murrow High School
Brooklyn, NY

James Dock
Guilford High School
Rockford, IL

Richard Elkins
Nevin Platt Middle School
Boulder, CO

Kathryn Finn
Charles S. Pierce Middle School
Milton, MA

Robert Foulis
Stratford High School
Houston, TX

Lorrain García
Luther Burbank High School
Sacramento, CA

Katie Hagen
Ionia High School
Ionia, MI

Steven Hailey
Davis Drive School
Apex, NC

Eli Harel
Thomas Edison Intermediate School
Westfield, NJ

Cheryl Kim
Dr. Leo Cigarroa High School
Laredo, TX

Jennifer Kim
Kellogg Middle School
Seattle, WA

Jordan Leitner
Scripps Ranch High School
San Diego, CA

Courtney McPherson
Miramar High School
Miramar, FL

Zachary Nelson
Warsaw Community High School
Warsaw, IN

Diana Parrish
Oak Crest Junior High School
Encinitas, CA

Kimberly Robinson
Perryville Senior High School
Perryville, AR

John Roland
Mountain Pointe High School
Phoenix, AZ

Nichole Ryan
Bermudian Springs High School
York Springs, PA

Ryan Shore
West Miami Middle School
Miami, FL

Tiffany Stadler
Titusville High School
Titusville, FL

Michael Szymanski
West Seneca East High School
West Seneca, NY

Anela Talic
Soldan International Studies High School
St. Louis, MO

Gary Thompson
Fort Dorchester High School
Charleston, SC

Bethany Traynor
Glen Este High School
Cincinnati, OH

Gerard White
Paramount High School
Paramount, CA

Nichols Wilson
Waubonsie Valley High School
Aurora, IL

Amy Wyron
Robert Frost Intermediate School
Rockville, MD

Karina Zepeda
West Mecklenburg High School
Charlotte, NC

CONTENIDO

OBJECTIVES

- Greet people
- Introduce yourself
- Say where you are from
- Exchange phone numbers
- Say which day it is

UNIDAD 1

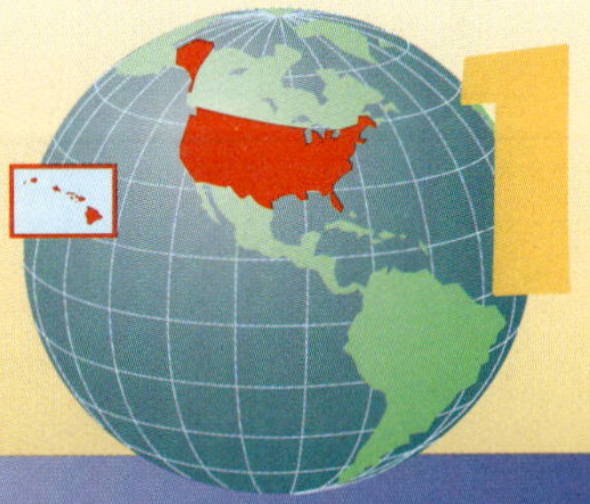

ESTADOS UNIDOS

MI MUNDO

Visit Miami, San Antonio, and Los Angeles with Francisco and his friend Alma.

ETAPA 1

OBJECTIVES

- Greet others
- Introduce others
- Say where people are from
- Express likes

UNIDAD 1

ETAPA 2

OBJECTIVES

- Describe others
- Give others' likes and dislikes
- Describe clothing

SAN ANTONIO - Mis buenos amigos 48

UNIDAD 1

ETAPA 3

Los Ángeles - Te presento a mi familia 70

OBJECTIVES

- Describe family
- Ask and tell ages
- Talk about birthdays
- Give dates
- Express possession

UNIDAD

2

CIUDAD DE MÉXICO

MÉXICO

UNA SEMANA TÍPICA

Explore exciting Mexico City with Isabel and Ricardo, two Mexican teenagers.

ETAPA 1

OBJECTIVES

- Describe classes and classroom objects
- Say how often you do something
- Discuss obligations

UNIDAD 2

ETAPA 2

¡Un horario difícil! 122

OBJECTIVES

- Talk about schedules
- Ask and tell time
- Ask questions
- Say where you are going
- Request food

UNIDAD 2

ETAPA 3

OBJECTIVES

- Discuss plans
- Sequence events
- Talk about places and people you know

Mis actividades 144

UNIDAD

3

SAN JUAN
PUERTO RICO

EL FIN DE SEMANA

Enjoy the weather and the landscape of Puerto Rico with three friends.

ETAPA 1

OBJECTIVES

- Extend invitations
- Talk on the phone
- Express feelings
- Say where you are coming from
- Say what just happened

UNIDAD 3

ETAPA 2

OBJECTIVES

- Talk about sports
- Express preferences
- Say what you know
- Make comparisons

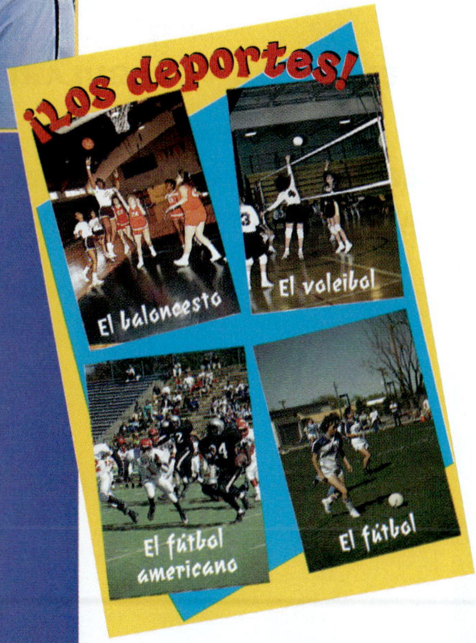

UNIDAD 3

ETAPA 3

OBJECTIVES

- Describe the weather
- Discuss clothing and accessories
- State an opinion
- Describe how you feel
- Say what is happening

El tiempo en El Yunque 218

UNIDAD 4

OAXACA
MÉXICO

¡DE VISITA!

Enjoy regional handicrafts and food with Rosa, Carlos, and Sofía.

ETAPA 1

OBJECTIVES

- Identify places
- Give addresses
- Choose transportation
- Request directions
- Give instructions

UNIDAD 4

ETAPA 2

OBJECTIVES

- Talk about shopping
- Make purchases
- Talk about giving gifts
- Bargain

En el mercado 270

UNIDAD 4

ETAPA 3

OBJECTIVES

- Order food
- Request the check
- Talk about food
- Express extremes
- Say where you went

¿Qué hacer en Oaxaca? 292

UNIDAD

5

BARCELONA
ESPAÑA

PREPARACIONES ESPECIALES

Have fun organizing a surprise birthday party for Luis.

ETAPA 1

OBJECTIVES

- Describe daily routine
- Talk about grooming
- Tell others to do something
- Discuss daily chores

UNIDAD 5

ETAPA 2

¿Qué debo hacer? 344

OBJECTIVES

- Say what people are doing
- Persuade others
- Describe a house
- Negotiate responsibilities

UNIDAD 5

ETAPA 3

OBJECTIVES

- Plan a party
- Describe past activities
- Express extremes
- Purchase food

¡Qué buena celebración! 366

UNIDAD 6

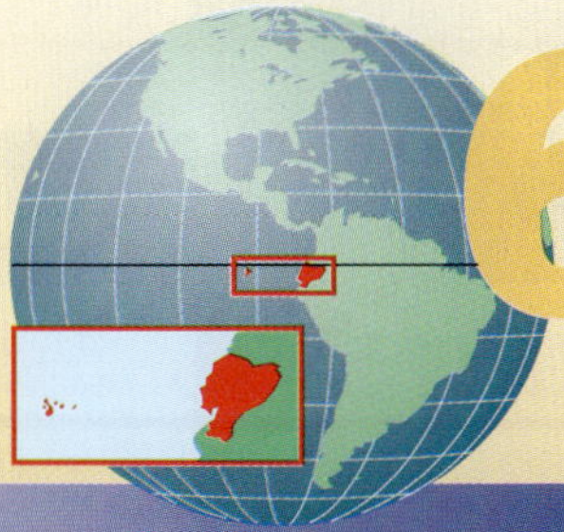

QUITO
ECUADOR

LA CIUDAD Y EL CAMPO

Compare life in the city to life in the countryside with Patricia and Miguel and his family.

ETAPA 1

OBJECTIVES

- Tell what happened
- Make suggestions to a group
- Describe city buildings
- Talk about professions

UNIDAD 6

ETAPA 2

OBJECTIVES

- Point out specific people and things
- Tell where things are located
- Talk about the past

A conocer el campo 418

UNIDAD 6

ETAPA 3

OBJECTIVES

- Talk about the present and future
- Give instructions to someone
- Discuss the past

¡A ganar el concurso! 440

El español en Texas

A brief history

Spanish-speaking peoples have been an integral part of the history and culture of Texas from the arrival of the European explorers to the present day. You see Spanish in the names of Texas's cities and towns and on many of its street signs. In the next pages you can read about a few important ways in which speakers of Spanish have influenced Texas and contributed to the identity of the United States.

El español en Texas

Juan de Oñate

1598
On behalf of King Phillip II of Spain, Mexican explorer Juan de Oñate leads an expedition into what is now Mexico, New Mexico, and Texas.

Battle of the Alamo

1821–1836
Texas becomes part of Mexico in 1821 and revolts against Mexican rule in 1835. Texan rebels are defeated in **San Antonio** by Mexican forces at the Battle of the Alamo in 1836. Inspired by the bravery and sacrifice of the defenders of the Alamo, the Texas army wins the Battle of San Jacinto, after which Texas gains independence from Mexico.

1500 1600 1700 1800

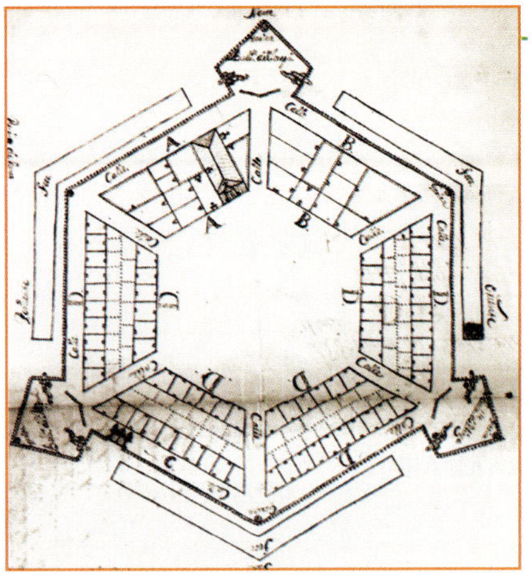

Plan of the fortress at Los Adaes

1729
Spain designates **Los Adaes** the capital of the province of Texas and establishes a fortress there. Los Adaes remains the easternmost settlement and military post in Spanish Texas for the next fifty years. Later, it becomes part of the state of Louisiana.

1835
When Antonio López de Santa Anna takes a dictatorial role in Mexico, Lorenzo de Zavala, a Mexican politician, resigns from his political duties in France and goes to Texas in 1835. Zavala is elected vice-president of the temporary government of the new Texas Republic. Because of his political experience with the Mexican government, his education, and his ability with language, he has a major role in the drafting of the Texas Constitution.

Lorenzo de Zavala

1935

Texan entrepreneur and civic leader María Torres Reyna becomes the first secretary of Ladies LULAC (League of United Latin American Citizens), a national civil rights organization. The Mexican-American Chamber of Commerce in **Houston** names her Businesswoman of the Year in 1980.

1993

Selena wins a Grammy Award for Best Mexican-American Album for *Live.* Born Selena Quintanilla Pérez in **Lake Jackson,** she is nominated for a second Grammy in 1995 for her album *Amor Prohibido.*

2005

The city of **Laredo** in South Texas will commemorate its 250th anniversary. Laredo began as a small Spanish settlement established by Tomás Sánchez de la Barrera y Garza in 1755 and is now the largest inland port in the United States and a center of world trade. Four international bridges crossing the Rio Grande connect **Laredo** with Nuevo Laredo, Mexico. The monument in this photo commemorates the establishment of the city.

1900 — 2000

1977

Oceanographer Frank González of **San Antonio** joins the National Oceanic and Atmospheric Administration. Dr. González is part of a team that studies very large ocean waves called tsunamis. He works with deep-ocean stations that track wave patterns to identify coastal communities at risk of being struck by tsunami waves.

2002

Sandra Cisneros, author of the popular book *The House on Mango Street,* publishes her second novel, *Caramelo,* to critical acclaim. She is a resident of **San Antonio.**

Why Learn Spanish?

To Appreciate the Importance of Spanish in the U.S.

The influence of Spanish is everywhere. Spanish words like **plaza** and **tornado** have become part of the English language. Just think of U.S. place names that come from Spanish: **Colorado, Florida, Nevada, Los Angeles, San Antonio, La Villita,** etc. You can see Spanish on signs. There are Spanish radio and television stations. Singers such as Jon Secada perform in Spanish as well as English.

To Connect

Spanish will help you **communicate** with other people. Spanish is the second most common language in the U.S. and the third most common in the world.

You will be able do things like **ask someone for directions, bargain at a market,** and **order in a restaurant** in Spanish.

To Have Fun

Taking Spanish is a new experience that will expose you to the **food,** the **music,** the **celebrations,** and other aspects of Spanish-speaking cultures. It will make travel to other countries as well as to different places in the United States much more enjoyable and more meaningful.

To Be Challenged

Studying Spanish is a challenge. There is a lot to learn, but it's not just vocabulary and grammar in a textbook. In the future you **will be able to read** Spanish-language **newspapers, magazines,** and **books.** Imagine reading *Don Quijote de la Mancha* by Miguel de Cervantes in the original Spanish someday!

To Help You in the Future

Taking a foreign language like Spanish is an accomplishment to be emphasized on college and job applications. It can also help you fulfill college language requirements. Spanish can be **useful in many careers,** from doctor, bank teller, and social worker to teacher, tour guide, and translator.

How to Study Spanish

Use Strategies

Listening strategies provide a starting point to help you understand.

Speaking strategies will help you express yourself in Spanish.

Reading strategies will show you different ways to approach reading.

Writing strategies help you out with your writing skills.

Cultural strategies help you compare Spanish-speaking cultures of the world to your own culture.

STRATEGY: SPEAKING

Use all you know It is easy to rely on what you learned most recently. But it is important to reuse what you've learned before. Try to include activities you learned in Unit 1, such as **cantar** and **nadar,** in your answers.

Use Study Hints

The **Apoyo para estudiar** feature provides study hints that will help you learn Spanish.

Apoyo para estudiar

Gender

Knowing the gender of nouns that refer to people is easy. But how do you learn the gender of things? When learning a new word, such as **camiseta,** say it with the definite article: **la camiseta.** Say it to yourself and say it aloud several times. That will help you remember its gender.

Build Your Confidence

Everyone learns differently, and there are different ways to achieve a goal. Find out what works for you. Grammar boxes are set up with an explanation, a visual representation, and examples from real-life contexts. Use this combination of words and graphics to help you learn Spanish. Focus on whatever helps you most.

GRAMÁTICA Expressing Feelings with **estar** and Adjectives

¿RECUERDAS? *p. 134* You learned that the verb **estar** is used to say where someone or something is located.

Estar is also used with **adjectives** to describe how someone feels at a given moment.

estoy	estamos
estás	estáis
está	están

agrees

Diana **está preocupada** por Ignacio.

*Diana **is worried** about Ignacio.*

agrees

Ignacio **está preocupado** por Roberto.

*Ignacio **is worried** about Roberto.*

Remember that **adjectives** must **agree** in gender and number with the nouns they describe.

Practice: Actividades 6 7

Más práctica *cuaderno p. 61*

Para hispanohablantes *cuaderno p. 59*

Online Workbook CLASSZONE.COM

Have Fun

Taking a foreign language does not have to be all serious work. The dialogs in this book present the Spanish language in **entertaining, real-life contexts.**

- Pair and group activities give you a chance to **interact with your classmates.**
- Vocabulary and grammar puzzles will test your knowledge, but will also be **fun to do.**

Listen to Spanish Inside and Outside of Class

Listening to Spanish will help you understand it. Pay attention to the **dialogs** and the **listening activities** in class.

Take advantage of opportunities to **hear Spanish outside of class** as well.

- Do you know someone who speaks Spanish?
- Are there any Spanish-language radio and/or television stations in your area?
- Does your video store have any Spanish-language movies?

Take Risks

The goal of studying a foreign language like Spanish is to **communicate.**

Don't be afraid to **speak.**

Everyone makes mistakes, so don't worry if you make a few. When you do make a mistake, **pause and then try again.**

El mundo
Países hispanohablantes
Países con alto número de hispanohablantes
GROENLANDIA (DINAMARCA)
Bahía de Baffin
Mar de Siberia Oriental
Mar de Beaufort
RUSIA
Alaska (EE.UU.)
Mar de Bering
Bahía de Hudson
Mar del Labrador
CANADÁ
ESTADOS UNIDOS
OCÉANO ATLÁNTICO
Golfo de México
ISLAS BAHAMAS
REP. DOMINICANA
PUERTO RICO (EE.UU.)
SAN CRISTÓBAL Y NEVIS
ANTIGUA Y BARBUDA
GUADALUPE (FRANCIA)
DOMINICA
MARTINICA (FRANCIA)
SAN VICENTE Y GRANADINAS
BARBADOS
TRINIDAD Y TOBAGO
HAITÍ
CUBA
JAMAICA
Mar Caribe
SANTA LUCÍA
GRANADA
MÉXICO
BELICE
GUATEMALA
EL SALVADOR
HONDURAS
NICARAGUA
COSTA RICA
PANAMÁ
VENEZUELA
COLOMBIA
GUAYANA FRANCESA (FRANCIA)
GUYANA
SURINAM
ECUADOR
Islas Galápagos (Ecuador)
PERÚ
BRASIL
BOLIVIA
PARAGUAY
CHILE
URUGUAY
ARGENTINA
Islas Malvinas (R.U.)
Islas Hawai (EE.UU.)
OCÉANO PACÍFICO
ISLAS MARSHALL
VANUATÚ
KIRIBATI
NAURU
ISLAS TUVALU
ISLAS SALOMÓN
SAMOA OCCIDENTAL
SAMOA (EE.UU.)
FIDJI
TONGA
NUEVA CALEDONIA (FRANCIA)
NUEVA ZELANDA
180°
150°
120°
90°
60°
30°

OCÉANO ÁRTICO
Mar de Barents
Mar de Kara
Mar de Laptev
Mar de Noruega
ISLANDIA
SUECIA
FINLANDIA
NORUEGA
ESTONIA
LETONIA
LITUANIA
REINO UNIDO
Mar del Norte
Mar Báltico
IRLANDA
ALEMANIA
POLONIA
BIELORRUSIA
UCRANIA
MOLDAVIA
FRANCIA
AUSTRIA
RUMANIA
ANDORRA
ESPAÑA
PORTUGAL
ITALIA
GIBRALTAR (R.U.)
GRECIA
TÚNEZ
Mar Mediterráneo
Mar Negro
TURQUÍA
GEORGIA
ARMENIA
Mar Caspio
CHIPRE
LÍBANO
SIRIA
ISRAEL
IRAQ
AZERBAIYÁN
IRÁN
JORDANIA
KUWAIT
QATAR
BAHREIN
E.A.U.
OMÁN
ARABIA SAUDITA
YEMEN
1 DINAMARCA
2 HOLANDA
3 BÉLGICA
4 LUXEMBURGO
5 SUIZA
6 REPÚBLICA CHECA
7 ESLOVAQUIA
8 HUNGRÍA
9 ESLOVENIA
10 CROACIA
11 BOSNIA Y HERZEGOVINA
12 SERBIA Y MONTENEGRO
13 ALBANIA
14 MACEDONIA
15 BULGARIA
16 MALTA
RUSIA
Lago Baikal
Mar de Ojotsk
Mar de Aral
KAZAKSTÁN
MONGOLIA
UZBEKISTÁN
KIRGUISTÁN
TURKMENISTÁN
TADJIKISTÁN
AFGANISTÁN
PAQUISTÁN
CHINA
COREA DEL NORTE
COREA DEL SUR
Mar de Japón
JAPÓN
NEPAL
BHUTÁN
INDIA
Trópico de Cáncer
TAIWÁN
MYANMAR
BANGLADESH
LAOS
TAILANDIA
VIETNAM
CAMBOYA
Mar de China
FILIPINAS
GUAM (EE.UU.)
Mar Arábigo
Golfo de Bengala
SRI LANKA
ISLAS MALDIVAS
BRUNEI
MALAYSIA
PALAU
MICRONESIA
Ecuador
SINGAPUR
INDONESIA
PAPUASIA NUEVA GUINEA
TIMOR ORIENTAL
Islas Canarias (Esp.)
MARRUECOS
ARGELIA
LIBIA
EGIPTO
SAHARA OCCIDENTAL
CABO VERDE
MAURITANIA
MALÍ
NÍGER
CHAD
SUDÁN
Mar Rojo
ERITREA
JIBUTI
SENEGAL
GAMBIA
GUINEA
GUINEA BISSAU
SIERRA LEONA
LIBERIA
COSTA DE MARFIL
BURKINA FASO
GHANA
TOGO
BENIN
NIGERIA
CAMERÚN
GUINEA ECUATORIAL
REP. CENTRO-AFRICANA
ETIOPÍA
SOMALIA
UGANDA
KENIA
CONGO
GABÓN
REP. DEM. DEL CONGO
RUANDA
BURUNDI
TANZANIA
CABINDA (ANGOLA)
SEYCHELLES
ANGOLA
MALAWI
ZAMBIA
COMORES
MOZAMBIQUE
NAMIBIA
ZIMBABWE
MADAGASCAR
MAURICIO
BOTSWANA
OCÉANO ÍNDICO
SUAZILANDIA
SUDÁFRICA
LESOTHO
AUSTRALIA
Trópico de Capricornio
N
0 1000 2000 kilómetros
0 1000 2000 millas
ANTÁRTIDA
0
30
60
90
120

México y Centroamérica
ESTADOS UNIDOS
Washington, D.C.
OCÉANO ATLÁNTICO
ISLAS BAHAMAS
Nassau
Tijuana
Mexicali
Ciudad Juárez
Baja California
Hermosillo
SIERRA MADRE OCCIDENTAL
Chihuahua
SIERRA MADRE ORIENTAL
Nuevo Laredo
MÉXICO
Monterrey
Golfo de México
Durango
San Luis Potosí
Tampico
La Habana
CUBA
Guadalajara
Mérida
Veracruz
México, D.F.
Puebla
Kingston
JAMAICA
Belice
BELICE
Belmopan
Oaxaca
Acapulco
HONDURAS
MAR CARIBE
Guatemala
Tegucigalpa
GUATEMALA
San Salvador
NICARAGUA
EL SALVADOR
Managua
San José
Colón
Panamá
COSTA RICA
PANAMÁ
COLOMBIA
OCÉANO PACÍFICO
Quito
ECUADOR
PERÚ
0 250 500 kilómetros
0 250 500 millas

El Caribe
ESTADOS UNIDOS
N
Estrecho de Florida
Nassau
ISLAS BAHAMAS
OCÉANO ATLÁNTICO
La Habana
Santa Clara
CUBA
Nueva Gerona
Camagüey
Holguín
Manzanillo
Guantánamo
Santiago de Cuba
ISLAS DE TURCOS Y CAICOS (R.U.)
REPÚBLICA DOMINICANA
HAITÍ
La Española
Puerto Príncipe
Santo Domingo
Arecibo
San Juan
Mayagüez
Ponce
Humacao
PUERTO RICO
ANTILLAS MAYORES
Kingston
JAMAICA
HONDURAS
MAR CARIBE
NICARAGUA
Aruba (Hol.)
Curaçao (Hol.)
Bonaire (Hol.)
Caracas
San José
COSTA RICA
Panamá
PANAMÁ
Golfo de Panamá
VENEZUELA
COLOMBIA
Bogotá
OCÉANO PACÍFICO
0 250 500 kilómetros
0 250 500 millas

Sudamérica

MAR CARIBE
OCÉANO ATLÁNTICO
Barranquilla
Cartagena
Maracaibo
Lago Maracaibo
Caracas
TRINIDAD Y TOBAGO
Puerto España
VENEZUELA
Georgetown
GUYANA
Paramaribo
SURINAM
Cayena
GUAYANA FRANCESA (FRANCIA)
N
Medellín
Manizales
Bogotá
Cali
COLOMBIA
Ecuador
Otavalo
Quito
ECUADOR
Guayaquil
Cuenca
Río Negro
Río Amazonas
Río Madeira
Río Tapajóz
Río Xingú
Río Tocantins
Río São Francisco
PERÚ
CORDILLERA DE LOS ANDES
Trujillo
Lima
Callao
BRASIL
Lago Titicaca
BOLIVIA
La Paz
Cochabamba
Santa Cruz
Sucre
Brasilia
GRAN CHACO
PARAGUAY
Asunción
Trópico de Capricornio
Islas Galápagos (Ecuador)
OCÉANO PACÍFICO
0 250 kilómetros
0 250 millas
Salta
San Miguel de Tucumán
CHILE
Resistencia
Córdoba
Valparaíso
Santiago
Mendoza
Rosario
URUGUAY
OCÉANO PACÍFICO
Buenos Aires
Montevideo
ARGENTINA
La Plata
Concepción
PAMPAS
Bahía Blanca
Mar del Plata
Temuco
PATAGONIA
OCÉANO ATLÁNTICO
Estrecho de Magallanes
0 250 500 kilómetros
0 250 500 millas
Tierra del Fuego
Islas Malvinas (R.U.)
Cabo de Hornos

España
OCÉANO ATLÁNTICO
MAR CANTÁBRICO
FRANCIA
La Coruña
ASTURIAS
CANTABRIA
Bilbao
PAÍS VASCO
GALICIA
CORDILLERA CANTÁBRICA
LOS PIRINEOS
ANDORRA
Pamplona
León
NAVARRA
Río Ebro
CASTILLA-LEÓN
CATALUÑA
Valladolid
Río Duero
Zaragoza
Barcelona
ESPAÑA
ARAGÓN
Salamanca
SIERRA DE GUADARRAMA
MADRID
Río Tajo
Madrid
PORTUGAL
COMUNIDAD VALENCIANA
Islas Baleares
Menorca
Palma
Mallorca
CASTILLA-LA MANCHA
Valencia
Ibiza
Lisboa
Río Guadiana
EXTREMADURA
MAR MEDITERRÁNEO
Córdoba
MURCIA
Sevilla
Río Guadalquivir
Granada
ANDALUCÍA
SIERRA NEVADA
Málaga
Gibraltar (R.U.)
Estrecho de Gibraltar
Ceuta (España)
Melilla (España)
OCÉANO ATLÁNTICO
MARRUECOS
Islas Canarias (España)
OCÉANO ATLÁNTICO
La Palma
Santa Cruz de Tenerife
Tenerife
Las Palmas
Gran Canaria
ÁFRICA
0 50 kilómetros
0 50 millas
0 50 100 kilómetros
0 50 100 millas
África
CAMERÚN
Malabo
GUINEA ECUATORIAL
Golfo de Guinea
Bata
GABÓN
0 200 kilómetros
0 200 millas
N

ETAPA PRELIMINAR

¡Hola, bienvenidos!

OBJECTIVES

- Greet people
- Introduce yourself
- Say where you are from
- Exchange phone numbers
- Say which day it is

¿Qué ves?

Look at the photo of the first day of school.

1. How might the students be greeting one another?
2. What are they carrying?
3. Where should new students go? At what time?

¡Hola!

When greeting, it is customary to shake hands. Many people also exchange a kiss on the cheek or a hug. The greeting changes with the time of day. **Hola** can be used anytime. **Buenos días** is used in the morning, **Buenas tardes** in the afternoon and early evening, and **Buenas noches** at night.

Hola.

Buenos días.

Buenas tardes.

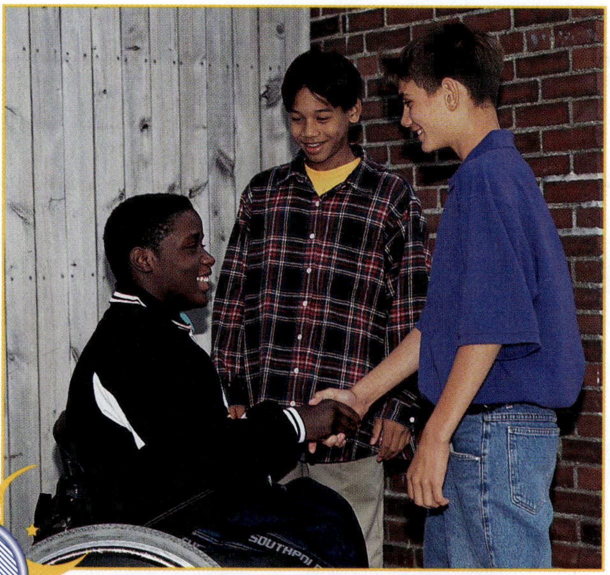

Buenas noches.

Adiós

These expressions are all used to say good-bye. **Adiós** means *Good-bye*. **Hasta mañana** literally means *Until tomorrow*. You can say **Hasta luego** or **Nos vemos** if you expect to see the person later that day or in the near future.

Adiós.

Hasta luego.

Hasta mañana.

Nos vemos.

1 Buenos días

How would you greet a friend at these times?

modelo

5:00 p.m. — *Buenas tardes.*

1. 8:00 P.M.
2. 10:45 A.M.
3. 2:00 P.M.
4. 8:30 A.M.
5. anytime
6. 9:00 P.M.

2 Hasta mañana

Use different expressions to say good-bye to these people.

1. Ana
2. Señor Ruiz
3. Señora Díaz
4. Alfredo

3 ¿Saludo o despedida?

Imagine that you are in a Spanish-speaking community. Identify what you hear as a greeting (**saludo**) or a farewell (**despedida**) for these eight phrases.

4 Nos vemos

Greet and say good-bye to your partner, according to these situations.

1. Greet each other in the afternoon. You will see each other tomorrow.
2. Greet each other in the evening. You don't expect to see each other anytime soon.
3. Greet each other in the morning. You will see each other later today.

More Practice:
Más práctica *cuaderno p. 1*
Para hispanohablantes *cuaderno p. 1*

¿Cómo te llamas?

Me llamo Tomás.

Chicos

Adán	Fernando	Marcos
Alejandro	Francisco	Mateo
Álvaro	Gerardo	Miguel
Andrés	Gilberto	Nicolás
Arturo	Gregorio	Pablo
Benjamín	Guillermo	Patricio
Carlos	Ignacio	Pedro
Cristóbal	Iván	Rafael
Daniel	Jaime	Ramón
David	Javier	Raúl
Diego	Jorge	Ricardo
Eduardo	José	Roberto
Enrique	Juan	Teodoro
Esteban	Julio	Timoteo
Federico	Leonardo	Tomás
Felipe	Luis	Vicente

Me llamo Alma.

Chicas

Alejandra	Elena	Mercedes
Alicia	Emilia	Micaela
Alma	Estefanía	Mónica
Ana	Estela	Natalia
Andrea	Eva	Patricia
Anita	Francisca	Raquel
Bárbara	Graciela	Rosa
Beatriz	Isabel	Rosalinda
Carlota	Juana	Rosana
Carmen	Julia	Sofía
Carolina	Luisa	Susana
Claudia	Margarita	Teresa
Consuelo	María	Verónica
Cristina	Mariana	Victoria
Diana	Marta	Yolanda

Francisco: Hola. ¿Cómo te llamas?

Alma: Me llamo Alma.

Francisco: Encantado, Alma. Me llamo Francisco.

Alma: Es un placer, Francisco.

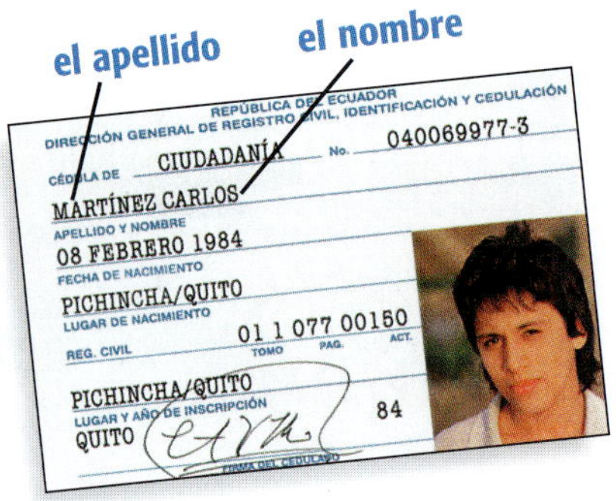

Apoyo para estudiar

Chico, chica

In Spanish, all nouns have either a masculine or feminine gender. Masculine nouns usually end in **-o** and feminine nouns usually end in **-a**.

Raquel: Hola. Me llamo Raquel.

Susana: Me llamo Susana. Encantada.

Raquel: Igualmente.

Susana: ¿Cómo se llama el chico?

Raquel: Se llama Jorge.

Jorge: ¿Cómo se llama la chica?

Enrique: Se llama Ana.

Rosa: Buenos días. Me llamo Rosa. ¿Cómo te llamas?

Carlos: Mucho gusto, Rosa. Me llamo Carlos.

Rosa: El gusto es mío.

5 Me llamo...

How do these people introduce themselves?

modelo

Marcos García — *Me llamo **Marcos García.***

1. Marta Blanco
2. Raúl Morales
3. Rosa Vivas
4. Felipe Estrada
5. Ana Martínez
6. Ricardo Herrera
7. Arturo Cruz
8. Sofía Ponce

6 ¿Cómo te llamas en español?

Find out the Spanish names of five classmates.

modelo

You: *¿Cómo te llamas?* **Classmate:** *Me llamo Ana.*

7 ¿Cómo se llama?

- Greet and introduce yourself to a classmate.
- Point to others and find out their names.
- Say good-bye.

modelo

You: *Buenos días. Me llamo… ¿Cómo te llamas?*
Classmate: *Me llamo Mónica. Encantada.*

You: *Es un placer. ¿Cómo se llama la chica?*
Classmate: *Se llama Mariana.*

You: *Adiós. Hasta luego.*
Classmate: *Nos vemos.*

Nota: Vocabulario

Boys say **encantado.** Girls say **encantada.**

More Practice:
Más práctica *cuaderno* p. 2
Para hispanohablantes *cuaderno* p. 2

¿De dónde es?

Es de México.

Es de Estados Unidos.

Es de Ecuador.

Es de Perú.

Nota cultural

Spanish speakers sometimes use the articles **el, la, las,** or **los** before these country names. Their use is optional.

(la) Argentina
(el) Ecuador
(los) Estados Unidos
(las) Filipinas
(el) Paraguay
(el) Perú
(la) República Dominicana
(el) Uruguay

LOS PAÍSES DEL MUNDO HISPANOHABLANTE

- Argentina 21
- Belice 4
- Bolivia 17
- Chile 18
- Colombia 14
- Costa Rica 8
- Cuba 10
- Ecuador 15
- El Salvador 5
- España 22
- Estados Unidos 1
- Filipinas 24
- Guam 25
- Guatemala 3
- Guinea Ecuatorial 23
- Honduras 6
- México 2
- Nicaragua 7
- Panamá 9
- Paraguay 19
- Perú 16
- Puerto Rico 12
- República Dominicana 11
- Uruguay 20
- Venezuela 13

Soy de...

Raquel: ¿De dónde es?

Susana: Es de Uruguay.

Ricardo: ¿De dónde eres?

Manuel: Soy de Guatemala.

8 ¿De dónde es?

You and your partner have made some new friends. Tell where they are from. Change roles.

modelo

Tomás: España

You: *¿De dónde es **Tomás**?*

Partner: *Es de **España**.*

1. Estefanía: Panamá
2. Graciela: Cuba
3. Vicente: Costa Rica
4. Ignacio: Honduras
5. Mercedes: México
6. Alejandro: Nicaragua
7. Iván: Puerto Rico
8. Claudia: El Salvador

9 ¿De dónde eres?

You meet several South Americans. Role-play the situation with a partner, following the model.

modelo

1

You: *¿De dónde eres?* **Partner:** *Soy de Ecuador.*

10 Nuevos amigos

Listen as several people introduce themselves to you. Say their country of origin.

modelo

Álvaro: ¿Cuba o Colombia?

***Álvaro** es de Colombia.*

1. Alma: ¿Puerto Rico o Costa Rica?
2. Guillermo: ¿Honduras o Estados Unidos?
3. Carmen: ¿Uruguay o Paraguay?
4. Eduardo: ¿México o España?
5. Yolanda: ¿Venezuela o Guatemala?
6. Adán: ¿Argentina o Nicaragua?

11 ¿Eres de...?

Imagine that everyone in your class is from different Spanish-speaking countries. Choose a country. Ask other students questions to find out which country each person is from. Follow the model.

modelo

Student 1: *¿Eres de Honduras?*

You: *No.*

Student 2: *¿Eres de Guatemala?*

You: *Sí, soy de Guatemala.*

Nota: Vocabulario

To say yes, use **sí. No** is the same as in English.

More Practice:

Más práctica *cuaderno pp. 3–4*
Para hispanohablantes *cuaderno pp. 3–4*

El abecedario (El alfabeto)

avión

bota

cerdo

dinero

escalera

flor

gafas

huevo

imán

jarra

kiwi

lápiz

maleta

nieve

ñu

oso

paraguas

queso

Apoyo para estudiar

Dictionary

Dictionaries published before 1994 include **ch** and **ll** as separate letters in the Spanish alphabet.

reloj

guitarra

sombrero

tijeras

unicornio

video

wafle

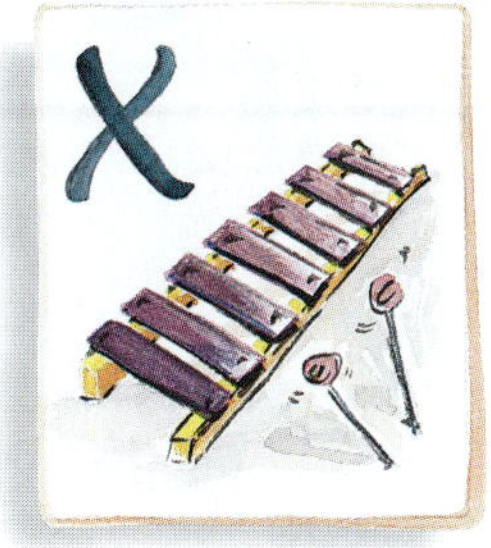

xilófono

yogur

zanahoria

12 Información

Listen to two people introduce themselves. Complete the information, writing down their first and last names as they are spelled.

1. **a.** nombre
   b. apellido
2. **a.** nombre
   b. apellido

13 ¿Cómo te llamas?

Find out the Spanish names of five classmates. Write the names down as they spell them.

modelo

You: *¿Cómo te llamas?*

Classmate: *Me llamo Esteban, E - S - T - E - B - A - N.*
(e, ese, te, e, be, a, ene)

Pronunciación

Here is how to say the name of each letter of the Spanish alphabet.

a = a	k = ka	rr = erre
b = be, be larga	l = ele	s = ese
c = ce	m = eme	t = te
d = de	n = ene	u = u
e = e	ñ = eñe	v = ve, uve, ve corta
f = efe	o = o	w = doble ve, doble uve
g = ge	p = pe	x = equis
h = hache	q = cu	y = i griega, ye
i = i	r = ere	z = zeta
j = jota		

More Practice:
Más práctica *cuaderno* p. 5
Para hispanohablantes *cuaderno* p. 5

Los números de cero a diez

cero uno dos tres cuatro

cinco seis siete ocho nueve

diez

Roberto: ¿Cuál es tu teléfono?

Ignacio: 8–9–7–3–1–4–2.

¿Qué día es hoy?

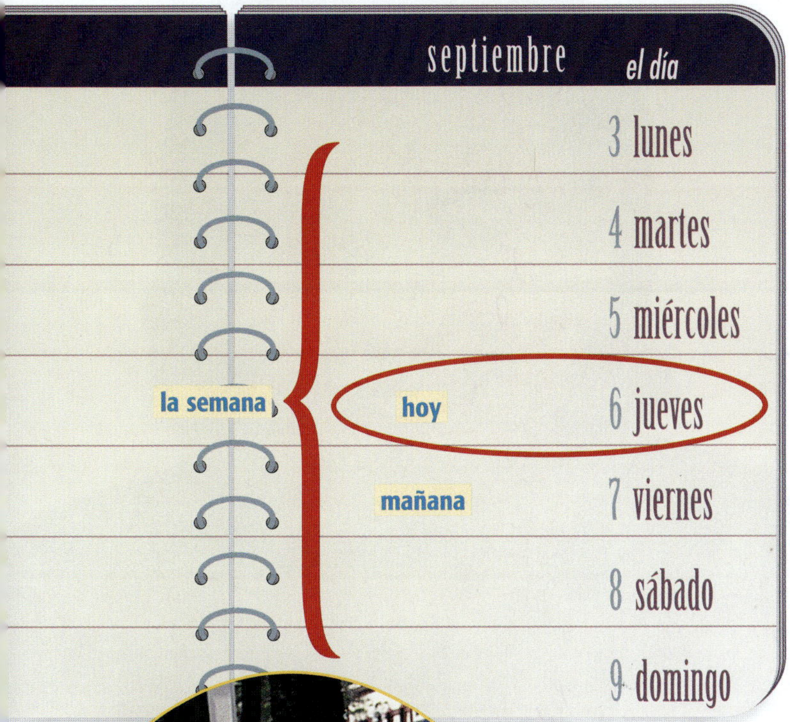

Sofía: Hoy es jueves.

Rosa: Mañana es viernes. ¡Fantástico!

Apoyo para estudiar

Days of the week

In Spanish the days of the week are not capitalized.

14 ¿Cuál es tu teléfono?

Ask for and write down the telephone numbers of five classmates.

modelo

You: *Carolina, ¿cuál es tu teléfono?*

Classmate: *Seis - seis - tres - seis - nueve - cinco - siete.*

15 El día

Tell what day it is today and tomorrow.

modelo

jueves — *Hoy es **jueves.** Mañana es viernes.*

1. lunes
2. sábado
3. miércoles
4. martes
5. domingo
6. viernes

16 ¿Qué día?

You often forget what day it is. Ask your partner for help. Change roles.

modelo

lunes

You: *¿Qué día es hoy?*

Partner: *Hoy es **lunes.***

You: *¡Sí! Mañana es martes.*

1. sábado
2. miércoles
3. viernes
4. domingo
5. jueves
6. martes

More Practice:

Más práctica *cuaderno p. 6*
Para hispanohablantes *cuaderno p. 6*

Frases útiles

In the Classroom

Abran los libros.	Open your books.
Cierren los libros.	Close your books.
Escriban…	Write…
Escuchen…	Listen (to)…
Lean…	Read…
Levanten la mano.	Raise your hand.
Miren el pizarrón. **la foto.**	Look at the chalkboard. the photo.
Pásenme la tarea.	Pass in the homework.
Repitan.	Repeat.
Saquen un lápiz.	Take out a pencil.
Siéntense.	Sit down.

Skills

Escuchar

Hablar

Leer

Escribir

Helpful Spanish Phrases

¿Cómo se dice…?	How do you say…?
Más despacio, por favor.	More slowly, please.
No sé.	I don't know.
¿Qué quiere decir…?	What does… mean?
Repita, por favor.	Repeat, please.

In the Text

Cambien de papel.
Change roles.

Completa la conversación.
Complete the conversation.

Contesta las preguntas.
Answer the questions.

Di quién habla.
Say who is speaking.

¿Es cierto o falso?
True or false?

Escoge la respuesta correcta.
Choose the correct response.

- **la palabra**
  word
- **la frase**
  phrase
- **la oración**
  sentence

Escucha...
Listen to...

Explica...
Explain...

Lee...
Read...

Pregúntale a otro(a) estudiante...
Ask another student...

Trabaja con otro(a) estudiante...
Work with another student...

Trabaja en un grupo de...
Work in a group of...

17 Instrucciones

Repond to your teacher's classroom instructions.

18 En la clase

What is the teacher telling the students? Match the picture with the instructions below.

1. 2. 3. 4.

a. Abran los libros.
b. Pásenme la tarea.
c. Miren el pizarrón.
d. Levanten la mano.

19 ¡Atención, clase!

Take turns giving classroom instructions to partners, who respond appropriately.

20 ¡Abran los libros!

In groups, look through your book to find examples of the instructions you have learned. Write down the page number for each one.

More Practice:
Más práctica *cuaderno* p. 7
Para hispanohablantes *cuaderno* p. 7

Onda Internacional

VIDEO DVD

El concurso

In this book you will get to know teens from different parts of the Spanish-speaking world. Many of these young people are interested in a contest sponsored by a Spanish magazine for teens called *Onda Internacional.* Why are they interested? Read on!

"Hi! I've got the new edition of **Onda Internacional** *magazine. It has many different articles. There are articles about Spanish-speaking countries, sports, fashion, food, school, leisure activities, and much more. And look! There's a contest. Write an article or prepare a photo essay about what it means to you to be latino or latina. The two winners will travel to parts of the Spanish-speaking world and work for the magazine. Well, get out your cameras, pencils, paper, and ideas, and take part in the contest!"*

Apoyo para estudiar

Reading a poster

When you read a poster, look at the size of lettering, kinds of words, colors, visuals, and any other items it contains. Based on what you already know about *Onda Internacional* and what you see on this poster, why might someone use a poster? Give as many reasons as you can.

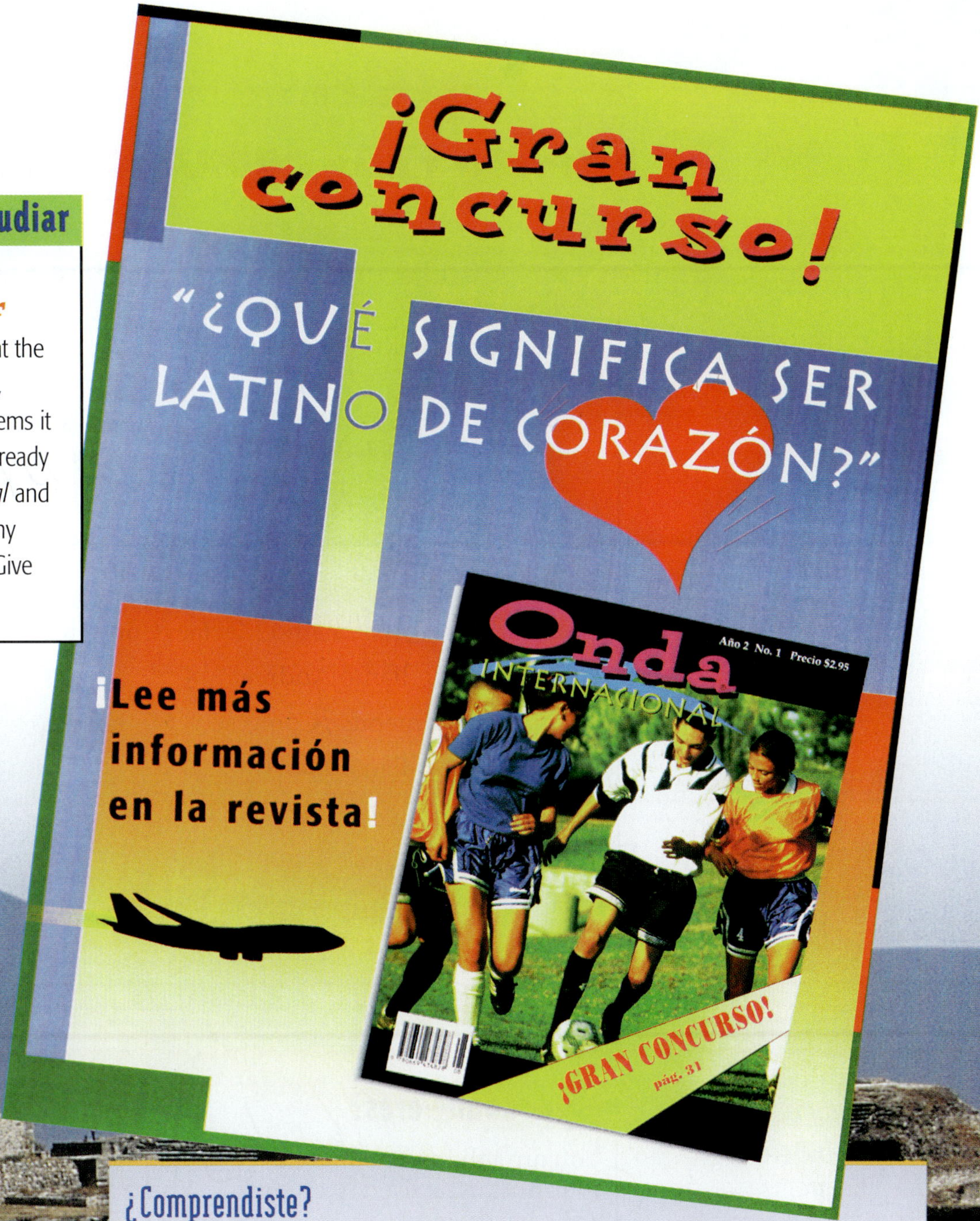

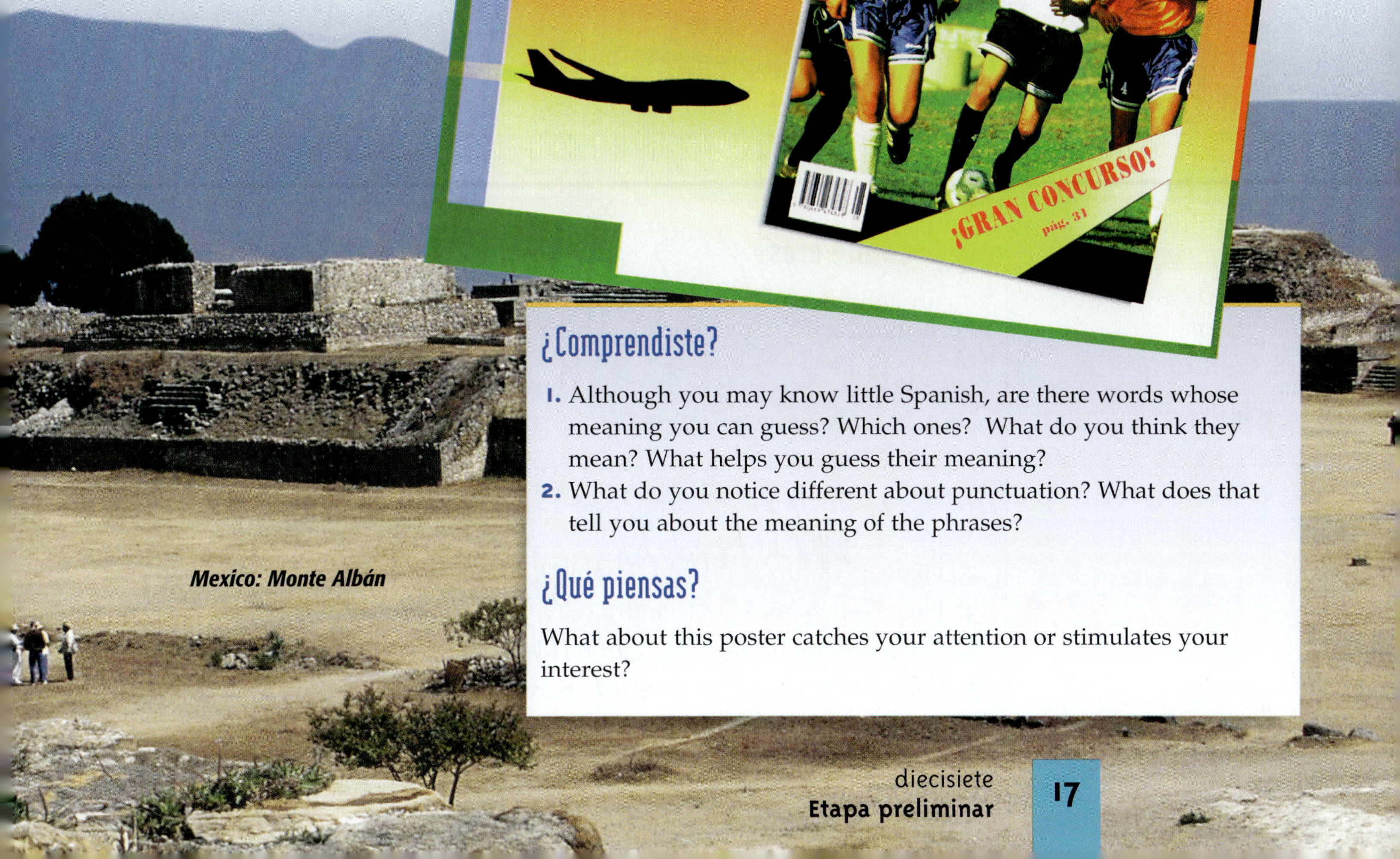

Mexico: Monte Albán

¿Comprendiste?

1. Although you may know little Spanish, are there words whose meaning you can guess? Which ones? What do you think they mean? What helps you guess their meaning?
2. What do you notice different about punctuation? What does that tell you about the meaning of the phrases?

¿Qué piensas?

What about this poster catches your attention or stimulates your interest?

ETAPA PRELIMINAR

En uso

REPASO Y MÁS COMUNICACIÓN

OBJECTIVES

- Greet people
- Introduce yourself
- Say where you are from
- Exchange phone numbers
- Say which day it is

Now you can...

- greet people.
- introduce yourself.

To review

- greetings and introductions, see pp. 2–5.

1 En la clase

Marta speaks with two people. Complete the conversations with the words given.

adiós | hasta | llamo | se | placer | llama | llamas | encantada | hola | mañana | tardes | vemos | mío | mucho | me

Marta: ¡__1__! Me llamo Marta. ¿Cómo te __2__?

Andrea: __3__ llamo Andrea. __4__.

Marta: Igualmente. ¿Cómo se __5__ el chico?

Andrea: __6__ llama Mateo.

Marta: Es un __7__, Andrea. Nos __8__.

Andrea: __9__, Marta. __10__ luego.

Marta: Buenas __11__, Mateo. Me __12__ Marta.

Mateo: __13__ gusto, Marta.

Marta: El gusto es __14__. Hasta __15__.

Now you can...

- say where you are from.

To review

- saying where you are from, see pp. 6–8.

2 ¿De dónde eres?

You are talking to some international students who say where they and their friends are from. Where are they from?

modelo

Luisa (Chile) / Jorge (Puerto Rico)

*Me llamo **Luisa.** Soy de **Chile. Jorge** es de **Puerto Rico.***

1. Julio (Panamá) / Mónica (Bolivia)
2. Diana (Estados Unidos) / Rafael (Uruguay)
3. Patricio (España) / Alejandra (Guatemala)
4. Natalia (Argentina) / Benjamín (México)
5. Gregorio (Cuba) / Verónica (El Salvador)

Self-Check Quiz
CLASSZONE.COM

Now you can...
- exchange phone numbers.

To review
- numbers, see p. 12.

3 Teléfonos

You need some phone numbers. With a partner, role-play conversations asking for friends' numbers. Follow the model.

modelo

Rosana: 530-4401

You: *Rosana, ¿cuál es tu número de teléfono?*

Rosana: *Cinco - tres - cero - cuatro - cuatro - cero - uno.*

1. Timoteo: 927-2296
2. Mariana: 820-3981
3. Cristóbal: 450-5649
4. Emilia: 392-4100
5. Leonardo: 758-3141
6. otro(a) estudiante: ¿?

Now you can...
- say which day it is.

To review
- days of the week, see p. 13.

4 ¿Qué día es hoy?

Tell what day it is today, based on what tomorrow is.

modelo

Mañana es viernes.

Hoy es jueves.

1. Mañana es domingo.
2. Mañana es miércoles.
3. Mañana es lunes.
4. Mañana es jueves.
5. Mañana es martes.
6. Mañana es sábado.

5 Hola

Greet a partner and introduce yourself. Talk about which day it is today and tomorrow. Say good-bye.

modelo

You: *Hola. Me llamo… ¿Cómo te llamas?*

Partner: *Mucho gusto. Me llamo…*

You: *¿Qué día es…?*

6 Mucha información

Imagine that everyone has a new identity. Ask three classmates for the information needed to complete the chart.

modelo

You: *Hola. Me llamo… ¿Cómo te llamas?*

Student 1: *Es un placer. Me llamo Carolina. Soy de Perú. ¿De dónde eres?*

You: *Soy de Honduras. ¿Cuál es tu teléfono?*

Student 1: *Siete - tres - cero - siete - seis - seis - dos. ¿Cuál es tu…?*

Nombre	País	Teléfono
1. Carolina	Perú	730-7662
2.		
3.		

7 *En tu propia voz*

ESCRITURA Write to your new pen pal. Include the following information.

- Write a greeting.
- Introduce yourself.
- Say where you are from.
- Write three questions for your new pen pal to answer.

En resumen

REPASO DE VOCABULARIO

GREETINGS

Greeting People

Buenos días.	*Good morning.*
Buenas tardes.	*Good afternoon.*
Buenas noches.	*Good evening.*
Hola.	*Hello.*

Responding

El gusto es mío.	*The pleasure is mine.*
Encantado(a).	*Delighted/Pleased to meet you.*
Es un placer.	*It's a pleasure.*
Igualmente.	*Same here.*
Mucho gusto.	*Nice to meet you.*

Saying Good-bye

Adiós.	*Good-bye.*
Hasta luego.	*See you later.*
Hasta mañana.	*See you tomorrow.*
Nos vemos.	*See you later.*

INTRODUCING YOURSELF

el apellido	*last name, surname*
el nombre	*name, first name*
¿Cómo te llamas?	*What is your name?*
¿Cómo se llama?	*What is his/her name?*
Me llamo...	*My name is...*
Se llama...	*His/Her name is...*

SAYING WHERE YOU ARE FROM

¿De dónde eres?	*Where are you from?*
¿De dónde es?	*Where is he/she from?*
Soy de...	*I am from...*
Es de...	*He/She is from...*

EXCHANGING PHONE NUMBERS

¿Cuál es tu teléfono?	*What is your phone number?*

Numbers from Zero to Ten

cero	*zero*
uno	*one*
dos	*two*
tres	*three*
cuatro	*four*
cinco	*five*
seis	*six*
siete	*seven*
ocho	*eight*
nueve	*nine*
diez	*ten*

SAYING WHICH DAY IT IS

¿Qué día es hoy?	*What day is today?*
Hoy es...	*Today is...*
Mañana es...	*Tomorrow is...*
el día	*day*
hoy	*today*
mañana	*tomorrow*
la semana	*week*

Days of the Week

lunes	*Monday*
martes	*Tuesday*
miércoles	*Wednesday*
jueves	*Thursday*
viernes	*Friday*
sábado	*Saturday*
domingo	*Sunday*

OTHER WORDS AND PHRASES

no	*no*
sí	*yes*

Skills

escribir	*to write*
escuchar	*to listen*
hablar	*to talk, to speak*
leer	*to read*

SPANISH IS THE OFFICIAL LANGUAGE OF THESE COUNTRIES:

Argentina	*Argentina*
Bolivia	*Bolivia*
Chile	*Chile*
Colombia	*Colombia*
Costa Rica	*Costa Rica*
Cuba	*Cuba*
Ecuador	*Ecuador*
El Salvador	*El Salvador*
España	*Spain*
Guatemala	*Guatemala*
Guinea Ecuatorial	*Equatorial Guinea*
Honduras	*Honduras*
México	*Mexico*
Nicaragua	*Nicaragua*
Panamá	*Panama*
Paraguay	*Paraguay*
Perú	*Peru*
Puerto Rico	*Puerto Rico*
República Dominicana	*Dominican Republic*
Uruguay	*Uruguay*
Venezuela	*Venezuela*

UNIDAD 1

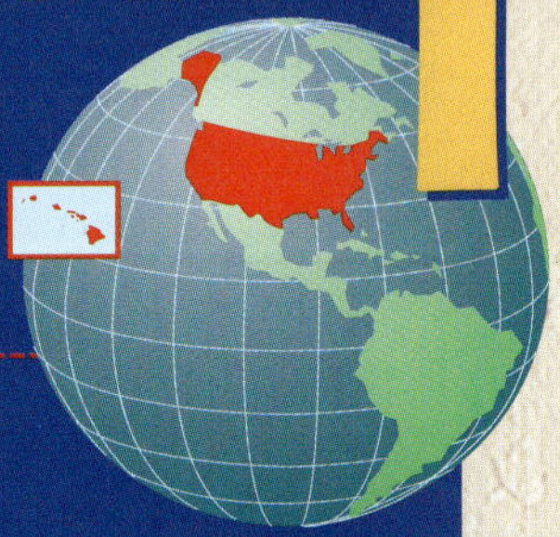

ESTADOS UNIDOS

MI MUNDO

TEXAS Essential Knowledge and Skills

1 Communication

- **A Engage in exchanges**
  - *Greeting and introducing others*
- **B Demonstrate understanding**
  - *Expressing likes and dislikes*
  - *Expressing possession*
  - *Identifying family members, their ages, and their birthdays*
- **C Present information**
  - *Saying where people live and are from*
  - *Describing people and their clothing*

2 Cultures

- **A Practices**
  - *The influence of Spanish speakers in the United States*
  - *A traditional birthday celebration*
  - *Traditional holidays*
- **B Products**
  - *Tejano music*

3 Connections

- **B Use the language**
  - *Social Studies: Hispanic traditions and events and those of other communities in the U.S.*
  - *Social Studies: Hispanic celebrations and those of other communities in the U.S.*

4 Comparisons

- **B Concept of culture**
  - *Events marking transition from childhood to adulthood*
  - *Important holidays*
- **C Influence**
  - *Unique music forms*

5 Communities

- **A Within and beyond school**
  - *Using Spanish in Spanish-speaking communities for personal enjoyment*
- **B Lifelong learner**
  - *Using Spanish in the workplace*

INTERNET Preview
CLASSZONE.COM

- More About Latinos
- Webquest
- Self-Check Quizzes
- Flashcards
- Writing Center
- Online Workbook
- eEdition Plus Online

MURALES are popular art sometimes found on the sides of buildings in L.A. Often their artists are Chicano, or Mexican American. What street art have you seen?

ALMANAQUE CULTURAL

POBLACIÓN: 281,421,906

POBLACIÓN DE DESCENDENCIA HISPANA: 35,305,818

CIUDAD CON MÁS LATINOS: Nueva York

CIUDAD CON MAYOR PORCENTAJE (%) DE LATINOS: El Paso

EN ESTADOS UNIDOS

Las ciudades que ves en el mapa tienen un gran número de latinos. En esta unidad vas a visitar Miami, San Antonio y Los Ángeles. ¡Vamos!

More About Latinos
CLASSZONE.COM

FAJITAS reflect the Mexican influence on Los Angeles cuisine. What Mexican dishes have you tried?

EL ÁLAMO, a former Spanish mission from 1718, reminds us how long Spanish influences have been in San Antonio. In what parts of the U.S. might someone be able to visit a former Spanish mission?

EL SÁNDWICH CUBANO, filled with ham, pork, and cheese, is a popular meal in Miami. Can you guess which ethnic group brought this food to Miami?

CASCARONES, eggshells filled with confetti, are used to celebrate the April **Fiesta.** People break them on each other's heads for good luck. What do you do to celebrate events in your community?

JON SECADA, Cuban American singer and songwriter, performs in English and Spanish. He has won Grammy awards for his work. What other Latino musicians do you know?

UNIDAD 1

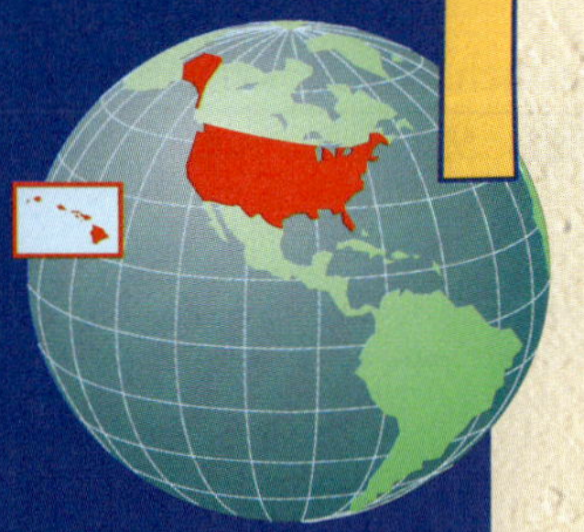

MI MUNDO

¡En español! **helps you become a competent learner of Spanish in these five ways:**

Texas Essential Knowledge and Skills

1 Comunicación

2 Culturas

3 Conexiones

4 Comparaciones

5 Comunidades

Communication

Communicate in another language!

How do we get acquainted with others? We converse, ask, explain, describe; we talk. In what other ways do we give and receive information that develops relationships?

Comparisons

Compare your culture and language to other ones.

Studying and learning Spanish give you a fresh understanding of your own language and culture. You discover comfortable similarities and interesting differences. For example, word order in Spanish and English sentences sometimes differs. What other differences in language have you found? The photo offers a clue.

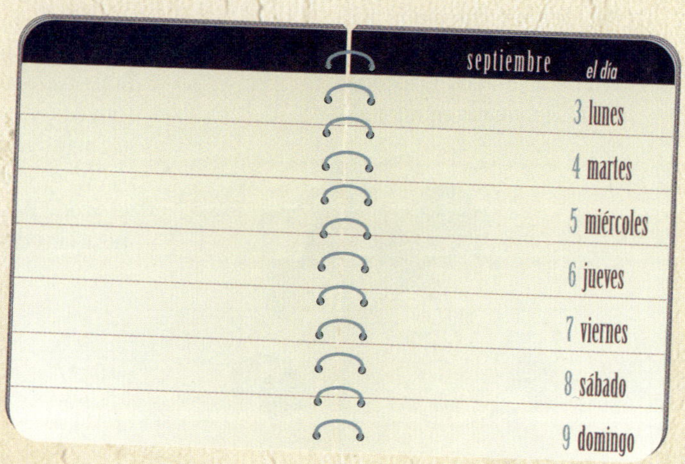

Webquest CLASSZONE.COM

Guided Web-based activities help you explore how Spanish is used in the United States.

Connections

Connect new information to other subjects.

Graphs and charts from mathematics or social studies can be used to report information. And Spanish can help you learn about other subjects. The photo offers a clue to one subject. What is it? Can you think of others?

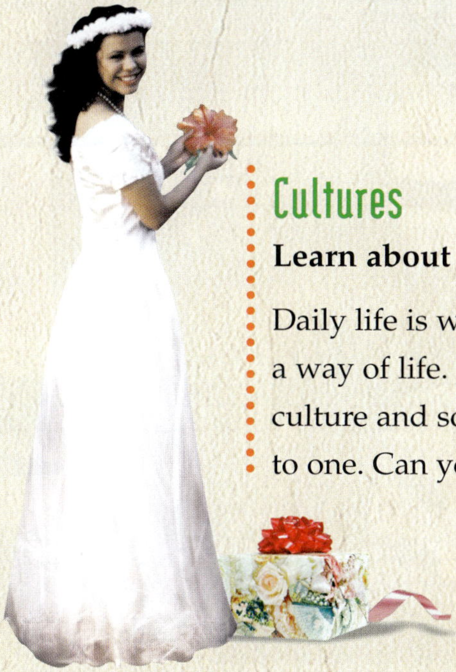

Cultures

Learn about other cultures.

Daily life is woven into each language and Spanish reflects a way of life. What celebrations might differ between your culture and someone else's culture? The photo offers a clue to one. Can you think of others?

Communities

Use Spanish in your community!

A group of people who share common interests and a common location make a community. Identify different communities in your area. Are there any where you can practice your Spanish?

Fíjate

Each of the following statements relates to one of the areas described (Communication, Comparisons, Connections, Cultures, Communities). Determine which area is best represented by each statement.

1. Writing to pen pals, listening to music with Spanish lyrics, and reading information in Spanish on the Internet are ways to use Spanish language skills.
2. Calendars printed in Spanish usually end each week with Sunday, not Saturday.
3. Murals painted by chicanos in Los Angeles would be interesting subject matter for an art class.
4. For their 15th birthday, many Hispanic girls celebrate a formal event known as a *quinceañera*.
5. As a student of Spanish, you may be able to help Spanish-speaking clients shopping in stores in your neighborhood.

UNIDAD 1

ETAPA 1

¡Bienvenido a Miami!

OBJECTIVES

- Greet others
- Introduce others
- Say where people are from
- Express likes

¿Qué ves?

Look at the photo of Máximo Gómez Park in Miami.

1. Which people do you think are the main characters in this **Etapa**?
2. Look at their gestures. What are they doing?
3. What do the photos tell you about the community?

En contexto

VIDEO DVD AUDIO

VOCABULARIO

Francisco García Flores has just moved into his new community in Miami. He is getting to know the people there. Look at the illustrations. They will help you understand the meanings of the words in blue and answer the questions on the next page.

A La chica es Alma Cifuentes. El chico es Francisco García. Son amigos.

Alma: ¿Qué tal?
Francisco: Estoy bien, ¿y tú?
Alma: Regular.

B El policía vive en el apartamento.

C **Mujer:** Gracias.
Francisco: De nada.

CD-ROM Take-Home Tutor

D **La familia** García vive en **una casa. La señora** García es **doctora.**

Francisco: Alma, **te presento a** mi familia.
Señor García: Mucho gusto. **¿Cómo estás?**
Alma: **Bien, gracias. ¿Cómo está usted?**
Señor García: **No muy bien** hoy.

E **La mujer** es **maestra** y **la muchacha** es **estudiante.**

F **El hombre** es **el señor** Estrada. Alma es **una amiga.**

Alma: **Le presento a** mi amigo, Francisco.
Señor Estrada: Encantado. ¿Cómo estás?
Francisco: **Muy bien, gracias, ¿y usted?**
Señor Estrada: Si es lunes, **estoy terrible.**

Online Workbook
CLASSZONE.COM

Preguntas personales

1. ¿Tienes amigos?
2. ¿Eres maestro(a) o estudiante?
3. ¿Vives en un apartamento o en una casa?
4. ¿Cómo se llaman las personas de tu familia?
5. ¿Cómo estás hoy?

En vivo

VIDEO DVD AUDIO

DIÁLOGO

Alma | Francisco | David | Arturo | Sr. Estrada

PARA ESCUCHAR • STRATEGY: LISTENING

Listen to intonation A rising or falling voice (intonation) helps a listener understand meaning as much as individual words do. The voice often rises at the end of a question and falls at the end of a statement. Listen carefully. Can you tell which sentences are questions? Being a good listener will help you become a good speaker. When you speak, try to imitate the intonation.

¡Bienvenido!

1► **Alma:** Hola, me llamo Alma Cifuentes. Soy tu vecina. Ésa es mi casa.
Francisco: Mucho gusto, Alma.

5► **Francisco:** ¡Ay, David! Alma, te presento a David. David es el monstruo de Miami.
David: ¡No soy monstruo! ¡Y no soy de Miami!
Alma: Es un placer, señor David.

6► **Alma:** Pues, ¿de dónde son ustedes?
Francisco: Nosotros somos de muchos lugares. Mamá es de Puerto Rico. Papá es de México. Yo soy de Puerto Rico y David es de San Antonio.
Alma: Entonces, ¡bienvenido a Miami!

7► **Arturo:** ¡Alma, chica! ¿Qué tal?
Alma: Muy bien, gracias, Arturo. Arturo, te presento a Francisco García. Él es mi vecino.
Arturo: Francisco, es un placer.
Francisco: Igualmente, Arturo.

CD-ROM Take-Home Tutor

2► **Alma:** Y tú, ¿cómo te llamas?
Francisco: ¿Yo? Yo me llamo Francisco García Flores.
Alma: Encantada, Francisco.

3► **Francisco:** Papá, te presento a Alma Cifuentes. Alma, mi papá.
Sr. García: Es un placer, Alma.
Alma: Mucho gusto, señor García.

4► **Francisco:** Mamá, Alma Cifuentes. Alma, mi mamá.
Sra. García: Mucho gusto, Alma.
Alma: El gusto es mío, señora.

8► **Alma:** A Arturo le gusta mucho correr. A mí me gusta también. ¿Te gusta correr, Francisco?
Francisco: No, no me gusta mucho correr.

9► **Sr. Estrada:** ¡Alma! ¿Cómo estás hoy?
Alma: Muy bien, señor Estrada, ¿y usted?
Sr. Estrada: Hoy es lunes, ¿no? Si es lunes, estoy terrible.
Alma: Le presento a mi amigo Francisco.
Francisco: Es un placer, señor Estrada.

10► **Francisco:** Este concurso es muy interesante.

En acción

PARTE A Comprensión del diálogo

For Activities 1–2, refer to the dialog on pages 30–31.

Alma | Francisco | David | Arturo | Sr. Estrada

1 ¿Quién?

Escuchar ¿Quién habla: Alma, Francisco o el señor Estrada? *(Hint: Say who speaks.)*

1. «Soy tu vecina. Ésa es mi casa.»
2. «Nosotros somos de muchos lugares.»
3. «A Arturo le gusta mucho correr.»
4. «Si es lunes, estoy terrible.»
5. «Este concurso es muy interesante.»

2 ¿Cierto o falso?

Escuchar ¿Es cierto o falso? Si es falso, di lo que es cierto. *(Hint: True or false? If it is false, say what is true.)*

1. Alma es de San Antonio.
2. Francisco es el vecino de Arturo.
3. David no es de Miami.
4. Francisco dice: «Me gusta correr.»
5. Francisco dice que el concurso es interesante.
6. El señor Estrada está muy bien.

PARTE B Práctica del vocabulario

Objectives for Activities 3–5
- Introduce others

3 ¿Quién es?

Hablar Describe a las personas de la comunidad: **una chica, un chico, un muchacho, un hombre** o **una mujer.** *(Hint: Describe the people from the community.)*

modelo

*Es **un hombre.***

1.

2.

3.

4.

5.

Estados Unidos

También se dice

There are different ways to say *boy* and *girl* in Spanish.

- **chaval(a):** Spain
- **chavo(a):** Mexico
- **chico(a):** many countries
- **joven:** many countries
- **muchacho(a):** many countries
- **niño(a):** many countries
- **pibe(a):** Argentina

4 ¿Qué son?

Leer ¿Qué es cada persona de la comunidad de Alma: **estudiante, señora, maestra, mujer, doctora, policía** o **chica**? *(Hint: Say who each person from Alma's community is.)*

modelo

La __mujer__ *es doctora.*

1. La mujer es la _____ Durán.
2. La _____ es una vecina.
3. La señorita Galdós es _____.
4. El señor Durán es _____.
5. La muchacha es _____.
6. La mujer es _____.

5 ¿Quiénes son?

Escribir Escribe quién es y dónde vive. *(Hint: Write who each one is and where he or she lives.)*

modelo

la señorita Álvarez: 

***La señorita Álvarez** es maestra.*
*Vive en **un apartamento**.*

1. el señor Gómez: 
2. Alma: 
3. la señora García: 

PARTE C

Práctica: gramática y vocabulario

Objectives for Activities 6–19
- Greet others
- Introduce others
- Say where people are from
- Express likes

GRAMÁTICA Familiar and Formal Greetings

There are different ways to say *How are you?* in Spanish.

Familiar:

Mr. Estrada greets Alma by saying:

—¡Alma!
¿Cómo estás hoy?
Alma! ***How are you*** *today?*

¿Cómo estás? is a familiar greeting.

Use with:
- a friend
- a family member
- someone younger

Another familiar greeting: **¿Qué tal?**

Formal:

If Alma had spoken first, she might have said:

—¡Señor Estrada!
¿Cómo está usted?
Mr. Estrada! ***How are you?***

¿Cómo está usted? is a formal greeting.

Use with:
- a person you don't know
- someone older
- someone for whom you want to show respect

Tú is a familiar way to say *you*.

Usted is a formal way to say *you*.

Practice: Actividades 6 7 8

Más práctica *cuaderno p. 13*
Para hispanohablantes *cuaderno p. 11*

Online Workbook CLASSZONE.COM

6 ¿Quién dice qué?

Hablar ¿Quién habla? Trabaja con otro(a) estudiante para practicar las conversaciones. *(Hint: Who is speaking? Work with another student to practice the conversations.)*

1. Francisco y Arturo
2. Alma y el señor Estrada
3. David y el señor García
4. el señor Estrada y la señora García

a. —¿Cómo está usted?
—Muy bien, ¿y tú?

b. —¿Qué tal?
—Regular. ¿Y tú?

c. —¿Cómo está usted?
—Bien, ¿y usted?

d. —¿Cómo estás, papá?
—Muy bien, ¿y tú?

7 ¿Cómo estás? o ¿Cómo está usted?

Hablar/*Escribir* Pregúntale a cada persona cómo está. *(Hint: Ask each person how he or she is.)*

modelo
Juan
¿Cómo estás, ***Juan****?*

1. Antonio
2. señorita Díaz
3. Felipe
4. señor Castro
5. Luisa
6. señora Ramos
7. Paquita
8. doctora Flores

8 ¿Tú o usted?

Hablar Practica los saludos con otro(a) estudiante. Cambien de papel.
(Hint: Practice the greetings with another student. Change roles.)

STRATEGY: SPEAKING

Practice To become a good speaker, practice aloud—to yourself and with a partner. When talking with a partner, make it sound like a real conversation. Soon you'll be a good speaker of Spanish.

modelo

Juan–señor Álvarez

Juan: *¿Cómo está usted, señor Álvarez?*

Sr. Álvarez: *Bien, gracias, ¿y tú, Juan?*

Juan: *Regular.*

1. Pablo–Felipe
2. señora Ruiz–señor Muñoz
3. Francisco–señor Fernández
4. Juan–Julia
5. señora Campos–Susana
6. doctor Galindo–Pedro
7. Paulina–Ricardo
8. profesor Romero–Eva

GRAMÁTICA Describing People: Subject Pronouns and the Verb ser

To discuss people in Spanish, you will often use **subject pronouns**. When you want to describe a person or explain who he or she is, use the verb **ser.**

When Alma introduces Francisco to Arturo, she uses a **subject pronoun** with **ser.**

—**Él es** mi vecino.
He is *my neighbor.*

Francisco uses other examples.

—**Nosotros somos** de muchos lugares.
We are *from many places.*

—**Yo soy** de Puerto Rico.
I am *from Puerto Rico.*

Singular		Plural
yo soy *I am*		**nosotros(as) somos** *we are*
tú eres *you are*	*familiar*	**vosotros(as) sois** *you are*
usted es *you are*	*formal*	**ustedes son** *you are*
él, ella es *he, she is*		**ellos(as) son** *they are*

Vosotros(as) is only used in Spain.
Ustedes is formal in Spain; formal and familiar in Latin America.

If Alma were to say that someone is a neighbor, she would say:

—**Él es un** vecino.

However, if she were to say that someone is a policeman, she would say:

—**Él es** policía.

The word **un** or **una** does not appear before a profession.

Practice: Actividades 9 10 11 12

Más práctica *cuaderno p. 14*
Para hispanohablantes *cuaderno p. 12*

Online Workbook CLASSZONE.COM

9 ¡Descríbelos!

Leer Explica quién es cada persona de la comunidad. Usa cada pronombre sólo una vez. *(Hint: Explain who each person from the community is. Use each pronoun only once.)*

1. _____ eres doctora.	a. yo
2. _____ somos amigas.	b. tú
3. _____ es doctor.	c. usted
4. _____ son amigas.	d. él
5. _____ somos estudiantes.	e. ella
6. _____ son amigos.	f. nosotros
7. _____ es maestra.	g. nosotras
8. _____ soy estudiante.	h. ustedes
9. _____ son maestros.	i. ellos
10. _____ es policía.	j. ellas

10 ¡Escucha! ¿Quién es?

Escuchar Escoge la oración correcta para indicar quién es la persona. *(Hint: Choose the correct sentence to indicate who the person is.)*

1. **a.** Ella se llama Francisca.
   b. Él se llama Francisco.
2. **a.** Ellas son policías.
   b. Ellos son policías.
3. **a.** A él le gusta correr.
   b. A ella le gusta correr.
4. **a.** Ella no está bien.
   b. Él no está bien.
5. **a.** Ellos son estudiantes.
   b. Ellas son estudiantes.

11 ¿Quién es Francisco?

Hablar/Escribir Explica quiénes son las personas. *(Hint: Explain who the people are.)*

modelo

Francisco: estudiante

*Él es **Francisco.** Es **estudiante.***

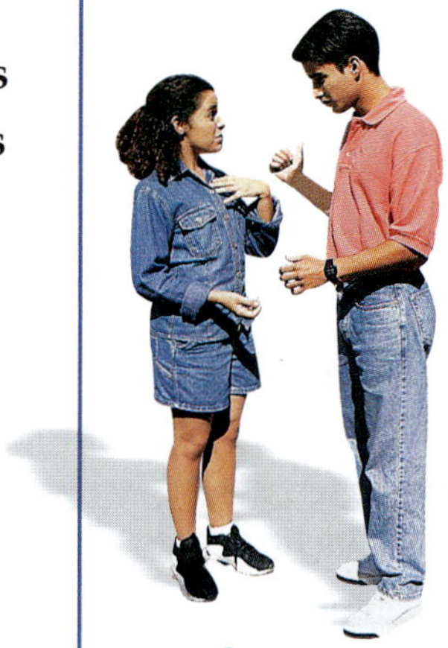

1.

2.

3.

4.

5.

6.

1. Francisco y Alma: amigos
2. la señora García: doctora
3. el señor Gómez: policía
4. Arturo: un amigo
5. Alma: estudiante
6. la señora Díaz y la señora Castro: maestras

12 Yo soy...

Escribir Decide la profesión de las personas de tu comunidad. Escribe cinco oraciones.
(Hint: Decide the profession of the people in your community. Write five sentences.)

modelo
Ella es doctora.

Nota: Gramática

To make a noun plural, add **-s** if it ends in a vowel, **-es** if it ends in a consonant: amiga**s**, doctor**es**.

1	2	3
yo él nosotros ellas tú ella ellos ustedes	eres soy somos es son	¿?

Estados Unidos

Nota cultural

Spanish is the native language of about half the residents of Miami. Cubans are the majority group within Spanish-speaking Miami, but there are people from all over the Spanish-speaking world here. When in Miami, you can use your Spanish to make new friends from all over the world without leaving the United States!

More Practice: **Más comunicación** *p. R1*

GRAMÁTICA Using ser de to Express Origin

To say where a person is from use: **ser** + **de** + **place**

—David **es de San Antonio.**

—Papá **es de México.**

Francisco says:
—Nosotros **somos de muchos lugares.**
*We **are from** many places.*

—Mamá **es de Puerto Rico.**
—Yo **soy de Puerto Rico.**

Practice: **Actividades** 13 14 15
Más práctica *cuaderno p. 15*
Para hispanohablantes *cuaderno p. 13*
Online Workbook CLASSZONE.COM

13 ¿De dónde son?

Hablar/Escribir ¿De dónde son los estudiantes de intercambio? *(Hint: Where are the exchange students from?)*

modelo

Elena / Argentina

Elena** es de **Argentina.

1. Carlos / España
2. tú / Panamá
3. Luisa / Colombia
4. nosotros / México
5. Ana y Felipe / Bolivia
6. Rita / Argentina
7. ellos / Chile
8. Carmen y yo / Costa Rica
9. ella / Miami
10. él / Los Ángeles

14 ¡Son de muchos lugares!

Hablar Estás en una comunidad nueva. Pregúntale a otro(a) estudiante de dónde son las personas. Cambien de papel. *(Hint: You are in a new community. Ask another student where the people are from. Change roles.)*

modelo

Ana: México

Estudiante A: *¿De dónde es **Ana**?*

Estudiante B: *Ella es de **México**.*

los policías: Chile

Estudiante B: *¿De dónde son los **policías**?*

Estudiante A: *Ellos son de **Chile**.*

1. los muchachos: Bolivia
2. la muchacha: Perú
3. Elena: Los Ángeles
4. Luisa: Ecuador
5. Ramón: Estados Unidos
6. las mujeres: Panamá
7. Paco: Bolivia
8. las estudiantes: San Antonio
9. Inés: Colombia
10. los hombres: Argentina

Estados Unidos

Nota cultural

Spanish influences are seen in Miami's architecture. The tower of this hotel was modeled after La Giralda, part of the cathedral in Sevilla, Spain.

15 ¡Somos de lugares diferentes!

Hablar/Escribir Imagínate que eres de otro lugar. Pregúntales a otros estudiantes de dónde son. Escribe una lista. *(Hint: Imagine you are from another place. Ask other students where they are from. Write a list.)*

modelo

Tú: *¿De dónde eres, Juan?*

Juan: *Soy de San Francisco.*

Nombre	Es de...
1. Juan	San Francisco
2.	
3.	
4.	
5.	

GRAMÁTICA Using Verbs to Talk About What You Like to Do

When you want to talk about what you like to do, use the phrase:

Me gusta + ***infinitive***

The ***infinitive*** is the basic form of a verb.

Other helpful phrases to talk about what people like:

Te gusta correr. *You like to run.*
Le gusta correr. *He/She likes to run.*
¿Te gusta correr? *Do you like to run?*
¿Le gusta correr? *Does he/she like to run?*

Arturo would say: —**Me gusta correr.**
I like to run.

To say someone doesn't like something, use **no** before the phrase.

—**No me gusta correr.**
*I **don't like** to run.*

Practice: 16 17 18

Más práctica *cuaderno p. 16*
Para hispanohablantes *cuaderno p. 14*

Online Workbook
CLASSZONE.COM

Vocabulario

Infinitives

bailar

leer

cantar

nadar

comer

patinar

escribir

trabajar

¿Qué te gusta?

16 Le gusta...

Hablar/Escribir Explica lo que le gusta o no le gusta hacer a cada persona. *(Hint: Explain what each person likes or doesn't like to do.)*

modelo

Marisol: correr (sí) — *Le gusta **correr**.*

tú: trabajar (no) — ***No** te gusta **trabajar**.*

1. Mario: comer (sí)
2. tú: escribir (no)
3. Susana: patinar (no)
4. yo: cantar (sí)
5. él: nadar (sí)
6. Elena: bailar (no)
7. tú: leer (sí)
8. yo: trabajar (sí)
9. ella: nadar (no)
10. tú: bailar (sí)

17 Preferencias

Hablar Pregúntale a otro(a) estudiante qué le gusta hacer. Cambien de papel. *(Hint: Ask another student what he or she likes to do. Change roles.)*

modelo

Estudiante A: *¿Te gusta patinar?*

Estudiante B: *Sí, me gusta **patinar**.*

Estudiante A
PREGUNTAS

¿Te gusta...?

1.

2.

3.

4.

5.

6.

Estudiante B
RESPUESTAS

Sí, me gusta...

No, no me gusta...

18 Me gusta

Hablar/*Escribir* Explica lo que te gusta y lo que no te gusta hacer. *(Hint: Explain what you like and don't like to do.)*

modelo

escribir

*Me gusta **escribir**.*

1. cantar
2. trabajar
3. patinar
4. comer
5. nadar
6. correr
7. bailar
8. leer
9. escribir
10. hablar

Apoyo para estudiar

Cracking the language code

Spanish is not translated English. Spanish has its own way of expressing ideas. Grammar is the rules for putting words together in order to make sense. How many expressions can you find where Spanish and English express the same idea differently? Think about these when practicing so you prepare yourself for real communication. Read Spanish examples carefully. Read English equivalents when you need help.

PARTE D Todo en acción

Activities 20–21 bring together all concepts presented.

19 Presentaciones

Hablar Trabaja en un grupo de tres. Tus amigos no se conocen. Preséntalos. *(**Hint:** Work in a group of three. Your friends don't know each other. Introduce them.)*

modelo

señor Estrada–David

Tú: *Señor Estrada, le presento a mi amigo, David.*

Señor Estrada: *Mucho gusto, David.*

David: *Igualmente, señor Estrada.*

Nota: Vocabulario

To make a formal introduction, use **Le presento a…**
To make a familiar introduction, use **Te presento a…**

1. Alma–Jorge
2. señora Delgado–Emilio
3. señora Blanco–Marcos
4. señorita Álvarez–Manuel
5. señor Gómez–Carlos
6. Diana–Timoteo
7. Arturo–David
8. Mónica–Carlos

Pronunciación

Refrán

Pronunciación de las vocales The vowels **a, e, i, o, u** are always pronounced the same way. One word in Spanish that uses all the vowels is the word for the animal known as a bat. It is **murciélago.** Try to pronounce it.

Here is a popular nonsense rhyme that children use when playing games. It is the Spanish version of "Eeny, meeny, miney, moe." Use it to practice vowels.

Tin, marín
de dos Pingüés
cúcara, mácara
títere, fue.

20 ¡Un nuevo amigo!

Escuchar Escucha lo que dice tu nuevo amigo. Contesta las preguntas. *(**Hint:** Listen to what your new friend says. Answer the questions.)*

1. ¿Cómo se llama el chico?
   a. Ángel
   b. Enrique
2. ¿De dónde es?
   a. Los Ángeles
   b. Miami
3. ¿Cómo está hoy?
   a. Muy bien.
   b. Bien.
4. ¿Qué le gusta hacer?
   a. bailar y patinar
   b. bailar y cantar
5. ¿Le gusta trabajar?
   a. sí
   b. no

21 ¿Quién eres tú?

Escribir Escribe algo de ti. *(**Hint:** Write about yourself.)*

modelo

¡Hola! Me llamo Elena. Yo soy de Miami. Vivo en un apartamento. Me gusta leer, bailar y cantar.

Nota: Vocabulario

To say what kind of home you live in, use the phrase **Vivo en…**

More Practice:

Más comunicación *p. R1*

Online Workbook
CLASSZONE.COM

AUDIO

En voces

LECTURA

PARA LEER • STRATEGY: READING

Preview graphics Think about how you read English. Do you check photos or other graphics before reading an article? View these graphics, then predict what this reading is about. After reading it, decide whether your prediction was on target or needs adjustment.

Los latinos de Estados Unidos

En Estados Unidos hay personas de muchos países de Latinoamérica.

Francisco: ¿Qué tal? Me llamo Francisco García Flores. Soy de Puerto Rico, pero vivo en Miami. El hombre de México es mi papá. La mujer es mi mamá.

PUERTO RICO

Sra. García: Me llamo Anita García. También soy de Puerto Rico pero trabajo como doctora en Miami.

MÉXICO

Sr. García: Buenos días. Yo me llamo Juan García. Soy de México. Vivo en Miami con mi familia.

CUBA

Sr. Estrada: Hola. Me llamo Felipe Estrada. Yo soy de Cuba, pero vivo en Miami.

CENTRO Y SUDAMÉRICA

Alma: Mi nombre es Alma. Soy de Colombia, pero también vivo en Miami.

Estados Unidos

Nota cultural

Francisco introduces himself as **Francisco García Flores. García** is his father's last name, and **Flores** is his mother's. In Spanish-speaking cultures most people use both last names. Some women add their husband's name after the word **de.** So Francisco's mother's name might be **Anita Flores de García** in many countries. In the U.S. some Spanish-speaking women use just their husband's name, as **Anita García** does here.

REPÚBLICA DOMINICANA

Arturo: Hola. Me llamo Arturo. Soy estudiante en Miami, pero soy de la República Dominicana.

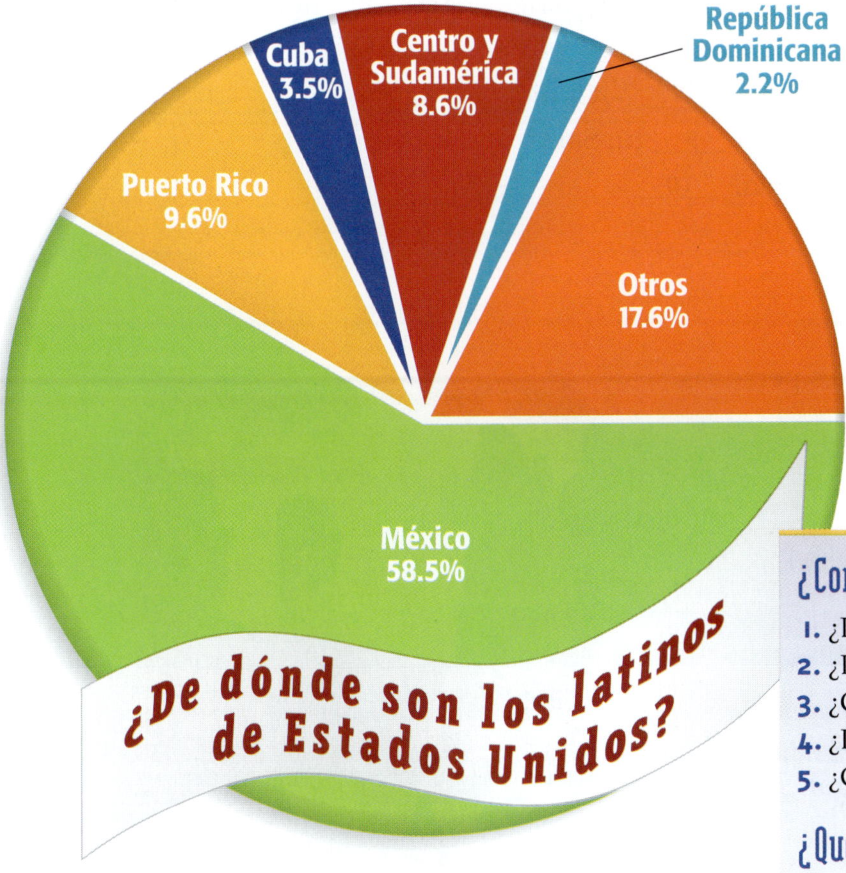

Online Workbook
CLASSZONE.COM

¿Comprendiste?

1. ¿De dónde es la doctora? ¿Cómo se llama?
2. ¿De dónde es el señor García?
3. ¿Cómo se llama el señor de Cuba?
4. ¿De dónde es la chica?
5. ¿Cómo se llama el estudiante? ¿De dónde es?

¿Qué piensas?

¿De dónde son los latinos de Estados Unidos? ¿De dónde son las personas de tu comunidad? Compara tu comunidad con la comunidad de Francisco.

ETAPA 1

En uso

REPASO Y MÁS COMUNICACIÓN

OBJECTIVES
- Greet others
- Introduce others
- Say where people are from
- Express likes

Now you can...
- greet others.

To review
- vocabulary for greetings, see p. 28.
- familiar and formal greetings, see p. 34.

1 ¡Hola!

Escuchas esta conversación en tu comunidad. Completa la conversación con las palabras apropiadas. *(Hint: You hear this conversation in your community. Complete the conversation with the appropriate words.)*

bien gusto está usted estás cómo tal tú gracias presento

Carlos: Hola, Sara. ¿Qué __1__?
Sara: Muy bien, gracias, ¿y __2__?
Carlos: No muy __3__. Hoy es lunes.
Sara: Carlos, te __4__ a mi maestro de español, el señor Sánchez.
Sr. Sánchez: Mucho __5__, Carlos. ¿__6__ estás?
Carlos: Estoy terrible. ¿Y __7__? ¿Cómo __8__ hoy?
Sr. Sánchez: Regular. ¿Cómo __9__ tú, Sara?
Sara: Estoy muy bien, __10__.

Now you can...
- introduce others.

To review
- making introductions, see p. 29 and p. 41.

2 Te presento a...

Presenta a las siguientes personas. *(Hint: Introduce the following people.)*

modelo
Daniela–Antonio
Daniela,** te presento a **Antonio.

1. doctora Cruz–Miguel
2. Jorge–Gabriel
3. señora Ramos–Eva
4. señor Orozco–Víctor
5. Celia–Yolanda
6. Pablo–Juan
7. señorita Quintana–Ana
8. Mónica–Octavio

Self-Check Quiz
CLASSZONE.COM

Now you can...
- say where people are from.

To review
- subject pronouns and the verb **ser,** see p. 35.
- **ser de** to express origin, see p. 37.

3 ¿Quiénes son?

Hay una fiesta. ¿Quiénes son y de dónde son estas personas?
*(**Hint:** Who are these people at a party and where are they from?)*

modelo

la señora Moreno: policía (Bolivia)
*Ella es **policía.** Es de **Bolivia.***

1. el señor Ortiz: maestro (Venezuela)
2. Julia: mi amiga (Paraguay)
3. tú: estudiante (Miami)
4. María y Rosa: amigas (Colombia)
5. Roberto y yo: vecinos (Chile)
6. usted: doctor (Puerto Rico)
7. la señora Romero: mi vecina (Los Ángeles)
8. José y yo: amigos (Guatemala)
9. yo: estudiante (Estados Unidos)
10. las mujeres: doctoras (Costa Rica)

Now you can...
- express likes.

To review
- verbs to talk about what you like to do, see p. 39.

4 Preferencias

¿Qué le gusta o no le gusta hacer? *(**Hint:** What does the person like or not like to do?)*

modelo

Marta: sí
Le gusta correr.

tú: no
No te gusta patinar.

1. Adriana: sí

2. la maestra: sí

3. tú: sí

4. ella: no

5. Raúl: no

6. yo: sí

7. yo: no

8. tú: sí

5 Nuevos amigos

STRATEGY: SPEAKING

Understand, then speak Make sure you understand what your partner says. If you don't, say **Repite, por favor** (Please repeat). Once you understand, speaking clearly helps make you understood.

Imagínate que eres un(a) nuevo(a) estudiante. Contesta las preguntas de otro(a) estudiante. Cambien de papel. *(**Hint:** Imagine you are a new student. Answer the questions of another student. Change roles.)*

1. ¿Cómo te llamas?
2. ¿Cómo estás hoy?
3. ¿De dónde eres?
4. ¿Te gusta...?

6 ¡Mucho gusto!

Usando la información de la Actividad 5, preséntale tu nuevo(a) amigo(a) a otro(a) estudiante o a tu maestro(a). *(**Hint:** Using the information from Activity 5, introduce your new friend to another student or to your teacher.)*

7 En tu propia voz

ESCRITURA Le escribes a un(a) amigo(a). Explícale quiénes son y de dónde son las personas de tu comunidad. ¡Usa la imaginación! *(**Hint:** Explain who the people in your community are and where they are from. Use your imagination!)*

¿Qué le gusta?

¿Quién?

¿De dónde es?

CONEXIONES

Los estudios sociales Compare Francisco's community with your own. Draw two intersecting circles. In one circle, write about the people in Francisco's new community. For example, Arturo is a student. Who are the people in your community? What do they do and where are they from originally? If they were all born in the U.S., do you know what country their families were originally from? Write about them in the second circle. What things does your circle have in common with Francisco's? List them where the two circles overlap.

Venn diagram

Flashcards
CLASSZONE.COM

En resumen

REPASO DE VOCABULARIO

SAYING WHERE PEOPLE ARE FROM

¿De dónde + ser...?	*Where is... from?*
ser de...	*to be from...*

People

el (la) amigo(a)	*friend*
la chica	*girl*
el chico	*boy*
la familia	*family*
el hombre	*man*
la muchacha	*girl*
el muchacho	*boy*
la mujer	*woman*
el señor	*Mr.*
la señora	*Mrs.*
la señorita	*Miss*

Professions

el (la) doctor(a)	*doctor*
el (la) estudiante	*student*
el (la) maestro(a)	*teacher*
el (la) policía	*police officer*

Subject Pronouns

yo	*I*
tú	*you (familiar singular)*
él	*he*
ella	*she*
usted	*you (formal singular)*
ustedes	*you (plural)*
nosotros(as)	*we*
vosotros(as)	*you (familiar plural)*
ellos(as)	*they*

Places

la comunidad	*community*
el mundo	*world*
el país	*country*

GREETING OTHERS

¿Cómo está usted?	*How are you? (formal)*
¿Cómo estás?	*How are you? (familiar)*
¿Qué tal?	*How is it going?*
Estoy...	*I am...*
(No muy) Bien, ¿y tú/usted?	*(Not very) Well, and you (familiar/formal)?*
Regular.	*So-so.*
Terrible.	*Terrible./Awful.*
Gracias.	*Thank you.*
De nada.	*You're welcome.*

INTRODUCING OTHERS

Te/Le presento a...	*Let me introduce you (familiar/formal) to...*

SAYING WHERE YOU LIVE

Vivo en...	*I live in...*
Vive en...	*He/She lives in...*
el apartamento	*apartment*
la casa	*house*

EXPRESSING LIKES

¿Te gusta...?	*Do you like...?*
¿Le gusta...?	*Does he/she like...?*
Me gusta...	*I like...*
Te gusta...	*You like...*
Le gusta...	*He/She likes...*

Activities

bailar	*to dance*
cantar	*to sing*
comer	*to eat*
correr	*to run*
escribir	*to write*
leer	*to read*
nadar	*to swim*
patinar	*to skate*
trabajar	*to work*

OTHER WORDS AND PHRASES

bienvenido(a)	*welcome*
el concurso	*contest*
el lugar	*place*
mucho/s(a/s)	*much, many*
no	*not*
o	*or*
pero	*but*
también	*also, too*
y	*and*

Juego

Le gusta bailar pero no le gusta correr. Le gusta leer pero no le gusta cantar. Le gusta nadar pero no le gusta comer mucho. ¿Qué actividades no le gusta hacer a Marisol?

UNIDAD 1

ETAPA 2

Mis buenos amigos

OBJECTIVES

- Describe others
- Give others' likes and dislikes
- Describe clothing

¿Qué ves?

Look at the photo of the River Walk in San Antonio.

1. What do the teenagers look like?
2. What have they been buying?
3. What handicrafts do you see in the photo?
4. Which street name do you think comes from Spanish?

SOY

En contexto

VIDEO DVD AUDIO

VOCABULARIO

Francisco's friends back in San Antonio are waiting to go to a Tejano music concert. Look at the illustrations. They will help you understand the meanings of the words in blue and answer the questions on the next page.

A Raúl, Rosalinda, Bill y Graciela son los amigos de Francisco.

Raúl es **cómico.**

Rosalinda es **bonita** y muy **inteligente.**

Bill (o Guillermo en español) es muy **simpático.** Tiene **un perro** que se llama Bud. Bud es **gordo.**

Graciela es **guapa.**

CD-ROM Take-Home Tutor

B Los mariachis llevan chaquetas y **pantalones negros.** Los sombreros son **grandes.**

C El hombre trabaja en el bote. Es muy **trabajador.** No es **perezoso.**

D El sombrero es grande. Los cascarones son **pequeños.** ¡Hay cascarones **azules** y **verdes**!

La chica es **paciente** y **seria.** **El gato** es **feo.**

Preguntas personales

Online Workbook CLASSZONE.COM

1. ¿Eres alto(a)?
2. ¿Tu pelo es largo o corto?
3. ¿Eres trabajador(a) o perezoso(a)?
4. ¿Eres rubio(a), moreno(a), castaño(a) o pelirrojo(a)?
5. ¿Cómo eres tú?

En vivo

VIDEO DVD AUDIO

DIÁLOGO

Raúl

Rosalinda

Graciela

Guillermo

PARA ESCUCHAR • STRATEGY: LISTENING

Listen to stress Voice emphasis (stress) helps you understand sentences with extra emotion. Listen for greater emphasis on the first word of the sentence. Can you hear that emphasis? When these stressed sentences are written, they have exclamation points. Don't look at the written words. Can you guess which sentences are being written with exclamation points as you listen?

Con los amigos...

1► **Alma:** ¡Paco! ¡Cuántas fotos!
Francisco: Son fotos de mis amigos y de mi familia. Son para el concurso.

5► **Alma:** Y la chica que lleva la blusa morada, ¿cómo se llama?
Francisco: Ella es mi amiga Rosalinda.
Alma: ¡Tiene el pelo largo!

6► **Alma:** Es muy bonita.
Francisco: También es muy inteligente. En el colegio, es seria y trabajadora. Le gusta mucho estudiar.

7► **Alma:** Y tu amiga pelirroja, ¿cómo se llama?
Francisco: Es Graciela. Graciela es muy simpática. Es mi mejor amiga.

CD-ROM Take-Home Tutor

2 ▶ **Francisco:** Tengo un video de mis amigos. ¿Te interesa?
Alma: ¡Claro que sí, cómo no!

3 ▶ **Alma:** ¡Qué divertidos son!
Francisco: Es verdad. Raúl es muy cómico. Raúl lleva jeans y una camiseta roja.

4 ▶ **Raúl:** Paco, ¿te gusta mi camiseta?
Alma: Raúl es muy guapo.
Francisco: ¡Por favor! ¡No digas eso! Es muy egoísta.

8 ▶ **Francisco:** Guillermo es rubio. Y su perro Bud, ¡es gordo! A Guillermo le gusta caminar con el perro.

9 ▶ **Francisco:** ¡Guillermo es fuerte! Pero es un poco perezoso.

10 ▶ **Alma:** ¡Qué buen amigo eres! ¡Y qué buenos amigos tienes! Pues, ahora tienes una nueva amiga…
Francisco: ¡Sí! ¡A los nuevos amigos!

En acción

PARTE B Práctica del vocabulario

Objectives for Activities 3–5
- Give others' likes and dislikes
- Describe others

PARTE A Comprensión del diálogo

For Activities 1–2, refer to the dialog on pages 52–53.

Raúl Rosalinda Graciela Guillermo

1 ¿Cierto o falso?

Escuchar ¿Es cierto o falso? Si es falso, di lo que es cierto. *(**Hint**: True or false? If it is false, say what is true.)*

1. Francisco tiene un video de sus amigos.
2. Los amigos de Francisco son de Miami.
3. Raúl no es cómico.
4. Alma dice: «Ahora tienes una nueva amiga.»
5. Para Francisco, los nuevos amigos son importantes.

2 ¿Quién es?

Escuchar ¿Quién es: Rosalinda, Graciela, Guillermo o Raúl? *(**Hint**: Who is it?)*

1. Es cómico y guapo.
2. Es seria y trabajadora.
3. Es pelirroja y simpática.
4. Es fuerte pero un poco perezoso.

3 ¿Te gusta?

Hablar/Escribir Habla con cinco estudiantes. ¿Qué le gusta hacer a cada uno? Completa un cuadro. *(**Hint**: Talk with five students. What does each one like to do? Complete a chart.)*

modelo

Tú: *Rosa, ¿te gusta **leer**?*
Rosa: *Sí, me gusta **leer**.*

Persona	Rosa	
patinar	sí	
leer	sí	
correr	no	
nadar	sí	
cantar	sí	
bailar	sí	

Estados Unidos

También se dice

Did you notice that Alma calls Francisco **Paco**? **Paco** is a nickname (**apodo**) for **Francisco.** Some other Spanish nicknames you might hear are **Beto** for **Alberto** or **Noberto, Tito** for **Antonio** or **Modesto, Lola** for **Dolores, Paquita** for **Francisca, Chela** for **Isabela** or **Mabel, Pepe** or **Cheo** for **José,** and **Cacho** for **Óscar.**

4 ¿Cómo es?

Hablar Describe a cada persona o animal, usando la palabra correcta. *(Hint: Describe each person or animal, using the correct word.)*

modelo

El gato es feo *. (bonito, feo)*

1.

2.

3.

4.

5.

6.

1. Ella tiene el pelo _____. (largo, corto)
2. El perro es _____. (grande, pequeño)
3. Él es _____. (gordo, delgado)
4. Ella es _____. (rubia, pelirroja)
5. El perro es _____. (trabajador, perezoso)
6. Él es _____. (alto, bajo)

5 La verdad es...

Hablar Tu amigo(a) no dice la verdad. Explica cómo es cada uno en realidad. Cambien de papel. *(Hint: Your friend doesn't tell the truth. Explain what each one is really like. Change roles.)*

modelo

Bud / delgado

Estudiante A: ***Bud** es **delgado.***

Estudiante B: *No es **delgado.** Es gordo.*

1. Raúl / rubio
2. Guillermo / moreno
3. Bud / trabajador
4. Rosalinda / alta
5. Graciela / rubia
6. Raúl / serio
7. el gato / guapo
8. Guillermo / castaño
9. Rosalinda / pelirroja
10. Graciela / fea
11. Raúl / bajo
12. Guillermo / gordo

PARTE C

Práctica: gramática y vocabulario

Objectives for Activities 6–18
- Describe others
- Describe clothing
- Give others' likes and dislikes

GRAMÁTICA Definite Articles with Specific Things

Nouns name people, animals, places, or things.

- All Spanish nouns have **masculine** or **feminine** gender.

  el chico **la chica**

- When nouns identify one item, they are **singular**.

  el amigo **la amiga**

- When they identify more than one item, they are **plural**.

  los amigos

In Spanish, the **definite article** that accompanies a noun will match its gender and number.

		Definite Article	Noun
Masculine	Singular	**el** *the*	chic**o** *boy*
	Plural	**los** *the*	chic**os** *boys*
Feminine	Singular	**la** *the*	chic**a** *girl*
	Plural	**las** *the*	chic**as** *girls*

(Article and noun: *matches gender*; *matches number*.)

Francisco says:

matches

—Son para **el** concurs**o**.
They are for the contest.

matches

—¡A **los** nuevos amig**os**!
To new friends!

To help you learn the gender of a noun, each **noun** is given with its definite article.

The gender of a noun must be learned. Usually
- nouns ending with **-o** are **masculine.**
- nouns ending with **-a** are **feminine.**

Practice:
Actividades 6 7

Más práctica
cuaderno p. 21
Para hispanohablantes
cuaderno p. 19

Online Workbook
CLASSZONE.COM

Apoyo para estudiar

Gender

Knowing the gender of nouns that refer to people is easy. But how do you learn the gender of things? When learning a new word, such as **camiseta,** say it with the definite article: **la camiseta.** Say it to yourself and say it aloud several times. That will help you remember its gender.

Vocabulario

La ropa

los calcetines

el sombrero

la camisa

el suéter

la chaqueta

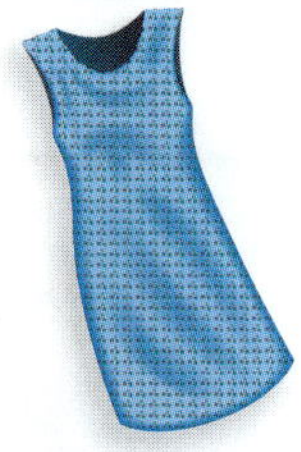
el vestido

los jeans

¿Cuál es tu ropa favorita?

6 Los vecinos de Raúl

Leer Raúl describe a sus vecinos. Completa sus oraciones con **el, la, los** o **las.** *(Hint: Raúl is describing his neighbors. Complete his sentences with the correct article.)*

1. _____ chicas son Ana y Luisa.
2. _____ señorita Madrigal es maestra.
3. _____ muchacho es Juan.
4. _____ hombres son doctores.
5. _____ muchachos son estudiantes.
6. _____ mujer es la señora Ramos.
7. _____ muchacha es estudiante.
8. _____ señoras son doctoras.
9. _____ señor Robles es policía.
10. _____ señores Suárez son maestros.

7 ¿Qué llevan?

Hablar/*Escribir* Explica lo que llevan Graciela y Rosalinda en su viaje. *(Hint: Explain what Graciela and Rosalinda are taking on their trip.)*

modelo

1. *el vestido*
2. *las blusas*

Graciela

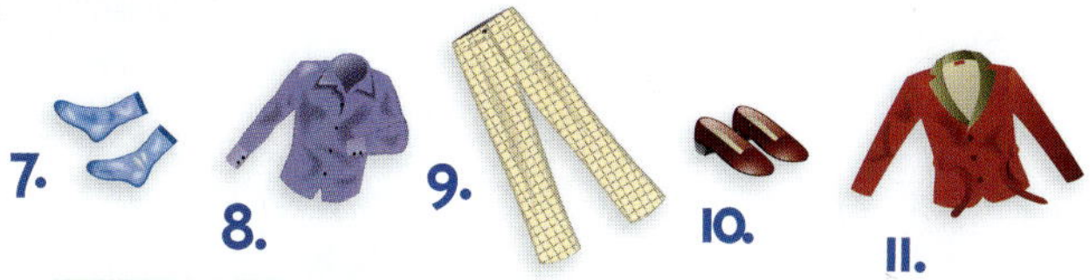

Rosalinda

GRAMÁTICA Indefinite Articles with Unspecified Things

A noun may sometimes appear with an indefinite article. The **indefinite article** that accompanies a noun will also match its gender and number.

		Indefinite Article	Noun
Masculine	Singular	**un** *a*	chic**o** *boy*
	Plural	**unos** *some*	chic**os** *boys*
Feminine	Singular	**una** *a*	chic**a** *girl*
	Plural	**unas** *some*	chic**as** *girls*

matches gender (un — chico); *matches number* (unos — chicos)

Francisco says:

—Raúl lleva **una** camiset**a**... (*matches gender*)

*Raúl wears **a** T-shirt...*

Practice: **Actividades** 8 9

Más práctica *cuaderno p. 22*
Para hispanohablantes *cuaderno p. 20*

Online Workbook CLASSZONE.COM

8 ¿Qué lleva?

Hablar Pregúntale a otro(a) estudiante qué lleva cada persona. Cambien de papel. *(Hint: Ask another student what each person is wearing. Change roles.)*

modelo

la chica

Estudiante A: *¿Qué lleva **la chica**?*

Estudiante B: *Ella lleva unos jeans y una camiseta.*

Nota: Vocabulario

To ask what a person is wearing, say **¿Qué lleva?** To answer, use **lleva.**

1. Guillermo

2. Rosalinda

3. el chico

4. Graciela

9 ¿Qué llevas tú?

Hablar/*Escribir* Explica lo que llevas para ir a cada lugar. *(Hint: Explain what you wear to each place.)*

modelo

Llevo unos jeans y un suéter.

Nota: Vocabulario

To say what you wear, use **llevo.**

1.

2.

3.

4.

Estados Unidos

También se dice

Different Spanish words can be used to talk about jeans. Sometimes the word **jeans** is used, just as in English. This is called a loan word. Other words are:

bluyines: many countries
mahones: Caribbean countries
mezclillas: Mexico
vaqueros: Argentina, Spain
tejanos: Spain

GRAMÁTICA Using Adjectives to Describe: Gender

Adjectives describe nouns. Like articles, they match the gender of the nouns they describe. In Spanish, adjectives usually follow the noun.

Masculine adjectives often end in **-o**.

agrees

el chico **guapo**

the good-looking boy

Feminine adjectives often end in **-a**.

agrees

la chica **guapa**

the good-looking girl

Most adjectives that end with **-e** match both genders.

el chico **paciente** ← *same word* → la chica **paciente**

Many adjectives that end with a **consonant** match both genders.

el chico **fenomenal** ← *same word* → la chica **fenomenal**

Some add **-a** to become feminine. These adjectives must be learned.

el chico **trabajador** —*becomes*→ la chica **trabajadora**

the hard-working boy / *the hard-working girl*

Practice:
Actividades 10 11

Más práctica
cuaderno p. 23
Para hispanohablantes
cuaderno p. 21

Online Workbook
CLASSZONE.COM

10 Los amigos de Francisco

Leer Tu amigo(a) es curioso(a). Descríbele a los amigos de Francisco. *(Hint: Your friend is curious. Describe Francisco's friends to him or her.)*

1. Graciela es una amiga _____ [simpático(a)].
2. Mónica es _____ [malo(a)].
3. Javier no es un chico muy _____ [interesante].
4. Rosalinda es una chica _____ [bonito(a)].
5. Felipe es un amigo _____ [aburrido(a)].
6. ¡Qué _____ [cómico(a)] es Raúl!
7. Linda es _____ [divertido(a)].
8. Es un perro muy _____ [inteligente].
9. ¡Qué _____ [fuerte] es Guillermo!
10. Alma es _____ [bueno(a)].

Vocabulario

Adjectives

aburrido(a) *boring*
bueno(a) *good*
divertido(a) *enjoyable*
fuerte *strong*
interesante *interesting*
malo(a) *bad*

¿Cómo eres?

11 ¡Todos son diferentes!

Hablar Tu amigo(a) no conoce a estas personas. Explícale cómo son. *(Hint: Your friend doesn't know these people. Explain what they're like.)*

modelo

Ana: interesante y guapo(a)

Estudiante A: *¿Cómo es **Ana**?*

Estudiante B: *Ella es **interesante y guapa.***

1. Graciela: interesante y divertido(a)
2. Guillermo: fuerte y trabajador(a)
3. Raúl: delgado(a) y simpático(a)
4. Rosalinda: moreno(a) y bonito(a)
5. tu amigo: ¿?
6. tu amiga: ¿?
7. tu vecina: ¿?
8. el (la) maestro(a): ¿?

Nota: Vocabulario

To ask what someone is like, use:
¿Cómo + ser + noun?

¿Cómo es Guillermo?

***What is** Guillermo **like**?*

More Practice: **Más comunicación** *p. R2*

Estados Unidos — Nota cultural

During **Fiesta** week in San Antonio, there is a **charreada,** or Mexican-style rodeo. The contestants, **los charros,** display equestrian skills developed from ranch work.

GRAMÁTICA Using Adjectives to Describe: Number

Adjectives must also match the number of the nouns they describe. To make an adjective plural, add **-s** if it ends with a vowel, **-es** if it ends with a consonant.

los chico**s**:
guapos, divertidos y **fenomenales**

las chica**s**:
guapas, divertidas y **fenomenales**

When an adjective describes a group with both genders, the **masculine** form of the adjective is used.

El chico y la chica son **guapos**.

Practice: 12 13 14 15 16 17 18

Más práctica *cuaderno p. 24*
Para hispanohablantes *cuaderno p. 22*

Online Workbook
CLASSZONE.COM

Vocabulario

Los colores

To ask what color something is, ask **¿De qué color es…?**

- **amarillo(a)**
- **anaranjado(a)**
- **azul**
- **blanco(a)**
- **marrón**
- **morado(a)**
- **negro(a)**
- **rojo(a)**
- **rosado(a)**
- **verde**

The plural of **marrón** is **marrones. Café** and **pardo(a)** are also *brown.*

¿Cuál es tu color favorito?

12 ¿De qué color es?

Hablar Tu amigo(a) está en una fiesta y tú estás en casa. Hablan por teléfono de la ropa que llevan las personas. Tu amigo(a) dice qué ropa llevan y de qué color es. Cambien de papel. *(Hint: Your friend at a party tells you over the phone about the clothing people are wearing. Work with a partner to say what the item is and its color. Change roles.)*

Roberto

modelo

Estudiante A: ***Roberto*** *lleva* ***una camisa*** *interesante.*

Estudiante B: *¿De qué color es* ***la camisa?***

Estudiante A: *Es roja.*

1. Guillermo

2. Francisco

3. Raúl

4. Alma

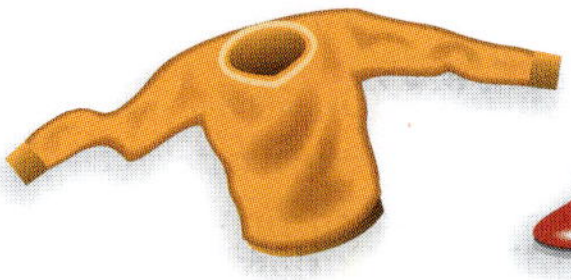

5. David

6. Rosalinda

7. Graciela

8. Ana

13 ¡Muchos colores!

Escuchar Raúl lleva ropa de muchos colores. Escucha y escribe los colores de la ropa. *(Hint: Raúl wears colorful clothing. Listen and write the color of the clothing.)*

1. los pantalones
2. la camisa
3. la chaqueta
4. los calcetines
5. los zapatos

14 Los ojos y el pelo

Hablar/Escribir Descríbele a un(a) amigo(a) los ojos y el pelo de Francisco y de sus amigos. *(Hint: Describe for a friend the eyes and hair of Francisco and his friends.)*

modelo

Francisco tiene los ojos marrones y el pelo corto. Es moreno.

Nota: Vocabulario

Tener means *to have*. Use **tiene** to talk about the features a person has.

1.

2.

3.

4.

15 ¿Qué lleva y qué le gusta?

Hablar/*Escribir* Estás con un(a) amigo(a). Él (Ella) quiere saber algo de estas personas. Describe qué lleva cada persona y qué le gusta hacer. *(Hint: You are with a friend. He/She wants to know something about these people. Describe what each person is wearing and what he or she likes to do.)*

modelo

Graciela: escribir

***Graciela** lleva una blusa blanca, una falda morada y zapatos negros. Le gusta **escribir**.*

1. Alma: correr

2. la Sra. García: trabajar

3. Guillermo: leer

4. Raúl: nadar

5. Rosalinda: cantar

16 ¿Qué lleva hoy?

Hablar/*Escribir* Descríbele a la clase la ropa que llevan cinco estudiantes. *(Hint: Describe for the class the clothing that five students have on.)*

Nombre	Lleva...
1. Juana	una falda marrón, una camisa blanca, unos zapatos marrones
2.	

17 Es...

Hablar Describe a una persona de la clase. Otro(a) estudiante tiene que adivinar quién es. *(Hint: Describe a person from your class. Another student must guess who it is.)*

modelo

Estudiante A: *Tiene el pelo corto y castaño. Tiene los ojos azules. Lleva una falda marrón, una camisa blanca y unos zapatos marrones.*

Estudiante B: *Es Juana.*

PARTE D

Todo en acción

Activities 19–20 bring together all concepts presented.

18 ¿Cómo son?

STRATEGY: SPEAKING

Trust your first impulse When speaking, your first impulse will usually be right. Speak! Making mistakes is natural, and you will make some when speaking. When you make a mistake, pause and correct yourself. Don't worry if you make a few mistakes!

Hablar Da tu opinión de cada persona. Cambien de papel. *(Hint: Give your opinion of each person. Change roles.)*

modelo

el señor Álvarez: el maestro / bueno

Estudiante A: *¿Cómo es **el señor Álvarez**?*

Estudiante B: *No es un **buen maestro.***
*o: Es un **buen maestro.***

Nota: Gramática

Sometimes an adjective may precede a noun. When the words **bueno** or **malo** precede a masculine singular noun, they are shortened to **buen** and **mal.** When **grande** precedes any singular noun, it becomes **gran** and its meaning changes to *great.*

1. Francisco: el estudiante / malo
2. la señorita Álvarez: la maestra / grande
3. Raúl: el amigo / grande
4. el señor Gómez: el policía / bueno
5. Alma: la vecina / malo
6. Rosalinda: la estudiante / bueno

Pronunciación

Trabalenguas

Pronunciación de la *f*, la *s* y la *ch* The letters **f** and **s**, and the combination **ch**, are pronounced the same in Spanish as they are in English. To practice the sounds, repeat these tongue twisters.

—¡Qué falda fantástica! —dice Sara Sánchez.

¿Con cuántas planchas plancha Pancha?

19 ¿Cómo es Teresa?

Escuchar Escucha el párrafo. ¿Son las oraciones ciertas o falsas? Si una oración es falsa, di lo que es cierto. *(Hint: Listen to the paragraph. Are the sentences true or false? If a sentence is false, say what is true.)*

1. Teresa es baja y rubia.
2. Ella tiene los ojos azules y el pelo largo.
3. En el colegio, es cómica y divertida.
4. Es una chica muy inteligente.
5. Le gusta bailar, pero no le gusta patinar.

20 ¿Cómo es tu amigo(a)?

Escribir Describe a un(a) amigo(a). Otro(a) estudiante va a dibujar según tu descripción. *(Hint: Describe a friend. Another student will draw your description.)*

modelo

Mi amiga Marta es baja y rubia. Tiene el pelo corto y los ojos azules. Lleva un vestido rojo. Ella es trabajadora y paciente. Le gusta leer y bailar. Es una buena estudiante.

More Practice:

Más comunicación *p. R2*

Online Workbook
CLASSZONE.COM

En colores

VIDEO DVD

CULTURA Y COMPARACIONES

PARA CONOCERNOS

STRATEGY: CONNECTING CULTURES

When learning about another language, you also learn about the people who speak it—their way of life, traditions, and contributions to the world. In addition, you learn to think about your own culture.

Recognize regional music Is there a kind of music unique to your area or that you like a lot? What people or events influenced its development? What instruments are used? (See p. R20 for the names of instruments in Spanish.) Compare this music to Tejano music, using a Venn diagram.

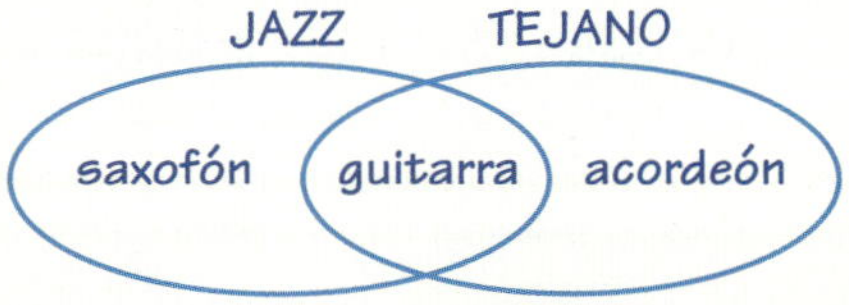

EL CONJUNTO

Un instrumento típico es el bajo sexto. Es una guitarra española grande. Tiene doce cuerdas[3].

[3] twelve strings

TEJANO 107 FM KXTN

Hay mucha música tejana en las estaciones de radio de San Antonio. También hay información en revistas[1] y periódicos[2].

[1] magazines [2] newspapers

Selena: una artista famosa de la música tejana

TEJANO

Los músicos de la foto llevan camisas negras, chaquetas y sombreros.

En San Antonio hay muchos grupos de música tejana. Un grupo de música tejana se llama «un conjunto tejano».

La música tejana tiene influencias de la música de Europa y de México. También tiene influencias de la música de Estados Unidos.

Otro instrumento típico es el acordeón. Tiene teclas[4] blancas y negras y un sonido[5] divertido.

[4] keys [5] sound

More About Latinos
CLASSZONE.COM

¿Comprendiste?

1. ¿Cómo se llama un grupo de música tejana?
2. ¿De dónde tiene influencias la música tejana?
3. ¿Cuáles son los instrumentos típicos?
4. ¿Qué es un bajo sexto?

¿Qué piensas?

1. ¿Cuál es tu música favorita?
2. ¿Cómo se llama tu grupo favorito? Compara el grupo con un conjunto tejano.

ETAPA 2

En uso

REPASO Y MÁS COMUNICACIÓN

OBJECTIVES

- Describe others
- Give others' likes and dislikes
- Describe clothing

Now you can...

- describe others.

To review

- definite and indefinite articles, see p. 56 and p. 57.
- adjectives, see p. 59 and p. 60.

1 La comunidad

Describe a las personas de la comunidad. *(Hint: Describe the people of the community.)*

modelo

ella: bueno(a) / amigo(a)

Ella** es una **buena amiga.

muchachos: estudiante / inteligente / trabajador(a)

*Los **muchachos** son **estudiantes inteligentes** y **trabajadores**.*

1. señora: maestro(a) / paciente / cómico(a)
2. muchacho: bueno(a) / amigo(a)
3. señores: policía / fuerte / simpático(a)
4. yo: estudiante / trabajador(a)
5. él: grande / maestro(a)
6. nosotros: estudiante / interesante / serio(a)
7. chico: malo(a) / estudiante
8. señoras: vecino(a) / aburrido(a) / perezoso(a)
9. tú: estudiante / inteligente
10. señor: bueno(a) / doctor(a)

Now you can...

- give others' likes and dislikes.

To review

- verbs to talk about what others like to do, see p. 54.

2 ¡Muy diferentes!

El señor García y la señora García son muy diferentes. Lee lo que al señor le gusta hacer y di lo que a la señora le gusta hacer. *(Hint: Mr. and Mrs. García are very different. Read what he likes to do and then tell what she likes to do.)*

modelo

Le gusta leer. (cantar)

*No **le gusta leer**. Le gusta **cantar**.*

1. Le gusta trabajar. (escuchar música)
2. Le gusta correr. (nadar)
3. Le gusta patinar. (bailar)
4. Le gusta llevar jeans. (llevar pantalones)
5. Le gusta comer pizza. (comer un sándwich)
6. Le gusta hablar. (escuchar)
7. Le gusta leer. (escribir)
8. Le gusta llevar una camiseta. (llevar una blusa)

Self-Check Quiz
CLASSZONE.COM

Now you can...
- describe clothing.

To review
- vocabulary for clothing, see p. 56.
- definite and indefinite articles, see p. 56 and p. 57.
- colors, see p. 60.

3 ¿Qué llevan?

¿Qué llevan estas personas hoy? *(**Hint**: Tell what they are wearing today.)*

modelo

chico

*El **chico** lleva **una camiseta amarilla** y **unos pantalones blancos.***

1. mujer

2. hombre

3. muchacho

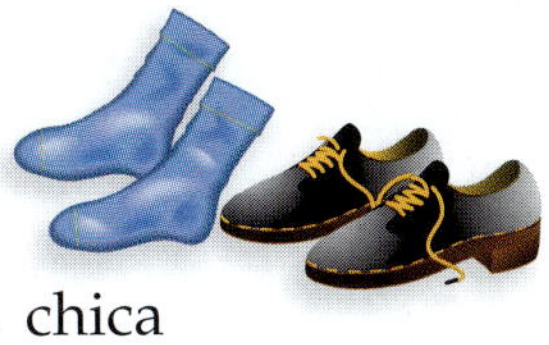

4. chica

5. señorita

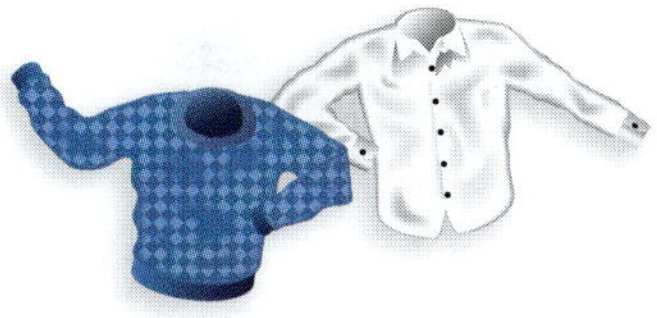

6. señor

Now you can...
- describe others.
- describe clothing.

To review
- vocabulary for clothing, see p. 56.
- adjectives, see p. 59 and p. 60.
- colors, see p. 60.

4 Mis amigos

Alma habla de sus amigos. ¿A quién describe?
*(**Hint**: Tell which friend Alma describes.)*

1. Es alto y tiene el pelo corto y negro.
2. Es bajo, feo y anaranjado.
3. Lleva una blusa blanca, una falda anaranjada y calcetines blancos.
4. Es pelirrojo y tiene una camisa blanca.
5. Tiene el pelo largo y rubio.
6. Lleva una chaqueta azul y pantalones negros.
7. Lleva una camiseta roja, jeans y zapatos blancos.
8. Es gordo y perezoso.
9. Lleva un suéter morado, pantalones amarillos y zapatos marrones.
10. Es alta y rubia.

5 Amigos

STRATEGY: SPEAKING

Think, plan, then speak Think about what you want to say. Rely on what you have practiced and memorized. Plan, then speak, using what you know.

Describe a uno de los amigos de Francisco. Incluye características y ropa. Otro(a) estudiante tiene que adivinar quién es. *(**Hint:** Describe one of Francisco's friends, including characteristics and clothing. Another student will guess who it is.)*

Raúl
Arturo
Guillermo
Alma
Rosalinda
Graciela

6 Los estudiantes de la clase

Describe a un(a) estudiante de la clase. Incluye características y ropa. Di lo que le gusta. La clase tiene que adivinar quién es. *(**Hint:** Describe a student in the class, including characteristics and clothing. Say what he or she likes. The class will guess who it is.)*

7 En tu propia voz

ESCRITURA Escribe una descripción de una persona famosa o popular. Incluye sus características, la ropa que lleva y las actividades que le gusta o no le gusta hacer. Lee la descripción mientras los otros estudiantes la dibujan y adivinan quién es. *(**Hint:** Write a description of a famous or popular person. Include characteristics, clothing, and what he or she likes to do. Read your description while other students draw it and guess who the person is.)*

modelo

Es gordo. Lleva una chaqueta roja y unos pantalones rojos. Tiene el pelo blanco. Es un hombre simpático. Le gusta comer.

Es Santa Claus.

CONEXIONES

La música Research music of the Spanish-speaking country of your choice. Report to the class. Your presentation may use writing, drawing, and/or music recordings. To learn the names of common instruments, see p. R20. Use **ser** and **tiene** to describe the music. For example, **Es música interesante y divertida.** As you hear your classmates' reports, write down the characteristics of the different types of music. Which ones are similar?

	MÚSICA TEJANA
INFLUENCIAS	Europa, México, Estados Unidos
¿CÓMO ES?	divertida
LOS MÚSICOS LLEVAN...	jeans
INSTRUMENTOS	acordeón, bajo sexto

En resumen

REPASO DE VOCABULARIO

DESCRIBING OTHERS

¿Cómo es?	*What is he/she like?*

Appearance

alto(a)	*tall*
bajo(a)	*short (height)*
bonito(a)	*pretty*
castaño(a)	*brown (hair)*
corto(a)	*short (length)*
delgado(a)	*thin*
feo(a)	*ugly*
fuerte	*strong*
gordo(a)	*fat*
grande	*big, large; great*
guapo(a)	*good-looking*
largo(a)	*long*
moreno(a)	*dark hair and skin*
pelirrojo(a)	*redhead*
pequeño(a)	*small*
rubio(a)	*blond*

Features

Tiene...	*He/She has...*
los ojos (verdes, azules)	*(green, blue) eyes*
el pelo (rubio, castaño)	*(blond, brown) hair*

Personality

aburrido(a)	*boring*
bueno(a)	*good*
cómico(a)	*funny, comical*
divertido(a)	*enjoyable, fun*
inteligente	*intelligent*
interesante	*interesting*
malo(a)	*bad*
paciente	*patient*
perezoso(a)	*lazy*
serio(a)	*serious*
simpático(a)	*nice*
trabajador(a)	*hard-working*

DESCRIBING CLOTHING

What one is wearing

¿De qué color...?	*What color...?*
Llevo.../Lleva...	*I wear...He/She wears...*
¿Qué lleva?	*What is he/she wearing?*

Clothing

la blusa	*blouse*
el calcetín	*sock*
la camisa	*shirt*
la camiseta	*T-shirt*
la chaqueta	*jacket*
la falda	*skirt*
los jeans	*jeans*
los pantalones	*pants*
la ropa	*clothing*
el sombrero	*hat*
el suéter	*sweater*
el vestido	*dress*
el zapato	*shoe*

Colors

amarillo(a)	*yellow*
anaranjado(a)	*orange*
azul	*blue*
blanco(a)	*white*
marrón	*brown*
morado(a)	*purple*
negro(a)	*black*
rojo(a)	*red*
rosado(a)	*pink*
verde	*green*

OTHER WORDS AND PHRASES

la bolsa	*bag*
el (la) gato(a)	*cat*
el (la) perro(a)	*dog*
nuevo(a)	*new*
otro(a)	*other, another*
pues	*well*
¡No digas eso!	*Don't say that!*
¡Qué (divertido)!	*How (fun)!*
Es verdad.	*It's true.*

Juego

La mujer alta tiene el pelo corto y negro. Lleva una chaqueta azul y una falda larga. ¿Quién es?

a.

b.

c.

UNIDAD 1

ETAPA 3

Te presento a mi familia

OBJECTIVES

- Describe family
- Ask and tell ages
- Talk about birthdays
- Give dates
- Express possession

¿Qué ves?

Look at the photo of a home in Los Angeles.

1. Describe the people.
2. What do you think their relationships are?
3. What is each person doing?
4. Where in the United States might you see houses like this one?

En contexto

VIDEO DVD AUDIO

VOCABULARIO

Francisco's cousin Verónica is having a party for her fifteenth birthday. Look at the illustrations. They will help you understand the meanings of the words in blue and answer the questions on the next page.

A Hoy es **una fecha** muy especial. Es **el cumpleaños** de Verónica. Ella está **feliz. ¿Cuántos años tiene** ella? Tiene **quince años** de **edad.** ¡Tiene una fiesta quinceañera!

B Los señores García son los más **viejos** de la familia. Son **los abuelos** de Verónica. Javier y Juan García son **los hijos** de ellos.

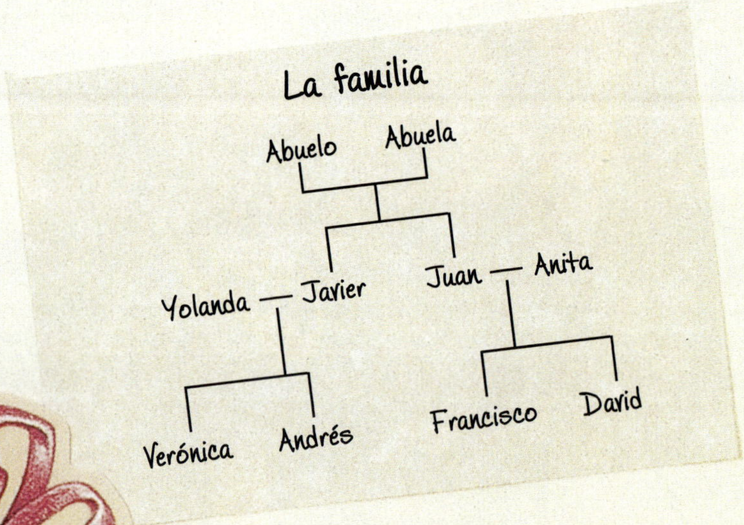

CD-ROM Take-Home Tutor

C **Los padres** de Verónica tienen una familia simpática. Verónica y Andrés son **hermanos.** Andrés es **joven.** Es **el hermano menor** de Verónica. Verónica es **la hija** y Andrés es **el hijo** de Javier y Yolanda. Verónica es la hija **mayor.**

D Los padres de Francisco son **los tíos** de Verónica. Verónica es **la prima** de Francisco y de David.

Otras palabras para hablar de la familia:

el (la) esposo(a) husband (wife)
el (la) hermanastro(a) stepbrother (stepsister)
la madrastra stepmother
el (la) medio(a) hermano(a) half-brother (half-sister)
el (la) nieto(a) grandson (granddaughter)
el padrastro stepfather

Online Workbook CLASSZONE.COM

Preguntas personales

1. ¿Tienes primos? ¿Tíos? ¿Abuelos?
2. ¿Tu familia es grande o pequeña?
3. ¿Tienes hermanos mayores o menores?
4. ¿Cuántos hermanos tienes?
5. ¿Cómo se llaman tus padres? ¿Tus hermanos?

En vivo

VIDEO DVD AUDIO

DIÁLOGO

Javier

Verónica

Yolanda

Andrés

PARA ESCUCHAR • STRATEGIES: LISTENING

Visualize As you listen, point to the images that you hear named. Link the image and the name. This helps you learn and remember.

Get the main idea In order to understand, listen first to try to get the general idea of what is happening. What is the general topic of conversation between Francisco and Alma here?

Con la familia...

1 ▸ **Alma:** ¿Y quién es este señor?
Francisco: Es mi tío Javier. La foto es de su cumpleaños. Tiene ahora 39 años. Es el hermano menor de mi papá.

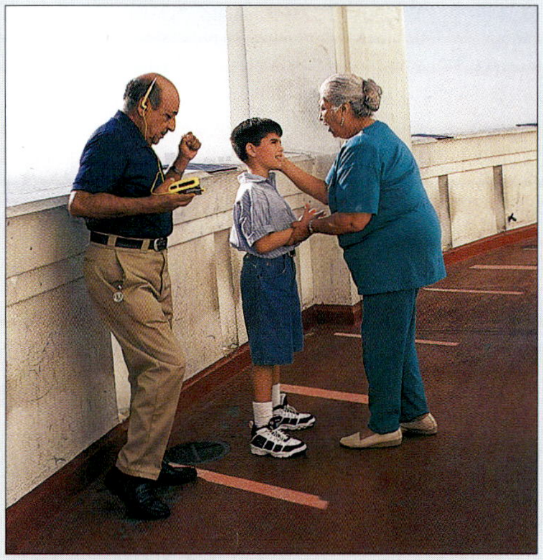

5 ▸ **Alma:** Y esta familia, ¿quién es?
Francisco: Bueno, éstos son mis abuelos.

6 ▸ **Alma:** ¡Qué simpáticos son tus abuelos!
Francisco: Son muy activos. Mi abuelo siempre dice: «Soy viejo por fuera pero soy joven por dentro.»

7 ▸ **Alma:** Y tu abuela, ¿cómo es?
Francisco: Mi abuela es muy paciente, especialmente con sus queridos nietos. Ella adora a sus nietos.

CD-ROM Take-Home Tutor

2 ► **Francisco:** Es artista. Le gusta pintar murales. Hay muchos murales en la ciudad de Los Ángeles.

Alma: ¡Ay! ¡Qué chévere!

3 ► **Alma:** Y esta chica, ¿quién es?

Francisco: ¡Oh!, ¿esa chica? Esa chica es mi prima Verónica. Verónica es muy divertida.

4 ► **Alma:** ¿Qué edad tiene Verónica?

Francisco: Pues, su cumpleaños es en octubre. Así que ahora tiene quince años. Verónica es muy atlética.

8 ► **Alma:** ¿Quién es la mujer que está con tu tío Javier?

Francisco: Ella es su esposa. Es mi tía Yolanda.

9 ► **Francisco:** Ellos son los hijos de mi tío Javier y mi tía Yolanda.

Alma: ¡Ah, sí!, ésa es tu prima.

Francisco: Sí, y él es Andrés, mi primo.

Alma: ¿Cuántos años tiene Andrés?

Francisco: Andrés tiene siete años.

10 ► **Alma:** Tu familia es muy fotogénica.

Francisco: Gracias, Alma. Oye, ¿cuál es la fecha de hoy?

Alma: El once de noviembre. ¿Por qué?

Francisco: ¡Ay! Sólo tengo diez días más para el concurso.

En acción

PARTE B Práctica del vocabulario

Objectives for Activities 3–5
- Describe family
- Talk about birthdays

PARTE A Comprensión del diálogo

For Activities 1–2, refer to the dialog on pages 74–75.

Javier

Verónica

Yolanda

Andrés

1 ¿Quién es?

Escuchar ¿Quién es cada persona? *(Hint: Who is each person?)*

1. Le gusta pintar murales.
2. Es muy atlética.
3. Tiene siete años.
4. Es la tía de Francisco.
5. Tiene quince años.

2 ¿Cierto o falso?

Escuchar ¿Es cierto o falso? Si es falso, di lo que es cierto. *(Hint: True or false? If it is false, say what is true.)*

1. Javier es el tío de Andrés.
2. Verónica es la prima de Francisco.
3. Andrés es el hermano mayor de Verónica.
4. Yolanda es la abuela de Javier.
5. Verónica y Andrés son los hijos de Javier y Yolanda.

3 La familia

Leer Explica quiénes son los miembros de la familia de Francisco, usando la palabra correcta: **abuelos, primo, prima, hermano, tía, tío, tíos, madre, padre, padres.** *(Hint: Explain who the members of Francisco's family are.)*

1. Verónica es la _____ de Francisco.
2. Yolanda y Javier son los _____ de él.
3. David es su _____.
4. Andrés es su _____.
5. Juan y Anita son sus _____.
6. Los señores García mayores son sus _____.
7. Anita es su _____.
8. Yolanda es su _____.
9. Javier es su _____.
10. Juan es su _____.

Estados Unidos

También se dice

Alma says **¡Qué chévere!** in the dialog. There are many ways to say *How awesome!* in Spanish.

- **¡Qué bárbaro!:** Argentina
- **¡Qué guay!:** Spain
- **¡Qué buena nota!:** Ecuador
- **¡Qué padre!:** Mexico

4 ¿Cómo son?

Hablar/*Escribir* Describe a las personas de Los Ángeles. *(Hint: Describe the people from Los Angeles.)*

modelo

Francisco

Francisco es alto, delgado y moreno. Es joven y simpático. Tiene el pelo corto.

1. Andrés **2.** Verónica **3.** Rafael

4. el abuelo **5.** la abuela **6.** Yolanda **7.** Javier

5 ¡Una familia simpática!

Leer Describe a la familia de Verónica, usando **los padres, el cumpleaños, la hermana, los hijos, el hermano, la familia, mayor, quince, los abuelos** o **menor.** *(Hint: Describe Veronica's family.)*

1. _____ García es pequeña.
2. Los señores García son _____ de Verónica.
3. Verónica es _____ de Andrés.
4. Ella es la hermana _____.
5. Yolanda y Javier son _____ de Andrés.
6. Andrés es _____ de Verónica.
7. Él es el hermano _____ de ella.
8. Verónica y Andrés son ____ de Yolanda y Javier.
9. Hoy es _____ de Verónica.
10. Ella tiene _____ años.

Práctica: gramática y vocabulario

Objectives for Activities 6–18

• Describe family • Ask and tell ages • Express possession • Give dates • Talk about birthdays

GRAMÁTICA Saying What You Have: The Verb **tener**

When you want to talk about what you have, use the verb **tener.**

yo	**tengo**	nosotros(as)	**tenemos**
tú	**tienes**	vosotros(as)	**tenéis**
usted, él, ella	**tiene**	ustedes, ellos(as)	**tienen**

Francisco says:

—¡Sólo **tengo** diez días más!
*I **have** only ten more days!*

Tener is also used to talk about how old a person is.

—**¿Cuántos años tiene** Verónica?
*How old **is** Veronica?*

—**Tiene** quince **años.**
***She is** fifteen years old.*

Practice: **Actividades** 6 7 8 9

Más práctica *cuaderno p. 29*
Para hispanohablantes *cuaderno p. 27*

Online Workbook CLASSZONE.COM

6 ¡Unas familias interesantes!

Hablar Explica cómo son los miembros de las familias de estas personas. *(Hint: Explain what the family members of these people are like.)*

modelo

ella: hermana / inteligente ***Ella** tiene una **hermana inteligente.***

1. Paco: prima / cómico(a)
2. Alma: hermana / trabajador(a)
3. Verónica: tía / bonito(a)
4. los señores García: hijo / activo(a)
5. Verónica y Andrés: primos / aburrido(a)
6. nosotros: padres / ¿?
7. yo: tío / ¿?
8. mi familia y yo: abuelos / ¿?
9. tú: hermano(a) / ¿?
10. yo: familia / ¿?

Estados Unidos

Nota cultural

The oldest house currently standing in Los Angeles is the Avila Adobe, located on Olvera Street, in the city's historic center. It was built as a home for the rancher Francisco Abela in 1818, a time when California was part of Mexico, not the United States!

7 ¿Qué edad?

Escribir Explica cuántos años tiene cada persona. *(Hint: Explain how old each person is.)*

modelo

la abuela: 70 — ***La abuela** tiene **setenta** años.*

1. Andrés: 7
2. Verónica: 15
3. Javier: 39
4. yo: ¿?
5. mis padres: ¿?
6. mi amigo(a): ¿?

Vocabulario

Los números de 11 a 100

11	**once**	25	**veinticinco**
12	**doce**	26	**veintiséis**
13	**trece**	27	**veintisiete**
14	**catorce**	28	**veintiocho**
15	**quince**	29	**veintinueve**
16	**dieciséis**	30	**treinta**
17	**diecisiete**	31	**treinta y uno**
18	**dieciocho**	40	**cuarenta**
19	**diecinueve**	50	**cincuenta**
20	**veinte**	60	**sesenta**
21	**veintiuno**	70	**setenta**
22	**veintidós**	80	**ochenta**
23	**veintitrés**	90	**noventa**
24	**veinticuatro**	100	**cien**

For 21, 31, and so on, use **veintiún, treinta y un,** and so on before a masculine noun and **veintiuna, treinta y una,** and so on before a feminine noun.

Tengo **veintiún** años. Tienes **treinta y una** camisetas.

¿Cuántos años tienes?

8 La familia de Antonio

Escuchar Lee las preguntas. Luego, escucha lo que dice Antonio de su familia. Escoge la respuesta correcta. *(Hint: Listen to what Antonio says about his family. Then answer the questions.)*

1. ¿Cómo se llama el hermano menor de Antonio?
   a. Alberto **b.** Andrés
2. ¿Cuántos años tiene Andrés?
   a. 8 **b.** 17
3. ¿Quién es Luisa?
   a. su madre **b.** su hermana
4. ¿Quiénes son Rosa y Alberto?
   a. sus abuelos **b.** sus padres
5. ¿Cómo son Marta y Rafael?
   a. viejos y divertidos **b.** jóvenes y divertidos

9 ¿Cuántos años?

Hablar Pregúntale a otro(a) estudiante cuántos años tiene cada persona. *(Hint: Ask another student how old each person is.)*

modelo

tu madre

Estudiante A: *¿Cuántos años tiene **tu madre**?*

Estudiante B: *Tiene cuarenta años.*

1. tu padre
2. tú
3. tu abuelo(a)
4. tu tío(a)
5. tu amigo(a)
6. tu madre

More Practice: **Más comunicación** *p. R3*

GRAMÁTICA Expressing Possession Using de

In English, you express possession by adding **'s** to the **noun** that refers to the possessor. In Spanish, you use the preposition **de** to refer to the **possessor.**

el hermano **de papá**
Dad's brother

los hijos **de Javier**
Javier's children

Practice: Actividades 10 11 12

Más práctica *cuaderno p. 30*
Para hispanohablantes *cuaderno p. 28*

Online Workbook
CLASSZONE.COM

10 La ropa de...

Hablar Cada persona escoge su ropa para una fiesta. Di de quién es cada cosa. *(Hint: Everyone is choosing clothing for a party. Say whose each item is.)*

Andrés

modelo
*Es **la camisa** de **Andrés.***

1. Verónica

2. Javier

3. Juan

4. Anita

5. Yolanda

6. David

Estados Unidos

Nota cultural

The early Spanish settlers of Los Angeles developed land into ranches, or **haciendas.** The names of many **haciendas** have survived as street names, such as **Los Feliz, Verdugos,** and **Sepúlveda.**

11 La familia de Rafael Ramos

Hablar/*Escribir* Explica la relación entre las personas. *(Hint: Explain the relationship between the people.)*

modelo

Teresa–Rafael y Lucía

Teresa** es la abuela de **Rafael y Lucía.

Javier y Yolanda–Rafael

Javier y Yolanda** son los tíos de **Rafael.

1. Carolina–Andrés
2. Carlos–Yolanda y Guillermo
3. Lucía–Verónica
4. Rafael–Lucía
5. Teresa y Carlos–Rafael y Lucía
6. Rafael y Lucía–Guillermo y Carolina
7. Guillermo y Carolina–Rafael y Lucía
8. Rafael y Lucía–Andrés y Verónica

12 ¿De quién es?

STRATEGY: SPEAKING

Rehearse Practicing with a partner is a rehearsal for real conversation, so make the most of it. Think of real situations where you can use what you are practicing, such as asking about what people in the class are wearing.

Hablar Trabaja con otro(a) estudiante para explicar de quién es la ropa. Cambien de papel. *(Hint: Work with another person to explain whose clothing it is. Change roles.)*

modelo

Estudiante A: *¿De quién es la **chaqueta**?*

Estudiante B: *Es de **Francisco.***

Nota: Vocabulario

Use the expression **¿De quién es...?** to ask who owns something. To answer, use **Es de...**

1. falda: Verónica
2. vestido: Anita
3. suéter: Andrés
4. camiseta: Javier
5. blusa: la abuela
6. ¿?

GRAMÁTICA Expressing Possession: Possessive Adjectives

Possessive adjectives tell you who owns something or describe a relationship between people or things. In Spanish, possessive adjectives agree in number with the nouns they describe.

Singular Possessive Adjectives		Plural Possessive Adjectives	
mi *my*	**nuestro(a)** *our*	**mis** *my*	**nuestros(as)** *our*
tu *your (familiar)*	**vuestro(a)** *your (familiar)*	**tus** *your (familiar)*	**vuestros(as)** *your (familiar)*
su *your*	**su** *your*	**sus** *your*	**sus** *your*
su *his, her, its*	**su** *their*	**sus** *his, her, its*	**sus** *their*

Francisco would say: —Es **mi** tío.
*He is **my** uncle.*

—Son **mis** abuelos.
*They are **my** grandparents.*

The adjectives **nuestro(a)** and **vuestro(a)** must also agree in gender with the nouns they describe.

agrees
nuestr**o** abuel**o**

agrees
nuestr**a** abuel**a**

agrees
nuestr**os** abuel**os**

agrees
nuestr**as** abuel**as**

If you need to emphasize, substitute the adjective with:

de + **pronoun** or the person's name

This also helps to clarify the meaning of **su** and **sus.**

Es **su** tío. —*becomes*→ Es el tío **de él**.

de usted, él, ella
de nosotros(as)
de vosotros(as)
de ustedes, ellos(as)

Practice: **Actividades** 13 14 15

Más práctica *cuaderno p. 31*
Para hispanohablantes *cuaderno p. 29*

Online Workbook CLASSZONE.COM

13 ¿De quién es la ropa?

Hablar Ves mucha ropa. No sabes de quién es. Pregúntale a otro(a) estudiante si es de él o ella. Cambien de papel. *(Hint: You see some clothing. You don't know whose it is. Ask another student if it's his or hers. Change roles.)*

modelo

chaqueta (no)

Estudiante A: *¿Es tu **chaqueta**?*

Estudiante B: ***No, no** es mi **chaqueta.***

1. suéter (sí)
2. camisas (sí)
3. blusa (no)
4. pantalones (no)
5. zapatos (sí)
6. falda (no)
7. camiseta (no)
8. calcetines (sí)
9. vestido (no)
10. jeans (sí)

14 ¿Quiénes son?

Hablar Estás en la casa de tus amigos para una fiesta. Pregúntale a uno de ellos quién es cada persona. Cambien de papel. *(Hint: You're at your friends' house for a party. Ask one of them who everyone is. Change roles.)*

modelo

abuelo

Estudiante A: *¿Quién es?*

Estudiante B: *Es nuestro abuelo.*

abuelos

Estudiante B: *¿Quiénes son?*

Estudiante A: *Son nuestros **abuelos**.*

Nota: Vocabulario

When you want to ask who a person is, use the expression **¿Quién es?** When you want to ask who several people are, use **¿Quiénes son?**

1. tía
2. primo
3. hermanas
4. padres
5. tío
6. primas
7. abuela
8. vecinos
9. vecina
10. hermano

15 ¿De quién es la camisa?

Hablar En tu casa tienes ropa de muchas personas. Otro(a) estudiante te pregunta de quién es. *(Hint: You have many people's clothes in your house. Another student asks you whose they are.)*

modelo

camisa / tu hermano

Estudiante: *¿**La camisa** es de **tu hermano**?*

Tú: *Sí, es su camisa.*

1. pantalones / David
2. vestido / tu tía
3. blusas / ellas
4. calcetines / tu padre
5. falda / tu abuela
6. chaquetas / tus abuelos
7. zapatos / Susana
8. camisetas / Rafael

Juego

Marco tiene un hermano. José tiene un año. El hermano de Marco se llama José. ¿Cuántos años tiene el hermano de Marco?

16 En la clase

Hablar/*Escribir* Explica cuántas personas de cada tipo hay en la clase. *(Hint: Explain how many of each type of person there are in the class.)*

Nota: Vocabulario

The word **hay** is used to mean *there is* or *there are*.

Hay muchos murales en la ciudad de Los Ángeles.
***There are** many murals in the city of Los Angeles.*

Hay un concurso muy interesante.
***There is** a very interesting contest.*

To say that there are none, use **No hay...**

1. chicas castañas
2. chicos castaños
3. chicos rubios
4. chicas rubias
5. chicos morenos
6. chicas morenas
7. chicos pelirrojos
8. chicas pelirrojas
9. chicos
10. maestros

Estados Unidos

Nota cultural

In Spanish-speaking countries, the date is written with the number of the day first, then the number of the month.

el dos de mayo = 2/5

GRAMÁTICA Giving Dates: Day and Month

When you want to give the date, use the following phrase:

Es el + **number** + **de** + month.

—¿Cuál es la fecha de hoy?
What is the date today?

—Hoy **es el once de** noviembre.
*Today **is the eleventh of** November.*

Notice that the names of months are not capitalized in Spanish.

In Spanish, the only date that does not follow this pattern is the first of the month.

Es el primero de noviembre.
***It is** November **first**.*

Practice: Actividades 17 18

Más práctica *cuaderno* p. 32
Para hispanohablantes *cuaderno* p. 30

Online Workbook CLASSZONE.COM

Vocabulario

Los meses del año

¿Cuál es tu mes favorito?

PARTE D

Todo en acción

Activities 19–20 bring together all concepts presented.

17 La familia de de Francisco

Escribir Explica cuándo son los cumpleaños. *(**Hint:** Explain when their birthdays are.)*

modelo

Francisco: 15/3

*El cumpleaños de **Francisco** es el **quince de marzo.***

1. Alma: 4/1
2. Verónica: 22/10
3. Andrés: 5/5
4. la abuela: 23/7
5. yo: ¿?
6. mi madre: ¿?
7. mi padre: ¿?
8. mi amigo(a): ¿?

18 ¿Cuál es la fecha de tu cumpleaños?

Hablar Pregúntales a otros estudiantes la fecha de su cumpleaños. ¿Cuántos cumpleaños hay en cada mes? *(**Hint:** Ask other students their birthdays. How many are in each month?)*

Nombre	Su cumpleaños es
Ramón	el 13 de junio

19 ¿Cuál es la respuesta?

Escuchar Escoge la respuesta correcta. *(**Hint:** Choose the correct answer.)*

1. **a.** Tiene cinco años.
   b. Tiene setenta años.
   c. Tiene veinte años.
2. **a.** Son viejas.
   b. Son grandes.
   c. Son jóvenes.
3. **a.** Soy policía.
   b. Soy estudiante.
   c. Soy maestro.
4. **a.** Llevo un suéter.
   b. Llevo una camiseta.
   c. Llevo una chaqueta.

20 Mi madre

Escribir Describe a un miembro de tu familia. *(**Hint:** Describe a family member.)*

modelo

Mi madre se llama Elena. Es alta y castaña. Tiene los ojos verdes. Le gusta cantar y leer. Es muy inteligente. Tiene cuarenta años. Su cumpleaños es el cuatro de mayo.

More Practice: **Más comunicación** *p. R3*

Online Workbook CLASSZONE.COM

Pronunciación

Trabalenguas

Pronunciación de la *m* y la *n* The letters **m** and **n** are pronounced in Spanish just as they are in English. Try the following tongue twisters.

Nueve nenes nadan.

Mi mamá me mima.

En voces

AUDIO

LECTURA

PARA LEER

STRATEGY: READING

Look for cognates These are words that look alike and have similar meanings in both English and Spanish, such as **europeo** and **artificiales**. What other cognates can you find in **«Las celebraciones del año»**?

Las celebraciones del año

Hay muchas fechas importantes durante el año. Los países hispanohablantes celebran estas fechas de varias formas. Algunas[1] celebraciones son iguales que las de Estados Unidos, pero también hay tradiciones diferentes.

octubre

12/10 El Día de la Raza En este día no hay trabajo. Hay muchos desfiles[2]. El día celebra el encuentro[3] del indígena[4] con el europeo y el africano. Hoy esta mezcla[5] de razas[6] y tradiciones forma la cultura latinoamericana.

noviembre

1/11 El Día de Todos los Santos y 2/11 el Día de los Muertos[7] En estos días todos honran a las personas de su familia. En México las familias decoran las tumbas de sus antepasados[8] con flores bonitas.

[1] some
[2] parades
[3] meeting
[4] native (Indian)
[5] mixture
[6] races
[7] Dead
[8] ancestors

diciembre y enero

31/12 La Nochevieja y 1/1 el Año Nuevo
Hay fuegos artificiales[9], desfiles o celebraciones en todos los países. En Ecuador los años viejos se representan con figuras grandes de personas famosas de ese año. A medianoche[10] los años viejos se queman[11]. En España es tradicional comer doce uvas[12] a la medianoche.

enero

6/1 El Día de los Reyes
Es el día tradicional para dar regalos[13] de Navidad en los países latinos.

Estados Unidos

También se dice

To talk about U.S. holidays not mentioned in this reading, use these phrases:

Valentine's Day: **Día de los Enamorados, Día de San Valentín**
Mother's Day: **Día de la Madre**
Father's Day: **Día del Padre**
Memorial Day: **Día Conmemorativo**
July 4th: **Día de la Independencia**
Labor Day: **Día del Trabajador**
Halloween: **Noche de Brujas**
Thanksgiving: **Día de Acción de Gracias**
Christmas Eve: **Nochebuena**
Christmas: **Navidad**

Online Workbook
CLASSZONE.COM

¿Comprendiste?

1. ¿Cómo celebran los latinoamericanos el Día de la Raza?
2. ¿Cuáles son las fechas en que los mexicanos honran a su familia?
3. Describe dos tradiciones del Año Nuevo.
4. ¿En qué fecha dan regalos de Navidad las personas de los países latinos? ¿Cómo se llama ese día?

¿Qué piensas?

¿Hay una celebración especial en tu casa para un día festivo? ¿Cómo es?

[9] fireworks
[10] midnight
[11] are burned
[12] grapes
[13] give gifts

En colores

CULTURA Y COMPARACIONES

PARA CONOCERNOS

STRATEGY: CONNECTING CULTURES

Compare rites of passage In your community what are some events, formal or informal, that mark a young person's transition from childhood to adulthood? What are they called and when do they occur? How are they celebrated? If you could design your own event, how would it be celebrated? Use a word web to record your thoughts. Think of its components as you read **«La quinceañera».**

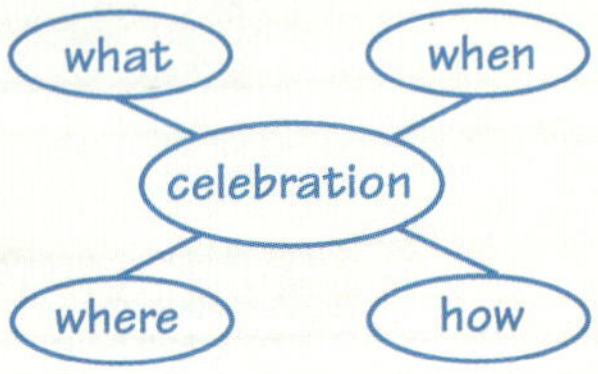

La palabra *quinceañera* se refiere a[1] dos conceptos. Una quinceañera es una chica de quince años. Una quinceañera también es una fiesta en que se celebra el cumpleaños de una chica de quince años.

La quinceañera lleva un vestido especial. Es tradicional llevar un vestido rosado.

Hay mucha preparación para la quinceañera. Hay muchas decoraciones.

La quinceañera

La tradición más importante es que la familia acompaña a la quinceañera en su día especial.

La quinceañera es una tradición especial de la cultura latina. Representa el momento en que una chica llega a ser[2] una mujer. Las tradiciones son diferentes en cada región. Una tradición es tener una ceremonia religiosa. Algunas fiestas se celebran en la casa de la familia. Otras se celebran en un hotel o un restaurante. La familia de la quinceañera invita a todos sus primos, sus tíos, sus abuelos y sus buenos amigos.

More About Latinos
CLASSZONE.COM

¿Comprendiste?

1. ¿Qué es una quinceañera?
2. ¿Cuál es una tradición de la quinceañera?
3. ¿Dónde se celebran las fiestas?
4. ¿Qué lleva la quinceañera?

¿Qué piensas?

1. ¿Qué fiestas hay en tu comunidad?
2. ¿Hay otras fiestas similares para una chica en tu comunidad? ¿Para un chico?

---

[1] refers to
[2] becomes

En uso

REPASO Y MÁS COMUNICACIÓN

OBJECTIVES
- Describe family
- Ask and tell ages
- Talk about birthdays
- Give dates
- Express possession

Now you can...
- describe family.

To review
- vocabulary for family, see p. 72.

1 Una familia feliz

Mónica, una amiga de Verónica, describe a su familia. Completa el párrafo. *(Hint: Complete Monica's description of her family.)*

modelo

Tengo tres __primos__. *Lucas es mi primo* __mayor__.

Mi familia es muy interesante. Mis __1__ son Gregorio y Berta. Tengo una __2__ que se llama Rosita. Ella es mi hermana __3__. Mi padre tiene un hermano. Es mi __4__ Carlos. Es muy cómico. Sus tres __5__ son Paquita, Lucas y Pepe. Ellos son mis __6__. La __7__ de ellos es mi tía Amalia. Mis primos y yo tenemos unos __8__ muy simpáticos: Rafael y Esperanza Santana.

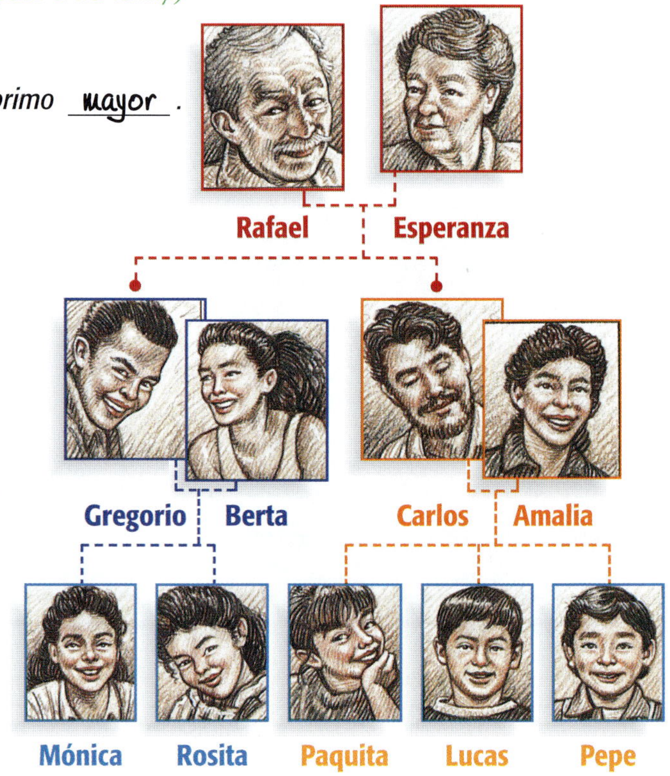

Now you can...
- tell ages.

To review
- the verb **tener,** see p. 78.
- vocabulary for numbers, see p. 79.

2 ¿Cuántos años tienen?

Di la edad de cada persona que Verónica conoce. *(Hint: Tell the ages of the people Veronica knows.)*

modelo

Yolanda: 44 — ***Yolanda** tiene **cuarenta y cuatro años.***

1. Juan y Anita: 42
2. el señor Uribe: 100
3. su prima: 28
4. yo: 15
5. los amigos de los García: 70
6. tú: 13
7. la señora Quiroga: 91
8. su tío: 67
9. nosotros: 38
10. usted: 83
11. Rafael: 17
12. Carlota: 21

Self-Check Quiz
CLASSZONE.COM

Now you can...
- talk about birthdays.

To review
- possession using **de,** see p. 80.
- dates and months, see p. 84.

3 ¿Cuándo cumplen años?

¿Cuál es la fecha de cumpleaños de cada persona? *(Hint: What is each person's birthday?)*

modelo

Antonio: 19/7

*El cumpleaños de **Antonio** es el **diecinueve de julio.***

1. Rafael: 23/12
2. Francisco: 15/3
3. Rosalinda: 6/2
4. la señora García: 1/10
5. David: 30/6
6. Yolanda: 25/11

Un pastel para la quinceañera

Now you can...
- give dates.

To review
- dates and months, see p. 84.

4 Las fiestas

¿Cuáles son las fechas de estos días festivos? *(Hint: What are the dates of these holidays?)*

modelo

17/3

el diecisiete de marzo

1. 25/12
2. 4/7
3. 1/1
4. 11/11
5. 14/6
6. 12/10
7. 5/5
8. 6/1
9. 2/2
10. 14/2
11. 17/3
12. 31/10

Now you can...
- express possession.

To review
- the verb **tener,** see p. 78.
- possessive adjectives, see p. 82.

5 Amigos internacionales

Estas personas tienen amigos y familia de otros países. ¿Cómo son? *(Hint: Describe people's international friends and family members.)*

modelo

Inés: amiga de México (bonito)

Inés** tiene **una amiga de México.** Su amiga es **bonita.

1. Víctor: vecinos de Cuba (viejo)
2. yo: doctor de Guatemala (joven)
3. ustedes: amigos de Argentina (simpático)
4. nosotras: maestra de la República Dominicana (cómico)
5. tú: tíos de Chile (trabajador)
6. Raquel y Mario: prima de Puerto Rico (moreno)
7. Lisa y yo: amigo de España (guapo)

6 ¡Tenemos unas preguntas!

STRATEGY: SPEAKING

Practice speaking smoothly Speaking smoothly without starts and stops helps others understand you. So first think about what you want to say, then practice saying it smoothly and naturally.

Trabajando en grupos, escriban preguntas para su maestro(a). Incluyan preguntas sobre su familia y su cumpleaños. *(Hint: Work together to write questions for your teacher. Include questions about his or her family and birthday.)*

modelo

¿Quién es su madre?

¿Tiene usted...?

¿Cuántos años...?

¿De dónde...?

¿Cuál es la fecha de...?

¿Cómo es...?

¿Cómo se llama...?

7 Su familia

Dibuja tu árbol genealógico. Incluye nombres y edades. Usando el árbol genealógico de otro(a) estudiante, descríbele la familia a otro grupo de la clase. *(Hint: Draw your family tree. Include names and ages. Using another student's family tree, describe his or her family to a group from the class.)*

modelo

La familia de Julio es pequeña. Él tiene un hermano mayor. No tiene hermanas. Su padre se llama Víctor y su madre se llama Lisa...

8 En tu propia voz

ESCRITURA Escribe un poema de cinco líneas describiendo a un miembro de tu familia. *(Hint: Write a five-line poem (cinquain) describing a family member.)*

modelo

Abuelo
Delgado, moreno
Inteligente
Le gusta leer
Persona divertida

TÚ EN LA COMUNIDAD

Theresa is a student in Massachusetts. Spanish comes in handy when she and a friend help two fifth-grade Guatemalan girls learn English. At home, she practices speaking Spanish with her brother, who also studies it in school. She also writes letters in Spanish to a little girl in Guatemala, and she is able to read the letters the girl writes back. Do you correspond with anyone in Spanish?

Flashcards CLASSZONE.COM

En resumen

REPASO DE VOCABULARIO

DESCRIBING FAMILY

Family Members

la abuela	*grandmother*
el abuelo	*grandfather*
los abuelos	*grandparents*
la hermana	*sister*
el hermano	*brother*
los hermanos	*brother(s) and sister(s)*
la hija	*daughter*
el hijo	*son*
los hijos	*son(s) and daughter(s), children*
la madre	*mother*
el padre	*father*
los padres	*parents*
el (la) primo(a)	*cousin*
la tía	*aunt*
el tío	*uncle*
los tíos	*uncle(s) and aunt(s)*

Descriptions

joven	*young*
mayor	*older*
menor	*younger*
viejo(a)	*old*

EXPRESSING POSSESSION

¿De quién es...?	*Whose is...?*
el (la)... de...	*(someone)'s...*
Es de...	*It's...*
mi	*my*
tu	*your (familiar)*
su	*your, his, her, its, their*
nuestro(a)	*our*
vuestro(a)	*your (plural familiar)*

ASKING AND TELLING AGES

Asking About Age

la edad	*age*
¿Cuántos años tiene...?	*How old is...?*
Tiene... años.	*He/She is...years old.*

Numbers from 11 to 100

once	*eleven*
doce	*twelve*
trece	*thirteen*
catorce	*fourteen*
quince	*fifteen*
dieciséis	*sixteen*
diecisiete	*seventeen*
dieciocho	*eighteen*
diecinueve	*nineteen*
veinte	*twenty*
veintiuno	*twenty-one*
treinta	*thirty*
cuarenta	*forty*
cincuenta	*fifty*
sesenta	*sixty*
setenta	*seventy*
ochenta	*eighty*
noventa	*ninety*
cien	*one hundred*

Juego

El abuelo tiene 24 años más que su hijo Carlos. Carlos tiene 35 años más que su hijo Antonio. Los tres combinados tienen 100 años. ¿Cuántos años tiene...

1. el abuelo?
2. Carlos?
3. Antonio?

GIVING DATES

Asking the Date

el año	*year*
la fecha	*date*
¿Cuál es la fecha?	*What is the date?*
Es el... de...	*It's the...of...*

Months

el mes	*month*
enero	*January*
febrero	*February*
marzo	*March*
abril	*April*
mayo	*May*
junio	*June*
julio	*July*
agosto	*August*
septiembre	*September*
octubre	*October*
noviembre	*November*
diciembre	*December*

TALKING ABOUT BIRTHDAYS

el cumpleaños	*birthday*
felicidades	*congratulations*
feliz	*happy*

OTHER WORDS AND PHRASES

ahora	*now*
la ciudad	*city*
con	*with*
dentro	*inside*
fuera	*outside*
hay	*there is, there are*
más	*more*
muy	*very*
¡Qué chévere!	*How awesome!*
¿Quién es?	*Who is it?*
¿Quiénes son?	*Who are they?*
sólo	*only*
tener	*to have*
todo(a)	*all*

En tu propia voz

ESCRITURA

¡Estudia en otro país!

You have the opportunity to study in a Spanish-speaking country and live with a family there. The program requires you to write a description of yourself so that you can be placed in a home. Your description will be the family's introduction to their guest, you!

Function: Tell others about yourself
Context: Application for placement with a Spanish-speaking family
Content: Self-description
Text type: Descriptive paragraph

PARA ESCRIBIR • STRATEGY: WRITING

Use different kinds of descriptive words Help your readers get to know you and understand what kind of person you are by giving a variety of descriptions. Include biographical data, physical traits, personal characteristics, and interests.

Modelo del estudiante

The writer begins by offering basic biographical data about herself.

The author tells what she looks like. This strengthens the portrait she is creating.

The writer uses descriptive adjectives with **ser** to tell what kind of person she is.

The author talks about her interests that are relevant to the program. This completes her introduction.

Me llamo Kristin Garza. Soy de Waco, Texas. Tengo 15 años. Soy castaña. Tengo el pelo largo y los ojos verdes. Soy alta y muy fuerte. Soy inteligente y atlética. No soy perezosa. Me gusta correr con mi perro y bailar con mis amigos. Vivo en una casa con mi familia. Tengo dos hermanos y una hermana. Mi padre es policía y mi madre es maestra. Mis abuelos viven en Waco también. Ellos son de México. Yo soy buena estudiante. Me gusta estudiar español y la historia de Latinoamérica.

Writing Center
CLASSZONE.COM

Estrategias para escribir

Antes de escribir...

Prepare to write your descriptive paragraph by brainstorming ideas in these categories: biographical data, physical traits, personal characteristics, and interests. Do all of your brainstorming in Spanish. Use a concept web to organize your ideas. Then select the most interesting and descriptive words about yourself from your web. Decide what order to arrange them in your paragraph, and start writing.

Revisiones

When you finish your first draft, exchange paragraphs with a friend. Then ask:

- *Does the paragraph include name, age, and hometown?*
- *Are there enough descriptive adjectives?*
- *Is there a variety of information—family, activities, school, etc.?*

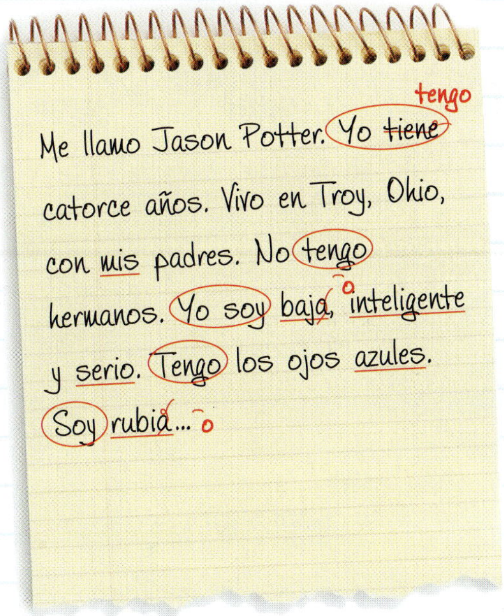

La versión final

Look at your revised paragraph and ask yourself these questions:

- *Are adjectives used correctly?*

Try this: Underline every adjective. Check to make sure that each one agrees in number and gender with its noun.

- *Did I use the right forms of **ser** and **tener**?*

Try this: Circle each form of **ser** and **tener** and their subjects (when given). Check to make sure that they match.

UNIDAD 2

CIUDAD DE MÉXICO
MÉXICO

UNA SEMANA TÍPICA

TEXAS Essential Knowledge and Skills

1 Communication

- **A Engage in exchanges**
  - *Requesting snack and lunch food*
  - *Discussing after-school plans*
- **B Demonstrate understanding**
  - *Asking and telling time*
  - *Saying how often you do something*
- **C Present information**
  - *Describing classes, classroom objects, and schedules*
  - *Talking about places and people you know*

2 Cultures

- **A Practices**
  - *School in Mexico City*
  - *Regional vocabulary*
  - *The importance of parks to life in Mexico*
- **B Products**
  - *The history of Mexico City*

3 Connections

- **A Use resources**
  - *Health: Researching the nutritional value of Mexican foods*
- **B Use the language**
  - *Mathematics: Using pie charts to summarize survey results in Spanish*

4 Comparisons

- **A Nature of language**
  - *Snack foods of Mexico City and the U.S.*
- **B Concept of culture**
  - *Daily schedules of young people in Mexico City and the U.S.*
  - *Historical areas in Mexico City and the U.S.*

5 Communities

- **A Within and beyond school**
  - *Using Spanish beyond the school experience*
- **B Lifelong learner**
  - *Using Spanish for personal enjoyment*

INTERNET Preview
CLASSZONE.COM

- More About Mexico
- Webquest
- Self-Check Quizzes
- Flashcards
- Writing Center
- Online Workbook
- eEdition Plus Online

DIEGO RIVERA (1886–1957) painted *La vendedora de flores* (1942) as well as many other paintings and murals. What paintings by Mexican artists have you seen?

ALMANAQUE CULTURAL

POBLACIÓN: 8.591.309

ALTURA: 2.309 metros (7.575 pies)

CLIMA: 19° C (66° F)

COMIDA TÍPICA: tortillas, frijoles, tacos

GENTE FAMOSA DE MÉXICO: Lázaro Cárdenas (político), Carlos Fuentes (escritor), Amalia Hernández (bailarina), Frida Kahlo (pintora), Diego Rivera (pintor)

¿VAS A MÉXICO, D.F.? Generalmente los mexicanos usan la palabra *México* para hablar del país. Para hablar de la Ciudad de México, usan las frases *la capital, el distrito federal* o simplemente *el D.F.* El distrito federal está en el centro de la ciudad.

More About Mexico
CLASSZONE.COM

EL PALACIO DE BELLAS ARTES, begun in 1904 by an Italian architect, was finished 30 years later by a Mexican one. The Ballet Folklórico performs here. What do you think its name means?

EL BALLET FOLKLÓRICO has communicated the spirit of Mexico through dance since 1959. It was founded by Amalia Hernández. What traditional dances of the United States do you know?

TORTILLAS are traditionally made by hand. The price of tortillas is set by the government. What Mexican dishes made with tortillas have you tried?

EL METRO opened in 1969 to combat pollution. It serves over 4 million people a day. To ride it, ask for a **billete!** Why might you ride a subway?

LÁZARO CÁRDENAS (1895–1970), president 1934–1940, made great improvements in Mexico. The Department of Tourism was created during his presidency, and Mexico became internationally influential. Who is the current president of Mexico?

UNIDAD 2

UNA SEMANA TÍPICA

Texas Essential Knowledge and Skills

1 Comunicación

The student communicates in Spanish using the skills of listening, speaking, reading, and writing.

2 Culturas

3 Conexiones

4 Comparaciones

5 Comunidades

Webquest CLASSZONE.COM

Explore communication in Mexico City through guided Web activities.

Comunicación

As a student of Spanish, you will have the opportunity to communicate in another language. This means engaging in new kinds of conversations, giving and finding out new information, and expressing your ideas in new ways.

Comunicación en acción **Describe a las personas de la foto. ¿Es el chico rubio o moreno? ¿Qué lleva? ¿Tiene la chica el pelo largo o corto? ¿Qué lleva ella? ¿Son estudiantes?**

Comunidades

In this unit you will learn how one student uses Spanish in his own community. He helps Spanish-speaking children with their homework and uses Spanish in his part-time job.

Conexiones

You will be able to understand spoken and written Spanish that informs you about many school subjects. You will also be able to present information and talk about your own ideas as well as write different types of reports.

Este mural es de la Universidad Autónoma de México. Es de Orozco, un artista mexicano famoso.

Culturas

By learning to read Spanish and to understand spoken Spanish, you will have the opportunity to learn about different aspects of culture. In this unit you will learn about places in Mexico . . .

. . . and Mexican food.

A muchos mexicanos les gusta comer tacos al pastor. Es una comida típica de México.

Comparaciones

You will also learn what Mexican teens do in a typical week. Do you think they enjoy some of the same activities you do?

A algunos adolescentes les gusta jugar al básquetbol, cantar con los amigos o leer.

Fíjate

Look closely at the photo captions. You probably don't understand every word, but by looking at the pictures and at the words you do know, you probably understand the information they convey.

1. Where are the two students eating?
2. Who created the design on the university building?
3. Name the food shown that is typical of Mexico.
4. Name an activity that Mexican teens do that you also do.

UNIDAD 2

ETAPA 1

Un día de clases

OBJECTIVES

- Describe classes and classroom objects
- Say how often you do something
- Discuss obligations

Horario: Isabel Palacios

Hora	lunes	martes	miércoles	jueves	viernes
12:30	computación	inglés	computación	inglés	computación
1:30	literatura	matemáticas	literatura	matemáticas	literatura
2:30	arte	educación física	arte	educación física	arte
3:30	receso	receso	receso	receso	receso
4:00	historia	música	historia	música	historia
5:00		ciencias naturales		ciencias naturales	

¿Qué ves?

Mira la foto del centro de la Ciudad de México.

1. ¿Tiene pelo corto la chica?
2. ¿Son rubios o morenos los chicos?
3. ¿Es roja o rosada la chaqueta del chico?
4. ¿Isabel tiene clases el sábado?

PRODUCTOS PARA

En contexto

VOCABULARIO

VIDEO DVD AUDIO

Isabel spends most of the week in school. Here Isabel describes the things she uses there.

A

Bienvenidos a mi **escuela.** En **la clase** el maestro **habla** mucho. Los estudiantes **escuchan** al maestro. Las lecciones son interesantes.

B

Para **estudiar,** tengo **un escritorio.** En mi escritorio, tengo **un cuaderno, un diccionario, un lápiz** y **papel.**

C

En mi **mochila,** tengo mi **libro** de **ciencias,** mi **calculadora** y mi **pluma.** También tengo mi tarea. ¡Siempre **saco una buena nota** en la tarea!

CD-ROM Take-Home Tutor

D En la clase, hay **una computadora.** Me gusta escribir con **un teclado.** La computadora tiene **una pantalla, un ratón** y **una impresora.**

E El profesor escribe en **el pizarrón** con **tiza.** Si hay un error, usa **el borrador.**

Online Workbook
CLASSZONE.COM

Preguntas personales

1. ¿Hay una computadora en tu clase?
2. ¿Te gusta usar la computadora o una pluma?
3. ¿Practicas mucho o no en la clase de español?
4. ¿Qué tienes en tu mochila?
5. ¿Qué tienes en tu escritorio?

En vivo

VIDEO DVD AUDIO

DIÁLOGO

Isabel | Mamá | Ricardo | Prof. Martínez

PARA ESCUCHAR • STRATEGY: LISTENING

Listen for feelings Many things happen to Isabel in this scene. How does she feel? What do you hear that makes you think she feels that way?

¡A la escuela!

1 ▶ **Isabel:** ¿Qué pasa con la computadora? ¡Y la pantalla! ¿Qué pasa con el ratón? Con razón. Hay que conectar el ratón al teclado.

5 ▶ **Isabel:** Necesito sacar una buena nota en esta clase.
Ricardo: Yo también. Estudio todos los días, pero la clase es difícil.

6 ▶ **Profesor:** Good morning, class.
Clase: Good morning, Professor Martínez.

7 ▶ **Isabel:** Tengo que sacar una buena nota. ¡Es muy importante!
Profesor: Miss, would you like to share your ideas with the class?

CD-ROM Take-Home Tutor

2 ▶ **Isabel:** ¡Papel! ¡La impresora no tiene papel!

Mamá: ¡Pronto! ¡Siempre llegas tarde a la escuela!

3 ▶ **Mamá:** ¿Necesitas tu cuaderno? ¿Y tus libros? ¿Y la calculadora?

Isabel: Sí, mamá, claro.

4 ▶ **Mamá:** ¿Y tu tarea, Isabel? ¿Tu tarea para la clase de ciencias naturales?

8 ▶ **Isabel:** Lo siento. No hablo más.

Profesor: This is English class.

Isabel: I'm sorry, teacher. I won't talk anymore.

9 ▶ **Isabel:** ¡Qué vergüenza! Siempre escucho con atención en la clase de inglés.

Ricardo: Cálmate, Isabel. ¿Qué clases tienes hoy?

Isabel: Tengo matemáticas y ciencias naturales.

10 ▶ **Isabel:** ¡Qué horror!

Ricardo: ¿Qué?

Isabel: ¡Mi tarea para la clase de ciencias naturales! ¡Está en la impresora, en mi casa! ¡Tengo que hablar con la profesora Díaz! ¡Ahora mismo!

En acción

PARTE A Comprensión del diálogo

For Activities 1–2, refer to the dialog on pages 104–105.

Isabel

Mamá

Ricardo

Prof. Martínez

1 ¿Cuál es?

Escuchar Escoge la respuesta correcta. *(Hint: Choose the best answer.)*

1. Este semestre Isabel necesita sacar una buena nota en la clase de _____.
   a. matemáticas
   b. español
   c. inglés
2. Isabel prepara su tarea en _____.
   a. la computadora
   b. la clase
   c. el cuaderno
3. Isabel no tiene su tarea para la clase de _____.
   a. inglés
   b. ciencias naturales
   c. matemáticas
4. La tarea de Isabel está en _____.
   a. su mochila
   b. la impresora
   c. la clase
5. Isabel tiene que hablar con _____.
   a. la profesora Díaz
   b. Ricardo
   c. su mamá

2 ¿Qué dicen?

Escuchar Escoge lo que dice cada persona según la foto. *(Hint: Choose what each person is saying.)*

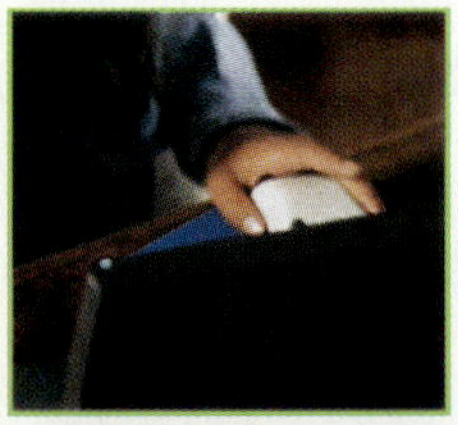

1. **a.** ¿Qué pasa con el ratón?
   b. Éste es mi escritorio.
   c. Ésta es la computadora.

2. **a.** ¡La impresora no tiene papel!
   b. ¡Todos los días lo mismo!
   c. ¡Y la pantalla!

3. **a.** Usas la calculadora en la clase de matemáticas, ¿no?
   b. ¿Necesitas tu cuaderno?
   c. Yo siempre preparo mi tarea en la computadora.

4. **a.** Yo también tengo ciencias naturales hoy.
   b. Preparo mi tarea en la computadora.
   c. Cálmate, Isabel.

5. **a.** ¡Mi tarea! ¡Está en la impresora en mi casa!
   b. Tengo matemáticas y ciencias naturales.
   c. Tengo mis libros.

PARTE B

Práctica del vocabulario

Objectives for Activities 3–6

- Describe classes and classroom objects

3 ¿Qué hay en la clase?

Hablar Trabaja con otro(a) estudiante para decir si hay o no hay estas cosas en la clase. Cambien de papel. *(**Hint:** Say if these things are in the classroom.)*

modelo

Tú: *¿Hay una mochila azul?*

Otro(a) estudiante: *No, no hay una mochila azul. Hay una mochila roja.*

1. un libro
2. un cuaderno
3. un pizarrón
4. una mochila roja
5. un escritorio
6. un borrador
7. dos computadoras
8. dos ratones
9. una impresora
10. ¿?

México

También se dice

Mexico is a country with a lot of distinctive regional vocabulary. Many Mexicans would say **calificaciones** instead of **notas, gis** instead of **tiza,** and **libreta** instead of **cuaderno.** In many countries you may hear the word **pizarra** instead of **pizarrón,** and **mouse** instead of **ratón. Mouse** is a loan word from English.

4 ¿Qué hay?

Hablar/*Escribir* ¿Qué hay en el escritorio de Isabel? *(**Hint:** What's on Isabel's desk?)*

modelo

Hay tres libros.

5 ¿Qué clases tienes?

Hablar Habla con otro(a) estudiante sobre las clases que tienes este semestre. Cambien de papel. *(Hint: Talk about your classes.)*

modelo

arte **Tú:** *¿Tienes clases de **arte** este semestre?*
Otro(a) estudiante: *Sí, tengo arte.*
o: *No, no tengo arte.*

1. ciencias
2. literatura
3. matemáticas
4. computación
5. música
6. estudios sociales
7. educación física
8. historia

6 ¿Cómo son las clases?

STRATEGY: SPEAKING

Develop more than one way of expressing an idea
It adds variety and interest to your speech. For example, in addition to saying what something *is*, you can say what it is *not*.

—¿Cómo es tu clase de historia?

—No es interesante.

Hablar Descríbele tus clases a otro(a) estudiante. Contesta sus preguntas. Cambien de papel. *(Hint: Describe your classes. Answer the questions.)*

modelo

Tú: *¿Qué clases tienes?*
Otro(a) estudiante: *Tengo historia, español, literatura…*
Tú: *¿Cómo es la clase de…?*
Otro(a) estudiante: *Es… No es…*
Tú: *¿Qué te gusta estudiar?*

Vocabulario

Las materias

el arte

la historia

las ciencias
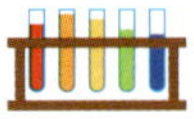

el inglés

la computación

la literatura

la educación física

las matemáticas
x+y=z

el español

la música

los estudios sociales

For more class subjects, see p. R21.

Here are other words to talk about classes.

fácil *easy*
difícil *difficult, hard*
el examen *test*
la lección *lesson*
la prueba *quiz*

Remember that you can use these adjectives you've learned, too.

aburrido(a)
interesante
bueno(a)
malo(a)

¿Qué clase tiene mucha tarea?

PARTE C

Práctica: gramática y vocabulario

Objectives for Activities 7–18

- Say how often you do something
- Discuss obligations

GRAMÁTICA Saying What You Do: Present of -ar Verbs

To talk about things you do, you use the present tense. To form the present tense of a regular verb that ends in **-ar**,

drop the **-ar** and add the appropriate ending.

estudiar ← **o, as, a, amos, áis,** or **an**

The verb **estudiar** means *to study*.

yo	**estudio**	nosotros(as)	**estudiamos**
tú	**estudias**	vosotros(as)	**estudiáis**
usted, él, ella	**estudia**	ustedes, ellos(as)	**estudian**

Isabel's mother says:

—¿**Necesitas** tu cuaderno?

***Do you need** your notebook?*

Vocabulario

Verbs Ending in -ar

ayudar (a) *to help*

buscar *to look for, to search*

contestar *to answer*

enseñar *to teach*

entrar (a, en) *to enter*

esperar *to wait for, to expect*

llegar *to arrive*

llevar *to wear, to carry*

mirar *to look at, to watch*

necesitar *to need*

pasar *to happen, to pass, to pass by*

preparar *to prepare*

usar *to use*

¿Qué pasa cada día?

Practice:
Actividades 7 8 9 10 11

Más práctica *cuaderno pp. 37–38*

Para hispanohablantes *cuaderno pp. 35–36*

Online Workbook CLASSZONE.COM

7 ¿Qué estudian?

Hablar/*Escribir* Describe lo que estudia cada persona.

*(**Hint:** Describe what each person studies.)*

modelo

Elena: 

Elena** estudia **historia.

1. yo: 

2. mis amigos: x+y=z
3. nosotros: 

4. Federico: 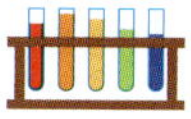
5. tú: 
6. Juana y Miguel: 
7. ella: 
8. Lorenzo y yo: 
9. ellas: 
10. ustedes: 

8 ¿Qué hacen en la escuela?

Hablar Tu amigo(a) está equivocado(a). Decide lo que hace cada persona en la escuela de Isabel y Ricardo en realidad. Cambien de papel. *(Hint: Your friend is mistaken. Decide what each person is really doing.)*

modelo

Ricardo / estudiar francés (¿?)

Estudiante A: *Ricardo estudia francés.*

Estudiante B: *No, no estudia francés. Estudia inglés.*

1. Isabel / buscar su libro (¿?)
2. las muchachas / esperar a Ricardo (¿?)
3. su amigo / usar una computadora (¿?)
4. la profesora Díaz / enseñar historia (¿?)
5. los estudiantes / sacar malas notas (¿?)
6. la muchacha / mirar el libro (¿?)
7. el profesor Romero / ayudar a Luis (¿?)
8. su amiga / necesitar un cuaderno (¿?)

Apoyo para estudiar

Verb Conjugations

Using the right ending on a verb is very important. Often verbs are used without subject pronouns (**yo, tú, él, ella, usted,** and so on). To help remember verb endings, practice each **-ar** verb with a partner in a question/answer exercise:

¿Estudias...?	–Sí, estudio...
¿Miran ustedes...?	–Sí, miramos...
¿Enseña ella...?	–Sí, ella enseña...
¿Preparan ellos...?	–Sí, ellos preparan...

9 ¿Qué haces?

Hablar Pregúntale a otro(a) estudiante si hace estas actividades. *(Hint: Ask another student if he or she does these activities.)*

modelo

sacar buenas notas

Tú: *¿Sacas buenas notas?*

Otro(a) estudiante: *Sí, saco buenas notas.*

1. hablar mucho
2. usar un diccionario
3. escuchar en clase
4. preparar la tarea en la computadora
5. llegar tarde a la clase
6. usar una calculadora en la clase de matemáticas
7. mirar el pizarrón
8. estudiar mucho
9. llevar una mochila
10. ayudar en casa

10 ¿Qué hacen?

Hablar Pregúntale a otro(a) estudiante qué actividades él o ella y su amigo(a) hacen. *(Hint: Ask if another student and a friend do these activities.)*

bailar	**hablar**	**preparar**
cantar	**nadar**	**trabajar**
estudiar	**patinar**	**usar**

modelo

Tú: *¿Tú y tu amigo(a)* ***estudian*** *mucho?*

Otro(a) estudiante: *Sí, (No, no)* ***estudiamos...***

More Practice: **Más comunicación** *p. R4*

11 ¡Lógicamente!

Escuchar Escucha la oración e indica la respuesta más lógica. *(Hint: Listen and indicate the most logical response.)*

1. a. No estudia.
   b. Ayuda a sus padres.
   c. Necesita un lápiz.
2. a. Tiene un examen mañana.
   b. Habla mucho en clase.
   c. No escucha a la maestra.
3. a. Enseña ciencias naturales.
   b. Necesita estudiar.
   c. Espera a su amigo.
4. a. Usa una calculadora.
   b. No estudia mucho.
   c. Ayuda a su abuelo.
5. a. Necesita estudiar mucho.
   b. Estudia en casa.
   c. Busca su diccionario.

GRAMÁTICA Expressing Frequency with Adverbs

To talk about how often someone does something, you use expressions of frequency. Expressions of frequency are adverbs or adverbial phrases.

siempre	*always*
todos los días	*every day*
mucho	*often*
a veces	*sometimes*
de vez en cuando	*once in a while*
poco	*a little*
rara vez	*rarely*
nunca	*never*

Ricardo and Isabel might say:

—Estudio **todos los días.**
*I study **every day**.*

—Yo **siempre** estudio.
*I **always** study.*

Different adverbs are placed in different parts of a sentence.

These expressions are usually placed **before** the **verb**:

siempre	Isabel **siempre llega** tarde a la escuela.
rara vez	Isabel **rara vez habla** en la clase.
nunca	Isabel **nunca usa** un diccionario.

These expressions are usually placed **after** the **verb**:

mucho	Ricardo **estudia mucho.**
poco	Isabel **habla poco** en la clase.

Longer phrases can be placed at the **beginning** or the **end** of the sentence:

todos los días	**Todos los días** Isabel llega tarde. Isabel llega tarde **todos los días.**
a veces	**A veces** Isabel llega tarde. Isabel llega tarde **a veces.**
de vez en cuando	**De vez en cuando** Isabel llega tarde. Isabel llega tarde **de vez en cuando.**

Practice:
Actividades
12 13 14

Más práctica
cuaderno p. 39
Para hispanohablantes
cuaderno p. 37

Online Workbook
CLASSZONE.COM

12 Los estudiantes diferentes

Leer María es buena estudiante. Felipe no es buen estudiante. Lee las oraciones y explica quién dice probablemente cada una. *(Hint: Explain if María or Felipe most likely says each of these sentences.)*

modelo

Estudio mucho. *María*

1. Nunca escucho en clase.
2. Rara vez saco malas notas.
3. Preparo mi tarea todos los días.
4. Estudio poco para los exámenes.
5. A veces entro en la clase tarde.
6. Miro poco el pizarrón.
7. Siempre estudio para las pruebas.
8. Estudio de vez en cuando.
9. Hablo mucho con mi amigo en clase.
10. Siempre ayudo a mis amigos con su tarea.

13 ¿Siempre o nunca?

Hablar Pregúntale a otro(a) estudiante si siempre hace estas actividades. *(Hint: Ask another student if he or she always does these activities.)*

modelo

Tú: *¿Siempre* ***usas la computadora****?*

Otro(a) estudiante: *Sí, siempre uso la computadora.*
o: *No, nunca uso la computadora.*

1. usar la computadora
2. llegar tarde a la escuela
3. estudiar
4. escuchar a la maestra
5. hablar en clase
6. preparar tu tarea en la computadora
7. sacar buenas notas
8. ayudar a tus amigos
9. necesitar una calculadora
10. llevar un sombrero en clase

siempre
todos los días
mucho
a veces
de vez en cuando
poco
rara vez
nunca

14 El estudiante ideal

Hablar/*Escribir* Trabaja en un grupo de tres para hacer un póster. Describe al estudiante ideal. Usa las expresiones **siempre, todos los días, mucho, a veces, de vez en cuando, poco, rara vez, nunca.** *(Hint: Work in groups of three to make a poster that describes the ideal student. Use expressions of frequency.)*

Un estudiante ideal

Prepara su tarea todos los días.

Nunca llega tarde a clase.

GRAMÁTICA Expressing Obligation with hay que and tener que

To talk about things someone must do, you can use two different phrases that express obligation.

- Use the impersonal phrase

  hay que + ***infinitive***

  if there is **no specific subject.**

- Use a form of **tener** in the phrase

  tener que + ***infinitive***

  if there is a **specific subject.**

—**Hay que conectar** el ratón al teclado.

*You have to (one must) **connect** the mouse to the keyboard.*

—**Tengo que sacar** una buena nota.

*I have to **get** a good grade.*

Practice:
Actividades
15 16 17 18

Más práctica *cuaderno p. 40*
Para hispanohablantes *cuaderno p. 38*

Online Workbook
CLASSZONE.COM

15 Las necesidades

Hablar/*Escribir* Explica lo que los amigos de Ricardo tienen que hacer hoy. Di si tú tienes que hacer las mismas cosas. *(Hint: Explain what Ricardo's friends have to do and say if you have to do these things too.)*

modelo

Juan / estudiar

***Juan** tiene que **estudiar.** Yo (no) tengo que estudiar.*

1. Elena / esperar a su hermano
2. Ana y Luis / usar la computadora
3. Antonio / preparar su tarea para mañana
4. Isabel y María / ayudar a su abuela
5. Andrés / hablar con el maestro
6. Felipe y yo / correr
7. Ramón y tú / trabajar
8. Patricia / buscar su cuaderno

México

Nota cultural

La Universidad Autónoma de México, founded in 1551, is the oldest university in the continental Americas. Its modern campus covers almost three square miles.

16 Buenas notas...

Hablar/*Escribir* ¿Qué hay que hacer para sacar buenas notas en la clase de matemáticas? Menciona un mínimo de cuatro cosas. *(Hint: Mention at least four things one must do to get a good math grade.)*

modelo

Hay que escuchar en clase.

practicar

usar

preparar

estudiar

escuchar

17 ¿Qué tienes que hacer?

Hablar/*Escribir* Pregúntales a cinco estudiantes qué tienen que hacer después de clases. Da un resumen. *(Hint: Ask five students what they have to do after classes. Give a summary.)*

modelo

Tú: *José, ¿qué tienes que hacer después de clases hoy?*

José: *Tengo que estudiar.*

Resumen: *Tres estudiantes tienen que estudiar.*

Nombre	Tiene que...
José	estudiar
Estudiante 1	
Estudiante 2	

18 ¡Pobre Isabel!

Leer Lee sobre Isabel y su profesora de ciencias naturales. Explica si **el** o **la** es necesario. *(Hint: Read about Isabel and her science teacher. Explain if **el** or **la** is necessary.)*

Nota: Gramática

Use **el** and **la** before titles like **profesor(a)** and **señor(a)** when talking *about* someone.

—¡Tengo que hablar con ***la*** **profesora Díaz**!

El **señor Martínez** es el profesor de inglés.

Do not use articles when talking *to* someone.

—No tengo mi tarea, **profesora Díaz.**

Isabel habla con __1__ profesora Díaz, su profesora de ciencias naturales.

«Buenos días, __2__ profesora Díaz. ¿Cómo está usted hoy?»

«Muy bien, Isabel, ¿y tú?»

«Pues, no estoy muy bien, __3__ profesora. No tengo mi tarea para hoy.»

__4__ profesora Díaz no está muy feliz.

«Isabel, para sacar una buena nota, ¡hay que preparar la tarea todos los días!»

México

Nota cultural

Pluma is the word for *feather*. It has come to mean *pen* because birds' feathers were once used with ink to serve as pens. **Bolígrafo** is a modern word for *pen*. Technically **bolígrafo**, or **boli**, refers to a ballpoint pen, but **pluma** is also used.

PARTE D

Todo en acción

Activities 19–20 bring together all concepts presented.

19 La clase de tu amiga

Escuchar Una amiga describe su clase de español. Escucha la descripción. Luego, contesta las preguntas. *(Hint: Listen to a friend describe her Spanish class, and then answer the questions.)*

1. La clase de español es _____.
   a. fácil y divertida
   b. difícil pero interesante
   c. fácil pero aburrida
2. La profesora de la clase es de _____.
   a. España
   b. México
   c. Estados Unidos
3. La señorita Casas habla español en clase _____.
   a. rara vez
   b. de vez en cuando
   c. todos los días
4. Tu amiga tiene que _____ cuando la señorita Casas habla.
   a. escribir
   b. escuchar
   c. estudiar
5. Tiene que preparar su tarea todos los días para _____.
   a. practicar mucho
   b. sacar una buena nota
   c. usar la computadora

20 Mi clase favorita es...

Escribir Escribe un párrafo sobre tu clase favorita, y explica lo que tienes que hacer para sacar una buena nota. Luego, léele tu párrafo a la clase. *(Hint: Write about your favorite class and what you have to do to get a good grade. Read your paragraph to the class.)*

modelo

Mi clase favorita es historia. Me gusta escuchar a la maestra, la señorita Sánchez. Enseña bien. Habla mucho y es muy interesante. Todos los días escuchamos muy bien. Hay que estudiar para sacar una buena nota. Tengo que preparar la tarea todos los días. Siempre preparo la tarea con la computadora.

More Practice: **Más comunicación** *p. R4*

Online Workbook
CLASSZONE.COM

Pronunciación

Trabalenguas

Pronunciación de la *y* y la *ll* The **ll** and **y** have the same sounds in Spanish. At the beginning and middle of words they sound like the *y* in the English word *yes*. At the end of a word the **y** sounds like the Spanish **i**, as in **muy. Ll** does not occur at the end of words. To practice these sounds, say the tongue twisters.

Yolanda ya vive en una casa amarilla.

¿Cómo se llama la llama llorona?

En voces

AUDIO

LECTURA

PARA LEER

STRATEGY: READING

Use context clues You can use the context to guess the meaning of unfamiliar words. Context includes what is written before and after the word. Pictures often contribute to the context too. What do you think the highlighted words mean?

- Una encuesta **escolar**
- El papel sale de la impresora con los **resultados** de la encuesta.

Una encuesta[1] escolar

Ricardo tiene que hacer una encuesta en la escuela. Él prepara una lista de preguntas. Ricardo habla con los otros estudiantes y escribe sus respuestas en un cuaderno. En casa escribe las respuestas en la computadora. Con una calculadora suma[2] el total de respuestas. El papel sale[3] de la impresora con los resultados de la encuesta. Ricardo usa los resultados de la encuesta para hacer un proyecto en la clase de matemáticas.

[1] survey [2] he adds [3] comes out

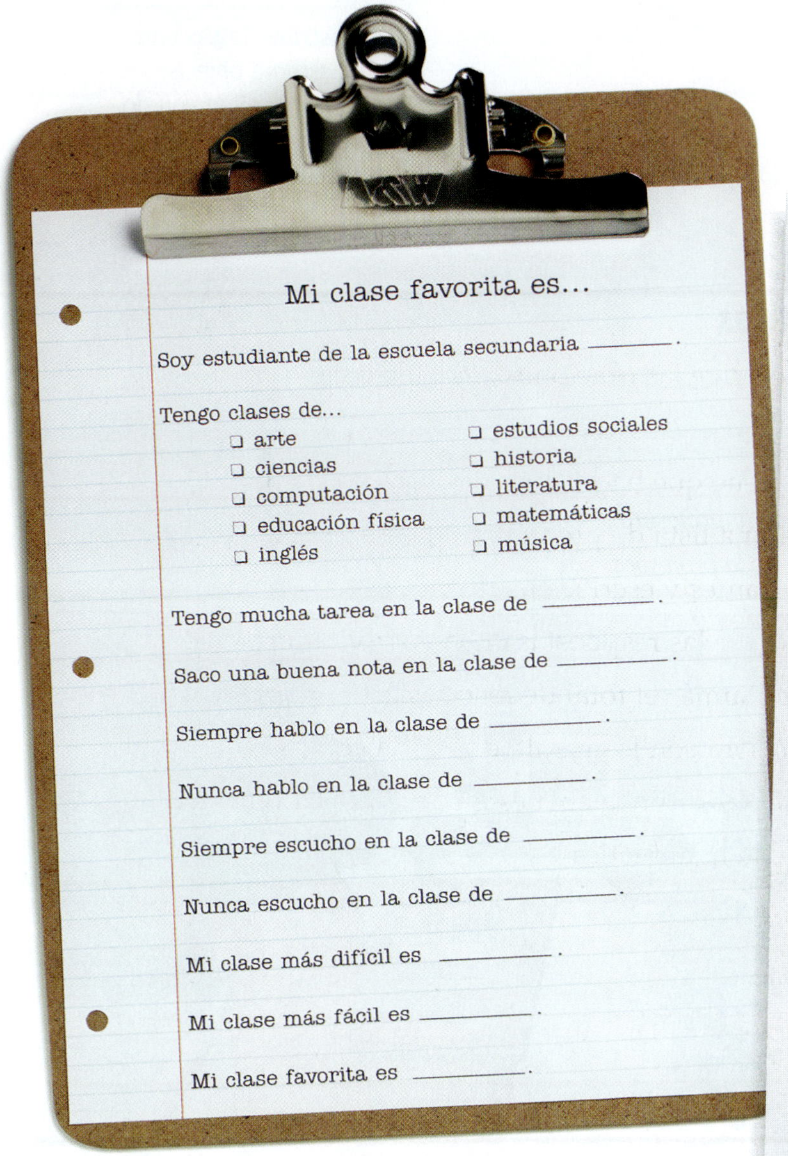
Mi clase favorita es...

Soy estudiante de la escuela secundaria ________.

Tengo clases de...

- ❑ arte
- ❑ ciencias
- ❑ computación
- ❑ educación física
- ❑ inglés
- ❑ estudios sociales
- ❑ historia
- ❑ literatura
- ❑ matemáticas
- ❑ música

Tengo mucha tarea en la clase de ________.

Saco una buena nota en la clase de ________.

Siempre hablo en la clase de ________.

Nunca hablo en la clase de ________.

Siempre escucho en la clase de ________.

Nunca escucho en la clase de ________.

Mi clase más difícil es ________.

Mi clase más fácil es ________.

Mi clase favorita es ________.

Los resultados

Una encuesta a 50 estudiantes

Clase con más tarea: matemáticas
(25 estudiantes)

Los estudiantes sacan más buenas notas en la clase de: música
(35 estudiantes)

Los estudiantes hablan más en la clase de: literatura
(30 estudiantes)

Los estudiantes nunca hablan en la clase de: inglés
(25 estudiantes)

Los estudiantes escuchan más en la clase de: ciencias
(40 estudiantes)

Los estudiantes nunca escuchan en la clase de: historia
(20 estudiantes)

La clase más difícil es: ciencias
(35 estudiantes)

La clase más fácil es: arte
(45 estudiantes)

La clase favorita es: literatura
(30 estudiantes)

Online Workbook
CLASSZONE.COM

¿Comprendiste?

1. ¿Qué tiene que hacer Ricardo?
2. ¿Qué usa Ricardo para escribir la encuesta?
3. ¿Los estudiantes hablan mucho o poco en la clase de inglés?
4. ¿Es difícil la clase de música o arte en la escuela de Ricardo?
5. ¿Qué clase es la clase favorita de los estudiantes?

¿Qué piensas?

Escribe tus respuestas para la encuesta de Ricardo.

ETAPA 1

En uso

REPASO Y MÁS COMUNICACIÓN

OBJECTIVES

- Describe classes and classroom objects
- Say how often you do something
- Discuss obligations

Now you can...

- describe classes and classroom objects.

To review

- vocabulary for classroom objects, see pp. 102–103.
- the present tense of regular **-ar** verbs, see p. 109.

1 En la clase de matemáticas

Mira el dibujo de la clase y corrige las oraciones. *(Hint: Correct the statements to match the drawing.)*

modelo

Hay siete libros en el escritorio de la profesora.

Hay cinco libros en el escritorio de la profesora.

1. Tres muchachas hablan y no escuchan a la profesora.
2. Hay tres cuadernos en el escritorio de la profesora.
3. La profesora usa una calculadora.
4. Hay tres computadoras y dos impresoras.
5. No hay borradores.
6. Las computadoras no tienen ratones.
7. Hay tres pizarrones en la clase.
8. Todos los estudiantes tienen lápices.

Self-Check Quiz
CLASSZONE.COM

Now you can...
- describe classes.
- say how often you do something.

To review
- **-ar** verbs, see p. 109.
- adverbs of frequency, see p. 111.

2 ¿Cómo es cada clase?

Una amiga de Isabel describe las acciones de unos estudiantes. ¿Cómo es cada clase que describe? Escoge la opción apropiada.
(Hint: Choose the option that describes each class.)

1. Nosotros siempre escuchamos en la clase de música.
2. Isabel estudia mucho para la clase de inglés.
3. Isabel y Ricardo sacan buenas notas en la clase de arte.
4. Muchos estudiantes llegan tarde a la clase de matemáticas.

a. Es difícil.
b. Es fácil.
c. Es interesante.
d. Es aburrida.

Now you can...
- say how often you do something.

To review
- the present tense of regular **-ar** verbs, see p. 109.
- adverbs of frequency, see p. 111.

3 ¡Unos estudiantes excelentes!

Todos estos estudiantes son excelentes. ¿Por qué?
(Hint: Tell why they are excellent.)

modelo

nosotros / preparar la tarea: ¿siempre o nunca?
Nosotros siempre preparamos la tarea.

1. Isabel y Ricardo / llegar tarde: ¿todos los días o rara vez?
2. tú / sacar buenas notas: ¿siempre o nunca?
3. Alma / ayudar a sus amigos: ¿mucho o poco?
4. yo / escuchar al profesor: ¿de vez en cuando o todos los días?
5. Arturo y yo / hablar inglés en la clase de español: ¿a veces o nunca?
6. ellas / mirar el pizarrón: ¿mucho o poco?

Now you can...
- discuss obligations.

To review
- **tener que**, see p. 113.

4 Una fiesta pequeña

Explica por qué estas personas no están en la fiesta de Alberto.
(Hint: Tell why these people aren't at Alberto's party.)

modelo

Sonia: habla con su madre — ***Sonia** tiene que **hablar con su madre**.*

1. ustedes: estudian
2. yo: preparo la tarea
3. mis amigos y yo: trabajamos
4. tú: esperas a tus padres
5. Samuel: ayuda a su hermano
6. Soledad y Raúl: usan la computadora

5 ¿Cómo son tus clases?

STRATEGY: SPEAKING

Expand the conversation How do you keep a conversation going? Be interested. Find out more about your partner by asking either/or questions to prompt him or her when words don't come. Also, it's hard to keep a conversation going with just **sí** or **no** answers. So, say more rather than less.

¿Te gusta... o...?

¿Cómo es...?

Prepara cinco preguntas para hablar con otro(a) estudiante sobre sus clases. *(Hint: Prepare five questions to talk with another student about classes.)*

modelo

Tú: *¿Tienes clase de historia?*

Otro(a) estudiante: *Sí, tengo clase de historia.*

Tú: *¿Cómo es la clase?*

Otro(a) estudiante: *Es buena. El profesor enseña bien...*

6 Una visita a la clase

Imagínate que tus compañeros son nuevos estudiantes. Háblales de ocho cosas que hay en la clase y de cinco actividades que hacen los estudiantes. *(Hint: Give new students a "tour" of the class, pointing out items and discussing activities.)*

modelo

En la clase hay veinte escritorios y un pizarrón...

Los estudiantes estudian y...

7 En tu propia voz

ESCRITURA Describe tu clase favorita con muchos detalles. Incluye información sobre las cosas que hay en la clase y las actividades que hacen los estudiantes. *(Hint: Describe your favorite class.)*

Mi clase favorita es...

En la clase hay...

El maestro siempre...

A veces yo...

Nosotros nunca...

Todos los días hay que...

Los estudiantes siempre...

La maestra se llama...

CONEXIONES

Las matemáticas Remember Ricardo's survey that polled students about their classes? Use his survey to interview students who are studying Spanish at your school. Interview twenty students to find out which class they like best, which class they find hardest, and so on. Summarize your results. Create a pie chart for each question, showing the percentage of students that voted for each class named. Compare your results with Ricardo's.

Clase favorita

Resultados de 20 estudiantes

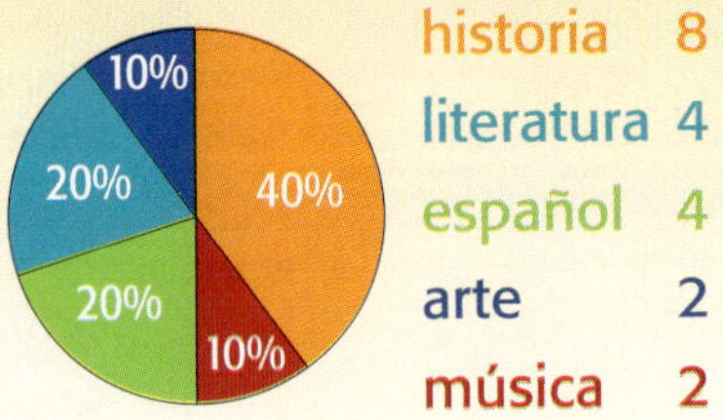

Flashcards
CLASSZONE.COM

En resumen

REPASO DE VOCABULARIO

DESCRIBING CLASSES

At School

la clase	*class, classroom*
la escuela	*school*
el examen	*test*
la lección	*lesson*
la prueba	*quiz*
la tarea	*homework*

School Subjects

el arte	*art*
las ciencias	*science*
la computación	*computer science*
la educación física	*physical education*
el español	*Spanish*
los estudios sociales	*social studies*
la historia	*history*
el inglés	*English*
la literatura	*literature*
las matemáticas	*mathematics*
la materia	*subject*
la música	*music*

Classroom Activities

enseñar	*to teach*
escuchar	*to listen (to)*
estudiar	*to study*
hablar	*to talk, to speak*
mirar	*to watch, to look at*
preparar	*to prepare*
sacar una buena nota	*to get a good grade*

DESCRIBING CLASS OBJECTS

el borrador	*eraser*
la calculadora	*calculator*
el cuaderno	*notebook*
el diccionario	*dictionary*
el escritorio	*desk*
el lápiz	*pencil*
el libro	*book*
la mochila	*backpack*
el papel	*paper*
el pizarrón	*chalkboard*
la pluma	*pen*
la tiza	*chalk*

At the Computer

la computadora	*computer*
la impresora	*printer*
la pantalla	*screen*
el ratón	*mouse*
el teclado	*keyboard*

SAYING HOW OFTEN

a veces	*sometimes*
de vez en cuando	*once in a while*
mucho	*often*
nunca	*never*
poco	*a little*
rara vez	*rarely*
siempre	*always*
todos los días	*every day*

DISCUSSING OBLIGATIONS

hay que	*one has to, one must*
tener que	*to have to*

Actions

ayudar (a)	*to help*
buscar	*to look for, to search*
contestar	*to answer*
entrar (a, en)	*to enter*
esperar	*to wait for, to expect*
llegar	*to arrive*
llevar	*to wear, to carry*
necesitar	*to need*
pasar	*to happen, to pass, to pass by*
usar	*to use*

OTHER WORDS AND PHRASES

¡Ahora mismo!	*Right now!*
Con razón.	*That's why.*
difícil	*difficult, hard*
fácil	*easy*
mismo(a)	*same*
pronto	*soon*
la razón	*reason*
tarde	*late*

Juego

Jorge tiene que preparar la tarea de cada clase. ¿En qué materias tiene tarea?

1. Usa una calculadora.
2. Estudia un libro sobre computadoras.
3. Busca una palabra en inglés en su diccionario.
4. Canta.

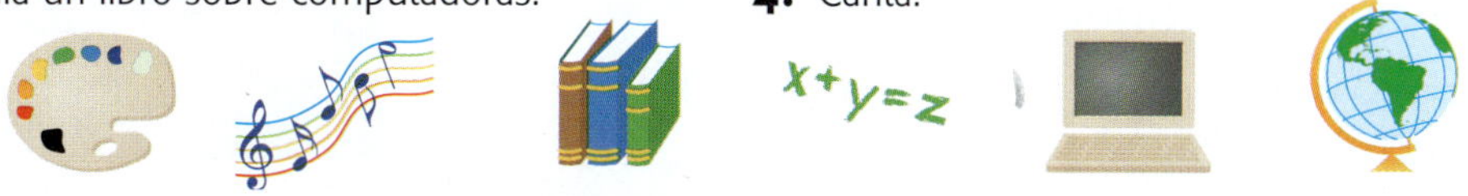

UNIDAD 2

ETAPA 2

¡Un horario difícil!

OBJECTIVES

- Talk about schedules
- Ask and tell time
- Ask questions
- Say where you are going
- Request food

¿Qué ves?

Mira la foto del patio de una escuela mexicana. **¡Ojo!** El símbolo **$** representa pesos mexicanos, **no** dólares.

1. ¿Llevan jeans todos?
2. ¿Hay aguas en el menú?
3. ¿Es verde o azul la mochila de Ricardo?
4. ¿Es roja o rosada la mochila de Isabel?

En contexto

VIDEO DVD AUDIO

VOCABULARIO

Isabel and Ricardo have a lot to do at school today. Let's see where they go at different times during the day.

A

Isabel: Hola, Ricardo. **¿Qué hora es?**
Ricardo: **Son las once.**
Isabel: ¿**A qué hora** está la maestra en **la oficina**?
Ricardo: **A la una.**

B

Son las once y media. Todos los días Ricardo estudia en **la biblioteca.** Hay muchos libros en la biblioteca.

C

Son las dos. Isabel y Ricardo están en **el auditorio.** ¡Qué bien actúan!

Take-Home Tutor

D

Son las cuatro. Ricardo está en **el gimnasio** de la escuela con unos amigos.

E

Son las cinco. Durante **el receso,** Isabel y Ricardo toman **una merienda** en **la cafetería.**

Isabel: Para la merienda siempre **quiero comer una torta** o **fruta.** A veces quiero **tomar un refresco.**

Ricardo: Para la merienda yo quiero comer **una hamburguesa** y **papas fritas. Quiero beber agua.**

Online Workbook
CLASSZONE.COM

Preguntas personales

1. ¿Tu escuela tiene un gimnasio? ¿Un auditorio?
2. ¿Estudias en la biblioteca o en casa?
3. ¿Te gusta comer en la cafetería de la escuela o en casa?
4. ¿Qué te gusta beber: un refresco o agua?
5. Para la merienda, ¿qué te gusta comer?

VIDEO DVD AUDIO

En vivo
DIÁLOGO

Isabel

Maestra

Ricardo

PARA ESCUCHAR • STRATEGY: LISTENING

Listen for the main idea It is important first to understand the main idea without getting lost in the details. Here Isabel is looking for a teacher. What do you hear that tells you that?

Horas y horarios

1 ▶ **Isabel:** Busco a la profesora Díaz.
Maestra: No está en este momento.
Isabel: ¿A qué hora llega?
Maestra: A las diez y media.

5 ▶ **Ricardo:** Quiero comer unas papas fritas, y quiero beber un refresco.
Isabel: Quiero beber un refresco también.

6 ▶ **Isabel:** ¡Este semestre es horrible! Tengo un horario difícil. Los lunes, miércoles y viernes tengo inglés, historia, matemáticas y literatura. Y los martes y jueves música, geografía, computación y ciencias naturales.

7 ▶ **Ricardo:** ¿A qué hora es tu clase de computación?
Isabel: A la una de la tarde, con el profesor García.
Ricardo: Mi clase de computación es a las cuatro, con el profesor Anaya.

CD-ROM Take-Home Tutor

2 ▶ **Isabel:** Profesora, ¿qué hora es?
Maestra: Son las once menos cuarto.

3 ▶ **Maestra:** A veces la profesora Díaz está en su oficina durante el almuerzo, y a las tres.
Isabel: Muchas gracias, profesora. Hasta luego.

4 ▶ **Isabel:** ¿Adónde vas, Ricardo?
Ricardo: Voy a la cafetería. ¿Me acompañas?
Isabel: Sí, vamos. Tengo tiempo.

8 ▶ **Isabel:** Mira, ¿qué es eso?
Ricardo: ¡De verdad es interesante! ¿Te gusta escribir?
Isabel: Sí, me gusta mucho.
Ricardo: ¿Por qué no participamos?

9 ▶ **Isabel:** Quiero participar… pero con mi horario…
Ricardo: Isabel, por la noche hay tiempo para trabajar en el concurso…
Isabel: Por la noche tengo que trabajar en mi tarea. ¡Tengo mucha tarea!

10 ▶ **Ricardo:** ¿Por qué no vamos a la cafetería para hablar más tranquilos?
Isabel: ¿Cuándo?
Ricardo: A las cinco y veinte.
Isabel: De acuerdo. Voy a las cinco y veinte. ¡Ay! ¡Ya es tarde!

En acción

PARTE B Práctica del vocabulario

Objectives for Activities 3–5
- Say where you are going
- Request food

PARTE A Comprensión del diálogo

For Activities 1–2, refer to the dialog on pages 126–127.

Isabel Maestra Ricardo

1 ¿Cierto o falso?

Escuchar ¿Es cierto o falso? Si es falso, di lo que es cierto. *(Hint: True or false? If it is false, say what is true.)*

1. La profesora Díaz está en su oficina.
2. Ricardo quiere comer una hamburguesa.
3. Isabel tiene un horario muy difícil.
4. Isabel y Ricardo tienen la clase de computación con el profesor Anaya.
5. Isabel tiene mucha tarea.

2 ¿Qué pasa?

Escuchar Escoge la respuesta correcta según el diálogo. *(Hint: Choose the correct answer.)*

1. Isabel busca _____.
   a. a Ricardo **b.** su libro de matemáticas **c.** a la profesora Díaz
2. La profesora Díaz normalmente llega a su oficina _____.
   a. a las diez y media **b.** tarde **c.** a las dos
3. Ricardo va _____.
   a. a la cafetería **b.** al gimnasio **c.** a la clase
4. Ricardo quiere beber _____.
   a. unas papas fritas **b.** un refresco **c.** agua
5. Isabel va a la cafetería _____.
   a. a las cinco y veinte **b.** a las diez y media **c.** a las tres

3 Los amigos de Isabel

Leer Isabel dice lo que ella y sus amigos hacen en clase. Completa sus oraciones con la forma correcta del verbo. *(Hint: Complete Isabel's sentences, telling what she and her friends do.)*

1. Elena _____ (hablar) poco.
2. Antonio y Marisol siempre _____ (ayudar) al profesor.
3. Ana y yo _____ (buscar) un libro.
4. Yo _____ (escuchar) al profesor en la clase de inglés.
5. Nosotros _____ (usar) la calculadora en la clase de matemáticas.
6. Mis amigos _____ (hablar) mucho en la clase de inglés.
7. Yo _____ (mirar) la pantalla de la computadora para leer.
8. Tú _____ (estudiar) mucho.

México

También se dice

If you visit Mexico, you will notice that **tomar** is used more often than **beber** to mean *to drink.* In Latin America, a potato is **una papa,** but in Spain it is **una patata. Papas fritas** and **patatas fritas** are both french fries and potato chips.

4 ¡Una buena merienda!

Hablar Trabajas en la cafetería. Un(a) estudiante quiere comprar algo. ¿Qué dicen ustedes? Cambien de papel. *(Hint: A student asks for a snack as you work in the cafeteria. Change roles.)*

modelo

Estudiante: *¿Qué hay para la merienda?*

Tú: *¿Quieres comer* ***una torta*** *o* ***fruta****?*

Estudiante: *Una torta, por favor.*

Nota: Vocabulario

To ask what someone wants to eat, say **¿Quieres comer…?;** to ask what someone wants to drink, say **¿Quieres beber…?** Use **por favor** when you want to say *please*.

1.

2.

3.

4.

5 ¿Qué es?

Hablar/*Escribir* Isabel le muestra la escuela a una nueva estudiante. ¿Qué dice? *(Hint: Isabel shows a new student the school. What does she say?)*

modelo

Es ***el gimnasio.***

1.

2.

3.

4.

PARTE C

Práctica: gramática y vocabulario

Objectives for Activities 6–19

- Say where you are going
- Talk about schedules
- Ask and tell time
- Ask questions

GRAMÁTICA Saying Where You Are Going: The Verb ir

When you talk about where someone is going, use the verb **ir.**

The verb **ir** means *to go.*

yo	**voy**	nosotros(as)	**vamos**
tú	**vas**	vosotros(as)	**vais**
usted, él, ella	**va**	ustedes, ellos(as)	**van**

As a question, **vamos** can mean ***Shall we...?*** But if stated definitely it means ***Let's go!***

Isabel and Ricardo say:

—**¿Adónde vas,** Ricardo?
Where are you going, *Ricardo?*

—**Voy** a la cafetería.
I'm going *to the cafeteria.*

Isabel uses the word **adónde** to ask where Ricardo is going. This word means *where.* **Dónde** also means *where.*

- Use **adónde** to mean *where* when there is a verb indicating motion, such as **ir**.

¿Adónde va Ricardo?
(To) ***Where*** *is Ricardo going?*

Notice how asking **¿adónde...?** is similar to asking ***to where...?***

- Use **dónde** to ask where someone or something is.

¿Dónde está Ricardo?
Where *is Ricardo?*

Practice: Actividades 6 7 8
Más práctica *cuaderno p. 45*
Para hispanohablantes *cuaderno p. 43*
Online Workbook CLASSZONE.COM

Vocabulario

La vida diaria

- **el almuerzo** *lunch*
- **la cita** *appointment*
- **comprar** *to buy*
- **descansar** *to rest*
- **terminar** *to finish*
- **tomar** *to take, to eat or drink*
- **visitar** *to visit*

¿Qué te gusta?

6 ¿Adónde van?

Leer Isabel y Ricardo hablan en la escuela. Completa su conversación con **ir**. *(Hint: Complete what Isabel and Ricardo say, using* ***ir****.)*

Isabel: ¡Hola, Ricardo! ¿Adónde __1__?
Ricardo: __2__ a la cafetería a tomar un refresco.
Isabel: Yo __3__ a la oficina de la profesora Díaz. Tengo una cita con ella ahora mismo.
Ricardo: Y después, ¿adónde __4__?
Isabel: Después, Andrea y yo __5__ a la biblioteca para estudiar.
Ricardo: Es un semestre difícil, ¿verdad?
Isabel: ¡Sí! ¡Tengo un horario horrible!

7 Un horario difícil

Hablar/*Escribir* Éste es el horario de Isabel. ¿Qué días va a sus clases? *(Hint: On what days does Isabel go to her classes?)*

modelo

inglés

*Isabel va a la clase de **inglés** los martes y jueves.*

Nota: Vocabulario

Use **el** with a day of the week to say an event will happen on a specific day. Use **los** with a day of the week to say an event happens every week on that day. Add an **s** to **sábado** and **domingo** when you use **los**.

El lunes voy a la biblioteca.
***On** Monday I am going to the library.*

Los martes y jueves tengo estudios sociales.
***On** Tuesdays and Thursdays I have social studies.*

Los sábado**s** y domingo**s** no tengo clase.
***On** Saturdays and Sundays I don't have class.*

Horario: Isabel Palacios

lunes	martes	miércoles	jueves	viernes
computación	inglés	computación	inglés	computación
literatura	matemáticas	literatura	matemáticas	literatura
arte	educación física	arte	educación física	arte
receso	receso	receso	receso	receso
historia	música	historia	música	historia
	ciencias naturales		ciencias naturales	

1. educación física
2. historia
3. computación
4. literatura
5. ciencias naturales
6. matemáticas
7. música
8. arte

8 ¿Adónde vas para...?

Hablar Pregúntales a cinco estudiantes adónde van para hacer estas actividades. Léele un resumen de las respuestas a la clase. *(Hint: Ask five others where they go to do these things and report your results.)*

modelo

Tú: *¿Adónde vas para **estudiar**?*

Estudiante 1: *Voy a **casa.***

Resumen: *Cuatro estudiantes van a casa para estudiar. Un estudiante va a la biblioteca.*

Nota: Gramática

When **a** is placed before the definite article **el**, the two words form the contraction **al**.

a + **el** = **al** Voy **al** gimnasio.

Las actividades

1. estudiar
2. visitar al (a la) profesor(a) de español
3. comprar una hamburguesa
4. tomar un refresco
5. descansar
6. usar la computadora
7. buscar un diccionario
8. preparar tu tarea
9. hablar español
10. comer

¿Adónde?

el auditorio
la biblioteca
la cafetería
casa
la clase
el apartamento
la escuela
el gimnasio
su oficina
México
¿otro lugar?

GRAMÁTICA Telling Time

There are several useful phrases for talking about the current time. Use:

¿Qué hora es?	to ask what time it is.
Son las + ***hour***.	to give the time for every hour except one o'clock.
Es la una.	to say it is one o'clock.

Use **cuarto** for a quarter of an hour and **media** for half an hour.

Son las doce y *minutes*

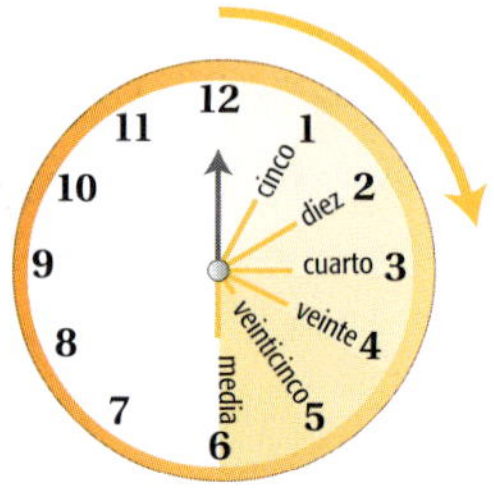

Use **y** + ***minutes*** for the number of minutes **after** the hour.

12:00	Son las doce.
12:10	Son las doce **y diez.**
12:15	Son las doce **y cuarto.**
12:30	Son las doce **y media.**

Es la una menos *minutes*

Use **menos** + ***minutes*** for the number of minutes **before** the hour.

1:00	Es la una.
12:50	Es la una **menos diez.**
12:45	Es la una **menos cuarto.**

To talk about when something will happen, use:

¿A qué hora + ***verb*** + ***event?***	¿A qué hora es la clase? *What time is the class?*
A las + ***hour***	A las (dos, tres). *At (two o'clock, three o'clock).*
A la + ***one o'clock***	A la una. *At one o'clock.*

Practice: **Actividades** 9 10 11

Más práctica *cuaderno* p. 46
Para hispanohablantes *cuaderno* p. 44

Online Workbook CLASSZONE.COM

9 ¿Qué hora es?

Hablar El padre de Isabel tiene una colección de relojes. Trabaja con otro(a) estudiante para preguntar y decir la hora que da cada uno. Cambien de papel. *(Hint: Isabel's father has a collection of clocks. Tell the time for each.)*

modelo

Estudiante A: *¿Qué hora es?*

Estudiante B: *Son las cinco menos cuarto.*

1. 
2. 
3. 
4. 
5. 

6. 

10 ¿A qué hora?

Escuchar/*Escribir* Escucha al profesor para completar el horario de Ana, una amiga de Isabel. Luego, escribe cuándo tiene cada clase. *(**Hint:** Listen and complete Ana's schedule. Then write when each class is.)*

modelo

arte - 7:30

Ana tiene la clase de arte a las siete y media de la mañana.

1. matemáticas
2. inglés
3. receso
4. ciencias naturales
5. estudios sociales
6. literatura

Vocabulario

Para hablar de la hora

Use these phrases when telling time.

A la una **de la mañana/tarde/noche** *At one in the morning/afternoon/night*

la medianoche *midnight*

el mediodía *noon*

el reloj *clock, watch*

por la mañana/tarde/noche *during the morning/afternoon/night*

¿Cuándo estudias?

11 Tu horario

STRATEGY: SPEAKING

Take risks You learn faster when you are willing to take chances. Don't worry about sounding foolish. Your desire to communicate in Spanish encourages others and helps you.

Hablar Habla con otro(a) estudiante de tu horario, usando las preguntas como guía. Cambien de papel. *(**Hint:** Take turns with another student to ask questions about your schedules.)*

1. ¿Qué clases tienes por la mañana?
2. ¿Qué clases tienes por la tarde?
3. ¿A qué hora tienes inglés?
4. ¿A qué hora tienes el almuerzo?
5. ¿A qué hora tienes...?
6. ¿Qué días tienes la clase de...?

More Practice: **Más comunicación** *p. R5*

México

Nota cultural

In Mexico the word **torta** is used to describe a large sandwich on crusty bread. In Spain **bocadillo** is used. In other countries, **torta** usually means *cake*. In Mexico, the word **pastel** is used to mean *cake*. In Spain, **tarta** is used for *cake*.

torta / bocadillo

pastel / tarta / torta

GRAMÁTICA Describing Location with the Verb estar

To say where people or things are located, use the verb **estar**. Here are its forms in the present tense.

yo	**estoy**	nosotros(as)	**estamos**
tú	**estás**	vosotros(as)	**estáis**
usted, él, ella	**está**	ustedes, ellos(as)	**están**

The teacher says:

—La profesora Díaz **está** en su oficina durante el almuerzo…
*Professor Díaz **is** in her office during lunch…*

Practice: Actividades 12 13 14

Más práctica *cuaderno p. 47*
Para hispanohablantes *cuaderno p. 45*

Online Workbook
CLASSZONE.COM

12 ¿Dónde están?

Leer/Escribir Lee las oraciones y explica dónde están los estudiantes. *(Hint: Read the sentences and explain where the students are.)*

modelo
Carlos habla español.
Está en la clase de español.

1. Nosotros miramos el pizarrón.
2. Ella usa una calculadora.
3. Ellas toman un refresco.
4. Él escucha música.
5. Tú buscas un libro.
6. Juana corre.
7. Pedro usa un ratón.
8. La profesora y Ana hablan.
9. Tú compras papas fritas.
10. Los estudiantes cantan.

13 ¡Cuántos lugares!

Hablar Isabel, Ricardo y sus amigos están en varios lugares durante el día. Con otro(a) estudiante, di dónde están. *(Hint: Take turns saying where Isabel, Ricardo, and friends are in the pictures.)*

modelo
Tú: *¿Dónde están Isabel y Ricardo?*
Otro(a) estudiante: *Están en la clase.*

1.

2.

3.

4.

5.

14 ¿Dónde estás?

Hablar/*Escribir* Son las diez de la mañana del lunes. Explica dónde están estas personas.
(Hint: It's ten o'clock Monday morning. Explain where these people are.)

1. yo
2. mi maestro(a) de español
3. los maestros de educación física
4. los estudiantes de drama
5. mi hermano(a)
6. los estudiantes de mi clase y yo

GRAMÁTICA Asking Questions: Interrogative Words

There are many ways to ask questions. This is how you create a simple question that has a *yes* or *no* answer.

Statement	Technique	Question
Isabel va a la escuela.	Use rising intonation to imply a question.	¿Isabel va a la escuela?
Isabel va a la escuela.	Switch the position of the **subject** and **verb.**	¿**Va Isabel** a la escuela?

You've already learned the interrogative words **(a)dónde** and **cuántos(as).**

Here are more interrogative words.

Some questions are formed by putting a **conjugated verb** after the **question word.**

cómo	*how*	¿**Cómo está** Ricardo?
cuál(es)	*which or what*	¿**Cuál es** el libro?
cuándo	*when*	¿**Cuándo estudia** Ricardo?
por qué	*why*	¿**Por qué va** Ricardo a casa?
qué	*what*	¿**Qué es**?
quién(es)	*who*	¿**Quién(es) habla(n)** con el profesor?

Each interrogative word has an **accent** on the appropriate vowel.

All questions are **preceded** by an **inverted question mark** and **followed** by a **question mark.**

Sometimes **qué** and **cuál(es)** are followed by words other than verbs. **Qué** can be followed directly by a **noun,** but **cuál** or **cuáles** cannot. Use **cuál** for one item and **cuáles** for more than one.

¿**Qué libro** mira Isabel?
*What **book** is Isabel looking at?*

¿**Cuáles de los libros** mira Isabel?
*Which **books** is Isabel looking at?*

Practice: Actividades 15 16 17 18 19

Más práctica *cuaderno p. 48*
Para hispanohablantes *cuaderno p. 46*

Online Workbook CLASSZONE.COM

15 Un día típico

Hablar Una amiga de Isabel te habla de un día típico, pero tú no escuchas. Tienes que verificar lo que dice. Cambia la posición del verbo para formar una pregunta. Sigue el modelo. *(Hint: Make sure of what Isabel's friend is telling you. Ask a question by changing the position of the verb.)*

modelo

Isabel y Ricardo van a la escuela a la una.

¿Van Isabel y Ricardo a la escuela a la una?

1. Ellos tienen clases difíciles hoy.
2. Ricardo habla con su profesora a las dos.
3. Isabel y Ricardo tienen una prueba.
4. Isabel y sus amigas estudian en la biblioteca.
5. Ellos terminan las clases a las cinco.
6. Isabel va a casa para estudiar.

16 La amiga curiosa

Leer/*Escribir* Isabel tiene una amiga curiosa. Le hace muchas preguntas sobre su clase de ciencias naturales. Escribe la palabra interrogativa para completar sus preguntas. *(Hint: Write the appropriate question word.)*

1. ¿A _____ hora tienes la clase?	A las cuatro.
2. ¿ _____ es la clase?	Difícil.
3. ¿ _____ enseña la clase?	La profesora Díaz.
4. ¿ _____ es la profesora?	Simpática.
5. ¿ _____ tienes que hablar con la profesora?	No tengo mi tarea.
6. ¿ _____ preparas tu tarea?	Por la noche.

17 ¿Qué o cuál?

Leer Necesitas más información sobre Isabel y Ricardo. Completa las preguntas con **qué** o **cuál(es)** para informarte. *(Hint: Complete each question with **qué** or **cuál(es)** to ask for more information.)*

1. Ricardo tiene ocho materias este semestre.
   ¿_____ materia le gusta más?
2. Hoy es el cumpleaños de Isabel.
   ¿_____ es la fecha de hoy?
3. Ricardo tiene una clase a la una.
   ¿_____ clase tiene a la una?
4. Hay dos señores en la clase.
   ¿_____ es el profesor?
5. Hay cinco libros en la clase de matemáticas.
   ¿_____ de los libros son de Ricardo?
6. No es una calculadora.
   ¿_____ es?
7. Paco, Ricardo, Ana y Marcela son estudiantes en la clase de matemáticas.
   ¿_____ de ellos sacan buenas notas?
8. Ricardo busca unos libros en su mochila.
   ¿_____ libros busca?

México

Nota cultural

Public high schools in Mexico City have two daily schedules. The students attend classes either during the morning, from around 7:30 to 12:30, or during the afternoon, from around 1:00 to 6:00.

Activity 20 brings together all concepts presented.

18 ¿Quién?

Hablar/*Escribir* A veces Isabel no escucha cuando sus amigos le hablan. Ayúdala a hacer preguntas basadas en lo que dicen. *(Hint: Help Isabel ask questions based on what her friends say.)*

modelo

Elena estudia español. (¿Quién?)

¿Quién estudia español?

1. El inglés es fácil. (¿Cómo?)
2. Paco y sus amigos tienen el receso a las tres. (¿Cuándo?)
3. La clase de música es divertida. (¿Cuál?)
4. Ana está en clase. (¿Dónde?)
5. Margarita compra una computadora. (¿Qué?)
6. Luisa descansa. (¿Quién?)
7. Estudio por la mañana. (¿Cuándo?)
8. Rita tiene una computadora nueva. (¿Qué?)
9. El libro de arte es interesante. (¿Cuál?)
10. Es un diccionario. (¿Qué?)

19 ¡Pobre Luis!

Escuchar Escucha la conversación entre Ernesto y Luis. Luego, contesta las preguntas. *(Hint: Listen to the conversation. Then answer the questions.)*

1. ¿Por qué no está bien Luis?
   - **a.** Tiene que ayudar a su padre.
   - **b.** Está muy bien.
   - **c.** Tiene un semestre difícil.
2. ¿Qué hora es?
   - **a.** Es la una y veinticinco.
   - **b.** Son las dos y media.
   - **c.** A la una y veinticinco.
3. ¿A qué hora tiene la cita con la señora García?
   - **a.** A las ocho.
   - **b.** A la una y media.
   - **c.** Es la una y media.
4. ¿Cuándo tiene un examen de literatura?
   - **a.** mañana
   - **b.** el lunes
   - **c.** hoy

20 ¿Cómo es tu horario?

Hablar Pregúntale a otro(a) estudiante sobre los detalles de su horario, como los días y las horas de sus clases, cómo son y adónde va para las clases. Cambien de papel. *(Hint: Ask another student about his or her schedule. Change roles.)*

modelo

Tú: *¿Qué clases tienes por la mañana?*

Otro(a): *Tengo español, matemáticas y…*

Tú: *¿A qué hora tienes la clase de…?*

Otro(a): *A las diez menos cuarto.*

Tú: *¿Adónde vas para esta clase?*

Otro(a): *Voy al…*

More Practice:

Más comunicación *p. R5*

Online Workbook
CLASSZONE.COM

Pronunciación

Trabalenguas

Pronunciación de la *h* y la *j* The **h** in Spanish is always silent, like the *h* in the English word *honest.* The **j** in Spanish sounds like the English *h* in *Ha, ha!* To practice these sounds, try this tongue twister.

Hoy Juanita hace de jinete.

En colores
CULTURA Y COMPARACIONES

PARA CONOCERNOS
STRATEGY: CONNECTING CULTURES

Compare snack foods Make a list of your favorite snack foods. Then read to find out about typical snack foods in Mexico City. Based on this, how would you compare snack foods in the U.S. with those in Mexico?

Las meriendas populares

Estados Unidos	México
1.	1.
2.	2.
3.	3.

¿Quieres comer una merienda mexicana?

Aquí tenemos dos tipos de meriendas típicas de México. En México la merienda grande se llama **una torta.** La torta tiene pan redondo[1] y muchos ingredientes. La merienda pequeña se llama **un sándwich.** En Estados Unidos, ¿cómo se llama una torta?

Una merienda típica de México es **el taco al pastor.** Tiene carne asada[2], normalmente puerco[3], en una tortilla de maíz[4]. ¿Es diferente de los tacos que tú comes?

[1] round bread
[2] roasted meat
[3] pork
[4] corn

Si te gusta comer fruta para la merienda, hay una variedad increíble. O tal vez te interesa[5] un **agua de fruta** en vez de[6] agua. En México es común beber aguas de frutas tropicales. Hay aguas de papaya, piña[7] y muchas otras frutas. ¡Y si no te gustan las frutas, siempre es posible comprar **una hamburguesa y papas fritas**!

[5] you are interested in
[6] instead of
[7] pineapple

More About Mexico
CLASSZONE.COM

¿Comprendiste?

1. ¿Qué diferencia hay entre un sándwich y una torta en México?
2. ¿Cómo es el taco al pastor?
3. ¿Qué hay en un agua de fruta?
4. ¿Cuáles de las meriendas mexicanas comes?

¿Qué piensas?

Estás en México y quieres comer. ¿Qué vas a comprar, una hamburguesa o una merienda típica de México? ¿Por qué?

ETAPA 2

En uso

REPASO Y MÁS COMUNICACIÓN

OBJECTIVES

- Talk about schedules
- Ask and tell time
- Ask questions
- Say where you are going
- Request food

Now you can...

- talk about schedules.

To review

- telling time, see p. 132.

1 ¡Qué horario!

Sara habla de su horario. ¿Qué dice?
(Hint: Tell what Sara says about her schedule.)

modelo

inglés

Tengo inglés los lunes, miércoles y viernes a las siete y media.

Sara Blanco	lunes	martes	miércoles	jueves	viernes
7:30	inglés	—	inglés	—	inglés
8:15	—	computación	—	computación	—
9:00	literatura	música	literatura	música	literatura
9:45	receso	receso	receso	receso	receso
10:30	educación física	ciencias naturales	educación física	ciencias naturales	educación física
11:15	historia	—	historia	—	historia
12:00	matemáticas	arte	matemáticas	arte	matemáticas

1. arte
2. literatura
3. música
4. ciencias naturales
5. receso
6. historia
7. matemáticas
8. computación

Now you can...

- ask and tell time.

To review

- telling time, see p. 132.
- location with the verb **estar**, see p. 134.

2 Un día ocupado

Hablas por teléfono con un(a) amigo(a). Hablen de la hora y expliquen dónde están estas personas. Cambien de papel.
(Hint: You're on the phone. Tell the time and where people are.)

modelo

9:05: Isabel (cafetería)

Tú: *¿Qué hora es?*

Otro(a) estudiante: *Son las **nueve y cinco** de la mañana.*

Tú: *¿Dónde está **Isabel**?*

Otro(a) estudiante: *Está en **la cafetería**.*

1. 8:15: Gloria (clase de arte)
2. 11:30: Ricardo (gimnasio)
3. 12:50: la profesora (oficina)
4. 1:00: Manuel y Eva (auditorio)
5. 2:40: Isabel (oficina del maestro)
6. 4:25: ustedes (gimnasio)
7. 7:30: René (biblioteca)
8. 9:45: tú (casa)

Self-Check Quiz
CLASSZONE.COM

Now you can...
- ask questions.

To review
- interrogative words, see p. 135.

3 ¡Muchas preguntas!

Los amigos de Ricardo le hacen preguntas. Complétalas con palabras interrogativas según las respuestas entre paréntesis.
*(**Hint:** Complete Ricardo's friends' questions with the correct interrogative word.)*

1. ¿ _____ estudias? (En mi casa.)
2. ¿ _____ es tu clase favorita? (La clase de literatura.)
3. ¿ _____ vas al gimnasio? (Por la tarde.)
4. ¿ _____ estás hoy? (Bien.)
5. ¿ _____ es el profesor de computación? (El profesor Anaya.)
6. ¿ _____ vas? (A la cafetería.)
7. ¿ _____ estudias inglés? (Me gusta el inglés.)
8. ¿ _____ están en la biblioteca? (Isabel y Andrea.)
9. ¿ _____ de estos libros necesitas? (El diccionario y el libro de inglés.)

Now you can...
- say where you are going.

To review
- the verb **ir**, see p. 130.

4 En la escuela

Es la una de la tarde. ¿Adónde van estas personas?
*(**Hint:** Tell where everyone is going.)*

modelo

Miguel y Ana tienen que correer.

Van al gimnasio.

1. Necesito buscar unos libros.
2. Isabel tiene que hablar con sus profesores.
3. Tú quieres comprar una torta.
4. Mis amigos tienen que cantar en un programa.
5. Nosotros tenemos un examen de español.

Now you can...
- request food.

To review
- vocabulary for snacks, see p. 125.

5 En la cafetería

¿Qué dices cuando quieres una de estas meriendas?
*(**Hint:** What do you say when you want one of these snacks?)*

modelo

Un taco, por favor.

1.

2.

3.

4.

5.

6.

6 El horario

STRATEGY: SPEAKING
Help your partner Make an effort to discover what you have in common. If you think of an activity that you have learned to say but don't remember the word, ask **¿Cómo se dice...?** Help each other out.

Conversa con otro(a) estudiante sobre su horario. *(Hint: Discuss your schedule with a partner.)*

¿A qué hora...?

- estar en la clase de inglés
- ir a la cafetería
- estar en el gimnasio
- preparar la tarea
- usar la computadora
- descansar

7 ¿Dónde estoy?

Describe una situación. Incluye información sobre la hora y las actividades de las personas. Tus amigos tienen que adivinar dónde estás. *(Hint: Describe a situation. Your partners have to guess where you are.)*

modelo

Tú: *Son las diez. Uso mi calculadora y escucho al profesor.*

Otro(a) estudiante: *Estás en la clase de matemáticas.*

8 En tu propia voz

ESCRITURA Prepara siete preguntas para un(a) nuevo(a) estudiante. Incluye preguntas sobre su horario, sus clases y sus actividades. *(Hint: List seven questions for a new student.)*

¿A qué hora...?	¿Cuál es...?	¿Qué...?
¿Dónde estás a las...?	¿Cómo es...?	¿Cuándo...?
¿Adónde vas para...?	¿Por qué...?	¿Quién...?

CONEXIONES

La salud You can learn about the nutrition in Mexican food from cookbooks, a menu from a Mexican restaurant, or the grocery store. Choose three foods and a beverage and find out about their nutritional value. Read their packaging, request nutritional information from a restaurant, or check a book that lists nutritional values. Create a chart. Which is the most nutritious? Why?

	Calorías	Grasa	Carbohidratos	Vitaminas
1.				
2.				

Flashcards
CLASSZONE.COM

En resumen

REPASO DE VOCABULARIO

TALKING ABOUT SCHEDULES

el almuerzo	*lunch*
la cita	*appointment*
el horario	*schedule*
el receso	*break*
el semestre	*semester*

Activities

comprar	*to buy*
descansar	*to rest*
estar	*to be*
terminar	*to finish*
tomar	*to take, to eat or drink*
visitar	*to visit*

ASKING AND TELLING TIME

¿A qué hora es...?	*(At)What time is...?*
¿Qué hora es?	*What time is it?*
A la(s)...	*At... o'clock.*
Es la.../Son las...	*It is... o'clock.*
de la mañana	*in the morning*
de la noche	*at night*
de la tarde	*in the afternoon*
la medianoche	*midnight*
el mediodía	*noon*
menos	*to, before*
por la mañana	*during the morning*
por la noche	*during the evening*
por la tarde	*during the afternoon*
el reloj	*clock, watch*
y cuarto	*quarter past*
y media	*half past*

ASKING QUESTIONS

adónde	*(to) where*
cómo	*how*
cuál(es)	*which (ones), what*
cuándo	*when*
dónde	*where*
por qué	*why*
qué	*what*
quién(es)	*who*

REQUESTING FOOD

¿Quieres beber...?	*Do you want to drink...?*
¿Quieres comer...?	*Do you want to eat...?*
Quiero beber...	*I want to drink...*
Quiero comer...	*I want to eat...*

Snacks

el agua (fem.)	*water*
la fruta	*fruit*
la hamburguesa	*hamburger*
la merienda	*snack*
las papas fritas	*french fries*
el refresco	*soft drink*
la torta	*sandwich*
el vaso de	*glass of*

SAYING WHERE YOU ARE GOING

ir	*to go*
al	*to the*

Places

el auditorio	*auditorium*
la biblioteca	*library*
la cafetería	*cafeteria, coffee shop*
el gimnasio	*gymnasium*
la oficina	*office*

OTHER WORDS AND PHRASES

durante	*during*
por favor	*please*
la verdad	*truth*

Juego

¿Adónde van?

Marco: Me gusta escuchar música.

Maricarmen: Necesito buscar unos libros.

Josefina: Voy a hablar con la maestra.
Ella no está en clase.

¿Adónde va Marco? ¿Maricarmen? ¿Josefina?

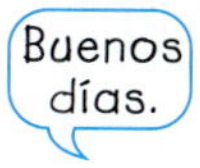

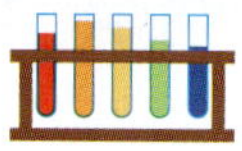

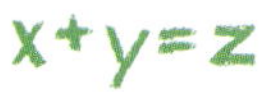

UNIDAD 2

ETAPA 3

Mis actividades

OBJECTIVES

- Discuss plans
- Sequence events
- Talk about places and people you know

¿Qué ves?

Mira la foto del centro de Coyoacán, en la Ciudad de México. *Coyoacán* significa «lugar de los coyotes».

1. ¿Hay muchas personas en el parque?
2. ¿La familia de la foto quiere comer o beber?
3. ¿Hay una universidad en la Ciudad de México?

En contexto

VIDEO DVD AUDIO

VOCABULARIO

Ricardo is taking a walk through a park where he and his friends spend a lot of time after school.

¡Hola! Después de clases voy al **parque.** Hay mucho que **hacer.** Me gusta **caminar con el perro.** Mi perro **tiene sed** y quiere **beber** agua. **Voy a** buscar a mis amigos.

A Me gusta **pasar un rato con mis amigos** en el parque. **Tocan la guitarra** y cantan.

B A veces me gusta **andar en bicicleta.**

CD-ROM Take-Home Tutor

D A Isabel le gusta leer **una revista.** A mí me gusta leer **el periódico.** ¿Quieres ir al **museo** o al **teatro** por la tarde?

E Cuando **tenemos hambre** y sed, compramos una merienda, como fruta y un refresco, en **la tienda.** ¡También me gusta **comer chicharrones!**

C La chica **cuida a su hermano.** Ellos **pasean** por el parque.

Online Workbook
CLASSZONE.COM

Preguntas personales

1. ¿Hay un parque en tu comunidad?
2. ¿Qué te gusta más, andar en bicicleta o correr?
3. ¿Te gusta leer el periódico o una revista?
4. ¿De vez en cuando vas a un museo o al teatro? ¿Vas con tus padres o con amigos?
5. ¿Tocas la guitarra u otro instrumento? ¿Uno(a) de tus amigos(as) toca un instrumento? ¿Cuál?

VIDEO DVD AUDIO

En vivo

DIÁLOGO

Ricardo

Isabel

PARA ESCUCHAR • STRATEGY: LISTENING

Listen and observe During a conversation, it is just as important to observe physical actions as it is to listen to the words spoken. Body language supports what is being said and sometimes better expresses meaning. What do you see and hear in this segment that influences Isabel's decision?

En el parque

1 ▶ **Ricardo:** ¡Hola, Isabel! ¿Qué tal?
Isabel: Bien, no tengo problemas con la clase de ciencias naturales.
Ricardo: ¡Qué bueno!

5 ▶ **Ricardo:** También toco el piano.
Isabel: ¡Mira nada más!
Ricardo: La verdad es que… no toco el piano muy bien.
Isabel: ¡Conozco a alguien muy modesto!

6 ▶ **Ricardo:** ¿Tienes hambre? ¿Comemos unos chicharrones? Esa señora vende unos chicharrones deliciosos.
Isabel: Sí, buena idea. Voy contigo.

7 ▶ **Ricardo:** Vamos a hablar del concurso. ¿Vas a participar?
Isabel: ¿Con mi horario?
Ricardo: Si no haces algo muy complicado, no hay problema.
Isabel: Pero, ¿qué?, ¿qué hago?

CD-ROM Take-Home Tutor

2 ▶ **Isabel:** ¿Adónde vamos? Quiero hablar del concurso.
Ricardo: ¿Tienes hambre?
Isabel: No, la verdad, no.

3 ▶ **Ricardo:** ¿Qué haces después de clases?
Isabel: Veo la televisión o paso un rato con mis amigos.
Ricardo: ¿Por qué no vamos al parque?

4 ▶ **Isabel:** Y tú, ¿qué haces después de las clases y antes de cenar?
Ricardo: Si no tengo que cuidar a mi hermano, ando en bicicleta.

8 ▶ **Ricardo:** No te preocupes. Las personas con inspiración no tienen problemas en México.
Isabel: Ricardo, ya es tarde. ¡Es hora de ir a casa!
Ricardo: Sí, es verdad.

9 ▶ **Isabel:** ¡La plaza! ¡La gente! ¡Los animales! ¡Los muchachos! ¡Las actividades! ¡La gente vive en una plaza! ¡Es mi proyecto para el concurso! La plaza es el corazón de la vida mexicana.

10 ▶ **Isabel:** ¡Voy a participar en el concurso! Para conocer a los mexicanos, hay que ir a una plaza. La plaza es un poema.

En acción

PARTE A Comprensión del diálogo

For Activities 1–2, refer to the dialog on pages 148–149.

Ricardo

Isabel

1 ¿En qué orden?

Escuchar ¿Cuándo pasan estas cosas? Pon las oraciones en el orden correcto según el diálogo. *(Hint: Put the sentences in order.)*

a. Isabel y Ricardo comen chicharrones.

b. Isabel pasa por la plaza.

c. Isabel y Ricardo van al parque.

d. Isabel decide participar en el concurso.

e. Ricardo habla de sus actividades después de las clases.

2 ¿Qué pasa?

Escuchar Escoge la(s) respuesta(s) correcta(s) según el diálogo. ¡Ojo! Algunas oraciones tienen más de una respuesta correcta. *(Hint: Choose the correct answer or answers.)*

1. Normalmente, después de las clases, Isabel _____.
a. va al parque
b. ve la televisión
c. pasa un rato con los amigos

2. Después de las clases, Ricardo _____.
a. cuida a su hermano
b. toca la guitarra
c. anda en bicicleta

3. En el parque, los dos comen _____.
a. papas fritas
b. chicharrones
c. tacos

4. El proyecto de Isabel para el concurso va a ser sobre la vida en _____.
a. el parque
b. la plaza
c. la ciudad

México

También se dice

There are different ways to say *Wow!* when you are amazed by something or someone. Isabel uses one in the dialog. Do you recognize which?

- **¡Anda!:** Spain
- **¡Mira nada más!:** Mexico
- **¡Mirá vos!:** Argentina

México

Nota cultural

El Museo Nacional de Antropología, in Mexico City's **Parque Chapultepec,** contains objects from Mexico's native cultures. It is a popular place for school groups to visit.

PARTE B Práctica del vocabulario

Objectives for Activities 3–6

• Discuss plans • Talk about places and people you know

3 ¿Dónde están?

Hablar ¿Dónde están Isabel y Ricardo? *(Hint: Say where they are.)*

modelo

Están en la cafetería.

1.

2.

3.

4.

4 ¿Qué hacen?

Hablar Explica lo que hacen después de las clases. ¿Lo haces también? *(Hint: Say what these people do after class. Do you do it too?)*

modelo

Estudiante A: *La muchacha cuida a su hermano. ¿Cuidas a tu hermano también?*

Estudiante B: *Sí, yo cuido a mi hermano.*

1.

2.

3.

4.

5.

5 ¿Qué haces?

STRATEGY: SPEAKING

Use all you know It is easy to rely on what you learned most recently. But it is important to reuse what you've learned before. Try to include activities you learned in Unit 1, such as **cantar** and **nadar**, in your answers.

Hablar/*Escribir* Escribe dos cosas que haces después de clases. Luego, habla con cinco estudiantes y escribe sus respuestas. *(Hint: Write two things you do and ask five others what they do.)*

modelo

Tú: *Normalmente, ¿qué haces después de clases, Marco?*

Marco: *Paso un rato con mis amigos.*

Nombre	Actividad
yo	Ando en bicicleta.
	. . . .
Marco	Pasa un rato con sus amigos.
	. . . .

Juego

Paco tiene un vaso de agua. Pepe tiene sed. ¿Qué tiene el perro?

6 ¡Qué hambre y sed!

Hablar Trabaja con otro(a) estudiante para hacer y contestar preguntas basadas en cada dibujo. Cambien de papel. *(Hint: Take turns answering questions based on each picture.)*

modelo

Estudiante A: *¿Tienes sed?*

Estudiante B: *Sí, tengo sed. Voy a beber un vaso de agua.*

Estudiante B: *¿Tienes hambre?*

Estudiante A: *Sí, tengo hambre. Voy a comer una hamburguesa.*

Nota: Vocabulario

To say that someone is thirsty, use the phrase **tener sed;** if the person is hungry, use **tener hambre.**

1. 
2. 
3. 
4. 
5. 
6. 

PARTE C

Práctica: gramática y vocabulario

Objectives for Activities 7–19
- Discuss plans • Sequence events • Talk about places and people you know

GRAMÁTICA Saying What You Are Going to Do: ir a ...

When you talk about things you are planning to do in the future, you say what you are *going to* do. To talk about activities you are going to do, use the phrase:

ir + a + *infinitive*

yo	**voy a...**	nosotros(as)	**vamos a...**
tú	**vas a...**	vosotros(as)	**vais a...**
usted, él, ella	**va a...**	ustedes, ellos(as)	**van a...**

Isabel says:

—¡**Voy a participar** en el concurso!

***I'm going to participate** in the contest!*

Practice: **Actividades** 7 8 9 10 11

Más práctica *cuaderno p. 53*
Para hispanohablantes *cuaderno p. 51*

Online Workbook CLASSZONE.COM

7 ¿A qué hora?

Hablar Isabel y Ricardo tienen mucho que hacer hoy. Explica lo que van a hacer y a qué hora. ¿Cuándo vas a hacer tú estas actividades?
(Hint: Say when they are going to do these things and when you will do them.)

modelo

Isabel y Ricardo / estudiar en la escuela / 10:00

Isabel y Ricardo** van a **estudiar en la escuela** a las **diez.

Yo voy a estudiar a las seis.

1. Isabel / usar la computadora / 11:20
2. Ricardo / ir a la biblioteca / 12:45
3. Isabel y Ricardo / tomar un refresco / 1:55
4. Ricardo / hacer ejercicio / 3:00
5. Isabel / pasear con su amiga / 6:30
6. Ricardo / ayudar a su padre / 7:45
7. Ricardo / preparar su tarea / 8:15
8. Isabel y Ricardo / cenar / 9:00
9. Isabel / ver la televisión / 9:35

Vocabulario

Más para hacer después de clases

cuidar (a) *to take care of*
un animal

pintar

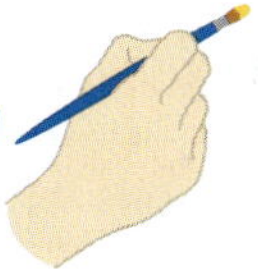

el pájaro

tocar el piano

el pez

ver la televisión

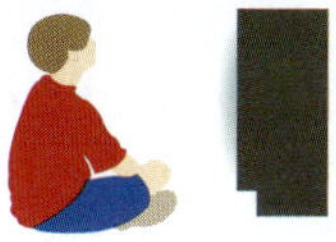

See the words for more pets on p. R20.

mandar una carta

cenar *to have dinner, supper*
hacer ejercicio *to exercise*
preparar *to prepare*
la cena *supper, dinner*
(la) comida *food, a meal*
ir al supermercado *to go to the supermarket*

leer *to read*
un poema *poem*
(la) poesía *poetry*
una novela *novel*

¿Qué te gusta hacer?

8 ¿Adónde vas?

Hablar Un(a) estudiante te pregunta sobre las actividades que tú y tus amigos van a hacer después de clases. *(Hint: Say what you and your friends are going to do after school.)*

modelo

tú y tus amigos: museo (¿ver arte o hacer ejercicio?)

Estudiante: *¿Adónde van ustedes?*

Tú: *Vamos al museo.*

Estudiante: *¿Qué van a hacer allí?*

Tú: *Vamos a ver arte.*

1. tú y tus amigos: parque (¿comprar libros o pasear?)
2. tú: casa (¿ver la televisión o hablar con el maestro?)
3. tú: biblioteca (¿estudiar o tocar la guitarra?)
4. tú y tus amigos: tienda (¿caminar con el perro o comprar ropa?)
5. tú: supermercado (¿mandar una carta o comprar una merienda?)
6. tú y tus amigos: cafetería (¿comer chicharrones o usar la computadora?)
7. tú: gimnasio (¿leer una revista o hacer ejercicio?)

9 ¡Lógicamente!

Hablar/*Escribir* ¿Adónde van y qué van a hacer tus amigos y tu familia? *(Hint: What are the people going to do?)*

modelo

Yo voy a la plaza. Voy a caminar con el perro.

¿Quién?	¿Adónde?	¿Qué va a hacer?
1. yo	auditorio	beber un refresco
2. mi amigo(a)	biblioteca	buscar un libro
3. mi amiga y yo	cafetería	pasear
4. mis padres	plaza	comprar una revista
5. ellas	tienda	escuchar música
6. mi hermano(a)	¿otro lugar?	¿otra actividad?

Vocabulario

Sequencing Events

To sequence events, use these words.

primero *first*

entonces *then, so*

luego *later*

por fin *finally*

antes *before*

después *after, afterward*

When a **noun** or an **infinitive** follows **antes** or **después**, use the preposition **de**.

¿Qué haces **después de las clases** y **antes de cenar**?

*What do you do **after** classes and **before** eating dinner?*

¿Qué pasa cada día?

México

También se dice

Plaza is a word that refers to any public square in the Spanish-speaking world. The main square in a city or town might be called the **plaza principal** or **plaza mayor.** In Mexico, the main square is called the **zócalo.** The **Zócalo** in Mexico City is where the cathedral and many government buildings are.

10 Primero...

Escuchar Lee las oraciones. Luego, escucha el párrafo. ¿En qué orden va a hacer Ricardo estas actividades? *(Hint: Listen and indicate the order in which Ricardo plans to do things.)*

a. Va a hacer ejercicio en el gimnasio.

b. Va a cenar.

c. Va a pasar un rato con sus amigos.

d. Va a ir a la biblioteca a buscar un libro.

11 Después de clases...

Escribir Escribe un párrafo sobre lo que *te gusta hacer* y lo que *tienes que hacer*. Usa **primero, antes (de), después (de), entonces, luego.** *(Hint: Write about what you **like to do** and **have to do**.)*

modelo

Después de las clases, me gusta hacer muchas cosas. Primero, me gusta ir al gimnasio. Luego, paso un rato con mis amigos. Hablamos o escuchamos música. A las seis voy a casa. ¿Y entonces? Siempre tengo que ayudar a mi madre y cuidar a mi hermana. Después de cenar, tengo que preparar mi tarea. ¡Por fin estudio!

More Practice: **Más comunicación** *p. R6*

GRAMÁTICA Present Tense of Regular -er and -ir Verbs

¿RECUERDAS? *p. 109* Remember how to conjugate present tense **-ar** verbs?

estudio	**estudiamos**
estudias	**estudiáis**
estudia	**estudian**

Regular verbs that end in **-er** or **-ir** work similarly. Regular **-er** verbs have the same endings as **-ir** verbs except in the **nosotros(as)** and **vosotros(as)** forms.

The letter change matches the verb ending:
-er verbs = **emos, éis**
-ir verbs = **imos, ís**

comer *to eat*

yo	**como**	nosotros(as)	**comemos**
tú	**comes**	vosotros(as)	**coméis**
usted, él, ella	**come**	ustedes, ellos(as)	**comen**

vivir *to live*

yo	**vivo**	nosotros(as)	**vivimos**
tú	**vives**	vosotros(as)	**vivís**
usted, él, ella	**vive**	ustedes, ellos(as)	**viven**

Ricardo says:

–Esa señora **vende** unos chicharrones deliciosos.
*That woman **sells** delicious pork rinds.*

Vocabulario

Verbs Ending in -er and -ir

You have seen the verbs **beber, comer, correr, escribir,** and **leer** before. Here are some others.

Verbs: **-er**
aprender *to learn*
comprender *to understand*
vender *to sell*
ver *to see* (**yo: veo**)

Verbs: **-ir**
abrir *to open*
compartir *to share*
recibir *to receive*
vivir *to live*

¿Qué pasa después de clases?

Practice: 12 13 14
Más práctica *cuaderno p. 54*
Para hispanohablantes *cuaderno p. 52*
Online Workbook CLASSZONE.COM

12 ¿Qué leen y escriben?

Hablar Explica lo que leen y escriben estas personas. *(**Hint:** Explain what these people are reading and writing.)*

modelo

Alberto / leer una novela

Alberto lee una novela.

1. Beatriz / leer un libro
2. los muchachos / leer el diccionario
3. tú / leer una revista
4. Horacio / escribir un poema
5. tú / escribir una carta
6. sus padres / escribir poesía
7. yo / leer ¿?
8. mi amigo(a) / escribir ¿?
9. mi amigo(a) y yo / leer ¿?
10. yo / escribir ¿?

México

Nota cultural

In Mexico mealtimes are much later than in the United States. Lunch is usually between 2:00 and 3:00 in the afternoon and dinner between 9:00 and 10:00 in the evening.

13 ¿Mucho o poco?

Hablar/*Escribir* ¿Las personas que tú conoces hacen mucho o poco estas cosas? *(**Hint:** Do the people you know do these things a lot or a little?)*

1. yo (aprender)
2. mis amigos y yo (comer)
3. mis amigos (compartir las meriendas)
4. mi amigo(a) (vender periódicos)
5. yo (ver la televisión)
6. mi hermano(a) (recibir cartas)
7. mi padre (leer)
8. los estudiantes (abrir los libros)
9. mis primos (comer y beber)
10. mi madre (comprender)

14 ¿Lo hacen o no?

Hablar/*Escribir* Pregúntales a cinco estudiantes si hacen lo siguiente. Dale un resumen de las respuestas a la clase. *(**Hint:** Ask five students whether they do the following. Report the results.)*

modelo

comer en la cafetería

Tú: *¿Comes en la cafetería?*

Pedro: *No, no como en la cafetería.*

Resumen: *Cristina, Ramón, Lidia y Tomás comen en la cafetería. Pedro no come en la cafetería.*

1. vivir en un apartamento
2. aprender mucho en la escuela
3. ver la televisión todos los días
4. recibir muchas cartas
5. comprender las matemáticas

GRAMÁTICA Regular Present Tense Verbs with Irregular yo Forms

These are verbs that have regular present tense forms except for an irregular **yo** form.

conocer *to know, to be familiar with (a person or a place)*

conozco	conocemos
conoces	conocéis
conoce	conocen

These verbs follow the form for regular **-er** verbs except in the **yo** form.

hacer *to do, to make*

hago	hacemos
haces	hacéis
hace	hacen

Isabel says:

—¡**Conozco a alguien** muy modesto!
***I know someone** very modest!*

Voy a cuidar **a mi hermano.**
*I am going to take care of **my brother.***

Voy a cuidar **mi gato.**
*I am going to take care of **my cat.***

Note that whenever a **person** is the object of a verb, the personal **a** must be used after the **verb** except when using the verb **tener.**

A may also be used when talking about animals that are pets, but it is not required.

Practice: **Actividades** 15 16 17

Más práctica *cuaderno p. 55*
Para hispanohablantes *cuaderno p. 53*

Online Workbook CLASSZONE.COM

15 En la biblioteca

Leer Completa la conversación de Isabel y Ricardo con el verbo **hacer**. *(Hint: Practice with the verb **hacer**.)*

Isabel: Ricardo, ¿qué __1__?
Ricardo: __2__ la tarea. Y tú, ¿qué __3__?
Isabel: Yo también __4__ la tarea.
Ricardo: ¿Vas a participar en el concurso?
Isabel: ¡Sí, y voy a __5__ algo muy interesante!

16 Un día típico

Hablar/Escribir Explica lo que hacen. Usa la **a** personal si es necesario. *(Hint: Explain what they're doing. Use the personal **a** if needed.)*

1. un amigo / cuidar / ¿?
2. yo / hacer / ¿?
3. nosotros / esperar / ¿?
4. mis padres / visitar / ¿?
5. tú / ayudar / ¿?
6. yo / conocer / ¿?

17 ¿A quién conocen?

Hablar/Escribir Tú, tus amigos y tu familia conocen a muchas personas. Explica a quiénes conocen. *(Hint: Explain who they know.)*

1. yo
2. mi amigo(a)
3. mi hermano(a)
4. mi familia y yo
5. mis padres
6. mis amigos

GRAMÁTICA Using the Verb oír

Like **hacer** and **conocer**, the verb **oír** *(to hear)* has an irregular **yo** form in the present tense.

- Some of its forms also require a spelling change where the **í** becomes a **y**.
- Note that the **nosotros(as)** and **vosotros(as)** forms have accents.

oigo	oímos
oyes	oís
oye	oyen

You may hear the expression **¡Oye!** used throughout the dialog. It is used to get someone's attention, the way *Hey!* is used in English.

To get Isabel's attention Ricardo might say: —¡**Oye,** Isabel!

Practice: Actividades 18 19

Más práctica *cuaderno p. 56*
Para hispanohablantes *cuaderno p. 54*

Online Workbook CLASSZONE.COM

18 ¿A quiénes oyen?

Escribir ¿A quién oye cada persona? Completa las oraciones con la forma correcta del verbo **oír**. *(Hint: Say whom each person hears.)*

modelo

Isabel / su madre

Isabel** oye a **su madre.

1. Anita / sus amigos
2. los estudiantes / la profesora
3. tú / tu amigo
4. yo / mi hermano
5. Felipe y yo / la señora Ruiz
6. ustedes / sus vecinos
7. Ricardo / el profesor Martínez
8. nosotros / papá

19 ¿Dónde oyes...?

Hablar Conversa con otro(a) estudiante sobre dónde oyes estas cosas. *(Hint: Say where you hear these things.)*

modelo

música **Estudiante A:** *¿Dónde oyes música?*
Estudiante B: *Oigo música en el auditorio.*

Estudiante A — PREGUNTAS

1. música
2. la profesora
3. tus amigos
4. la guitarra
5. el doctor
6. unos pájaros
7. el piano

Estudiante B — RESPUESTAS

- la casa
- la clase
- el auditorio
- el parque
- la oficina
- la tienda

PARTE D

Todo en acción

Activities 20–21 bring together all concepts presented.

20 ¡A oír bien!

Escuchar Escoge la respuesta más apropiada para cada oración. *(Hint: Choose the best response.)*

1. **a.** caminar con el perro
   b. tocar la guitarra
   c. hacer ejercicio
2. **a.** ir al parque
   b. comer una hamburguesa
   c. abrir el libro
3. **a.** mandar una carta
   b. ir al teatro
   c. comprar una novela
4. **a.** comer una torta
   b. beber un refresco
   c. visitar a los amigos

21 Una carta

Escribir Tu amigo(a) quiere saber qué haces todos los días. Escríbele una carta. *(Hint: Write a letter to your friend about your daily activities.)*

modelo

Querido Paco:

¿Cómo estás? Yo estoy muy bien. ¿Qué hago todos los días? Pues, hago muchas cosas. Primero, siempre camino con el perro en el parque. Después, paso un rato con mis amigos. A veces, andamos en bicicleta o vamos a casa para escuchar música. De vez en cuando, tengo que cuidar a mi hermano...

¿Y tú? ¿Qué haces después de las clases?

Tu amigo,

Daniel

More Practice: **Más comunicación** *p. R6*

Online Workbook
CLASSZONE.COM

Pronunciación

Refrán

La pronunciación y los acentos

1. Words ending in a vowel, or the letters **n** or **s**, are stressed on the next-to-last syllable.
2. Words ending in a consonant other than **n** or **s** are stressed on the last syllable.
3. Words that have written accents are stressed on the syllable with the accent.

A las diez en la cama estés,
mejor antes que después.

AUDIO

En voces

LECTURA

PARA LEER

STRATEGY: READING

Skim Before reading a long passage, it is helpful to read quickly to get a general idea of its content. Skim the paragraphs, noting clues that indicate the central theme or topic. By skimming, you can tell quickly what a reading is about. Then it will be easier to do a more careful reading.

México y sus jóvenes

¿Qué hacen los mexicanos jóvenes? De lunes a viernes los muchachos que tienen menos de[1] 18 años van a la escuela. Tienen muchas materias —a veces tienen hasta ocho clases en un día. Y también tienen mucha tarea. Por eso, después de clases muchos de los estudiantes van a sus casas para hacer la tarea y después descansar.

En la Ciudad de México hay muchos teatros, museos, tiendas y parques. En cada[2] lugar es posible ver a muchos jóvenes, especialmente los fines de semana.

[1] less than
[2] each, every

Los viernes por la tarde, los sábados y los domingos son los días principales en que los jóvenes mexicanos están libres[3]. Los domingos hay mucha gente en los parques. Andan en bicicleta, practican deportes[4] o tocan un instrumento. De vez en cuando, para el almuerzo, van a un restaurante con sus familias. El domingo es el día principal para pasear y descansar.

[3] free
[4] sports

Online Workbook
CLASSZONE.COM

¿Comprendiste?

1. ¿Qué hacen los jóvenes de lunes a viernes?
2. ¿Adónde van muchos jóvenes los fines de semana en la Ciudad de México?
3. ¿Qué actividades hacen los domingos?
4. ¿Qué hace a veces una familia los domingos?

¿Qué piensas?

Explica si tu vida es como la vida de un joven mexicano.

En colores

VIDEO DVD

CULTURA Y COMPARACIONES

PARA CONOCERNOS

STRATEGY: CONNECTING CULTURES

Compare places Have you lived in or visited a place that has a long history? Is there a special name for that historical area? How old is it? What can you see—buildings, sculptures, murals—that reveals its history? What is its historical importance? What comparisons can you make between it and places in «**El Zócalo: centro de México**»?

Conozco este lugar	Lugar histórico de México
Nombre del lugar: Edad del lugar: Pinturas/Murales: Otras cosas:	Nombre del lugar: Edad del lugar: Pinturas/Murales: Otras cosas:

El Zócalo:

Un canal del imperio azteca

El Zócalo es el centro de la Ciudad de México. Es la plaza principal de la ciudad. Allí estaban[1] la vieja capital colonial española y también la capital azteca de México, Tenochtitlán. En el tiempo de los aztecas, el Zócalo fue[2] un centro ceremonial con pirámides y palacios. Después de conquistar Tenochtitlán en 1521, los españoles construyeron[3] su capital encima de[4] la capital de los aztecas. La Catedral española está aquí, encima del Templo Mayor de los aztecas,

[1] there used to be [2] was [3] built [4] on top of

En el Zócalo están **la Catedral** y **el Sagrario**. Son dos símbolos religiosos y ejemplos importantes de la arquitectura y el arte colonial de México.

El Templo Mayor es la pirámide principal de Tenochtitlán. De esta excavación vienen descubrimientos[6] importantes sobre los aztecas.

El calendario azteca o la Piedra del Sol[7] fue descubierto[8] debajo del[9] Zócalo en 1790.

centro de México

una gran pirámide. El Palacio Nacional, el centro del gobierno[5] mexicano, está encima de las ruinas de un palacio azteca. Hoy el Zócalo es el centro de la vida social y religiosa de las personas de esta ciudad.

[5] government
[6] discoveries
[7] Sun Stone
[8] was discovered
[9] beneath

More About Mexico
CLASSZONE.COM

¿Comprendiste?

1. ¿Cómo se llama la capital azteca?
2. ¿Qué está encima de las ruinas de un palacio?
3. ¿Qué descubrimientos importantes hay en el Zócalo?
4. ¿Qué lugar del Zócalo representa la vida política de México?
5. ¿Cuáles representan la vida religiosa?

¿Qué piensas?

1. Si vas a la Ciudad de México, ¿por qué es importante ver el Zócalo?
2. ¿Qué importancia tiene el Zócalo en la historia de México?

ETAPA 3

En uso

REPASO Y MÁS COMUNICACIÓN

OBJECTIVES
- Discuss plans
- Sequence events
- Talk about places and people you know

Now you can...
- discuss plans.

To review
- **ir** + **a** + infinitive, see p. 153.

1 ¿Qué vas a hacer tú?

Todos tienen planes para esta tarde. ¿Qué van a hacer? *(**Hint**: Tell what people's afternoon plans are.)*

modelo

Victoria — *Victoria va a tocar la guitarra.*

1. Juan y Rubén

2. yo

3. la señora Estrada

4. nosotros

5. tú

6. Benjamín

Now you can...
- talk about places and people you know.

To review
- the verb **conocer**, see verbs with irregular **yo** forms, p. 157.

2 Nuestra comunidad

Todos hablan de las personas y de los lugares que conocen en la comunidad. ¿Qué dicen? *(**Hint:** Tell who is familiar with the people and places.)*

modelo

nosotros: la familia Méndez

Nosotros** conocemos a **la familia Méndez.

1. ellos: los maestros
2. yo: el museo de arte
3. tú: la tienda de música
4. Marcela: el doctor
5. nosotras: el teatro
6. yo: las policías

Self-Check Quiz
CLASSZONE.COM

Now you can...
- sequence events.

To review
- vocabulary for sequencing events, see p. 154.

3 Todos los sábados

¿Qué hace Miguel todos los sábados? Usa el horario para completar las oraciones. *(Hint: Tell what Miguel does every Saturday.)*

modelo

Primero, Miguel lee el periódico.

10:00 leer el periódico
10:30 correr en el gimnasio
11:30 escribir cartas
1:00 comer con los amigos
3:00 descansar en casa
5:00 pasear en el parque

1. _____ correr en el gimnasio, Miguel lee el periódico.
2. _____ correr, él escribe cartas.
3. _____, Miguel come con los amigos.
4. _____ comer, descansa en casa.
5. _____, él pasea en el parque.

Now you can...
- discuss plans.

To review
- the present tense of regular **-er** and **-ir** verbs, see p. 155.
- verbs with irregular **yo** forms, see p. 157.
- the verb **oír**, see p. 158.

4 ¡Muchas actividades!

¿Dónde hacen estas personas las siguientes actividades? *(Hint: Where do people do these activities?)*

modelo

Luz / correr (¿museo o parque?)
Luz corre en el parque.

1. Samuel y Sofía / leer unos libros (¿biblioteca o teatro?)
2. yo / ver la televisión (¿gimnasio o casa?)
3. usted / comer fruta (¿museo o cafetería?)
4. nosotros / hacer la tarea (¿supermercado o biblioteca?)
5. yo / oír música (¿auditorio o museo?)
6. la señora Santana / vender ropa (¿cafetería o tienda?)
7. tú / recibir cartas (¿casa o parque?)
8. yo / hacer ejercicio (¿gimnasio o museo?)
9. nosotros / comer chicharrones (¿parque o biblioteca?)
10. Eduardo / oír los pájaros (¿teatro o parque?)
11. Marcelo / comprender la lección (¿clase de matemáticas o cafetería?)
12. Cristina / aprender historia (¿escuela o gimnasio?)

5 Y luego...

STRATEGY: SPEAKING
Ask for clarification Show your interest by asking for clarification or verification: **Ah, sí, ¿tú vas al museo antes de comer?** Or use other words about the sequence of plans: **entonces, luego, después (de), antes (de),** or a specific time.

Imagínate que eres un(a) turista en una ciudad mexicana. Selecciona cuatro actividades. Luego, conversa con otro(a) estudiante sobre tus planes. *(Hint: You are a tourist. Select four activities and explain your plans.)*

modelo

Primero, voy al Zócalo...

9:00	Excursión al Zócalo
10:30	Museo de Arte Moderno
2:00	Almuerzo
3:30	Tienda de ropa típica
5:00	Paseo en el parque central
8:30	Cena mexicana en el hotel

6 En la plaza

Tú y tus compañeros están en esta plaza mexicana. Hablen sobre lo que ven y oyen y mencionen a las personas que conocen. ¡Usen la imaginación! *(Hint: You and your classmates are in this Mexican plaza. Talk about what you see and hear and the people you know.)*

7 En tu propia voz

ESCRITURA Imagínate que el sábado vas a hacer muchas cosas. Describe tus planes. *(Hint: Describe your plans.)*

Entonces...
Luego...
Por la tarde voy a...
Antes de...
Primero, voy a...
Después...

TÚ EN LA COMUNIDAD

Tim is a high school student in Wisconsin. He volunteers to help children with their homework, and he often speaks with them in Spanish. He also uses Spanish to understand some of the customers at his part-time job at a store. Do you speak Spanish at work?

Flashcards
CLASSZONE.COM

En resumen

REPASO DE VOCABULARIO

DISCUSSING PLANS

ir a...	*to be going to...*

After-school Plans

andar en bicicleta	*to ride a bike*
caminar con el perro	*to walk the dog*
cenar	*to have dinner, supper*
comer chicharrones	*to eat pork rinds*
cuidar (a)	*to take care of*
el animal	*animal*
mi hermano(a)	*my brother (sister)*
el pájaro	*bird*
el pez	*fish*
hacer ejercicio	*to exercise*
ir al supermercado	*to go to the supermarket*
leer	*to read*
la novela	*novel*
el periódico	*newspaper*
el poema	*poem*
la poesía	*poetry*
la revista	*magazine*
mandar una carta	*to send a letter*
pasar un rato con los amigos	*to spend time with friends*
pasear	*to go for a walk*
pintar	*to paint*
preparar	*to prepare*
la cena	*supper, dinner*
la comida	*food, a meal*
tocar el piano	*to play the piano*
tocar la guitarra	*to play the guitar*
ver la televisión	*to watch television*

SEQUENCING EVENTS

antes (de)	*before*
después (de)	*after, afterward*
entonces	*then, so*
luego	*later*
por fin	*finally*
primero	*first*

ACTIVITIES

abrir	*to open*
aprender	*to learn*
beber	*to drink*
compartir	*to share*
comprender	*to understand*
hacer	*to make, to do*
oír	*to hear*
recibir	*to receive*
tener hambre	*to be hungry*
tener sed	*to be thirsty*
vender	*to sell*
ver	*to see*
vivir	*to live*

PLACES AND PEOPLE YOU KNOW

conocer a alguien	*to know, to be familiar with someone*

Places

el museo	*museum*
el parque	*park*
el teatro	*theater*
la tienda	*store*

OTHER WORDS AND PHRASES

cada	*each, every*
el corazón	*heart*
la gente	*people*
el problema	*problem*
la vida	*life*

Juego

¿Qué actividades hacen las personas?

Adriana: Le gusta hacer ejercicio y tiene un perro.

José: Le gusta tocar un instrumento. Carlos Santana, Mary Chapin Carpenter y Melissa Etheridge tocan este instrumento.

Jorge: Es un hermano muy responsable. Tiene una familia grande.

UNIDAD 2

En tu propia voz

ESCRITURA

El horario de la escuela

Alicia and Álvaro are Spanish-speaking students who are coming to your school. Familiarize them with a typical school week by sending them their schedule, which is the same as yours.

Function: Acquaint new students with school schedule
Context: Informing Spanish-speaking students
Content: Description of a school day
Text type: School schedule

PARA ESCRIBIR • STRATEGY: WRITING

Organize information chronologically and by category A clear and detailed schedule is important for any student. Alicia and Álvaro will need to know the school hours, class subjects and times, and after-school activities in chronological order.

Modelo del estudiante

Franklin High School

FHS

El horario escolar

The writer organizes information chronologically, using appropriate times.

7:40 Llegamos a la escuela.

7:45–11:00 Tenemos las clases de historia, música (lunes, miércoles y viernes), arte (martes y jueves), inglés y biología por la mañana.

The author groups classes according to the morning or afternoon, noting that not all classes meet every day.

11:05–12:05 Almuerzo. Comemos en la cafetería.

12:10–2:35 Tenemos las clases de español, matemáticas, educación física (lunes y jueves) y computación (martes, miércoles y viernes) por la tarde.

2:50–4:00 Siempre hay actividades después de las clases. Los lunes vamos al club de español. Los martes y jueves nadamos. Los miércoles usamos las computadoras. Los viernes bailamos en el gimnasio.

The writer describes a variety of extracurricular activities (common in U.S. schools but not Latin ones) and tells on which days they take place.

Writing Center
CLASSZONE.COM

Estrategias para escribir

Antes de escribir...

Before you begin the first draft of your schedule, brainstorm the elements of your school week. Good writers always begin by thinking about their audience, the people who will be reading their work. So think about the Spanish-speaking students. What kinds of things would you want to know if you were in their place? Use a chart to help you organize your ideas. Be sure to include your class subjects and times, lunch time, and after-school activities. Then write your schedule in chronological order, including complete-sentence descriptions for each block of time.

mi horario

hora	lunes	martes	miércoles	jueves	viernes
7:45	llegar →				
8:00	matemáticas →				
8:45	educación física	música	música	educación física	música

Revisiones

Share your draft with a partner. Then ask:

- *Is the schedule complete and accurate?*
- *Is the schedule organized chronologically?*
- *Would any other information be useful?*

La versión final

Review what you have written, asking yourself these questions:

- *Did I use the appropriate verb forms?*

Try this: Circle every verb. Check to make sure that each verb has the appropriate subject.

- *Are articles used correctly?*

Try this: Underline every article/noun combination. Check to make sure that each article agrees in number and gender with its noun.

7:45
Llegamos a la escuela.
8:00–11:15 tenemos
Nosotros ~~tiene~~ las clases de matemáticas, educación física, música, literatura y español por ~~el~~ la mañana.

UNIDAD 3

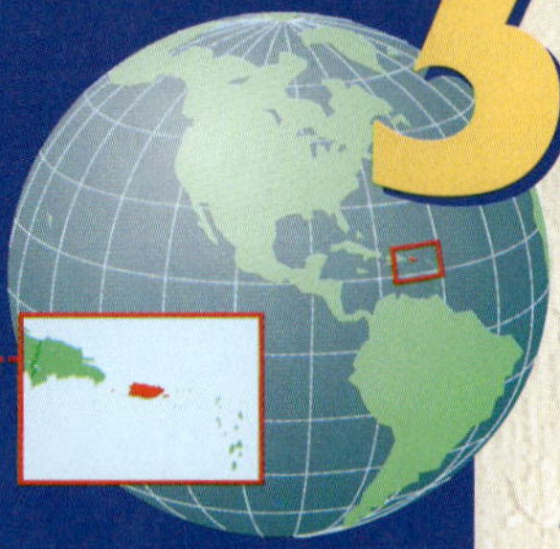

SAN JUAN
PUERTO RICO

EL FIN DE SEMANA

TEXAS Essential Knowledge and Skills

1 Communication

A Engage in exchanges
Discussing what just happened
Talking on the telephone
Discussing sports

B Demonstrate understanding
Expressing feelings and emotions
Stating preferences and opinions

C Present information
Talking about clothes and accessories
Describing the weather

2 Cultures

A Practices
Regional vocabulary
Leisure activities in Puerto Rico
The history, geography, and wildlife of Puerto Rico
Some important people from Puerto Rico

3 Connections

A Use resources
Music: Music and dance in Puerto Rico and the U.S.

B Use the language
Science: Using the Celsius scale in Spanish-speaking countries and learning the conversion formula

4 Comparisons

B Concept of culture
Sports traditions in Puerto Rico and the U.S.
Tourist attractions in Puerto Rico and the U.S.

C Influence
Music and dance in Puerto Rico and the U.S.

5 Communities

A Within and beyond school
Using Spanish for personal interest

B Lifelong learner
Using Spanish to help others

GIGI FERNÁNDEZ won the gold medal in women's tennis (doubles) in the 1992 and 1996 Summer Olympics. What other Latin American athletes do you know?

INTERNET Preview

CLASSZONE.COM

- More About Puerto Rico
- Flashcards
- Webquest
- Writing Center
- Self-Check Quizzes
- Online Workbook
- eEdition Plus Online

ALMANAQUE CULTURAL

POBLACIÓN: 3.808.610

ALTURA: 0 metros (el nivel del mar)

CLIMA: 27° C (80° F)

COMIDA TÍPICA: pasta de guayaba, tostones, pernil

GENTE FAMOSA DE PUERTO RICO: Gigi Fernández (tenista), Luis Muñoz Marín (político), Luis Rafael Sánchez (escritor), Chayanne (cantante)

¿VAS A PUERTO RICO? No necesitas pasaporte. Puerto Rico es una parte de Estados Unidos.

More About Puerto Rico
CLASSZONE.COM

EL MORRO is a fortress that the Spanish began in 1539 and finished in 1787. How could such a fortress protect the city of San Juan?

EL LORO PUERTORRIQUEÑO became an endangered species in 1971, when only twenty of these parrots were left. Their numbers have now increased. You might see one in El Yunque, the tropical rain forest. What other animals have been saved from extinction?

LUIS MUÑOZ MARÍN (1898–1980) became the island's first elected governor in 1948. In 1952 he signed an agreement making Puerto Rico a commonwealth of the U.S. What other U.S. territories do you know that aren't states?

PASTA DE GUAYABA is a popular dessert. This sweet, thick paste made from the guava fruit is usually eaten with white cheese. What tropical fruits have you eaten?

LOS TAÍNOS were the people living on the island when Columbus arrived in 1493. They left these glyphs. Their language survived in words like **huracán** *(hurricane)*. What other Native American cultures can you name?

UNIDAD 3

EL FIN DE SEMANA

Texas Essential Knowledge and Skills

1 Comunicación

2 Culturas

The student gains knowledge and understanding of other cultures.

3 Conexiones

4 Comparaciones

5 Comunidades

Culturas

Have you ever wondered what pastimes young people enjoy most in other countries? What things people there build or create? The things they do and make—from music to monuments—tell you a lot about the people in a culture. In this unit, you will get to know young people and special places in San Juan, Puerto Rico.

Culturas en acción **Estás de vacaciones en Puerto Rico. Habla de tus planes para hoy. ¿Vas a escuchar música puertorriqueña? ¿Vas a comer en un restaurante puertorriqueño?**

Comunicación

If you were to invite new friends to join you in getting acquainted with Puerto Rico, what would you say to them? Would you use any of the following questions?

¿Comemos algo?

¿Vamos a caminar?

¿Hay tiendas en el Viejo San Juan?

¿Qué te gusta hacer?

Webquest
CLASSZONE.COM

Explore cultures in Puerto Rico through guided Web activities.

Comunidades

You can enjoy contributions made by Puerto Ricans in your own community. They may be your neighbors, or famous athletes and entertainers on television.

¿Conoces puertorriqueños famosos? ¿Por qué son famosos?

Comparaciones

Puerto Rico and the United States have some pastimes in common. What do you think are some popular ones, based on the photos you see here?

¿Te gusta el béisbol? ¿Escuchas la música de Puerto Rico?

Conexiones

Knowing what to expect about geography, climate, animal life, and earth sciences would help you enjoy a visit to Puerto Rico. Consider these questions:

¿Qué ropa necesitas en un clima tropical?

¿Hay animales exóticos en el bosque tropical?

¿Leemos la temperatura en *Celsius* o *Fahrenheit* en Puerto Rico?

Fíjate

Each of the following statements relates to one or more of the areas described (**Culturas, Comunicación, Comunidades, Comparaciones, Conexiones**). Determine which one each statement best represents.

1. El loro puertorriqueño es un pájaro bonito.
2. El béisbol es muy popular en Puerto Rico y en Estados Unidos.
3. A los jóvenes les gustan la música y el baile tradicionales de la isla.
4. Vamos a invitar a nuestros amigos a conocer las tradiciones puertorriqueñas.
5. Si visitas Puerto Rico, tienes que visitar la interesante comunidad del Viejo San Juan.

UNIDAD 3

ETAPA 1

¡Me gusta el tiempo libre!

OBJECTIVES

- Extend invitations
- Talk on the phone
- Express feelings
- Say where you are coming from
- Say what just happened

¿Qué ves?

Mira la foto de la calle de San Sebastián en el Viejo San Juan, Puerto Rico.

1. ¿Las casas son viejas?
2. ¿Qué llevan las personas, ropa formal o casual?
3. ¿Cómo se llama la plaza de la calle San Sebastián?

En contexto

VIDEO DVD AUDIO

VOCABULARIO

Look at the illustrations to see what Diana and Ignacio do in their free time. This will help you understand the meaning of the words in blue. It will also help you answer the questions on the next page.

A

Ignacio y Diana tienen **tiempo libre.** Hoy van a unas tiendas para **ir de compras.**

Diana: **¿Quieres acompañarme a** comprar unas cosas?
Ignacio: **Sí, me encantaría.**

B El muchacho de la tienda trabaja mucho. Él está muy **ocupado.**

Diana: ¿Por qué no **alquilamos un video? ¿Te gustaría** ver algo?
Ignacio: **¡Claro que sí!**

C ¡Para Ignacio y Diana es divertido tomar fotos! Expresan muchas emociones. Primero, Diana está **alegre,** pero Ignacio está **triste.** Luego, Diana está **enojada,** pero Ignacio no. Él está **tranquilo.** Al final Ignacio está **preocupado,** pero Diana no. Ella está **contenta.**

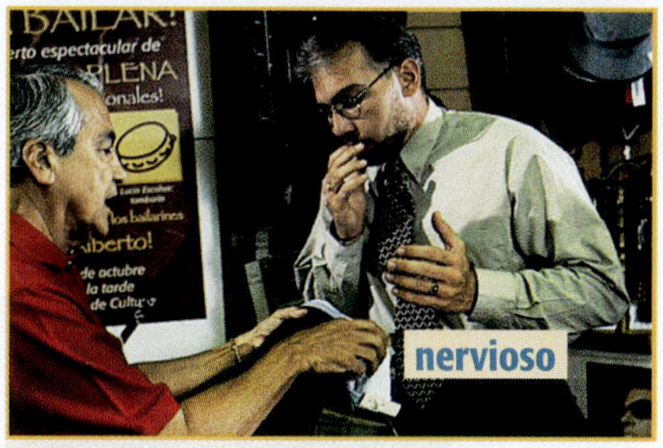

Take-Home Tutor

D El hombre que trabaja en la tienda está **nervioso.** ¡El cliente de la camisa roja está enojado! La madre cuida a su niño. Él está **enfermo.**

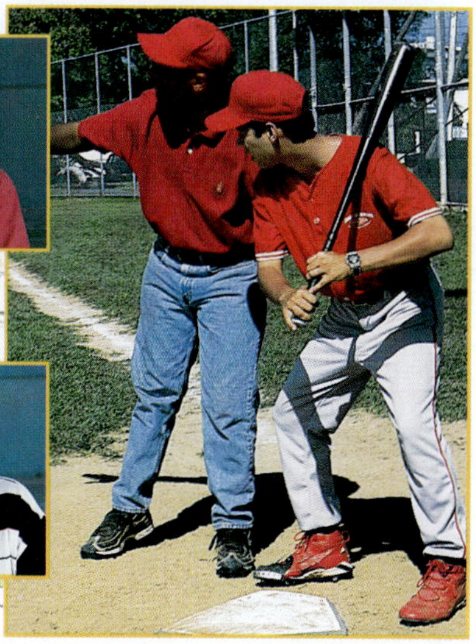

F En el estadio la comunidad **practica deportes.** En Puerto Rico el deporte favorito es el béisbol. Muchas personas miran. Unas están **emocionadas,** otras están **deprimidas.**

G **Ignacio:** **Te invito** a ir a **un concierto.**

Diana: ¡Gracias!

E Ignacio y Diana **van al cine.** Después de ver **la película,** Diana está **cansada.**

Online Workbook
CLASSZONE.COM

Preguntas personales

1. ¿Tienes mucho tiempo libre?
2. ¿Te gusta más ir al cine o alquilar un video?
3. ¿Te gusta ir de compras o practicar deportes?
4. ¿Te gusta ir a conciertos? ¿Cómo estás cuando escuchas un concierto?
5. ¿Cuál es tu actividad favorita? ¿Cómo estás cuando haces la actividad?

VIDEO DVD AUDIO

En vivo
DIÁLOGO

Diana

Ignacio

Roberto

PARA ESCUCHAR • STRATEGY: LISTENING

Listen for a purpose Listening for specific information is like scanning when reading. Practice listening for one idea. What is the exact day and time of an important event for Ignacio? Why is it important?

El evento	El día	La hora

La llamada

1 ▶ **Diana:** Oye, hermano, voy de compras. ¿Quieres acompañarme?
Ignacio: No, tal vez otro día.
Diana: ¡Qué aburrido!

5 ▶ **Roberto:** Tengo muy buenas noticias. ¡Estoy muy emocionado! ¡Mi familia y yo vamos a Puerto Rico a vivir! Llegamos el viernes. ¿Cuándo hablamos?

6 ▶ **Ignacio:** Te invito a mi práctica de béisbol. Es el sábado, a las dos. ¿Te gustaría venir?
Roberto: ¡Claro que sí! En el lugar de siempre, ¿no?
Ignacio: Sí, en el mismo lugar de siempre.
Roberto: Bueno, ¡adiós!

7 ▶ **Diana:** ¿Tu pana Roberto?
Ignacio: Roberto y su familia vienen a vivir a Puerto Rico de nuevo.
Diana: Estás contento, ¿no?
Ignacio: Sí, pero también estoy nervioso.

CD-ROM Take-Home Tutor

2 ▶ **Ignacio:** ¡El teléfono!
Diana: Ay, Ignacio. No tienes que contestar; la máquina contesta.

3 ▶ **Mensaje:** Es la casa de la familia Ortiz. Deja un mensaje después del tono. ¡Gracias!
Roberto: ¡Oye, Ignacio! Habla tu viejo amigo Roberto. Si estás allí, ¡por favor, contesta!

4 ▶ **Ignacio:** ¡Sí, Roberto, estoy aquí! ¡Qué sorpresa! ¿Cómo estás? ¿Dónde estás? En Minnesota, ¿no?

8 ▶ **Diana:** Va a ser el Roberto de siempre. Bueno, ¿quieres ir de compras, o no?
Ignacio: Pues, sí, hermanita. Ya no quiero ver más deportes. Vamos.

9 ▶ **Diana:** Acabo de comprar unos zapatos.
Ignacio: Yo vengo del cine.
Diana: ¿Hay una película interesante?
Ignacio: A las muchachas sólo les gusta ver las películas de romance, ¿no es verdad?
Diana: ¡No! ¡También nos gusta ver otras!

10 ▶ **Diana:** ¿Qué pasa? ¿Estás preocupado?
Ignacio: Es que… dos años en Minnesota… ya no conozco a Roberto.
Diana: ¡No te preocupes! Los buenos amigos son amigos para siempre.

En acción

PARTE A Comprensión del diálogo

For Activities 1–2, refer to the dialog on pages 178–179.

1 ¿Cierto o falso?

Escuchar ¿Es cierto o falso? Si es falso, di lo que es cierto. *(Hint: Say what is true.)*

1. Roberto es un viejo amigo.
2. Roberto está en San Juan.
3. Diana compra unos calcetines.
4. Ignacio pasa por el cine.
5. A Diana sólo le gusta ver las películas de romance.
6. Ignacio está muy tranquilo.

2 ¿Quién?

Escuchar ¿Qué persona del diálogo habla: Diana, Ignacio o Roberto? *(Hint: Say who speaks.)*

1. «Oye, hermano, voy de compras.»
2. «Tengo muy buenas noticias.»
3. «¡Mi familia y yo vamos a Puerto Rico a vivir!»
4. «Te invito a mi práctica de béisbol.»
5. «Yo vengo del cine.»
6. «¡También nos gusta ver otras!»

PARTE B Práctica del vocabulario

Objectives for Activities 3–5
- Express feelings

3 El tiempo libre

Hablar Explica lo que Ignacio y Diana hacen en su tiempo libre. Pregúntale a otro(a) estudiante si también hace la actividad. *(Hint: Say what they do. Ask another student if he or she does it, too.)*

alquilar un video **leer una novela** **ir de compras** **escribir una carta** **ver la televisión** **ir al cine** **practicar deportes**

modelo

Estudiante A: *En su tiempo libre, Ignacio y Diana ven la televisión. ¿Te gusta ver la televisión en tu tiempo libre?*

Estudiante B: *Sí, me gusta ver la televisión en mi tiempo libre.*

1.

2.

3.

4.

5.

6.

4 El tiempo libre de su amiga

Escuchar Escucha lo que dice la amiga de Diana. Ella habla de lo que hace los sábados. Luego, indica el orden en que ocurren las actividades. *(Hint: Put Diana's friend's activities in order.)*

a. Alquila un video.
b. Prepara el almuerzo.
c. Hace la tarea.
d. Cuida a su hermano.
e. Va de compras.

Puerto Rico

También se dice

There are many ways to talk about **un buen amigo.** Diana uses one of them, **pana.**

- **colega:** Spain
- **cuadro:** Colombia
- **cuate:** Mexico
- **pana:** Puerto Rico, Ecuador, parts of Latin America
- **pata:** Peru
- **vale:** Venezuela

Ignacio uses the word **hermanita** when talking to Diana. The ending **-ito(a)** adds meaning to a word. It can mean *very small* or express a special relationship. **Hermanita** means *little sister*, but it also expresses Ignacio's close relationship with his sister. This ending is used in most Spanish-speaking countries.

5 ¿Cómo están?

Leer ¿Cómo están Diana, Ignacio y Roberto en estas situaciones? Completa cada oración con los adjetivos de la lista. *(Hint: How do they feel?)*

alegre
deprimido(a)
nervioso(a)
preocupado(a)
tranquilo(a)
ocupado(a)
triste
enfermo(a)
emocionado(a)
cansado(a)
enojado(a)
contento(a)

1. Cuando Diana trabaja mucho, ella está ______.
2. Cuando Roberto habla con Ignacio, ellos están ______.
3. Cuando Ignacio y Diana sacan una buena nota, ellos están ______.
4. Cuando Ignacio y Diana sacan una mala nota, ellos están ______.
5. Cuando Roberto no está bien, él está ______.
6. Cuando no hay clases, Diana está ______.
7. Cuando Ignacio tiene mucha tarea, él está ______.
8. Cuando Roberto está en la clase y no tiene su tarea, él está ______.
9. Cuando su abuelo está enfermo, Diana está ______.
10. Cuando Ignacio come la comida de Diana, ella está ______.

PARTE C

Práctica: gramática y vocabulario

Objectives for Activities 6–18

- Express feelings • Extend invitations • Say what just happened • Say where you are coming from • Talk on the phone

GRAMÁTICA Expressing Feelings with estar and Adjectives

¿RECUERDAS? *p. 134* You learned that the verb **estar** is used to say where someone or something is located.

estoy	estamos
estás	estáis
está	están

Estar is also used with **adjectives** to describe how someone feels at a given moment.

Diana **está preocupada** por Ignacio. (agrees)
*Diana **is worried** about Ignacio.*

Ignacio **está preocupado** por Roberto. (agrees)
*Ignacio **is worried** about Roberto.*

Remember that **adjectives** must **agree** in gender and number with the nouns they describe.

Practice: Actividades 6 7

Más práctica *cuaderno p. 61*
Para hispanohablantes *cuaderno p. 59*

Online Workbook CLASSZONE.COM

6 Una reacción típica

Hablar ¿Cómo están estas personas en estas situaciones?
(Hint: How are they?)

modelo

Cuando mi tía está enferma… *ella está deprimida.*

Nota: Gramática

When **cuando** is not used as a question word, it does not have an accent.

1. Cuando mis amigos(as) y yo vamos de compras…
2. Cuando vemos una película muy divertida…
3. Cuando tengo un examen de inglés…
4. Cuando mi amigo(a) saca una mala nota…
5. Cuando no recibes una carta de tu buen amigo…
6. Cuando mis amigos(as) no tienen clases…
7. Cuando oigo música alegre…
8. Cuando es tu cumpleaños…
9. Cuando tengo mi clase favorita…
10. Cuando haces mucho ejercicio…

7 ¿Cuándo estás…?

Hablar Con otro(a) estudiante, explica cuándo te sientes así.
(Hint: Say when you feel this way.)

modelo

deprimido(a)

Tú: *¿Cuándo estás **deprimido(a)**?*

Otro(a): *Estoy **deprimido(a)** cuando no tengo tiempo para pasar un rato con mis amigos. ¿Y tú?*

Tú: *Estoy **deprimido(a)** cuando tengo mucho trabajo.*

1. alegre
2. triste
3. nervioso(a)
4. cansado(a)
5. enojado(a)
6. contento(a)
7. tranquilo(a)
8. preocupado(a)
9. emocionado(a)
10. deprimido(a)

8 ¿Te gustaría...?

Hablar Pregúntale a otro(a) estudiante si le gustaría hacer estas actividades contigo el sábado. Cambien de papel. *(Hint: Invite a classmate to do things with you.)*

modelo

Estudiante A: *¿Te gustaría ir conmigo al museo el sábado?*

Estudiante B: *¡Claro que sí!*

Nota: Gramática

When you use **mí** and **ti** after **con**, they combine with **con** to form the words **conmigo** and **contigo.**

¿Te gustaría venir **conmigo**?
*Would you like to come **with me**?*

Sí, me gustaría ir **contigo.**
*Yes, I'd like to go **with you.***

Vocabulario

Para aceptar o no una invitación

Gracias, pero no puedo. *Thanks, but I can't.*

Me gustaría... *I would like...*

¡Qué lástima! *What a shame!*

Tal vez otro día. *Maybe another day.*

Other useful words:

porque *because*

solo(a) *alone*

temprano *early*

¿Cuándo usas estas frases?

Estudiante A
PREGUNTAS

¿Quieres acompañarme a...?

Te invito a...

¿Te gustaría venir conmigo a...?

1.

2.

3.

4.

5.

¿?

Estudiante B
RESPUESTAS

¡Claro que sí!

Sí, me encantaría.

Me gustaría ir contigo a...

Gracias, pero no puedo.

Tal vez otro día.

¡Qué lástima! Gracias, pero no puedo.

GRAMÁTICA Saying What Just Happened with acabar de

When you want to say that something just happened, use the present tense of

acabar + **de** + ***infinitive***

acabo de comer *I just ate*	**acabamos de comer** *we just ate*
acabas de comer *you just ate*	**acabáis de comer** *you just ate*
acaba de comer *he, she, you just ate*	**acaban de comer** *they, you just ate*

Diana says:

—**Acabo de comprar** unos zapatos.
I just bought *some shoes.*

Practice: Actividades 9 10 11

Más práctica *cuaderno p. 62*
Para hispanohablantes *cuaderno p. 60*

9 ¿Qué acaban de hacer?

Hablar Ignacio y sus amigos acaban de hacer muchas cosas. ¿Qué acaban de hacer? *(Hint: Say what they just did.)*

modelo

Ignacio y yo: ver una película interesante

Ignacio y yo** acabamos de **ver una película interesante.

1. Ignacio y Pedro: escuchar un concierto
2. yo: correr en el parque
3. Raquel: bailar con Juan
4. Lucía y Pilar: alquilar un video
5. tú: comprar una novela nueva
6. mi hermano y yo: visitar a nuestro primo
7. Ana: sacar una buena nota en el examen
8. Alma y Dorotea: comer tacos
9. yo: ir al supermercado
10. Iván: caminar con el perro

10 ¿Por qué están así?

Escribir Diana explica cómo están sus amigos. Escribe por qué están así. *(Hint: Diana explains how her friends are. Tell why they feel that way.)*

modelo

Ignacio y yo / triste

Ignacio y yo** estamos **tristes** porque acabamos de **leer una novela triste.

1. Roberto / ocupado(a)
2. unas amigas / preocupado(a)
3. yo / tranquilo(a)
4. Antonio / cansado(a)
5. ellos / enojado(a)
6. Ana / enfermo(a)
7. Ignacio / contento(a)
8. mis amigas y yo / emocionado(a)

leer una novela triste
sacar una mala nota
ir a un concierto
llegar a San Juan
comer mucho
terminar un examen
ver su programa favorito
trabajar mucho
leer poesía

11 ¿Cómo están?

STRATEGY: SPEAKING
Personalize After completing this activity, make the expressions your own by describing how you feel after doing these things.

Hablar ¿Cómo están estas personas cuando acaban de hacer lo siguiente? *(Hint: How are these people when they just did the following?)*

modelo

¿Cómo está tu padre...? (trabajar mucho)

Estudiante A: *¿**Cómo está tu padre** cuando acaba de **trabajar mucho**?*

Estudiante B: *Está cansado.*

1. ¿Cómo está tu amigo(a)...? (estudiar mucho)
2. ¿Cómo está tu amigo(a)...? (pasear por el parque)
3. ¿Cómo estás tú...? (terminar un examen)
4. ¿Cómo están tus padres...? (escuchar un concierto)
5. ¿Cómo estás tú...? (leer una revista)
6. ¿Cómo está tu maestro(a)...? (hablar mucho)

More Practice: **Más comunicación** *p. R7*

Puerto Rico

Nota cultural

The name **Puerto Rico** was given to the island by the Spanish. Its port is one of the world's busiest. Guess what **Puerto Rico** means in English.

GRAMÁTICA Saying Where You Are Coming From with venir

¿RECUERDAS? *p. 78* Do you remember the forms of the verb **tener?**

tengo	tenemos
tienes	tenéis
tiene	tienen

Venir (*to come*) is similar to **tener,** except that the **nosotros(as)** and **vosotros(as)** forms have **-ir** endings, while **tener** uses **-er** endings.

vengo	ven**imos**
vienes	ven**ís**
viene	vienen

Ignacio says:
—Roberto y su familia **vienen** a Puerto Rico...
*Roberto and his family **are coming** to Puerto Rico...*

Later he says:
—Yo **vengo** del cine.
*I'm **coming** from the movie theater.*

Practice: **Actividades** 12 13 14

Más práctica *cuaderno p. 63*
Para hispanohablantes *cuaderno p. 61*

Online Workbook
CLASSZONE.COM

12 Vienen de...

Leer Roberto está en el aeropuerto de San Juan. Él viene de Minneapolis. ¿De dónde vienen los otros pasajeros? *(Hint: Where are these passengers coming from?)*

modelo

Tomás __viene__ de Miami.

1. Yo _____ de Nueva York.
2. Antonio _____ de Quito, Ecuador.
3. Nosotros _____ de San Antonio.
4. Tú _____ de la Ciudad de México.
5. Las señoras _____ de Los Ángeles.

13 ¿Por qué no vienen?

Hablar/*Escribir* Diana va al cine, pero sus amigos no van. Ella explica por qué. *(Hint: What does Diana say about her friends not coming with her?)*

modelo

Julio

Julio** no viene conmigo porque va a **practicar deportes.

1. tú
2. Ignacio
3. mis primos
4. Emiliana
5. Ana
6. Jorge
7. Marta y Rosa
8. Sofía
9. Angelina
10. Ricardo

hacer la tarea
leer el periódico
preparar la cena
cuidar a su hermano
andar en bicicleta
ver la televisión
practicar deportes
escribir una carta

14 ¿De dónde vienen?

Hablar/Leer Lee las oraciones. Explica de dónde vienen estas personas. *(Hint: Explain where the people are coming from.)*

tienda **cine** **museo** **cafetería** **gimnasio** **concierto** **escuela** **biblioteca** **parque**

modelo

Ignacio y Diana acaban de escuchar música.

*Vienen **del concierto.***

Nota: Gramática

Remember how **a** contracts with **el** to form **al**? The preposition **de** also contracts with **el** to form **del.**

1. Mis amigos acaban de hacer ejercicio.
2. Ustedes acaban de ver una exhibición de arte.
3. Ignacio y Diana acaban de comer.
4. Acabo de buscar un libro.
5. Acabas de comprar una falda.
6. Roberto acaba de ver una película.
7. Acabas de tomar un examen de historia.
8. Acabo de caminar con el perro.

Puerto Rico

Nota cultural

Ricky Martin, already an international music star, catapulted to fame in the U.S. with his debut English single "Livin' la Vida Loca." Born in Puerto Rico in 1971, he began singing professionally at age twelve. His album *Vuelve,* "Come Back," won the 1998 Grammy Award for Latin pop. He has also acted on TV and on Broadway.

GRAMÁTICA Saying What Someone Likes to Do Using gustar + infinitive

¿RECUERDAS? *p. 39* You learned to use **me gusta, te gusta,** and **le gusta** + ***infinitive*** to talk about the activities a person likes to do.

me gusta correr
te gusta correr
le gusta correr

Here are more phrases to use to talk about what people like to do.

nos gusta correr	***we like to run***
os gusta correr	***you*** *(familiar plural)* ***like to run***
les gusta correr	***they/you*** *(plural)* ***like to run***

When you want to emphasize or identify the person that you are talking about, use:

a + **name** / **noun** / **pronoun** →

A Diana le gusta ir de compras.
Diana *likes to shop.*

A su **hermana le gusta ir** de compras.
His ***sister*** *likes to shop.*

A ella le gusta ir de compras.
She *likes to shop.*

These are the **pronouns** that follow **a**.

a mí → **me gusta**	**a nosotros(as)** → **nos gusta**
a ti → **te gusta**	**a vosotros(as)** → **os gusta**
a usted, él, ella → **le gusta**	**a ustedes, ellos(as)** → **les gusta**

Practice: **Actividades** 15 16 17

Más práctica *cuaderno p. 64*
Para hispanohablantes *cuaderno p. 62*

Online Workbook
CLASSZONE.COM

15 ¿A quién le gusta?

Leer Diana le escribe una carta a su amiga Elena, contándole las actividades que ella y sus amigos hacen. Completa su carta con **a mí, a ti, a él, a ella, a nosotros, a ustedes.**
(Hint: Complete Diana's letter to her friend.)

Querida Elena:

¿Qué hago aquí en San Juan? Bueno, primero estudio mucho porque __1__ me gusta sacar buenas notas. Después de las clases, normalmente voy a la cafetería con mis amigos Pablo y Linda. Pablo siempre compra dos hamburguesas. ¡__2__ le gusta mucho comer!

Cuando tenemos tiempo libre, vamos al cine. __3__ nos gusta ver películas de acción. A veces, Pablo y yo vamos al museo. Linda no va porque __4__ no le gusta el arte.

Y tú, ¿qué haces? ¿__5__ te gusta estudiar? ¿Qué haces con tus amigos? ¿__6__ les gusta ir al cine o a un museo?

Bueno, espero tu carta.

Tu amiga,

Diana

16 ¿A quién le gusta ir a...?

Hablar/*Escribir* ¿A quién le gusta hacer estas actividades? *(Hint: Who likes to do the following?)*

a mis abuelos **a mi amigo y a mí** **a mis padres** **a mi amigo(a)** **a mí** **a mi profesor(a) de...** **a mis amigos(as)** **a mi hermano(a)**

modelo

ir a los museos

*A mis padres les gusta **ir a los museos.***

1. ir a los museos
2. ir de compras
3. hacer la tarea
4. ir al cine
5. bailar
6. llegar temprano
7. ir a conciertos
8. alquilar videos
9. practicar deportes
10. cantar solo(a)

17 ¿Qué les gusta hacer?

Hablar Pregúntales a otros estudiantes lo que a ellos y a sus amigos les gusta hacer. *(Hint: Ask others what they and their friends like to do.)*

modelo

nadar

Tú: *¿A ustedes les gusta **nadar**?*

Otro(a): *No, no nos gusta **nadar,** pero nos gusta bailar.*

1. andar en bicicleta
2. escribir poesía
3. practicar deportes
4. alquilar videos
5. patinar
6. leer novelas
7. ir de compras
8. cantar
9. ver la televisión
10. ¿?

18 Una conversación telefónica

Escuchar Escucha la conversación de Ignacio y Roberto. Luego, di si las oraciones son ciertas o falsas. Corrige las falsas. *(Hint: Say if the sentences are true or false. Correct the false ones.)*

1. El señor Campos contesta el teléfono.
2. Roberto no está en casa.
3. Ignacio invita a Roberto a ir a un concierto.
4. Roberto no tiene tiempo libre el sábado.
5. El sábado es el cumpleaños de su hermano.
6. Ignacio y Roberto van al cine el domingo.
7. La película es a las cuatro.

Vocabulario

El teléfono

contestar *to answer*

dejar un mensaje *to leave a message*

la guía telefónica *phone book*

la llamada *call*

llamar *to call*

la máquina contestadora *answering machine*

marcar *to dial*

Speaking on the phone:

¿Puedo hablar con…?	*May I speak with…?*
Un momento.	*One moment.*
Regresa más tarde.	*He/She will return later.*
Dile/Dígale que me llame.	*Tell (familiar/formal) him or her to call me.*
Quiero dejar un mensaje para…	*I want to leave a message for…*
Deje/a un mensaje después del tono.	*Leave (formal/familiar) a message after the tone.*

¿Qué dices cuando hablas por teléfono?

PARTE D Todo en acción

Activities 19–20 bring together all concepts presented.

19 ¿Puedo hablar con...?

Hablar/Leer Practica con otro(a) estudiante la llamada de Diana. Contesta las preguntas. *(Hint: Practice the conversation and answer the questions.)*

Señor Ruiz: Hola.

Diana: Buenas tardes, señor Ruiz. Soy Diana.

Señor Ruiz: ¡Ah! Diana, ¿cómo estás?

Diana: Muy bien, gracias, señor. ¿Puedo hablar con Gloria, por favor?

Señor Ruiz: Pues, Gloria no está en este momento. Está en la biblioteca. Regresa más tarde.

Diana: Dígale que me llame, por favor.

Señor Ruiz: Sí, cómo no.

Diana: Gracias, adiós.

Señor Ruiz: Hasta luego.

1. ¿Quién hace la llamada?
2. ¿Quién contesta?
3. ¿Cómo está Diana?
4. ¿Dónde está Gloria?
5. ¿Cuándo regresa Gloria?

20 Te invito a...

Hablar/Escribir Trabaja en un grupo de tres. Tú llamas a casa de un(a) amigo(a) para hablar de su tiempo libre y hacerle una invitación. *(Hint: Work in a group of three to create two telephone conversations.)*

Conversación 1:
Tu amigo(a) no puede aceptar tu invitación. Explica por qué.

Conversación 2:
Tu amigo(a) acepta tu invitación. Deciden la hora y el día.

modelo

Señor Cano: *Hola.*

Luis: *Buenas tardes. Soy Luis. ¿Puedo hablar con Ana?*

Señor Cano: *Sí, Luis. Un momento.*

Ana: *Hola, Luis…*

More Practice:
Más comunicación p. R7

Online Workbook
CLASSZONE.COM

Puerto Rico

También se dice

There are many ways to answer the phone.

- **Hola:** Puerto Rico
- **Aló:** Chile, Colombia, Venezuela
- **Bueno:** Mexico
- **Diga:** Spain
- **Hable:** Argentina
- **Oigo:** Uruguay

Pronunciación

Refrán

Pronunciación de la *b* y la *v* The **b** and **v** are pronounced alike. At the beginning of a phrase and after the letters **m** or **n**, they are pronounced like the English *b* in the word *boy*. In the middle of a word, a softer sound is made by vibrating the lips. Practice the following words.

bueno vamos acaba novela hombre

La **b** es de **burro.** La **v** es de **vaca.**

Now try this **refrán.** Can you guess what it means?

No hay mal que por bien no venga.

En voces

LECTURA

AUDIO

PARA LEER

STRATEGY: READING

Scan Reading very quickly to get a specific piece of information, like a football score or a movie time, is called scanning. Scan this poster and decide whether Ignacio and Roberto can attend the festival. (Remember their plans for Saturday.)

Bomba y plena

La bomba y la plena son danzas típicas de Puerto Rico. Tienen sus orígenes en la música africana. Los instrumentos originales para tocar esta música alegre son los tambores[1], las panderetas[2], las maracas y el cuatro. El cuatro es un tipo de guitarra española pequeña, originalmente con cuatro cuerdas[3]. Las personas que bailan estas danzas llevan ropa de muchos colores. La música tiene mucho ritmo[4] y las personas ¡mueven todo el cuerpo[5]!

[1] drums
[2] type of tambourine
[3] strings
[4] rhythm
[5] body

Online Workbook
CLASSZONE.COM

¿Comprendiste?

1. ¿Cuándo es el concierto?
2. ¿En qué tienen sus orígenes la bomba y la plena?
3. ¿Es una música triste o alegre?
4. ¿Qué es el cuatro?
5. ¿Qué otros instrumentos hay?
6. ¿Qué ropa llevan las personas que bailan?

¿Qué piensas?

1. Hoy hay un concierto de bomba y plena en tu ciudad. ¿Qué ropa llevas y por qué?
2. ¿Un concierto de bomba y plena es divertido? ¿Por qué sí o por qué no?

ETAPA 1

En uso

REPASO Y MÁS COMUNICACIÓN

OBJECTIVES

- Extend invitations
- Talk on the phone
- Express feelings
- Say where you are coming from
- Say what just happened

Now you can...

- extend invitations.
- talk on the phone.

To review

- vocabulary for invitations, see p. 176 and p. 183.
- vocabulary for talking on the phone, see p. 188.

1 Una invitación por teléfono

Mateo, un amigo de Ignacio, habla por teléfono. Completa las dos conversaciones con las palabras apropiadas. *(Hint: Complete Mateo's conversations.)*

conmigo · contigo · lástima · mensaje · puedo · gracias · dígale · regresa · tal vez

Sra. Ruiz: Hola.

Mateo: Buenas tardes, señora. Soy Mateo. ¿__1__ hablar con Laura?

Sra. Ruiz: No está en este momento. __2__ más tarde. ¿Quieres dejar un __3__?

Mateo: Sí, gracias. __4__ que me llame, por favor.

Más tarde...

Mateo: Hola.

Laura: Hola, Mateo. Soy Laura.

Mateo: Oye, ¿te gustaría ir al cine __5__ mañana?

Laura: __6__, pero no puedo. Tengo que trabajar. __7__ otro día.

Mateo: ¡Qué __8__! ¿Y el sábado?

Laura: Sí, me encantaría ir __9__.

Now you can...

- express feelings.

To review

- **gustar** with infinitives, see p. 187.

2 Están contentos

Todos están contentos porque hacen las actividades que les gusta hacer. ¿Qué les gusta hacer? *(Hint: Say what they like to do.)*

modelo

Carlos: pasear

*A **Carlos** le gusta **pasear**.*

1. mis padres: alquilar un video
2. tú: escuchar un concierto
3. mis hermanos y yo: practicar deportes
4. la vecina: ir al cine
5. yo: ver la televisión
6. Berta y José: ir de compras
7. Ignacio: pasear
8. nosotros: hablar por teléfono

Self-Check Quiz
CLASSZONE.COM

Now you can...
- express feelings.

To review
- **estar** with adjectives, see p. 182.

3 Un festival internacional

Hay un festival internacional el sábado. ¿Cómo reaccionan estas personas? *(Hint: Tell how these people are feeling.)*

alegre | emocionado(a) | triste | nervioso(a) | enojado(a)

modelo
Julia: le gusta bailar
Julia** está alegre porque **le gusta bailar.

1. Ignacio y Diana: tienen que estudiar

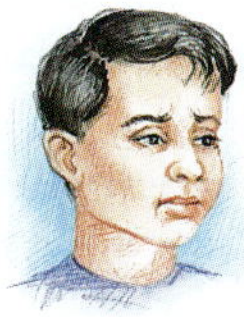

2. Rogelio: sus amigos no van

3. tú: vas a cantar

4. yo: tengo que trabajar

5. ustedes: su grupo favorito va a tocar

6. nosotros: vamos a ver a nuestros amigos

Now you can...
- say what just happened.
- say where you are coming from.

To review
- **acabar de,** see p. 184.
- the verb **venir**, see p. 185.

4 Muchas actividades

Todos estos amigos de Diana están muy ocupados hoy. ¿Qué acaban de hacer? ¿De dónde vienen? *(Hint: Tell what these people have just done and where they are coming from.)*

modelo
mis amigos: hacer ejercicio
***Mis amigos** acaban de **hacer ejercicio**. Vienen del gimnasio.*

1. yo: ver una exhibición de arte
2. tú: practicar deportes
3. Ernesto: leer revistas y periódicos
4. Hugo y Raquel: escuchar música
5. mi madre y yo: comprar comida
6. los Fernández: ver una película
7. usted: ir de compras
8. nosotros: comer papas fritas

5 Por teléfono

STRATEGY: SPEAKING

Use your tone to convey meaning Words alone do not reveal meaning. Your tone of voice makes a difference. In both your invitations and answers, express different feelings (happy, nervous, worried, angry, etc.).

Imagínate que vas a invitar a un(a) amigo(a) a hacer algo contigo. Llama a dos amigos. Un(a) amigo(a) no acepta la invitación, pero el (la) otro(a) sí. Decidan la hora y el día. *(**Hint:** Call two friends. One refuses your invitation, but the other accepts. Agree on the time and day.)*

6 ¡De visita!

Imagínate que estás de visita en Puerto Rico en la casa de una amiga. Los amigos de tu amiga vienen a conocerte. Conversen para aprender quiénes son, cómo están, por qué y de dónde vienen. *(**Hint:** Find out more about the people your friend knows.)*

modelo

Tú: *¿Quién es la muchacha?*

Tu amigo(a): *Es mi amiga Rosa. Está cansada porque acaba de practicar deportes. Viene del gimnasio.*

¿Quién es?	¿Cómo está?	¿Por qué?	¿De dónde viene?
un(a) amigo(a)	alegre	acaba de ¿ ?	la escuela
¿ ?	¿ ?	acaba de ¿ ?	¿ ?

7 En tu propia voz

ESCRITURA Imagínate que tienes un(a) amigo(a) puertorriqueño(a) por correspondencia. Escribe una carta sobre tus actividades y pregúntale sobre sus actividades. Sigue las instrucciones. *(**Hint:** Write a letter about your leisure activities to your pen pal.)*

- ¿Cuáles son tres de tus actividades favoritas?
- Pregúntale a tu amigo(a) sobre tres actividades específicas.

CONEXIONES

La música Would you like to hear **bomba y plena** music? Check your local library or the international section of a music store for recordings. You can probably find many kinds of music with Spanish influences. What other kinds of music do you like? You can check the Internet to find out what is popular in Spain. Listen to five songs from any source and complete the following chart. Then say why you do or don't like the songs.

Título	Sí, me gusta/No, no me gusta	¿Por qué?

Flashcards
CLASSZONE.COM

En resumen

REPASO DE VOCABULARIO

EXTENDING INVITATIONS

¿Quieres acompañarme a...?	*Would you like to come with me to...?*
Te invito.	*I'll treat you. I invite you.*
¿Te gustaría...?	*Would you like...?*

Accepting

¡Claro que sí!	*Of course.*
Me gustaría...	*I would like...*
Sí, me encantaría.	*Yes, I would love to.*

Declining

Gracias, pero no puedo.	*Thanks, but I can't.*
¡Qué lástima!	*What a shame!*
Tal vez otro día.	*Maybe another day.*

Activities

alquilar un video	*to rent a video*
el concierto	*concert*
ir al cine	*to go to a movie theater*
ir de compras	*to go shopping*
la película	*movie*
practicar deportes	*to play sports*
el tiempo libre	*free time*

EXPRESSING FEELINGS

alegre	*happy*
cansado(a)	*tired*
contento(a)	*content, happy, pleased*
deprimido(a)	*depressed*
emocionado(a)	*excited*
enfermo(a)	*sick*
enojado(a)	*angry*
nervioso(a)	*nervous*
ocupado(a)	*busy*
preocupado(a)	*worried*
tranquilo(a)	*calm*
triste	*sad*

TALKING ON THE PHONE

contestar	*to answer*
dejar un mensaje	*to leave a message*
la guía telefónica	*phone book*
la llamada	*call*
llamar	*to call*
la máquina contestadora	*answering machine*
marcar	*to dial*
el teléfono	*telephone*

Phrases for talking on the phone

Deje/a un mensaje después del tono.	*Leave (formal/familiar) a message after the tone.*
Dile/Dígale que me llame.	*Tell (familiar/formal) him or her to call me.*
¿Puedo hablar con...?	*May I speak with...?*
Quiero dejar un mensaje para...	*I want to leave a message for...*
Regresa más tarde.	*He/She will return later.*
Un momento.	*One moment.*

WHERE YOU ARE COMING FROM

del	*from the*
venir	*to come*

SAYING WHAT JUST HAPPENED

acabar de...	*to have just...*

OTHER WORDS AND PHRASES

conmigo	*with me*
contigo	*with you*
cuando	*when, whenever*
¡No te preocupes!	*Don't worry!*
porque	*because*
solo(a)	*alone*
temprano	*early*
ya no	*no longer*

Juego

¿Adónde van en su tiempo libre?

1. A Miguel le gusta escuchar música.
2. A Mariela le gusta ver las películas de Antonio Banderas.
3. *A Martina y a Martín les gusta comprar ropa.*

UNIDAD 3

ETAPA 2

¡Deportes para todos!

OBJECTIVES

- Talk about sports
- Express preferences
- Say what you know
- Make comparisons

¿Qué ves?

Mira la foto de un campo de béisbol en San Juan.

1. Para ti, ¿el béisbol es interesante?
2. ¿Quién practica, Ignacio o Roberto?
3. ¿Cuál es la fecha del campeonato de béisbol?
4. ¿En qué día de la semana es el campeonato?

VIDEO DVD AUDIO

En contexto

VOCABULARIO

Diana and Ignacio are looking at equipment in a sporting goods store. Look at the illustrations to understand the meaning of the words in blue. This will help you answer the questions on the next page.

¡Hola! Ignacio y yo estamos en **la tienda de deportes.** ¡Vamos a ver qué hay!

A

A mí me gusta andar en **patineta.** Uso **un casco** cuando ando en patineta y cuando uso **patines.**

B

Aquí hay de todo para practicar deportes como **el baloncesto, el voleibol, el fútbol** y **el fútbol americano.** ¡Y hay **una bola** especial para cada deporte! El baloncesto y el voleibol se practican en **una cancha.** El fútbol y el fútbol americano se practican en **un campo.** A veces se practican en **un estadio.**

D ¿Te gusta **levantar pesas?**

E Para practicar **el tenis** usas **una raqueta** y una bola.

F En Puerto Rico, es divertido **esquiar** en el agua o practicar **el surfing.**

C Practicas **el béisbol** con **un guante, un bate** y **una pelota.** Ésta es una foto del **equipo** de béisbol de Ignacio.

Preguntas personales

1. ¿Practicas deportes?
2. ¿Practicas el baloncesto o el voleibol?
3. ¿Te gusta más mirar el fútbol o el fútbol americano?
4. ¿Cuál es tu deporte favorito?
5. ¿Qué usas cuando practicas tu deporte favorito?

En vivo

VIDEO DVD AUDIO

DIÁLOGO

Ignacio

Claudio

Roberto

Sr. Castillo

PARA ESCUCHAR • STRATEGY: LISTENING

Listen for "turn-taking" tactics In English conversation we often say *uh, yeah, well, say,* or *listen* to signal that we are getting ready to speak. Listen carefully to the Spanish. What words or expressions do you hear that signal, "It's my turn to talk"?

El campo de béisbol

1 ▶ **Claudio:** Oye, ¿qué haces?
Ignacio: Espero a mi amigo.
Claudio: ¡Ah! ¿Sabe él a qué hora empieza la práctica?
Ignacio: Sí.

5 ▶ **Ignacio:** Sr. Castillo, le presento a Roberto. Viene de Minneapolis.
Sr. Castillo: Mucho gusto. ¿Qué deportes juegan en Minneapolis?
Roberto: ¡Son locos con el fútbol americano!

6 ▶ **Ignacio:** ¿Les gusta jugar al fútbol?
Roberto: Sí, pero no es tan popular como el fútbol americano. Mucha gente en los Estados Unidos piensa que el fútbol americano es más interesante que el fútbol.

7 ▶ **Roberto:** Me gusta jugar al baloncesto y al tenis. Pienso que el tenis es menos divertido que el baloncesto. También me gusta nadar.
Ignacio: Me gusta correr más que nadar.

CD-ROM Take-Home Tutor

2 ▶ **Claudio:** ¿Quieres practicar un poco conmigo?
Ignacio: No, gracias. Prefiero esperar a Roberto aquí.

3 ▶ **Roberto:** ¡Ignacio! ¡Qué gusto!
Ignacio: ¡Roberto! ¡Cuánto tiempo!
Roberto: ¡Ahora tengo un amigo para hablar de deportes!

4 ▶ **Roberto:** ¿Prefieres este bate o éste?
Ignacio: Yo prefiero este bate. ¿Juegas al béisbol en Minneapolis?
Roberto: Sí.

8 ▶ **Sr. Castillo:** ¿Piensas jugar en el equipo de baloncesto?
Roberto: Sí. También quiero jugar en el equipo de béisbol. ¿Puedo practicar con ustedes?
Sr. Castillo: ¡Claro! ¡Vamos!

9 ▶ **Ignacio:** Necesito tu ayuda. Quiero participar en un concurso.
Roberto: ¿Y qué piensas hacer?
Ignacio: Tengo una idea. Me gustaría hablar contigo sobre el proyecto.

10 ▶ **Roberto:** Claro, está bien. ¿Por qué no vienes a casa mañana por la mañana?
Ignacio: Así también saludo a tu familia.
Roberto: ¿Por qué no invitas a Diana?
Ignacio: Está bien. Nos vemos como a las diez.

En acción

PARTE A Comprensión del diálogo

Ignacio | Claudio | Roberto | Sr. Castillo

For Activities 1–2, refer to the dialog on pages 200–201.

1 ¿Qué dicen?

Escuchar ¿Qué dice una de las personas de la foto? Escoge la oración correcta. *(Hint: Choose what they would be saying.)*

1.

a. ¡Ignacio! ¡Qué gusto!
b. Espero a mi amigo.
c. Necesito tu ayuda.

2.

a. No, gracias.
b. Necesito tu ayuda.
c. Sr. Castillo, le presento a Roberto.

3.

a. ¡Cuánto tiempo!
b. ¡Vamos a jugar!
c. ¿Piensas jugar al baloncesto?

4.

a. ¿Prefieres este bate o éste?
b. ¿Y qué piensas hacer?
c. ¿Qué deportes juegan en Minneapolis?

2 ¿Qué pasa?

Escuchar Explica lo que hacen las personas del diálogo. Escoge la respuesta correcta. *(Hint: Explain what they do.)*

1. Ignacio espera _____.
   a. a Diana
   b. a su amigo Roberto
   c. al señor Castillo
2. Roberto viene de _____.
   a. Minneapolis
   b. Miami
   c. Puerto Rico
3. Roberto piensa que el _____ es muy popular en Minneapolis.
   a. béisbol
   b. fútbol americano
   c. baloncesto
4. A Ignacio le gusta _____ más que nadar.
   a. jugar al béisbol
   b. correr
   c. patinar
5. Ignacio necesita la ayuda de Roberto para el _____.
   a. béisbol
   b. tenis
   c. concurso

Práctica del vocabulario

Objectives for Activities 3–4
- Talk about sports

3 ¡Los deportes son buenos!

Escribir Completa el póster para tu clase de educación física. Da el nombre del deporte correspondiente a cada foto. *(Hint: Give the name of each sport.)*

4 ¡Organízalos!

Hablar Trabajas en una tienda de deportes. Explícale a otro(a) trabajador(a) dónde poner los artículos. ¡Ojo! Algunos artículos van en más de una sección. *(Hint: Tell your coworker the appropriate section for each article.)*

modelo

los bates

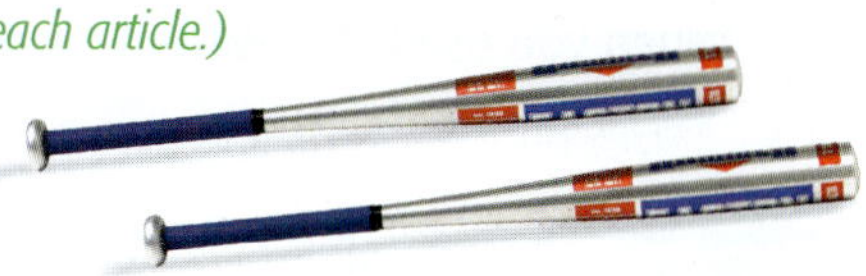

***Los bates** van en la sección de béisbol.*

EL BALONCESTO | EL BÉISBOL | EL VOLEIBOL | EL FÚTBOL AMERICANO | EL FÚTBOL | EL TENIS

1. las raquetas 
2. las pelotas 
3. los cascos 
4. los guantes 
5. las bolas 

Puerto Rico

También se dice

There are different ways to say *ball*.

- **bola:** Puerto Rico
- **balón:** Spain
- **pelota:** Latin America, Spain

In Puerto Rico, **una pelota** is a baseball. **Balón** and **cesto** *(basket)* are combined as **baloncesto** to mean *basketball*. **Básquetbol** is also sometimes used as a name for this sport.

PARTE C

Práctica: gramática y vocabulario

Objectives for Activities 5–17
- Talk about sports
- Express preferences
- Say what you know
- Make comparisons

GRAMÁTICA Talking About Playing a Sport: The Verb jugar

When you talk about playing a sport, you use the verb **jugar**. The forms of **jugar** are unique. In some of them, the **u** changes to **ue**.

jugar *to play*

juego	**ju**gamos
juegas	**ju**gáis
juega	**jue**gan

When you use **jugar** with the name of a sport, use

jugar a + ***sport***

Ignacio asks Roberto:

—¿**Juegas al béisbol** en Minneapolis?
*Do **you play** baseball in Minneapolis?*

Coach Castillo asks:

—¿Qué deportes **juegan** en Minneapolis?
*What sports do **they play** in Minneapolis?*

Vocabulario

Más sobre los deportes

al aire libre *outdoors*
andar en patineta *to skateboard*
ganar *to win*
el gol *goal*
la gorra *baseball cap*
el hockey *hockey*
el partido *game*
la piscina *pool*
sobre hielo *on ice*

Use these adjectives and others you know to describe sports.

favorito(a) *favorite*
peligroso(a) *dangerous*

¿Qué frase usas para hablar de tu deporte favorito?

Practice: Actividades 5 6 7 — **Más práctica** *cuaderno p. 69* — **Para hispanohablantes** *cuaderno p. 67* — Online Workbook CLASSZONE.COM

5 ¿A qué juegan?

Leer La nueva amiga de Diana quiere saber a qué deportes juegan ella y sus amigos. Completa sus oraciones con una forma de **jugar.** *(Hint: Use the correct form of jugar.)*

Mis amigos y yo __1__ a muchos deportes. Yo __2__ al voleibol. No ganamos siempre, pero me gusta mucho __3__. Yo también __4__ al baloncesto, y ¡sí! ganamos mucho. Antonio y Marco __5__ al fútbol americano y al béisbol. Andrea __6__ al tenis y al voleibol conmigo. Bueno, ¿a qué __7__ tú?

6 ¿Quién juega a qué?

Hablar ¿A qué deportes juegan tú, tus amigos y tus familiares? *(Hint: What sports do you and your friends and family play?)*

modelo

mi hermana

***Mi hermana** juega al voleibol.*

1. yo
2. mi hermano(a)
3. mis amigos(as)
4. mi amigo(a)
5. mis amigos(as) y yo
6. mi primo(a)
7. mis primos(as)
8. ¿ ?

7 La tienda de deportes

Hablar Acabas de recibir este anuncio de una tienda de deportes. Habla con tres estudiantes sobre los artículos que van a comprar. Luego, da un resumen de cuatro de los artículos. *(Hint: Discuss with several classmates what they want to buy.)*

modelo

Tú: *¿Juegas al fútbol?*

Sara: *Sí, juego al fútbol.*

Tú: *¿Vas a comprar una bola nueva?*

Sara: *No, no necesito una bola nueva.*

Resumen: *Sara y Pablo juegan al fútbol. Carlos no juega al fútbol. Pablo va a comprar una bola de fútbol nueva.*

GRAMÁTICA Stem-Changing Verbs: e → ie

You learned that the **u** in **jugar** sometimes changes to **ue**. When you use the verb **pensar** (*to think, to plan*), the **e** in its **stem** sometimes changes to **ie**. **Pensar** means *to plan* only when followed by an infinitive.

stem changes to

pensar → **pienso**

In stem-changing verbs, it is always the next-to-last syllable that changes.

pensar *to think, to plan*

pienso	pensamos
piensas	pensáis
piensa	piensan

Roberto says:

—Yo **prefiero** este bate.

***I prefer** this bat.*

The coach asks:

—¿**Piensas jugar** en el equipo de baloncesto?

***Do you plan** to play on the basketball team?*

Note that when one verb follows another, the first verb is **conjugated** and the second is in its **infinitive** form.

Vocabulario

Stem-Changing Verbs: e → ie

cerrar *to close*
empezar *to begin*
entender *to understand*
merendar *to have a snack*
perder *to lose*
preferir *to prefer*
querer *to want*

¿Cuándo usas una de estas palabras?

Practice: Actividades 8 9 10 11

Más práctica *cuaderno* p. 70
Para hispanohablantes *cuaderno* p. 68

Online Workbook CLASSZONE.COM

8 ¡Todos piensan jugar!

Hablar Explícale a un(a) amigo(a) quién piensa jugar a la pelota. *(Hint: Explain who plans to play ball.)*

modelo

ustedes — ***Ustedes** piensan jugar.*

1. Diana
2. yo
3. ella
4. los chicos
5. nosotros
6. tú
7. Ignacio
8. usted
9. Roberto y yo
10. ustedes

9 ¿Qué hacen?

STRATEGY: SPEAKING

Monitor yourself Listen to yourself. How do you sound? Do you hear errors? If so, stop and correct yourself. It is OK to do so.

Hablar/*Escribir* Explica lo que pasa un día en la escuela. *(Hint: Say what's happening.)*

1. los estudiantes / cerrar / libro
2. nosotras / perder / partido
3. el equipo / querer hacer / gol
4. tú / querer jugar / tenis
5. yo / entender / matemáticas
6. el partido / empezar / a las cuatro
7. ellos / merendar / cafetería
8. yo / preferir nadar / piscina
9. él / perder / gorra
10. tú / preferir estudiar / al aire libre

10 ¿Qué pasa aquí?

Hablar/*Escribir* Describe los dibujos con dos oraciones, usando las palabras. *(Hint: Use the words to describe what is happening.)*

1. entender/preferir

2. entender/querer

3. empezar/jugar

4. cerrar/querer

11 Un día de clases

Escribir Describe tu día de clases. Usa las palabras como guía. *(Hint: Describe your day, using the words as a guide.)*

1. yo / querer
2. mi maestro(a) / preferir
3. yo / empezar
4. mi amigo(a) / pensar
5. la clase de... / empezar
6. mis amigos y yo / merendar
7. el equipo de... / perder
8. los estudiantes / entender

GRAMÁTICA Saying What You Know: The Verb saber

¿RECUERDAS? *pp. 157, 158* You learned that some verbs have irregular **yo** forms.

conocer → **conozco**
hacer → **hago**
oír → **oigo**

Saber is another verb that has an irregular **yo** form. You use **saber** when you talk about factual information you know.

saber *to know*

sé	**sabemos**
sabes	**sabéis**
sabe	**saben**

Claudio asks Ignacio:

—¿**Sabe** él a qué hora empieza la práctica?
*Does **he know** what time practice starts?*

To say that someone knows how to do something, use: **saber** + ***infinitive***.

Sé patinar muy bien.
***I know how to skate** very well.*

Practice: Actividades 12 13 14

Más práctica *cuaderno p. 71*
Para hispanohablantes *cuaderno p. 69*

Online Workbook CLASSZONE.COM

Puerto Rico

Nota cultural

La Fortaleza is the oldest continuously inhabited executive mansion in the Americas. Built in 1532 to protect the island against invasion by sea, it is the residence of Puerto Rico's governor. Can you guess what **fortaleza** means?

12 ¡Saben hacer mucho!

Leer Estas personas saben hacer muchas cosas. Completa las oraciones con la forma correcta del verbo **saber.** *(Hint: Complete each sentence with the correct form of **saber**.)*

1. María _____ jugar al tenis.
2. Tú _____ nadar.
3. Nosotros _____ hablar español.
4. Yo _____ patinar.
5. Ustedes _____ bailar.
6. Él _____ cantar.
7. Los chicos _____ jugar al voleibol.
8. Ella _____ tocar el piano.
9. Mi hermanita _____ andar en bicicleta.
10. Nosotras _____ tocar la guitarra.

13 Los deportistas

Escuchar Muchos amigos de Diana saben jugar a varios deportes. Escucha las descripciones de Diana y explica a lo que saben jugar.
(Hint: Explain what sports her friends know.)

1. Gisela y César
2. Pablo
3. ella y su hermano
4. Roberto y su hermano
5. Diana

14 ¿Qué saben hacer?

Hablar ¿Qué saben hacer las personas que tú conoces?
(Hint: Say what they know how to do.)

modelo

tu hermano(a)

Tú: *¿Qué sabe hacer **tu hermana**?*

Otro(a) estudiante: *Mi hermana sabe cantar y bailar.*

1. tu amigo(a)
2. tus amigos(as)
3. tú
4. tú y tus amigos(as)
5. tu maestro(a) de español

More Practice:

Más comunicación *p. R8*

GRAMÁTICA Phrases for Making Comparisons

Several phrases are used to compare things. Roberto and Ignacio use these when they discuss sports.

- **más... que** *more... than*

...el fútbol americano es **más** interesante **que** el fútbol.
*...football is **more** interesting **than** soccer.*

- **menos... que** *less... than*

agrees

...**el tenis** es **menos** divertid**o** **que** el baloncesto.
*...tennis is **less** entertaining **than** basketball.*

Adjectives must agree in gender and number with the **nouns** that precede them.

- **tan... como** *as... as*

...el fútbol no es **tan** popular **como** el fútbol americano.
*...soccer is not **as** popular **as** football.*

These phrases are also used to compare things.

- **más que...** *more than...*

Me gusta correr **más que** nadar.
*I like to run **more than** (I like to) swim.*

- **menos que...** *less than...*

Me gusta usar un guante nuevo **menos que** un bate nuevo.
*I like to use a new glove **less than** a new bat.*

- **tanto como...** *as much as...*

A él le gusta jugar al fútbol **tanto como** al béisbol.
*He likes to play soccer **as much as** baseball.*

When you talk about numbers, you must use **más de** or **menos de**.

más de dos o tres minutos
***more than** two or three minutes*

en **menos de** cinco minutos
*in **less than** five minutes*

There are a few irregular comparative words.

mayor	**menor**	**mejor**	**peor**
older	*younger*	*better*	*worse*

Practice:
Actividades 15 16 17

Más práctica *cuaderno p. 72*
Para hispanohablantes *cuaderno p. 70*

Online Workbook
CLASSZONE.COM

15 ¿De o que?

Escribir Usa la palabra apropiada para describir a los deportistas de la escuela. *(Hint: Describe the athletes.)*

1. Hay más _____ siete personas en el equipo de béisbol.
2. Los chicos corren más _____ las chicas.
3. Las chicas saben jugar mejor _____ las maestras.
4. Hay menos _____ ocho personas en el equipo de baloncesto.
5. La chica rubia quiere jugar menos _____ la morena.
6. Ignacio tiene más _____ cinco bates.
7. Roberto juega peor _____ Diana.
8. Todas las semanas Ignacio practica más _____ cinco veces.

16 Las comparaciones

Hablar/Escribir Haz comparaciones usando **más que, menos que, tan… como** o **tanto como.** *(Hint: Use the correct phrase for making comparisons.)*

1. El gato es _____ gordo _____ el perro.

2. Las camisetas azules son _____ grandes _____ las camisetas rojas.

3. Le gusta estudiar _____ bailar.

4. Carmen es _____ seria _____ José.

5. Las muchachas son ____ altas _____ los chicos.

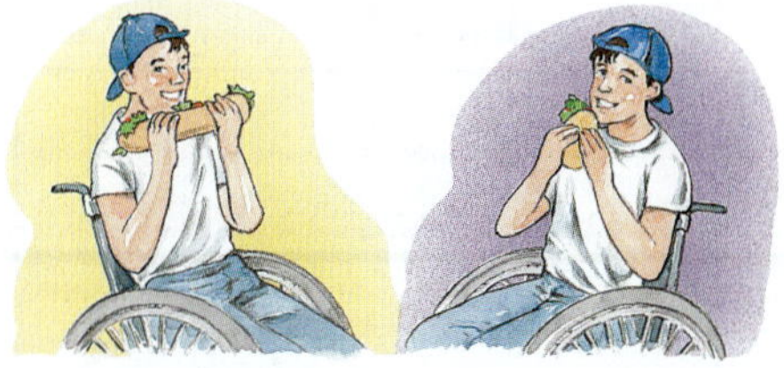

6. Le gusta comer un sándwich _____ un taco.

7. Paco es _____ trabajador _____ María Luisa.
8. yo / mi amigo(a): ¿?
9. las casas / los apartamentos: ¿?
10. la clase de historia / la clase de inglés: ¿?

Puerto Rico

Nota cultural

Puerto Ricans periodically vote on the relationship they want with the U.S. They rejected both statehood and independence in 1998. They are currently a commonwealth.

17 ¿Qué piensas tú? 

Hablar Trabaja con otro(a) estudiante para comparar los deportes. Cambien de papel. *(Hint: Compare sports with a classmate.)*

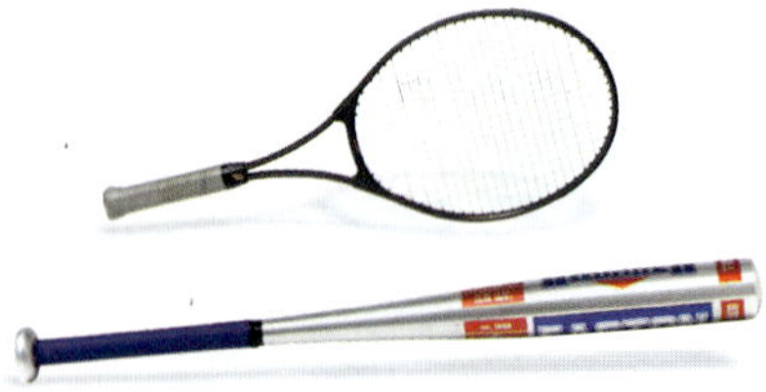

interesante

modelo

Estudiante A: *Para ti, ¿qué deporte es más* ***interesante, el tenis*** *o* ***el béisbol****?*

Estudiante B: *Para mí, el tenis es más interesante que el béisbol.*

Estudiante A: *Para mí, el tenis es tan interesante como el béisbol.*

Estudiante A PREGUNTAS

1. 

divertido

2. 

peligroso

3. 

difícil

4. 

malo

5. 

bueno

6. 

interesante

Estudiante B RESPUESTAS

Para mí, ... es más... que...
Para mí, ... es menos... que...
Para mí, ... es tan... como...

Apoyo para estudiar

Comparatives

When comparing, picture these visual cues:

(+) más… que
(–) menos… que
(=) tan… como

Think about extremes that would illustrate **más** and **menos**, such as **UN ELEFANTE [(+) más grande]** and **un ratón [(–) menos grande]**. Now think of two very different athletes or performers about whom you have an opinion. How would you compare them?

PARTE D

Todo en acción

Activities 18–19 bring together all concepts presented.

18 ¡Lógicamente!

Escuchar Todos hablan de los deportes. Escucha lo que dicen. Luego, indica la respuesta más lógica. *(Hint: Listen and indicate the most logical response.)*

1. **a.** ¡Qué bien! Tenemos más de cinco minutos.
   b. ¡Ay! Tenemos menos de cinco minutos.
2. **a.** ¿Tienes tu raqueta?
   b. ¿Tienes tu tarea?
3. **a.** Sí, me gusta nadar.
   b. ¡Claro que sí! Me gusta patinar.
4. **a.** No necesita un guante.
   b. ¿Va a la tienda de deportes?
5. **a.** Prefiere nadar.
   b. Prefiere levantar pesas.

19 ¿Cuál es tu deporte favorito?

Hablar/*Escribir* Habla con otros estudiantes sobre los deportes. Escribe sus respuestas. Prepara un resumen para la clase. *(Hint: Ask classmates about sports. Record responses and report them.)*

La encuesta	Estudiante 1	Estudiante 2
1. ¿A qué deportes sabes jugar?		
2. ¿A qué deportes juegas mucho?		
3. ¿A qué deporte prefieres jugar?		
4. ¿Cómo es?		
5. ¿Qué deporte prefieres ver?		
6. Compara el deporte que prefieres ver con el deporte que prefieres jugar.		
7. ¿Cuál es tu equipo favorito?		
8. ¿Cómo es?		
9. ¿Pierde mucho?		

More Practice: **Más comunicación** *p. R8*

Online Workbook
CLASSZONE.COM

Pronunciación

Trabalenguas

Pronunciación de la *ñ* The letter ñ does not exist in English, but the sound does. It is the sound made by the combination of the letters *ny* in the English word *canyon*. To practice the sound, pronounce the following tongue twister.

ñ

La ñ *es la **n** con bigote.*

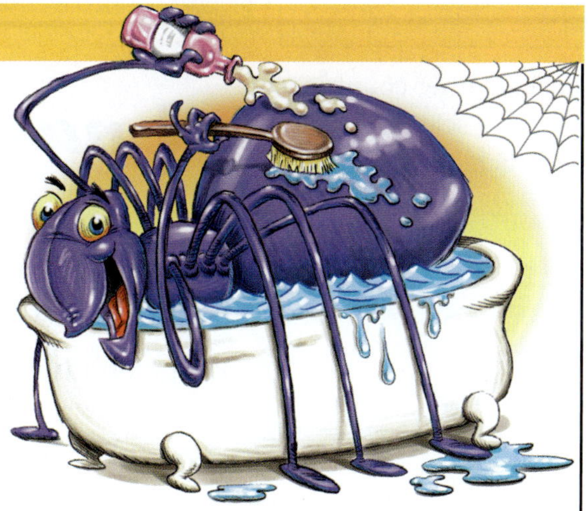

¡La araña se baña mañana!

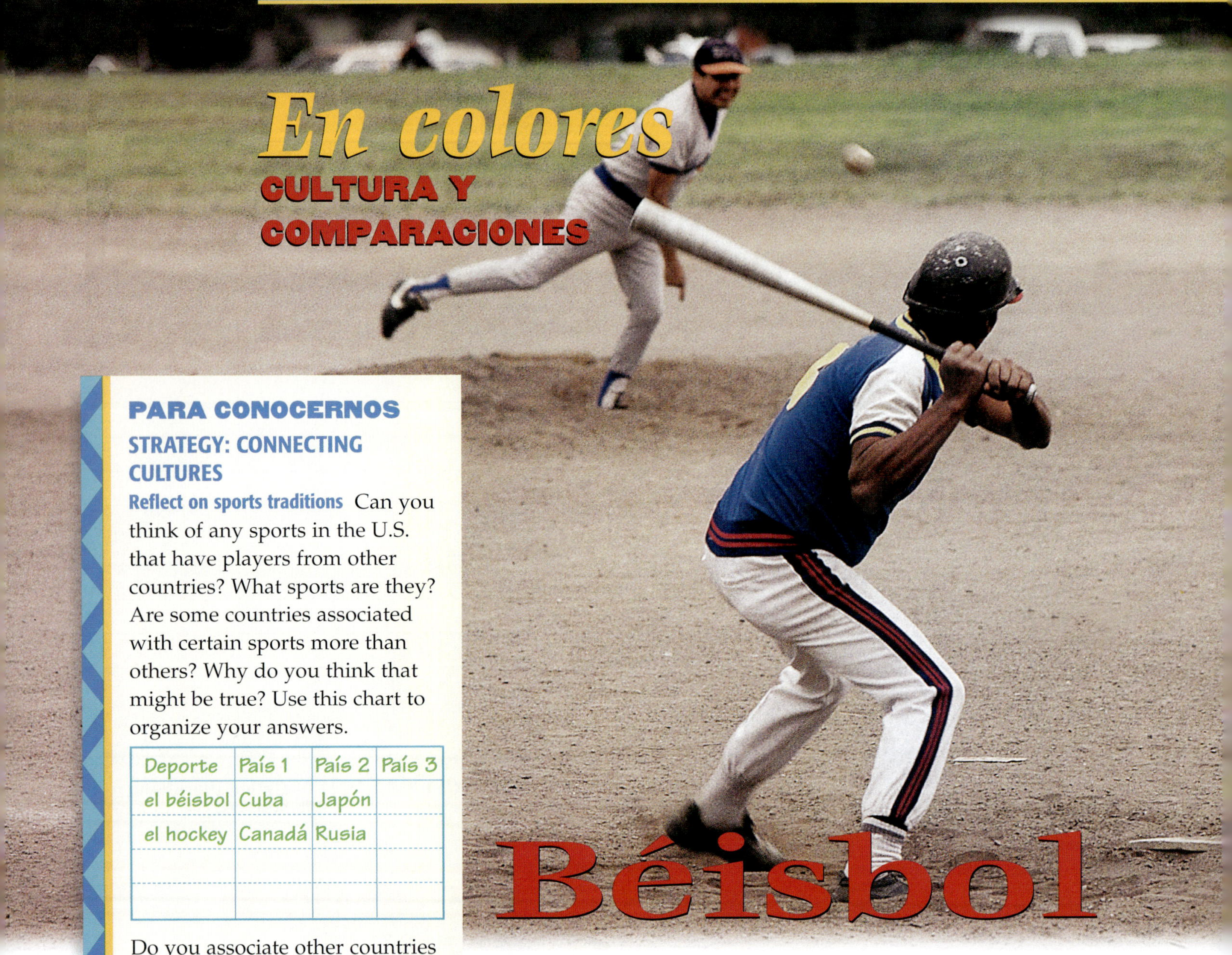

En colores

CULTURA Y COMPARACIONES

PARA CONOCERNOS

STRATEGY: CONNECTING CULTURES

Reflect on sports traditions Can you think of any sports in the U.S. that have players from other countries? What sports are they? Are some countries associated with certain sports more than others? Why do you think that might be true? Use this chart to organize your answers.

Deporte	País 1	País 2	País 3
el béisbol	Cuba	Japón	
el hockey	Canadá	Rusia	

Do you associate other countries with areas such as science, music, or art? If so, which ones? Why?

Béisbol

El pasatiempo nacional

En Puerto Rico el béisbol es muy popular. La temporada[1] de béisbol es de octubre a marzo. Los equipos que juegan forman la liga de invierno[2] y hay un partido casi todos los días.

Cada ciudad principal tiene un equipo. Unos jugadores[3] de las ligas mayores y menores[4] de Estados Unidos participan junto con los jugadores puertorriqueños.

[1] season [2] winter league [3] players [4] major and minor leagues

Roberto Clemente (1934–1972), jugador de los Piratas de Pittsburgh, es el puertorriqueño más famoso del béisbol. El primer latino elegido[5] para el Salón de la Fama[6] en 1973, Clemente empezó[7] su carrera con el equipo de Santurce, Puerto Rico. Hoy, en la ciudad de San Juan, el estadio principal de béisbol se llama Coliseo Roberto Clemente.

[5] elected [6] Hall of Fame [7] began

En el resto del Caribe el béisbol es tan importante como en Puerto Rico. Muchos jugadores importantes vienen de esta región. Juan Marichal de la República Dominicana está en el Salón de la Fama. Andrés Galarraga de Venezuela, Edgar Rentería de Colombia, Liván Hernández de Cuba y Fernando Valenzuela de México son otras figuras latinoamericanas importantes de las ligas mayores de béisbol de Estados Unidos.

José Cruz, Jr. e Iván Rodríguez son dos jugadores de Puerto Rico.

Nota cultural

On December 31, 1972, Roberto Clemente was about to deliver supplies to earthquake survivors in Nicaragua when his plane crashed. He is remembered not only as a great baseball player, but also as an outstanding humanitarian.

More About Puerto Rico
CLASSZONE.COM

¿Comprendiste?

1. ¿En qué meses juegan los equipos de la liga de invierno?
2. ¿De dónde vienen los jugadores de la liga de invierno?
3. ¿Quién es el primer latino elegido para el Salón de la Fama?
4. ¿Qué países latinos tienen jugadores en las ligas mayores?

¿Qué piensas?

1. ¿Por qué juegan en Puerto Rico los jugadores de las ligas mayores y menores de Estados Unidos?
2. ¿Por qué vienen a Estados Unidos los jugadores de otros países?

ETAPA 2

En uso

REPASO Y MÁS COMUNICACIÓN

OBJECTIVES

- Talk about sports
- Express preferences
- Say what you know
- Make comparisons

Now you can...

- talk about sports.

To review

- the verb **jugar**, see p. 204.

1 ¿Dónde juegas?

Todos hablan de su deporte favorito. ¿Dónde lo juegan?
(Hint: Tell where people play their favorite sports.)

modelo

mi padre: tenis (¿en la piscina o en la cancha?)

***Mi padre** juega al **tenis** en la cancha.*

1. tú: baloncesto (¿en el campo o en la cancha?)
2. usted: voleibol (¿en la cancha o sobre hielo?)
3. yo: fútbol (¿en la cancha o en el campo?)
4. los vecinos: béisbol (¿al aire libre o en el gimnasio?)
5. Tomás y yo: fútbol americano (¿en el estadio o en la piscina?)
6. mi hermano: hockey (¿en la cancha o sobre hielo?)

Now you can...

- express preferences.

To review

- stem-changing verbs: **e→ie**, see p. 205.

2 ¡Vamos a jugar!

Las amigas de Diana hablan de los deportes. Completa su conversación con los verbos apropiados en la forma correcta.
(Hint: Complete the conversation with the appropriate verbs in the correct form.)

cerrar pensar querer entender preferir empezar

Eva: Rita, ¿ __1__ ir a un partido de béisbol conmigo mañana? El partido __2__ a las siete.

Rita: Gracias, pero no me gusta ver el béisbol. Yo __3__ los deportes individuales, como el surfing. Para mí, el béisbol es aburrido. No __4__ por qué te gusta.

Eva: Pues, yo __5__ que el béisbol es muy interesante. Y mañana mi equipo favorito, los Cardenales, va a jugar.

Rita: Mis hermanos también __6__ ver jugar a los Cardenales mañana, pero yo no. Mi mamá y yo __7__ pasar los sábados en las tiendas. Pero, a veces vamos al nuevo gimnasio. Abre a las siete de la mañana y __8__ a las nueve de la noche.

Self-Check Quiz
CLASSZONE.COM

Now you can...
- say what you know.

To review
- the verb **saber**, see p. 207.

3 Somos deportistas

¿A qué deportes saben jugar estas personas? ¿Qué usan para jugar? *(Hint: Describe the sports these people know.)*

modelo

Bárbara

***Bárbara** sabe patinar.*
*Usa **patines.***

ustedes

***Ustedes** saben jugar al voleibol.*
*Usan **una bola.***

1. Guillermo

2. nosotros

3. yo

4. mis amigos

5. tú

6. yo

Now you can...
- make comparisons.

To review
- phrases for making comparisons, see p. 208.

4 Comparaciones

Expresa tus opiniones acerca de los deportes.
(Hint: Express your opinions about sports.)

modelo

correr / nadar (menos / divertido)

Correr es menos divertido que nadar.
o: *Nadar es menos divertido que correr.*
o: *Correr es tan divertido como nadar.*

1. el baloncesto / el tenis (menos / interesante)
2. el surfing / el béisbol (más / aburrido)
3. nadar / levantar pesas (más /bueno)
4. esquiar / patinar (más / peligroso)
5. el fútbol americano / el baloncesto (más / popular)
6. el voleibol / el fútbol (menos / difícil)
7. el tenis / el béisbol (más / malo)
8. patinar / levantar pesas (menos / fácil)

5 ¿Qué opinas tú?

STRATEGY: SPEAKING

Give reasons for your preferences Support your choices in different ways. Compare (1) how you feel about the sports, (2) what you know or don't know about them, or (3) basic similarities and differences among them. Think of different ways of explaining your choices.

Habla con otro(a) estudiante sobre los deportes. Explícale cuáles son tus preferencias y por qué. *(Hint: Talk about sports.)*

modelo

Tú: *¿Prefieres levantar pesas o jugar al voleibol?*

Otro(a) estudiante: *Prefiero jugar al voleibol. El voleibol es más interesante que levantar pesas.*

Tú: *Para mí, levantar pesas es más divertido.*

6 Un paseo por el club

Imagínate que trabajas en un nuevo club de deportes. Muéstrales el club a tus amigos, describiendo las actividades. *(Hint: Show your friends the new sports club where you work.)*

- Hay equipos de...
- Muchas personas juegan al...
- Tenemos cancha de...
- El club abre...
- Para jugar al voleibol, hay...
- Los sábados jugamos al...
- Al aire libre jugamos...
- Los viernes hay clases de...
- Para las personas que les gusta nadar, hay...

7 En tu propia voz

ESCRITURA Imagínate que tienes que preparar un folleto para promover el club nuevo de la Actividad 6. Incluye información sobre las actividades y el horario del club. *(Hint: Write a brochure promoting the new sports club.)*

TÚ EN LA COMUNIDAD

Sarah is a Florida student who uses Spanish at her job as a restaurant hostess and sends e-mails in Spanish. She also used her Spanish when she went to Venezuela as a volunteer with a medical mission group. Sarah spoke Spanish to the patients and translated doctors' questions and instructions. Do you use Spanish to help others?

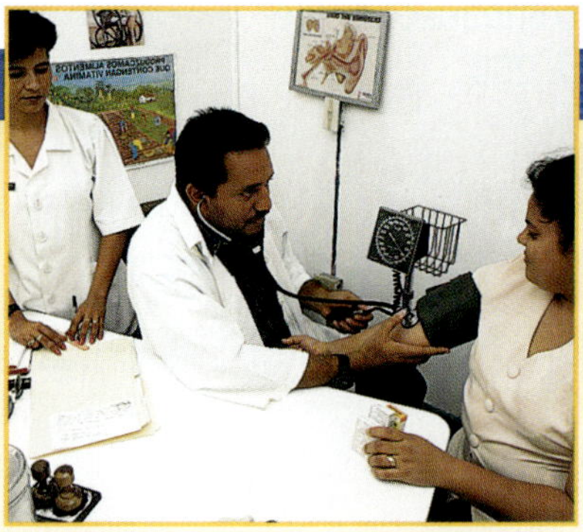

Flashcards
CLASSZONE.COM

En resumen

REPASO DE VOCABULARIO

TALKING ABOUT SPORTS

el equipo	*team*
ganar	*to win*
el gol	*goal*
jugar (ue)	*to play*
el partido	*game*
la tienda de deportes	*sporting goods store*

Sports

andar en patineta	*to skateboard*
el baloncesto	*basketball*
el béisbol	*baseball*
esquiar	*to ski*
el fútbol	*soccer*
el fútbol americano	*football*
el hockey	*hockey*
levantar pesas	*to lift weights*
el surfing	*surfing*
el tenis	*tennis*
el voleibol	*volleyball*

Equipment

el bate	*bat*
la bola	*ball*
el casco	*helmet*
la gorra	*baseball cap*
el guante	*glove*
los patines	*skates*
la patineta	*skateboard*
la pelota	*baseball*
la raqueta	*racket*

Locations

al aire libre	*outdoors*
el campo	*field*
la cancha	*court*
el estadio	*stadium*
la piscina	*swimming pool*
sobre hielo	*on ice*

EXPRESSING PREFERENCES

preferir (ie)	*to prefer*
querer (ie)	*to want*

SAYING WHAT YOU KNOW

saber	*to know*

MAKING COMPARISONS

más de	*more than*
más… que	*more…than*
mayor	*older*
mejor	*better*
menor	*younger*
menos de	*less than*
menos… que	*less…than*
peor	*worse*
tan… como	*as…as*
tanto como	*as much as*

OTHER WORDS AND PHRASES

cerrar (ie)	*to close*
empezar (ie)	*to begin*
entender (ie)	*to understand*
favorito(a)	*favorite*
loco(a)	*crazy*
merendar (ie)	*to have a snack*
peligroso(a)	*dangerous*
pensar (ie)	*to think, to plan*
perder (ie)	*to lose*

Juego

A Ángela, a Marco y a Juanito les gusta practicar diferentes deportes. ¿Cuáles son? Busca sus nombres. Con las otras letras, identifica su deporte preferido.

1. ALSAEGSPENARALEVANT
2. GINAMURFSOCR
3. NIAUJOTTBLOFU

UNIDAD 3

ETAPA 3

El tiempo en El Yunque

OBJECTIVES

- Describe the weather
- Discuss clothing and accessories
- State an opinion
- Describe how you feel
- Say what is happening

¿Qué ves?

Mira la foto de El Yunque, el bosque tropical.

1. ¿Hay muchas plantas verdes?
2. ¿Ignacio está ocupado o no?
3. ¿Diana y Roberto están alegres o preocupados?
4. ¿Cómo se llama el lugar?

VEREDA
EL YUNQUE
EL YUNQUE TRAIL
BOSQUE NACIONAL
DEL CARIBE
BAÑO GRANDE
CUERPOS CIVILES DE CONSERVACION
CIVILIAN CONSERVATION CORPS

En contexto

VIDEO DVD AUDIO

VOCABULARIO

Roberto has experienced all kinds of weather in Minnesota and Puerto Rico. Take a look at the pictures in his scrapbook to understand the meaning of the words in blue. This will also help you answer the questions on the next page.

A ¿**Qué tiempo hace** en Minnesota? En **el invierno** hace mal **tiempo.** ¡**Hace frío** y hay mucha **nieve**! Cuando va a **nevar,** necesitas **un gorro, una bufanda** y **un abrigo.**

B Cuando va a **llover,** necesitas **un paraguas.** A la madre de Roberto le gusta caminar bajo **la lluvia** con su paraguas **de cuadros.**

C En Puerto Rico, en **el verano hace calor.** Cuando **hay sol,** es divertido ir a **la playa** y nadar en **el mar.**

E A Roberto le gusta llevar estas **gafas de sol.**

D La chica lleva una camisa **con rayas.** Es verano.

F En **el bosque** tropical El Yunque, hay **árboles, plantas** y **flores** muy interesantes.

EL TIEMPO

Temperaturas

9 de marzo

	ALTA	BAJA
San Juan	87°	73°
Minneapolis	30°	15°

Preguntas personales

1. Cuando va a llover, ¿llevas un paraguas?
2. En el lugar donde vives, ¿hace calor o hace frío en el invierno?
3. ¿Prefieres ropa de cuadros o ropa con rayas?
4. ¿Qué ropa llevas en el invierno?
5. ¿Qué hay en un bosque tropical?

En vivo

DIÁLOGO

Diana

Roberto

Ignacio

PARA ESCUCHAR • STRATEGY: LISTENING

Sort and categorize details Minneapolis and San Juan are a world apart, yet in at least one way they are similar. How? What does Roberto say? What differences are mentioned? Use a Venn diagram to sort these details.

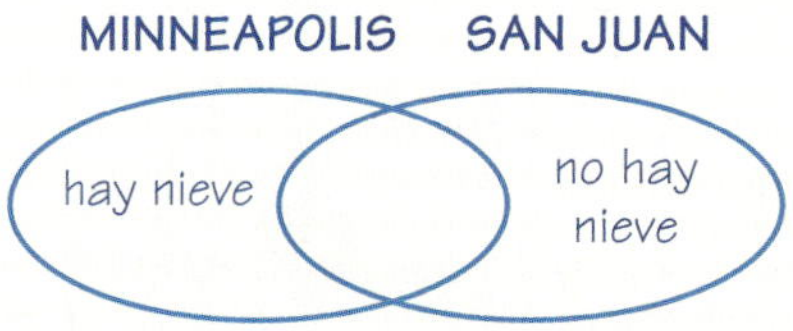

¡Qué tiempo!

1 ► **Diana:** ¡Qué mona tu bufanda! Me gusta tu gorro. ¿Hace mucho frío en Minneapolis?

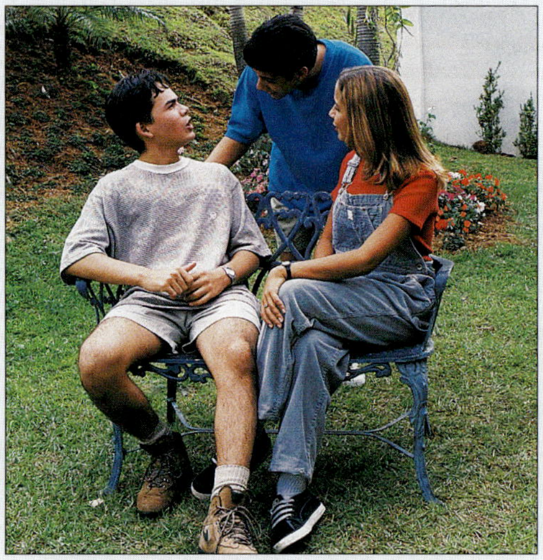

5 ► **Diana:** ¡Ay! Pues, ya tienes ropa de verano.
Roberto: Claro que la tengo. ¡En Minneapolis no es invierno todo el año!

6 ► **Roberto:** ¡Qué día bonito! Hace muy buen tiempo. Tengo ganas de ir a El Yunque.
Diana: Perfecto, porque el proyecto de Ignacio para el concurso es sobre el bosque tropical. Y está preparando el proyecto este mes.

7 ► **Ignacio:** Sí, y necesito sacar fotos del bosque. Y las quiero sacar hoy mismo.
Roberto: Tengo suerte, ¿no lo creen?
Diana: Creo que tienes mucha suerte.
Ignacio: Tengo prisa. Es buena hora para sacar fotos porque hay sol.

CD-ROM Take-Home Tutor

2 ▶ **Roberto:** En el invierno, sí, ¡hace mucho frío! ¡Brrr! Tengo frío cuando pienso en los inviernos de Minneapolis.

3 ▶ **Diana:** ¿Nieva mucho?

Roberto: Bueno, en el invierno, nieva casi todas las semanas. Pero en verano, es como aquí. Hace mucho calor.

4 ▶ **Ignacio:** ¿Qué vas a hacer con toda esta ropa de invierno? Aquí nadie la necesita.

Roberto: Tienes razón. Voy a necesitar shorts, trajes de baño y gafas de sol.

8 ▶ **Ignacio:** ¡Qué bonito! Los árboles, las flores…

Roberto: Sí, muy bonita.

Ignacio: No es como Minneapolis, ¿verdad, Roberto?

Roberto: Tienes razón, Ignacio.

9 ▶ **Ignacio:** Mi proyecto va a estar bien chévere, ¿no creen?… ¿No creen?…

…Sí, Ignacio, creo que tu proyecto va a ser muy impresionante.

10 ▶ **Ignacio:** ¡Está lloviendo! ¡Y no tengo paraguas!

Roberto: Te estamos esperando, hombre.

En acción

PARTE A Comprensión del diálogo

For Activities 1–2, refer to the dialog on pages 222–223.

1 ¿Qué lugar?

Escuchar ¿Qué lugar describe cada oración, Puerto Rico o Minnesota? ¡Ojo! Algunas oraciones describen los dos lugares. *(Hint: Which place is described?)*

1. En el invierno, hace mucho frío.
2. La gente no necesita ropa de invierno.
3. Nieva casi todas las semanas en el invierno.
4. En el verano, hace calor.
5. Necesitas shorts, traje de baño y gafas de sol.
6. Hay un bosque tropical.

2 Oraciones revueltas

Escuchar Completa las siguientes oraciones según el diálogo, combinando frases de las dos columnas. *(Hint: Complete the sentences by matching.)*

1. El proyecto de Ignacio para el concurso es sobre _____.
2. Tengo frío cuando pienso en _____.
3. ¿Qué vas a hacer con _____?
4. Es buena hora para _____.

a. sacar fotos
b. toda esta ropa de invierno
c. el bosque tropical
d. los inviernos de Minneapolis

PARTE B Práctica del vocabulario

Objectives for Activities 3–5
- Discuss clothing and accessories

3 ¿Qué hay en la maleta?

Hablar/*Escribir* Describe lo que hay en la maleta de Roberto. *(Hint: Describe what's in Roberto's suitcase.)*

modelo

1. Hay un abrigo marrón.

Puerto Rico

También se dice

There are different ways to say *cute*.

- **bonito:** Mexico and other countries
- **mono(a):** Puerto Rico, Spain
- **lindo(a):** many countries

Vocabulario

Las estaciones

el verano

el otoño

el invierno

la primavera

¿Qué actividad te gusta hacer en cada estación?

4 ¡Todos van de vacaciones!

Hablar/*Escribir* Todas las personas van de vacaciones. Explica adónde van, usando elementos de cada columna. ¿Qué van a llevar y qué van a hacer? *(**Hint:** Explain where people are vacationing, what they're taking with them, and what they'll be doing.)*

modelo

Yo voy a la playa en el verano.

Voy a llevar un traje de baño, gafas de sol y bronceador porque voy a tomar el sol.

Ignacio y Diana
Roberto
tú
yo
mi amigo(a)
mis amigos
mi familia y yo

la playa
las montañas
el desierto
el lago
el bosque tropical
¿otro lugar?

primavera
verano
otoño
invierno

la bufanda
el traje de baño
el paraguas
las gafas de sol
el abrigo
el bronceador
los shorts
el gorro
el impermeable

tomar el sol
andar en bicicleta
nadar
jugar a (¿qué deporte?)
esquiar
patinar sobre hielo
descansar
ver las plantas y las flores
sacar fotos
¿?

Práctica: gramática y vocabulario

Objectives for Activities 6–20 • Describe the weather • State an opinion • Describe how you feel • Say what is happening

5 ¡Organízalos!

Escribir Trabajas en una tienda. Organiza los artículos según la estación. *(Hint: Group the articles according to the season.)*

modelo

Las gorras van en la sección de verano.

LA PRIMAVERA

EL OTOÑO

EL VERANO

EL INVIERNO

1. 

2. 

3. 

4. 

5. 

6. 

7. 

8. 

9. 

GRAMÁTICA Describing the Weather

To talk about weather, you will often use the verb **hacer.**

¿Qué tiempo hace?
What's it like out?

Hace… *It's…*	**(mucho) calor.** *(very) hot.*	**(mucho) viento.** *(very) windy.*
	(mucho) fresco. *(very) cool.*	**(muy) buen tiempo.** *(very) nice outside.*
	(mucho) frío. *(very) cold.*	**(muy) mal tiempo.** *(very) bad outside.*
	(mucho) sol. *(very) sunny.*	

Diana asks Roberto:

—¿**Hace mucho frío** en Minneapolis?
***Is it very cold** in Minneapolis?*

Roberto replies:

—En el invierno, sí, **¡hace mucho frío!**
*In the winter, yes, **it's very cold**!*

When you talk about wind or sun, you can also use **hay.**

Hay… *It's…*	**(mucho) sol.** *(very) sunny.*
	(mucho) viento. *(very) windy.*

Use the verbs **llover** and **nevar** to say it is raining or snowing. They are verbs with stem changes, just like **jugar** and **pensar.**

Llueve mucho en el bosque tropical.
***It rains** a lot in the tropical rain forest.*

Nieva mucho en Minnesota.
***It snows** a lot in Minnesota.*

To say that it's cloudy, use the expression **está nublado.**

No vamos a la playa porque **está nublado.**
*We're not going to the beach because **it's cloudy.***

Practice: Actividades 6 7 8 9 10

Más práctica *cuaderno p. 77*

Para hispanohablantes *cuaderno p. 75*

Online Workbook CLASSZONE.COM

6 El tiempo

Escuchar Escucha las descripciones. ¿Qué estación es? Escoge el número de la oración que corresponde a cada estación. *(Hint: Match the number of the description with the season.)*

a. primavera
b. verano
c. otoño
d. invierno

7 ¿Qué tiempo hace?

Hablar/*Escribir* Usa un mínimo de dos expresiones para describir el tiempo en cada dibujo. ¿Qué estación es? *(Hint: Describe the weather and season.)*

modelo

Hace frío. Hay sol. Es invierno.

1.

2.

3.

4.

8 ¿Qué prefieres hacer?

Hablar Trabaja con otro(a) estudiante para explicar tus preferencias. Cambien de papel. *(Hint: Take turns giving your preferences.)*

modelo

preferir / hacer frío: ¿ir a la playa o patinar sobre hielo?

Estudiante A: *¿Qué **prefieres** hacer cuando **hace frío,** ir a la playa o patinar sobre hielo?*

Estudiante B: *Prefiero **patinar sobre hielo.***

1. querer / hay sol: ¿jugar al tenis o ver la televisión?
2. preferir / hacer mucho calor: ¿nadar en el mar o cuidar a tu hermano?
3. preferir / llover: ¿ir a la montaña o tocar la guitarra?
4. querer / nevar: ¿esquiar en las montañas o correr en el parque?
5. querer / hacer buen tiempo: ¿ir al cine o sacar fotos en el parque?
6. preferir / hacer mal tiempo: ¿ir de compras o pasear por el parque?
7. preferir / estar nublado: ¿practicar el surfing o ir al museo?
8. ¿?

9 ¿Qué vas a llevar?

STRATEGY: SPEAKING
Say how often Generalize by saying how often you wear an item in this weather. **(Siempre / A veces) llevo shorts cuando hace calor.**

Hablar La ropa que llevas depende mucho del tiempo. Trabaja con otro(a) estudiante para explicar qué vas a llevar según el tiempo. *(Hint: Explain what you'll be wearing.)*

modelo

hace calor

Estudiante A: ***Hace calor.*** *¿Qué vas a llevar hoy?*

Estudiante B: *Voy a llevar una camiseta y shorts. Siempre llevo shorts cuando hace calor.*

1. hace mucho frío
2. hace fresco
3. hace mucho calor
4. hay sol
5. llueve
6. la temperatura es de 70°
7. nieva
8. ¿?

10 El tiempo hoy

Hablar/Leer Tienes un periódico de San Juan. Tus amigos quieren saber qué tiempo hace en varias ciudades. Trabaja en un grupo de tres para hacer y contestar las preguntas sobre el tiempo. *(Hint: Say what the weather is in various places.)*

¿Qué tiempo hace en…?

¿Cuál es la temperatura en…?

¿Hace buen/mal tiempo en…?

¿Dónde hace/hay…?

EL TIEMPO

4 de enero	Tiempo	Temperatura mínima	Temperatura máxima
San Juan		70°	82°
Buenos Aires		75°	90°
Los Ángeles		50°	64°
Madrid		37°	46°
México		48°	61°
Miami		59°	70°
Nueva York		28°	32°
Quito		50°	59°
San Antonio		39°	51°

Clave: sol  lluvia  nieve  nublado  viento 

Puerto Rico

También se dice

Puerto Rico, like other countries, has its own way of saying the following:

sunglasses
- **gafas de sol:** Puerto Rico, Spain, Ecuador
- **lentes de sol:** many countries

T-shirt
- **camiseta:** Puerto Rico and many countries
- **playera:** Mexico
- **polera:** Chile
- **remera:** Argentina

shorts
- **shorts:** Puerto Rico
- **pantalones cortos:** many countries
- **pantalonetas:** Colombia, Ecuador

GRAMÁTICA Special Expressions Using tener

¿RECUERDAS? *p. 152* You learned to say that someone is hungry or thirsty using the verb **tener**. You also learned how to tell age using **tener**.

tener hambre
tener sed
tener... años

You can use the verb **tener** in many expressions.

tener... *to be...*

- **calor** *hot*
- **cuidado** *careful*
- **frío** *cold*
- **miedo** *afraid*
- **prisa** *in a hurry*
- **razón** *right*
- **sueño** *sleepy*
- **suerte** *lucky*

tener ganas de + ***infinitive*** *to feel like...*

- **bailar** *dancing*
- **cantar** *singing*

Roberto says:
—**Tengo suerte.**
I'm lucky.

Ignacio says:
—**Tengo prisa.**
I'm in a hurry.

Practice:
Actividades 11 12 13

Más práctica
cuaderno p. 78
Para hispanohablantes
cuaderno p. 76

Online Workbook
CLASSZONE.COM

11 Tiene ganas de...

Hablar/*Escribir* ¿Qué tienen ganas de hacer estas personas?
(Hint: What do they feel like doing?)

modelo
Diana: ir a la playa
Diana** tiene ganas de **ir a la playa.

1. nosotras: caminar
2. usted: ver la televisión
3. ellos: practicar deportes
4. tú: patinar
5. ustedes: ir de compras
6. Emilia y yo: jugar al tenis
7. Tomás: levantar pesas
8. tú: leer una novela
9. ella: tocar la guitarra
10. yo: ¿?

12 ¿Qué pasa aquí?

Hablar ¿Cómo se sienten estas personas? Describe cada dibujo, usando una expresión con **tener**. *(Hint: Describe each picture with a **tener** expression.)*

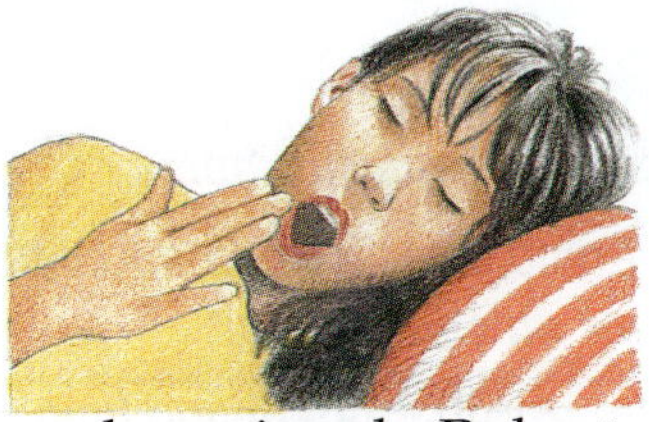

1. la amiga de Roberto

2. su prima

3. su hermana

4. su vecino

5. su amigo

13 Yo tengo...

Hablar Dile a otro(a) estudiante cómo te sientes en cada situación. Usa estas palabras: **calor, frío, miedo, prisa, razón, suerte.** Cambien de papel.
(Hint: Say how you feel.)

modelo

no comer por muchas horas

Tú: *¿Cómo estás cuando **no comes por muchas horas**?*

Otro(a) estudiante: *¡Tengo hambre!*

1. correr a la escuela
2. jugar al tenis en el sol
3. ver una película de horror
4. caminar en la nieve
5. saber hacer un examen
6. ganar mucho

More Practice: **Más comunicación** *p. R9*

Puerto Rico

Nota cultural

El Yunque is a rain forest. All rain forests have four zones. They are (from lowest to highest) the floor, the understory, the canopy, and the emergent layer. Some zones are more humid than others; some get more sunlight. Each is a habitat for different kinds of animals and plants.

GRAMÁTICA Direct Object Pronouns

The **direct object** in a sentence receives the action of the verb. Direct objects answer the question *whom?* or *what?* about the verb. Nouns used as **direct objects** can be replaced by **pronouns.**

Singular	Plural
me *me*	**nos** *us*
te *you (familiar)*	**os** *you (familiar)*
lo ← ***masculine*** *you (formal), him, it*	**los** ← ***masculine*** *you, them*
la ← ***feminine*** *you (formal), her, it*	**las** ← ***feminine*** *you, them*

The **direct object** noun is placed after the **conjugated verb**.

Diana says:

—Pues, ya **tienes ropa de verano.**
*You already have **summer clothing.***

replaced by

Roberto answers:

—Claro que **la tengo**.
*Of course I have **it**.*

The direct object **pronoun** is placed directly **before** the **conjugated verb**.

When an infinitive follows the conjugated verb, the direct object **pronoun** can be placed:

before the **conjugated verb** or **attached** to the **infinitive**

Ignacio says: ***replaced by***

—Necesito sacar **fotos** del bosque. Y **las quiero sacar** hoy mismo. *I need to take pictures of the rain forest. I want to take **them** today.*

He could also have said: ***replaced by***

—Necesito sacar **fotos** del bosque. Y **quiero sacarlas** hoy mismo.

Practice: 14 15 16 17 18

Más práctica *cuaderno p. 79*
Para hispanohablantes *cuaderno p. 77*

Online Workbook CLASSZONE.COM

14 ¿Qué compran?

Hablar Habla con otro(a) estudiante para explicar qué compran. *(Hint: Say what they buy.)*

modelo

Roberto: el guante de béisbol

Tú: *¿**Roberto** compra **el guante de béisbol**?*

Otro(a) estudiante: *Sí, lo compra.*

1. Diana: los patines
2. Ignacio: la raqueta
3. Roberto: las pelotas
4. Diana: las pesas
5. Roberto: el casco
6. Roberto: los bates
7. Diana: la patineta
8. Diana: el traje de baño
9. Ignacio: la bola
10. Ignacio: las gorras

15 La fiesta

Leer Diana y su amiga se escriben por Internet. Completa su conversación con el pronombre apropiado. *(Hint: Complete their conversation.)*

Diana: Sara, ¿Juan ____1____ invita a ti a su fiesta?

Sara: Sí, ____2____ invita. ¿A ustedes ____3____ invita?

Diana: Sí, ____4____ invita.

Sara: ¿Invita a Tina y a Graciela?

Diana: No, no ____5____ conoce.

Sara: ¿Y a Roberto?

Diana: Sí, ____6____ invita.

Sara: ¿Invita a Julio y a Fernando?

Diana: Sí, ____7____ invita. Son sus mejores amigos.

Sara: ¿Y a Mónica?

Diana: No, no ____8____ invita. Ella es su hermana.

16 Una visita

Hablar Tú y un(a) amigo(a) van a San Juan. Pregúntense qué van a llevar en el viaje. *(Hint: Tell your friend what you are taking on the trip.)*

modelo

tu traje de baño

Tu amigo(a): *¿Vas a llevar **tu traje de baño**?*

Tú: *Sí, voy a llevarlo.* **o** *Sí, lo voy a llevar.*

Nota: Vocabulario

You learned that **llevar** means *to wear.* In this example, **llevar** means *to take along.*

1. tus gafas de sol
2. tu abrigo
3. tu bufanda
4. tus shorts
5. tu gorro
6. tu impermeable
7. tu raqueta de tenis
8. tus camisetas
9. tus libros de español
10. ¿?

17 ¿Qué pasa?

Escuchar Escucha la conversación. Luego, decide si las oraciones son ciertas o falsas. Corrige las falsas. *(Hint: True or false?)*

1. Cuando llueve, Raúl ve la televisión.
2. Raúl lee revistas. Las lee cuando llueve.
3. María lleva paraguas. Lo lleva cuando llueve.
4. Raúl necesita gafas de sol para ir a la playa.
5. María tiene bronceador. Va a llevarlo a la playa.

18 Creo que...

Hablar Tienes que pensar en el tiempo. ¿Qué necesitas llevar? Cambien de papel. *(Hint: Say if you think so.)*

modelo

calor (chaqueta)

Tú: *Hace **calor**.*

Tu amigo(a): *¿Necesito **chaqueta**?*

Tú: *Creo que no. No la necesitas.*

Nota: Vocabulario

Creer *(to think, to believe)* can be used to state an opinion.

Creo que sí. **Creo que no.**

1. sol (gafas de sol)
2. llover (bronceador)
3. nevar (traje de baño)
4. buen tiempo (impermeable)
5. frío (bufanda)
6. fresco (suéter)
7. sol (¿?)
8. llover (¿?)

Juego

¿Qué describe la oración?

Hace buen tiempo.

a.

b.

GRAMÁTICA Say What Is Happening: Present Progressive

When you want to say that an action is happening now, use the **present progressive**.

estoy esperando	**estamos esperando**
estás esperando	**estáis esperando**
está esperando	**están esperando**

Ignacio says: —¡**Está lloviendo**!
It's raining!

Roberto replies: —Te **estamos esperando**...
We're waiting for you...

To form this tense, use:

the present tense of **estar** + ***present participle***

To form the present participle of a verb, drop the **ending** of the infinitive and add **-ando** or **-iendo**.

-ar verbs	esper**ar**	**ando**	esper**ando**
-er verbs	com**er**	**iendo**	com**iendo**
-ir verbs	escrib**ir**	**iendo**	escrib**iendo**

When the **stem** of an **-er** or **-ir** verb ends in a vowel, change the **-iendo** to **-yendo**.

le**er** → le**yendo**

o**ír** → o**yendo**

cre**er** → cre**yendo**

Practice:
Actividades
19 20

Más práctica
cuaderno p. 80
Para hispanohablantes
cuaderno p. 78

Online Workbook
CLASSZONE.COM

Activity 21 brings together all concepts presented.

19 ¡Están ocupados!

Hablar Todos están haciendo sus actividades favoritas. ¿Qué están haciendo? *(Hint: Say what everyone is doing.)*

1. Diana: comprar ropa
2. Roberto y su hermano: hablar
3. Luis: abrir un libro
4. Paco y yo: pasar un rato con los amigos
5. tú: bailar con tus amigos
6. nosotros: leer una novela
7. yo: ver la televisión
8. sus amigos: oír música
9. Carlos: escribir una carta
10. la familia: comer

20 ¿Qué están haciendo?

Hablar Es sábado por la tarde. ¿Qué están haciendo estas personas? *(Hint: Say what everyone's doing.)*

1. tus padres
2. tú y tus amigos
3. tu hermano(a)
4. tu amigo(a)
5. tú

21 ¡Qué buenas vacaciones!

Escribir Elena y su familia están de vacaciones en la playa. Describe lo que está pasando. Usa las preguntas como guía. *(Hint: Describe what is happening. Use the questions as a guide.)*

- ¿Qué tiempo hace?
- ¿Qué están haciendo las personas?
- ¿Cómo están? ¿Tienen frío? ¿Tienen hambre?

More Practice: **Más comunicación** *p. R9*

Online Workbook
CLASSZONE.COM

Pronunciación

Trabalenguas

Pronunciación de la *j* y la *g* The letter **j** is pronounced somewhat like the *h* in the English word *hope*, but a bit stronger. Before the letters **e** and **i**, the Spanish **g** is pronounced just like the **j**. Listen to this tongue twister, then try it yourself to practice.

«Ji, ji, ji» ríen Javier y Jorge cuando miran a Jazmín la jirafa ingerir jarabe.

En voces

AUDIO

LECTURA

PARA LEER • STRATEGY: READING

Distinguish details Find out what **coquíes** are. What features do they have? Use the word web to describe a **coquí** and name its identifying characteristics.

El coquí

No muy lejos de[1] San Juan está el Bosque Nacional del Caribe. En este bosque tropical, El Yunque, hay animales y plantas que no ves en ninguna otra parte[2] del mundo. El coquí, el animal más conocido de todo Puerto Rico, vive protegido[3] en El Yunque.

[1] Not far from [2] any other part [3] protected

El Yunque, el Bosque Nacional del Caribe

Si visitas Puerto Rico, vas a ver imágenes del coquí en muchos lugares —en nombres de tiendas, artículos de promoción y libros. La tradición puertorriqueña es que si ves un coquí vas a tener mucha suerte. Y si quieres tener un bonito recuerdo[9] de Puerto Rico es posible comprar un coquí verde de juguete[10], símbolo de la isla.

[9] souvenir [10] toy

El coquí es una rana[4] de tamaño[5] pequeño que vive en los árboles. Los coquíes son de diferentes colores. Hay coquíes grises[6], marrones, amarillos y verdes. Reciben su nombre por su canto[7] característico. Hay 16 especies de coquíes en Puerto Rico, pero sólo dos producen el canto típico «coquí». Dos están en peligro[8] de extinción. Casi todos los coquíes empiezan a cantar cuando llega la noche.

[4] frog [5] size [6] grey [7] song [8] danger

Online Workbook
CLASSZONE.COM

¿Comprendiste?

1. ¿Dónde vive el coquí?
2. ¿Qué es el coquí? ¿Por qué se llama coquí?
3. ¿Cómo es el coquí?
4. ¿Cuándo canta el coquí?
5. ¿Por qué es bueno ver un coquí?

¿Qué piensas?

¿Por qué piensas que dos especies de coquí están en peligro de extinción?

Hazlo tú

Estudia más sobre el coquí y dibuja o describe las plantas típicas donde vive.

En colores

VIDEO DVD

CULTURA Y COMPARACIONES

PARA CONOCERNOS

STRATEGY: CONNECTING CULTURES

Define travel and tourism Look at a travel brochure. (Get one from a travel agency or hotel.) What does it contain? What does it *not* contain? Do you think there is a difference between being a *traveler* and being a *tourist*? List the interests of each. Explain your ideas.

Viajero	Turista

Una excursión por la isla

Roberto tiene ganas de pasear por Puerto Rico otra vez. Diana e Ignacio lo llevan de excursión por la isla. En la Oficina de Turismo ven este folleto[1].

[1] brochure

Descubra la isla de Puerto Rico

¡La hija del mar y del sol!

El mar y Puerto Rico tienen una unión fuerte. Las primeras personas de la isla, los taínos, llegan en canoas. Cristóbal Colón también llega a la isla por el mar. Y por el mar Puerto Rico sufre[2] ataques por muchos años. Los españoles construyen[3] El Morro en el siglo XVI[4] como protección contra los ingleses, los holandeses y los piratas. Hoy una excursión por San Juan siempre incluye[5] una visita a esta gran fortaleza.

[2] suffers
[3] build
[4] 16th century
[5] includes
[6] waves
[7] national anthem
[8] indigenous, native
[9] land

Puerto Rico: Diversión para todos

Tanto para el turista como para el puertorriqueño, el mar ofrece muchas actividades. En las playas es posible practicar muchos deportes: nadar, practicar el surfing o esquiar. El surfing es muy popular. En Puerto Rico hay playas que tienen olas[6] grandes, donde hay competiciones internacionales.

El himno nacional[7] de Puerto Rico, «La Borinqueña», habla de Borinquen, una palabra que viene del nombre indígena[8] de la isla. Sus palabras explican la relación entre la tierra[9], el mar y el sol.

«Ésta es la linda tierra,
que busco yo.
Es Borinquen la hija,
la hija del mar y del sol.»

More About Puerto Rico
CLASSZONE.COM

¿Comprendiste?

1. ¿Cuál es el grupo que llega primero a Puerto Rico?
2. ¿De quiénes vienen los ataques contra los españoles de Puerto Rico?
3. ¿Cuáles son unos deportes populares en las playas de Puerto Rico?
4. ¿De qué deporte hacen competiciones internacionales?
5. En el himno nacional de Puerto Rico, ¿qué es Borinquen?

¿Qué piensas?

1. Si algún día vas a Puerto Rico, ¿qué vas a hacer? ¿Te gustaría visitar lugares históricos o pasar toda tu visita en la playa? ¿Por qué?
2. ¿Cómo imaginas tu vacación perfecta? ¿Adónde vas? ¿Qué tiempo hace?

Hazlo tú

¿Cuáles son los deportes más populares en tu comunidad? Trabaja con otro(a) estudiante para preparar un folleto sobre las atracciones de tu estado.

ETAPA 3

En uso

REPASO Y MÁS COMUNICACIÓN

OBJECTIVES

- Describe the weather
- Discuss clothing and accessories
- State an opinion
- Describe how you feel
- Say what is happening

Now you can...
- describe the weather.

To review
- weather expressions, see p. 226.

1 ¿Qué tiempo hace?

Estás leyendo el periódico. Explica qué tiempo hace en cada lugar. *(Hint: Explain what the weather is like.)*

1.  Miami 92°
2.  Boston 31°
3.  Portland 34°
4.  San Juan 85°
5.  Washington 67°
6.  Los Ángeles 75°

Now you can...
- describe the weather.
- discuss clothing and accessories.

To review
- direct object pronouns, see p. 230.

2 ¿Cuándo lo usas?

Otro(a) estudiante quiere saber cuándo usas las siguientes cosas. ¿Qué le dices? Cambien de papel. *(Hint: Tell when you use the following items.)*

modelo

¿el traje de baño?: verano

Tú: *¿Cuándo usas **el traje de baño**?*

Otro(a) estudiante: *Lo uso en el **verano** porque hace calor.*

1. ¿los shorts?: verano
2. ¿el gorro?: invierno
3. ¿los suéteres?: otoño
4. ¿la bufanda?: invierno
5. ¿el paraguas?: primavera
6. ¿las gafas de sol?: verano

Now you can...
- state an opinion.

To review
- weather expressions, see p. 226.

3 Opiniones

¿Qué sabes de Puerto Rico? Expresa tu opinión. *(Hint: Express your opinion.)*

modelo

Hace mal tiempo todo el año.
Creo que no.

Hay playas bonitas.
Creo que sí.

1. En el invierno hay mucha nieve.
2. En El Yunque hay plantas y animales muy interesantes.
3. Cuando está nublado, los puertorriqueños toman el sol.
4. El surfing es popular en Puerto Rico.

Self-Check Quiz
CLASSZONE.COM

Now you can...
- describe how you feel.

To review
- **tener** expressions, see p. 229.

4 Los problemas de Roberto

Roberto siempre tiene problemas. Descríbelos. *(Hint: Describe Roberto's problems.)*

calor frío ganas prisa sed
hambre miedo sueño razón suerte

1. Cuando Roberto tiene _____, nunca hay comida.
2. Roberto siempre tiene _____, pero siempre llega tarde.
3. Cuando hay una tormenta, Roberto tiene mucho _____.
4. En el invierno en Minnesota, Roberto no lleva un abrigo y siempre tiene _____.
5. Cuando Roberto tiene _____ de nadar, siempre llueve.
6. Roberto tiene mucha _____, pero no hay agua.
7. Cuando camina en el desierto, Roberto tiene mucho _____.
8. Cuando Roberto participa en un concurso, nunca tiene _____.
9. Roberto piensa que 2 + 2 = 5. No tiene _____.
10. A las once de la noche Roberto siempre tiene _____.

Now you can...
- say what is happening.

To review
- the present progressive, see p. 232.

5 ¡Está lloviendo!

La familia de Josefina, una amiga de Diana, está en casa. Según Josefina, ¿qué están haciendo ahora? *(Hint: What are they doing?)*

1. Emilio y yo
2. Dani y Pati
3. mi padre
4. yo
5. mi madre
6. Emilio

6 ¿Adónde voy?

STRATEGY: SPEAKING

Get specific information To find out someone's vacation plans ask questions about all the specifics. Ask about weather **(el tiempo)**, clothing **(la ropa)**, or activities **(actividades y deportes)** at their destination. The model shows you how.

Imagínate que vas a uno de estos lugares. Los otros estudiantes tienen que adivinar adónde vas. Contesta sus preguntas. *(**Hint:** Answer your classmates' questions as they try to guess where you are going.)*

el desierto
el bosque tropical
la playa en verano
las montañas en invierno
el lago en otoño

modelo

Otro(a): *¿Va a nevar?*
Tú: *No, no va a nevar.*
Otro(a): *¿Vas a llevar el traje de baño?*
Tú: *Sí, voy a llevarlo.*
Otro(a): *¿Vas a practicar el surfing?*
Tú: *Sí, voy a practicarlo.*
Otro(a): *¿Vas a la playa?*
Tú: *Sí, voy a la playa.*

7 Por teléfono

Estás de vacaciones. Hablas con tu amigo(a) por teléfono. Describe el tiempo que hace, cómo estás y lo que está haciendo tu familia en ese momento. *(**Hint:** Describe the weather, how you feel, and what your family is doing on your vacation.)*

8 En tu propia voz

ESCRITURA Tu amigo(a) puertorriqueño(a) viene a vivir con tu familia por un año. Escríbele una carta describiendo qué tiempo hace durante cada estación del año, la ropa que necesita llevar y las actividades que él o ella puede hacer en cada estación. *(**Hint:** Write your Puerto Rican friend a letter describing the weather and items he or she should bring when visiting.)*

En la primavera hace...

Para el frío, necesitas llevar...

En el verano hace...

Llueve mucho en...

CONEXIONES

Las ciencias The Fahrenheit temperature scale is used in Puerto Rico. However, most Spanish-speaking countries use the Celsius scale. On this scale, water freezes at 0° and boils at 100°. To convert, use these formulas.

$100°C \times 9/5 + 32 = 212°F$ $\qquad$ $212°F - 32 \times 5/9 = 100°C$

Convert the temperatures in the chart and write what seasons they might represent. Explain the other weather conditions. Choose a location in the Spanish-speaking world. Find out its average temperature and weather conditions in each season.

C	F	Estación	Tiempo
0°			
10°			
	68°		
25°			
30°			
	95°		

Flashcards
CLASSZONE.COM

En resumen

REPASO DE VOCABULARIO

DESCRIBING THE WEATHER

¿Qué tiempo hace?	*What is the weather like?*
Está nublado.	*It is cloudy.*
Hace...	*It is...*
buen tiempo	*nice outside*
calor	*hot*
fresco	*cool*
frío	*cold*
mal tiempo	*bad outside*
sol	*sunny*
viento	*windy*
Hay...	*It's...*
sol	*sunny*
viento	*windy*
el grado	*degree*
llover (ue)	*to rain*
la lluvia	*rain*
nevar (ie)	*to snow*
la nieve	*snow*
el sol	*sun*
la temperatura	*temperature*
el tiempo	*weather*
la tormenta	*storm*
el viento	*wind*

Seasons

las estaciones	*seasons*
el invierno	*winter*
el otoño	*fall*
la primavera	*spring*
el verano	*summer*

DESCRIBING HOW YOU FEEL

tener...	*to be...*
calor	*hot*
cuidado	*careful*
frío	*cold*
miedo	*afraid*
prisa	*in a hurry*
razón	*right*
sueño	*sleepy*
suerte	*lucky*
tener ganas de...	*to feel like...*

STATING AN OPINION

creer	*to think, to believe*
Creo que sí/no.	*I think so. / I don't think so.*

CLOTHING AND ACCESSORIES

Clothing

el abrigo	*coat*
la bufanda	*scarf*
el gorro	*cap*
el impermeable	*raincoat*
los shorts	*shorts*
el traje de baño	*bathing suit*

Styles

con rayas	*striped*
de cuadros	*plaid, checked*

Accessories

el bronceador	*suntan lotion*
las gafas de sol	*sunglasses*
el paraguas	*umbrella*

OTHER WORDS AND PHRASES

sacar fotos	*to take pictures*
tomar el sol	*to sunbathe*

Places

el bosque	*forest*
el desierto	*desert*
el lago	*lake*
el mar	*sea*
la montaña	*mountain*
la playa	*beach*
el río	*river*

Vegetation

el árbol	*tree*
la flor	*flower*
la planta	*plant*

Juego

Es julio. Hace frío y nieva mucho. Mucha gente esquía en las montañas. ¿En qué país están?

a. México

b. Estados Unidos

c. Chile

En tu propia voz

ESCRITURA

Una fiesta puertorriqueña

The Spanish classes at your school are sponsoring an all-school celebration of Puerto Rican culture. It is your job to design the posters. Use the student model as your guide.

Function: Announce an all-school party
Context: Inviting students and faculty
Content: Puerto Rican celebration
Text type: Poster

PARA ESCRIBIR • STRATEGY: WRITING

Appeal to the senses A well-constructed poster will entice people to attend the party. One way to do so is to include details that appeal to the senses: sight **(la vista)**, hearing **(el oído)**, touch **(el tacto)**, taste **(el gusto)**, and smell **(el olfato)**.

Modelo del estudiante

The writer keeps herself focused by generating categories (**fecha, hora,** etc.) under which specific information will be listed.

The writer appeals to **sight** when she shows that students will "tour" Puerto Rico via photos.

The writer addresses the students' sense of **hearing** by mentioning music.

The invitation appeals to **taste** and **smell** by mentioning various Puerto Rican foods.

Writing Center
CLASSZONE.COM

Estrategias para escribir

Antes de escribir...

With another student, discuss what you have learned about Puerto Rico. Use an observation chart to help organize your thoughts. Short on ideas? Review this unit, or use the library or Internet to find more information. Then bring the details together to make an exciting poster (and party). Be sure to include: date, time, and place of the party; activities; food and drink; suggested dress; decorations.

Una fiesta puertorriqueña

la vista	el oído	el tacto	el gusto	el olfato
el sol	música bomba y plena	la playa	tostones	las flores
el Viejo San Juan	el mar			la comida

Revisiones

Once you have a draft, share it with a partner. Then ask:

- *Can you tell where/when the party takes place?*
- *Does the poster appeal to the senses?*
- *Does it make you want to go to the party?*
- *Does it communicate the island theme?*

La versión final

Before you create the final draft of your invitation, look over your work with the following questions in mind:

- *Did I use* ***gustar*** *correctly?*

Try this: Underline each use of **gustar.** Check to make sure that it is used with an infinitive and the correct pronoun: **me, te, le, nos, os,** or **les.**

- *Are adjectives used correctly?*

Try this: Circle every noun/adjective combination. Check to make sure that each adjective matches the gender and number of the noun it modifies.

UNIDAD 4

OAXACA MÉXICO

¡DE VISITA!

TEXAS Essential Knowledge and Skills

1 Communication

- **A Engage in exchanges**
  - *Asking for and giving directions*
  - *Making purchases and bargaining*
  - *Discussing gift ideas*
  - *Ordering food*
- **B Demonstrate understanding**
  - *Identifying places to visit in the city*
- **C Present information**
  - *Choosing means of transportation*
  - *Talking about shopping*
  - *Saying where you went*

2 Cultures

- **A Practices**
  - *The history of Oaxaca and its surroundings*
  - *Bargaining in a marketplace*
- **B Products**
  - *Traditional arts, crafts, and architecture in Oaxaca*
  - *Regional foods*

3 Connections

- **A Use Resources**
  - *Physical Education: Mexican folk dancing*
- **B Use the language**
  - *Mathematics: Calculating prices in a Mexican* ***mercado***

4 Comparisons

- **B Concept of culture**
  - *Shopping in Mexico and the U.S.*
  - *Modes of transportation*
  - *City/town structure*

5 Communities

- **B Lifelong learner**
  - *Using Spanish in the workplace*
  - *Using Spanish in volunteer activities*

ANIMALITOS are popular forms for Oaxacan wood carvings. Notice the colorful painting. What other Oaxacan carving is on this page?

INTERNET Preview
CLASSZONE.COM

- More About Mexico
- Webquest
- Self-Check Quizzes
- Flashcards
- Writing Center
- Online Workbook
- eEdition Plus Onlne

ALMANAQUE CULTURAL

POBLACIÓN: 256.130
ALTURA: 1.550 metros (5.084 pies)
CLIMA: 21° C (69,1° F)
COMIDA TÍPICA: mole negro, tasajo
GENTE FAMOSA DE OAXACA: Francisco Toledo (pintor), Benito Juárez (político), Rufino Tamayo (pintor)

¿VAS A OAXACA? La gente de México usa la palabra *Oaxaca* para referirse al estado de Oaxaca, la ciudad de Oaxaca y el valle de Oaxaca. Cuando escuches «Oaxaca», pregunta a qué parte se refiere.

More About Mexico
CLASSZONE.COM

MONTE ALBÁN

MONTE ALBÁN This city was built by the Zapotecs around 600 B.C. high upon a hill. What do you think the word **monte** means?

BENITO JUÁREZ was one of Mexico's presidents. From the clothing in this picture, can you guess when he lived? Check your idea on p. 286.

PESOS are Mexican money. How are they different from dollars?

MOLE NEGRO Many ingredients, including chiles and chocolate, make up black **mole** sauce. What have you eaten that is made from chocolate?

RUFINO TAMAYO (1899–1991), Oaxacan artist, completed *Mujer tendiendo la mano a la luna* in 1946. Can you guess what that means?

UNIDAD

4

¡DE VISITA!

Texas Essential Knowledge and Skills

1 Comunicación

2 Culturas

3 Conexiones

The student uses Spanish to make connections with other subject areas and to acquire information.

4 Comparaciones

5 Comunidades

Webquest
CLASSZONE.COM

Explore connections in Oaxaca through guided Web activities.

CASA LINDA

ENSALADAS Y SOPAS	
Ensalada mixta	$25
Sopa de pollo	$20
COMIDAS	
Servidas con arroz y frijoles	
Arroz con pollo	$45
Bistec asado	$60
Enchiladas	$40
Pollo	$50
Tacos	$35
Tamales	$40
Tortas	$35

Conexiones

Calculations are usually done in a math class, not in a Spanish class. However, when you learn Spanish, you can use it with skills you already know to get new information. Connect your math skills with your new language skills to change dollars into pesos, to pay your restaurant bill, or to bargain for prices in a market in Oaxaca. In this unit you will learn how to bargain and how to request a check.

Conexiones en acción **Imagínate que trabajas en el restaurante Casa Linda. Una turista tiene noventa pesos. ¿Puede comprar una ensalada mixta y dos tacos?**

Comunicación

When traveling, you need to understand and interpret spoken and written Spanish. You also need to ask for help politely. Remembering useful phrases will help you obtain information while observing customs of politeness.

Señora, por favor, ¿dónde queda...?

Repita, por favor.

Perdone, señorita, ¿cómo llego a...?

Perdone, señor, ¿puede usted decirme...?

Culturas

Oaxaca and Mexico City are as different as San Antonio and New York City. Near Oaxaca mysterious ruins hold the secrets of ancient peoples. Their customs, traditions, arts, and crafts continue in the lives of their modern descendants who are residents of that region.

En Oaxaca puedes visitar los mercados, el museo arqueológico y las pirámides de Monte Albán.

¿Qué hay en los museos de tu comunidad? ¿De dónde viene?

Comparaciones

Do you ever bargain in your community? It is important to know when it is appropriate to bargain. It is also important to be able to read prices.

¿Cuál es el símbolo de dólares? ¿De pesos? ¿Cuánto cuestan las jarras de la foto?

Comunidades

Does your local newspaper have an arts or cultural section? There you might be able to find out about exhibits and performances in your own community of the art, crafts, music, and dance of other cultures.

Fíjate

Each of the following statements relates to one or more of the areas described (**Conexiones, Comunicación, Culturas, Comparaciones, Comunidades**). Determine which one each statement best represents.

1. El Ballet Folklórico viene a nuestro auditorio el sábado.
2. Los mercados al aire libre son más comunes en México que en Estados Unidos.
3. Si hay aproximadamente diez pesos en un dólar, ¿cuántos pesos recibo por veinte dólares?
4. Perdone, ¿puede usted decirme dónde queda la calle Alcalá?
5. Las pirámides zapotecas tienen una forma diferente de las pirámides de Egipto.

UNIDAD 4

ETAPA 1

¡A visitar a mi prima!

OBJECTIVES

- Identify places
- Give addresses
- Choose transportation
- Request directions
- Give instructions

¿Qué ves?

Mira la foto del Zócalo de Oaxaca.

1. ¿La chica vive en Oaxaca o está visitando Oaxaca?
2. ¿Qué tiempo hace?
3. ¿Cuántos museos ves en el mapa?

En contexto

VOCABULARIO

VIDEO DVD AUDIO

Rosa is taking a walk through the city of Oaxaca. She looks at a map in order to find her way around.

B Allí está **el correo,** de donde mando cartas. **La iglesia** es muy bonita.

A Hay mucho que ver en Oaxaca. ¡Mira **el mapa**! Es divertido pasear. Primero, voy a **una plaza.** Después, descanso en **un café** y tomo un refresco.

C Si estoy enferma y necesito medicina, voy a **la farmacia.** Está en **la calle** Bustamante.

CD-ROM Take-Home Tutor

D Voy al **banco** por la tarde. Si quieres visitar la ciudad, hay **un hotel** muy bonito para pasar la noche.

E Llego a **la estación de autobuses** de Oaxaca. Acabo de venir de la capital.

F Para ir del **centro** al **aeropuerto** voy por esta **avenida.** Hay un taxi en **la esquina.**

Online Workbook
CLASSZONE.COM

Preguntas personales

1. ¿Te gusta ir al centro?
2. ¿Usas la estación de autobuses o el aeropuerto?
3. ¿Prefieres pasar un rato en un café o en una plaza?
4. ¿Dónde compras medicina?
5. ¿Adónde vas si estás en otra ciudad y tienes sueño?

En vivo

VIDEO DVD AUDIO

DIÁLOGO

Rosa

Carlos

Sofía

PARA ESCUCHAR • STRATEGY: LISTENING

Listen and follow directions How you remember directions gives clues about the ways you prefer to learn. Listen to Carlos's directions. Which is most natural for you, to (1) repeat key words, (2) write key words, (3) use gestures, (4) draw a map, or (5) do something else? Your choices indicate how you prefer to learn. Use them to help you follow directions as you listen.

Visita a Oaxaca

1 ▶ **Rosa:** Perdone, ¿puede usted decirme dónde queda la calle Morelos?
Hombre: No, señorita. Perdone, pero no sé dónde queda esa calle.

5 ▶ **Carlos:** Ésta es la avenida Constitución. Camina por esta calle. Allí vas a ver un banco.
Rosa: ¿Dices que hay un banco?
Carlos: Sí, hay un banco al lado de una farmacia.

6 ▶ **Carlos:** Vas a llegar a un parque. Cruza el parque. Enfrente de la estatua está la calle Morelos.
Rosa: Muchas gracias, eh…
Carlos: Carlos, me llamo Carlos.
Rosa: Rosa, soy Rosa.

7 ▶ **Carlos:** Salgo del trabajo a las siete. Si quieres, salimos a comer con tu prima.
Rosa: Me gustaría. A ver qué dice mi prima. ¿Puedo llevar el mapa?
Carlos: Sí, claro que sí.

CD-ROM Take-Home Tutor

2 ▶ **Rosa:** Buenos días. Vengo a visitar a mi prima. No sé dónde queda su nueva casa. Busco esta dirección.

3 ▶ **Carlos:** ¡Ah, sí!, claro, la calle Morelos. Desde aquí es muy fácil llegar.

Rosa: ¡Ay, qué bueno! ¿Queda lejos de aquí?

4 ▶ **Carlos:** A pie llegas en diez minutos. Pero llegas más rápido en taxi.

Rosa: Prefiero caminar. ¿Puedes decirme cómo llego?

8 ▶ **Sofía:** ¡Rosa!

Rosa: ¡Sofía! ¿Cómo estás?

Sofía: ¡Qué sorpresa! ¿Qué haces por aquí?

Rosa: ¡Vengo a visitarte!

Sofía: Pasa, pasa, prima.

9 ▶ **Rosa:** ¡Qué bonita es la nueva casa de tu familia! ¿Dónde está mi tía?

Sofía: Está haciendo algunas compras.

Rosa: Yo también quiero ir de compras. Es el cumpleaños de mi mamá y quiero comprar algo bonito para ella.

10 ▶ **Sofía:** Yo digo que el mercado tiene las cosas más bonitas. ¿Por qué no vamos mañana por la mañana? ¿Qué dices?

Rosa: Me encantaría.

Sofía: Entonces, mañana, ¡al mercado! Y después, salimos a pasear por la plaza.

En acción

PARTE A — Comprensión del diálogo

For Activities 1–2, refer to the dialog on pages 252–253.

1 ¿Cierto o falso?

Escuchar ¿Es cierto o falso? Si es falso, di lo que es cierto. *(Hint: Say what is true.)*

1. Sofía no sabe que Rosa viene a visitarla.
2. El hombre de la calle no sabe dónde vive Sofía.
3. Es difícil llegar a la casa de Sofía.
4. Rosa quiere ir al mercado, pero Sofía no quiere ir.
5. Rosa quiere comprar algo para su padre.

2 ¿En qué orden?

Escuchar Di en qué orden pasan los sucesos. *(Hint: Give the order of events.)*

a. Rosa habla con Carlos.
b. Rosa llega a Oaxaca.
c. Rosa camina a la casa de su prima.
d. Sofía habla con Rosa sobre el mercado.
e. Rosa habla con un hombre en la calle.
f. Rosa recibe el mapa de Carlos.

PARTE B — Práctica del vocabulario

Objectives for Activities 3–5
- Identify places

3 La nueva comunidad

Hablar Una muchacha quiere saber qué hay en su nueva comunidad. ¿Qué pregunta? *(Hint: Ask about places.)*

modelo

¿Hay un correo por aquí?

Nota: Vocabulario

Por, which most often means *for*, has many uses and meanings.

Camina **por** esta calle.	*Walk **along/down** this street.*
Pasa **por** la tienda.	*Come (Pass) **by** the store.*
¿Qué haces **por** aquí?	*What are you doing **around** here?*

1.

2.

3.

4.

5.

6.

4 ¿Adónde van?

Hablar Rosa y Sofía van de compras. Di adónde van para comprar las siguientes cosas. *(Hint: Say where they go to buy things.)*

modelo

Van a la pastelería.

1.

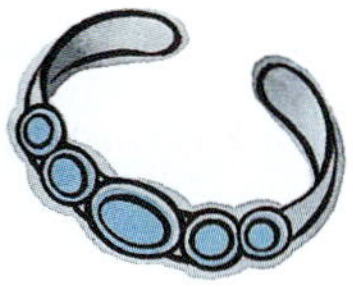
2.

3.

4.

5.

6.

7.

8.

9.

10.

5 ¿En qué estación?

Escuchar Escucha las descripciones. ¿Qué estación describe cada una? *(Hint: Say which season.)*

a. la primavera
b. el verano
c. el otoño
d. el invierno

Vocabulario

Las tiendas

el centro comercial

la carnicería

la joyería

la librería

la panadería

la papelería

la pastelería

la tienda de música y videos

la zapatería

¿A qué tiendas vas de compras?

PARTE C

Práctica: gramática y vocabulario

Objectives for Activities 6–18

• Identify places • Give addresses • Choose transportation • Request directions • Give instructions

GRAMÁTICA The Verb decir

To talk about what someone says, use the verb **decir.** The verb **decir** means *to say* or *to tell*. It has several irregular forms in the present tense.

digo	**decimos**
dices	**decís**
dice	**dicen**

Only the **nosotros(as)** and **vosotros(as)** forms are regular.

Note that **decir que** means *to say* ***that***...

Sofía says: —Yo **digo que** el mercado tiene las cosas más bonitas.
I say that *the market has the prettiest things.*

Practice: **Actividades** 6 9

Más práctica *cuaderno p. 85*
Para hispanohablantes *cuaderno p. 83*

Online Workbook CLASSZONE.COM

6 ¿Quién lo dice?

Hablar Muchos dicen que Oaxaca tiene mucho de interés. ¿Quién lo dice? *(Hint: Who says what?)*

modelo

yo / la ciudad / calles bonitas

*Yo digo que **la ciudad** tiene **calles bonitas.***

1. Carlos / las iglesias / arte regional
2. Rosa y Sofía / el Zócalo / gente interesante
3. tú / las joyerías / cosas bonitas
4. Roberto y yo / los cafés / comida regional
5. yo / los museos / artículos interesantes

México

También se dice

There are different ways to talk about a car.

- **el auto(móvil):** many countries
- **el coche:** Spain, parts of South America
- **el carro:** Mexico, Central America

7 ¿De dónde salen?

Escribir Rosa y Sofía ven a muchas personas. ¿De dónde salen todos? Usa la forma correcta de **salir.** *(Hint: Say from where people are leaving.)*

Nota: Vocabulario

Salir means *to leave* or *to go out.* It has an irregular **yo** form: **salgo.**

1. Rosa y Sofía _____ del café.
2. Carlos _____ de la tienda de música y videos.
3. Yo _____ de la panadería.
4. Nosotros _____ de la farmacia.
5. Juan y Pedro _____ de la librería.
6. Beatriz _____ del cine.
7. Tú _____ del correo.
8. Ustedes _____ del banco.
9. Diego y yo _____ de la plaza.
10. La señora _____ de la carnicería.

8 De viaje

Hablar/*Escribir* Todos salen. ¿Para dónde salen y qué transporte van a usar? *(Hint: Say where they are headed and what transportation they use.)*

modelo

Sofía / el café

***Sofía** sale para **el café**. Va en **taxi**.*

1. Rosa y Sofía / el centro comercial
2. nosotros / la Ciudad de México
3. tú / San Juan
4. ellos / Miami

¿?

5. Félix / el banco
6. ustedes / el correo
7. Carlos / Monte Albán
8. yo / ¿?

9 ¿Qué dicen?

Hablar Pregúntale a un(a) amigo(a) cómo les gusta viajar a estas personas. Cambien de papel. *(Hint: Explain what they say about traveling.)*

modelo

tus padres

Tú: *¿Cómo les gusta viajar a **tus padres**?*

Tu amigo(a): *Mis padres siempre dicen que les gusta viajar en avión.*

1. tu hermano(a)
2. tus abuelos
3. tú
4. tus amigos
5. tú y tu familia

Vocabulario

De viaje

manejar *to drive*
viajar *to travel*
el viaje *trip*

a pie

en autobús

en avión

en barco

en carro

en metro

en moto(cicleta)

en taxi

en tren

¿Cómo prefieres viajar?

GRAMÁTICA Using Prepositional Phrases to Express Location

When you talk about where things are located, use **prepositions.** Here are some common ones.

- Rosa está **cerca del taxi.**
  *Rosa is **near** the taxi.*
- El banco está **detrás del taxi.**
  *The bank is **behind** the taxi.*
- El taxi está **delante del banco.**
  *The taxi is **in front of** the bank.*
- El policía está **al lado del banco.**
  *The policeman is **beside** the bank.*
- La farmacia está **a la izquierda de la carnicería.**
  *The pharmacy is **to the left of** the butcher's shop.*
- La carnicería está **entre la farmacia y la panadería.**
  *The butcher's shop is **between** the pharmacy and the bakery.*
- La panadería está **a la derecha de la carnicería.**
  *The bakery is **to the right of** the butcher's shop.*
- El aeropuerto está **lejos.**
  *The airport is **far.***

Use **de** when the preposition is followed by a **specific location.**

Practice: Actividades 10 11 12

Más práctica *cuaderno pp. 86–87*
Para hispanohablantes *cuaderno pp. 84–85*

Online Workbook CLASSZONE.COM

10 ¿Dónde está?

Hablar/*Escribir* Explica dónde están las tiendas de la foto. *(Hint: Explain where they are.)*

1. La carnicería está (a la izquierda / a la derecha) de la farmacia.
2. El taxi está (cerca / lejos) de Rosa.
3. El banco está (entre / detrás) del taxi.
4. La panadería está (cerca / lejos) del aeropuerto.
5. La carnicería está (a la izquierda / a la derecha) de la panadería.
6. La farmacia está (entre / al lado de) la carnicería y el banco.
7. La panadería está (entre / al lado de) la carnicería.

11 En el centro comercial

Hablar Rosa y Sofía van al centro comercial. Sofía explica dónde están las tiendas. *(Hint: Say where the stores are.)*

modelo

la farmacia

Rosa: *¿Dónde está **la farmacia**?*

Sofía: *La farmacia está enfrente del café. Está a la derecha de …*

Nota: Vocabulario

When one building is facing another, use **enfrente de.**

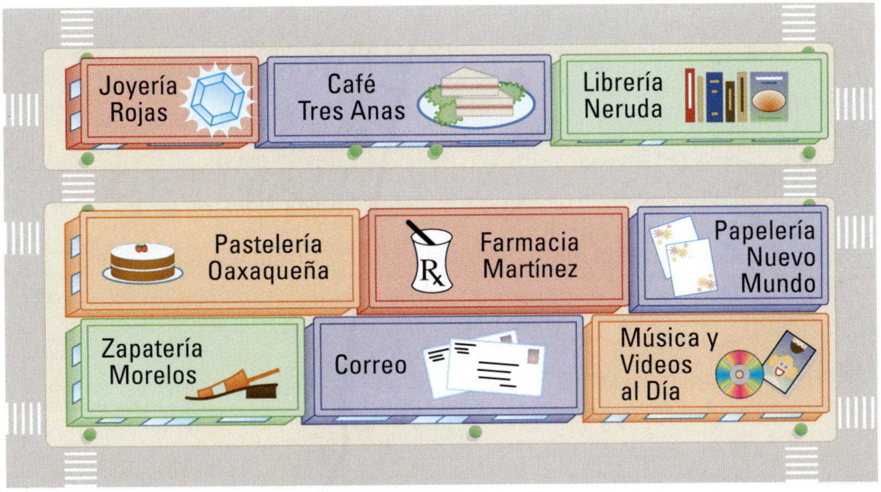

1. correo
2. librería
3. café
4. papelería
5. zapatería
6. joyería
7. pastelería
8. tienda de música y videos

México

Nota cultural

The Zapotecs, Mixtecs, and 16 other Native American groups live in Oaxaca, each with its own language and culture. In July they celebrate the **Guelaguetza,** wearing their native costumes, dancing, and exchanging gifts. **Guelaguetza** is a Zapotec word that means *gift*.

12 Las tiendas

STRATEGY: SPEAKING

Recognize and use set phrases

Think of the expressions you use as a whole instead of constructing them a word at a time. This helps you think in Spanish instead of translating from English.

Hablar/*Escribir* Explica dónde están las tiendas de tu comunidad. ¿Cómo vas? *(Hint: Explain where stores are and how you go there.)*

a pie	**en carro**
en autobús	**en moto**
en metro	**en bicicleta**
en taxi	

modelo

la librería

***La librería** está lejos de mi casa. Está al lado de una farmacia grande. Voy a la librería en autobús.*

1. farmacia
2. librería
3. zapatería
4. joyería
5. pastelería
6. centro comercial
7. tienda de música y videos
8. supermercado

More Practice: **Más comunicación** *p. R10*

GRAMÁTICA Regular Affirmative tú Commands

To tell a person to do something, use an affirmative command. **Tú commands** are used with friends or family. The regular affirmative **tú command** is the same as the **él/ella** form of the present tense.

Infinitive	Present	Affirmative tú Command
caminar	(él, ella) **camina**	**¡Camina!**
comer	(él, ella) **come**	**¡Come!**
abrir	(él, ella) **abre**	**¡Abre!**

Carlos says:

—**Camina** por esta calle… **Cruza** el parque…
__Walk__ down this street… __Cross__ the park…

If you use a **command** with a **direct object pronoun**, attach the pronoun to the end of the command.

Cruza el parque. → **¡Crúzalo!**
__Cross__ the park. → ***Cross it!***

If needed, add an **accent** when you attach a pronoun to retain the original stress. See p. 159.

Vocabulario

Las direcciones

cruzar *to cross*
doblar *to turn*
quedar (en) *to be (in a specific place), to agree on*
la cuadra *city block*
derecho *straight ahead*
desde *from*
hasta *until, as far as*

¿Cómo vas a la escuela?

Practice: Actividades 13 14 15 16 17 18
Más práctica *cuaderno p. 88*
Para hispanohablantes *cuaderno p. 86*

Online Workbook CLASSZONE.COM

13 ¿Qué hacer en Oaxaca?

Escribir Sofía le explica a Rosa qué hacer en Oaxaca. *(Hint: Explain what Sofía suggests Rosa should do.)*

modelo

jugar al tenis
Juega al tenis.

1. correr
2. sacar fotos
3. hablar con Carlos
4. escribir una carta
5. escuchar música
6. pasear por la plaza
7. leer revistas
8. visitar el museo
9. comprar un libro
10. ver una película

14 ¡Invita a todos!

Hablar La amiga de Sofía organiza una fiesta y quiere saber a quién invitar. Sofía le dice su opinión. *(Hint: Tell whom Sofía says to invite.)*

modelo

Carlos — **Su amiga:** *¿Invito a **Carlos**?*
Sofía: *Sí, ¡invítalo!*

1. Sandra
2. las muchachas
3. Jorge, Pepe y Alicia
4. Fernando y Marta
5. Juan y Diego
6. Amalia
7. Julio
8. Tomás y David
9. Gregorio
10. Alicia y Claudia

15 ¿Qué hago primero?

Hablar Carlos tiene que hacer muchas cosas hoy. Le pregunta a Rosa qué debe hacer primero. *(Hint: Say what Rosa tells Carlos to do.)*

modelo

¿trabajar en la tienda o comer?

Carlos: *¿Qué hago primero,* ***trabajo en la tienda o como****?*

Rosa: *Primero, come. Después, trabaja.*

1. ¿escribir una carta o estudiar para un examen?
2. ¿leer el periódico o abrir la tienda?
3. ¿correr en el parque o cenar?
4. ¿ver la televisión o terminar mi tarea?
5. ¿caminar con el perro o alquilar un video?

16 ¡Mañana es otro día!

Hablar Tu amigo(a) quiere hacer muchas cosas, pero no tiene tiempo. Tú le dices cuándo hacer todo. *(Hint: Say when your friend should do things.)*

modelo

comprar unos jeans

Tu amigo(a): *Quiero* ***comprar unos jeans,*** *pero no tengo tiempo.*

Tú: *¡Cómpralos el lunes!*

1. buscar las gafas de sol
2. visitar el museo del centro
3. leer un libro sobre un viaje
4. vender los libros
5. preparar el almuerzo para la familia
6. escribir una carta
7. usar la computadora
8. estudiar la lección

17 ¡A la fiesta!

Hablar/*Escribir* Sofía explica cómo llegar a su casa para una fiesta. Su amiga Amalia la llama para confirmar las direcciones. Completa su conversación, usando un pronombre si es posible. *(Hint: Give directions.)*

modelo

Amalia: *¿Primero, camino derecho tres cuadras por la calle González Ortega? ¿Cruzo la calle?*

Sofía: *Sí, camina derecho tres cuadras por la calle González Ortega. Crúzala.*

1. **Amalia:** ¿Entonces, doblo a la izquierda y camino seis cuadras más?
2. **Amalia:** Allí veo una plaza. ¿Cruzo la plaza y camino una cuadra más por la calle Guerrero?
3. **Amalia:** ¿Entonces, doblo a la derecha y camino una cuadra por la calle 20 de Noviembre?
4. **Amalia:** Entonces, llego a la avenida Hidalgo. ¿La cruzo?
5. **Amalia:** Entonces, veo el Parque Alameda. ¿Cruzo el parque?

México

Nota cultural

Oaxaca means "place of the **guaje**" in Nahuatl, a language of Mexico. The **guaje** is a large tree with pods and flowers. The pods sometimes look like gourds. Some say *Oaxaca* means "place of the gourds."

18 Una visita a Oaxaca

Hablar Estás de visita en Oaxaca. Quieres saber cómo llegar a varios lugares. Hablas con dos jóvenes. ¿Qué dicen? Cambien de papel. *(Hint: Ask directions to various places.)*

modelo

el parque → el teatro (Estás en el parque. Vas al teatro.)

Tú: *Perdona. ¿Cómo llego al teatro?*

Joven 1: *Lo siento, pero no sé. No vivo por aquí.*

Tú: *Perdona. ¿Puedes decirme dónde queda el teatro?*

Joven 2: *Cómo no. Camina derecho dos cuadras por la avenida Independencia hasta la calle 5 de Mayo. El teatro está en la esquina.*

1. el Zócalo → la tienda de artesanías
2. la tienda de artesanías → el correo
3. el correo → el mercado
4. el mercado → la catedral
5. la catedral → la iglesia
6. la iglesia → el parque

Vocabulario

Direcciones, por favor

Perdona(e), ¿cómo llego a…? *Pardon, how do I get to…?*

¿Puedes (Puede usted) decirme dónde queda…? *Could you tell me where…is?*

¿Queda lejos? *Is it far?*

Las respuestas

¡Cómo no! *Of course!*

Lo siento… *I'm sorry…*

acá/aquí *here*

allá/allí *there*

el camino *road*

la dirección *address, direction*

¿Cómo explicas las direcciones?

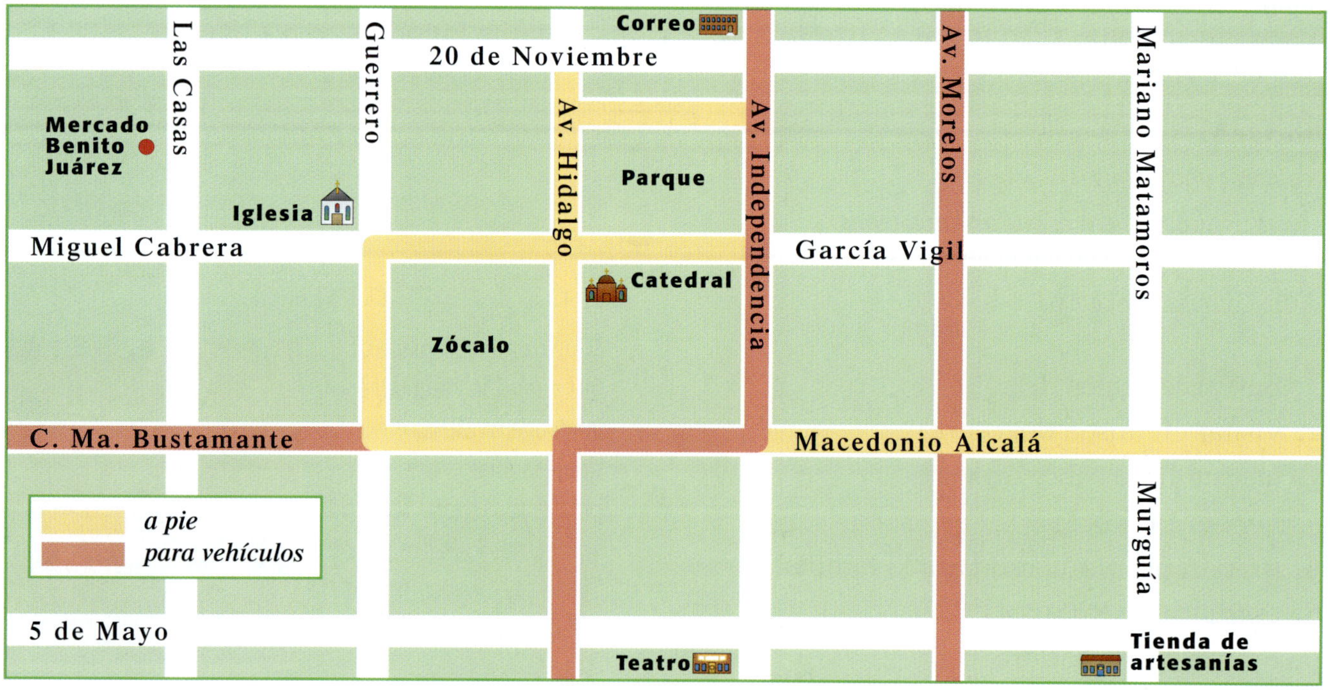

Todo en acción

Activities 19–20 bring together all concepts presented.

19 ¿Puede usted decirme...?

Escuchar Rosa le pregunta a un policía cómo llegar a la librería. Escucha su conversación. Indica en qué cuadra del mapa están la librería, la papelería y el correo. *(Hint: Say where each place is.)*

20 Tu comunidad

Escribir Vas a dar una fiesta. Escribe las direcciones para ir a tu casa desde la escuela. *(Hint: Give directions to your house from school.)*

modelo

Mi casa está a seis cuadras de la escuela. Camina dos cuadras por la calle Wilson. Vas a ver un banco. Dobla a la izquierda y camina dos cuadras por la calle Metropolitan. Hay una farmacia en la esquina. Dobla a la derecha y camina una cuadra. En la avenida Connecticut, dobla a la izquierda y camina una cuadra más. Yo vivo en la avenida Connecticut 284. Mi casa está enfrente de la pastelería.

Nota: Vocabulario

Addresses with numbers that have more than two digits can be expressed by pairing digits.

284 Connecticut Avenue

–Vivo en la avenida Connecticut, dos ochenta y cuatro.

1340 Main Street

–Vivo en la calle Main, trece cuarenta.

More Practice:

Más comunicación *p. R10*

Online Workbook CLASSZONE.COM

Pronunciación

Refrán

Pronunciación de la *r* When the letter **r** occurs in the middle of a word and between two vowels, it is pronounced by a single tap of your tongue just behind your teeth. It feels like the English *d* when you say the words *buddy* or *ladder*. To practice the tap **r**, pronounce these words. Then try the **refrán**. Can you guess what it means?

la joyería la panadería la papelería la pastelería la zapatería

AUDIO

En voces

LECTURA

PARA LEER

STRATEGY: READING

Combine strategies Put together the reading strategies you have practiced.

1. Look at the title, photos, and graphics to predict the reading's theme.
2. Skim the reading to get a general idea of the content.
3. Use context clues to help you make intelligent guesses about new words.

These steps make it easier for you to read Spanish.

Predict	Theme:
Skim	General Idea:
Use context clues	New Words:

¡VISITA OAXACA!

UN PASEO[1] A PIE

La ciudad de Oaxaca es un monumento histórico nacional. Hay arquitectura colonial, iglesias y museos muy importantes. Para verla mejor tienes que conocer Oaxaca a pie.

1 Empieza en el Zócalo, el centro de Oaxaca. Es el lugar ideal para ver a los oaxaqueños. Hay muchos cafés y restaurantes aquí.

2 Ahora cruza la calle Guerrero y entra en el Palacio de Gobierno[2]. Mira el mural sobre la historia y la cultura de Oaxaca.

[1] walk [2] Government Palace, State Capitol

3 Al salir del Palacio, camina hasta llegar a la avenida Hidalgo. Cruza la avenida para ver la catedral. A veces hay conciertos aquí.

4 Detrás de la catedral está la avenida Independencia. Sigue por la avenida y dobla a la izquierda en la calle Macedonio Alcalá. Allí hay unas tiendas excelentes y varias casas coloniales. Sigue derecho cuatro cuadras para ver la iglesia de Santo Domingo. Mira el interior.

5 Al lado de la iglesia queda el Museo Regional de Oaxaca. En el museo hay objetos arqueológicos de Monte Albán. También hay ropa, artículos textiles y otros artículos de las primeras culturas de la región.

6 Regresa al Zócalo. Si hace buen tiempo, hay conciertos aquí a las siete de la tarde. ¿Tienes hambre? Entonces, cena en uno de los restaurantes oaxaqueños. ¡Come algo típico y pasa un rato con tus amigos!

¿Comprendiste?

1. ¿Por qué es importante visitar Oaxaca?
2. ¿Dónde empieza el paseo?
3. ¿Dónde ves un mural sobre la historia y la cultura de Oaxaca?
4. ¿Dónde está la catedral?
5. ¿Qué hay en la calle Macedonio Alcalá?
6. ¿Dónde está el Museo Regional de Oaxaca?

Online Workbook
CLASSZONE.COM

¿Qué piensas?

Eres un(a) turista en Oaxaca, pero tienes sólo cuatro horas para visitarla. ¿Qué vas a hacer?

Hazlo tú

Estás en Oaxaca. Escríbele una postal a un(a) amigo(a). Explícale qué vas a hacer mañana. ¿Qué haces primero? ¿Adónde vas después?

ETAPA 1

En uso

REPASO Y MÁS COMUNICACIÓN

OBJECTIVES

- Identify places
- Give addresses
- Choose transportation
- Request directions
- Give instructions

Now you can...

- identify places.
- give addresses.

To review

- prepositions of location, see p. 258.

1 ¡Al centro!

Hay un nuevo estudiante en la comunidad. Usando el mapa, explícale adónde vas cuando quieres hacer las siguientes cosas. *(Hint: Say where to go.)*

modelo

comprar zapatos (detrás de)

*Cuando quiero **comprar zapatos,** voy a la zapatería. Está **detrás de** la tienda de música y videos. La dirección es avenida Flores setenta y nueve.*

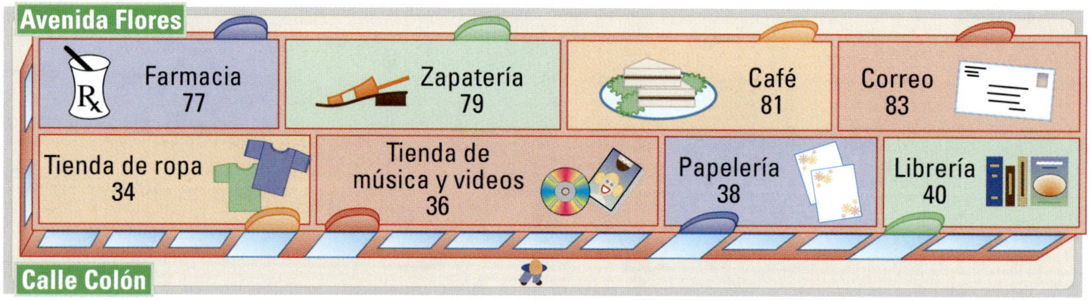

1. comprar papel (a la derecha de)
2. comprar jeans (a la izquierda de)
3. tomar un refresco (entre)
4. comprar medicina (detrás de)
5. mandar una carta (al lado de)
6. comprar un libro (a la derecha de)
7. alquilar un video (entre)
8. comprar zapatos (a la izquierda de)

Now you can...

- give instructions.

To review

- regular affirmative **tú** commands, see p. 260.

2 Para sacar buenas notas...

Tu amigo(a) quiere sacar buenas notas. Contesta sus preguntas con mandatos afirmativos. *(Hint: Say what to do.)*

modelo

¿Uso el diccionario? *Sí, úsalo.*

1. ¿Preparo la tarea?
2. ¿Leo el libro?
3. ¿Miro los videos?
4. ¿Aprendo el vocabulario?
5. ¿Estudio las lecciones?
6. ¿Escribo un poema?
7. ¿Compro una calculadora?
8. ¿Tomo los exámenes?

Self-Check Quiz
CLASSZONE.COM

Now you can...
- request directions.

To review
- prepositions of location, see p. 258.

3 ¿Dónde queda?

Estás visitando un pueblo y necesitas direcciones para llegar a un banco. Hablas con un policía. Completa la conversación con las expresiones correctas. *(Hint: Ask for directions.)*

Tú: **(Oye / Perdone)**. Señor, ¿**(puede / puedo)** usted decirme dónde está el banco?

Policía: ¡Cómo **(no / sí)**! El banco no queda **(cerca / lejos)**. Está a sólo tres **(lados / cuadras)** de aquí. Primero, hay que caminar **(derecho / detrás)** por la avenida Olmos hasta llegar a la plaza. Allí, **(dobla / llega)** a la derecha en la calle San Juan y **(queda / camina)** una cuadra. Entonces, **(cruza / camina)** la calle Sonora. El banco queda en la esquina.

Tú: Muchas gracias, señor. ¿Y **(hay / puede)** un café cerca del banco?

Policía: Sí. El Café Romano está **(al lado / entre)** del banco. Es excelente. Y si necesitas mandar cartas, el correo queda **(derecho / a la izquierda)** del café.

Now you can...
- choose transportation.

To review
- the verb **salir**, see p. 256.
- the verb **decir**, see p. 256.

4 ¡Salgo hoy!

Todos salen para diferentes lugares. Explica adónde van, qué dicen del lugar adónde van y cómo van a viajar. *(Hint: Tell where they go, what they say, and how they go.)*

modelo

mi vecino: México (es muy interesante)

***Mi vecino** sale para **México.** Dice que **es muy interesante.** Va en carro.*

1. mi primo: España (es muy especial) 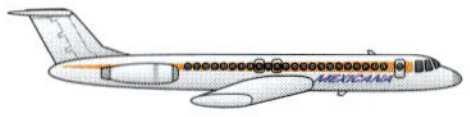
2. nosotros: Los Ángeles (es fantástico) 
3. ustedes: la Ciudad de México (es muy divertida) 
4. yo: Puerto Rico (es muy bonito) 
5. Marta y Ramón: la playa (es divertida) 
6. usted: el centro (no es aburrido) 

5 ¿Cómo llego?

STRATEGY: SPEAKING

Use variety to give directions When you give directions, don't just speak. Make your directions clear by using gestures, pointing to a map, and repeating key information. This helps others make sense of your words.

Trabajas en una tienda. Explícale a un(a) turista cómo llegar a tres lugares. Antes de explicar, haz un mapa como ayuda. (Mira el ejemplo de abajo.) Cambien de papel. *(Hint: Say how to get to three places.)*

modelo

Turista: *Perdone, señor(ita), ¿cómo llego a la iglesia?*

Tú: *Camina tres cuadras por la avenida Juárez. La iglesia está a la izquierda en la esquina.*

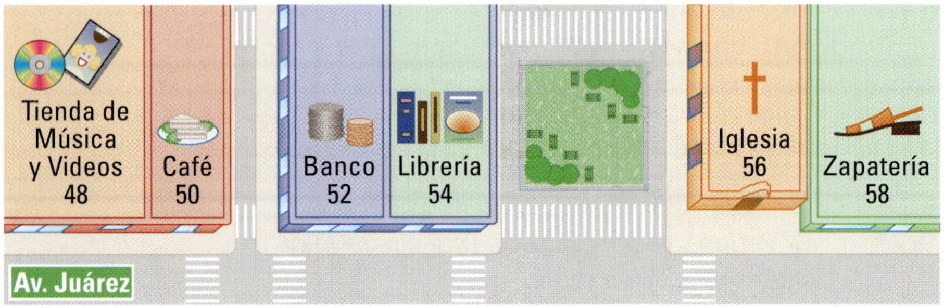

6 En tu propia voz

ESCRITURA Hay una nueva estudiante que no conoce tu comunidad. Usa las siguientes expresiones para darle siete recomendaciones. *(Hint: Write recommendations for a new student.)*

comer	caminar
visitar	practicar deportes
nadar	jugar
correr	ver películas
patinar	alquilar videos
comprar	mandar cartas
pasear	buscar libros

modelo

Compra ropa en el centro comercial Park Plaza.

CONEXIONES

La educación física Different regions in Mexico have their own special folk music, dances, and costumes. For example, in one Oaxacan folk dance, women balance filled glasses on their heads! Research other Mexican folk dances in the library and/or on the Internet. Then teach a dance to your class. Answer these questions about the dance.

- ¿De qué región es la danza?
- ¿Qué representa la danza?
- ¿En qué ocasión la bailan?
- ¿Cómo es la música?
- ¿Qué ropa llevan los danzantes?

Flashcards
CLASSZONE.COM

En resumen

REPASO DE VOCABULARIO

IDENTIFYING PLACES

el aeropuerto	*airport*
el banco	*bank*
el café	*café*
la carnicería	*butcher's shop*
el centro	*center, downtown*
el centro comercial	*shopping center*
el correo	*post office*
la estación de autobuses	*bus station*
la farmacia	*pharmacy, drugstore*
el hotel	*hotel*
la iglesia	*church*
la joyería	*jewelry store*
la librería	*bookstore*
la panadería	*bread bakery*
la papelería	*stationery store*
la pastelería	*pastry shop*
la plaza	*town square*
la tienda de música y videos	*music and video store*
la zapatería	*shoe store*

GIVING ADDRESSES

la avenida	*avenue*
la calle	*street*
el camino	*road*
la dirección	*address, direction*

CHOOSING TRANSPORTATION

a pie	*on foot*
el autobús	*bus*
el avión	*airplane*
el barco	*ship*
el carro	*car*
el metro	*subway*
la moto(cicleta)	*motorcycle*
el taxi	*taxi, cab*
el tren	*train*

REQUESTING DIRECTIONS

Requesting

Perdona(e), ¿cómo llego a...?	*Pardon, how do I get to...?*
¿Puedes (Puede usted) decirme dónde queda...?	*Could you tell me where ... is?*
¿Queda lejos?	*Is it far?*
acá/aquí	*here*
allá/allí	*there*

Replying

¡Cómo no!	*Of course!*
Lo siento...	*I'm sorry...*
cerca (de)	*near (to)*
cruzar	*to cross*
la cuadra	*city block*
delante (de)	*in front (of)*
a la derecha (de)	*to the right (of)*
derecho	*straight ahead*
desde	*from*
detrás (de)	*behind*
doblar	*to turn*
enfrente (de)	*facing*
entre	*between*
la esquina	*corner*
hasta	*until, as far as*
a la izquierda (de)	*to the left (of)*
al lado (de)	*beside, next to*
lejos (de)	*far (from)*
quedar (en)	*to be (in a specific place), to agree on*

OTHER WORDS AND PHRASES

la cosa	*thing*
decir	*to say, to tell*
manejar	*to drive*
el mapa	*map*
por	*for, by, around*
salir	*to go out, to leave*
viajar	*to travel*
el viaje	*trip*

Juego

¿Adónde van los jóvenes?

UNIDAD 4

ETAPA 2

En el mercado

OBJECTIVES

- Talk about shopping
- Make purchases
- Talk about giving gifts
- Bargain

¿Qué ves?

Mira la foto del centro de Oaxaca.

1. ¿Hace buen tiempo?
2. ¿Quiénes llevan camisetas azules?
3. ¿Quiénes llevan vestidos?
4. ¿Qué hace la mujer?

PRIMAVERA

En contexto

VIDEO DVD AUDIO

VOCABULARIO

Sofía is going shopping at the market in Oaxaca. She sees all kinds of things. Find out what items interest her the most.

A

¡Hola! Voy al **Mercado Benito Juárez**. Allí compro **el regalo** perfecto.

B Hay **artículos de cuero,** como **botas, una bolsa, un cinturón** y **una cartera.** ¿Qué voy a comprar?

C Me gusta usar **las joyas** de **oro** y de **plata.** Voy a **poder** comprar **aretes, anillos, pulseras** y **collares** aquí.

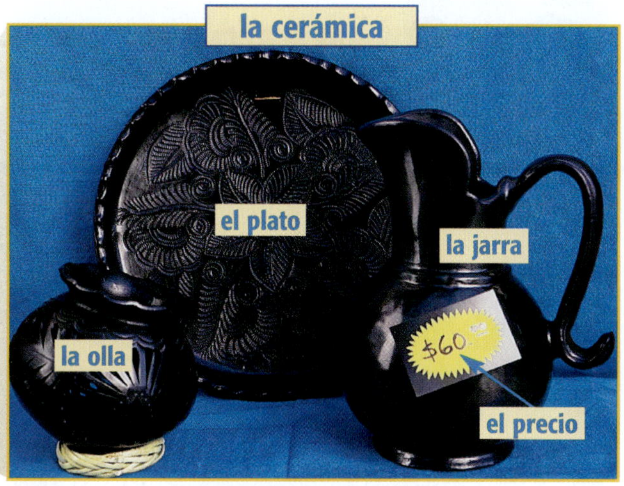

D Hay muchas **artesanías** aquí. Hay **cerámica,** como **jarras, ollas** y **platos. El precio** de la jarra es 60 pesos.

E En el mercado es divertido **regatear.**

Sofía: ¿**Me deja ver** la jarra? **¿Cuánto cuesta?**
Vendedor: Cincuenta pesos.
Sofía: **¡Es muy cara!** No tengo suficiente **dinero.** **Le puedo ofrecer** treinta y cinco pesos.
Vendedor: **Le dejo** la jarra **en** cuarenta pesos.
Sofía: Bueno.
Vendedor: ¿Cómo va a **pagar**?

Preguntas personales

1. ¿Te gustan las artesanías?
2. ¿Prefieres las joyas o las artesanías?
3. Cuando vas a un mercado, ¿regateas o pagas el precio?
4. ¿Qué joya quieres comprar?
5. ¿Tienes un artículo de cuero? ¿Cuál?

En vivo

VIDEO DVD AUDIO

DIÁLOGO

Rosa

Sofía

Carlos

Vendedor

PARA ESCUCHAR • STRATEGY: LISTENING

Observe as you listen Look carefully as you listen to understand meaning from visual cues. Look for items that belong in specific categories. Write the items in the appropriate column in a chart.

cerámica	cuero	música	joyas

¡A regatear!

1 ► **Sofía:** ¿Qué le vas a comprar a tu mamá?
Rosa: Quiere una olla de barro negro. Los mercados son muy interesantes y puedes regatear.

5 ► **Carlos:** ¿Almorzamos juntos mañana? Podemos ir a mi restaurante favorito. Almuerzo allí cada ocho días. Voy a participar en un concurso y quiero sus opiniones.
Rosa: Me parece ideal.

6 ► **Carlos:** Entonces hasta mañana, a la una, en el restaurante La Madre Tierra. ¿Recuerdas cómo llegar al restaurante?
Sofía: Sí, Carlos, recuerdo dónde está.
Carlos: ¡Adiós!
Rosa: ¡Hasta mañana!

7 ► **Vendedor:** ¡Ollas, platos, jarras! Aquí encuentra el regalo perfecto…
Rosa: ¿Me deja ver esta olla grande? ¿Cuánto cuesta?
Vendedor: Las ollas grandes cuestan 70 pesos cada una.

CD-ROM Take-Home Tutor

2 ► **Rosa:** Mira, es el nuevo disco compacto de mi grupo favorito.

Sofía: Tienes que comprarle un regalo a tu mamá.

3 ► **Rosa:** Vuelvo si me queda dinero.

Sofía: ¡Carlos! ¡Qué sorpresa! Te presento a mi prima. Es de la Ciudad de México.

4 ► **Carlos:** Sí, ya lo sé. Hola, Rosa. ¿Qué onda?

Sofía: ¿Tú conoces a Rosa? ¿Cómo?

Carlos: Es nuestro secreto, ¿verdad?

8 ► **Rosa:** ¡Es muy cara! Le puedo ofrecer 50 pesos.

Vendedor: Ay, señorita, tengo que ganarme la vida, ¿no? Le dejo la olla en 65.

9 ► **Rosa:** ¿Por qué no me da la olla por 60?

Vendedor: Muy bien. Quedamos en 60.

Rosa: Muchísimas gracias, muy amable.

Vendedor: De nada.

Sofía: Muy bien, Rosa. Ahora tienes el regalo para tu mamá.

10 ► **Sofía:** ¿Tienes dinero suficiente para el disco compacto?

Rosa: Sí, creo que sí. ¿Sabes?, quiero comprarle un regalo a Carlos. Le doy el disco compacto mañana. ¿Por qué no volvemos a esa tienda de música?

En acción

PARTE A Comprensión del diálogo

For Activities 1–2, refer to the dialog on pages 274–275.

Rosa | Sofía | Carlos | Vendedor

1 ¿Cierto o falso?

Escuchar ¿Es cierto o falso? Si es falso, di lo que es cierto. *(Hint: Say what is true.)*

1. Rosa quiere comprar un regalo para Sofía.
2. La mamá de Rosa quiere un disco compacto.
3. Rosa cree que los mercados son interesantes.
4. Rosa, Sofía y Carlos van a comer juntos mañana.
5. Rosa paga cincuenta pesos por la olla.

2 ¿Quién habla?

Escuchar ¿Quién habla: Rosa, Sofía, Carlos o el vendedor? *(Hint: Say who speaks.)*

1. «¿Qué le vas a comprar a tu mamá?»
2. «Te presento a mi prima.»
3. «Podemos ir a mi restaurante favorito.»
4. «¡Ollas, platos, jarras!»
5. «Quiero comprarle un regalo a Carlos.»

PARTE B Práctica del vocabulario

Objectives for Activities 3–5
- Talk about shopping • Make purchases
- Talk about giving gifts

3 Los planes

Leer/*Escribir* Completa la carta de Rosa con una de las expresiones. *(Hint: Complete Rosa's letter.)*

artículos de cuero | pagar | precio | cartera | mercado | para | cinturón | olla | regalo

Nota: Vocabulario

Use **para** *(for, in order to)* to indicate…

• the recipient of items	…el regalo **para** tu mamá.
• purpose	Vamos al restaurante **para** comer.
• implied purpose	Tengo dinero **para** [comprar] algo.

Querida Emiliana:

Hoy voy al __1__ con mi prima Sofía. Tengo que comprar un __2__ de cumpleaños __3__ mi mamá. Ella quiere una __4__ negra. No sé qué __5__ tiene una olla, pero Sofía dice que no voy a __6__ más de setenta pesos. Si Sofía tiene razón, voy a tener suficiente dinero __7__ comprar algo para mi papá también. Él prefiere los __8__. Entonces, voy a comprar una __9__ o un __10__ para él. ¡Ay! Son las ocho. Me tengo que ir. Sofía me está esperando.

Hasta pronto,

Rosa

4 La tienda

Hablar Trabajas en una tienda grande. Acaban de llegar algunos artículos nuevos. Dile a otro(a) vendedor(a) adónde llevar los artículos. Cambien de papel. *(Hint: Tell where the items go.)*

modelo

botas

Tú: *¿Adónde llevo **las botas**?*

Otro(a): *Al departamento de **artículos de cuero,** por favor.*

1. carteras
2. pulseras de oro
3. jarras
4. ollas
5. aretes de plata
6. cinturones
7. pantalones
8. collares de oro
9. bolsas
10. platos
11. anillos de plata
12. cerámica

5 ¿Cuánto cuestan?

Hablar Rosa quiere saber los precios de unas joyas. ¿Qué dice el vendedor? Cambien de papel. *(Hint: Ask prices.)*

modelo

Rosa: *¿Cuánto cuesta **el anillo**?*

Vendedor: *Cuesta **cuarenta y ocho** pesos.*

Nota: Gramática

When asking or giving the price of a single item, use **cuesta.** When asking or giving the price of more than one item, use **cuestan.**

¿Cuánto cuesta el anillo? **¿Cuánto cuestan** los aretes?

1.

2.

3.

4.

5.

6.

México

También se dice

There are many ways to ask people what's happening or what's going on. In many countries you may hear

- **¿Qué hay?**
- **¿Qué pasa?**
- **¿Qué tal?**

In Mexico you may hear

- **¿Qué hubo?**
- **¿Qué onda?**

PARTE C Práctica: gramática y vocabulario

Objectives for Activities 6–17

• Talk about shopping • Make purchases • Talk about giving gifts • Bargain

GRAMÁTICA Stem-Changing Verbs: o → ue

¿RECUERDAS? *p. 205* Remember verbs like **pensar**, where the stem alternates between **e** and **ie**?

pensar *to think, to plan*

pienso	pensamos
piensas	pensáis
piensa	piensan

Something similar happens with verbs like **almorzar** *(to eat lunch)*. The stem alternates between **o** and **ue**.

almorzar *to eat lunch*

almuerzo	almorzamos
almuerzas	almorzáis
almuerza	almuerzan

The stem doesn't change for the **nosotros** *(we)* or **vosotros** *(you)* form.

Carlos says:

—**Almuerzo** allí cada ocho días.
***I eat lunch** there every week.*

Many other verbs have this same kind of change in their stem.

The vendor says:

—Aquí **encuentra** el regalo perfecto.
*Here **you'll find** the perfect gift.*

—Las ollas grandes **cuestan** 70 pesos...
*The big pots **cost** 70 pesos...*

Practice: 6 7 8 9 11

Más práctica *cuaderno p. 93*

Para hispanohablantes *cuaderno p. 91*

Online Workbook CLASSZONE.COM

6 ¿Qué pueden hacer?

Escribir Escribe lo que estas personas pueden hacer. Completa las frases con la forma correcta de **poder.**
(Hint: Write what they can do.)

modelo

los chicos: jugar al béisbol

Los chicos** pueden **jugar al béisbol.

1. tú: tocar el piano
2. Rosa y Sofía: patinar
3. Carlos: manejar
4. yo: hablar español
5. Andrea y yo: nadar
6. ellos: escribir poesía
7. nosotros: correr
8. Rodrigo: bailar
9. ustedes: cantar
10. nosotras: esquiar

Vocabulario

Stem-Changing Verbs: o → ue

almorzar *to eat lunch*
contar *to count, to tell or retell*
costar *to cost*
devolver *to return (an item)*
dormir *to sleep*
encontrar *to find, to meet*
poder *to be able, can*
recordar *to remember*
volver *to return, to come back*

¿Qué haces cada día? ¿Cada semana?

7 ¡Al mercado!

Leer/*Escribir* Sofía y Rosa hablan con la madre de Sofía antes de ir al mercado. Completa su conversación con la forma correcta de cada verbo. *(Hint: Complete what they say.)*

almorzar	**encontrar**	**recordar**
devolver	**poder**	**volver**

Rosa: Vamos al mercado para ver si yo ___1___ un regalo para mamá.

Mamá: ¿ ___2___ ustedes para almorzar?

Sofía: No. Nosotras ___3___ en un café.

Mamá: Entonces yo voy a la zapatería para ___4___ mis zapatos nuevos.

Sofía: ¿Por qué los ___5___?

Mamá: Porque son pequeños.

Rosa: Tía, si yo ___6___ bien, la zapatería está cerca del correo, ¿no?

Mamá: Sí, tú ___7___ muy bien.

Rosa: ¿ ___8___ mandar una carta?

Mamá: ¡Sí! ¡Cómo no!

8 ¿A qué hora almuerzas tú?

Hablar Pregúntales a cuatro estudiantes a qué hora almuerzan. *(Hint: Ask when they eat lunch.)*

Nombre	Hora
1. María	12:00

9 ¿Podemos ir?

Hablar Tus primas están de visita. Ustedes quieren ir a varios lugares. Tú le preguntas a tu mamá si pueden ir. Sigue el modelo. *(Hint: Ask for permission.)*

modelo

mis primas y yo → cine (9:30)

Tú: *Mamá, ¿podemos ir al cine?*

Mamá: *¿A qué hora vuelven?*

Tú: *Volvemos a las nueve y media.*

1. yo → centro comercial (4:00)
2. Elena → joyería (2:30)
3. Ana y yo → librería (4:30)
4. nosotros(as) → café (8:30)
5. Ana y Elena → tienda de ropa (1:30)
6. Micaela → banco (8:00)
7. Elena y yo → pastelería (5:00)
8. Micaela y yo → zapatería (5:30)
9. Elena y Micaela → correo (12:30)
10. Ana y Micaela → panadería (3:30)

10 ¿Qué usa?

Escuchar Rosa le explica a Sofía cómo va a varios lugares en la capital. ¿Qué transporte usa para ir a cada lugar? *(Hint: Say what transportation she uses.)*

1. carro	a. la escuela
2. metro	b. la clase de piano
3. taxi	c. el parque
4. a pie	d. el museo
5. autobús	e. la casa de los abuelos

11 Le puedo ofrecer...

STRATEGY: SPEAKING

Express emotion Bargaining is the art of compromise with a little emotion.

React: ¡Qué bonito! ¡Qué chévere! ¡Qué bien!

Get someone's attention: Perdone…

Agree: Creo que sí. Claro que sí. Está bien.

Disagree: Creo que no. Gracias, pero no puedo.

Hablar Estás en un mercado. Necesitas comprar unas cosas. Con otro(a) estudiante, regatea. Cambien de papel. ¡La conversación puede variar mucho! *(Hint: Bargain.)*

modelo

Tú: *¿Me deja ver los aretes? ¿Cuánto cuestan?*

Vendedor(a): *Ochenta pesos.*

Tú: *¡Es demasiado! Le puedo ofrecer setenta pesos.*

Vendedor(a): *¡Son muy baratos! Son de buena calidad. Le dejo los aretes en setenta y cinco pesos.*

Tú: *Bueno, los llevo.*

Vendedor(a): *¿Cómo paga usted?*

Tú: *En efectivo.*

Vendedor(a): *¡Perfecto!*

1.

2.

3.

4.

5.

More Practice: **Más comunicación** *p. R11*

Vocabulario

Expresiones para regatear

Use these along with the expressions you learned in **En contexto** to complete **Actividad 11.**

barato(a) *cheap, inexpensive*
la calidad *quality*
cambiar *to change, to exchange*
el cambio *change, money exchange*
caro(a) *expensive*
demasiado(a) *too much*
el dólar *dollar*
el efectivo *cash*
perfecto(a) *perfect*
la tarjeta de crédito *credit card*

¿Qué palabras usas cuando regateas?

GRAMÁTICA Indirect Object Pronouns

¿RECUERDAS? *p. 230* You learned that **direct object pronouns** can be used to avoid repetition of the noun and answer the question *whom?* or *what?* about the verb.

replaces

—Pues, ya tienes **ropa de verano.**
*You already have summer **clothing.***

—Claro que **la** tengo.
*Of course I have **it.***

Indirect objects are **nouns** that tell *to whom/what* or *for whom/what.*
Indirect object pronouns replace or accompany **indirect objects.**

Singular	Plural
me *me*	**nos** *us*
te *you (familiar)*	**os** *you (familiar)*
le *you (formal), him, her*	**les** *you, them*

Notice that **indirect object pronouns** use the same words as **direct object pronouns** except for **le** and **les.**

accompanies ***replaces***

Rosa **le** compra una olla **a su madre.**
*Rosa buys a pot **for her mother.***

Rosa **le** compra una olla.
*Rosa buys a pot **for her.***

The pronouns **le** and **les** can refer to different **indirect objects.** To clarify what they mean, they are often accompanied by:

a + **name, noun,** or **pronoun**

Rosa **le** compra una olla.
*Rosa buys a pot **for her.***

Rosa **le** compra una olla **a su madre.**
*Rosa buys a pot **for her mother.***

To add emphasis use

a + **pronoun**

A mí me compro unos aretes.
*I'm buying **myself** some earrings.*

To review the pronouns that follow **a,** see **Gramática,** p. 187.

Practice: **Actividades** 12 13 14 15

Más práctica *cuaderno pp. 94–95*
Para hispanohablantes *cuaderno pp. 92–93*

Online Workbook CLASSZONE.COM

12 El mercado

Leer Los padres de Sofía van al mercado. Completa las oraciones de Sofía con **me, te, le, les** o **nos.** *(Hint: Say for whom they buy things.)*

1. Mis padres _____ compran unas botas de cuero a mi hermano.
2. Ellos _____ compran unos aretes a mí.
3. Ellos _____ compran unos discos compactos a mi hermano y a mí.
4. Mi mamá _____ compra una cartera a mi papá.
5. Mi papá _____ compra una pulsera a mi mamá.
6. Mis padres _____ compran un plato a mis abuelos.
7. Ellos _____ compran una jarra a sus amigos.
8. Mis padres _____ compran un videojuego a mis hermanitos.
9. Mi mamá _____ compra un collar a su amiga.
10. Rosa, ¡ellos _____ compran algo a ti también!

13 ¡Cuántos regalos!

Escribir Es el cumpleaños de la mamá de Rosa. Muchas personas le dan regalos. ¿Qué le dan? *(Hint: What do they give her?)*

modelo

Rosa: una olla

Rosa** le da **una olla.

Nota: Vocabulario

Dar means *to give*. It has an irregular **yo** form: **doy.** Its other forms are regular, except the **vosotros** form, which has no accent.

1. su esposo: un collar de oro
2. nosotros: una bolsa
3. sus hijos: una pulsera
4. su hermano: una jarra de barro negro
5. yo: un disco compacto
6. tú: un video
7. Sofía: unos aretes
8. su hermana: un anillo de plata

Juego

¿Lidia le da la lila a Lola, o quiere darle Lola la lila a Lidia?

México

Nota cultural

El Museo Regional de Oaxaca contains gold jewelry from tomb 7 at Monte Albán. Mexican archaeologists Alfonso Caso and Ignacio Bernal discovered the tomb in 1932. You can buy reproductions of the jewelry at the museum or at shops in Oaxaca.

Figura mixteca de la tumba 7

14 Regalos para todos

Escuchar Rosa va a la tienda de música y videos. ¡Compra muchos regalos! Escucha a Rosa y escribe lo que les compra a las personas. *(Hint: Say for whom Rosa buys what.)*

modelo

*Rosa le compra **un disco compacto** a la profesora Díaz.*

a. 

b. 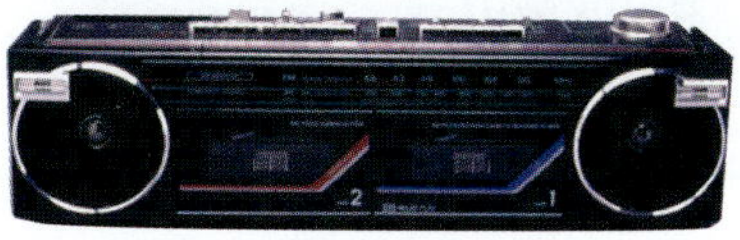

c. 

d. 

e. 

15 ¿Qué te dan a ti?

Hablar ¿Qué te dan estas personas para tu cumpleaños? *(Hint: Who gives what?)*

modelo

tus padres

Tú: *¿Qué te dan **tus padres** para tu cumpleaños?*

Otro(a): *Mis padres me dan un radiocasete.*

1. tu hermano(a)
2. tus primos
3. tus abuelos
4. tus tíos
5. tus amigos
6. tu mejor amigo(a)
7. tu mamá
8. tu papá

Vocabulario

En la tienda de música y videos

el casete

el disco compacto

el radio

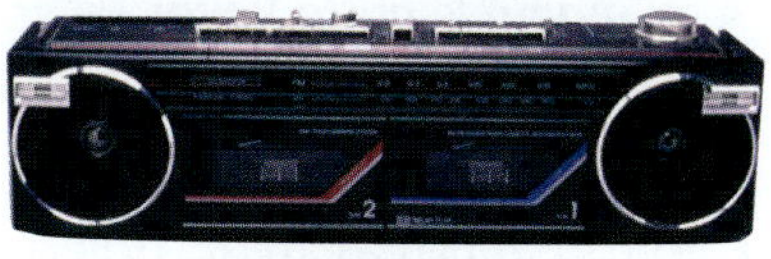

el radiocasete

el video

la videograbadora

el videojuego

¿Qué te gusta usar?

GRAMÁTICA Placement of Indirect Object Pronouns

How do you know where **indirect object pronouns** go in a sentence? They work just like **direct object pronouns.**

- When the pronoun accompanies a **conjugated verb**, the **pronoun** comes **before** the verb.

before

Rosa **le** **compra** una olla a su madre.
Rosa buys her mother a pot.

- But when the **pronoun** accompanies a sentence with an **infinitive**, it can either go **before** the **conjugated verb** or be **attached** to the end of the **infinitive**:

attached

Rosa **quiere** **comprarle** una olla a su madre.
Rosa wants to buy her mother a pot.

Practice: Actividades 16 17 — **Más práctica** *cuaderno p. 96* — **Para hispanohablantes** *cuaderno p. 94* — **Online Workbook** CLASSZONE.COM

16 ¿Qué quieres darles?

Escribir Ya sabes qué les gusta hacer a varias personas. ¿Qué quieres darles? *(Hint: Say what you want to give.)*

modelo

mamá / llevar joyas

*A mi **mamá** le gusta **llevar joyas.** Quiero darle un collar.*
***o:** Le quiero dar un collar.*

1. papá / llevar artículos de cuero
2. hermano / jugar al béisbol
3. hermana / usar la cerámica
4. abuela / escuchar música
5. mejor amigo / ver videos
6. prima / jugar al tenis
7. amiga / escuchar el radiocasete
8. tía / comprar joyas de oro

17 En la tienda

Hablar/*Escribir* Carlos está muy ocupado hoy. Acaba de vender muchas cosas en la tienda de su papá. ¿A quiénes les vendió cosas? *(Hint: To whom has Carlos sold things?)*

modelo

Carlos acaba de venderle una revista a Rosa.

***o:** Carlos le acaba de vender una revista a Rosa.*

un refresco
un mapa
un periódico
una revista
¿?

a Rosa
a Rosa y a Sofía
a mí
a su vecino
¿?

PARTE D

Todo en acción

Activity 18 brings together all concepts presented.

18 Almacén SuperGanga

Hablar Tú y un(a) amigo(a) van de compras. ¿Cuál es un buen regalo para cada persona de la familia? ¿Cuánto cuesta? ¿Es caro o barato? Hablen de las posibilidades.
(Hint: Choose gifts.)

modelo

hermanito

Tú: *Quiero comprarle un regalo a mi **hermanito.***

Tu amigo(a): *¿Por qué no le compras el videojuego «El dragón gigante»?*

Tú: *Busco algo más barato.*

Tu amigo(a): *...*

1. hermano(a)
2. amigo(a)
3. primo(a)

More Practice: **Más comunicación** *p. R11*

Online Workbook
CLASSZONE.COM

Pronunciación

Trabalenguas

Pronunciación de la *rr* The sound of **rr** in Spanish is produced by rapidly tapping the roof of the mouth with the tip of the tongue. Practice **rr** by repeating this tongue twister aloud. Use the pictures to help you figure out what it means.

Erre con erre, guitarra,

erre con erre, barril;

¡qué rápido corren los carros, los carros del ferrocarril!

En colores
CULTURA Y COMPARACIONES

PARA CONOCERNOS

STRATEGY: CONNECTING CULTURES

Compare bargaining customs Where does bargaining take place? How do people act when they bargain? Use a Venn diagram to compare bargaining in the United States to the kind of bargaining that Rosa did in the Mercado Benito Juárez in Oaxaca.

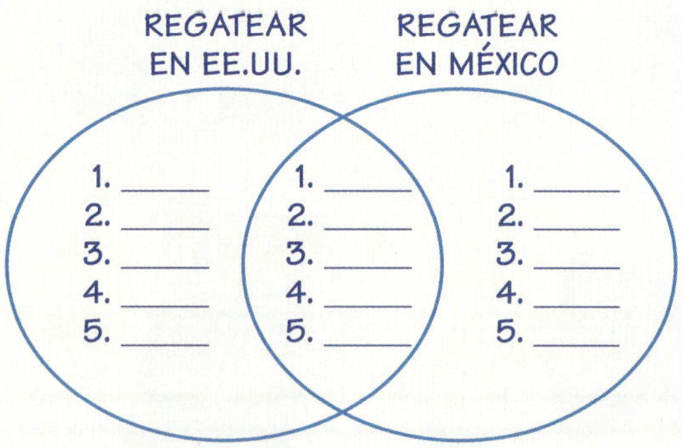

What do they have in common?

México

Nota cultural

Benito Juárez (1806–1872) is the most famous Oaxacan in the history of Mexico. Of Zapotec origin, he was elected governor of Oaxaca and later president of Mexico. The market is named in his honor.

El Mercado Benito Juárez

El mercado tiene una gran variedad de cerámica y otras artesanías regionales. También hay plantas medicinales, productos textiles, frutas, verduras[1] y carnes[2]. El mercado es un festival de colores, texturas y aromas. Como[3] todos los mercados, el Benito Juárez es un lugar ideal para regatear.

[1] vegetables [2] meats [3] As, Like

Las cinco reglas[4] fundamentales para regatear

Regatear es un arte que necesitas practicar.
Estas reglas te van a ayudar.

1 **Habla sólo español.**

2 **Actúa[5] como un(a) estudiante con poco dinero, no como un(a) turista rico(a)[6].**

3 **Escucha el primer precio. Después contesta: «¡Es demasiado!»**

4 **Pasa por otras tiendas para comparar los precios.**

5 **Siempre sonríe[7] al regatear. No cuesta dinero y a veces recibes mejores precios.**

[4] rules [5] Act [6] rich [7] smile

More About Mexico
CLASSZONE.COM

¿Comprendiste?

1. ¿Qué hay para comprar en el Mercado Benito Juárez?
2. ¿Cómo es el mercado?
3. ¿Cómo compras en este mercado?

¿Qué piensas?

1. En tu opinión, ¿cuál es la regla más importante para recibir un buen precio? ¿Por qué?
2. ¿Cuáles de estas reglas son efectivas? ¿Piensas que algunas reglas no son efectivas? Explica tu opinión.
3. Ya sabes unas reglas para regatear. Mira tu diagrama de Venn. ¿Quieres escribir algo más? ¿Quieres cambiar algo?

Hazlo tú

Con otro(a) estudiante prepara un diálogo. Van a regatear. Una persona puede ser el (la) vendedor(a). La otra puede ser el (la) cliente(a).

ETAPA 2

En uso
REPASO Y MÁS COMUNICACIÓN

OBJECTIVES
- Talk about shopping
- Make purchases
- Talk about giving gifts
- Bargain

Now you can...
- talk about shopping.

To review
- indirect object pronouns, see p. 281 and p. 284.

1 ¿Qué nos va a comprar?

La abuela de Carlos conoce bien a su familia. ¿Qué les va a comprar a todos? *(Hint: Say what she'll buy.)*

modelo

Héctor y Eloísa: ver películas

*A **Héctor y a Eloísa les** gusta **ver películas**. Entonces, ella va a comprar**les un video**. Cuesta **cincuenta y tres pesos.***

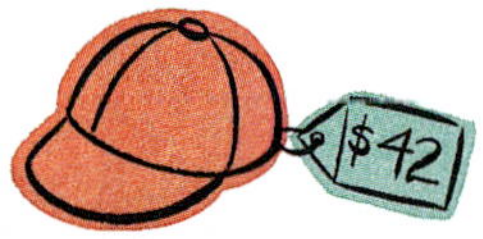

1. yo: usar artículos de cuero
2. mamá: llevar joyas
3. nosotros: escuchar música
4. tú: leer
5. papá: jugar al béisbol
6. los vecinos: tener cosas de cerámica

Now you can...
- make purchases.

To review
- stem-changing verbs: **o** → **ue**, see p. 278.

2 ¡De compras!

Rosa y Sofía están de compras. Completa su conversación con el vendedor. *(Hint: Complete the conversation.)*

Rosa: ¿Cuánto __1__ (costar) los aretes?

Vendedor: __2__ (recordar, yo) el precio. Los aretes __3__ (costar) sólo 75 pesos.

Sofía: Rosa, ¿por qué no __4__ (volver, nosotras) más tarde? __5__ (poder, nosotras) almorzar en el Café Sol.

Rosa: ¿El Café Sol otra vez? Tú y yo siempre __6__ (almorzar) allí.

Vendedor: Yo les __7__ (poder) recomendar el nuevo Café Florida.

Rosa: Gracias, señor. Compro los aretes.

Sofía: ¡Qué suerte! Tú siempre __8__ (encontrar) regalos baratos.

Self-Check Quiz
CLASSZONE.COM

Now you can…
- talk about giving gifts.

To review
- the verb **dar**, see p. 282.
- indirect object pronouns, see p. 281 and p. 284.

3 ¡Feliz cumpleaños!

Hoy la señora Juárez celebra su cumpleaños. ¿Qué le dan todos? *(Hint: Say what people give.)*

modelo

Gustavo

Gustavo** le da **una bolsa.

1. yo

2. su esposo

3. tú

4. Sara y yo

5. sus hijos

6. nosotros

Now you can…
- bargain.

To review
- vocabulary for bargaining, see p. 273 and p. 280.
- stem-changing verbs: **o** → **ue**, see p. 278.
- indirect object pronouns, see p. 281 and p. 284.

4 ¡A regatear!

Tú quieres comprar un cinturón en el mercado y tienes que regatear. Completa la conversación. *(Hint: Bargain.)*

Tú: Perdone, señora. ¿(Te / Me) deja ver el cinturón de cuero, por favor?

Vendedora: ¡Cómo no! Usted (podemos / puede) ver que es de muy buena (calidad / oro).

Tú: Es muy bonito. Busco un (precio / regalo) para mi papá, a quien (les / le) gusta usar artículos de cuero. ¿Cuánto (cuesta / cuestan) el cinturón?

Vendedora: Para usted, joven, sólo cien pesos.

Tú: ¡Uy! ¡Es muy (barato / caro)! (Le / Nos) puedo ofrecer setenta pesos.

Vendedora: Bueno, (me / le) dejo el cinturón en ochenta y cinco.

Tú: No (puedes / puedo) pagar tanto. ¿Por qué no (me / les) da el cinturón por ochenta?

Vendedora: Está bien. Quedamos en ochenta.

5 El mercado

STRATEGY: SPEAKING
Disagree politely Find ways to disagree with the seller about the quality of the article or how it compares with another one. You can contradict politely or express a negative opinion in these ways: **no me gusta/gustaría..., no puedo...**

Estás en un mercado al aire libre. Compra tres cosas. Regatea para pagar el mejor precio. Después, cambien de papel. *(**Hint:** Bargain for three items.)*

¿Cuánto cuesta(n)?

¿Me deja ver...?

Le dejo... en...

¡Es muy caro!
Le puedo ofrecer...

6 ¡A comprar regalos!

Completa la tabla con los regalos que vas a comprarles a estas personas. No puedes pagar más de cien dólares. Luego, en grupos de tres, hablen de sus compras. *(**Hint:** Say what you'll buy.)*

modelo

Voy a comprarle un videojuego a mi amigo Daniel. Lo puedo encontrar en la tienda Super Max. Cuesta veinte dólares.

¿Para quién?	¿Qué?	¿Dónde?	¿Cuánto?
mi amigo(a)	un videojuego	Super Max	$20
todos mis amigos			
el (la) profesor(a)			
mi familia y yo			
yo			

7 *En tu propia voz*

ESCRITURA Una joven de Oaxaca está de visita en tu comunidad. En un párrafo, explícale dónde y cómo comprar regalos para cinco miembros de su familia. *(**Hint:** Explain where and how to shop.)*

modelo

¿A tu mamá le gusta usar joyas? Puedes encontrar joyas bonitas en la joyería Sparkles. Queda en la calle Main. Venden collares muy baratos. Cuestan veinte dólares. No puedes regatear, pero puedes pagar con tarjeta de crédito...

CONEXIONES

Las matemáticas Create your own **mercado** in your Spanish classroom with objects donated by your classmates. You will **regatear**. Make a chart of the objects for sale and the prices they sell for. Calculate the total amount of money raised. Donate all proceeds to a community organization on behalf of the Spanish classes in your school.

Objeto	Precio
disco compacto	$5

Flashcards
CLASSZONE.COM

En resumen

REPASO DE VOCABULARIO

MAKING PURCHASES

Jewelry

el anillo	*ring*
el arete	*earring*
el collar	*necklace*
las joyas	*jewelry*
el oro	*gold*
la plata	*silver*
la pulsera	*bracelet*

Music and Videos

el casete	*cassette*
el disco compacto	*compact disc*
el radio	*radio*
el radiocasete	*radio-tape player*
el video	*video*
la videograbadora	*VCR*
el videojuego	*video game*

Handicrafts

la artesanía	*handicraft*
los artículos de cuero	*leather goods*
la bolsa	*handbag*
las botas	*boots*
la cartera	*wallet*
la cerámica	*ceramics*
el cinturón	*belt*
la jarra	*pitcher*
la olla	*pot*
el plato	*plate*

BARGAINING

¿Cuánto cuesta(n)...?	*How much is (are) ...?*
¡Es muy caro(a)!	*It's very expensive!*
Le dejo... en...	*I'll give ... to you for ...*
Le puedo ofrecer...	*I can offer you ...*
¿Me deja ver...?	*May I see ...?*
regatear	*to bargain*

TALKING ABOUT GIVING GIFTS

dar	*to give*
el regalo	*gift*

TALKING ABOUT SHOPPING

barato(a)	*cheap, inexpensive*
la calidad	*quality*
cambiar	*to change, to exchange*
caro(a)	*expensive*
demasiado(a)	*too much*
el mercado	*market*
perfecto(a)	*perfect*

Money and Payment

el cambio	*change, money exchange*
el dinero	*money*
el dólar	*dollar*
el efectivo	*cash*
pagar	*to pay*
el precio	*price*
la tarjeta de crédito	*credit card*

OTHER WORDS AND PHRASES

juntos	*together*
para	*for, in order to*

Stem-Changing Verbs: o → ue

almorzar	*to eat lunch*
contar	*to count, to tell or retell*
costar	*to cost*
devolver	*to return (an item)*
dormir	*to sleep*
encontrar	*to find, to meet*
poder	*to be able, can*
recordar	*to remember*
volver	*to return, to come back*

Juego

¿Qué cosa compras por pocos pesos, una olla de plata o un plato barato?

UNIDAD 4

ETAPA 3

¿Qué hacer en Oaxaca?

OBJECTIVES

- Order food
- Request the check
- Talk about food
- Express extremes
- Say where you went

¿Qué ves?

Mira la foto de Monte Albán.

1. ¿Alguien lleva una gorra?
2. ¿Quién es la persona principal?
3. ¿Qué hace?
4. ¿Cuánto cuesta un refresco en el restaurante?

En contexto

VIDEO DVD AUDIO

VOCABULARIO

Carlos is at a restaurant in Oaxaca. Take a look at what he likes to eat.

A

Carlos tiene mucha hambre y va a **un restaurante.** Lee **el menú** y decide comer **una enchilada**. Es **deliciosa.** ¡Pero **la salsa** es **picante**! **El mesero** va a **servir**le **una limonada.**

B

Otras personas comen en el restaurante también. Una persona come **arroz** y **bistec.** Usa **un tenedor** y **un cuchillo** para comer.

C Otra persona come **sopa, pollo** y **ensalada.** Usa **una cuchara** para tomar la sopa.

CD-ROM Take-Home Tutor

D Una persona quiere **café** con **azúcar.** Otra quiere **una taza** de **té.**

E ¿Qué tienen de **postre**? ¡**Un flan** muy **rico**!

Preguntas personales

Online Workbook CLASSZONE.COM

1. ¿Te gusta comer comida picante?
2. ¿Prefieres comer en un restaurante o en casa?
3. ¿Prefieres un bistec o pollo?
4. ¿Qué te gusta más: la sopa, la ensalada o el postre?
5. ¿Cuál es tu comida favorita?

VIDEO DVD AUDIO

En vivo

DIÁLOGO

Sofía

Rosa

Carlos

Mesero

PARA ESCUCHAR • STRATEGY: LISTENING

Integrate your skills Combine what you know.

1. Identify the main idea. Is it (1) explaining relationships, (2) ordering in a restaurant, or (3) learning about Oaxaca?
2. Listen for specifics. What word(s) describe(s) Monte Albán?
3. Listen for feelings. Who expresses curiosity? Pleasure? Other emotions?

¡Al restaurante!

1 ▶ **Sofía:** Tienes que decirme. ¿Cómo conoces a Carlos?
Rosa: ¡Es un secreto!
Sofía: ¡Por favor, Rosa!

5 ▶ **Carlos:** Un bistec asado.
Mesero: ¿Algo de tomar?
Sofía: Una limonada para mí.
Rosa: Agua mineral, por favor.
Carlos: Un refresco de naranja.

6 ▶ **Mesero:** Muy bien. ¿Y de postre? Los postres ricos son otra especialidad de la casa. Son buenísimos.
Sofía: Por ahora, nada más. El postre lo pedimos después, gracias.
Mesero: Para servirles.

7 ▶ **Sofía:** Oye, Carlos, ¿cómo va tu proyecto para el concurso?
Carlos: Muy bien. Es sobre las ruinas de Monte Albán.
Rosa: ¿Ya fuiste a Monte Albán?
Carlos: Sí, fui para sacar fotos.

CD-ROM Take-Home Tutor

2 ▶ **Rosa:** Está bien. Conozco a Carlos porque fui a la tienda de su papá para pedir direcciones para llegar a tu casa.

3 ▶ **Carlos:** ¿Nos puede traer pan, por favor?
Mesero: Enseguida se lo traigo.
Rosa: Yo quiero un plato tradicional.
Carlos: La especialidad de la casa tiene mole negro y tasajo. Es riquísima.

4 ▶ **Carlos:** Me gustan las enchiladas, pero voy a pedir bistec. Viene con arroz y frijoles.
Mesero: ¿Listos para pedir?
Sofía: Para mí, una ensalada mixta y pollo.
Rosa: Para mí, la especialidad.

8 ▶ **Carlos:** Hay unas vistas fabulosas. Y el Juego de Pelota es antiguo e interesante.
Rosa: Me gusta mucho tu idea para el concurso.

9 ▶ **Mesero:** ¿Algo más, jóvenes?
Sofía: ¿Pido un postre y lo compartimos?
Mesero: ¿Un flan, señoritas? Lo sirvo en dos platos con dos cucharas.
Sofía: Perfecto, señor. Muchas gracias.
Mesero: ¿Y para usted?

10 ▶ **Carlos:** No quiero ningún postre, pero ¿me puede traer la cuenta, por favor?
Mesero: Sí, cómo no.
Sofía: El mesero sirve muy bien.
Carlos: Me gusta este restaurante. ¡Quisiera comer aquí todos los días!

En acción

PARTE A Comprensión del diálogo

For Activities 1–2, refer to the dialog on pages 296–297.

1 ¿Quién habla?

Escuchar ¿Quién habla: Sofía, Carlos, Rosa o el mesero? *(Hint: Say who speaks.)*

1. «¿Cómo conoces a Carlos?»
2. «Yo quiero un plato tradicional.»
3. «Me gustan las enchiladas, pero voy a pedir bistec.»
4. «¿Un flan, señoritas? Lo sirvo en dos platos…»
5. «No quiero ningún postre, pero ¿me puede traer la cuenta, por favor?»

2 ¿Quién lo come?

Escuchar ¿Quién come o bebe estas cosas: Rosa, Sofía o Carlos? ¡Ojo! Dos personas comparten una cosa. *(Hint: Who orders what?)*

1. el mole negro y tasajo
2. una ensalada mixta y pollo
3. un agua mineral
4. un bistec
5. un refresco de naranja
6. una limonada
7. un flan

PARTE B Práctica del vocabulario

Objectives for Activities 3–6
• Talk about food • Say where you went

3 En la cafetería

STRATEGY: SPEAKING

Vary ways to express preferences Use **querer** or **preferir** to vary your sentences about their choices.

Hablar Carlos y sus amigos van a comer. ¿Qué va a comer cada persona? Piensa en las palabras que sabes, las de esta etapa y las del siguiente vocabulario. *(Hint: Say what each one eats.)*

modelo

Ana: postre

***Ana** prefiere comer flan, pan dulce o pastel.*

1. Carlos: comida mexicana
2. Diego: carne
3. Elena: comida picante
4. Marta: comida vegetariana
5. Daniel: algo típico de Estados Unidos

Vocabulario

La comida

las bebidas

la carne

la lechuga

el pan

el pan dulce

el pastel

el queso

caliente *hot, warm* **dulce** *sweet* **sin** *without* **vegetariano(a)** *vegetarian*

¿Prefieres una cena con carne o sin carne? ¿Qué te gusta comer?

4 ¿Qué pasa?

Escuchar Escucha las descripciones. ¿Qué foto se relaciona con cada descripción?
(Hint: Which description matches each photo?)

a.

b.

c.

d.

5 A poner la mesa

Hablar Trabajas en un restaurante. El (La) nuevo(a) mesero(a) no sabe cómo poner la mesa. Ayúdalo(a).
(Hint: Help the waiter/waitress set the table.)

modelo

el tenedor

Mesero(a): *¿Dónde pongo **el tenedor**?*

Tú: *Al lado del plato, a la izquierda.*

Nota: Vocabulario

Poner means *to put*. It has an irregular **yo** form: **pongo.** The expression **poner la mesa** means *to set the table*.

1. el cuchillo
2. la cuchara
3. el vaso
4. la taza
5. el plato

También se dice

Spanish speakers use different words for *waiter/waitress.*

- **mesero(a):** Mexico, Puerto Rico
- **camarero(a):** Spain
- **mozo(a):** Argentina, Puerto Rico
- **caballero/señorita:** many countries

To describe Mexico's spicy cuisine, **picante** is used by all Spanish speakers. In Mexico, **picoso(a)** describes especially spicy food!

salsa picante

PARTE C

Práctica: gramática y vocabulario

Objectives for Activities 7–21
- Talk about food • Order food • Request the check • Express extremes

6 ¿Fuiste?

Hablar Sofía y Rosa hablan de muchas tiendas. Trabaja con otro(a) estudiante. Cambien de papel. *(Hint: Talk about where they went.)*

modelo

tienda de música

Sofía: *¿Fuiste a la **tienda de música**?*

Rosa: *Sí, fui para comprar un disco compacto.*

Nota: Vocabulario

Fui means *I went*; **fuiste** means *you* **(tú)** *went*.

1. zapatería
2. joyería
3. librería
4. pastelería
5. carnicería
6. panadería
7. tienda de ropa
8. papelería

México

Nota cultural

Oaxaca's cuisine blends pre-Hispanic and Spanish traditions. Visitors should try the many **mole** sauces, the string cheese **quesillo,** the giant tortillas known as **tlayudas,** and **tasajo,** strips of grilled spicy meat.

GRAMÁTICA Using gustar to Talk About Things You Like

¿RECUERDAS? *p. 187* Remember how to express what **activities** people like to do? You use these phrases with an infinitive.

me gusta...	**nos gusta...**
te gusta...	**os gusta...**
le gusta...	**les gusta...**

When you want to talk about **things** that people like, change the form of **gustar** to match the **singular** or **plural** nouns for those things.

Singular

me gusta la idea	**nos gusta la idea**
te gusta la idea	**os gusta la idea**
le gusta la idea	**les gusta la idea**

Plural

me gustan las personas	**nos gustan las personas**
te gustan las personas	**os gustan las personas**
le gustan las personas	**les gustan las personas**

Notice that the form of **gustar** matches the **noun,** not the speaker.

Rosa says: *matches singular noun*

—¡**Me gusta** mucho tu **idea** para el concurso!

***I like** your idea for the contest a lot!*

Carlos says: *matches plural noun*

—**Me gustan las enchiladas.**

***I like** enchiladas.*

Practice: 7 8 9

Más práctica *cuaderno p. 101*

Para hispanohablantes *cuaderno p. 99*

Online Workbook CLASSZONE.COM

7 ¿Qué les gusta(n)?

Hablar Rosa habla de la comida que a ella y a sus amigos les gusta. ¿Qué dice? *(Hint: Say what food people like.)*

modelos

a mí: las enchiladas

*Me gustan **las enchiladas.***

a Pedro y a Juan: el flan

*Les gusta **el flan.***

1. a Diego: el arroz
2. a Arturo: las papas fritas
3. a mí: el flan
4. a ustedes: los postres
5. a nosotros: la comida picante
6. a Paco y a Enrique: el pollo
7. a nosotras: el pan dulce
8. a ti: las ensaladas
9. a Carlos: el mole negro
10. a los chicos: los tacos

Apoyo para estudiar

¿Me gusta o me gustan?

How do you say *I like it* or *I like them* when talking about nouns? When you use **gustar** with nouns, think of the phrase *to please* in English. *I like something* means *Something is pleasing to me.* So, how do you say *I like it* or *I like them*? Look at the title of this study hint!

8 ¿Te gusta(n)...?

Hablar Pregúntales a cinco estudiantes si les gustan estas comidas. Da un resumen de los resultados. *(Hint: Say who likes what.)*

modelo

las enchiladas

Tú: *¿Te gustan **las enchiladas**?*

Otro(a) estudiante: *Sí, me gustan mucho.*

Resumen: *A cuatro personas les gustan las enchiladas. A una persona no le gustan.*

1. las hamburguesas
2. los postres
3. el arroz con pollo
4. las papas fritas
5. el flan
6. la carne
7. la salsa
8. los tacos
9. el queso
10. las sopas

9 ¡Nos gusta la ropa!

Hablar/*Escribir* Estás en una tienda de ropa. Explica a quién le gusta cada prenda. *(Hint: Say what they like.)*

blusa	gorra	shorts
camiseta	falda	zapatos
calcetines	pantalones	suéter
camisa		

modelo

a mí *Me gustan los zapatos negros.*

1. a mí
2. a mi hermano(a)
3. a mi amigo(a)
4. a mis padres
5. a mis amigos
6. a mi mamá
7. a nosotros
8. a mis abuelos
9. a mi tío(a)
10. a mi primo(a)

More Practice: **Más comunicación** *p. R12*

GRAMÁTICA Affirmative and Negative Words

When you want to talk about an indefinite or negative situation, you use an **affirmative** or a **negative** word.

Affirmative Words	Negative Words
algo *something*	**nada** *nothing*
alguien *someone*	**nadie** *no one*
algún/alguno(a) *some*	**ningún/ninguno(a)** *none, not any*
siempre *always*	**nunca** *never*
también *also*	**tampoco** *neither, either*

The waiter asks:

—¿**Algo** de tomar?

***Something** to drink?*

Sofía says:

—Por ahora, **nada** más.

*For now, **nothing** more.*

Notice that **alguno(a)** and **ninguno(a)** must match the gender of the noun they replace or modify. **Alguno** and **ninguno** have different forms when used before masculine singular nouns.

alguno → **algún** **ninguno** → **ningún**

Las chicas quieren **algún** postre, pero Carlos no quiere **ningún** postre.

*The girls want **some** dessert, but Carlos **doesn't** want **any** dessert.*

If a verb is preceded by **no**, words that follow must be negative. A **double negative** is required in Spanish when **no** precedes the verb.

No quiero **nada.**

*I **don't** want **anything.***

Carlos **no** quiere **ninguno** (de los postres).

*Carlos does **not** want **any** (of the desserts).*

However, if a negative word, such as **nunca** or **nadie,** comes before the verb, a second negative is not needed.

Nadie quiere postre.

***No one** wants dessert.*

Las chicas **nunca** comen en casa.

*The girls **never** eat at home.*

Practice: 10 11 12 13

Más práctica
cuaderno pp. 102–103
Para hispanohablantes
cuaderno pp. 100–101

Online Workbook
CLASSZONE.COM

10 De mal humor

Leer Estás de mal humor. Tu amigo(a) te hace muchas invitaciones pero no quieres hacer nada. Completa el diálogo con la forma correcta de **alguno(a)** o **ninguno(a)**.
(Hint: Complete the conversation.)

Nota: Gramática

Ningunos(as) is almost never used. It is used only with items that are usually plural, such as **pantalones.**

No tengo **ningunos** pantalones.

1. ¿Quieres ir a _____ restaurante?
2. No quiero ir a _____ restaurante.
3. ¿Quieres comer _____ fruta?
4. No quiero comer _____ fruta.
5. ¿Quieres ir a _____ tienda?
6. No quiero ir a _____ tienda.
7. ¿Quieres alquilar _____ videos?
8. No, no quiero alquilar _____ video.
9. ¿Quieres leer _____ revistas?
10. No quiero leer _____ revista.
11. ¿Quieres escuchar _____ discos compactos?
12. No quiero escuchar _____ disco compacto.

11 El sábado por la noche

Hablar Pregúntale a otro(a) estudiante si va a hacer varias cosas el sábado por la noche. Te dice que no las va a hacer. *(Hint: Say what someone won't do.)*

modelos

invitar a alguien al cine

Tú: *¿Vas a **invitar a alguien al cine**?*
Otro(a) estudiante: *No, no voy a invitar a nadie.*

leer algo

Tú: *¿Vas a **leer algo**?*
Otro(a) estudiante: *No, no voy a leer nada.*

Nota: Gramática

When **alguien** or **nadie** is the object of a verb, it is preceded by the personal **a.**

1. visitar a alguien
2. hablar con alguien
3. escribir algo
4. ver a alguien
5. estudiar algo
6. llamar a alguien
7. comprar algo
8. esperar a alguien
9. comer algo
10. conocer a alguien

12 ¿Sí o no?

Hablar/*Escribir* Usa una palabra de cada columna para decir si van a hacer algo o no. *(Hint: Say if someone will do something or not.)*

modelo

***Yo** voy a beber **algo**.*

1. yo
2. mi hermano(a)
3. mi amigo(a)
4. mis padres
5. mis amigos

a. algo
b. alguien
c. nada
d. nadie

13 ¡No lo hago!

Escribir Lee la lista de Rosa. Luego, escribe cinco cosas que tú no haces, usando estas palabras. *(Hint: Write what you don't do.)*

1. nada
2. nadie
3. ninguno(a)
4. nunca
5. tampoco

Las cosas que no hago

No como nada picante.
No conozco a nadie aburrido.
No tengo ningún libro interesante.
Nunca hablo en clase.
Tampoco escribo en mis libros.

14 ¡Es buenísimo!

Hablar/*Escribir* Todos describen algo hoy. ¿Qué dicen? Sigue el modelo. *(Hint: Describe each item.)*

modelo

el postre (bueno) ***El postre** es **buenísimo.***

Nota: Gramática

To express extremes with most adjectives, drop the final vowel and add the ending **-ísimo(a).** The adjective must agree in gender and number with the noun it modifies.

La idea de Rosa es **interesantísima.**

*Rosa's idea is **very (extremely) interesting.***

When the last consonant is **c, g,** or **z,** spelling changes are required.

c → qu ri**c**o(a) → ri**qu**ísimo(a)
g → gu lar**g**o(a) → lar**gu**ísimo(a)
z → c feli**z** → feli**c**ísimo(a)

1. la maestra (simpático)
2. las enchiladas (rico)
3. el perro (malo)
4. la película (bueno)
5. las joyas (caro)
6. el libro (aburrido)

GRAMÁTICA Stem-Changing Verbs: e → i

¿RECUERDAS? *p. 205* You have already learned about **e** → **ie** stem-changing verbs like **pensar**.

pensar *to think, to plan*

pienso	**pensamos**
piensas	**pensáis**
piensa	**piensan**

The verb **pedir** also has a stem change. The stem alternates between **e** and **i**.

pedir *to ask for, to order*

pido	**pedimos**
pides	**pedís**
pide	**piden**

The stem doesn't change for the **nosotros** *(we)* or **vosotros** *(you)* form.

Sofía says:

–¿**Pido** un postre y lo compartimos?

*Should **I order** dessert and we'll share it?*

Vocabulario

Stem-Changing Verbs: e → i

servir *to serve* | **pedir** *to ask for, to order*

Other verbs that follow the pattern:

repetir *to repeat* | **seguir** *to follow, to continue*

The **yo** form of **seguir** drops the **u: yo sigo.**

¿Qué pides en un restaurante?

Practice: Actividades 15 16 17 18

Más práctica *cuaderno p. 104*

Para hispanohablantes *cuaderno p. 102*

Online Workbook CLASSZONE.COM

15 En el restaurante

Leer Rosa, Carlos y Sofía van a un restaurante. Completa su conversación con la forma correcta de **pedir.** *(Hint: Complete the conversation.)*

Carlos: Las enchiladas son riquísimas aquí. ¿Las __1__ ustedes?

Chicas: ¡Claro que sí!

Mesero: ¿Listos para __2__?

Carlos: Sí, queremos las enchiladas de carne para los tres.

Mesero: ¿Y de postre?

Rosa: Sofía, ¿ __3__ tú y yo un pastel y lo compartimos?

Sofía: Buenísima idea. Y tú, Carlos, ¿qué __4__?

Carlos: Yo __5__ un flan, ¡y no lo comparto con nadie!

México

Nota cultural

The artistic heritage of Oaxaca is known worldwide. There are baskets, pottery, hand-loomed clothing, and rugs with pre-Hispanic designs.

16 Sirven...

Hablar/*Escribir* Carlos almuerza mucho en las casas de sus amigos. ¿Qué sirven? *(Hint: Say what they serve.)*

modelo

Antonio: hamburguesas

Antonio** sirve **hamburguesas.

1. Patricia y Carla: ensalada
2. yo: enchiladas
3. nosotros: fruta
4. usted: tortas
5. tú: mole negro
6. mi hermana y yo: tacos
7. ustedes: pollo
8. la señora Ruiz: bistec
9. los señores Almeida: carne
10. Jaime: arroz
11. Regina y yo: sopa
12. ellos: tamales

17 Pido...

Hablar Pregúntale a otro(a) estudiante qué bebida pide normalmente. Cambien de papel. *(Hint: Say what drink you ask for.)*

modelo

desayunas

Estudiante A: *¿Qué bebida pides cuando **desayunas**?*

Estudiante B: *Pido una taza de té.*

Nota: Vocabulario

Desayunar means *to have breakfast*. **El desayuno** is *breakfast*.

ESTUDIANTE A

¿Qué bebida pides cuando...?

1. desayunas
2. tienes mucha sed
3. estás enfermo(a)
4. no puedes dormir
5. cenas con tu familia en un restaurante
6. tienes frío
7. tienes calor

ESTUDIANTE B

Pido...

18 ¿A quién?

Escuchar Lee las oraciones. Carlos y su amiga Elena están en un restaurante. Escucha y decide si cada oración es cierta o falsa. Corrige las falsas. *(Hint: Say if each sentence is true or false.)*

1. Carlos tiene hambre.
2. Elena va a pedir enchiladas de pollo.
3. Carlos va a pedir un bistec.
4. Los dos van a pedir algún refresco.
5. Carlos no va a pedir ningún postre.

Vocabulario

En el restaurante

Para pedir comida

¿Me ayuda a pedir? *Could you help me order?*

¿Me trae…? *Could you bring me…?*

Quisiera… *I would like…*

Para pedir la cuenta

¿Cuánto es? *How much is it?*

La cuenta, por favor. *The check, please.*

Es aparte. *Separate checks.*

¿Está incluido(a)…? *Is … included?*

¿Cuánto le doy de propina? *How much do I tip?*

¿Cómo pides en un restaurante?

19 La fiesta

Hablar Estás organizando una fiesta. Tu amigo(a) te pregunta quién trae ciertas cosas. *(Hint: Who brings what?)*

modelo

Antonio: platos

Tu amigo(a): *¿**Antonio** trae los **platos**?*

Tú: *Sí, él los trae.*

Nota: Vocabulario

Traer means *to bring*. It has an irregular **yo** form: **traigo.** Its other forms are regular.

1. tú: tenedores
2. Marta: postre
3. la señorita Díaz: refrescos
4. Margarita y yo: ensalada
5. Enrique y Pablo: pollo
6. yo: enchiladas
7. tú: limonada
8. Sara y Ángel: pastel
9. Raúl: cuchillos
10. yo: arroz

20 ¿Listos para pedir?

Hablar Eres mesero(a) en un restaurante mexicano. Tres personas llegan y quieren comer. ¿Qué dicen? Trabaja con tres estudiantes para representar la escena. Cambien de papel. *(Hint: Order food.)*

modelo

Mesero(a): *¿Listos para pedir?*

Persona A: *Sí, quisiera un bistec asado con papas fritas.*

Mesero(a): *¿Algo para tomar?*

Persona A: *Una limonada, por favor.*

Mesero(a): *¿Y usted?*

Persona B: *¿Me trae una enchilada de pollo y un refresco?*

Mesero(a): *¿Y usted, señorita?*

Persona C: *Me gustaría…*

Activity 22 brings together all concepts presented.

21 ¡La cuenta, por favor!

Hablar Acaban de comer y quieren la cuenta. ¿Qué dicen? La conversación puede variar. *(Hint: Request the check.)*

modelo

Persona A: *Perdone. La cuenta, por favor.*

Mesero(a): *¿Para los dos?*

Persona B: *No, mi cuenta es aparte.*

Persona A: *¿Está incluida la propina?*

Mesero(a): *No, señor. Bueno, ahora traigo las dos cuentas.*

1. Las cuentas son aparte.
2. Las cuentas no son aparte.
3. La propina está incluida.
4. La propina no está incluida.

22 ¡A comer!

Hablar/*Escribir* Vas a un restaurante con unos amigos. Trabaja en un grupo de cuatro para escribir un diálogo en tres partes, usando las expresiones de la lista. Luego, preséntenle los diálogos a la clase. *(Hint: Write a restaurant dialog.)*

Parte 1: Llegan al restaurante. El (La) mesero(a) les trae el menú. Piden la comida.

Parte 2: El (La) mesero(a) les trae la comida. Hablan de la calidad de la comida y del servicio.

Parte 3: Acaban de comer. Piden la cuenta. Pagan la cuenta y dan una propina.

modelo

Persona A: *¿Nos puede traer el menú, por favor?*

Mesero(a): *Sí, ahora mismo lo traigo.*

Persona B: *Bueno, ¿qué vamos a pedir?*

Persona C: *¿Sirven buenas enchiladas de pollo aquí?*

Persona A: *Creo que sí.*

Persona C: *Entonces, voy a pedirlas.*

Persona B: *A mí no me gustan las enchiladas. Yo voy a pedir arroz con pollo.*

Persona A: *Y yo bistec.*

Mesero(a): *¿Listos para pedir?...*

More Practice: **Más comunicación** *p. R12*

Online Workbook CLASSZONE.COM

Pronunciación

Trabalenguas

Pronunciación de la *g* The letter **g** in Spanish has a soft sound before the vowels **i** and **e.** It sounds somewhat like the *h* in the English word *he*, but a little harder. Practice by pronouncing the following words:

gimnasio biolo**gí**a **ge**neral **Ge**raldo

When it precedes other vowels, the **g** has a different sound, like in the word *go*. To produce this sound with **i** or **e**, a **u** must be inserted. Practice the following words:

gato **gu**sto **go**rdo abri**go** **gui**tarra hambur**gue**sa

Now try the tongue twister.

En voces

VIDEO DVD AUDIO

LECTURA

PARA LEER

STRATEGY: READING

Gather and sort information as you read

Do you and your friends have jobs after school or on weekends? Fill out this chart about jobs by interviewing two people. Then use this chart to gather information about Andrés as you read.

Preguntas	Persona 1	Persona 2	Andrés
¿Dónde trabajas?			
¿Cuándo?			
¿Qué haces?			
¿Trabajas en algo que te puede servir en el futuro?			

Andrés, joven aprendiz de alfarero[1]

¡Hola! Me llamo Andrés Real. Vivo en San Bartolo Coyotepec, un pueblo cerca de la ciudad de Oaxaca. *Coyotepec* significa[2] «montaña de los coyotes». La verdad es que ya no hay muchos de estos animales. Mi pueblo no es muy grande, pero es muy famoso. La cerámica negra que ves en tiendas y mercados por todo México es de aquí. Si algún día ves una olla de barro[3] negro que parece[4] metal, probablemente es de San Bartolo Coyotepec.

La *Alfarería Doña Rosa* es donde yo trabajo después de salir de la escuela. En la alfarería hacemos la cerámica de barro. Esta alfarería se llama *Doña Rosa* en honor a mi abuela doña Rosa Valente Nieto de Real. Ella inventó[5] este tipo de cerámica. Mi abuela murió[6] en 1979, pero mi familia todavía[7] usa su método para hacer la cerámica.

---

[1] potter
[2] means
[3] clay
[4] that looks like
[5] invented
[6] died
[7] still

Yo soy aprendiz, o estudiante, de alfarero. Mi papá, mi mamá y mis tíos me enseñan este arte. No hago ollas grandes pero hago animalitos, como coyotes. Mis animalitos no siempre salen bien porque estoy aprendiendo. Como mi abuela, algún día voy a vender los artículos de barro negro de Coyotepec por todo el mundo.

Online Workbook
CLASSZONE.COM

¿Comprendiste?

1. ¿Dónde vive Andrés?
2. ¿Por qué es famoso su pueblo?
3. ¿Quién es su abuela? ¿Por qué es famosa?
4. ¿Qué hace Andrés en la alfarería?
5. ¿Qué quiere hacer Andrés algún día?

¿Qué piensas?

Usa tu imaginación. En otra hoja de papel, escribe lo que hace Andrés en un día típico. También escribe lo que tú haces antes o después de clases.

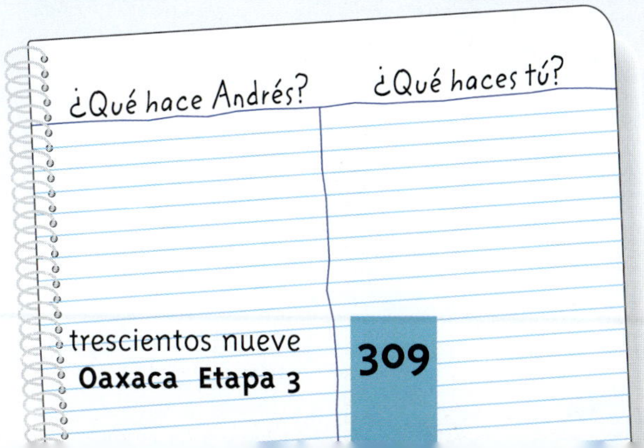

En colores
CULTURA Y COMPARACIONES

PARA CONOCERNOS
STRATEGY: CONNECTING CULTURES

Analyze and recommend Some areas depend on tourism for income, but sometimes local people are against it. Why is that so? Think of reasons for and against tourism.

Turismo: no	Turismo: sí
1.	1.
2.	2.
3.	3.

Based on your analysis, write three or more rules for being a good tourist.

México

Nota cultural
Today many Zapotec Indians support themselves through farming and traditional handicrafts such as weaving.

Monte Albán:

Para el concurso de Onda Internacional, *Carlos visita Monte Albán. Saca fotos y escribe este artículo sobre una de las primeras culturas de Oaxaca.*

El estado de Oaxaca es una importante región arqueológica. El lugar más famoso es Monte Albán, una de las primeras ciudades de Mesoamérica[1] y la vieja capital de los zapotecas[2]. Sabemos que la civilización de Monte Albán empieza por el año 500 a.C.[3] Pero los orígenes y el fin de esta civilización son un misterio fascinante.

[1] Middle America (Mexico and Central America)
[2] Zapotec Indians
[3] B.C.

Los Danzantes

ruinas misteriosas

Muchos turistas visitan Monte Albán todos los años para conocer sus pirámides, terrazas, tumbas y esculturas. La parte donde hay más exploración es la Plaza Central, centro de la vida social y religiosa de los zapotecas. Allí hay grandes plataformas, como el Juego de Pelota y la Galería de los Danzantes. Los arqueólogos no saben mucho sobre el Juego de Pelota. Tampoco saben qué representan los Danzantes. ¿Son figuras de hombres que danzan o son prisioneros[4]?

El Juego de Pelota

Aproximadamente entre los años 700 y 800 d.C.[5], los zapotecas abandonan Monte Albán. Luego, los mixtecas[6] usan el lugar. Hoy, descendientes de los dos grupos viven en las montañas y el valle de Oaxaca. Su cultura sigue presente en la lengua y las costumbres[7].

[4] prisoners
[5] A.D.
[6] Mixtec Indians
[7] customs

More About Mexico
CLASSZONE.COM

¿Comprendiste?

1. ¿Qué importancia tiene Monte Albán?
2. ¿Qué sabemos del fin de la civilización de Monte Albán?
3. ¿Qué pueden ver los turistas aquí?
4. ¿Qué saben los arqueólogos del Juego de Pelota o de los Danzantes?
5. ¿Hay zapotecas hoy en Oaxaca?

¿Qué piensas?

Eres un(a) turista en Monte Albán. En una hoja de papel, describe tu visita y tus reacciones. Mira las fotos para inspirarte.

ETAPA 3

En uso

REPASO Y MÁS COMUNICACIÓN

OBJECTIVES
- Order food
- Request the check
- Talk about food
- Express extremes
- Say where you went

Now you can...
- order food.
- request the check.

To review
- affirmative and negative words, see p. 302.

1 En el restaurante

Lucía y Emilio están en un restaurante. Completa su diálogo con el mesero con la forma correcta de las siguientes palabras: **alguno, ninguno, algo, nada, alguien, nadie.** *(Hint: Complete the conversation.)*

Lucía: Emilio, conozco a __1__ que trabaja en este restaurante.
Emilio: ¿De verdad? Yo no conozco a __2__ aquí. ¿Quién es?
Lucía: Un vecino. Prepara los postres.
Mesero: La especialidad es el bistec. No hay __3__ bistec tan delicioso como el nuestro. Les doy __4__ minutos para mirar el menú.

Mesero: ¿Están listos para pedir?
Emilio: Sí, para mí, la especialidad.
Lucía: Y yo quisiera las enchiladas y una ensalada.
Mesero: ¿Quieren __5__ de tomar?
Emilio: Por ahora, __6__ más. Después, vamos a compartir __7__ postre.

Emilio: La cuenta, por favor.
Mesero: Sí, señor. Un momento.
Lucía: ¿Le dejamos __8__ propina?
Emilio: No. Está incluida.

Now you can...
- talk about food.

To review
- stem-changing verbs: **e** → **i**, see p. 304.

2 El nuevo mesero

El nuevo mesero está aprendiendo. ¿Qué sirve? *(Hint: Say what he serves.)*

modelo

Isabel: arroz (lechuga)

Isabel** pide **arroz,** pero el mesero le sirve **lechuga.

1. Andrés y yo: enchiladas (pollo)
2. tú: una ensalada (pastel)
3. los señores Gálvez: un flan (pan)
4. yo: carne (un postre)
5. ella: una sopa (un sándwich)
6. nosotros: té (café)

Self-Check Quiz
CLASSZONE.COM

Now you can...
- talk about food.
- express extremes.

To review
- the verb **gustar** + nouns, see p. 300.
- extremes, see p. 303.

3 ¡La comida es buenísima!

A todos les gusta comer. ¿Qué opinan de la comida?
(Hint: Describe their reactions.)

modelo

yo: enchiladas (bueno)

A mí me** gustan **las enchiladas.** Son **buenísimas.

1. mis hermanos: flan (rico)
2. Jaime: papas fritas (bueno)
3. tú: salsa (rico)
4. yo: limonada (bueno)
5. la señorita Anaya: arroz (bueno)
6. nosotros: tacos (rico)

Now you can...
- talk about food.

To review
- the verb **traer**, see p. 306.

4 ¡Una fiesta mexicana!

Hay una fiesta mexicana hoy. ¿Qué traen todos?
(Hint: Say what people bring.)

modelo

Dolores: salsa

Dolores** trae **la salsa.

1. yo: tenedores
2. Salvador: platos
3. nosotros: enchiladas
4. el profesor: arroz
5. Alex y Tito: ensalada
6. la directora: flan
7. tú: pastel
8. René y yo: limonada

Now you can...
- say where you went.

To review
- **fui/fuiste**, see p. 300.

5 ¿Adónde fuiste?

Tu amigo(a) acaba de ir de compras. Escribe tus preguntas y sus respuestas según el modelo. Tiene las siguientes cosas: **un disco compacto, pan, un collar, carne, un pastel, unos artículos de cuero** y **una novela.** *(Hint: Say where you went.)*

modelo

pastelería

Tú: *¿Fuiste a la **pastelería**?*

Tu amigo(a): *Sí, fui para comprar un pastel.*

1. joyería
2. librería
3. panadería
4. carnicería
5. tienda de música
6. mercado

6 ¡Tengo hambre!

STRATEGY: SPEAKING

Borrow useful expressions Here are some useful expressions for agreeing and accepting **(está bien, perfecto)** and for refusing **(no quiero…, por ahora nada más)**. Use them in your conversation in the restaurant.

Estás en un restaurante. Pide un mínimo de tres cosas. Después, habla de la comida y pide la cuenta. Otro(a) estudiante va a ser el (la) mesero(a). Cambien de papel. *(Hint: Order food.)*

Quisiera…

Me gustaría…

¿Me trae…?

¿Está incluido(a)…?

7 ¡Una fiesta!

Trabajando en grupos, hablen de dos cosas que cada persona va a traer a una fiesta. *(Hint: Plan a party.)*

modelo

Sara: *Me gusta la limonada. Traigo limonada y algunos vasos.*

José: *Me gustan las enchiladas y la música. Traigo enchiladas y una guitarra.*

8 En tu propia voz

ESCRITURA Trabajas en un restaurante mexicano. Escribe un párrafo para una guía turística. *(Hint: Describe a Mexican restaurant.)*

modelo

Restaurante Azteca *¿Le gusta la salsa picante? En el Restaurante Azteca servimos una salsa deliciosa y muy picante. La especialidad de la casa es…*

TÚ EN LA COMUNIDAD

Grendale is a high school student in Nevada. He sometimes speaks Spanish with coworkers when he volunteers at a nursing home. At his part-time job, he uses Spanish with Mexican, South American, and Spanish tourists who come to the store. He has a friend from Uruguay who is an exchange student, and they often speak in Spanish. Do you speak Spanish with any of your friends?

En resumen

REPASO DE VOCABULARIO

ORDERING FOOD

¿Me ayuda a pedir?	*Could you help me order?*
¿Me trae…?	*Could you bring me…?*
el menú	*menu*
pedir (i)	*to ask for, to order*
Quisiera…	*I would like…*

At the Restaurant

el (la) mesero(a)	*waiter (waitress)*
el restaurante	*restaurant*
servir (i)	*to serve*
traer	*to bring*

Place Setting

la cuchara	*spoon*
el cuchillo	*knife*
la taza	*cup*
el tenedor	*fork*

EXPRESSING EXTREMES

riquísimo(a)	*very tasty*

REQUESTING THE CHECK

¿Cuánto es?	*How much is it?*
¿Cuánto le doy de propina?	*How much do I tip?*
la cuenta	*bill, check*
La cuenta, por favor.	*The check, please.*
Es aparte.	*Separate checks.*
¿Está incluido(a)…?	*Is… included?*
la propina	*tip*

SAYING WHERE YOU WENT

Fui…/Fuiste…	*I went…/You went…*

TALKING ABOUT FOOD

caliente	*hot, warm*
delicioso(a)	*delicious*
dulce	*sweet*
picante	*spicy*
rico(a)	*tasty*
vegetariano(a)	*vegetarian*

Food

el arroz	*rice*
el azúcar	*sugar*
el bistec	*steak*
la carne	*meat*
la enchilada	*enchilada*
la ensalada	*salad*
la lechuga	*lettuce*
el pan	*bread*
el pollo	*chicken*
el queso	*cheese*
la salsa	*salsa*
la sopa	*soup*

Beverages

la bebida	*beverage, drink*
el café	*coffee*
la limonada	*lemonade*
el té	*tea*

Desserts

el flan	*caramel custard dessert*
el pan dulce	*sweet roll*
el pastel	*cake*
el postre	*dessert*

OTHER WORDS AND PHRASES

algo	*something*
alguien	*someone*
alguno(a)	*some*
desayunar	*to have breakfast*
el desayuno	*breakfast*
la lengua	*language*
listo(a)	*ready*
nada	*nothing*
nadie	*no one*
ninguno(a)	*none, not any*
poner	*to put*
poner la mesa	*to set the table*
el pueblo	*town, village*
sin	*without*
tampoco	*neither, either*
todavía	*still, yet*

Juego

Cada miembro de la familia Martínez quiere algo diferente. ¡Pobre Pablo, el mesero! Pablo es inteligente y trae lo que quieren. ¿Qué les sirve a 1) Marco, 2) Martina y 3) Marisol?

Marco Martínez: Quiero algo líquido y caliente con proteínas.

Martina Martínez: Quiero algo verde y vegetariano.

Marisol Martínez: Quiero algo dulce para mi café.

UNIDAD 4

En tu propia voz

ESCRITURA

¡A viajar!

You and your family are planning a vacation. Write a letter to a Spanish-speaking friend, detailing your plans for the trip.

Function: Explain plans for a trip
Context: Writing to a friend
Content: Your upcoming vacation
Text type: Personal letter

PARA ESCRIBIR • STRATEGY: WRITING

Tell who, what, where, when, why, and how A well-written, friendly letter uses many details to communicate information. Cover all the details by answering these interrogatives: **¿Quién? ¿Qué? ¿Dónde? ¿Cuándo? ¿Por qué? ¿Cómo?**

Modelo del estudiante

Who is indicated by the salutation. Friendly letters usually start with **Querido(a)** *(dear)*, followed by a colon.

Querida Ana:

In the first paragraph, the writer tells **where, when,** and **why** she is going.

¿Cómo estás? Yo estoy muy emocionada. ¡Mi familia y yo vamos de vacaciones a México en agosto! Vamos a estar en Oaxaca por tres días. Estamos estudiando México en mi clase de español y ayer fui a la biblioteca para aprender más. Nuestros planes para el viaje son muy interesantes. ¡Vamos a hacer muchas cosas!

In the remaining paragraphs, the writer tells **what** she will do on each day of her trip. She also says **how** she will be traveling.

Día 1: Salimos en avión por la mañana y llegamos al Hostal de La Noria al mediodía. Por la tarde hacemos una excursión por la ciudad. Cenamos en el restaurante La Casa de la Abuela, en el centro de Oaxaca.

Día 2: Por la mañana vamos en autobús a Monte Albán. ¡Voy a sacar muchas fotos! Por la tarde vamos de compras al Mercado Benito Juárez. ¿Prefieres un collar o unos aretes?

The author keeps herself organized and on task by constructing each paragraph around what she will do on a specific day.

Día 3: Quiero conocer los museos y caminar por la ciudad. No tenemos planes especiales.

¿Qué haces tú durante las vacaciones? ¡Escríbeme!

She adds a closing, followed by a comma, and signs her name.

Hasta luego,

Susana

Writing Center
CLASSZONE.COM

Estrategias para escribir

Antes de escribir...

Think about a trip you will take, or one that you'd like to take. Remember that you will need to tell who, what, where, when, why, and how. To help you organize your details, fill in a chart like this one.

¿A quién le escribes? **a mi amigo Carlos**

¿Adónde vas de viaje? **a Oaxaca**

¿Cómo vas a viajar? ________

¿Qué vas a hacer allí? ________

¿Día 1? ________

¿Día 2? ________

¿Día 3? ________

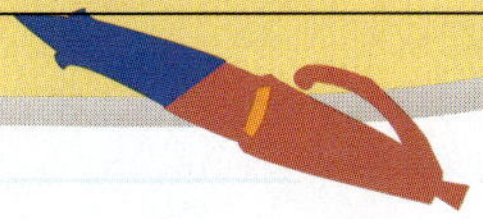

Revisiones

Read your letter aloud to a partner. Then ask:

- *How did I make my letter clear?*
- *When, where, and how are we going on vacation?*
- *What, if anything, is confusing?*
- *What other details may be helpful?*

La versión final

Before you create the final draft of your letter, look over your work with the following questions in mind:

- *Are verbs correct? Have I included necessary stem changes?*

Circle the verbs in your letter. Remember the special spellings of stem-changing verbs.

- *Is punctuation accurate?*

Underline all punctuation. Check that the salutation has a colon, the closing has a comma, sentences end with periods, and question marks and exclamation points are in place.

To insert or delete words, letters, or punctuation, use the editorial marks shown.

Querido Carlos,
¿ Qué tal? Estoy muy feliz. Mañana voy a viajar a México y volvo vuelvo en dos semanas. ¡No puedo creerlo! Viajo con mi hermano mayor. Primero, vamos a la Ciudad de México. Después quiero haser c una excursión en autobús a Oaxaca.
Día 1
Primero, pensamos ir al Mercado Benito Juárez...

EDITORIAL MARKS

^ = insert   ⁞ = insert colon

—ᘓ = delete

UNIDAD 5

BARCELONA ESPAÑA

PREPARACIONES ESPECIALES

TEXAS Essential Knowledge and Skills

1 Communication

- **A Engage in exchanges**
  - *Telling others to do something*
  - *Persuading others*
  - *Negotiating responsibilities*
  - *Planning a party and purchasing food*
- **B Demonstrate understanding**
  - *Expressing extremes*
- **C Present information**
  - *Describing daily routines, grooming, and chores*
  - *Saying what people are doing*
  - *Describing a house*
  - *Describing past activities*

2 Cultures

- **A Practices**
  - *Well-known people from Barcelona*
  - *Cooking*
- **B Products**
  - *Barcelona and its architecture*
  - *Regional foods*

3 Connections

- **B Use the language**
  - *Art: Comparing painting styles*
  - *Health: Planning a meal*

4 Comparisons

- **B Concept of culture**
  - *Daily routines and chores in Spain and the U.S.*
  - *Homes in Spain and the U.S.*
- **C Influence**
  - *Appetizers*

5 Communities

- **A Within and beyond school**
  - *Using Spanish with family and friends*
- **B Lifelong learner**
  - *Using Spanish in the workplace*

LA SAGRADA FAMILIA is a church begun by architect Antonio Gaudí (1852–1926). It is not yet finished. What do you think about the style of architecture you see in the photo?

INTERNET Preview
CLASSZONE.COM

- More About Spain
- Webquest
- Self-Check Quizzes
- Flashcards
- Writing Center
- Online Workbook
- eEdition Plus Online

ALMANAQUE CULTURAL

POBLACIÓN: 2.819.000

ALTURA: 12 metros (39 pies)

CLIMA: 10°C (54°F), invierno; 25°C (75°F), verano

COMIDA TÍPICA: mariscos, tapas, paella

GENTE FAMOSA DE BARCELONA: José Carreras (cantante), Antonio Gaudí (arquitecto), Joan Miró (pintor), Pablo Picasso (pintor), Arantxa Sánchez Vicario (tenista)

¿VAS A BARCELONA? Barcelona es la capital de Cataluña, una región de España. Tiene una identidad catalana muy fuerte. La gente habla catalán y español.

More About Spain
CLASSZONE.COM

EL MONUMENTO DE CRISTÓBAL COLÓN commemorates Columbus's meeting with the king and queen of Spain after his first voyage to the Americas. They met in Barcelona in 1493. Who were the king and queen of Spain then?

JOAN MIRÓ (1893–1983) is one of Barcelona's most famous artists. You can see his surrealist works at the **Fundación Miró.** How would you describe this piece by Miró?

Tapestry of the Foundation, Miró Foundation on Montjuic

ACEITUNAS are one of Spain's most important products. Their oil is used to cook Spanish specialties such as **paella** and **tortilla española.** They are also often eaten as **tapas.** What dishes made with olives or olive oil have you eaten?

LAS RAMBLAS is a well-known street in the heart of Barcelona that has it all! Artisans, performers, and vendors sell everything from parakeets to newspapers here. Where might you find something similar in the U.S.?

MIGUEL DE CERVANTES SAAVEDRA (1547–1616) is the most well-known Spanish author. His classic *Don Quijote de la Mancha* is considered to be the first modern novel. What plays or movies are based on this book?

UNIDAD 5

PREPARACIONES ESPECIALES

Texas Essential Knowledge and Skills

1 Comunicación

2 Culturas

3 Conexiones

4 Comparaciones

The student develops insight into the nature of language and culture by comparing the student's own language and culture to another.

5 Comunidades

Comparaciones

If someone offered you pop, a hero, or a cruller, would you know what that meant? In different regions of the United States, pop is soda, a hero is a sandwich, and a cruller is a doughnut. Similar language variations exist among and within Spanish-speaking countries. In this unit, you will learn about and compare customs relating to food and daily life and discover that the same word may mean different things in different places.

Comparaciones en acción **¿Qué prefieres, una tortilla mexicana o una tortilla española? ¡Son muy diferentes! ¿En Estados Unidos hay algún plato similar a la tortilla española?**

Comunicación

An important part of communication is presenting your own ideas to others orally or in writing. Think of your favorite snack or dish. Can you tell a friend how to prepare it?

¿Cómo preparas tu merienda favorita?

Webquest
CLASSZONE.COM

Explore comparisons in Barcelona through guided Web activities.

Culturas

Barcelona is a commercial center, a major seaport, and a popular tourist destination. It was home to the artists Picasso and Miró and the famous architect Gaudí. Visitors will learn about the art, architecture, history, food, and customs of this important city.

Picasso completó esta pintura en 1938. Se llama *Maya con una muñeca.* ¿Qué piensas que es una muñeca?

Conexiones

You have probably learned about health and nutrition in school. In recent years much attention has focused on the healthful diet of the Mediterranean countries, such as Spain, Italy, and Greece. In this unit you will learn about some dishes typical of this region and their ingredients.

¿Qué tipo de productos venden en este mercado de Barcelona?

Comunidades

Does the food of other places interest you? Check the yellow pages of the telephone book for listings of restaurants or grocery stores that specialize in ethnic foods.

¿Qué comes tú si quieres *fast food*? En España comen tapas.

Fíjate

Using the photos and the captions, you can answer these questions and share your opinions.

1. Mira la pintura de Picasso. ¿Cómo se llama la chica?
2. ¿Cuáles son los platos típicos de España y de México que tienen el mismo nombre?
3. ¿Dónde puedes comprar productos frescos en Barcelona?
4. ¿Cuál de las tapas que ves en las fotos te gusta más?

UNIDAD 5

ETAPA 1

¿Cómo es tu rutina?

OBJECTIVES

- Describe daily routine
- Talk about grooming
- Tell others to do something
- Discuss daily chores

¿Qué ves?

Mira la foto del Parque Güell en Barcelona.

1. ¿Es interesante o no el parque?
2. ¿Qué hace la chica?
3. ¿Qué lleva la chica?
4. ¿De qué color es el animal?
5. ¿Cómo se llama el parque de atracciones de Barcelona?

Preparación para el diálogo

En contexto

VIDEO DVD AUDIO

VOCABULARIO

Luis is following his morning routine. Watch him get ready for the day.

A Luis oye **el despertador.** Pero está en **la cama.** ¡Quiere dormir más!

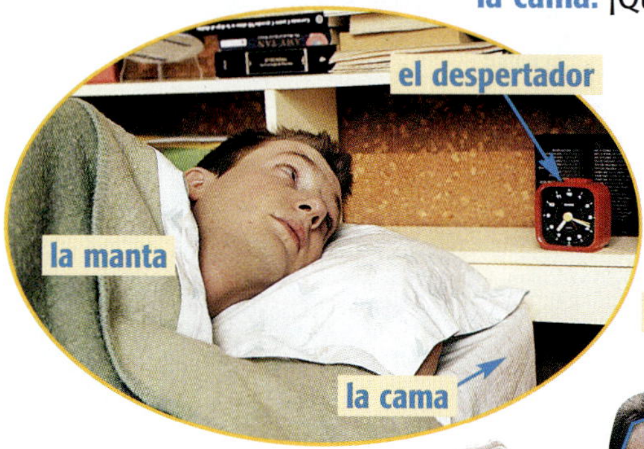

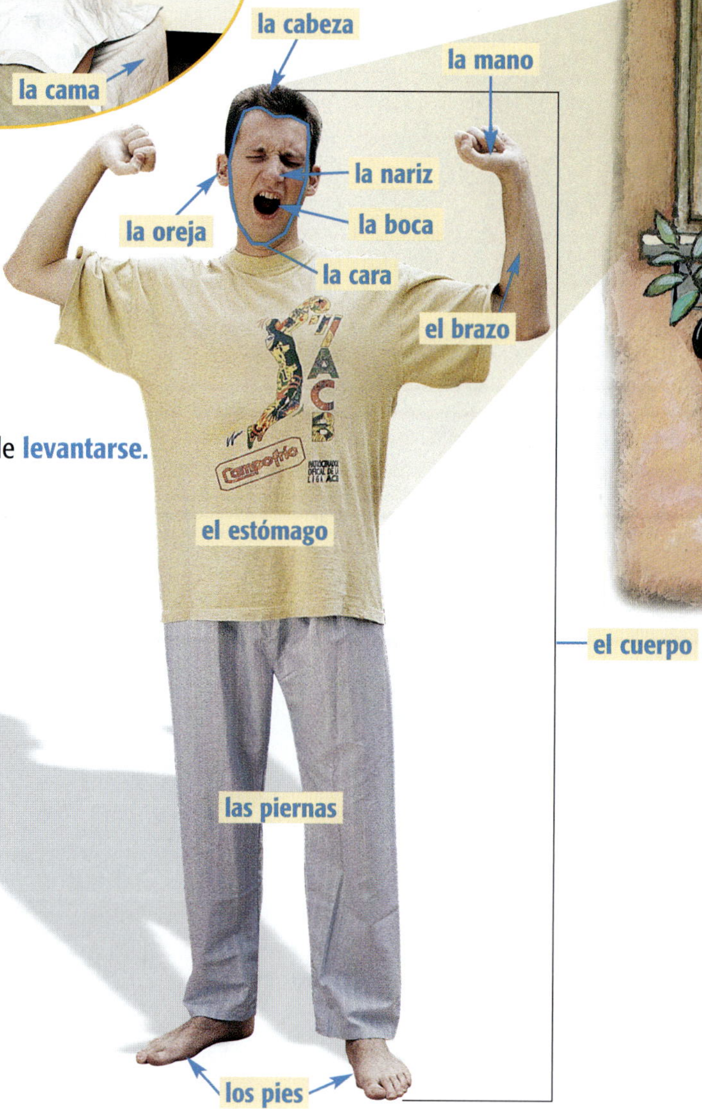

B Luis acaba de **levantarse.**

CD-ROM Take-Home Tutor

C Luis va a **lavarse.** Se lava **la cara** con **jabón** y va a **secarse** con **una toalla.**

D Esta mañana Luis tiene tiempo para **ducharse** y lavarse **la cabeza** con **champú.**

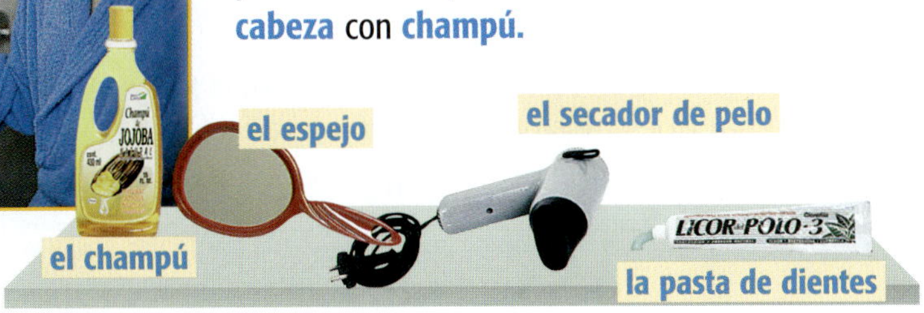

E Luis se lava **los dientes** con **el cepillo de dientes.** Después, va a **peinarse** con **un peine.** ¡Ya está listo!

Online Workbook CLASSZONE.COM

Preguntas personales

1. ¿Usas un despertador?
2. ¿Te lavas la cara por la mañana o por la noche?
3. ¿Usas un secador de pelo o una toalla para secarte el pelo?
4. ¿A qué hora te levantas?
5. ¿Cuándo te lavas los dientes?

VIDEO DVD AUDIO

En vivo

DIÁLOGO

PARA ESCUCHAR • **STRATEGY: LISTENING**

Listen for a mood or a feeling Nothing is going right for Luis. What does he say to show frustration? Jot down some of his expressions for protesting. When would you use them?

Muchos quehaceres

1 ▶ **Juan Carlos:** ¡Luis! ¡Mercedes llega en diez minutos!

Luis: ¡Sí, ya lo sé! ¡Ahora me ducho y salgo! ¡Necesito lavarme los dientes!

5 ▶ **Luis:** Necesito secarme el pelo.

Carmen: ¡Ponte otra camisa! Mírate en el espejo, ¡esta camisa está muy fea! ¡Y no uses mi secador de pelo! ¡Por favor, no lo uses!

6 ▶ **Juan Carlos:** Hijo. Por favor, haz todo lo que está en esta lista.

Luis: Pero, ¿tengo que hacerlo todo hoy?

Juan Carlos: Sí, hijo. Primero haz los quehaceres.

Luis: ¡Pero, papá!

7 ▶ **Lourdes:** Necesitamos varias cosas. Ve a la tienda. Aquí tienes mi lista.

Luis: Mamá, me espera Álvaro.

Lourdes: Pero esto es importante.

Luis: ¡No es justo! ¡Es mi cumpleaños!

2 ▶ **Carmen:** ¡Luis! ¡Luis! ¡Mercedes está aquí!
Luis: ¡Sí, sí, sí! ¡Pero primero me pongo la ropa! ¡Ya voy!

3 ▶ **Luis:** ¡Hola, Mercedes! ¿Cómo estás?
Mercedes: Bien, Luis. ¡Y feliz cumpleaños! ¿Qué tal tu mañana?
Luis: Muy tranquila, gracias.

4 ▶ **Luis:** ¿Qué haces? ¿Por qué me estás sacando fotos? ¡No hagas eso!
Mercedes: Son para un concurso.
Luis: ¿Para qué concurso son?
Mercedes: Te digo luego. Álvaro nos espera en una hora. ¿Estás listo?

8 ▶ **Juan Carlos:** Sí, pero también puedes celebrarlo después. También cuida a tu hermana.
Luis: ¡No puede ser!
Carmen: ¡Ja, ja! ¡Me tienes que cuidar!

9 ▶ **Luis:** Voy a llamar a Álvaro. Nunca vamos a llegar a tiempo.
Mercedes: ¡Pobre Luis! ¡No seas tan dura con él! Es su cumpleaños.
Carmen: ¡Le quiero ver la cara al llegar a su fiesta!

10 ▶ **Luis:** Está ocupado. Lo llamo más tarde. Bueno, vamos. Tenemos muchas cosas que hacer. ¡Carmen, Mercedes!, ¿me ayudáis con los quehaceres?

En acción

PARTE A — Comprensión del diálogo

For Activities 1–2, refer to the dialog on pages 326–327.

1 Frases revueltas

Escuchar Explica lo que pasa en el diálogo. Completa las oraciones, combinando frases de las dos columnas. *(Hint: Explain what happens.)*

1. Cuando Mercedes llega, Luis...
2. Mercedes...
3. Álvaro...
4. A Luis no le gusta...
5. Cuando Luis llama a Álvaro...

a. cuidar a su hermana.
b. no está en casa de Luis.
c. está ocupado.
d. está sacando fotos.
e. no está listo para salir.

2 ¿Qué pasa?

Escuchar Completa las oraciones para describir lo que pasa en el diálogo. *(Hint: Describe what happens.)*

1. Cuando Mercedes llega, Luis está...
2. Mercedes saca fotos para...
3. Cuando Mercedes llega, Luis acaba de...
4. Luis tiene planes para salir con...
5. Luis no está contento porque...

PARTE B — Práctica del vocabulario

Objectives for Activities 3–5
• Describe daily routine • Talk about grooming

3 Antonio va a...

Hablar/*Escribir* Hoy va a ser un día típico para Antonio, un amigo de Carmen. Explica a qué hora va a hacer cada actividad, según los dibujos. *(Hint: Explain when he is going to do each activity.)*

modelo

Antonio va a ***levantarse*** *a las* ***siete y cuarto.***

1.

2.
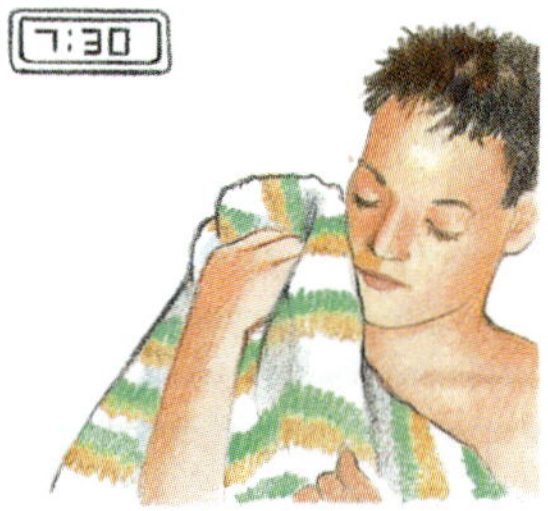

3.

4.

España

También se dice In this unit you will see and hear language that is typical of Spain.

Did you notice that Luis uses the word **ayudáis**? Remember that in Spain the **vosotros(as)** form of verbs is usually used with people one knows well.

In Spain people use certain expressions for daily routine.

to wash one's hair
- **lavarse la cabeza:** Spain
- **lavarse el pelo/el cabello:** many countries

to brush one's teeth
- **lavarse los dientes:** Spain
- **cepillarse los dientes:** many countries

4 En la droguería

Hablar Los padres de Luis están de compras y ven este anuncio. Hablan de lo que necesitan Luis y Carmen. ¿Qué dicen? *(Hint: Say what they need.)*

modelo

Luis (¿?): lavarse

Papá: *¿Necesita **Luis** jabón?*

Mamá: *Sí, lo necesita para **lavarse**.*

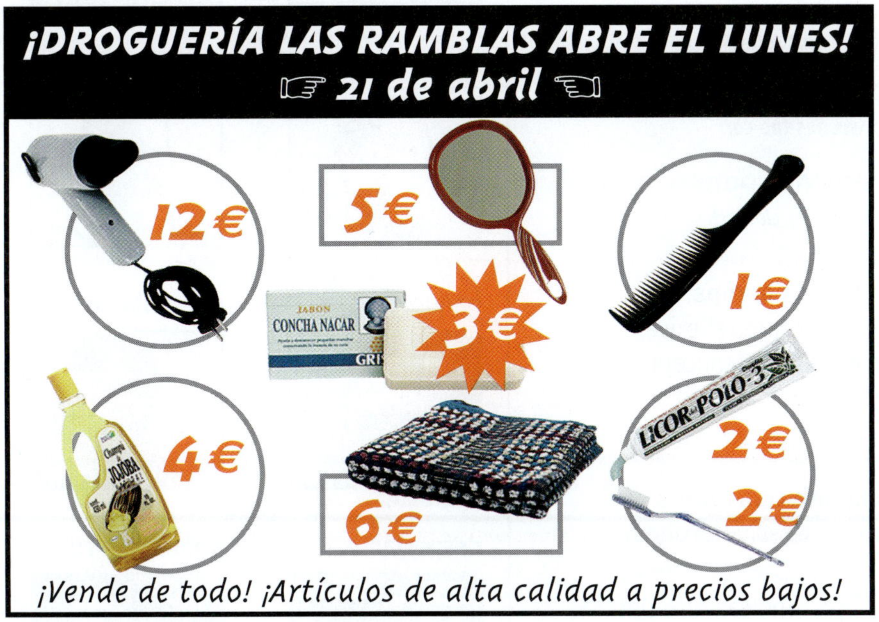

1. Luis (¿?): lavarse los dientes
2. Luis y Carmen (¿?): peinarse
3. Carmen (¿?): lavarse la cabeza
4. Luis y Carmen (¿?): secarse
5. Carmen (¿?): secarse el pelo

5 Para correr...

Hablar Imagínate que un extraterrestre llega a tu casa. Pregúntale cómo hace las siguientes actividades. *(Hint: Ask how the extraterrestrial does these activities.)*

modelo

correr

Tú: *¿Cómo **corres**?*

Extraterrestre: *Para **correr**, uso seis piernas y seis pies.*

1. comer
2. bailar
3. oír
4. escribir
5. pensar
6. nadar
7. caminar
8. tocar el piano
9. ver la televisión
10. jugar al béisbol

PARTE C

Práctica: gramática y vocabulario

Objectives for Activities 6–18
- Describe daily routine • Talk about grooming
- Tell others to do something • Discuss daily chores

GRAMÁTICA Describing Actions That Involve Oneself: Reflexive Verbs

To describe people doing things for themselves, use reflexive verbs. Examples of reflexive actions are *brushing one's teeth* or *combing one's hair.* **Reflexive pronouns** are used with **reflexive verbs** to indicate that the subject of the sentence receives the action of the verb.

lavarse
to wash oneself

me lavo	**nos lavamos**
te lavas	**os laváis**
se lava	**se lavan**

Many verbs can be used with or without **reflexive pronouns**. When there is **no** reflexive pronoun, the person doing the action does **not** receive the action.

reflexive
Pepa **se lava.**
*Pepa **washes herself.***

not reflexive
Pepa **lava el carro.**
*Pepa **washes the car.***

Luis says: —¡Primero **me pongo** la ropa!
*First **I put on** my clothes!*

Notice he says **la ropa,** not **mi ropa,** because reflexive pronouns include the concept of possession.

When you use the **infinitive form** of a reflexive verb **after** a **conjugated verb,** be sure to use the correct **reflexive pronoun**.

Quiero levantarme temprano.
I want to get up early.

Me quiero levantar temprano.

You can also put the **reflexive pronoun in front** of the **conjugated verb.**

Some verbs have different meanings when used reflexively.

dormir (ue) *to sleep*	**dormirse** *to fall asleep*
ir *to go*	**irse** *to leave, to go away*
poner *to put*	**ponerse** *to put on (clothes)*

Practice: 6 7 8 9

Más práctica *cuaderno p. 109*
Para hispanohablantes *cuaderno p. 107*

Online Workbook
CLASSZONE.COM

Vocabulario

Reflexive Verbs

acostarse: o→ue

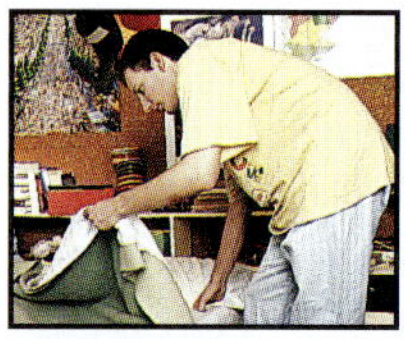

lavarse la cabeza

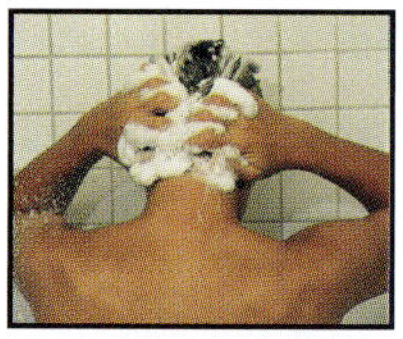

afeitarse

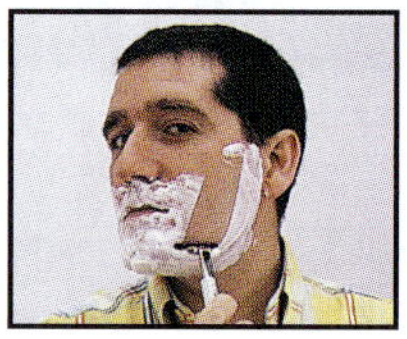

lavarse los dientes

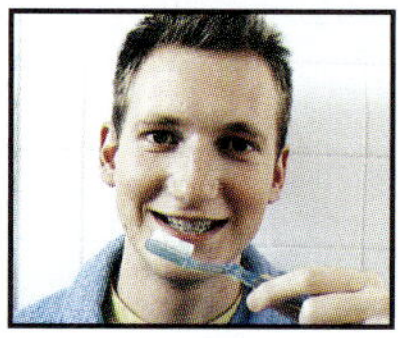

bañarse

maquillarse

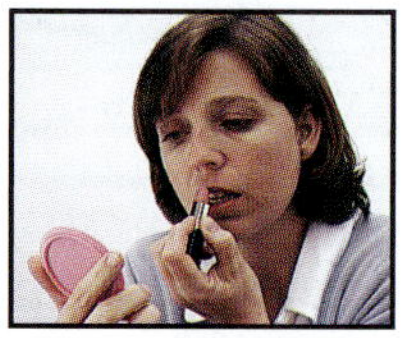

despertarse: e→ie

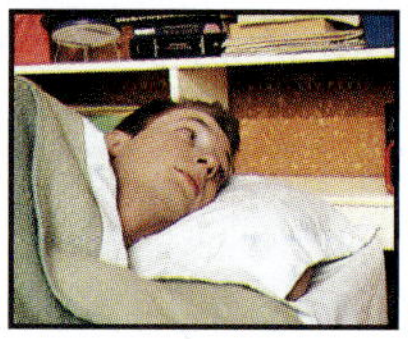

ponerse la ropa

Notice that **acostarse** and **despertarse** are stem-changing verbs.

¿Cuándo haces estas actividades, por la mañana o por la noche?

6 Se lavan...

Escuchar/*Escribir* Luis explica que todos tienen que lavarse después de trabajar mucho. ¿Qué se lavan? *(**Hint:** What is being washed?)*

1. Carmen / lavarse / ¿?
2. los padres de Luis / lavarse / ¿?
3. Mercedes y Luis / lavarse / ¿?
4. Luis / lavarse / ¿?
5. Álvaro / lavarse / ¿?

7 No están listos

Hablar Luis habla de sus amigos. Van a una fiesta. Nadie está listo. ¿Qué tiene que hacer cada uno? *(**Hint:** Say what they have to do.)*

modelo

Marta: lavarse la cabeza

Marta** tiene que **lavarse la cabeza.
o: Marta se** tiene que **lavar la cabeza.
*Siempre **se lava la cabeza** antes de ir a una fiesta.*

1. tú: afeitarse
2. vosotros(as): secarse el pelo
3. tú y Álvaro: lavarse los dientes
4. tú: ducharse
5. Emiliana: maquillarse
6. sus primos: ponerse la ropa nueva
7. Mercedes y Elena: peinarse
8. tu hermana: lavarse la cara
9. Yolanda: bañarse
10. Alfredo: ponerse otra camisa

8 Primero...

Hablar Pregúntale a otro(a) estudiante qué hace primero. *(**Hint:** Which activity do you do first?)*

modelo

¿ducharse o lavarse los dientes?

Estudiante A: *¿Qué haces primero, **te duchas** o **te lavas los dientes?***

Estudiante B: *Primero **me ducho** y luego **me lavo los dientes.***

1. ¿lavarse la cabeza o lavarse la cara?
2. ¿bañarse o lavarse los dientes?
3. ¿afeitarse/maquillarse o peinarse?
4. ¿lavarse la cara o ponerse la ropa?
5. ¿ponerse la ropa o peinarse?
6. ¿peinarse o secarse el pelo?
7. ¿lavarse los dientes o lavarse la cara?
8. ¿ponerse la ropa o maquillarse/afeitarse?

9 Tu día típico

STRATEGY: SPEAKING

Sequence events When telling about several events, make the order in which they occurred clear. Remember these expressions: **primero, entonces, luego, después, antes de..., después de..., por la mañana/tarde.**

Hablar/*Escribir* Describe tu día típico. Usa los verbos de esta lección. *(**Hint:** Describe a typical day.)*

modelo

Primero, me despierto y me levanto a las siete...

GRAMÁTICA Irregular Affirmative tú Commands

¿RECUERDAS? *p. 260* You've already learned how to give instructions to someone by using the **affirmative tú commands** of regular verbs.

caminar	**¡Camina!**
comer	**¡Come!**
abrir	**¡Abre!**

Some verbs have **irregular affirmative tú commands.** Here are the irregular affirmative **tú commands** of some verbs you know.

Infinitive	Affirmative tú Command
decir	**di**
hacer	**haz**
ir	**ve**
poner	**pon**
salir	**sal**
ser	**sé**
tener	**ten**
venir	**ven**

Luis's father says:

—Primero **haz** los quehaceres.
*First **do** the chores.*

Remember that when you use a **pronoun** with an **affirmative command,** the **pronoun attaches** to the **command.**

Carmen says:

—¡**Ponte** otra camisa!
***Put on** (yourself) another shirt!*

Practice: Actividades 10 11 12

Más práctica *cuaderno p. 110*
Para hispanohablantes *cuaderno p. 108*

Online Workbook CLASSZONE.COM

10 ¡Pobre Carmen!

Hablar/*Escribir* Luis siempre le dice a su hermana qué hacer. ¿Qué le dice? *(**Hint:** Give Luis's commands.)*

modelo
poner la mesa
Pon la mesa.

1. ser buena
2. decir la verdad
3. hacer la tarea
4. venir a casa a las seis
5. salir para comprar pan
6. tener paciencia
7. ir a la tienda
8. poner el libro en la mochila
9. tener cuidado
10. ir a la farmacia

Juego

Beto se despierta, se levanta, se ducha, desayuna y sale para la escuela. ¿Qué más necesita hacer esta mañana?

11 ¿Qué hago primero?

Hablar Tienes mucho que hacer hoy. Le preguntas a tu mamá qué debes hacer primero. ¿Qué te dice? *(Hint: Talk about chores.)*

modelo

¿poner la mesa o hacer las camas?

Tú: *¿Qué hago primero?* ***¿Pongo la mesa o hago las camas?***

Mamá: *Primero* ***haz las camas.*** *Después* ***pon la mesa.***

1. ¿hacer la cama o preparar el desayuno?
2. ¿limpiar el cuarto o comprar comida?
3. ¿ir a la tienda o hacer los otros quehaceres?
4. ¿quitar la mesa o lavar los platos?
5. ¿hacer ejercicio o lavar la ropa sucia?
6. ¿mandar la carta o ir al supermercado?
7. ¿poner la mesa o caminar con el perro?
8. ¿hacer la tarea o tocar el piano?

12 Los amigos ayudan

Hablar/*Escribir* Mercedes les pide mucho a sus amigos. ¿Qué les pide? *(Hint: What does Mercedes ask?)*

modelo

Ángela: poner ¿?

Ángela, pon *los libros en mi mochila, por favor.*

1. Luis: ser ¿?
2. Andrés: salir para ¿?
3. Marta: venir a ¿?
4. Álvaro: tener ¿?
5. Lucía: hacer ¿?
6. Paco: decir ¿?
7. Linda: ir ¿?
8. Carmen: poner ¿?
9. Andrés: tener ¿?
10. Teresa: hacer ¿?

More Practice: **Más comunicación** *p. R13*

Vocabulario

Para hablar de los quehaceres

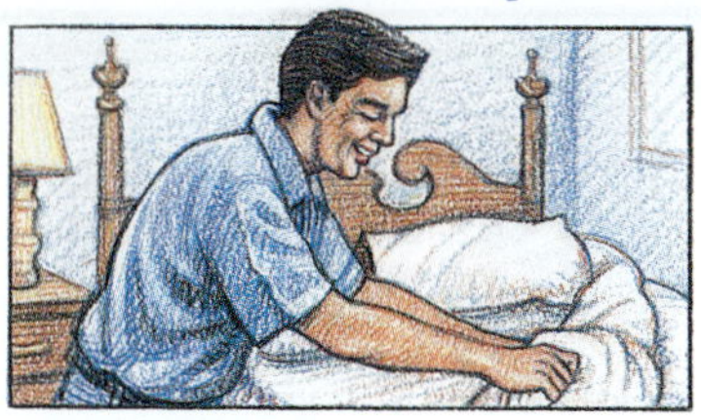

hacer la cama

lavar los platos

limpiar el cuarto

quitar la mesa

estar **limpio(a)**

estar **sucio(a)**

En tu familia, ¿quién hace estos quehaceres?

GRAMÁTICA Negative tú Commands

When you tell someone what **not** to do, use a **negative command.** **Negative tú commands** are formed by taking the **yo** form of the present tense, dropping the **-o**, and adding the appropriate ending.

hablo ← **-es** for **-ar** verbs

vuelvo ← **-as** for **-er** and **-ir** verbs

Infinitive	Yo Form	Negative tú Command
hablar	**hablo**	**¡No hables!**
volver	**vuelvo**	**¡No vuelvas!**
venir	**vengo**	**¡No vengas!**

Carmen says:

—¡Y **no uses** mi secador de pelo!
*And **don't use** my hair dryer!*

A few verbs have **irregular negative tú commands.** Notice that none of the **yo** forms of these verbs end in **-o**.

Infinitive (yo form)	Negative tú Command
dar (doy)	**No** le **des** mi dirección a nadie. *Don't give my address to anyone.*
estar (estoy)	**No estés** triste. *Don't be sad.*
ir (voy)	**No vayas** a la tienda. *Don't go to the store.*
ser (soy)	**No seas** mala. *Don't be bad.*

Practice:
Actividades
13 14 15

Más práctica
cuaderno p. 111
Para hispanohablantes
cuaderno p. 109

Online Workbook
CLASSZONE.COM

13 ¡No, no, no!

Hablar/*Escribir* Cuando Luis cuida a su hermana menor, ella hace cosas que no debe hacer. Luis siempre le dice que no. *(Hint: What does Luis say?)*

modelo
patinar en la calle
*Carmen, no **patines en la calle.***

1. correr en la casa
2. ver la televisión antes de hacer la tarea
3. hablar mucho por teléfono
4. abrir el libro de papá
5. mirar mis videos
6. comer muchos dulces
7. usar mis discos compactos
8. beber tantos refrescos
9. ir al parque muy tarde
10. venir tarde a comer

España

Nota cultural

Many people in Barcelona speak **catalán.** Can you guess what these **catalán** words mean?

Bon dia
Benvinguts
museu

14 Las instrucciones

Hablar/*Escribir* Estás cuidando a un niño de seis años. ¿Qué instrucciones le das?
*(**Hint:** What do you say to a six-year-old?)*

modelo

correr en la casa

***No corras en la casa.** Corre en el parque.*

1. poner los libros en el gimnasio
2. ser malo
3. salir de la casa solo
4. comer dulces antes de cenar
5. estar triste
6. decir malas palabras
7. llevar mi chaqueta
8. dormir en el sofá
9. hablar con personas que no conoces
10. escribir en tu libro

15 Cuando salgo, mis padres me dicen...

Hablar/*Escribir* ¿Cuáles son las instrucciones que te dan tus padres cuando sales? Habla con los otros estudiantes de la clase. Cada estudiante dice un mínimo de dos instrucciones. ¿Cuáles son las cinco instrucciones más comunes?
*(**Hint:** What instructions do your parents give you?)*

modelo

Tú: *Ana, ¿qué te dicen tus padres cuando sales?*

Ana: *Haz la tarea antes de salir. No salgas sola. Sé buena. No vayas lejos. Regresa a las ocho.*

Persona	Instrucciones afirmativas	Instrucciones negativas
Ana	Haz la tarea.	No salgas sola.
	Sé buena.	No vayas lejos.
	Regresa a las ocho.	

GRAMÁTICA Using Correct Pronoun Placement with Commands

¿RECUERDAS? *p. 260* Remember that when you use an **object pronoun** with an **affirmative command,** you **attach** the pronoun to the end of the command.

Cruza el parque. → **¡Crúzalo!**
Cross** the park.* → ***Cross it!

Object pronouns precede the verbs in **negative commands,** just as with other conjugated verbs.

Carmen says:

—**¡No lo uses!**
Don't use it (the hair dryer)!

Remember, you may need to add an **accent** when you attach a pronoun.

Practice: Actividades 16 17

Más práctica *cuaderno p. 112*
Para hispanohablantes *cuaderno p. 110*

Online Workbook
CLASSZONE.COM

16 En el restaurante

Hablar/Escribir Tu amigo(a) no puede decidir qué hacer en el restaurante. Contesta sus preguntas. *(Hint: Answer your friend's questions.)*

modelo

¿Bebo limonada? (sí) *¿Pido enchiladas? (no)*

Sí, bébela. *No, no las pidas.*

1. ¿Leo el menú? (sí)
2. ¿Como el arroz? (sí)
3. ¿Comparto los frijoles? (no)
4. ¿Pido las bebidas? (sí)
5. ¿Tomo el café? (no)
6. ¿Bebo el té? (sí)
7. ¿Uso el tenedor? (no)
8. ¿Pido un postre? (no)
9. ¿Pago la cuenta? (sí)
10. ¿Dejo la propina? (no)

17 ¡No lo hagas ahora!

Hablar Tu amigo(a) quiere salir pero tú tienes muchos quehaceres hoy. ¿Qué te dice? *(Hint: Give commands.)*

modelo

hacer la cama

Tú: *Tengo que **hacer la cama.***

Tu amigo(a): *No **la hagas** ahora. **Hazla** más tarde.*

1. limpiar el cuarto
2. poner la mesa
3. lavar los platos
4. preparar la cena
5. comprar pan
6. hacer la tarea
7. cuidar las plantas
8. escribir una carta
9. estudiar la lección
10. contestar el teléfono

18 ¡Las decisiones!

Hablar Quieres hacer algo, pero tienes que hacer otra cosa. Escoge una situación y pregúntales a cinco estudiantes qué hacer. *(Hint: Ask five students what to do.)*

modelo

Quieres ver la televisión pero tienes tarea.

Tú: *¿Veo la televisión o hago la tarea?*

Estudiante 1: *No veas la televisión. Haz la tarea.*

Estudiante 2: *Primero, haz la tarea y luego, ve la televisión.*

1. Quieres alquilar un video pero tienes que visitar a tus abuelos.
2. Quieres descansar pero tus amigos quieren andar en bicicleta.
3. Quieres cenar en un restaurante pero tienes que preparar la cena en casa.
4. Quieres acostarte pero tienes que estudiar para un examen.
5. Quieres ir a una tienda pero puedes regatear en el mercado.

España

Nota cultural

Rock con raíces, or Root-Rock, has become popular with urban youth in Spain. It blends traditional elements of **flamenco,** such as castanets and hand claps, with electric guitars and synthesizers. Rosario's music has many flamenco influences.

PARTE D

Todo en acción

Activities 19–20 bring together all concepts presented.

19 La rutina de Álvaro

Escuchar Lee las oraciones. Luego, escucha el diálogo y di si las oraciones son ciertas o falsas. Corrige las falsas. *(Hint: Say what is true.)*

1. Álvaro se despierta a las nueve los sábados.
2. Álvaro se queda en la cama un rato después de despertarse.
3. Álvaro se lava la cara y los dientes después de levantarse.
4. Álvaro no se baña los sábados.
5. Álvaro se afeita y se lava la cabeza por la noche.

20 La Farmacia Véndetodo

Escribir Trabajas en una farmacia. Escribe un anuncio sobre algunos productos. Usa los verbos reflexivos para describir los productos. Usa los mandatos (afirmativos y negativos) para decirles a los clientes qué comprar. *(Hint: Write an ad for a pharmacy.)*

More Practice:

Más comunicación *p. R13*

Online Workbook
CLASSZONE.COM

Pronunciación

Trabalenguas

Pronunciación de la *s*, la *z* y la *c* In the Spanish spoken in Latin America and southern Spain, the **s** and **z** always sound like the *s* in the English word *miss*. When **c** is followed by the vowel **i** or **e**, it has the same sound. In central and northern Spain, the **z** and **c** are not pronounced like an *s*, but like the *th* sound in the English word *thin,* when they are followed by **i** or **e.** So if you go to Barcelona, you may want to try the *th* sound! Practice the sounds by repeating the following words. Then try the tongue twister! From the picture, can you guess what it means?

cabeza **pasta de dientes**
cepillo **secador**
lápiz

¡El sapo del centro sirve zumo sabroso!

AUDIO

En voces

LECTURA

Una exhibición especial de Picasso

PARA LEER • STRATEGY: READING

Scan for crucial details Before you decide to visit the exhibit **«Picasso y los retratos»** there is some practical information you need to know. Look quickly to pick up certain details. Can you find the answers in the article? If you can, jot them down.

1. **¿En qué museo está la exhibición?**
2. **¿Cuándo termina?**

Si te levantas el sábado y tienes ganas de ir a un museo, hay una exhibición especial en el Museo Picasso de Barcelona. Es una colección de retratos[1] de Pablo Picasso. La exhibición se llama «Picasso y los retratos». Es posible verla hasta el 31 de julio.

Las pinturas de la exhibición «Picasso y los retratos» son de varios estilos. En algunos retratos, por ejemplo *Retrato de Jaime Sabatés*, usa un estilo tradicional. En otros retratos vemos el desarrollo[2] de la pintura moderna en la composición de las partes del cuerpo: la cara, las orejas, los brazos y las piernas. Un ejemplo es *Maya con una muñeca*.

[1] portraits [2] development

España

Nota cultural

Pablo Ruiz Picasso (1881–1973) was born in Málaga. In 1895 he moved with his family to Barcelona. He studied classical art there and later painted on his own. After several trips to France, Picasso moved there in 1904. This is one of his self-portraits.

En catalán la palabra **museo** se dice **museu.**

Retrato de Jaime Sabatés, *1899–1900 Un retrato de Jaime Sabatés, gran amigo de Picasso. Sabatés le dio*[5] *su importante colección de obras*[6] *de Picasso al museo.*

Maya con una muñeca, 1938

Los retratos de Picasso también nos dan una idea de su vida privada. Hay retratos de sus amigos, sus hijos y las mujeres importantes en su vida.

Si vas a la exhibición, aprovecha[3] tu visita para ver otras obras de este pintor español en nuestro Museo Picasso. ¡Hay más de tres mil[4]!

---

[3] take advantage of
[4] thousand
[5] gave
[6] works

Online Workbook
CLASSZONE.COM

¿Comprendiste?

1. ¿Cómo se llama la exhibición especial del Museo Picasso de Barcelona?
2. ¿Cuáles son dos estilos de retratos de la exhibición?
3. ¿De quiénes son los retratos de la exhibición?
4. ¿Cómo se llama el amigo que Picasso pintó?
5. ¿Cuántas obras de Picasso hay normalmente en el Museo Picasso de Barcelona?

¿Qué piensas?

Mira los dos retratos que están al lado del artículo. ¿Qué diferencias hay entre los dos?

ETAPA 1

En uso

REPASO Y MÁS COMUNICACIÓN

OBJECTIVES

- Describe daily routine
- Talk about grooming
- Tell others to do something
- Discuss daily chores

Now you can...

- describe daily routine.

To review

- reflexive verbs, see p. 330.

1 Nuestra rutina diaria

Un amigo de Luis describe la rutina diaria de su familia. ¿Qué dice? *(Hint: Describe his family's daily routine.)*

modelo

Todos los días yo __me despierto__ *a las siete.*

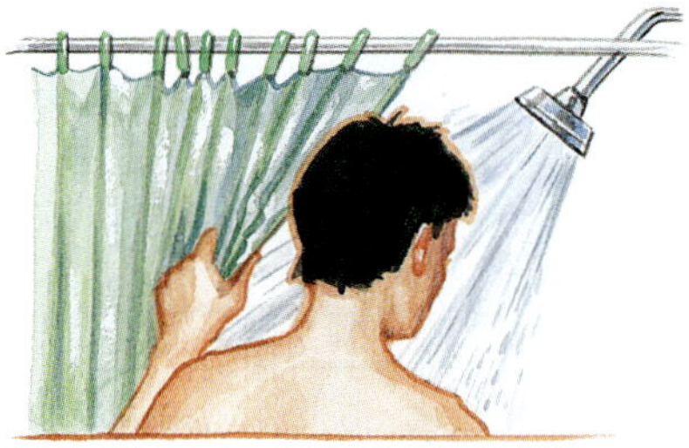

1. Mis padres _____ a las seis y media.
2. Yo _____ después de levantarme.

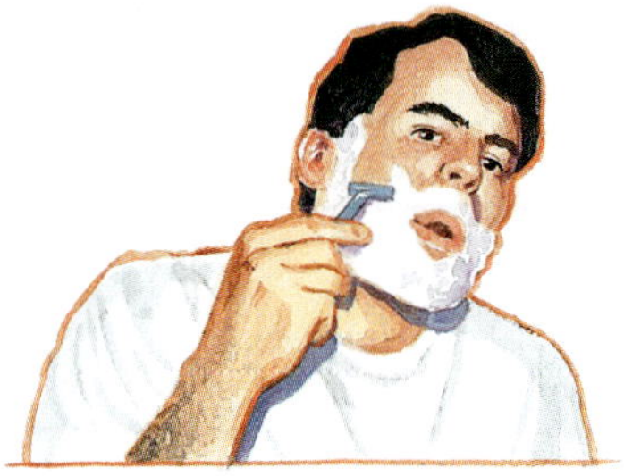

3. Papá _____ a las siete menos cuarto.
4. Mamá _____ antes de prepararnos el desayuno.

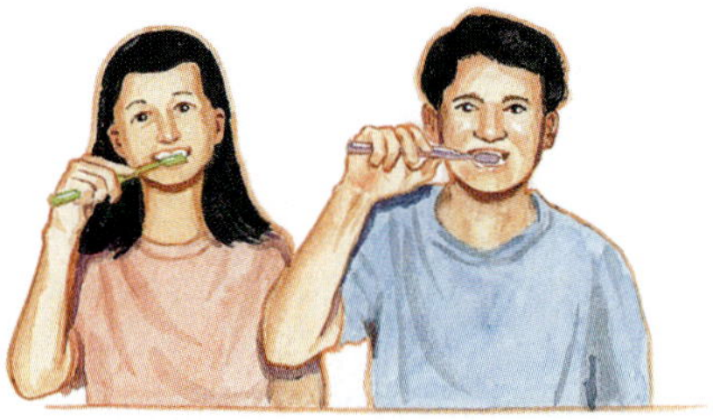

5. Nosotros _____ los dientes después del desayuno.
6. Mi hermana _____ por la noche.

Self-Check Quiz
CLASSZONE.COM

Now you can...
- talk about grooming.

To review
- reflexive verbs, see p. 330.

2 ¡De viaje!

Luis y su familia van a hacer un viaje. ¿Qué necesitan llevar todos? *(Hint: Say what they need.)*

modelo

lavarse la cara (yo)

Yo** necesito jabón para **lavarme la cara.

1. maquillarse (mamá)
2. lavarse los dientes (tú)
3. despertarse (nosotros)
4. secarse (tú)
5. lavarse la cabeza (yo)
6. secarse el pelo (Carmen y yo)
7. peinarse (papá)
8. lavarse las manos (ustedes)

Now you can...
- tell others to do something.

To review
- irregular affirmative **tú** commands, see p. 332.
- negative **tú** commands, see p. 334.

3 En casa de los abuelos

Vas a pasar el fin de semana con tus abuelos. ¿Qué te dice tu mamá? *(Hint: What does your mother say?)*

modelo

ser simpático(a)

Sé simpático(a).

levantarte muy tarde

No te levantes muy tarde.

1. hacer los quehaceres
2. ser perezoso(a)
3. salir con tus abuelos y no con tus amigos
4. ir a fiestas con tus amigos
5. decir cosas interesantes
6. ser bueno(a)
7. ponerte otra camisa
8. llevar ropa sucia
9. ir al supermercado con tu abuela
10. tener paciencia con tus abuelos

Now you can...
- tell others to do something.
- discuss daily chores.

To review
- pronoun placement with commands, see p. 335.

4 ¡A trabajar!

Un(a) amigo(a) quiere ayudarte con los quehaceres. Contesta sus preguntas. *(Hint: Answer a friend's questions.)*

modelo

¿Compro los refrescos? (sí)

Sí, cómpralos.

¿Preparo la cena? (no)

No, no la prepares.

1. ¿Hago las camas? (sí)
2. ¿Lavo los platos sucios? (sí)
3. ¿Cuido a tu hermano? (no)
4. ¿Quito la mesa? (no)
5. ¿Mando las cartas? (sí)
6. ¿Contesto el teléfono? (no)

5 Todos los días...

STRATEGY: SPEAKING

Use gestures Physical actions, gestures, and body language convey meaning too. Watch your partner's actions. Do they convey meaning? Observe others, especially native speakers, and mimic body language to enhance meaning when you speak.

Describe tu rutina diaria. Explica a qué hora haces las actividades. Mientras hablas, otro(a) estudiante tiene que hacer las acciones. Cambien de papel. *(Hint: Describe your routine as your partner acts it out.)*

modelo

Me levanto a las seis de la mañana. Después de levantarme, siempre me ducho. A las seis y media...

despertarse
bañarse
afeitarse
levantarse
lavarse la cabeza
ducharse
peinarse
maquillarse
ponerse la ropa

6 ¡Necesito consejos!

Imagínate que tienes uno de los problemas de la lista. ¿Qué consejo van a darte tus compañeros? *(Hint: What advice do they give?)*

modelo

Tú: *Siempre tengo sueño en mis clases. Estoy cansado todo el día.*

Estudiante 1: *Acuéstate más temprano.*

Estudiante 2: *No te levantes hasta las siete.*

- Tu casa es un desastre y tus padres tienen una fiesta esta noche.
- Estás enfermo(a).
- Siempre tienes sueño en tus clases.
- Sacas malas notas en la clase de español.
- Comes mucho y no haces ejercicio.
- Estás muy sucio(a) después de trabajar mucho.
- ¿?

7 En tu propia voz

ESCRITURA Describe un sábado típico en tu casa. Incluye las rutinas y los quehaceres de los miembros de tu familia. *(Hint: Describe a Saturday.)*

CONEXIONES

El arte Which kind of art do you prefer? Modern? Traditional? Still life? Portraits? Who is your favorite painter? Paint (or draw) a portrait (**un retrato**) or a still life (**una naturaleza muerta**) in the style you prefer. Then explain to a partner what is in your painting. Compare your painting (in terms of style, subject, and colors) with your partner's. Complete a Venn diagram.

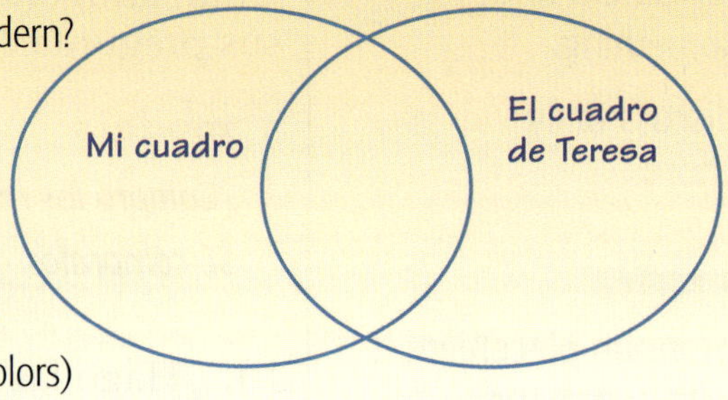

En resumen

REPASO DE VOCABULARIO

DESCRIBING DAILY ROUTINE

acostarse (ue)	*to go to bed*
afeitarse	*to shave oneself*
bañarse	*to take a bath*
despertarse (ie)	*to wake up*
dormirse (ue)	*to fall asleep*
ducharse	*to take a shower*
lavarse	*to wash oneself*
lavarse la cabeza	*to wash one's hair*
lavarse los dientes	*to brush one's teeth*
levantarse	*to get up*
maquillarse	*to put on makeup*
peinarse	*to comb one's hair*
ponerse la ropa	*to get dressed*
secarse	*to dry oneself*

TALKING ABOUT GROOMING

Items

el cepillo (de dientes)	*brush (toothbrush)*
el champú	*shampoo*
el espejo	*mirror*
el jabón	*soap*
la pasta de dientes	*toothpaste*
el peine	*comb*
el secador de pelo	*hair dryer*
la toalla	*towel*

Parts of the Body

la boca	*mouth*
el brazo	*arm*
la cabeza	*head*
la cara	*face*
el cuerpo	*body*
el diente	*tooth*
el estómago	*stomach*
la mano	*hand*
la nariz	*nose*
la oreja	*ear*
el pie	*foot*
la pierna	*leg*

DISCUSSING DAILY CHORES

hacer la cama	*to make the bed*
lavar los platos	*to wash the dishes*
limpiar el cuarto	*to clean the room*
limpio(a)	*clean*
los quehaceres	*chores*
quitar la mesa	*to clear the table*
sucio(a)	*dirty*

OTHER WORDS AND PHRASES

la cama	*bed*
el despertador	*alarm clock*
duro(a)	*hard, tough*
irse	*to leave, to go away*
la manta	*blanket*
ponerse	*to put on (clothes)*

Juego

Ya son las siete. ¿Qué necesitan estos chicos para prepararse y llegar a tiempo a la escuela?

1.

2.

3.

4.

UNIDAD 5

ETAPA 2

¿Qué debo hacer?

OBJECTIVES

- Say what people are doing
- Persuade others
- Describe a house
- Negotiate responsibilities

¿Qué ves?

Mira la foto de la tienda.

1. ¿La tienda vende muchas o pocas frutas?
2. ¿Quién compra muchas frutas: Carmen, Mercedes o Luis?
3. ¿Cuánto cuesta el pan?

AGUD

En contexto

VIDEO DVD AUDIO

VOCABULARIO

Luis and Carmen have a lot of chores to do! See what they do to clean up their house.

A Luis **barre el suelo** de **la cocina.**

B

En **la habitación** de Luis hay **una lámpara** y **un armario.** Aquí todo ya está limpio.

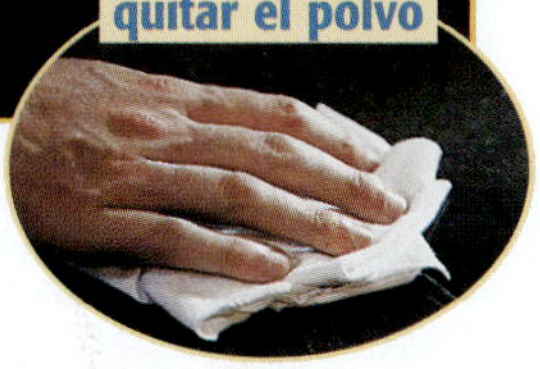

D Luis **quita el polvo** de **la mesa** del **comedor.** También tiene que quitar el polvo de **las sillas.**

E Cuando terminan, Luis cierra **la puerta** de la casa con **la llave** y sale con Carmen.

C En **la sala** Carmen **pasa la aspiradora.** Aquí hay **unos muebles,** como **el sofá** y **el sillón.** También hay un televisor.

Preguntas personales

1. ¿Tienes jardín?
2. ¿Prefieres barrer el suelo o pasar la aspiradora?
3. ¿Quitas el polvo en la sala o en tu habitación?
4. ¿Dónde hay una mesa en tu casa?
5. ¿Qué muebles hay en tu habitación?

VIDEO DVD AUDIO

En vivo
DIÁLOGO

Luis

Carmen

Mercedes

PARA ESCUCHAR • STRATEGY: LISTENING

Note and compare Jot down what you do to help around the house. Then listen and note what Luis, Carmen, and Mercedes are doing. How are your lists similar? How are they different? Who does more? What do you think of Carmen's approach to her chores?

Yo	Luis, Carmen y Mercedes

¡A limpiar la casa!

1 ▶ **Luis:** Carmen, Mercedes, ¿me ayudáis con los quehaceres?
Carmen: ¿Por qué te debo ayudar?
Luis: A ver. ¿Porque eres una hermana muy maja?

5 ▶ **Luis:** En vez de sacar fotos, debes ayudarme. Si no me ayudas, vamos a llegar tarde a casa de Álvaro.
Mercedes: Está bien, Luis. Ahora te estoy ayudando.

6 ▶ **Luis:** Carmen, ¿qué estás haciendo? ¿Por qué no estás pasando la aspiradora?
Carmen: Sí, sí, mira, estoy pasándola.

7 ▶ **Luis:** Pero, Carmen, debes pasarla cuidadosamente. Mira, hazlo como lo estoy haciendo yo, lentamente.
Carmen: ¡Ay, pero Luis! Quiero terminar rápidamente.

2► **Luis:** Porque si limpias la sala, te llevo al cine mañana.
Carmen: ¿Eso es todo?
Luis: Te doy un regalo.

3► **Carmen:** ¿Qué me vas a dar? ¡Dámelo ahora!
Luis: No, no, después. Primero quita el polvo de la mesa.
Carmen: Ya, ya, estoy quitándolo.

4► **Luis:** ¿Todavía estás sacando fotos?
Mercedes: Sí, estoy sacándolas para algo muy importante.
Luis: Estoy barriendo el suelo.
Mercedes: Claro, veo que estás barriéndolo. Pero necesito las fotos.

8► **Luis:** Todavía hay que lavar los platos y sacar la basura.
Mercedes: Tú debes sacar la basura. Yo ayudo a Carmen a lavar los platos. ¿Está bien, Carmen?

9► **Carmen:** ¡Sí, perfecto!
Luis: Bueno. Y después vamos a la tienda.

10► **Luis:** Pero, ¿qué hacéis? ¿Y los platos?
Mercedes: Estamos lavándolos, ¿no ves?

En acción

PARTE A — Comprensión del diálogo

For Activities 1–2, refer to the dialog on pages 348–349.

1 ¿Quién hace qué?

Escuchar ¿Quién(es) hace(n) cada quehacer según el diálogo: Carmen, Mercedes o Luis? *(Hint: Say who does each chore.)*

1. quita el polvo
2. barre el suelo
3. pasa la aspiradora
4. saca la basura
5. lava los platos

2 ¿Cierto o falso?

Escuchar ¿Es cierto o falso? Corrige las falsas. *(Hint: True or false? Correct the false ones.)*

1. Luis tiene muchos quehaceres.
2. Carmen no ayuda a Luis con los quehaceres.
3. Mercedes está sacando fotos.
4. Mercedes y Luis no van a salir esta tarde.
5. Mercedes ayuda a Carmen a lavar los platos.

España

También se dice

There are different ways to describe a really wonderful person. Luis uses **una hermana muy maja.**

Es muy **maja:** Spain
Es muy **buena onda:** Mexico
Es muy **buena gente:** many countries

PARTE B — Práctica del vocabulario

Objectives for Activities 3–6
• Describe a house • Negotiate responsibilities

3 ¿Dónde pongo...?

Hablar La señora Díaz acaba de entrar en su nueva casa. Su hijo le pregunta dónde poner los muebles y otras cosas. ¿Qué dicen? *(Hint: Say in which room these things belong.)*

modelo
Su hijo: *¿Dónde pongo **la mesa**?*
Señora Díaz: *Ponla en la cocina.*

1. 
2. 
3. 
4. 
5. 
6. 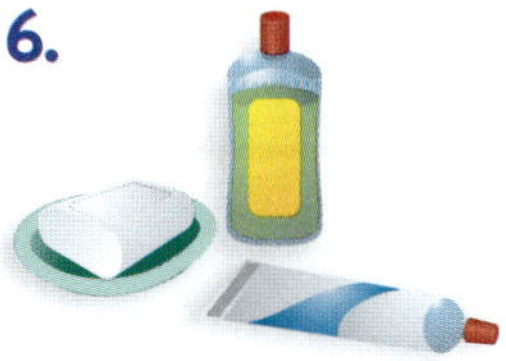
7. 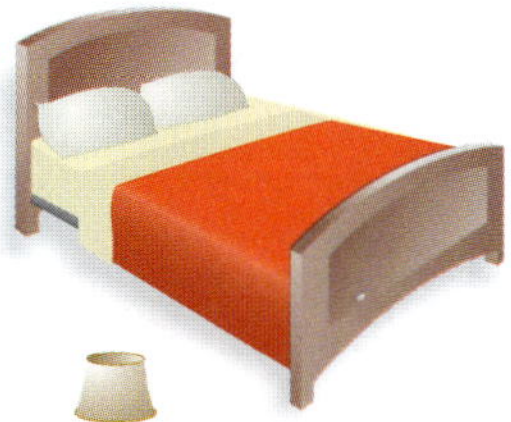
8. 
9. 
10. 

4 La casa

Leer/*Escribir* Todos hablan de la casa. ¿Qué dicen? Escoge la respuesta más apropiada para cada oración. *(Hint: Choose the appropriate answer.)*

1. Siempre dormimos en _____.
   a. el baño
   b. el comedor
   c. las habitaciones
2. Normalmente, veo la televisión en _____.
   a. la sala
   b. el baño
   c. el jardín
3. Mi abuela prepara un almuerzo rico en la _____.
   a. pared
   b. cocina
   c. puerta
4. Abro la puerta con _____.
   a. el suelo
   b. la llave
   c. la ventana
5. Comemos en el _____.
   a. baño
   b. suelo
   c. comedor
6. Hay flores y plantas bonitas en _____.
   a. el jardín
   b. la pared
   c. la puerta

5 El plano de la casa

Hablar/*Escribir* Imagínate que eres arquitecto(a). Indícale a tu cliente cada cuarto o lugar en el plano de la casa. *(Hint: What is in the house?)*

modelo

Aquí está la sala. La sala tiene una puerta y tres ventanas.

España

Nota cultural

When you ask for a **tortilla** in a restaurant in Spain, don't expect the kind of **tortilla** you eat in Mexico! In Spain, a **tortilla** is a dish made with eggs that is a lot like an omelet.

Práctica: gramática y vocabulario

Objectives for Activities 7–19
- Say what people are doing
- Persuade others

6 Si tú pones la mesa...

STRATEGY: SPEAKING
Negotiate Choose the chore you'd rather do. Then talk with your partner, who will express a preference. Decide who will do each.

Hablar Habla con un(a) amigo(a) sobre los quehaceres y escoge entre dos. *(Hint: Choose a chore.)*

modelo

poner la mesa / preparar la cena

Tú: *Si tú pones la mesa, yo preparo la cena.*

Amigo(a): *Prefiero preparar la cena.*

Tú: *Está bien. Yo pongo la mesa y tú preparas la cena.*

Nota: Vocabulario

Use **si** (with no accent!) to say *if*.

Si tú pones la mesa, yo preparo la cena.
If you set the table, I'll make dinner.

1. quitar la mesa / lavar los platos
2. hacer las camas / preparar el almuerzo
3. pasar la aspiradora / barrer el suelo
4. lavar la ropa / quitar el polvo
5. cuidar al hermano / ir al supermercado

GRAMÁTICA Pronouns with the Present Progressive

¿RECUERDAS? *p. 232* Remember how you use the **present progressive** to describe actions in progress?

estoy esper**ando**	estamos esper**ando**
estás esper**ando**	estáis esper**ando**
está esper**ando**	están esper**ando**

When you use **pronouns** with the **present progressive,** you can put them in one of two places.

- Put pronouns **before** the conjugated form of **estar...**
- or **attach** them to the end of the **present participle**.

Mercedes says:

attached

—**Estoy sacándolas** para algo muy importante.
***I'm taking them** (the pictures) for something very important.*

You need to add an **accent** when you attach a pronoun.
barriéndolo

She could have said:

before

—**Las estoy sacando** para algo muy importante.

Some verbs you know have **irregular present participle forms.**

- When the **stem** of an **-er** or **-ir** verb ends in a vowel, change the **-iendo** to **-yendo** to form the present participle.
- **e → i** stem-changing verbs have a vowel change in the stem.
- Some other verbs also have a vowel change in the stem.

Verb	Irregular Present Participle
leer	leyendo
oír	oyendo
traer	trayendo
pedir	pidiendo
servir	sirviendo
decir	diciendo
dormir	durmiendo
venir	viniendo

Practice:
Actividades 7 8 9 10 11

Más práctica
cuaderno pp. 117–118
Para hispanohablantes
cuaderno pp. 115–116

Online Workbook
CLASSZONE.COM

7 De compras

Hablar Mercedes y sus amigos están en un supermercado. Están comprando comida para una fiesta. Una prima la encuentra y quiere saber quién está comprando la comida con ella. *(Hint: Say who's buying the food.)*

modelo

las aceitunas (María)

Su prima: *¿Quién está comprando **las aceitunas**?*

Mercedes: ***María** las está comprando.*
***o:** **María** está comprándolas.*

1. el jamón (Enrique y Pedro)
2. la tortilla española (Marta)
3. los calamares (Isabel y Rocío)
4. el chorizo (Ana y yo)
5. el pan (Álvaro)

Vocabulario

Las tapas

las aceitunas *olives*

el chorizo *sausage*

los calamares *squid*

el jamón *ham*

la tortilla española *potato omelet*

Las tapas son porciones pequeñas de comida. ¿Cuáles te gustan?

8 ¡Todos están ocupados!

Hablar Tu mamá te deja una lista de quehaceres. Pides ayuda, pero todos están ocupados. *(Hint: Ask for help.)*

modelo

preparar la comida (lavarse la cabeza)

Estudiante A: *¿Me puedes ayudar a **preparar la comida?***

Estudiante B: *No puedo. Estoy **lavándome la cabeza**.*
***o:** No puedo. **Me** estoy **lavando** la cabeza.*

Nota: Gramática

When using the present progressive, place reflexive pronouns as you would place direct and indirect object pronouns.

1. hacer la cama (lavarse la cabeza)
2. poner la mesa (afeitarse)
3. pasar la aspiradora (secarse el pelo)
4. barrer el suelo (ponerse la ropa)
5. lavar la ropa (peinarse)
6. limpiar la cocina (ponerse la ropa)
7. hacer el almuerzo (lavarse las manos)
8. lavar los platos (maquillarse)
9. quitar la mesa (bañarse)
10. quitar el polvo (ducharse)

9 ¡Qué inteligente!

Escuchar Álvaro llama a una amiga para invitarla a salir. Escucha su conversación. Luego, explica lo que están haciendo las personas. *(Hint: Say what they are doing.)*

1. la madre de Ana
2. sus hermanos
3. sus hermanas
4. Ana

10 ¡Lo está haciendo ahora!

Hablar Álvaro y unos amigos están limpiando su casa. Su madre le pregunta si van a hacer algunos quehaceres. *(Hint: Say who's doing what.)*

modelo

1. vosotros

Su madre: *¿**Vosotros** vais a **limpiar el cuarto**?*

Álvaro: ***Lo estamos limpiando** ahora.*
***o: Estamos limpiándolo** ahora.*

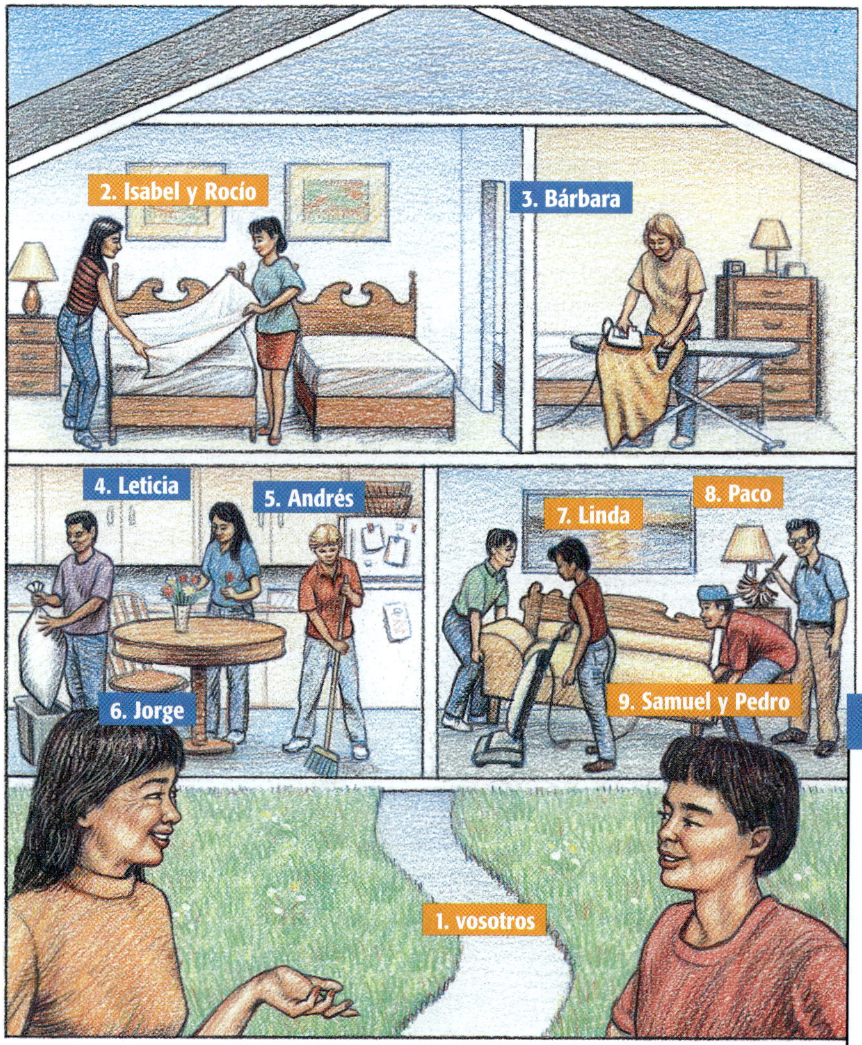

11 El sábado

Escribir Imagínate que es sábado a las nueve de la mañana. ¿Qué está haciendo cada miembro de tu familia? ¿Dónde están? *(Hint: Say what people are doing and where.)*

modelo

Mi mamá está preparando el desayuno. Lo está preparando en la cocina. Mi hermana mayor está leyendo una novela. La está leyendo en su habitación. Mi papá está trabajando en el jardín…

More Practice:
Más comunicación *p. R14*

Vocabulario

Más quehaceres

mover (o → ue) los muebles *to move the furniture*

ordenar (las flores, los libros) *to arrange (the flowers, books)*

planchar (la ropa) *to iron (the clothes)*

sacar la basura *to take out the trash*

¿Quién hace estos quehaceres en tu casa?

GRAMÁTICA Using the Verb deber

The verb **deber** means *should* or *ought to.* To say what people should do, use a **conjugated form of deber** with the **infinitive** of another verb.

deber *should, ought to*

debo	**debemos**
debes	**debéis**
debe	**deben**

Debo barrer el suelo.
I should sweep *the floor.*

Debes limpiar la cocina.
You should clean *the kitchen.*

Debe sacar la basura.
He should take out *the trash.*

Carmen asks Luis: ***before***

—¿Por qué **te debo ayudar**?
*Why **should I** help you?*

Luis tells Mercedes: ***attached***

—En vez de sacar fotos, **debes ayudarme**.
*Instead of taking pictures, **you should** help me.*

Remember you can put a **pronoun** in front of a conjugated verb or attach it to an infinitive.

Practice: **Actividades** 12 13 14 15 16

Más práctica *cuaderno p. 119*
Para hispanohablantes *cuaderno p. 117*

Online Workbook
CLASSZONE.COM

12 ¿Qué deben hacer todos para la fiesta?

Hablar/*Escribir* Mercedes explica lo que deben hacer sus amigos para una fiesta. *(Hint: Explain what they should do.)*

modelo

Luis / comprar platos ***Luis** debe **comprar platos**.*

1. Álvaro y sus amigos / limpiar la casa
2. Isabel / ordenar las flores
3. yo / hacer una tarta
4. mis amigos / comprar la comida
5. Yolanda y yo / escribir las invitaciones
6. tú / mandar las invitaciones

Vocabulario

La fiesta

una invitación cerrada **una invitación abierta**

¿Qué te gusta de una fiesta? ¿Las invitaciones? ¿Las sorpresas? ¿Los regalos?

13 ¿Me puedes ayudar?

Hablar Estás organizando una cena y necesitas la ayuda de unos amigos. Los llamas por teléfono. ¿Qué dicen? *(Hint: What do you say?)*

modelo

Carmen: salir para comprar el postre

Carmen: *¿Debo* ***salir para comprar el postre****?*

Tú: *Sí, sal para comprar el postre, por favor.*

1. Ana: ir a la tienda para comprar pan
2. Raúl: decirle a Pepe cómo llegar a la casa
3. Elena: hacer las tapas
4. Diego: venir a la casa a las cinco
5. Luisa: poner la mesa
6. Ramón: salir para comprar tenedores
7. Vicente: ir al supermercado para comprar café
8. Carlota: hacer una tortilla
9. Cristina: salir para comprar flores
10. Tito: decirle a Sara cuándo llegar

14 ¿Qué debes hacer?

Hablar Un(a) amigo(a) te pregunta si debe hacer algo o no. Contéstale. *(Hint: Say if a friend should do these things.)*

modelo

hacer la cama por la mañana

Estudiante A: *¿Debo* ***hacer la cama por la mañana****?*

Estudiante B: *Sí, debes hacer la cama por la mañana.*

1. nadar después de comer
2. estudiar mucho para sacar buenas notas
3. lavarse las manos antes de comer
4. lavarse los dientes después de comer
5. acostarse tarde
6. llevar un casco en bicicleta
7. hacer ejercicio
8. ayudar a mis padres con los quehaceres
9. comer mucho azúcar
10. levantarse antes del mediodía

15 ¿En qué orden?

Escuchar Liliana y su familia preparan una fiesta para su abuelo. Escucha lo que dice. Luego, indica el orden en que deben hacer las actividades. *(Hint: In what order should they do things?)*

a. preparar la comida
b. mandar las invitaciones
c. hacer la tarta
d. comprar el regalo

16 Para hacer una buena fiesta...

Escribir Un(a) amigo(a) te pregunta qué debe hacer para preparar una buena fiesta. Explícale todo. *(Hint: Explain what a friend should do.)*

Para hacer una buena fiesta...

1. Debes invitar a muchos amigos.
2. Debes servir comida rica.

GRAMÁTICA Using Adverbs That End in -mente

To describe how something is done, use **adverbs.** Many adverbs in Spanish are made by changing an existing **adjective.**

- When an adjective ends in **e, l,** or **z,** simply add **-mente** to the end.

Adjective	Adverb
reciente *recent*	**recientemente** *recently, lately*
frecuente *frequent*	**frecuentemente** *frequently, often*
fácil *easy*	**fácilmente** *easily*
normal *normal*	**normalmente** *normally*
especial *special*	**especialmente** *specially, especially*
feliz *happy*	**felizmente** *happily*

- For adjectives with **-o** or **-a** endings, add **-mente** to the **feminine** form.

Adjective	Adverb
cuidadoso(a) *careful*	**cuidadosamente** *carefully*
rápido(a) *fast, quick*	**rápidamente** *quickly*
lento(a) *slow*	**lentamente** *slowly*
tranquilo(a) *calm*	**tranquilamente** *calmly*

Luis says:

—Pero, Carmen, debes pasarla **cuidadosamente.**

*But Carmen, you should vacuum **carefully.***

Notice that you must keep an **accent** when an adjective is changed to an adverb.

rápido → **rápidamente**
fácil → **fácilmente**

When you use two adverbs, **drop** the **-mente** from the **first** one.

lenta y **tranquilamente**

Practice:
Actividades
17 18 19

Más práctica
cuaderno p. 120
Para hispanohablantes
cuaderno p. 118

Online Workbook
CLASSZONE.COM

17 En un restaurante

Leer Luis describe un restaurante. Completa sus oraciones con adverbios. Forma los adverbios de los adjetivos entre paréntesis.
(Hint: Complete the sentences with adverbs.)

Fui __1__ (reciente) con mi familia al restaurante Casa Paco. Es un restaurante buenísimo cerca de mi casa. Comemos allí __2__ (frecuente), ¡pues allí sirven cosas riquísimas! A mí me gustan __3__ (especial) los calamares y el chorizo. De postre, __4__ (normal) pido tarta. Ahora voy a Casa Paco con mis amigos. Vamos __5__ (rápido) porque tenemos mucha hambre. Allí todos comemos __6__ (tranquilo).

18 ¿Cómo lo hacen?

Hablar/*Escribir* Todos hacen algo hoy. ¿Cómo lo hacen? *(Hint: Say how everyone does each activity.)*

serio tranquilo paciente
frecuente cuidadoso fácil
rápido lento feliz

modelo

Carmen / barrer el suelo
***Carmen barre el suelo** rápidamente.*

1. Luis / hablar
2. Mercedes / trabajar
3. Álvaro / esperar
4. Jorge / terminar la tarea
5. Beto y Marta / cantar
6. Enrique / pasar la aspiradora
7. Rocío y Ana / quitar el polvo
8. Catalina / ir de compras
9. Pedro / desayunar
10. todos / bailar

19 ¡La buena limpieza!

Leer/*Escribir* Imagínate que recibes este anuncio de la compañía Buena Limpieza. Lee el anuncio y después contesta las preguntas. *(Hint: Answer the questions.)*

Buena Limpieza

¡Con diez años de experiencia, limpiamos fácilmente todo tipo de hogar!

Llegamos rápidamente a su hogar para ofrecerle un servicio completo de limpieza.

- Quitar completamente el polvo
- Pasar lentamente la aspiradora
- Limpiar cuidadosamente todos los cuartos, especialmente los baños y la cocina

¡Llámenos hoy al 86-25-54 para tener una casa bien limpia mañana!

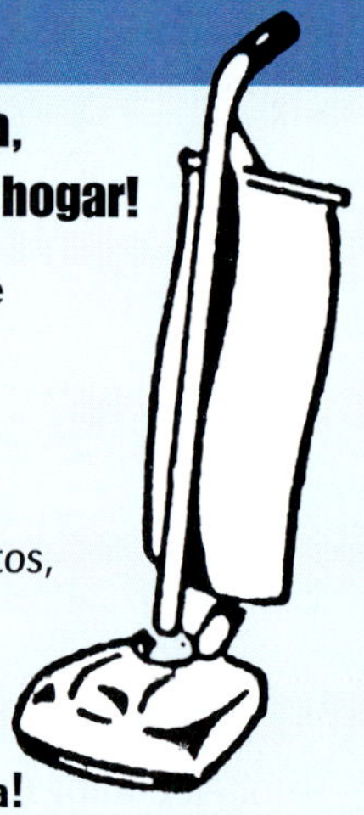

1. ¿Cómo limpia el servicio?
2. ¿Cómo llegan a la casa?
3. ¿Qué servicios ofrecen?
4. ¿Cómo pasan la aspiradora?
5. ¿Qué cuartos limpian especialmente bien?

España

También se dice

Many words are used to mean *bedroom.* Almost all are used in all countries. A few are used a bit more often in specific countries.

- **la habitación:** Spain
- **la pieza:** Argentina, Chile
- **la recámara:** Mexico
- **la alcoba:** many countries
- **el cuarto:** many countries
- **el dormitorio:** many countries

PARTE D Todo en acción

Activities 20–21 bring together all concepts presented.

20 Mi casa ideal

Hablar/*Escribir* Haz un plano de tu casa ideal. Después, muéstrale el plano a otro(a) estudiante y descríbele la casa. *(**Hint:** Design and describe your dream house.)*

modelo

Mi casa ideal es grande y bonita. Tiene un jardín con muchas flores y plantas. También tiene una piscina y una cancha de tenis. Hay una sala donde vemos la televisión. Hay una cocina muy grande donde comemos todos los días. La casa también tiene…

21 ¡Una buena fiesta!

Hablar/*Escribir* Trabaja en un grupo de tres para planear una fiesta. Luego, dale una invitación a cada estudiante de la clase. Para saber cuál es la mejor fiesta, haz una encuesta. ¿Cuántos estudiantes aceptan tu invitación? ¿Cuántos aceptan las invitaciones de los otros grupos? *(**Hint:** Plan a party.)*

- ¿Qué tipo de fiesta van a hacer?
- ¿Qué comida van a servir?
- ¿Qué van a celebrar?
- ¿Qué van a hacer en la fiesta?

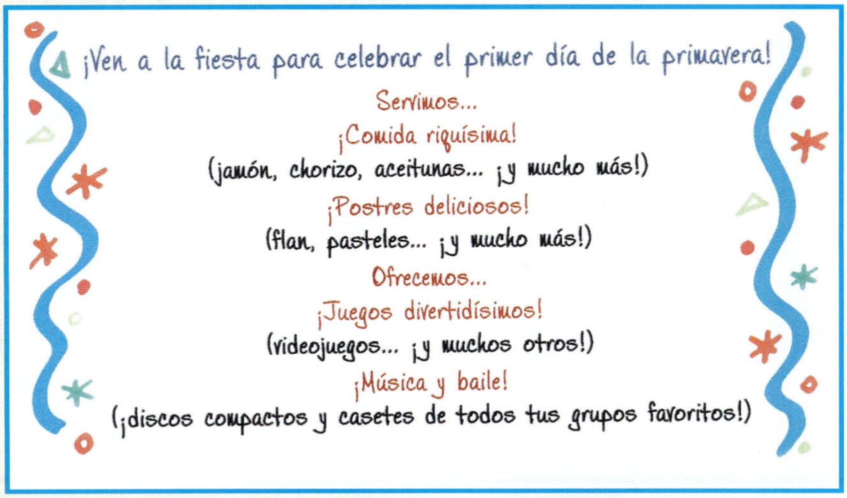

More Practice: **Más comunicación** *p. R14*

Online Workbook CLASSZONE.COM

Pronunciación

Trabalenguas

Pronunciación de la *c*, la *p* y la *t* When a **c** is followed by an **a**, **o**, or **u**, it sounds like the *c* in the English word *cat*. The letter combination **qu**, when followed by **e** or **i**, also makes this sound. This **c** sound and the letters **p** and **t** are pronounced similarly in Spanish and English. However, when you say them in English, a puff of air comes out of your mouth. In Spanish there is no puff of air. Try saying the following tongue twisters to practice these sounds.

Quince quiteños comen papas picantes.

No son tantas las tontas ni tantos los tontos muchachos.

En colores

CULTURA Y COMPARACIONES

PARA CONOCERNOS

STRATEGY: CONNECTING CULTURES

Predict reactions about restaurants Fast food chains are a U.S. invention being exported to other countries. Think about a favorite one and write down your answers to the questions in the chart.

	comida rápida	tapas
¿Qué comida sirven?		
¿Por qué vamos?		
¿Con quién vamos?		

As you read, answer the same questions about a place that serves **tapas.** Compare the two eating experiences. How do you think Luis or Mercedes would feel on their first trip to your favorite fast food restaurant?

Las tapas

¿Te gustarían unas tapas? Son muy típicas de España. ¿Sabes qué son? Una tapa es una porción pequeña de comida que la gente normalmente come con una bebida antes de la cena. ¡Vamos a probar[1] unas!

En el café ponen todas las tapas en el mostrador[2]. Hay tantas tapas diferentes. Mucha gente está buscando mesa, pero no hay. No es un problema porque es muy común comer las tapas de pie. Pagas un precio más barato si comes así[3].

[1] to try [2] counter [3] in this way

una experiencia muy española

Unos chicos están comiendo aceitunas, jamón y queso. Otros comen chorizo con pan. Las aceitunas, el jamón, el queso y el chorizo son tapas naturales[4]. También hay tapas cocidas[5], como la tortilla española y los calamares. La tortilla española es muy popular y es uno de los platos más famosos. Pero la especialidad de la casa es un plato típico de Barcelona y de toda Cataluña, el cocido catalán[6]. ¡Está riquísimo!

Comer tapas es una buena actividad para la familia o los amigos. A muchas personas les gusta conversar mientras comen las deliciosas tapas.

[4] served unheated [5] cooked [6] Catalonian stew

More About Spain
CLASSZONE.COM

¿Comprendiste?

1. ¿Qué sirven en este café?
2. ¿Por qué no hay problema si todas las mesas están ocupadas?
3. ¿Qué son las tapas naturales?
4. ¿Qué tapa cocida piden muchas personas? ¿Qué otras tapas cocidas hay?
5. ¿Cómo se llama la especialidad de la casa?

¿Qué piensas?

En España comer tapas es una actividad social. ¿Hay una actividad similar en Estados Unidos? Descríbela.

Hazlo tú

Eres camarero(a) en un café español. Dos personas llegan y piden tapas. ¿Qué dicen? ¿Qué les sirves?

ETAPA 2

En uso

REPASO Y MÁS COMUNICACIÓN

OBJECTIVES

- Say what people are doing
- Persuade others
- Describe a house
- Negotiate responsibilities

Now you can...

- say what people are doing.

To review

- pronouns with the present progressive, see p. 352.

1 ¡A limpiar!

Luis habla con su madre por teléfono. ¿Qué le dice sobre los quehaceres? *(**Hint:** Tell who is doing what.)*

modelo

¿quitar el polvo de la mesa? (yo)

Mamá: *¿Quién está **quitando el polvo de la mesa**?*

Luis: ***Yo** estoy quitándolo. o: **Yo** lo estoy quitando.*

1. ¿barrer el suelo? (yo)
2. ¿pasar la aspiradora? (Carmen)
3. ¿lavar los platos? (Mercedes y Carmen)
4. ¿sacar la basura? (yo)
5. ¿poner la mesa? (Carmen)
6. ¿limpiar los baños? (Mercedes y yo)
7. ¿hacer las camas? (yo)
8. ¿preparar las tapas? (nosotros)

Now you can...

- persuade others.

To review

- the verb **deber,** see p. 355.
- adverbs that end in **-mente,** see p. 357.

2 ¡Una fiesta!

Tú y tus amigos van a hacer una fiesta en tu casa en una hora. ¿Qué deben o no deben hacer todos? *(**Hint:** Tell what everyone should or should not do.)*

modelo

yo: poner la mesa (lento)

No debo poner la mesa lentamente.

1. ustedes: ordenar la casa (cuidadoso)
2. tú: hablar por teléfono (frecuente)
3. mis amigos y yo: preparar las tapas (rápido)
4. yo: ducharme (lento)
5. nosotros: hacer los quehaceres (tranquilo)
6. mis amigos: ayudarme (rápido)

Self-Check Quiz
CLASSZONE.COM

Now you can...
- describe a house.

To review
- house and furniture vocabulary, see pp. 346–347.

3 ¡Una nueva casa!

Imagínate que tú y tu familia acaban de llegar a esta nueva casa. Describe lo que hay en estos cuartos. *(Hint: Tell what is in these rooms.)*

modelo

En el baño hay una ventana y un armario.

Now you can...
- negotiate responsibilities.

To review
- **si** clauses with the present tense, see p. 352.

4 Si tú limpias...

Luis está hablando con Carmen sobre los quehaceres. ¿Qué le dice? *(Hint: Tell what Luis says.)*

modelo

quitar la mesa / lavar los platos
*Si tú **quitas la mesa,** yo **lavo los platos.***

1. lavar la ropa / planchar la ropa
2. barrer el suelo / sacar la basura
3. quitar el polvo / pasar la aspiradora
4. limpiar la sala / limpiar la cocina
5. poner la mesa / hacer las camas
6. limpiar las ventanas / ordenar los muebles

5 Mi casa es así

STRATEGY: SPEAKING

Detect misunderstandings Ask your partner questions about what he or she said to make sure you understand. To find out if you understood each other, you can restate what was said, do what was said, or draw what was said. Draw what is described, then compare your drawings. Together, identify where any misunderstandings occurred.

Dibuja un cuarto. Descríbeselo a otro(a) estudiante. Él o ella tiene que dibujar el cuarto que tú describes y decir qué cuarto es. *(Hint: Draw and describe a room.)*

modelo

Tú: *Hay una ventana grande a la derecha de la puerta. Cerca de la ventana hay un sofá y dos sillones. Hay una mesa entre los sillones…*

Otro(a) estudiante: *Es la sala.*

6 ¡Límpialo tú!

Tú y tus amigos tienen que preparar la casa para una fiesta esta noche. Hagan una lista de los quehaceres y después decidan quiénes van a hacerlos. *(Hint: List chores and decide who does what.)*

modelo

Tú: *Si ustedes limpian el baño, yo paso la aspiradora.*

Persona A: *¡No! Tú debes limpiar el baño. Yo prefiero pasar la aspiradora.*

Persona B: *Yo puedo limpiar el baño rápidamente si tú me ayudas.*

Tú: *Bueno. Yo te ayudo a limpiar el baño.*

7 En tu propia voz

ESCRITURA Imagínate que estás en una fiesta del Club de Español. Escribe una descripción de lo que están haciendo todos. *(Hint: Describe what people are doing.)*

modelo

La fiesta es muy alegre. Gregorio está tocando la guitarra y todos estamos cantando. La profesora está en la cocina. Está preparando las tapas cuidadosamente…

TÚ EN LA COMUNIDAD

Noemi is a high school student in New Jersey. A native Spanish speaker, she helps out Spanish-speaking customers in the clothing store where she works. She also speaks Spanish with family and friends. With whom do you speak Spanish?

Flashcards
CLASSZONE.COM

En resumen

REPASO DE VOCABULARIO

PERSUADING OTHERS

cuidadosamente	*carefully*
cuidadoso(a)	*careful*
deber	*should, ought to*
especial	*special*
especialmente	*specially, especially*
fácilmente	*easily*
felizmente	*happily*
frecuente	*frequent*
frecuentemente	*often, frequently*
lentamente	*slowly*
lento(a)	*slow*
normal	*normal*
normalmente	*normally*
rápidamente	*quickly*
rápido(a)	*fast, quick*
reciente	*recent*
recientemente	*lately, recently*
tranquilamente	*calmly*

DESCRIBING A HOUSE

The House

el baño	*bathroom*
la cocina	*kitchen*
el comedor	*dining room*
la habitación	*bedroom*
el jardín	*garden*
la pared	*wall*
la puerta	*door*
la sala	*living room*
el suelo	*floor*
la ventana	*window*

Furniture

el armario	*closet*
la lámpara	*lamp*
la mesa	*table*
los muebles	*furniture*
la silla	*chair*
el sillón	*armchair*
el sofá	*sofa, couch*
el televisor	*television set*

WHAT PEOPLE ARE DOING

barrer el suelo	*to sweep the floor*
mover (ue) los muebles	*to move the furniture*
ordenar (las flores, los libros)	*to arrange (the flowers, books)*
pasar la aspiradora	*to vacuum*
planchar (la ropa)	*to iron (the clothes)*
quitar el polvo	*to dust*
sacar la basura	*to take out the trash*

OTHER WORDS AND PHRASES

abierto(a)	*open*
cerrado(a)	*closed*
la llave	*key*
olvidar	*to forget*
si	*if*

Food

las aceitunas	*olives*
los calamares	*squid*
el chorizo	*sausage*
el jamón	*ham*
las tapas	*appetizers*
la tortilla española	*potato omelet*

Invitations

la fiesta	*party*
la invitación	*invitation*
sorprender	*to surprise*
la sorpresa	*surprise*

Juego

¿En qué cuarto están?

1. Sofía come.
2. Felipe ve la televisión.
3. Cristina lava los platos.

UNIDAD 5

ETAPA 3

¡Qué buena celebración!

OBJECTIVES

- Plan a party
- Describe past activities
- Express extremes
- Purchase food

¿Qué ves?

Mira la foto de la fiesta para Luis.

1. ¿Está contento Luis?
2. ¿Qué hay en la mesa?
3. ¿Cuántas personas están en la fiesta?
4. ¿En qué cuarto de la casa están?

CUMPLEAÑOS

En contexto

VIDEO DVD AUDIO

VOCABULARIO

Luis's friends are finishing their preparations for his surprise birthday party. Look at all of the food!

A Hay mucha comida para la fiesta. En **el frigorífico** hay **una lata de zumo** y **crema.** ¿Y en **el congelador**? **¡Helado!**

B Para hacer la tarta, Marta usa **harina, huevos, mantequilla** y **leche.** Acaba de hacer **galletas.**

C Hay **verduras, tomates** y **zanahorias.** También hay **salchichas.**

CD-ROM Take-Home Tutor

D

Iván **cocina** en **la estufa.** Cocina **carne de res** con **cebollas.**

E

Para **las patatas** alioli, Beto usa patatas, un poco de **aceite, sal** y **pimienta.** También usa mayonesa y otros ingredientes.

F

Cuando Luis llega, Marta **apaga la luz.** Beto le dice a Marta **«¡Cállate!».** ¡Quieren silencio para darle la sorpresa a Luis!

Online Workbook
CLASSZONE.COM

Preguntas personales

1. ¿Te gusta cocinar?
2. ¿Qué postre prefieres, helado o galletas?
3. ¿Cuál usas más, la estufa o el microondas?
4. ¿Qué preparas?
5. ¿Qué hay en tu frigorífico?

VIDEO DVD AUDIO

En vivo

DIÁLOGO

Álvaro Marta Iván Beto

PARA ESCUCHAR • STRATEGY: LISTENING

Listen and take notes There are many different ways to celebrate a birthday. Luis's friends have prepared a meal for him. Listen and write down the menu. Were all categories mentioned?

Bebidas	Carne	Verduras	Postre

¡De compras!

1 ▶ **Luis:** No lo puedo creer. Limpié la cocina, saqué la basura y tú, Carmen, pasaste la aspiradora.
Mercedes: ¿Y qué, Luis? ¿Qué es lo que no puedes creer?
Luis: Que es mi cumpleaños.

5 ▶ **Luis:** Trabajé en casa toda la mañana. Y ¡también tengo que cuidar a Carmen!
Álvaro: Ven a casa con Mercedes. Y trae a Carmen también.
Luis: Gracias. Nos vemos pronto.

6 ▶ **Marta:** ¡La tarta está lista, Álvaro! ¡Mírala!
Álvaro: ¡Quedó deliciosa! ¡Es la más deliciosa de Barcelona!
Marta: ¡Álvaro!
Álvaro: ¡Iván! ¿Está lista la carne de res?
Iván: Sí, claro.

7 ▶ **Álvaro:** ¡Beto! ¿Qué haces?
Beto: Estoy preparando un plato de verduras. ¡No te comas las zanahorias! ¿No ves que hay pocas?

CD-ROM Take-Home Tutor

2 ▶ **Luis:** ¡El día empezó con demasiados quehaceres!
Carmen: ¡Yo te ayudé, Luis!
Luis: Sí, Carmen, tú me ayudaste y Mercedes también me ayudó.

3 ▶ **Luis:** Lo más increíble es que son las dos y ¡todavía no terminamos!
Mercedes: No te preocupes, Luis. ¿Por qué no llamas a Álvaro?
Luis: Buena idea. Os veo en la tienda.

4 ▶ **Luis:** Hola, Álvaro, soy Luis.
Álvaro: ¡Hola, Luis! ¿Dónde estás?
Luis: Voy a la tienda con Mercedes y Carmen. Tengo que hacer unas compras.
Álvaro: ¿Ahora? Hombre, te estoy esperando.

8 ▶ **Luis:** Necesito comprar leche, zumo, huevos y mantequilla.
Carmen: ¡No olvides el helado! ¡Es lo más rico del mundo!
Luis: Tenemos que llevar estas cosas a casa. Vamos, pronto.

9 ▶ **Todos:** ¡Feliz cumpleaños, Luis!
Luis: ¿Cómo puede ser? ¡Mercedes! ¡Álvaro!
Álvaro: Sí, amigo. Lo planeamos todo.
Luis: Pues, por fin, dime, Mercedes, ¿para qué son esas fotos?

10 ▶ **Mercedes:** Son para un concurso. ¡Y tú eres la estrella de mi proyecto! Y el título de mi proyecto es «Un día especial en la vida de un joven español».
Luis: ¡Te voy a decir definitivamente que este día es muy especial!

En acción

PARTE B
Práctica del vocabulario

Objectives for Activities 3–5
• Plan a party • Purchase food

PARTE A
Comprensión del diálogo

For Activities 1–2, refer to the dialog on pages 370–371.

1 Frases revueltas

Escuchar Completa las oraciones para describir lo que pasa en el diálogo. *(Hint: Complete the sentences.)*

1. Luis tiene que cuidar a	a. helado
2. Luis va a hacer	b. su tarta
3. Carmen quiere comprar	c. la comida
4. Marta está feliz con	d. compras para su mamá
5. Los amigos de Luis están preparando	e. su hermana Carmen

2 ¿En qué orden?

Escuchar ¿En qué orden pasan estas cosas? *(Hint: In what order do they happen?)*

a. Luis entra en la tienda.
b. Luis, Mercedes y Carmen llegan a la casa de Álvaro.
c. Mercedes le dice a Luis que las fotos son para un concurso.
d. Los amigos de Luis le dicen «¡Feliz cumpleaños!».
e. Luis llama a Álvaro por teléfono.

España

También se dice

Sometimes **el frigorífico** is used in Spain to talk about the refrigerator. Other words are also used for this appliance.

- **la nevera:** Ecuador, Puerto Rico, parts of Spain
- **la heladera:** Argentina
- **el refrigerador:** Mexico

Spaniards say **zumo** for *juice*. Latin Americans use **jugo.**

3 Marta necesita...

Hablar Marta está haciendo una tarta para la fiesta de Luis. ¿Qué necesita? *(Hint: Say what Marta needs.)*

1.

2.

3.

4.

5.

4 ¿Qué cosa no debe estar?

Hablar Trabajas en un restaurante y tienes que poner todo en su lugar. Indica la cosa que no debe estar con las otras cosas. *(**Hint:** Say which item doesn't belong.)*

1.	zumo	leche	agua	harina
2.	galleta	cebolla	helado	flan
3.	chorizo	salchicha	aceite	carne de res
4.	crema	lechuga	tomate	zanahoria
5.	azúcar	sal	huevos	pimienta
6.	pescado	carne	puerco	zanahoria
7.	cereal	pasta	leche	arroz
8.	leche	puerco	yogur	crema
9.	pescado	cebolla	lechuga	patata
10.	helado	crema	leche	verduras

5 ¡Lógicamente!

Leer Todos están muy ocupados con las preparaciones para la fiesta de Luis. Explica lo que hacen. *(**Hint:** Explain what they do.)*

1. Álvaro pone el helado en (el congelador, la mantequilla, la pimienta).
2. Marta saca la leche (de la estufa, del frigorífico, del lavaplatos).
3. Iván empieza a cocinar (el helado, el zumo, la carne de res) a la una.
4. Marta hace (unos huevos, unas patatas, unas galletas) porque a Luis le gustan las cosas dulces.
5. La carne está muy (caliente, picante, dulce) porque Iván acaba de cocinarla.
6. Álvaro pone los platos sucios en (el lavaplatos, el microondas, la estufa).

Vocabulario

La comida

el cereal

la pasta

el puerco

el pescado

el yogur

¿Qué te gusta comer?

PARTE C

Práctica: gramática y vocabulario

Objectives for Activities 6–19
- Express extremes • Describe past activities
- Plan a party • Purchase food

GRAMÁTICA Talking About Extremes: Superlatives

¿RECUERDAS? *p. 208* Remember how you make comparisons? These phrases say that one item has **more** or **less** of a certain quality than another item has.

más... que

menos... que

When you want to say that something has the **most** or the **least** of a certain quality, use a **superlative.**

el más...	**el menos...**
los más...	**los menos...**
la más...	**la menos...**
las más...	**las menos...**

Luis es **el más alto.** Carmen es **la más pequeña.** Mercedes es **la menos cansada.**

*Luis is **the tallest.** Carmen is **the smallest.** Mercedes is **the least tired.***

To use a **noun** with the superlative form, put it **after** the article.

matches

Luis es **el chico más alto.** Mercedes es **la chica menos cansada.**

*Luis is **the tallest boy.** Mercedes is **the least tired girl.***

matches

Iván prepara **las comidas más sabrosas.**

*Iván makes **the tastiest meals.***

Be sure the adjective matches the noun in both gender and number.

When you refer to an idea or concept, use the neuter article **lo**.

Luis says: —**Lo más increíble** es que son las dos...

***The most incredible** (thing) is that it's two o'clock...*

Remember to use these **irregular** forms you learned with comparatives when referring to the *best, worst, oldest,* and *youngest.*

el/la mejor **el/la peor** **el/la mayor** **el/la menor**

Practice: **Actividades** 6 7 8

Más práctica *cuaderno p. 125*

Para hispanohablantes *cuaderno p. 123*

Online Workbook CLASSZONE.COM

6 Las comparaciones

Leer/*Escribir* ¿Qué dice Luis después de comparar todo? Lee la pregunta y contéstala.
(Hint: Explain what Luis decides.)

modelo

La galleta no es sabrosa, la fruta es sabrosa y la tarta es muy sabrosa. (¿Cuál es la más sabrosa?)

La tarta es la más sabrosa.

1. Mercedes tiene 16 años, Carmen tiene 12 años y Marta tiene 17 años. (¿Quién es la menor?)
2. La casa de Luis tiene diez cuartos, la casa de Marta tiene ocho cuartos y la casa de Beto tiene seis cuartos. (¿Quién tiene la casa más pequeña?)
3. Antonio no es muy alto, Andrés es alto y Álvaro es muy alto. (¿Quién es el más alto?)
4. El azúcar cuesta 36 céntimos, el helado cuesta 99 céntimos y el té cuesta 61 céntimos. (¿Cuál es el menos caro?)
5. Iván saca una A en arte, Enrique saca una B y Pepe saca una C. (¿Quién es el mejor estudiante?

7 Cosas para la casa

Hablar/*Escribir* Los padres de Luis van a un mercado al aire libre para comprar cosas para la casa. Comparan lo que ven. ¿Qué dicen? *(Hint: Compare the items.)*

modelo

pequeño, grande

*La silla roja es la más **pequeña.***

*La silla azul es la más **grande.***

1. caro, barato

2. largo, corto

3. alto, bajo

4. limpio, sucio

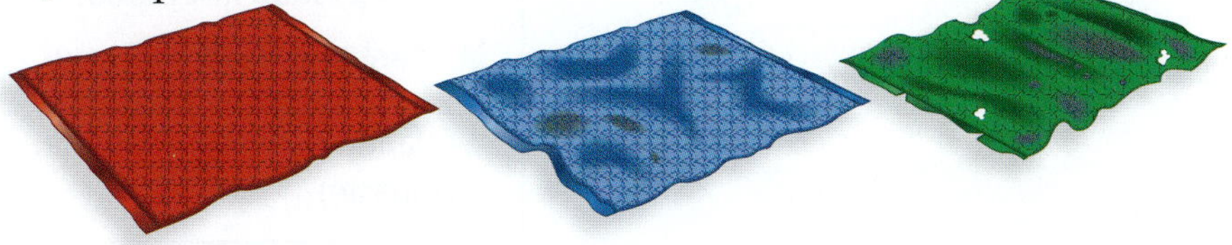

5. viejo, nuevo

8 En mi opinión...

STRATEGY: SPEAKING

Say what is the best and worst

Decide **el mejor** or **el peor** of any of these: **equipo de baloncesto o béisbol, cantante, actor o actriz, grupo musical, película del año,** or any other categories you want to make.

Hablar Todos tienen opiniones. Da tu opinión sobre las siguientes cosas. *(Hint: Give your opinion.)*

modelo

la comida más rica

Estudiante A: *¿Cuál es **la comida más rica** para ti?*

Estudiante B: *El bistec es **la comida más rica.***

1. la música más popular
2. el deporte menos divertido
3. la clase menos difícil
4. el peor quehacer
5. el lugar más bonito
6. la película menos interesante
7. el actor más guapo
8. la actriz más bonita
9. el mejor restaurante
10. el libro más fenomenal

More Practice:
Más comunicación *p. R15*

GRAMÁTICA Talking About the Past: The Preterite of Regular -ar Verbs

When you want to talk about actions completed in the past, use the **preterite tense.** To form the preterite of a regular **-ar** verb, add the appropriate preterite **ending** to the verb's **stem.**

limpiar *to clean*

Notice that the first and third person singular forms have an **accent** over the final vowel.

limpié	**limpiamos**
limpiaste	**limpiasteis**
limpió	**limpiaron**

The **nosotros(as)** form is the same in the **preterite** as in the **present** tense.

Luis says:

—**Limpié** la cocina…
—Sí, Carmen, tú me **ayudaste** y Mercedes también me **ayudó.**

***I cleaned** the kitchen…*
*Yes, Carmen, **you helped** me and Mercedes **helped** me also.*

Practice: Actividades 9 10 11 12

Más práctica *cuaderno pp. 126–127*
Para hispanohablantes *cuaderno pp. 124–125*

Online Workbook CLASSZONE.COM

9 Las compras

Leer Álvaro le explica a Beto qué compraron para la fiesta. Completa sus oraciones con la forma correcta de **comprar.**
(Hint: Complete what Álvaro explains.)

Nosotros __1__ cosas riquísimas para la fiesta de Luis, ¿verdad? Marta __2__ los huevos, la harina, la mantequilla y la leche para hacer la tarta. Iván __3__ la carne de res y las cebollas para hacer su plato riquísimo. Tú __4__ las patatas y el aceite para hacer las patatas alioli. Bárbara y Luisa __5__ los refrescos. ¿Y yo? Pues, yo __6__ lo más rico de todo, ¡el helado!

Vocabulario

El pasado

anoche *last night*
anteayer *the day before yesterday*
el año pasado *last year*
ayer *yesterday*
el mes pasado *last month*
la semana pasada *last week*

¿Cuándo patinaste (nadaste, cocinaste)?

10 ¿Qué terminaron ayer?

Hablar/*Escribir* Luis habla de los quehaceres que él y sus amigos hicieron ayer. ¿Qué dice? *(**Hint:** Explain what they did yesterday.)*

1. Ana y Marta

2. tú

3. yo

4. Sara y yo

5. ellos

6. Juana

Apoyo para estudiar

Preterite Tense

Since the **nosotros** form of a regular **-ar** verb is the same in both the preterite and the present tenses, how can you determine the tense? Use context clues to help you. Look for time indicators, like those in the vocabulary box, and the tense of other verbs.

11 ¿Por qué no me invitaste?

Escuchar Juana y su amigo Miguel hablan de una fiesta. Escucha su conversación. Luego, contesta las preguntas. *(**Hint:** Answer the questions.)*

1. ¿Qué celebraron las chicas?
2. ¿Cuándo celebraron?
3. ¿Por qué Juana no invitó a Miguel?
4. ¿A cuántas chicas invitó?
5. ¿Cómo pasaron la noche?

12 ¿Cuándo...?

Hablar/*Escribir* Pregúntales a cinco estudiantes cuándo hicieron estas actividades. Haz una lista. *(**Hint:** Ask when others did these activities.)*

modelo

terminar la tarea

Tú: *¿Cuándo **terminaste la tarea**?*

Pablo: ***Terminé la tarea** anteayer.*

Actividad	Pablo
1. terminar la tarea	anteayer
2. preparar una comida	
3. lavar los platos	
4. patinar sobre hielo	
5. usar la computadora	
6. escuchar un disco compacto	
7. limpiar tu habitación	
8. quitar la mesa	
9. mandar una carta	
10. hablar por teléfono	

GRAMÁTICA Preterite of Verbs Ending in -car, -gar, and -zar

Regular verbs that end in **-car, -gar,** or **-zar** have a spelling change in the **yo form** of the preterite to maintain the original sound of the verb stem.

	becomes		
sacar	**c**	**qu**	**(yo) saqué**
pagar	**g**	**gu**	**(yo) pagué**
empezar	**z**	**c**	**(yo) empecé**

Luis says:

—...**saqué** la basura...

...I took out the trash...

Practice: **Actividades** 13 14 15 16

Más práctica *cuaderno p. 128*
Para hispanohablantes *cuaderno p. 126*

Online Workbook
CLASSZONE.COM

13 ¡Una semana llena!

Leer Mercedes habla de sus actividades de la semana pasada. ¿Qué dice? Completa sus oraciones con el pretérito de cada verbo. *(Hint: Complete what Mercedes says.)*

El lunes yo __1__ (empezar) a leer un libro de historia muy largo. El martes __2__ (jugar) al voleibol con mis amigas. El miércoles fui al centro comercial con mi mamá y __3__ (buscar) unos jeans nuevos para la fiesta del sábado. El jueves __4__ (practicar) el tenis con Elena. El viernes __5__ (llegar) tarde a la escuela. ¡Por fin llegó el sábado! Fui a una fiesta donde __6__ (tocar) la guitarra y __7__ (sacar) muchas fotos. El domingo __8__ (almorzar) en casa de mis abuelos.

14 ¿Qué pasó en la fiesta?

Hablar/*Escribir* Álvaro explica lo que pasó en la fiesta. ¿Qué dice? *(Hint: What does Álvaro explain?)*

modelo

Luis / llegar / 3:00 *Luis llegó a las tres.*

1. yo / apagar / 
2. Mercedes / sacar / 
3. yo / tocar / 
4. Carmen y Samuel / jugar con / 
5. todos / almorzar / 
6. yo / empezar a / 

España

Nota cultural

On December 31, 2001, banks all over Europe scrambled to stock their automated teller machines with **euros.** On January 1, 2002, the euro became the new currency of twelve European countries including Spain, where it replaced the **peseta.** A euro is divided into 100 cents. In Spain, a cent is called a **céntimo.** The symbol for the euro is €.

15 ¿Tienes buena memoria?

Hablar/*Escribir* Pregúntales a cinco estudiantes sobre sus actividades. Escribe sus respuestas. *(Hint: Ask about activities.)*

modelo

Tú: *¿A qué hora llegaste a la escuela ayer?*

Otro(a) estudiante: *Llegué a la escuela a las siete y veinte.*
o: *No sé a qué hora llegué.*

	Estudiante 1	Estudiante 2
1. ¿Qué deporte practicaste el año pasado?		
2. ¿Qué buscaste en el centro comercial este año?		
3. ¿Qué almorzaste anteayer?		
4. ¿Cuándo empezaste a estudiar español?		
5. ¿Qué fotos sacaste en tus últimas vacaciones?		

Vocabulario

Los números de 200 a 1.000.000

doscientos(as) 200
trescientos(as) 300
cuatrocientos(as) 400
quinientos(as) 500
seiscientos(as) 600
setecientos(as) 700
ochocientos(as) 800
novecientos(as) 900
mil 1.000
un millón 1.000.000

Periods are used instead of commas for thousands and millions. The word **y** is used as you previously learned. It is *not* used after hundreds, thousands, or millions.

148 = ciento cuarenta **y** ocho
1.968 = mil novecientos sesenta **y** ocho
250 = doscientos cincuenta
1.000.562 = un millón quinientos sesenta **y** dos

The word **ciento** is used instead of **cien** in numbers greater than 100.

La bicicleta costó **cien** euros.
El radio costó **ciento cincuenta** euros.

Numbers ending in 200–900 agree in gender and number with nouns.

Costó doscient**os euros**.
Compré doscient**as galletas**.

Un millón is followed by **de** before nouns.
un millón de dólares

¿Qué cuesta más de cien dólares?

16 ¿Cuánto pagaron?

Escuchar Alicia, una amiga de Luis, habla de las cosas que ella y sus amigos compraron. Escucha lo que dice. ¿Cuánto pagaron por cada cosa? *(Hint: Say what it cost.)*

1.

2.

3.

4.

5.

Vocabulario

Las cantidades

la docena *dozen*	**el paquete** *package*
el gramo *gram*	**el pedazo** *piece*
el kilo *kilogram*	**cuarto(a)** *quarter*
el litro *liter*	**medio(a)** *half*

Use the definite article when talking about the price of a specific quantity of food.

Los huevos cuestan un euro **la** docena.

El pescado cuesta nueve euros **el** kilo.

¿Cuándo usas estas cantidades?

17 Compras para la fiesta

Hablar/Leer Imagínate que estás en España. Tú y un(a) amigo(a) van a hacer una fiesta. Tienen 45 euros para comprar comida y refrescos. Lee el anuncio. ¿Qué van a comprar? *(Hint: Say what you'll buy.)*

modelo

Estudiante A: *¿Compramos salchicha?*

Estudiante B: *¿A cuánto está?*

Estudiante A: *Está a cuatro euros cincuenta el kilo.*

Estudiante B: *Bueno, vamos a comprar dos kilos.*

Nota: Vocabulario

¿A cuánto está(n)…? is an expression used to ask how much something costs. It is often used with food items that may increase or decrease in price given a good or bad harvest. It may also indicate changing prices during a sale.

Activity 20 brings together all concepts presented.

18 Cosas nuevas

Hablar/*Escribir* El año pasado, los padres de Beto compraron algunas cosas nuevas. ¿Cuánto pagaron por cada una? *(Hint: How much did they pay?)*

modelo

Pagaron trescientos mil euros por la casa.

1.

2.

3.

4.

19 ¿Cuánto ganaron?

Hablar/*Escribir* Estas personas ganaron dinero en la lotería nacional de España. ¿Cuánto ganó cada una? *(Hint: How much did they win?)*

modelo

Alejandro Rey / 2.500 €

Alejandro Rey ganó dos mil quinientos euros.

1. Pedro Fatás / 500 €
2. Mateo García / 200 €
3. Sandra Mendoza / 800 €
4. Carmen Ruiz / 80.000 €
5. Arturo Blanco / 25.000 €
6. Teresa Fierros / 750 €
7. Iván Orozco / 1.500 €
8. Miguel Palacios / 3.000 €
9. Roberto Cruz / 1.000.000 €
10. Elena Sánchez / 900 €

20 Una fiesta

Escribir Describe una fiesta real o imaginaria. Incluye la siguiente información. *(Hint: Describe a party.)*

- ¿Cuándo y dónde celebrasteis la fiesta?
- ¿Cómo preparasteis la fiesta?
- ¿Quiénes ayudaron para hacer la fiesta?
- ¿Cómo pasasteis la noche?

modelo

El año pasado celebramos el cumpleaños de mi abuela con una fiesta en mi casa. Muchos ayudaron. Mis hermanos limpiaron la casa. Mi mamá preparó la comida: salchichas, verduras y carne de res. Yo preparé un pastel riquísimo. Apagué la luz y cuando mi abuela llegó por fin a la casa, todos le cantamos «Cumpleaños feliz». Saqué muchas fotos. Bailamos toda la noche y…

More Practice: **Más comunicación** *p. R5*

Online Workbook CLASSZONE.COM

Pronunciación

Refranes

Linking words Native speakers may seem to speak quickly when they link their words together in breath groups. Instead of pronouncing each word separately, they run some words together. This is common in all languages. Practice linking words in the following sentences.

Él que algo quiere, algo le cuesta.

Aceite de oliva, todo el mal quita.

La larga experiencia, más que los libros enseña.

AUDIO

En voces

LECTURA

PARA LEER • STRATEGY: READING

Reorganize information to check understanding A family friend gave you a copy of this recipe from her favorite cookbook. She has asked you to write it down as a recipe for her card file. Read **«Los favoritos de la cocina española»** and fill out the recipe card for her.

LA PAELLA VALENCIANA			
Paso	Ingredientes	Cantidad	Instrucciones
1.	Aceite	1/4 taza	Pon en la sartén
2.			
3.			
4.			

LOS FAVORITOS de la cocina española

De la cocina de Maruja Serrat, cocinera[6] del restaurante Tibidabo de Barcelona

Ésta es la receta[1] de un plato muy especial, la paella valenciana. Es importante usar los ingredientes más frescos[2] posibles. Y busca el mejor azafrán[3]. El azafrán da sabor[4] y color a la paella. Si no hay azafrán, no hay paella. A todo el mundo le gusta tanto la paella que generalmente no queda[5] nada. Pero si queda algo, ponlo en el frigorífico para mañana.

Paella valenciana

para cuatro personas

Ingredientes

1/4 taza de aceite de oliva
1/2 kilo de pollo
1/4 kilo de salchicha
1 cebolla
2 dientes de ajo[7]
1 tomate
1/2 taza de guisantes[8]
1 pimentón[9]
1/4 kilo de calamares
200 gramos de gambas[10]
sal y pimienta
1 1/2 taza de arroz
1/2 cucharadita de azafrán
3 tazas de agua

[1] recipe [2] freshest [3] saffron [4] flavor [5] remains [6] chef [7] cloves of garlic [8] green peas [9] sweet red pepper [10] shrimp

Instrucciones

Primero pon el aceite de oliva en la sartén[11]. Corta[12] el pollo y la salchicha en pedazos. Fríelos[13] por diez minutos. Luego corta la cebolla, el ajo, el tomate y el pimentón. Ponlos en la sartén junto con los guisantes. Ahora añade[14] los calamares y las gambas, la sal y la pimienta. En otra sartén o en una paellera[15], cocina el arroz en el agua. Luego añade el pollo, la salchicha, los calamares, las gambas, las verduras y el azafrán. Cocínalo otros veinte minutos. Sirve la paella en la paellera.

[11] frying pan [12] cut [13] fry them [14] add [15] paella pan

España

Nota cultural

Paella is a typical dish of Valencia, a region next to Cataluña. It is found throughout Spain.

Online Workbook
CLASSZONE.COM

¿Comprendiste?

1. ¿Por qué es importante el azafrán?
2. Si hay demasiada paella, ¿qué debes hacer?
3. ¿Qué haces con el pollo y la salchicha?
4. ¿Qué pones en la segunda sartén?
5. Después de poner el azafrán, ¿cuánto tiempo cocinas la paella?

¿Qué piensas?

1. ¿Es fácil o difícil hacer esta receta? ¿Por qué?
2. ¿Te gustaría comer paella? ¿Por qué?

Hazlo tú

¿Tienes una receta especial de tu familia? Explica cómo preparas este plato en tu casa.

En colores

VIDEO DVD

CULTURA Y COMPARACIONES

PARA CONOCERNOS

STRATEGY: CONNECTING CULTURES

Make a historical time line Place Barcelona's rich architectural history on a time line from ancient times to the present. First label each period with a word or two to identify it. Next add a word or pictorial symbol of an important detail from that time. Finally, use your time line to summarize for a classmate the main points of **«Barcelona: Joya de arquitectura».**

Casa Amatller

Barcelona
Joya de arquitectura

Escena típica del Barrio Gótico

Barcelona es una ciudad de muchos barrios[1] y de una gran variedad de estilos de arquitectura. Los romanos fueron los primeros en construir una ciudad aquí en el año 15 a.C.[2] Hoy no hay casi nada de la ciudad romana. Hay sólo unas ruinas y murallas[3] en el Barrio Gótico[4].

El Barrio Gótico de Barcelona es la ciudad vieja, un barrio de calles estrechas[5] y plazas pequeñas. Tiene muchos edificios[6] y monumentos impresionantes de los siglos XIII, XIV y XV, época[7] de la arquitectura gótica. Si caminas por la calle Montcada puedes ver las casas y los palacios de las

---

[1] districts [3] walls [5] narrow [7] period
[2] B.C. [4] Gothic Quarter [6] buildings

España

Nota cultural

Barcelona's Gothic Quarter was built when the Spanish Empire was at its height. The profits from Spain's colonies funded the construction of palaces, churches, and public buildings.

Casa Batlló

Casa Viçens

La Pedrera—apartamentos

Parque Güell

familias principales de Barcelona de la época medieval. Hoy estas casas están convertidas en museos y galerías de arte.

La ciudad moderna tiene grandes avenidas, como Las Ramblas. El arquitecto catalán Antonio Gaudí (1852–1926) construyó[8] edificios originales de estilo modernista. Trabajó con formas y estructuras experimentales. Gaudí trabajó primero en el Parque de la Ciudadela, donde actualmente[9] está el Museo de Arte Moderno. Años más tarde diseñó el Parque Güell, ciudad y parque dentro de Barcelona. Gaudí también diseñó casas privadas, cada una con un diseño único. Su obra maestra[10], nunca terminada, es una iglesia, La Sagrada Familia[11].

[8] built [9] nowadays [10] masterpiece [11] The Holy Family

More About Spain
CLASSZONE.COM

¿Comprendiste?

1. ¿Queda algo de la ciudad romana en Barcelona? Explica.
2. ¿Cómo se llama la ciudad vieja de Barcelona? ¿Por qué?
3. ¿Qué lugares de interés puedes ver en el Barrio Gótico?
4. ¿Cómo es la ciudad moderna?
5. ¿Qué importancia tiene Gaudí?

¿Qué piensas?

¿Es cierto que la historia de Barcelona empieza en la época medieval? Explica tus razones.

Hazlo tú

Eres guía y tienes que hablar de Barcelona. ¿Qué dices?

ETAPA 3

En uso

REPASO Y MÁS COMUNICACIÓN

OBJECTIVES

- Plan a party
- Describe past activities
- Express extremes
- Purchase food

Now you can...

- plan a party.

To review

- regular preterite **-ar** verbs, see p. 376.

1 ¡A preparar!

Explica quiénes ayudaron y quiénes no ayudaron a preparar la fiesta en la casa de Álvaro.
*(**Hint:** Tell who helped and who didn't help prepare for the party.)*

modelo

Luis: cuidar a Carmen

Luis** no ayudó. **Cuidó a Carmen.

tú: lavar los platos

Tú** ayudaste. **Lavaste los platos.

1. Álvaro: limpiar la casa
2. yo: nadar en la piscina
3. Iván: cocinar la carne de res
4. Elena y Arturo: escuchar música
5. tú: patinar en el parque
6. Beto: preparar las patatas y verduras
7. nosotros: hablar por teléfono
8. Marta: preparar la tarta

Now you can...

- describe past activities.

To review

- preterite of **-car, -gar, -zar** verbs, see p. 378.

2 ¡Una fiesta terrible!

Carmen habla con Luis sobre una fiesta muy mala que celebraron en su casa el mes pasado. ¿Qué dice? *(**Hint:** Tell what Carmen says about a terrible party.)*

modelo

yo (buscar) los vasos y no los (encontrar)

Yo busqué los vasos y no los encontré.

1. nadie (sacar) la basura antes de la fiesta
2. yo (pagar) todas las compras con mi dinero
3. pocas personas (llegar)
4. yo (tocar) el piano muy mal
5. yo no (almorzar) nada el día de la fiesta
6. nosotros (jugar) con unos videojuegos aburridos
7. yo (sacar) unas fotos terribles
8. tú (apagar) la luz durante la fiesta

Self-Check Quiz
CLASSZONE.COM

Now you can...
- express extremes.

To review
- superlatives, see p. 374.

3 Opiniones

Luis observa las siguientes cosas. ¿Qué dice?
(Hint: Give Luis's observations.)

modelo

Carmen: más / joven (de mi familia)

Carmen** es la **menor.

1. Mercedes: más / bonito (de mis amigas)
2. helado: más / bueno (de los postres)
3. papá: más / viejo (de mi familia)
4. zanahorias: menos / delicioso (de las verduras)
5. tarta: más / sabroso (de los postres)
6. tenis: más / malo (de los deportes)
7. limonada: más / dulce (de las bebidas)
8. calamares: menos / rico (de las tapas)

Now you can...
- purchase food.

To review
- prices and quantity, see p. 380.

4 ¿A cuánto están?

Imagínate que estás comprando comida en España. ¿Cuáles son los precios de hoy? *(Hint: Tell prices of foods.)*

modelo

Las zanahorias están a un euro cuarenta y cinco el kilo.

1. 

2. 

3. 

4. 

5. 

6. 

7. 

8. 

5 El fin de semana pasado

STRATEGY: SPEAKING

Maintain conversational flow To keep continuity in a conversation, acknowledge what was said, then add your own ideas. The model shows how this is done. You can build interest by withholding information: **Compré algo bonito. ¿Sabes qué es?**

Usando las actividades de la lista, habla con otro(a) estudiante sobre sus actividades del fin de semana pasado. *(Hint: Talk about what you did last weekend.)*

almorzar en un restaurante
limpiar la casa
comprar algo interesante
alquilar un video
tocar algún instrumento
practicar algún deporte
trabajar

modelo

Tú: *Compré algo interesante.*

Otro(a) estudiante: *¿Qué compraste?*

Tú: *Compré…*

6 En el supermercado

Imagínate que tú y un(a) amigo(a) están comprando comida en España. Hay tres papeles: un(a) comprador(a) optimista, un(a) comprador(a) pesimista y una persona que trabaja en el supermercado. Cambien de papel. *(Hint: Shop in the supermarket. One person is an optimist, another is a pessimist, and the third works at the supermarket.)*

modelo

Optimista: *¿A cuánto están los tomates?*

Trabajador(a): *Nuestros tomates son los más sabrosos de la comunidad. Hoy están a…*

Optimista: *¡Qué bien! Los compro.*

Pesimista: *¡No los compres! Los tomates de aquí son…*

7 En tu propia voz

ESCRITURA Imagínate que tú y tus amigos celebraron una fiesta el sábado pasado. ¿Cómo participaron todos? *(Hint: Describe how everyone participated in a class party.)*

modelo

Antes de la fiesta, todos limpiamos la casa. Sara pasó la aspiradora y yo lavé los platos. Durante la fiesta, Marcos tocó la guitarra y…

CONEXIONES

La salud What kind of food do you like the most? Which ethnic foods do you prefer? Is there a special dish from your region? Survey ten people at your school to find out their favorite food. Then create a menu featuring the foods chosen. Add prices and indicate the dishes that are good for your health.

Persona	La comida favorita

En resumen

REPASO DE VOCABULARIO

Flashcards CLASSZONE.COM

PLANNING A PARTY

apagar la luz	*to turn off the light*
¡Cállate!	*Be quiet!*

PURCHASING FOOD

¿A cuánto está(n)...?	*How much is (are)...?*

Food

el aceite	*oil*
la carne de res	*beef*
la cebolla	*onion*
el cereal	*cereal*
la crema	*cream*
la galleta	*cookie, cracker*
la harina	*flour*
el helado	*ice cream*
el huevo	*egg*
la leche	*milk*
la mantequilla	*butter*
la pasta	*pasta*
la patata	*potato*
el pescado	*fish*
la pimienta	*pepper*
el puerco	*pork*
la sal	*salt*
la salchicha	*sausage*
el tomate	*tomato*
la verdura	*vegetable*
el yogur	*yogurt*
la zanahoria	*carrot*
el zumo	*juice*

Packaging

la botella	*bottle*
la lata	*can*
el paquete	*package*

REQUESTING QUANTITIES

cuarto(a)	*quarter*
la docena	*dozen*
el gramo	*gram*
el kilo	*kilogram*
el litro	*liter*
medio(a)	*half*
el pedazo	*piece*
doscientos(as)	*two hundred*
trescientos(as)	*three hundred*
cuatrocientos(as)	*four hundred*
quinientos(as)	*five hundred*
seiscientos(as)	*six hundred*
setecientos(as)	*seven hundred*
ochocientos(as)	*eight hundred*
novecientos(as)	*nine hundred*
mil	*one thousand*
un millón	*one million*

DESCRIBING PAST ACTIVITIES

anoche	*last night*
anteayer	*the day before yesterday*
el año pasado	*last year*
ayer	*yesterday*
el mes pasado	*last month*
la semana pasada	*last week*

OTHER WORDS AND PHRASES

la estrella	*star*
sabroso(a)	*tasty*

In the Kitchen

cocinar	*to cook*
el congelador	*freezer*
la estufa	*stove*
el frigorífico	*refrigerator*
el horno	*oven*
el lavaplatos	*dishwasher*
el microondas	*microwave*

Juego

¿Qué son estas cosas? ¿Dónde las pones?

1. laheod
2. suplacitosos
3. elhce
4. neredecasr

En tu propia voz

ESCRITURA

Una buena rutina diaria

For a contest, design an educational pamphlet in Spanish for teens and young adults. Depict healthful habits, such as eating nutritious food and exercising. The winning pamphlets will be used in recreational facilities across the country.

Function: Inform teens about healthful habits
Context: Addressing Spanish-speaking young adults
Content: Recommendations for healthful routines and nutrition
Text type: Educational pamphlet

PARA ESCRIBIR • STRATEGY: WRITING

Engage the reader by addressing him or her personally Address your reader directly. Use commands that personally address the reader. Your educational pamphlet will tell the reader what to do and what not to do for a healthy lifestyle.

Modelo del estudiante

The writer addresses the reader personally with **questions** directed to him or her.

Here the writer uses **tú commands** to tell the reader exactly what to do.

Negative tú commands work well, too, to tell the reader what not to do.

Friendly words add a personal touch to your pamphlet.

¿Te despiertas cansadísimo? ¿Preocupado? ¿Deprimido? Tal vez no duermes bien. Para levantarte de buen humor, sigue esta lista:

- Prepara toda tu tarea antes de acostarte.
- Haz los quehaceres por la noche; no esperes hasta la mañana.
- Lee un poco, acuéstate y duerme 8 horas.

Vas a levantarte contentísimo.

Oye, amigo, ¿cómo estás después de comer? Por favor, ¡come mejor!

- Limpia bien los platos.
- Come comida buena, como pollo o pescado, fruta fresca, verduras y pan.
- Come tranquilamente.
- Toma mucha agua durante el día. Toma leche, agua o jugo con tus comidas.

¡Vas a estar fabuloso!

¿No tienes tiempo para hacer ejercicio?

- Organiza tus quehaceres.
- Reserva una hora cada día para practicar un deporte o hacer ejercicio.
- Llama a un amigo para hacer ejercicio contigo. Es mucho más divertido así.
- ¡No seas perezoso! Usa la hora que reservaste.

Vas a tener muchísima energía.

Writing Center
CLASSZONE.COM

Estrategias para escribir

Antes de escribir...

With another student, brainstorm the details of your pamphlet:

- *Possible health issues to address*
- *Personal questions*
- *What your reader should do*
- *What your reader should avoid doing*

Discuss issues of nutrition, energy, stress management, etc., that people your age might like to know more about. Then choose one or more issues to focus on in your pamphlet. Use a chart like this one to organize your ideas.

Una buena rutina diaria

Recomendación	Preguntas personales	Qué hacer	Qué no hacer
comer mejor	¿Comes muchos postres?	Compra fruta fresca.	No vayas a la pastelería.
organizar tu tiempo	¿Estás nervioso porque nunca terminas tu tarea?		

Revisiones

Share your draft with a partner. Then ask:

- *How are health issues addressed?*
- *How does the pamphlet "speak" directly to the reader?*
- *What phrases clearly tell the reader what to do?*

La versión final

Before you create the final draft, look over your work with the following questions in mind:

- *Are affirmative **tú** commands used correctly?*

Try this: Underline all affirmative commands. Check that each verb is regular. If not, use the appropriate irregular form. Do reflexive verbs include their pronouns?

- *Are negative commands constructed properly?*

Try this: Circle all negative commands. Do they include appropriate stems?

Note the marks you can use to insert a period or a comma.

¡Oye, amigo! ¿Tienes muy poca energía? ¿Pasas mucho tiempo viendo la televisión? ¿Estás perezoso y aburrido? ¡Mira, tengo algunas ideas fabulosas para ti!

- Apaga la televisión y no la pone más esta semana. pongas
- te Levánta y llama a tu mejor Dile amigo. Dícele que van a jugar a su deporte favorito.
- ¡Saca las cosas necesarias y hazlo!

EDITORIAL MARKS

⊙ = **period** ^ = **comma**

UNIDAD 6

QUITO ECUADOR

LA CIUDAD Y EL CAMPO

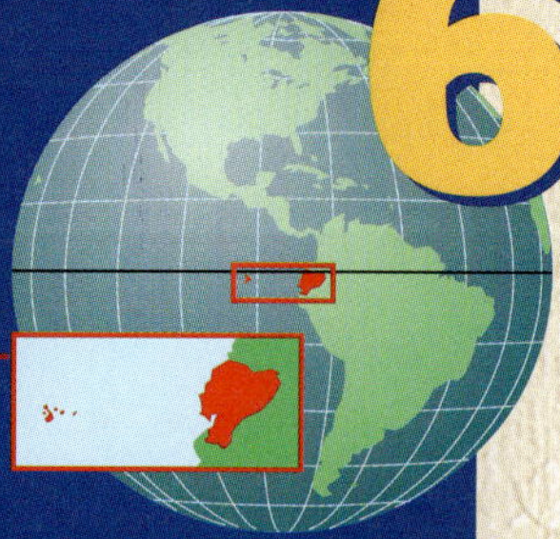

TEXAS Essential Knowledge and Skills

1 Communication

- **A Engage in exchanges**
  - *Talking about the past*
  - *Discussing the present and future*
  - *Giving instructions*
- **B Demonstrate understanding**
  - *Pointing out people and things and where they are located*
- **C Present information**
  - *Describing city buildings*
  - *Talking about professions*

2 Cultures

- **A Practices**
  - *The people of Otavalo, Ecuador*
  - *Other interesting places to visit in Ecuador*
- **B Products**
  - *Quito, Ecuador, and its buildings*
  - *International foods*

3 Connections

- **A Use resources**
  - *Health: Preparing a typical meal from a Spanish-speaking country*
- **B Use the language**
  - *Science: Finding out about animals*

4 Comparisons

- **A Nature of language**
  - *Place names in Ecuador and the U.S.*
- **B Concept of culture**
  - *Cultural groups in Ecuador and the U.S.*
- **C Influence**
  - *Foods and typical family meals in Ecuador and the U.S.*

5 Communities

- **B Lifelong learner**
  - *Using Spanish in the workplace*
  - *Using Spanish to help others*

LA MITAD DEL MUNDO is a monument built where the equator was measured. Ecuador's name comes from the fact that the equator **(el ecuador)** runs through it. What other countries of the world lie along the equator?

ALMANAQUE CULTURAL

POBLACIÓN: 1.610.800
ALTURA: 2.700 metros (8.775 pies)
CLIMA: 21° C (70° F) de día, 12° C (54° F) de noche
COMIDA TÍPICA: llapingachos, fritada
GENTE FAMOSA DE QUITO: Oswaldo Guayasamín (pintor), Jorge Icaza (escritor), Carlota Jaramillo (cantante)

¿VAS A QUITO? Quito es la capital de Ecuador. Su nombre viene de los indígenas quituas, un grupo muy antiguo.

More About Ecuador
CLASSZONE.COM

ATAHUALPA (1500–1533), son of the Incan king Huanya-Capac and grandson of Duchicela, king of Quito, is considered the first great Ecuadorian. He was heir to the kingdom of Quito and became leader of the Incan empire. Can you think of other Native American leaders?

PAPAS, a staple of the Ecuadorian diet, have been cultivated in the Andes since before the time of the Incas. This New World food was introduced by Spain to the European diet. What dishes made with potatoes do you eat?

UN RONDADOR is a wind instrument that has been used for more than 2000 years. It is made of cane or bamboo pieces of different widths and lengths. Each produces a distinct musical note. What other wind instruments do you know?

LA CASA DE SUCRE was once the home of independence leader Mariscal Antonio José de Sucre. It houses items from Quito's colonial and independence periods. What historic museums have you visited?

TAPICES are woven wall hangings and rugs made from the wool of sheep or alpaca. You will find these multicolored wall hangings in stores and outdoor markets. Where have you seen weavings?

UNIDAD 6

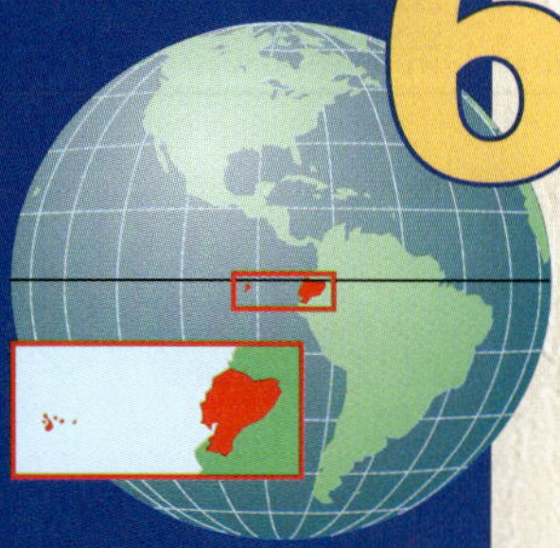

LA CIUDAD Y EL CAMPO

Texas Essential Knowledge and Skills

1 Comunicación

2 Culturas

3 Conexiones

4 Comparaciones

5 **Comunidades**

The student participates in communities at home and around the world by using Spanish.

Comunidades

Have you heard Spanish in your community? You may be able to use Spanish to tutor other students or to be a volunteer. In this unit you will learn about a student who uses Spanish to volunteer at a Boy Scout camp. There are also many paid professions in which Spanish skills are helpful. Health care, journalism, and teaching are just a few. What are some others?

Comunidades en acción **Describe una profesión que utilice el español. Tus compañeros de clase tienen que adivinar qué profesión es.**

Comunicación

Often you need to understand the words of others and pass them on. Perhaps you are interviewing someone from another country, or researching places to visit in the Spanish-speaking world. Or maybe you want to pass along an interesting story someone just told you. As a student of Spanish, you can understand and report what others have said.

Webquest
CLASSZONE.COM

Explore communities in Ecuador through guided Web activities.

Culturas

The indigenous people of Ecuador maintain strong cultural traditions and are talented artisans. Their textiles and other wares can be found in **mercados** surrounded by colonial churches and modern buildings, a colorful mix of old and new in Latin America.

Los mercados artesanales de Otavalo son muy populares entre los turistas. ¿Qué vende la mujer de esta foto?

Conexiones

Ecuador is one of the most geographically diverse countries in the world. The geography of Ecuador includes the Pacific coast, the Andes mountains, the Amazon jungle, and the Galápagos Islands. How does Ecuador's geography affect its climate? What different weather zones exist in this one country?

Quito está en un valle, con montañas por todas partes. Cuando hace sol es posible ver volcanes a la distancia, cubiertos de nieve.

Comparaciones

Your focus has been on learning Spanish, but you have probably begun to look at the English language differently. Have you learned anything about English that you didn't realize before? Do you think it would be easy or hard to learn English as a second language? Why?

Fíjate

Each of the following statements relates to one or more of the areas described (**Comunidades, Comunicación, Culturas, Conexiones, Comparaciones**). Determine which one each statement best represents.

1. El inglés y el español tienen muchas diferencias.
2. No hay **un** clima en Ecuador. ¡Hay muchos!
3. En Ecuador la vida moderna es una combinación de tradiciones indígenas y tradiciones europeas.
4. ¿Quién te llamó anoche? ¿De qué hablaron?
5. Una persona que sabe dos lenguas vale por dos personas.

UNIDAD 6

ETAPA 1

La vida de la ciudad

OBJECTIVES

- Tell what happened
- Make suggestions to a group
- Describe city buildings
- Talk about professions

¿Qué ves?

Mira la foto de un parque de Quito.

1. ¿Las montañas están cerca o lejos del parque?
2. ¿Qué hacen los dos jóvenes?
3. ¿Qué joyas lleva la señora?
4. ¿Cuántos parques hay en el mapa?

Negocios

En contexto
VOCABULARIO

VIDEO DVD AUDIO

Patricia is interviewing different people in Quito about their jobs. As she walks through old and new Quito, she describes different professions.

A *¡Hola!* Me llamo Patricia y voy a explicarles cómo son las profesiones de varias personas. Ahora estoy hablando con **un bombero.** Quiero saber algo de su trabajo. Con mi **grabadora** le hago **una entrevista.**

B Ella es **fotógrafa.** Saca fotos con **una cámara.** Está sacando una foto de **un edificio** muy **antiguo** y **tradicional.**

C **El cartero** lleva cartas a todos los edificios. A veces trabaja en el correo.

D Él es **taxista.** En su taxi lleva a la gente por toda la ciudad.

CD-ROM Take-Home Tutor

E **Mujer de negocios:** Me gusta vender y comprar productos. Ser una mujer de negocios es el trabajo perfecto para mí.

Hombre de negocios: Siempre leo todas las revistas de economía. Para ser un hombre de negocios hay que saber mucho.

F Él trabaja para un periódico. Le gusta escribir y hacer entrevistas. Por eso es **periodista.**

G Él es **arquitecto.** Hace planos de construcción. El edificio que planea aquí es el más grande de Quito. ¡Su oficina está en un edificio **enorme** y muy **moderno**!

Online Workbook
CLASSZONE.COM

Preguntas personales

1. ¿Te gusta hacer entrevistas?
2. ¿Prefieres edificios tradicionales o modernos?
3. ¿Tienes una cámara o una grabadora?
4. ¿Quién te lleva cartas?
5. ¿Cuál de estos trabajos te gustaría hacer?

En vivo

VIDEO DVD AUDIO

DIÁLOGO

Patricia | Miguel | Sra. Martínez | Sr. González

PARA ESCUCHAR • STRATEGY: LISTENING

Distinguish between what is said and not said Being a good listener means being careful and accurate. Which of these are mentioned in Patricia's interviews about city life? Which are not?

los trabajos	sí	mucha gente	
la calidad del aire		muchos vehículos	
el crimen		la vida aburrida	

En la ciudad

1 ▶ **Patricia:** Decidí participar en el concurso porque leí que los ganadores van a viajar. Quiero hacer entrevistas con personas en la ciudad y personas en el campo. Tú tienes familia en el campo, ¿no?

5 ▶ **Sra. Martínez:** Sí, pero también tiene sus problemas. La contaminación del aire, el tráfico…
Patricia: ¿Cómo se preparó para ser una mujer de negocios?

6 ▶ **Sra. Martínez:** Hice todo lo necesario. Fui a la universidad. Después me ofrecieron trabajo en el banco. Y llegué a ser gerente.
Patricia: ¿Y siempre vivió en Quito?
Sra. Martínez: Sí. Mis padres abrieron una panadería aquí.

7 ▶ **Patricia:** Buenas tardes, arquitecto González. Voy a escribir sobre el contraste entre la vida en la ciudad y en el campo.
Sr. González: ¿Qué quiere saber?
Patricia: ¿Le gusta vivir en la ciudad?

CD-ROM Take-Home Tutor

2 ▶ **Miguel:** Sí. ¿Los llamo?

Patricia: ¡Sí, muchas gracias, Miguel! Oye, vamos a pedir algo, ¿no? En un rato tengo que entrevistar a unas personas y no quiero llegar tarde.

3 ▶ **Patricia:** Buenos días. ¿Puede darme algunos minutos de su tiempo? Estoy preparando un artículo para un concurso.

Sra. Martínez: Claro que sí.

Patricia: Muy bien. ¿Cómo se llama y cuál es su profesión?

4 ▶ **Sra. Martínez:** Me llamo Ana Martínez. Soy una mujer de negocios. Trabajo en un banco aquí, en Quito.

Patricia: ¿Le gusta vivir en la ciudad?

8 ▶ **Sr. González:** La ciudad es interesante. Pero la vida en el campo es mucho más tranquila.

Patricia: ¿Vivió en el campo?

Sr. González: De niño viví en el campo, en casa de mis abuelos.

9 ▶ **Patricia:** ¿Y cuándo decidió venir a la ciudad?

Sr. González: Cuando entré a la universidad. Cuando recibí mi título de arquitecto, vi que en la ciudad hay más oportunidades que en el campo.

10 ▶ **Patricia:** ¿Miguel? Soy Patricia.

Miguel: ¿Cómo fueron las entrevistas?

Patricia: Excelente. Ya hice dos. ¿Llamaste a tu familia?

Miguel: Sí. Todo está listo para el sábado.

En acción

PARTE A Comprensión del diálogo

For Activities 1–2, refer to the dialog on pages 400–401.

1 ¿En qué orden?

Escuchar Según el diálogo, ¿en qué orden hace Patricia estas cosas? *(Hint: Put events in order.)*

- **a.** Patricia llama por teléfono a Miguel.
- **b.** Patricia le dice a Miguel por qué quiere participar en el concurso.
- **c.** Patricia va a la oficina del arquitecto.
- **d.** Patricia le hace una entrevista a la mujer de negocios.
- **e.** Patricia habla con Miguel sobre su familia del campo.

2 ¿Por qué?

Escuchar Explica por qué cada persona hace lo siguiente. *(Hint: Explain why.)*

1. ¿Por qué quiere Patricia participar en el concurso?
2. ¿Por qué habla Patricia con la mujer de negocios?
3. ¿Por qué vive el arquitecto en la ciudad?
4. ¿Por qué le gusta el campo al arquitecto?

PARTE B Práctica del vocabulario

Objectives for Activities 3–7
• Talk about professions • Describe city buildings

3 ¿Cuál es su profesión?

Hablar Todas estas personas trabajan en la ciudad. Tu amigo(a) quiere saber cuáles son sus profesiones. Cambien de papel. *(Hint: Say each profession.)*

modelo

Tú: *¿Cuál es la profesión del hombre?*

Tu amigo(a): *Es arquitecto.*

1.

2.

3.

4.

5.

6.

4 ¿Cómo son?

Escuchar Imagínate que haces una excursión de Quito. El guía describe los edificios. Indica el orden en que describe los edificios. *(Hint: Give the order.)*

a.

b.

c.

d.

Vocabulario

La ciudad

ancho(a) *wide*
estrecho(a) *narrow*
formal *formal*
informal *informal*
lujoso(a) *luxurious*
ordinario(a) *ordinary*
sencillo(a) *simple, plain*

¿Cómo son los edificios y las calles donde tú vives?

5 Un edificio interesante

Hablar Haz un dibujo de un edificio interesante de tu comunidad. Descríbelo. *(Hint: Draw a building and describe it.)*

modelo

La iglesia de mi comunidad es interesante. Es enorme y antigua. Cuando entras a la iglesia, ves que también es lujosa. Tiene muchos artículos de oro y ventanas de muchos colores.

6 Una ciudad grande

Escribir Imagínate que vas a visitar una ciudad grande. ¿Qué ciudad quieres visitar? ¿Qué sabes de la ciudad? Escribe un mínimo de seis oraciones para describirla. *(Hint: Describe a city.)*

modelo

Me gustaría visitar la ciudad de Nueva York. Sé que es una ciudad muy grande y divertida. En Nueva York hay muchos edificios enormes. Algunos son viejos y otros son muy modernos. Hay cosas interesantes en Nueva York. Hay…

PARTE C

Práctica: gramática y vocabulario

Objectives for Activities 8–20
- Tell what happened • Make suggestions to a group
- Talk about professions

7 ¿Cuál es tu opinión?

STRATEGY: SPEAKING
Exaggerate and react to exaggerations
As you discuss your opinions, you can be truthful or you can exaggerate. If you question the truth of what you hear, you can use these ways of expressing disbelief: **¿de veras?, ¿verdad?, ¡increíble!, ¡no me digas!, ¡no lo creo!** Use them when necessary.

Hablar Da tu opinión sobre las siguientes cosas. Luego, pregúntale a otro(a) estudiante cuál es su opinión. *(Hint: Give your opinion.)*

modelo

los edificios más interesantes

Tú: ***Los edificios más interesantes*** *son modernos. ¿Estás de acuerdo?*

Otro(a) estudiante: *No estoy de acuerdo. Para mí* ***los edificios más interesantes*** *son antiguos.*

Nota: Vocabulario

Estar de acuerdo means *to agree.* To say *I agree*, say **estoy de acuerdo.**

1. el edificio más bonito
2. la profesión más peligrosa
3. el actor más popular
4. el deporte menos aburrido
5. el mejor lugar para vivir
6. la profesión más interesante
7. la comida más rica
8. la peor estación del año

GRAMÁTICA The Preterite of -er and -ir Verbs

¿RECUERDAS? *p. 376* You've already learned to talk about completed past actions using regular **-ar** verbs.

limpiar *to clean*

limpié	**limpiamos**
limpiaste	**limpiasteis**
limpió	**limpiaron**

The **yo** forms and the **usted, él, ella** forms take **accents.**

Regular **-er** and **-ir** verbs follow a similar pattern. Notice that in the preterite, **-er** and **-ir** verb endings **match** each other.

ofrecer *to offer*

ofrecí	**ofrecimos**
ofreciste	**ofrecisteis**
ofreció	**ofrecieron**

decidir *to decide*

decidí	**decidimos**
decidiste	**decidisteis**
decidió	**decidieron**

Patricia asks:
—¿**Vivió** en el campo?
Did you live *in the country?*

Vocabulario

These verbs you know are regular in the preterite tense:

-er verbs

aprender, barrer, beber, comer, comprender, correr, devolver, entender, mover, perder, vender, volver

-ir verbs

abrir, compartir, escribir, recibir, salir, vivir

Practice: Actividades 8 9 10

Más práctica *cuaderno pp. 133–134*
Para hispanohablantes *cuaderno pp. 131–132*

Online Workbook CLASSZONE.COM

8 ¿Dónde vivieron?

Escribir Los amigos de Patricia comentan sobre las ciudades donde estudiaron durante un semestre. ¿Dónde vivieron? *(Hint: Where did they live?)*

modelo

Sam y Carlota: Barcelona

Sam y Carlota** vivieron en **Barcelona.

1. Enrique: Nueva York
2. nosotros: San Juan
3. tú: la Ciudad de México
4. Anita y yo: Miami
5. yo: San Antonio
6. ustedes: Los Ángeles
7. David: Madrid
8. Chela y yo: Oaxaca
9. Daniel y Jorge: Chicago
10. Victoria: Buenos Aires

Apoyo para estudiar

Preterite Tense

The **nosotros** forms of regular **-ir** verbs are the same in both the preterite and the present tenses, as are the **nosotros** forms of regular **-ar** verbs. Remember to use context clues to determine which tense is meant.

9 ¿Qué comiste?

Hablar Pregúntales a cinco estudiantes qué comieron y bebieron ayer. Preséntale a la clase un resumen de las respuestas. *(Hint: Ask what they ate and drank.)*

modelo

Tú: *¿Qué comiste y bebiste para el desayuno?*

Estudiante 1: *Comí cereal y bebí jugo.*

Resumen: *Para el desayuno, tres personas comieron cereal y dos comieron yogur. Cuatro personas bebieron jugo y una bebió leche.*

La comida	Estudiante 1	Estudiante 2
el desayuno	cereal, jugo	
el almuerzo		
la merienda		
la cena		

10 El otro día

Hablar/*Escribir* Explica qué hicieron tus amigos, tu familia y tú, usando las palabras indicadas como guía. *(Hint: Say what they did.)*

Nota: Gramática

The verb **ver** is regular in the preterite but does not have accents in any of its forms.

modelo

Yo salí con mis amigos anoche.

1. yo 2. mi hermano(a) 3. mis padres 4. mi amigo(a) 5. mis amigos y yo 6. ¿?	aprender compartir escribir recibir salir ver	¿?	anoche ayer anteayer la semana pasada el año pasado ¿?

GRAMÁTICA Talking About the Past: Verbs with a y Spelling Change

To write the third person **preterite** forms of **-er** and **-ir** verbs with **stems** that **end in a vowel,** change the **í** to **y**. Notice that all of these preterite forms require an accent, except the **ustedes, ellos(as)** forms.

oír *to hear*		**leer** *to read*		**creer** *to believe*	
oí	**oímos**	**leí**	**leímos**	**creí**	**creímos**
oíste	**oísteis**	**leíste**	**leísteis**	**creíste**	**creísteis**
oyó	**oyeron**	**leyó**	**leyeron**	**creyó**	**creyeron**

Patricia **leyó** algo del concurso.
*Patricia **read** something about the contest.*

Practice: Actividades 11 12 13
Más práctica *cuaderno p. 135*
Para hispanohablantes *cuaderno p. 133*
Online Workbook CLASSZONE.COM

11 Una conversación

Leer Dos amigos de Patricia están hablando de ella. Para saber lo que dicen, completa su conversación con la forma correcta del verbo **leer, oír** o **creer.** *(Hint: Complete their conversation.)*

Linda: ¿Por qué quiere participar Patricia en el concurso?

Raúl: __1__ en la revista que las personas que ganan van a viajar a diferentes países.

Linda: ¿Y __2__ ella la información que __3__?

Raúl: ¡Claro que sí! Mi hermana y yo también __4__ algo en la radio sobre el concurso.

Linda: ¿Qué __5__ ustedes?

Raúl: __6__ que las personas que ganan también van a trabajar como periodistas para la revista. ¿Y tú no __7__ nada en la radio sobre el concurso?

Linda: No, no __8__ nada en la radio. Tampoco __9__ nada en la revista.

12 ¡A leer!

Hablar/*Escribir* ¿Qué leyeron estas personas? *(Hint: What did they read?)*

la revista	el periódico
el poema	la tarea
el menú	el libro
la novela	

modelo

mi madre

Mi madre leyó una revista.

1. yo
2. mi amigo(a)
3. mis padres
4. mi padre
5. mi amigo(a) y yo
6. mis amigos
7. mi hermano(a)
8. mi maestro(a)
9. tú
10. ustedes

13 ¿Qué oyeron?

Hablar Todos fueron a un banquete y oyeron muchas cosas. Pregúntale a otro(a) estudiante lo que oyeron estas personas. *(Hint: Say what they heard.)*

modelo

tu amigo

Tú: *¿Qué oyó **tu amigo**?*

Otro(a) estudiante: *Oyó que Pedro no va a la fiesta.*

1. tu hermano(a)
2. tus amigos
3. tú
4. tu amigo(a)
5. tú y tu familia
6. tu padre
7. tus padres
8. tu maestro(a)
9. tu tío(a)
10. tus primos

More Practice: **Más comunicación** *p. R16*

Ecuador

Nota cultural

Quito is the second highest capital city in the world after La Paz, Bolivia. It is surrounded by mountains and volcanoes. The old city has colonial buildings with whitewashed walls and red-tiled roofs. The new city has many modern buildings.

GRAMÁTICA Using Irregular Verbs in the Preterite: hacer, ir, ser

¿RECUERDAS? *p. 300* Remember how to say *I went* and *you went* in Spanish?

fui fuiste

The verb **ir** is irregular in the **preterite.** Its preterite forms are exactly the **same** as the preterite forms of **ser. Hacer** also has irregular **preterite** forms. These verbs don't have any accents in the preterite.

ir/ser *to go/to be*

fui	fuimos
fuiste	fuisteis
fue	fueron

hacer *to make, to do*

hice	hicimos
hiciste	hicisteis
hizo	hicieron

Notice that the **c** becomes **z** before **o.**

The businesswoman says:

—**Hice** todo lo necesario. **Fui** a la universidad…

***I did** everything necessary. **I went** to the university…*

Practice: **Actividades** 14 15 16 17 18

Más práctica *cuaderno p. 136*

Para hispanohablantes *cuaderno p. 134*

Online Workbook CLASSZONE.COM

14 Hoy no, pero ayer sí

Leer Patricia explica lo que hacen hoy y lo que hicieron antes todas estas personas. Para saber qué hicieron, usa el pretérito del verbo **hacer.** *(Hint: Use the preterite of **hacer.**)*

modelo

Hoy no hago mi cama, pero ayer la hice *.*

1. Tú normalmente haces la tarea después de la cena, pero anoche la _____ antes.
2. Yo no voy a hacer la entrevista hoy porque la _____ ayer.
3. Anita y yo siempre hacemos ejercicio en el gimnasio, pero ayer no _____ nada.
4. Mamá y papá siempre me hacen un sándwich para el almuerzo, pero ayer no lo _____.
5. Normalmente no hago pasteles muy buenos, pero la semana pasada _____ uno riquísimo.
6. Mi mamá normalmente me hace vestidos muy bonitos, pero el año pasado no me _____ ninguno.
7. Normalmente hago los quehaceres los sábados, pero el sábado pasado no los _____.
8. A mamá le gusta hacer pan los domingos, pero el domingo pasado no lo _____.
9. No tengo que hacer las galletas hoy porque las _____ ayer.
10. Susana normalmente hace las camas, pero ayer las _____ Consuelo.

15 ¿Qué fueron?

Leer/*Escribir* Todos hablan hoy de sus antiguas profesiones. Lee las oraciones e indica qué profesión tuvo cada persona. *(Hint: Say what each person was.)*

modelo

Escribí una novela de romance.

Fui escritor(a).

1. Alfredo llevó muchísimas cartas.
2. La señora Rivera contestó el teléfono en la oficina y habló con los clientes que llegaron.
3. El señor Cano sacó muchas fotos de personas importantes.
4. Hiciste planos de casas buenísimos.
5. Llevaron a muchas personas al aeropuerto.
6. La señora Flores leyó los manuscritos de muchos escritores.
7. Ustedes trabajaron todo el día con números.
8. Escribí más de mil cartas para mi jefe.
9. Contestamos los teléfonos de toda la compañía.
10. Ellos hicieron muchas entrevistas.

Vocabulario

Las profesiones

la arquitectura *architecture*
la compañía *company*
el (la) contador(a) *accountant*
el (la) editor(a) *editor*
el (la) recepcionista *receptionist*
el (la) escritor(a) *writer*
el (la) gerente *manager*
el (la) jefe(a) *boss*
el (la) operador(a) *operator*
el (la) secretario(a) *secretary*

¿Cuándo visitas a estas personas?

16 ¿Adónde fueron?

Hablar/*Escribir* Todos salieron ayer. Explica adónde fue cada persona y cómo fue el día. *(**Hint**: Explain where they went.)*

modelo

Patricia: interesante

***Patricia** fue a la oficina del arquitecto. Fue **interesante**.*

1. Miguel: divertido

2. ustedes: ¿?

3. tú: aburrido

4. yo: ¿?

5. Miguel y yo: ¿?

6. mi familia: ¿?

17 ¿Adónde fuiste?

Hablar Pregúntale a otro(a) estudiante adónde fueron y qué hicieron estas personas el fin de semana pasado. *(**Hint**: Ask where these people went and what they did.)*

modelo

tus amigos

Tú: *¿Adónde fueron y qué hicieron **tus amigos** el fin de semana pasado?*

Otro(a): *El sábado mis amigos fueron a la cancha. Vieron un partido de baloncesto. El domingo no salieron.*

1. tu hermano(a)
2. tus padres
3. tú
4. tus amigos
5. tú y tu mejor amigo(a)
6. tus hermanos
7. tu mejor amigo(a)
8. ¿?

Ecuador

Nota cultural

In 2000, Ecuador changed its currency from the **sucre** to the U.S. dollar. The **sucre** had been the national currency for 116 years.

18 Un sábado especial

Escuchar Lee lo que hicieron Patricia, Marta y Andrea. Luego, escucha la conversación y explica quién hizo cada actividad. *(Hint: Indicate who did what.)*

1. Vio una película de acción.
2. Corrió en el parque.
3. Escribió una carta.
4. Comió en el restaurante Casa Linda.
5. Fue a un partido de fútbol.
6. Fue de compras.

Ecuador

También se dice

Ecuador has its own regionalisms for many of the items you already know in Spanish.

- **chompa:** chaqueta
- **departamento:** apartamento
- **esfero:** pluma, bolígrafo
- **saco:** suéter

19 Vamos a...

Hablar/*Escribir* Ana siempre quiere hacer algo con sus amigos. ¿Cómo los invita? *(Hint: What does she say?)*

modelo

¡Vamos a comer!

Nota: Gramática

When you want to say *Let's...!* use **Vamos a** + an infinitive.

1.

2.

3.

4.

Activity 21 brings together all concepts presented.

20 Tu calendario

Hablar/*Escribir* Haz un calendario imaginario o real de la semana pasada. Habla con otro(a) estudiante sobre lo que hicieron. *(Hint: Say what you did.)*

modelo

Estudiante A: *¿Qué hiciste el lunes?*

Estudiante B: *Aprendí un poema.*

lunes – aprendí un poema
martes –
miércoles –
jueves –
viernes –
sábado –
domingo –

21 Una entrevista

Hablar/*Escribir* Imagínate que eres periodista y otro(a) estudiante es profesional. Haz una entrevista, según las instrucciones. Escribe un resumen. *(Hint: Interview someone and write a summary.)*

Estudiante A: Imagínate que eres una persona profesional y que acabas de empezar un nuevo trabajo. Escoge una profesión. Contesta las preguntas del periodista.

Estudiante B: Imagínate que eres periodista y que estás escribiendo un artículo sobre los profesionales de la ciudad. Haz las preguntas necesarias.

¿Cuál es su profesión?
¿Dónde trabaja usted?
¿Qué hizo...?
¿Adónde fue para...?
¿Cómo se preparó para ser...?
¿Qué le gusta más del trabajo?
¿Qué es lo que menos le gusta del trabajo?

More Practice: **Más comunicación** *p. R16*

Online Workbook
CLASSZONE.COM

Apoyo para estudiar

Preterite of ir and ser

Since these verbs are the same in the preterite, how can you tell which is meant? Look at the context. If you see words that say where, **ir** is intended; if you see a description, **ser** is intended.

–¿Adónde fuiste anoche?

–Fui al cine. Vi una película de Antonio Banderas.

–¿Fue interesante?

–Sí, y también fue muy divertida.

Pronunciación

Trabalenguas

Pronunciación de la *d* When **d** begins a word or follows the letters **n** or **l**, it is pronounced with a hard sound, as it is in English. When **d** is between two vowels or at the end of a word, it is pronounced like the *th* in the English word *they*. To practice the **d**, try the following tongue twister.

Alcalde Machado   Alcalde Amador

Dos alcaldes, David Machado y Daniela Amador, danzan el fandango el sábado.

En voces

AUDIO

LECTURA

PARA LEER

STRATEGY: READING

Recognize place names It is easy to be confused by unfamiliar place names, but often there are simple words nearby to explain them. As you read each of the following place names, identify the word nearby that explains what it is.

NOMBRE	LUGAR
Amazonas	
La Carolina	
La Compañía	
El Ejido	
Pichincha	volcán

Saludos desde Quito

Un grupo de estudiantes está de visita en Quito, Ecuador. Aquí hay unas tarjetas que ellos les escribieron a sus amigos.

¡Hola! Hoy llegamos a Quito. ¡Estamos a sólo 24 kilómetros de la línea ecuatorial[1]! Fuimos en taxi al Cerro[2] Panecillo. Allí fue posible ver toda la ciudad. La ciudad es bonita y el paisaje[3] es maravilloso. Quito queda al lado del volcán Pichincha. Hoy, la cima se cubrió[4] de nieve, ¡pero en la ciudad la temperatura fue de 80 grados!

Alfonso

John Vivas
4231 Avenue M
Galveston, TX 77550
EE.UU.

[1] equator
[2] hill
[3] landscape
[4] the peak was covered

Ecuador

Nota cultural

Colonial comes from the word **colonia,** just as the word *colonial* in English comes from the word *colony*. In the U.S. *colonial times* refers to the period when the colonies were ruled by England. Ecuador was a colony of what country? What group designed its colonial areas?

¡Saludos desde Quito! Ayer paseamos por el Quito Colonial. Fue bonito caminar por las calles estrechas y ver las casas antiguas. Fuimos a la Plaza de la Independencia para ver la Catedral y el Palacio de Gobierno. ¡Allí sacamos muchas fotos! Después fuimos a la iglesia jesuita de la Compañía. Es famosa por su arte y su decoración de oro. Luego, en el Museo Arqueológico aprendí mucho sobre el arte precolombino[5]. Mañana vamos al sector moderno. ¡Hasta pronto!
Lucila

Elena M
59 Col
Coron
E.E.U

¿Qué tal? Hoy paseamos por el norte de Quito. ¡Qué diferencia! Las avenidas son anchas y hay parques grandes, como El Ejido y La Carolina. En el sector de la avenida Amazonas está la mayor parte de los hoteles, bancos, restaurantes caros y tiendas finas. Mañana vamos a visitar la Mitad del Mundo, un complejo turístico en la línea ecuatorial. Allí hay un museo, tiendas y restaurantes. Los domingos hay música típica de los Andes. Me encanta escuchar la música andina.
¡Hasta luego!
Marisa

Jennifer Herrera
131 Edgewater Drive
Orlando, FL 32804
EE.UU.

Online Workbook
CLASSZONE.COM

¿Comprendiste?

1. ¿Dónde queda Quito?
2. ¿Cómo es el Quito Colonial?
3. ¿Qué lugares puedes visitar en el Quito Colonial?
4. ¿Dónde está la parte moderna de Quito?
5. ¿Adónde vas para caminar por la línea ecuatorial?

¿Qué piensas?

1. ¿Qué diferencias hay entre el Quito Colonial y la ciudad moderna?
2. ¿Qué influencias crees que hay en la arquitectura del Quito Colonial?

Hazlo tú

Lee sobre el Quito Colonial y la ciudad moderna de Quito en la biblioteca o en Internet. Describe una excursión por el Quito Colonial. Indica los monumentos y edificios más importantes.

[5] pre-Columbian

ETAPA 1

En uso

REPASO Y MÁS COMUNICACIÓN

OBJECTIVES
- Tell what happened
- Make suggestions to a group
- Describe city buildings
- Talk about professions

Now you can...
- tell what happened.

To review
- preterite of regular **-er** and **-ir** verbs, see p. 404.

1 ¡Muy ocupados!

Todos participaron en un festival internacional el domingo pasado. ¿Qué hicieron? *(Hint: Tell what people did at the international festival.)*

modelo

usted: barrer el suelo después del festival

Usted barrió el suelo después del festival.

1. tú: recibir un regalo
2. mis amigos y yo: aprender algunos bailes ecuatorianos
3. mi madre: vender unas tapas
4. los periodistas: escribir muchos artículos sobre el festival
5. yo: compartir un postre enorme con mis hermanos
6. nosotros: beber mucha limonada
7. los niños: correr por todas partes
8. el fotógrafo: decidir sacar fotos de todas las actividades
9. tú: comer muchos llapingachos
10. yo: ver artesanías muy interesantes

Now you can...
- tell what happened.

To review
- preterite of verbs with a **y** spelling change, see p. 406.

2 ¿Lo creíste tú?

Imagínate que Patricia ganó el concurso, pero nadie lo creyó. ¿Dónde oyeron o leyeron el anuncio? *(Hint: Tell where people heard or read about the contest winner.)*

modelo

Miguel: por teléfono

***Miguel** lo oyó **por teléfono,** pero no lo creyó.*

el arquitecto: en el periódico

***El arquitecto** lo leyó **en el periódico,** pero no lo creyó.*

1. Patricia: en una carta
2. tú: en la televisión
3. la mujer de negocios: en la radio
4. los tíos de Miguel: por teléfono
5. yo: en la revista
6. nosotros: en el periódico

Self-Check Quiz
CLASSZONE.COM

Now you can...
- describe city buildings.
- tell what happened.
- talk about professions.

To review
- preterite of **hacer, ir, ser,** see p. 407.

3 ¿Qué fuiste tú?

Todos hablan de sus antiguas profesiones. ¿Qué dicen?
(Hint: Talk about people's former jobs.)

modelo

ella / gerente de un restaurante lujoso: ¿trabajar en una oficina formal o informal?
Ella fue gerente de un restaurante lujoso. Trabajó en una oficina formal.

1. ellos / hombres de negocios: ¿hacer contratos o ejercicio?
2. nosotros / bomberos: ¿ir a muchos conciertos o edificios?
3. tú / recepcionista de una compañía grande: ¿trabajar en un edificio pequeño o enorme?
4. tú y yo / periodistas: ¿hacer muchas tareas o entrevistas?
5. él / taxista: ¿ir a muchos o pocos lugares diferentes?
6. yo / escritor(a): ¿escribir cartas o novelas?
7. tú / cartero(a): ¿ir a muchos parques o muchas casas?
8. usted / arquitecto(a): ¿hacer planos o preguntas?

Now you can...
- make suggestions to a group.

To review
- **vamos a** + infinitive, see p. 410.

4 ¡Vamos a divertirnos!

Tu amigo(a) te invita a participar en varias actividades hoy. ¿Qué dicen? *(Hint: Suggest activities.)*

modelo

nadar
Tu amigo(a): *¡Vamos a **nadar**!*
Tú: *No, gracias. Voy al cine.*

1. levantar pesas
2. ir al cine
3. escuchar música
4. comer en un restaurante lujoso
5. jugar al tenis
6. ver la televisión
7. escribirle una carta al editor del periódico
8. pasear en el parque

5 ¿Qué hiciste ayer?

STRATEGY: SPEAKING

Relate details When retelling a past event, tell more than what you did **(¿qué hiciste?)**. People like to know details, such as where **(¿dónde?)**, with whom **(¿con quién?)**, and how it was **(¿cómo fue?)**. If your partner doesn't tell you all of the details, ask for them by using these questions.

Quieres saber lo que hizo otro(a) estudiante ayer. Usando los verbos de la lista, hazle preguntas. *(Hint: Talk about yesterday's activities.)*

comer | ir | leer | oír | ver | escribir | hacer | salir

modelo

Tú: *¿Hiciste ejercicio ayer?*

Otro(a) estudiante: *Sí, hice ejercicio en el parque. Caminé con mi perro. ¿Y tú?*

Tú: *Yo jugué al tenis.*

Otro(a) estudiante: *¿Qué comiste anoche?*

Tú: *Comí…*

6 Profesiones interesantes

Eres una persona profesional que ya no trabaja. Ahora estás visitando la clase de español. Los estudiantes te hacen preguntas para identificar tu profesión. La persona que identifica la profesión correcta es el (la) nuevo(a) profesional. *(Hint: Classmates ask questions to determine professions.)*

modelo

Estudiante 1: *¿Sacó usted fotos en su trabajo?*

Profesional: *No, no saqué fotos.*

Estudiante 2: *¿Trabajó usted en una oficina?*

Profesional: *Sí. Trabajé en una oficina muy lujosa.*

Estudiante 2: *¿Fue usted jefe(a)?*

Profesional: *Sí. Fui jefe(a) de una compañía enorme.*

7 En tu propia voz

ESCRITURA ¿Cómo es la ciudad ideal para ti? Dibújala y descríbela con un mínimo de seis oraciones. *(Hint: Draw and describe the ideal city.)*

modelo

En la ciudad ideal…

TÚ EN LA COMUNIDAD

Maynor, a native speaker of Spanish, is a high school student in California. He sometimes interprets for Spanish-speaking people who don't speak English when he's at his part-time job with a construction company. He also uses Spanish at his volunteer job at a Boy Scout camp. This helps boys who are more comfortable speaking in their native language. Additionally, he helps his friends who are learning Spanish to practice speaking the language. When do you use Spanish?

Flashcards
CLASSZONE.COM

En resumen

REPASO DE VOCABULARIO

DESCRIBING CITY BUILDINGS

ancho(a)	*wide*
antiguo(a)	*old, ancient*
el edificio	*building*
enorme	*huge, enormous*
estrecho(a)	*narrow*
formal	*formal*
informal	*informal*
lujoso(a)	*luxurious*
moderno(a)	*modern*
ordinario(a)	*ordinary*
sencillo(a)	*simple, plain*
tradicional	*traditional*

TALKING ABOUT PROFESSIONS

el (la) arquitecto(a)	*architect*
la arquitectura	*architecture*
el bombero	*firefighter*
la cámara	*camera*
el (la) cartero(a)	*mail carrier*
la compañía	*company*
el (la) contador(a)	*accountant*
el (la) editor(a)	*editor*
la entrevista	*interview*
el (la) escritor(a)	*writer*
el (la) fotógrafo(a)	*photographer*
el (la) gerente	*manager*
la grabadora	*tape recorder*
el hombre de negocios	*businessman*
el (la) jefe(a)	*boss*
la mujer de negocios	*businesswoman*
el (la) operador(a)	*operator*
el (la) periodista	*journalist*
la profesión	*profession*
el (la) recepcionista	*receptionist*
el (la) secretario(a)	*secretary*
el (la) taxista	*taxi driver*

MAKING SUGGESTIONS TO A GROUP

Vamos a...	*Let's...*

OTHER WORDS AND PHRASES

la contaminación del aire	*air pollution*
decidir	*to decide*
estar de acuerdo	*to agree*
el (la) ganador(a)	*winner*
ofrecer	*to offer*
el tráfico	*traffic*

Juego

¿Qué hacen sus padres?

El padre de Susana usa una cámara. El Sr. Rodríguez tiene un trabajo peligroso. Al papá de Adriana le gusta trabajar con los números.

1. ¿Quién es contador?
2. ¿Quién es fotógrafo?
3. ¿Quién es bombero?

UNIDAD 6

ETAPA 2

A conocer el campo

OBJECTIVES

- Point out specific people and things
- Tell where things are located
- Talk about the past

¿Qué ves?

Mira la foto de un taller en el campo de Ecuador.

1. ¿Las personas de la foto están contentas o tristes?
2. ¿Hay muchos o pocos sacos?
3. ¿De qué colores son los sacos?
4. ¿Cuál es el teléfono del taller?

Preparación para el diálogo

En contexto

VOCABULARIO

VIDEO DVD AUDIO

Patricia has left the city and is visiting the country. Look at the sights she sees and the people she meets.

A Aquí, en **el taller, la artesana** hace mucha ropa. Usa **lana** de muchos colores. La lana azul está **encima de** la mesa. La lana roja está **debajo de** la mesa.

B La mujer quiere el saco de **arriba.** Patricia quiere un gorro de **abajo.**

C En **la granja** hay varios animales. **El ganadero** cuida **estas vacas** que están aquí muy cerca. **Ese** animal, que está al otro lado de **la cerca,** es **un toro.**

Take-Home Tutor
CD-ROM

E **Aquellos** animales, que están lejos, son **llamas. El pastor** cuida las llamas.

F Aquí hay unos **cerdos.** El ganadero también tiene **un caballo.**

D Aquí hay **unas gallinas** y **un gallo.** Las gallinas están **dentro del corral.** El gallo está **fuera.**

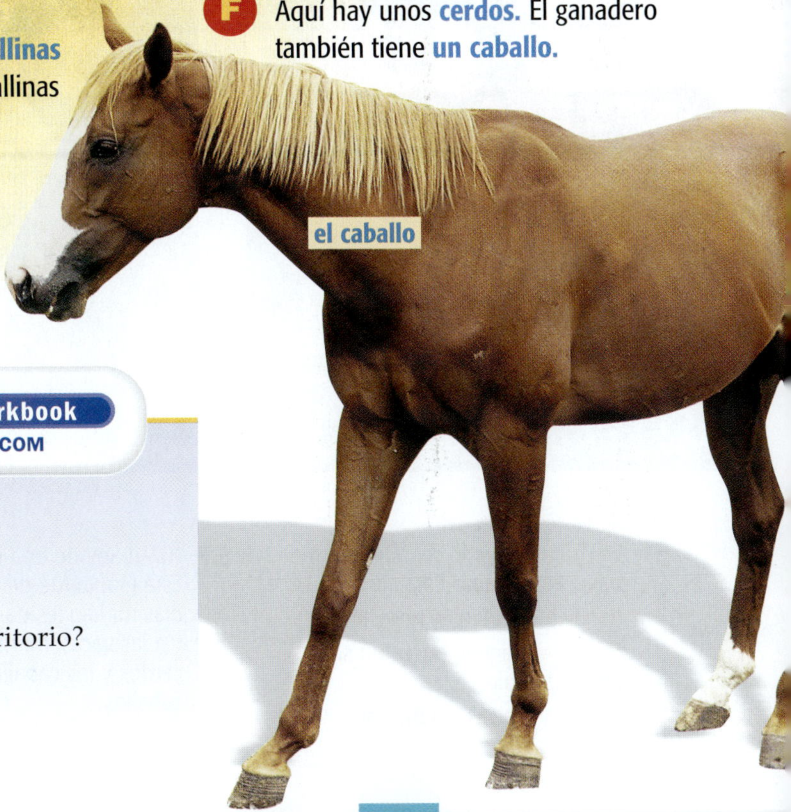

Online Workbook
CLASSZONE.COM

Preguntas personales

1. ¿Te gustan los caballos?
2. ¿Vives en el campo o en la ciudad?
3. ¿Te gustaría trabajar en una granja o en un taller?
4. ¿Qué hay encima de tu escritorio? ¿Debajo de tu escritorio?
5. ¿Qué ropa de lana tienes?

En vivo

VIDEO DVD AUDIO

DIÁLOGO

Patricia

Miguel

Bárbara

Julio

PARA ESCUCHAR • STRATEGY: LISTENING

Listen for implied statements Some things are said directly; others are suggested, but not stated. They are implied. Listen and decide which of the following are implied:

1. A slow, quiet life is boring.
2. Farm life requires hard work.
3. Life in both the city and the country is interesting.

What did you hear that influenced your decision?

En el campo

1► **Miguel:** ¡Buenos días, tía Bárbara!
Bárbara: ¡Miguel! ¡Bienvenidos! ¿Y tú eres Patricia?
Patricia: Sí. Es un placer.
Bárbara: ¿Te gusta mi taller?
Patricia: Sí, mucho.

5► **Bárbara:** Sí, ya lo sé. Miguel, ¿me bajas aquel saco? Está allí arriba.
Patricia: ¡Ay! No es necesario.
Bárbara: Miguel, busca un saco para ti también.
Miguel: Gracias, tía Bárbara.

6► **Julio:** Soy de una familia de ganaderos. Esta granja fue de mi abuelo. Todos los días mi hijo les da de comer a las gallinas y a las vacas. Mi hija menor cuida los cerdos y los caballos. Y hablando de caballos…

7► **Julio:** Miguel, ¿recuerdas la primera vez que viniste a visitarnos?
Miguel: Patricia no quiere oír esas viejas historias.
Julio: Pues, fue al corral, abrió la cerca y el caballo se escapó.

CD-ROM Take-Home Tutor

2 ▶ **Patricia:** ¿Cuándo vino usted a vivir aquí?
Bárbara: Vine en el año 1990.
Patricia: ¿Y le gusta vivir en el campo, en este pueblo pequeño?
Bárbara: Sí, es muy tranquilo.

3 ▶ **Bárbara:** A ver… ¿dónde están las tijeras? Ah, sí, allí están. Miguel, ¿me das las tijeras que están sobre la mesa?
Patricia: ¿Cómo fueron sus primeros años aquí?
Bárbara: Tuvimos que trabajar muchísimo.

4 ▶ **Patricia:** ¿Y venden los sacos y los gorros?
Bárbara: Sí, el mejor mercado es el mercado de Otavalo. Estuvimos ahí el domingo pasado.
Miguel: ¡A mí me gusta mucho ese mercado! ¡Vamos hoy!

8 ▶ **Julio:** Luego les dio de comer a las gallinas. ¡Les dio una bolsa de comida!
Miguel: ¡Tío Julio, por favor!
Julio: ¿Sabes, Patricia? ¡Miguel debe vivir en la ciudad!

9 ▶ **Patricia:** ¿Qué piensa usted de la ciudad?
Julio: Vamos a Quito todos los meses para visitar a mi hija mayor y su familia. Es muy interesante y hay mucho trabajo, pero vivimos aquí y estamos felices.
Patricia: Gracias, Julio.

10 ▶ **Julio:** Dice Miguel que ustedes van a Otavalo esta tarde.
Patricia: Sí.
Julio: ¿Te contó Miguel de la segunda vez que él nos acompañó a Otavalo?
Miguel: ¡Tío Julio!

En acción

PARTE A Comprensión del diálogo

For Activities 1–2, refer to the dialog on pages 422–423.

1 ¿En qué orden?

Escuchar ¿En qué orden pasaron estas cosas según el diálogo? *(Hint: Indicate the correct order.)*

a. Bárbara les da a Patricia y a Miguel unos sacos.
b. Patricia le hace una entrevista al tío Julio.
c. Patricia y Miguel van al mercado.
d. Patricia le hace una entrevista a Bárbara.
e. Patricia y Miguel llegan al campo.

2 ¿Qué pasa?

Escuchar Contesta las preguntas según el diálogo. *(Hint: Answer the questions.)*

1. ¿Por qué le gusta a Bárbara vivir en el campo?
2. ¿Dónde vende Bárbara la ropa que hace en su taller?
3. ¿Cómo fueron los primeros años de Bárbara en el campo?
4. ¿De quién fue la granja del tío Julio?
5. ¿Quiénes ayudan al tío Julio con su trabajo?
6. ¿Adónde van Patricia y Miguel después de visitar al tío Julio?

PARTE B Práctica del vocabulario

Objectives for Activities 3–5
- Point out specific people and things

3 Los animales de la granja

Hablar Patricia y Miguel vieron varios animales en el campo. ¿Qué vieron? *(Hint: Name the animals.)*

modelo
Vieron un caballo.

1.

2.

3.

4.

También se dice

In Spanish there are various words to describe people who work on farms or ranches. **Ganadero(a)** refers to a breeder of cattle or other livestock. **Granjero(a)** generally describes a worker on a poultry or dairy farm. To talk about a farmer who raises agricultural produce or plants, the word **agricultor(a)** is used. **Pastor(a)** describes someone who tends sheep.

4 Animales felices

Leer Patricia y Miguel ven este anuncio de alimento (comida) para animales en el camino al campo. Lee el anuncio y contesta las preguntas según la información.
(Hint: Answer questions.)

1. ¿Quién compra artículos de esta tienda?
2. ¿Qué vende la tienda?
3. ¿Qué animales ves en el anuncio?
4. ¿Qué días y horas está abierta la tienda?
5. ¿Dónde queda la tienda?

5 ¿Qué son?

Escuchar Todos hablan de su profesión. Escucha lo que dice cada persona e indica qué es, escogiendo la foto apropiada.
(Hint: Choose the correct picture.)

a.

b.

c.

d.

PARTE C

Práctica: gramática y vocabulario

Objectives for Activities 6–19

- Point out specific people and things
- Tell where things are located
- Talk about the past

GRAMÁTICA Saying Where Things Are Located

¿RECUERDAS? *p. 258* Remember prepositions of location?

cerca (de)	**entre**
delante (de)	**a la izquierda (de)**
a la derecha (de)	**al lado (de)**
detrás (de)	**lejos (de)**

You can also talk about the location of things using these words that you learned in **En contexto**:

abajo	**debajo (de)**	**encima (de)**
arriba	**dentro (de)**	**fuera (de)**

The words **arriba** and **abajo** are never followed by **de.**

Use **de** only when a **specific location** follows the expression.

Están **dentro del** taller.
*They are **inside** the workshop.*

—Miguel, ¿me bajas aquel saco? Está allí **arriba.**
*Miguel, (will you) get down that sweater for me? It's **up** there.*

Practice: Actividades 6 7 8

Más práctica *cuaderno p. 141*
Para hispanohablantes *cuaderno p. 139*

Online Workbook CLASSZONE.COM

6 ¿Dónde están?

Escribir Explica dónde están las personas y los animales. Completa cada oración con la palabra apropiada, según el dibujo. *(Hint: Explain where they are.)*

1. El cerdo está _____ del corral.

2. El gato está _____ de la cerca.

3. El artesano está _____ de su taller.

4. El pastor está _____.

5. El perro está _____ de la mesa.

7 Para el viaje

STRATEGY: SPEAKING

Recall what you know When describing where items are located, remember to use phrases that you learned earlier, such as **al lado de** and **a la derecha de,** as well as those you just learned.

Hablar Mira las cosas que Patricia va a llevar en su viaje al campo. Trabaja con otro(a) estudiante para preguntar dónde está cada cosa según el dibujo. Cambien de papel. *(Hint: Ask where things are.)*

modelo

1. el dinero

Estudiante A: *¿Dónde está **el dinero**?*

Estudiante B: *Está encima de la cama.*

8 Mi habitación

Escribir Piensa en tu habitación. ¿Qué hay allí? ¿Dónde está todo? Haz un dibujo y escribe un párrafo para describirla. *(Hint: Draw and describe your bedroom.)*

modelo

Hay muchísimas cosas en mi habitación. Hay muchos zapatos debajo de la cama y muchos libros encima del escritorio. Abajo, en el armario, hay ropa sucia y arriba hay...

Ecuador

También se dice

There are several words for *farm.*

- **la chacra:** many countries
- **la finca:** Colombia, Puerto Rico
- **la granja:** Argentina, Ecuador, Spain
- **la hacienda:** many countries
- **el rancho:** Mexico

GRAMÁTICA Pointing Out Specific Things Using Demonstratives

When you point out specific things, you use **demonstrative** adjectives and **pronouns.** In **En contexto** you saw how demonstrative adjectives are used. A **demonstrative** adjective describes the location of a **noun** in relation to a person.

Masculine Singular	Masculine Plural	Feminine Singular	Feminine Plural
este **cerdo** *this pig*	estos **cerdos** *these pigs*	esta **mesa** *this table*	estas **mesas** *these tables*
ese **cerdo** *that pig*	esos **cerdos** *those pigs*	esa **mesa** *that table*	esas **mesas** *those tables*
aquel **cerdo** *that pig (over there)*	aquellos **cerdos** *those pigs (over there)*	aquella **mesa** *that table (over there)*	aquellas **mesas** *those tables (over there)*

Bárbara says:

—Miguel, ¿me bajas aquel **saco**?
*Miguel, (will you) get down **that sweater** for me?*

Adjective relates location of the noun to a person

Demonstrative pronouns are used in place of the **adjective** and the **noun.** They are the same as the demonstrative adjectives except that they have an accent.

Masculine Singular	Masculine Plural	Feminine Singular	Feminine Plural
éste *this one*	**éstos** *these*	**ésta** *this one*	**éstas** *these*
ése *that one*	**ésos** *those*	**ésa** *that one*	**ésas** *those*
aquél *that one (over there)*	**aquéllos** *those (over there)*	**aquélla** *that one (over there)*	**aquéllas** *those (over there)*

Bárbara might have said: —Miguel, ¿me bajas **aquél** que está arriba?
*Miguel, would you get down **that one** up there for me?*

There are also **demonstrative** pronouns that refer to ideas or unidentified things that do not have a specific gender.

Esto es importante.
***This** is important.*

¿Qué es **eso?**
*What's **that?***

¿Qué es **aquello?**
*What's **that over there?***

Practice: Actividades 9 10 11

Más práctica *cuaderno p. 142*
Para hispanohablantes *cuaderno p. 140*

Online Workbook CLASSZONE.COM

9 En el mercado

Leer Patricia y Miguel están en una tienda. Completa sus oraciones con un adjetivo demostrativo. *(**Hint:** Complete what they say.)*

Patricia: ¿Te gusta __1__ bufanda amarilla?

Miguel: Prefiero __2__ bufanda blanca.

Patricia: ¿Y __3__ saco marrón?

Miguel: No es mi color favorito. Prefiero __4__ saco verde.

Patricia: Bueno, si te gusta el color verde, ¿por qué no compras __5__ mochila verde?

Miguel: La verdad es que prefiero __6__ mochila marrón.

Patricia: Ay, Miguel, ¡no te entiendo!

10 De compras

Hablar Imagínate que tú y un(a) amigo(a) van de compras. Habla de las cosas que ven según el modelo. Tú decides si están cerca o lejos. Cambien de papel. *(**Hint:** Talk about what you see.)*

modelo

las raquetas

Estudiante A: *¿Te gustan estas **raquetas**?*

Estudiante B: *Sí, pero prefiero ésas.*

1. la pelota
2. los pantalones
3. las gorras
4. el guante de béisbol
5. la falda
6. el abrigo
7. las gafas
8. los zapatos
9. la camiseta
10. los cascos

11 En la clase

Hablar/*Escribir* En grupos de tres, compara las cosas que tiene cada persona. Escribe las oraciones de tu grupo. *(**Hint:** Compare your possessions.)*

modelo

libro(s)

Estudiante A: *Estos **libros** son más grandes que ésos.*

1. libro(s)
2. pluma(s)
3. silla(s)
4. cuaderno(s)
5. mochila(s)
6. escritorio(s)
7. borrador(es)
8. calculadora(s)
9. diccionario(s)
10. ¿?

More Practice: **Más comunicación** *p. R17*

GRAMÁTICA Ordinal Numbers

When you talk about the order of items, use **ordinal numbers.** These are the first ten **ordinal numbers.**

- When used with nouns, they must agree in number and gender.
- Ordinals are placed **before nouns.**
- **Primero** and **tercero** drop the **o** before a **masculine singular** noun.

Patricia asks: *before the noun*

—¿Cómo fueron sus **primeros años** aquí?
*How were your **first** years here?*

Bárbara might say: *drops the o*

—Fue muy difícil hasta el **tercer** año.
*It was very difficult until the **third** year.*

To say *last,* use **último(a).**

La **última** vez que Miguel fue a Otavalo…
*The **last** time Miguel went to Otavalo…*

Practice: Actividades 12 13 14

Más práctica *cuaderno p. 143*
Para hispanohablantes *cuaderno p. 141*

Online Workbook CLASSZONE.COM

12 El orden

Hablar Patricia está con un grupo de amigos. Hacen cola para ver una película. Tú le preguntas a tu amigo(a) quiénes son. *(Hint: Ask who they are.)*

modelo

Patricia

Tú: *¿Quién es **Patricia**?*

Tu amigo(a): *Ella es la segunda.*

1. Felipe
2. Miguel
3. Carlos
4. Antonio
5. Marta
6. Ramona
7. Diego
8. Ana
9. Linda

13 ¿Quién llegó primero?

Hablar/*Escribir* Patricia y sus amigos participaron en una carrera. ¿En qué orden llegaron? *(Hint: Give their order in the race.)*

modelo

Patricia: 2 — ***Patricia** fue la **segunda** chica en llegar.*

1. Elena: 7
2. Antonio: 1
3. Ramón: 3
4. Linda: 8
5. Carlos: 10
6. Miguel: 4
7. Marta: 6
8. Alfredo: 9
9. Diego: 5

14 El primer día...

Escribir Explica en qué día hiciste las cosas durante las vacaciones. *(Hint: In what order did you do things?)*

modelo

***El segundo** día fui a un museo.*

1. primero(a)
2. segundo(a)
3. tercero(a)
4. cuarto(a)
5. quinto(a)
6. sexto(a)
7. séptimo(a)
8. último(a)

GRAMÁTICA Irregular Preterite Verbs

You've learned that **hacer, ir,** and **ser** are irregular in the preterite. Here are some other irregular preterite verbs. Notice that the forms for **dar** are similar to those for **ver. Decir** and **venir** have their own special forms.

dar *to give*		**decir** *to say, to tell*		**venir** *to come*	
di	dimos	dije	dijimos	vine	vinimos
diste	disteis	dijiste	dijisteis	viniste	vinisteis
dio	dieron	dijo	dijeron	vino	vinieron

Although the verbs **tener** and **estar** have irregular endings in the preterite, their forms follow similar patterns.

tener *to have*		**estar** *to be*	
tuve	tuvimos	estuve	estuvimos
tuviste	tuvisteis	estuviste	estuvisteis
tuvo	tuvieron	estuvo	estuvieron

Bárbara says: —**Vine** al campo en el año 1990.
***I came** to the country in 1990.*

—**Tuvimos** que trabajar muchísimo.
***We had** to work a whole lot.*

—**Estuvimos** ahí el domingo pasado.
***We were** there last Sunday.*

Do not use **estar** in the preterite to express feelings.

Practice: **Actividades** 15 16 17 18 19

Más práctica *cuaderno p. 144*
Para hispanohablantes *cuaderno p. 142*

Online Workbook CLASSZONE.COM

15 Todos ayudaron en la granja

Escribir Hay muchos animales en la granja del tío Julio. Muchas personas lo ayudaron con el trabajo. ¿A qué animales les dio de comer cada persona? *(Hint: Which animals did they feed?)*

modelo

Patricia: los cerdos — ***Patricia** les dio de comer a **los cerdos**.*

Nota: Vocabulario

The expression **darle(s) de comer** means *to feed.*

Le di de comer a mi gato. *I **fed** my cat.*

1. yo: el toro
2. ustedes: los gatos
3. Miguel: las llamas
4. tú: el gallo
5. mi hija: los caballos
6. mis hijos y yo: las vacas
7. mi esposa: el perro
8. mi hijo: las gallinas

16 ¿Por qué no vinieron?

Hablar Miguel invitó a varios amigos al campo el domingo, pero muchos no vinieron. Le pregunta a Patricia por qué. Cambien de papel. *(Hint: Explain why they didn't come.)*

modelo

Enrique (estudiar)

Miguel: *¿Por qué no vino **Enrique**?*

Patricia: *Enrique no vino porque tuvo que **estudiar.***

1. tú (hacer unos quehaceres)
2. Carlos y Alicia (trabajar)
3. tu hermana y tú (limpiar la casa)
4. Ana (ir a una fiesta de cumpleaños)
5. Felipe (hacer su tarea)
6. Juan y Jorge (visitar a sus abuelos)
7. Antonio (escribir una carta)
8. Cacho (ir al teatro)
9. Adán y Verónica (cuidar a sus hermanitos)
10. Marcos y Emiliano (jugar al fútbol)

17 ¿Dónde estuvo?

Hablar Pregúntales a tres estudiantes dónde estuvieron y qué hicieron estas personas el domingo. Luego, haz un resumen para la clase. *(Hint: Say where they were.)*

modelo

tu hermana

Tú: *¿Dónde estuvo y qué hizo **tu hermana** el domingo?*

Estudiante 1: *Estuvo en la cancha. Jugó al tenis.*

Resumen: *Un estudiante dijo que su hermana estuvo en la cancha el domingo. Jugó al tenis. Dos dijeron que sus hermanas estuvieron en la iglesia.*

	Estudiante 1
1. tú	
2. tu hermano(a)	
3. tus padres	
4. tú y tus amigos(as)	

Ecuador

Nota cultural

Quichua, an indigenous language, is still commonly spoken in certain regions of Ecuador, particularly in the mountains. Here is a Quichua expression used in Ecuador today.

¡Achachái!

(¡Qué frío!)

Activity 20 brings together all concepts presented.

18 Las cosas que nos pasan

Hablar/*Escribir* Describe algo que te pasó. Usa una forma de cada verbo por lo menos una vez. ¡Usa tu imaginación si es necesario! *(Hint: Describe something that happened.)*

dar	tener	decir
ver	hacer	ser
estar	venir	

modelo

Mis primas vinieron a visitarme. Me dieron un regalo. Fue una falda azul larga.

19 Un día bonito

Escuchar Escucha el párrafo sobre el viaje que hizo Luisa. Luego, ordena las fotos según lo que escuchaste. *(Hint: Put the pictures in order.)*

a.

b.

c.

d.

20 Un día en el campo

Escribir Escribe un párrafo sobre un viaje real o imaginario que hiciste al campo o a otro lugar. Usa las preguntas como ayuda. *(Hint: Write about a trip.)*

¿Adónde fuiste?
¿Qué oíste?
¿Qué viste?
¿Qué hiciste?
¿Con quién fuiste?

More Practice: **Más comunicación** *p. R17*

Online Workbook
CLASSZONE.COM

Pronunciación

Trabalenguas

Pronunciación de la *l* The letter **l** is pronounced like the *l* in the English word *lucky.* Practice its sound by saying this tongue twister.

Lana, Lena, Lina y Lulú
van y ven al león con el balón.
Al león con el balón ven
Lana, Lena, Lina y Lulú.

VIDEO DVD

En colores

CULTURA Y COMPARACIONES

PARA CONOCERNOS

STRATEGY: CONNECTING CULTURES

Research cultural groups The term *indigenous people* is used to refer to the original or native inhabitants of a region. Who were or are the indigenous people where you live? When researching, make sure to ask the five *W* questions: *who?, what?, when?, where?, why?* Make up five research questions about the original people of your area, using these words as prompts.

¿Quién?	
¿Qué?	
¿Cuándo?	
¿Dónde?	
¿Por qué?	

Use these questions to gather information as you read **«Los otavaleños».**

LOS OTAVALEÑOS

Si sales de Quito por la Carretera Panamericana[1] hacia el norte del país, vas a ver un paisaje[2] impresionante. Hay espléndidas vistas de montañas, volcanes y lagos. Entre Quito y la frontera[3] con Colombia hay un valle entre las montañas Imbabura y Cotacachi. Allí queda el pueblo de Otavalo.

Aquí viven los otavaleños. Este grupo indígena se conoce[4] por su artesanía, su éxito[5] económico y la preservación de sus costumbres folclóricas. Los sábados, los otavaleños organizan un mercado tradicional. Hay frutas y verduras, animales y lo más interesante para los turistas: tejidos[6] y artesanías. En este mercado

[1] Pan-American Highway
[2] landscape
[3] border
[4] is known
[5] success
[6] woven goods

puedes comprar ponchos, chompas y tapices de lana hechos[7] por los otavaleños. Los otavaleños también venden sombreros hechos a medida[8]. Como en todo mercado, ¡es importante regatear!

Hacer tejidos es una tradición de los indígenas de Otavalo. En 1917 empezaron a imitar los casimires[9] ingleses y así nació[10] la industria textil. Las personas que hacen los tejidos son de Otavalo y los pueblos cercanos, como Peguche, Ilumán, Carabuela y Quinchuqui.

Si visitas Otavalo, debes conocer la Plaza Bolívar, donde está la estatua del general inca Rumiñahui. También puedes aprender un poco de la historia y la arqueología de esta región en el Instituto Otavaleño de Antropología.

[7] made
[8] custom-made
[9] tweeds
[10] was born

Ropa tradicional otavaleña

More About Ecuador
CLASSZONE.COM

¿Comprendiste?

1. ¿Dónde queda Otavalo? ¿Cómo llegas?
2. ¿Qué importancia tiene Otavalo?
3. ¿Qué cosas venden en el mercado de Otavalo?
4. ¿Cómo y cuándo empezó la industria textil?
5. ¿Qué lugares puedes conocer en Otavalo?

¿Qué piensas?

1. ¿Por qué debes regatear si visitas Otavalo?
2. ¿Qué puedes hacer para aprender más de la vida de los otavaleños de hoy?

Hazlo tú

¿Hay artesanos en tu comunidad? Explica qué hacen. Si no hay, investiga alguna artesanía de Estados Unidos y haz un reportaje sobre esto.

ETAPA 2

En uso

REPASO Y MÁS COMUNICACIÓN

OBJECTIVES

- Point out specific people and things
- Tell where things are located
- Talk about the past

Now you can...

- tell where things are located.

To review

- location words, see p. 426.

1 En el campo

Imagínate que estás en el campo. ¿Qué ves? *(Hint: Tell what you see in the country.)*

modelo

dentro del corral, con los cerdos

El ganadero está ***dentro del corral, con los cerdos.***

1. debajo del árbol
2. arriba, con las llamas
3. encima de la cerca
4. abajo
5. fuera de su casa
6. dentro del corral, con el ganadero

Now you can...

- point out specific people and things.

To review

- ordinal numbers, see p. 430.

2 ¿Qué carro?

Estas personas participaron en una carrera. ¿Qué carro manejó cada uno? *(Hint: Say who drove what car in the race.)*

modelo

Campos: 4

Campos *manejó el cuarto carro.*

1. Molina: 2
2. Anaya: 7
3. Valencia: 9
4. Ibarra: 1
5. Quintana: 5
6. Blanco: 10
7. Rojas: 8
8. Espinoza: 3
9. Santana: 6

Self-Check Quiz
CLASSZONE.COM

Now you can...
- point out specific people and things.

To review
- demonstratives, see p. 428.

3 ¿Quiénes son?

Hay una fiesta de disfraces hoy. ¿Quiénes son estas personas?
*(**Hint:** Identify the people at the costume party.)*

modelo

maestra *Esa mujer es **maestra.***

1. policías
2. fotógrafa
3. bomberos
4. periodista
5. cartero
6. taxista
7. mujeres de negocios
8. doctor

Now you can...
- talk about the past.

To review
- irregular preterite verbs, see p. 431.

4 Un día especial

Patricia se encuentra con una amiga en Otavalo. Completa lo que dice con la forma correcta de los verbos **dar, decir, estar, tener** o **venir.** *(**Hint:** Complete with the preterite of the correct verb.)*

Hoy Miguel y yo __1__ en el campo toda la mañana. Yo __2__ tiempo de hacer algunas entrevistas para mi proyecto. Los parientes de Miguel me __3__ muchas cosas interesantes sobre la vida en el campo. El tío Julio también me __4__ algunas cosas cómicas sobre Miguel. Al final de la entrevista con Bárbara, ella me __5__ un regalo: este saco bonito. Después de la segunda entrevista, el tío Julio y su esposa nos __6__ de comer. Luego, nosotros __7__ aquí a Otavalo.

5 ¿Y aquel caballo?

STRATEGY: SPEAKING

Use words that direct others' attention You now have many ways to indicate one person, animal, or object among several. Remember to use them all.

- Indicate location (**al lado de,** etc.).
- Indicate order (**el segundo, el último**).
- Indicate distance (**este, ese, aquel**).

Imagínate que tienes dos mil dólares para comprar animales de la granja de un(a) ganadero(a). Regatea para recibir el mejor precio. *(**Hint**: Bargain for farm animals.)*

modelo

Tú: *¿Cuánto cuesta aquella vaca?*

Ganadero(a): *Aquélla es muy buena. Da mucha leche. Cuesta mil dólares.*

Tú: *¡Es demasiado! Le puedo ofrecer ochocientos.*

Ganadero(a): *No puedo vender aquélla por menos de novecientos, pero le dejo esta vaca más pequeña en setecientos.*

Tú: *Está bien. ¿Y ese cerdo que está en el corral?…*

6 ¿Dónde está?

Tus amigos buscan algo en la clase. Sólo tú sabes qué es y dónde está. Contesta sus preguntas. *(**Hint**: Classmates ask questions to find and identify objects.)*

modelo

Estudiante 1: *¿Está encima del escritorio de la maestra?*

Tú: *No, no está encima del escritorio de la maestra.*

Estudiante 2: *¿Está dentro de tu mochila?*

Tú: *Sí, está dentro de mi mochila.*

Estudiante 2: *¿Es tu libro de inglés?*

Tú: *Sí, es mi libro de inglés.*

7 En tu propia voz

ESCRITURA Haz una lista de diez cosas que pasaron en la escuela este año. Pon los sucesos en orden cronológico y escribe oraciones explicando cada uno. *(**Hint**: List ten things that happened at school this past year in chronological order.)*

modelo

Primero, las clases comenzaron en agosto y todos los estudiantes vinieron a la escuela. Segundo, tuvimos que aprender los nombres de los estudiantes en español durante la primera semana de clases. Tercero, en octubre…

CONEXIONES

Las ciencias Choose an animal whose name you've learned, such as the **llama**, or find out the Spanish name for another animal that is found in Ecuador. (**Vicuñas** and **alpacas** are close relatives of the **llama.**) Do some research on the animal. Draw a picture of it and write a short paragraph that answers the questions in the chart.

¿Cómo es el animal?
¿De qué color(es) es?
¿Dónde vive?
¿Qué come?
¿Es útil para la gente? ¿Para qué?

Flashcards
CLASSZONE.COM

En resumen

REPASO DE VOCABULARIO

POINTING OUT SPECIFIC PEOPLE AND THINGS

Indicating Which One

aquel(la)	*that (over there)*
aquél(la)	*that one (over there)*
aquello	*that (over there)*
ese(a)	*that*
ése(a)	*that one*
eso	*that*
este(a)	*this*
éste(a)	*this one*
esto	*this*

Ordinal Numbers

primero(a)	*first*
segundo(a)	*second*
tercero(a)	*third*
cuarto(a)	*fourth*
quinto(a)	*fifth*
sexto(a)	*sixth*
séptimo(a)	*seventh*
octavo(a)	*eighth*
noveno(a)	*ninth*
décimo(a)	*tenth*

People

el (la) artesano(a)	*artisan*
el (la) ganadero(a)	*rancher, farmer*
el (la) pastor(a)	*shepherd(ess)*

At the Farm

el caballo	*horse*
la cerca	*fence*
el cerdo	*pig*
el corral	*corral, pen*
la gallina	*hen*
el gallo	*rooster*
la granja	*farm*
la llama	*llama*
el toro	*bull*
la vaca	*cow*

TELLING WHERE THINGS ARE LOCATED

abajo	*down*
arriba	*up*
debajo (de)	*underneath, under*
dentro (de)	*inside (of)*
encima (de)	*on top (of)*
fuera (de)	*outside (of)*

OTHER WORDS AND PHRASES

el campo	*countryside, country*
darle(s) de comer	*to feed*
la lana	*wool*
el taller	*workshop*
las tijeras	*scissors*
último(a)	*last*

Juego

¿En qué orden terminaron la carrera?

UNIDAD 6

ETAPA 3

¡A ganar el concurso!

OBJECTIVES

- Talk about the present and future
- Give instructions to someone
- Discuss the past

¿Qué ves?

Mira la foto del mercado de Otavalo.

1. ¿Las vendedoras sólo venden ropa?
2. ¿Hace mucho calor o no? ¿Cómo lo sabes?
3. ¿De qué color es la blusa tradicional de las mujeres de Otavalo?
4. ¿Para qué es la carta que Patricia escribió?

En contexto

VIDEO DVD AUDIO

VOCABULARIO

Do you remember all that you have learned this year? You have learned to talk about the present, the future, and the past, and to give instructions. Take a look at these people and places for a quick review of what you have learned.

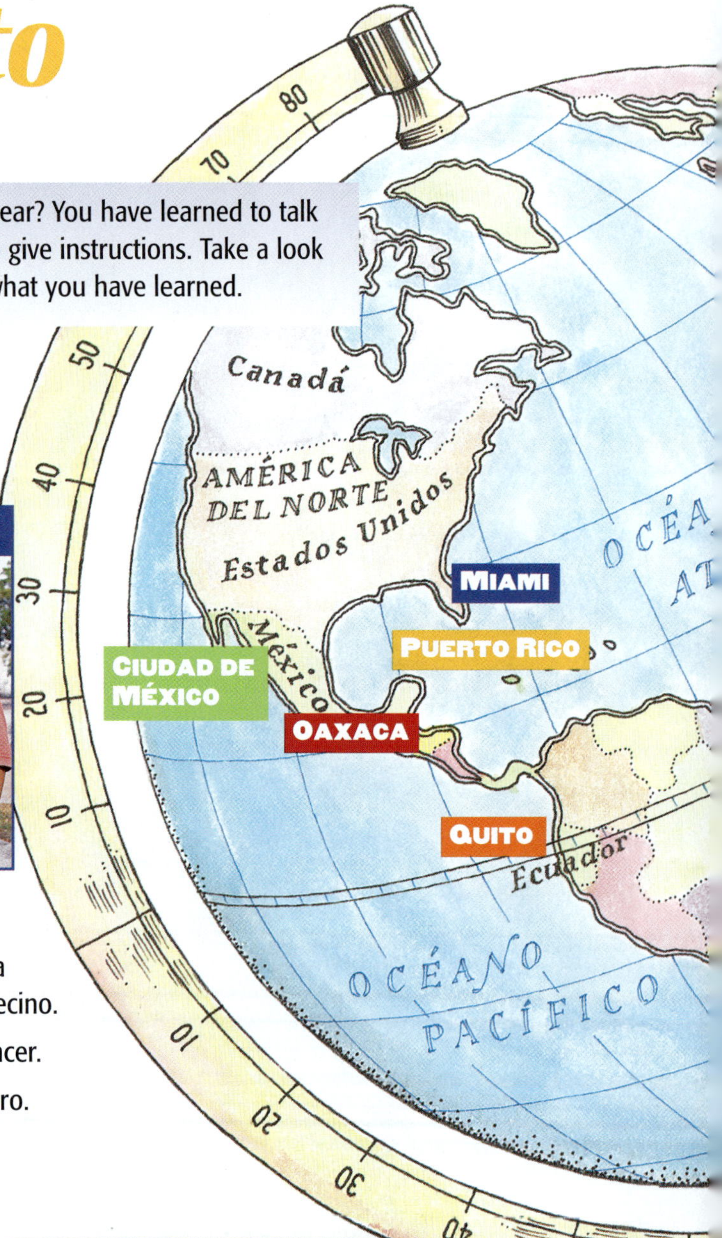

¡Hola! Aprendiste mucho este año. ¿Recuerdas todo lo que ves aquí?

MIAMI

A Talk about the present

Alma: Arturo, te **presento** a Francisco García. Él **es** mi vecino.

Arturo: Francisco, **es** un placer.

Francisco: Igualmente, Arturo.

CIUDAD DE MÉXICO

B Talk about the future

Isabel: **¡Voy a participar** en el concurso! Para conocer a los mexicanos, hay que ir a una plaza. La plaza es un poema.

PUERTO RICO

C **Say what is happening**

Ignacio: ¡Está lloviendo! ¡Y no tengo paraguas!

Roberto: Te estamos esperando, hombre.

OAXACA

D **Give instructions**

Carlos: Vas a llegar a un parque. Cruza el parque. Enfrente de la estatua está la calle Morelos.

Rosa: Muchas gracias…

E **Discuss the past**

Luis: ¡El día empezó con demasiados quehaceres!

Carmen: ¡Yo te ayudé, Luis!

Luis: Sí, Carmen, tú me ayudaste y Mercedes también me ayudó.

BARCELONA

QUITO

F **Discuss the past**

Miguel: ¿Cómo fueron las entrevistas?

Patricia: Excelente. Ya hice dos.

CD-ROM Take-Home Tutor

Online Workbook CLASSZONE.COM

Preguntas personales

1. ¿Quién es tu mejor amigo? ¿amiga?
2. ¿Qué vas a hacer este fin de semana?
3. ¿Qué está pasando en tu clase?
4. Explica cómo llegar a tu casa.
5. ¿Qué hiciste este año?

En vivo

VIDEO DVD AUDIO

DIÁLOGO

Patricia

Miguel

PARA ESCUCHAR • STRATEGY: LISTENING

Listen and take notes This conversation sums up Patricia's work on her project. What does she think about her work? As you jot down her ideas, listen for answers to *who? what? when? where?* and *why?* Use your notes to make a summary statement about Patricia's project.

¡Vamos a Otavalo!

1 ▶ **Miguel:** ¿Estás feliz con tus entrevistas?

Patricia: Sí, estoy muy feliz. Hice entrevistas con un arquitecto, la gerente de un banco y también con tu tío Julio y Bárbara.

5 ▶ **Patricia:** Pero aprendí algo mucho más importante también.

Miguel: ¿Sí? Dime.

Patricia: Aprendí que no tienes ni idea de lo que hay que hacer en una granja. ¡Abriste la cerca!

6 ▶ **Patricia:** ¡Mira, Miguel! ¡Es un mercado fenomenal! Voy a comprarle un regalo a mi hermana. Su cumpleaños es este mes.

Miguel: Cómprale una bolsa o un artículo de cuero. La artesanía de Otavalo es excelente.

7 ▶ **Patricia:** No sé si tengo suficiente dinero… a ver… ¿Crees que puedo regatear aquí?

Miguel: ¡Claro que sí! Es un mercado, ¿no? ¡Ven!

CD-ROM Take-Home Tutor

2 ▶ **Miguel:** ¿Cuál fue la mejor entrevista?

Patricia: No sé… Creo que fue la entrevista con tu tío Julio.

Miguel: ¿Y por qué? ¿Porque te habló de la vida en una granja?

3 ▶ **Patricia:** No, ¡porque me dijo qué hiciste tú la primera vez que estuviste en la granja!

Miguel: ¡Patricia!… ¿Y aprendiste algo de tus entrevistas?

4 ▶ **Patricia:** Sí, mucho. Sobre todo aprendí que la gente que vive en el campo no es tan diferente de la gente que vive en la ciudad. Es sólo el estilo de vida que es diferente. ¡A cada pájaro le gusta su nido!

8 ▶ **Miguel:** ¿Cuándo mandas tu proyecto a la revista?

Patricia: Después del fin de semana. Todavía tengo que escribir mucho.

9 ▶ **Miguel:** Hazme un favor… ¿Puedo leerlo antes? ¡Creo que va a salir muy bien y lo quiero ver! Y también…

Patricia: ¿Sí?

Miguel: ¡Quiero ver si escribiste algo de mi experiencia con la cerca y el caballo!

10 ▶ **Patricia:** Hice todo lo posible. Trabajé mucho. Espero tener buena suerte.

En acción

PARTE A Comprensión del diálogo

For Activities 1–2, refer to the dialog on pages 444–445.

Patricia Miguel

1 ¿En qué orden?

Escuchar ¿En qué orden pasaron estas cosas según el diálogo? *(Hint: What is the order?)*

a. Patricia mandó su proyecto a la revista.
b. Patricia y Miguel llegaron a Otavalo.
c. Patricia habló del cumpleaños de su hermana.
d. Patricia y Miguel entraron al mercado.

2 Frases revueltas

Escuchar Combina las frases para hacer oraciones basadas en el diálogo. *(Hint: Make sentences.)*

1. Patricia está contenta con
2. Miguel no tiene
3. Patricia va a comprarle
4. Patricia no sabe si tiene suficiente
5. Miguel quiere ver si Patricia escribe

a. dinero para comprar un regalo.
b. las entrevistas que hizo.
c. sobre su experiencia con el caballo.
d. ni idea de lo que hay que hacer en una granja.
e. un regalo a su hermana.

3 Juego de palabras

Hablar Patricia y Miguel juegan a este juego de palabras. Tú también puedes jugar. Di qué palabra no debe estar en cada grupo y por qué. *(Hint: Why doesn't one word belong?)*

modelo

abrigo bufanda gorro revista

***Una revista** no es ropa.*

1.	cerdo	jefe	vaca	gallo
2.	raqueta	bola	patines	cansado
3.	anillo	arete	casete	collar
4.	casco	cuchara	cuchillo	tenedor
5.	plato	bota	olla	jarra
6.	cancha	contento	campo	estadio
7.	hombre	chico	mujer	suelo
8.	café	té	cuenta	limonada
9.	espejos	orejas	piernas	brazos
10.	cepillo	jabón	jamón	champú

Ecuador

También se dice

There are many ways to say "To each his own." Each is used in many countries.

- **«A cada pájaro le gusta su nido.»** *Every bird likes its nest.*
- **«Zapatero, a tus zapatos.»** *Shoemaker, (attend) to your shoes!*
- **«A cada cual lo suyo.»** *To each his own.*
- **«Cada oveja con su pareja.»** *Every sheep has its mate.*

4 Las actividades

Escuchar Todas estas personas están ocupadas. ¿Qué oración describe lo que hace cada una? *(Hint: Describe each picture.)*

a.

b.

c.

d.

e.

f.

g.

h.

i.

j.

5 Entrevistas

Hablar/*Escribir* Imagínate que trabajas para una revista y que estás escribiendo un artículo sobre los jóvenes de hoy. Haz una entrevista con un(a) estudiante. Escribe las respuestas. *(Hint: Interview a student.)*

La vida familiar

1. ¿Cuántas personas hay en tu familia? ¿Quiénes son?
2. ¿Quién hace los quehaceres en tu casa?
3. ¿Cuál es la fecha de tu cumpleaños? ¿Cómo lo celebras normalmente?

La vida diaria

4. ¿A qué hora te levantas todos los días? ¿Qué haces después de levantarte?
5. ¿A qué hora te acuestas todos los días?
6. ¿Cómo es tu horario este semestre? ¿Cuántas materias tienes?

Los gustos

7. ¿Qué te gusta hacer después de las clases?
8. ¿Qué te gusta comer y beber?
9. ¿Cuál es tu deporte favorito? ¿Por qué?
10. ¿?

Práctica: gramática y vocabulario

Objectives for Activities 7–19 • Talk about the present and future • Give instructions to someone • Discuss the past

6 La ciudad y el campo

Hablar/*Escribir* Mira las fotos que sacó Patricia y describe lo que ves en cada una. *(Hint: Describe each picture.)*

1. 

2. 

3. 

4. 

5. 

REPASO Review: Present Progressive and **ir a** + infinitive

You have learned to use verbs in the present tense three different ways:

- **simple present** tense
- **present progressive** tense
- **ir a** + ***infinitive***

¿RECUERDAS? *pp. 232, 352* Remember the **present progressive?** The **present progressive** is used only to talk about actions that are **happening.** It is never used to refer to the future.

estoy	**hablando**	estamos	**hablando**
estás	**comiendo**	estáis	**comiendo**
está	**escribiendo**	están	**escribiendo**

Miguel y Patricia **están caminando** y **hablando**.
*Miguel and Patricia **are walking** and **talking.***

Remember to change **-iendo** to **-yendo** when the **stem** of an **-er** or an **-ir** verb ends in a **vowel.**

creer → **creyendo** **leer** → **leyendo** **oír** → **oyendo**

¿RECUERDAS? *p. 153* To talk about what you are going to do, use **ir a** + ***infinitive.*** Although this is a present tense, you are talking about something that is going to happen in the **future.**

voy a	**hablar**	vamos a	**hablar**
vas a	**comer**	vais a	**comer**
va a	**escribir**	van a	**escribir**

Patricia says:
—**Voy a comprar**le un regalo a mi hermana. *I'm **going to buy** a gift for my sister.*

Practice:
Actividades 7 8 9 10

Más práctica *cuaderno p. 149*
Para hispanohablantes *cuaderno p. 147*

Online Workbook
CLASSZONE.COM

7 ¿Qué están haciendo?

Hablar/*Escribir* Patricia y Miguel hacen muchas cosas. ¿Qué están haciendo en estas fotos? *(Hint: What are they doing?)*

modelo

Patricia y Miguel están caminando.

1.

2.

3.

4.

8 ¿Qué van a hacer?

Hablar/*Escribir* Todos van a hacer algo. ¿Qué van a hacer? *(Hint: Explain what they're going to do.)*

modelo

Patricia quiere hacer una entrevista con el tío Julio.

Va a viajar a la granja.

1. Los chicos piensan ver una película en casa.
2. Yo tengo un examen de matemáticas mañana.
3. Miguel quiere una mochila.
4. Tú quieres ir a la playa mañana.
5. Andrea y yo tenemos mucha sed.
6. Felipe y Enrique no quieren estar en casa.
7. Ustedes tienen hambre.
8. Diego piensa ir al gimnasio.
9. Estela está cansada.
10. José va a la cancha con su raqueta.

9 Los planes para el sábado

STRATEGY: SPEAKING

Use storytelling techniques Unexpected contrasts add interest to stories. Imagine an upside-down Saturday in which everyone decides to do spur-of-the-moment things. Example: **Mis padres no van a limpiar la casa. Van a buscar una nueva casa.**

Hablar ¿Qué van a hacer tú y estas personas el sábado por la mañana? Habla con otro(a) estudiante. Cambien de papel. *(Hint: What are they going to do?)*

1. tu mejor amigo(a)
2. tus padres
3. tu hermano(a)
4. tus amigos y tú
5. tú
6. ¿?

10 Una carta

Escribir Estás de vacaciones en el campo u otro lugar. Escríbele una carta a un(a) amigo(a) describiendo tus actividades. *(Hint: Write a letter.)*

- ¿Dónde estás?
- ¿Cómo es?
- ¿Qué están haciendo tu familia y tú?
- ¿Qué van a hacer mañana?

modelo

Querido Carlos:

Estamos en el campo. ¡Qué tranquilo es! Mis padres están tomando un refresco…

Mañana mis hermanos y yo vamos a…

Ecuador

Nota cultural

The Galápagos Islands contain some of the most unusual flora and fauna in the world. Their remote location off the coast of mainland Ecuador creates a unique habitat that is home to unusual animals, such as the blue-footed booby.

REPASO Review: Affirmative tú Commands

¿RECUERDAS? *pp. 260, 332* Remember that **tú commands** are used to give instructions to a friend or family member. The **affirmative tú command** form of a regular verb is the same as the **third person singular** of the simple present tense.

hablar → **Habla.** **comer** → **Come.** **escribir** → **Escribe.**

Remember to attach **direct object, indirect object,** and **reflexive pronouns** to **affirmative commands.** When you do, you usually need to add an accent.

Cómelo. *Eat it.* **Escríbeles.** *Write to them.* **Lávate.** *Wash yourself.*

Miguel says: —**Cómprale** una bolsa…
Buy her a handbag…

You also learned eight irregular **affirmative tú commands.**

decir → **di**	**ir** → **ve**	**salir** → **sal**	**tener** → **ten**
hacer → **haz**	**poner** → **pon**	**ser** → **sé**	**venir** → **ven**

Practice: Actividades 11 12 13

Más práctica *cuaderno p. 150*
Para hispanohablantes *cuaderno p. 148*

Online Workbook CLASSZONE.COM

11 ¡Cuántas órdenes!

Hablar/*Escribir* La mamá de Miguel le da muchas órdenes hoy. ¿Qué le dice? *(Hint: What does she say?)*

modelo

salir temprano para la escuela *Sal temprano para la escuela.*

1. venir a casa temprano
2. ir a la tienda
3. comer las verduras
4. ser bueno con tu hermano
5. lavar los platos
6. compartir con tu hermano
7. decir a qué hora vuelves
8. tener cuidado
9. poner la mesa
10. hacer la tarea

12 ¡Mañana es otro día!

Hablar Tu amigo(a) te invita al campo pero tienes otros planes. ¿Qué te dice tu amigo(a)? Cambien de papel. *(Hint: Say what to do.)*

modelo

limpiar

Tú: *Quiero **limpiar** el cuarto hoy.*

Tu amigo(a): *¡Límpialo mañana!*

1. leer
2. visitar
3. preparar
4. hacer
5. poner
6. escribir
7. hablar
8. comprar
9. buscar
10. ¿?

13 A preparar la fiesta

Escribir Estás preparando una fiesta y un amigo(a) te va a ayudar. Escribe un mensaje para él o ella explicándole lo que necesita hacer. Necesitas ayuda con cinco cosas. *(Hint: Write what to do.)*

modelo

Ana:
Gracias por ayudarme con la fiesta. Éstos son los quehaceres que debes hacer.
1) Ve de compras.
2) Compra una tarta para el postre.

More Practice: **Más comunicación** *p. R18*

REPASO Review: Regular Preterite

¿RECUERDAS? *pp. 376, 378, 404, 406* To talk about completed actions in the past, use the **preterite tense.**

-ar verbs		-er verbs		-ir verbs	
hablé	**hablamos**	**comí**	**comimos**	**escribí**	**escribimos**
hablaste	**hablasteis**	**comiste**	**comisteis**	**escribiste**	**escribisteis**
habló	**hablaron**	**comió**	**comieron**	**escribió**	**escribieron**

- Remember that the verb **ver** is regular in the **preterite** but has no accents.
- Remember that verbs ending in **-car, -gar,** and **-zar** have a spelling change in the **yo** form of the **preterite.**

  marcar → marqué **llegar → llegué** **cruzar → crucé**

- Third person forms of **-er** and **-ir** verbs with **stems** that end in a **vowel** require a **y** in the **preterite.**

leí	**leímos**
leíste	**leísteis**
leyó	**leyeron**

Miguel says: —¿Y **aprendiste** algo de tus entrevistas?
*And **did you learn** something from your interviews?*

Practice: **Actividades** 14 15 16

Más práctica *cuaderno p. 151*
Para hispanohablantes *cuaderno p. 149*

Online Workbook CLASSZONE.COM

14 El viaje

Leer Patricia escribió en su diario sobre su viaje al campo. Completa sus oraciones con uno de los verbos de abajo. *(Hint: Complete her diary.)*

Esta mañana, yo __1__ a las seis y media. Después de desayunar, __2__ mi grabadora y __3__ de la casa. Miguel y yo __4__ el autobús a las ocho.

Primero, nosotros __5__ el taller de Bárbara. ¡Qué interesante! Yo __6__ fotos y __7__ la entrevista. Bárbara __8__ mucho sobre la vida del campo.

Después, en la granja del tío Julio, Miguel y yo __9__ muchos animales. El tío Julio y Miguel __10__ de la primera vez que Miguel __11__ la granja. ¡Qué cómico! Después de la entrevista nosotros __12__.

Por fin, Miguel y yo __13__ a la ciudad después de ir al mercado en Otavalo. Yo __14__ un regalo allí. Yo __15__ a casa a las seis y media.

1–5	6–10	11–15
buscar	hablar	almorzar
levantarse	empezar	comprar
salir	sacar	llegar
tomar	ver	visitar
visitar	hablar	volver

15 ¿Quién lo hizo?

Hablar/Leer Habla con los otros estudiantes para saber quién hizo estas actividades el año pasado. Encuentra a tres personas que hicieron cada actividad. Escribe un resumen de las respuestas. *(Hint: Find people who did these activities.)*

modelo

Tú: *¿Sacaste una buena nota el año pasado?*

Otro(a) estudiante: *Sí, saqué una buena nota en matemáticas.*

Resumen: *Raúl, Sara y Ana sacaron una buena nota el año pasado.*

Actividad	Persona 1	Persona 2	Persona 3
sacar una buena nota	Raúl	Sara	Ana
viajar por una semana			
ver una película de horror			
comer comida mexicana			
escribir una carta			
oír un concierto			

Juego

Si tu mamá te dice «¡Sal para la escuela!», ¿qué vas a necesitar?

a.

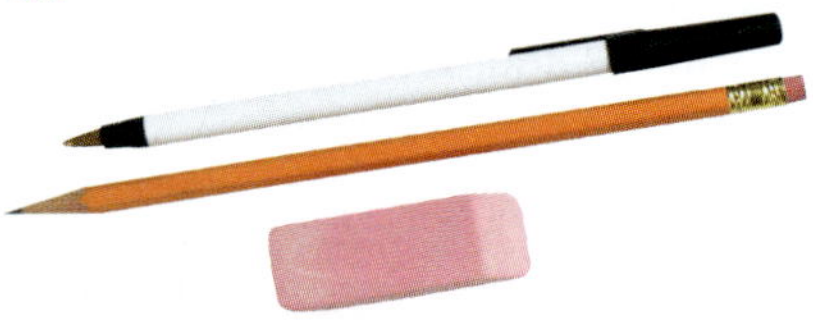

b.

16 ¿Qué hicieron?

Hablar/*Escribir* Describe qué hicieron todos. *(Hint: Describe what everyone did.)*

modelo

Patricia visitó una granja el sábado pasado.

Patricia y Miguel	almorzar	¿?	ayer
yo	comer		el sábado pasado
mi hermano(a)	compartir		anoche
mis padres	escribir		anteayer
mi mejor amigo(a)	jugar		el año pasado
mis amigos y yo	leer		el verano pasado
¿?	ver		la semana pasada
	visitar		

REPASO Review: Irregular Preterite

¿RECUERDAS? *pp. 407, 431* These are the **irregular preterite** verbs that you have learned.

dar *to give*		**decir** *to say, to tell*		**estar** *to be*		**hacer** *to make, to do*	
di	dimos	dije	dijimos	estuve	estuvimos	hice	hicimos
diste	disteis	dijiste	dijisteis	estuviste	estuvisteis	hiciste	hicisteis
dio	dieron	dijo	dijeron	estuvo	estuvieron	hizo	hicieron

ir *to go* / **ser** *to be*		**tener** *to have*		**venir** *to come*	
fui	fuimos	tuve	tuvimos	vine	vinimos
fuiste	fuisteis	tuviste	tuvisteis	viniste	vinisteis
fue	fueron	tuvo	tuvieron	vino	vinieron

Patricia might say:

—La entrevista con tu tío Julio **fue** la mejor porque él me **dijo** lo que **hiciste** tú la primera vez que **estuviste** en la granja.

*The interview with your Uncle Julio **was** the best because he **told** me what you **did** the first time you **were** on the farm.*

Practice: **Actividades** 17 18

Más práctica *cuaderno p. 152*
Para hispanohablantes *cuaderno p. 150*

Online Workbook CLASSZONE.COM

17 Un buen fin de semana

Escuchar Escucha la conversación entre María y Rosa y completa las oraciones. *(Hint: Complete the sentences.)*

1. El fin de semana pasado, Rosa…
2. Las gallinas…
3. Por la tarde, Rosa…
4. Rosa no compró el saco porque…
5. El sábado por la noche, Rosa…

18 ¿Quién hizo qué?

Escribir ¿Qué hicieron ayer? *(Hint: What did they do?)*

modelo

Patricia y Miguel / hacer…

Patricia y Miguel hicieron un viaje.

1. yo / ir…
2. mis padres / dar…
3. mis amigos(as) y yo / tener…
4. mi hermano(a) / hacer…
5. mi amigo(a) / venir…
6. mi familia y yo / estar…
7. mis amigos(as) / decir…
8. nosotros(as) / ir…
9. mi primo(a) / venir…
10. ustedes / hacer…

19 ¡Qué noticias!

Hablar/Leer Tú lees un artículo sobre algo que pasó en Quito y tu amigo(a) te pregunta sobre lo que leíste. Contesta las preguntas de tu amigo(a). *(Hint: Answer your friend's questions.)*

¿Cuándo? ¿Qué?

¿Quién? ¿Por qué? ¿Dónde?

Un turista contentísimo

Redacción Puyó

Quito— Ayer, en el centro de Quito, un turista mexicano pasó un día interesante. El turista perdió una bolsa con su pasaporte, su dinero, su tarjeta de crédito… y algo más.

«No sé cómo la perdí», dijo el turista, «pero hablé con un policía y me ayudó de una manera interesante».

El policía mandó al turista a un departamento especial. ¡Allí el turista encontró un perro con su bolsa! Otro policía le explicó todo:

«Salí con mi perro Nacho para hacer nuestra rutina diaria y, al llegar a la esquina, Nacho vio a otro perro con la bolsa. Cuando el perro sacó un sándwich de la bolsa, llegó Nacho y la tomó.

Afortunadamente Nacho sabe hacer bien su trabajo.

¡No hay ningún robo, solamente mucha hambre!»

Ecuador

Nota cultural

Ecuador is made up of three widely diverse regions: the Pacific coast, the Andes mountains, and the jungles of the Amazon. The variety of habitats makes Ecuador a popular ecotourism destination.

la Amazonia

PARTE D Todo en acción

Activities 20–21 bring together all concepts presented.

20 ¡Un año interesante!

Hablar/*Escribir* ¿Qué hiciste o qué te pasó este año? Preséntale tu historia a la clase. *(Hint: What did you do?)*

Este año en la clase de español

Este año aprendí mucho en la clase de español. Hablé con muchas personas y escribí mucho. Vimos un video interesante sobre unos jóvenes que hablan español. Fuimos a un museo para ver unos artículos de Latinoamérica...

21 Y el ganador es...

Hablar/*Escribir* Piensa en las personas de los diálogos. ¿Quién va a ganar el concurso? Escoge a una persona y explica por qué esa persona debe ganar. *(Hint: Explain who should win and why.)*

Francisco

Isabel

Ignacio

Carlos

Mercedes

Patricia

modelo

Pienso que Patricia debe ganar el concurso. Ella trabajó mucho…

More Practice: **Más comunicación** *p. R18*

Online Workbook
CLASSZONE.COM

Pronunciación

Refrán

Pronunciación de la *x* The letter **x** is pronounced several different ways. Before a vowel, before the letters **ce** or **ci**, or at the end of a word, **x** sounds like the English *x* in the word *taxi.* At the beginning of a word or before a consonant, the **x** is pronounced like the *s* in *same.* To practice these sounds, pronounce the following.

¡Es un examen excepcional! **Xochimilco y Taxco son lugares bonitos.**

In some words that come from other languages in Mexico and Central America, the letter **x** also has the following sounds:

j as in **jarra:** **México, Oaxaca, Xalapa**

sh as in *shoe:* **Ixtepec, Uxmal**

Now try the **refrán** about the taxi.

El taxi gratis no existe.

En voces

AUDIO LECTURA

UN PASEO POR ECUADOR

PARA LEER

STRATEGY: READING

Reflect on journal writing Have you ever kept a journal or a diary? How are diaries organized? As you read this article about a bus trip through Ecuador, notice the place and date given for each entry. This diary-style organization of the article helps you experience each day that the writer experiences. Use the chart to record an interesting experience you read from each day.

FECHA	LUGAR	EXPERIENCIA INTERESANTE
17 de abril		
18 de abril		
4 de mayo		
25 de mayo		

Para la mayoría[1] de los ecuatorianos, el autobús es el transporte más común. Para tener una experiencia muy ecuatoriana, decidí hacer un viaje en autobús.

GUAYAQUIL, 17 de abril:

Guayaquil es el puerto principal y la ciudad más grande del país. Para conocer la costa, decidí viajar a Machala. Compré mi boleto en la terminal moderna. Los buses de larga distancia tienen cortinas[2] y televisores con videograbadora. Paseamos por la costa del Pacífico. Hacía[3] mucho calor y mucha humedad. Vi los cultivos de arroz, caña de azúcar y plátanos[4]. Por el puerto de Machala pasan más de un millón de toneladas de plátanos y camarones[5] por año.

[1] majority [2] curtains [3] It was [4] bananas [5] shrimp

MACHALA, 18 de abril:

Decidí visitar los pueblitos. Viajé en un bus de transporte rural de colores muy alegres con personas muy animadas. El bus llevó todas sus posesiones encima. Fuimos a varios pueblos y plantaciones de café y cacao.

También se dice

The word *bus* has several forms.

- **el autobús:** many countries
- **el bus:** many countries
- **el colectivo:** Argentina
- **el ómnibus:** many countries
- **la guagua:** the Caribbean (In parts of South America, **la guagua** means *baby*!)

LA SIERRA, 4 de mayo:

Llegué a la sierra de Ecuador, la región central de los Andes. Hacía frío en las montañas. Me levanté a las cinco y subí a un antiguo bus de escuela para ir al mercado indígena de Saquisilí. Viajamos muy lentamente. ¡Qué frío en el bus! Todos los pasajeros llevaron saco o poncho. Algunos se durmieron. Muchas personas llevaron productos al mercado. Vimos los volcanes de Cotopaxi y Tungurahua. Llegamos al Saquisilí y todos salieron del bus para trabajar o hacer compras.

COCA, 25 de mayo:

La carretera terminó y tuve que seguir en barco por los ríos Napo y Coca, que van al río Amazonas. Vi barcos y canoas con muchos plátanos y pasajeros. En la selva[6] vive poca gente, la mayoría son indígenas. Como ven, ¡se puede conocer mucho viajando en autobús!

Online Workbook
CLASSZONE.COM

¿Comprendiste?

1. ¿Cuál es el transporte más común en Ecuador?
2. ¿En qué región empezó el autor?
3. ¿Qué productos son típicos de la costa?
4. ¿Cómo es el clima de la sierra?
5. ¿Adónde van los ríos Napo y Coca?

¿Qué piensas?

Compara el transporte de cada región. ¿En qué región te gustaría vivir? ¿Por qué?

Hazlo tú

¿Hay regiones como las de Ecuador en Estados Unidos? ¿Cómo son? Describe una de las regiones.

[6]jungle

En colores

CULTURA Y COMPARACIONES

Cómo las Américas cambiaron la comida europea

PARA CONOCERNOS

STRATEGY: CONNECTING CULTURES

Identify international foods Make a grocery list of fresh fruits and vegetables (4 or 5 items) that are regularly part of your family's diet. When is their growing season in the U.S.? Where do they come from when out-of-season? Check with the produce manager of your grocery store. Then decide which foods your family eats come from other countries.

Comida	Estación
naranja	marzo-abril

¿Puedes imaginarte tu dieta sin papas? Pues, en Europa no había[1] papas hasta que los conquistadores llegaron a las Américas. Los europeos comieron la papa por primera vez en América. La papa, planta nativa de Perú, era[2] la comida principal de los incas, indígenas de esa zona. La palabra *papa* es de origen quechua, la lengua de los incas.

Los españoles empezaron a llevar papas a España. Comida barata para los marineros[3], así llegó la papa a Europa. Hoy la papa es una de las comidas principales de Irlanda, Alemania, Rusia y Polonia.

[1] there were no [2] was [3] sailors

El maíz[4] también es de las Américas. El cultivo de maíz empezó en México alrededor del año 3500 a.C.[5] Llegó a Perú alrededor de 3200 a.C., pero no fue tan importante en la dieta de los peruanos como en la dieta de los mexicanos. En México se hicieron las tortillas del maíz.

Otro producto americano que cambió la comida europea es el tomate. No sabemos exactamente cómo y cuándo el tomate llegó a Europa, pero su cultivo era fácil en los países mediterráneos.

[4] corn [5] B.C.

Entonces, las papas fritas y la salsa de tomate para los espaguetis son de origen europeo, pero sus ingredientes principales llegaron a Europa de América. ¿Ves? Los viajes de Colón cambiaron muchas cosas, ¡entre ellas la comida europea!

More About Ecuador
CLASSZONE.COM

¿Comprendiste?

1. ¿De dónde vino la papa?
2. ¿Cómo llegó la papa a Europa?
3. ¿De dónde vino el maíz?
4. El maíz tuvo más importancia en la dieta de qué país, ¿Perú o México?
5. ¿Cómo llegó el tomate a Europa?

¿Qué piensas?

1. En tu opinión, ¿cómo sería la comida europea sin la papa y el tomate? ¿Y la comida norteamericana? ¿Por qué?
2. ¿Cómo crees que llegó la papa de España a otras partes de Europa?

Hazlo tú

Busca una receta con papas, tomates o maíz. Escribe la receta en español. Prepárala y comparte la comida con la clase. ¿Es una receta europea o americana? Explica su origen.

ETAPA 3

En uso

REPASO Y MÁS COMUNICACIÓN

OBJECTIVES

- Talk about the present and future
- Give instructions to someone
- Discuss the past

Now you can...

- talk about the present and future.

To review

- present progressive and **ir a** + infinitive, see p. 448.

1 ¡Muy ocupados!

Miguel y sus amigos hablan por teléfono de sus actividades. ¿Qué dicen? *(**Hint:** Tell present and future activities.)*

modelo

yo: estudiar matemáticas / ir al campo

*Ahora **yo** estoy estudiando **matemáticas,** pero más tarde voy a **ir al campo.***

1. Patricia: escribir cartas / hacer unas entrevistas
2. tú: hacer la tarea / alquilar un video
3. mis padres: limpiar la casa / caminar con el perro
4. yo: leer una novela / ir al cine
5. nosotros: ver la televisión / hacer ejercicio en el gimnasio
6. mi hermana: maquillarse / salir con Bernardo
7. ustedes: comer chicharrones / cenar en un restaurante elegante
8. tú: abrir unas cartas / andar en bicicleta

Now you can...

- give instructions to someone.

To review

- affirmative **tú** commands, see p. 450.

2 Una cena importante

El arquitecto que Patricia entrevistó viene a cenar con ella y su familia esta noche. La madre de Patricia necesita su ayuda. ¿Qué le dice? *(**Hint:** Say what Patricia's mother tells her to do.)*

modelo

limpiar el baño

Limpia el baño.

1. lavar los platos
2. barrer el suelo
3. poner la mesa
4. hacer los quehaceres cuidadosamente
5. tener cuidado
6. ir al supermercado a comprar más refrescos
7. ponerte un vestido
8. servir las bebidas
9. ser simpática durante la cena
10. pasar la aspiradora

Now you can...
- discuss the past.

To review
- regular preterite verbs, see p. 451.

3 ¿Qué hiciste?

Patricia habla con una amiga sobre el fin de semana pasado. ¿Qué dice? *(Hint: Tell what happened last weekend.)*

modelo

yo: tomar el autobús al campo — *Yo tomé el autobús al campo.*

1. yo: visitar una granja en el campo
2. Miguel: decidir acompañarme
3. Miguel y yo: ver muchos animales
4. yo: sacar muchas fotos
5. mi madre: escribir cartas
6. mi padre: leer unas revistas
7. mis hermanos: correr en el parque
8. yo: ver a Ana en el mercado de Otavalo
9. ella: comprar algunas artesanías a muy buen precio
10. yo: llegar a casa muy tarde

Now you can...
- discuss the past.

To review
- irregular preterite verbs, see p. 453.

4 Un día especial

Patricia habla con su madre. Completa lo que dicen con el pretérito de los verbos. *(Hint: Complete what they say.)*

Mamá: Patricia, tú __1__ (venir) a casa muy tarde ayer.

Patricia: Sí, mamá. Miguel y yo __2__ (ir) al campo.

Mamá: ¿Y qué __3__ (hacer) ustedes allí?

Patricia: Yo __4__ (hacer) entrevistas con el tío Julio y Bárbara.

Mamá: ¿Ellos te __5__ (decir) algo interesante?

Patricia: Sí. El tío Julio me __6__ (decir) mucho sobre la vida en una granja. La entrevista con Bárbara, la artesana, también __7__ (ser) interesante, y ella me __8__ (dar) este saco.

Mamá: ¡Qué bonito! ¿Ustedes __9__ (ir) a Otavalo por la tarde?

Patricia: Sí, mamá. Nosotros __10__ (estar) en el mercado por tres horas. Allí yo __11__ (tener) la oportunidad de entrevistar a un vendedor. Por eso, yo __12__ (venir) a casa tan tarde. Lo siento.

5 ¿Quién soy yo?

STRATEGY: SPEAKING

Rely on the basics You have practiced many speaking strategies for different contexts. These work in all situations. Keep them in mind as you speak.

1. Don't be afraid to make mistakes.
2. Encourage yourself; think positively.
3. Take your time.
4. Take risks; improvise.
5. Say more, rather than less.

And enjoy speaking… now that you have plenty you can say!

Imagínate que eres una de las personas de este libro. Dile a otro(a) estudiante qué hiciste ayer, qué estás haciendo ahora y qué vas a hacer mañana. Él o ella tiene que adivinar quién eres. *(Hint: Play the role of a character. Your partner must guess who you are.)*

Francisco, Ignacio, Mercedes, Ricardo, Alma, Patricia, Luis, Isabel, Carlos, Diana, Miguel, Sofía

6 ¿Qué hago?

Vas a uno de estos lugares por primera vez. Los otros estudiantes van a decirte qué debes hacer allí. *(Hint: Select a place; classmates will tell you what to do there.)*

la playa	**un mercado mexicano**
el campo	**una ciudad grande**
una granja	**un bosque tropical**
las montañas	**¿?**

modelo

Tú: *Voy a una ciudad grande por primera vez. ¿Qué hago?*

Estudiante 1: *Ve a un concierto.*

7 En tu propia voz

ESCRITURA Estás pensando en las vacaciones de verano. Escribe un párrafo sobre lo que hiciste el verano pasado y otro párrafo sobre lo que vas a hacer este verano. *(Hint: Write about summer activities.)*

CONEXIONES

La salud You have just read how New World foods changed European cuisine. Select a Spanish-speaking country and write a brief report about what people in that country typically eat. Prepare the food you would most like to taste. Was it difficult or easy to prepare? Is it nutritious?

- ¿Qué desayunan? ¿Almuerzan? ¿Cenan?
- ¿A qué hora almuerzan? ¿Cenan?
- ¿Qué meriendas hay?
- ¿Qué hay de postre?
- ¿Cuál es el plato más famoso de este país?

Flashcards
CLASSZONE.COM

En resumen

YA SABES

TALKING ABOUT THE PRESENT AND FUTURE

Simple Present

Estoy muy feliz.	*I am very happy.*
¡Es un mercado fenomenal!	*It's a phenomenal market!*
La artesanía de Otavalo es excelente.	*The handicrafts from Otavalo are excellent.*

Present Progressive

Miguel y Patricia están caminando y hablando.	*Miguel and Patricia are walking and talking.*

Ir a + *infinitive*

Voy a comprarle un regalo a mi hermana.	*I am going to buy a present for my sister.*
¡Creo que va a salir muy bien y lo quiero ver!	*I think that it is going to come out very well and I want to see it!*

DISCUSSING THE PAST

Regular Preterite

¿Porque te habló de la vida en una granja?	*Because he talked to you about life on a farm?*
¿Y aprendiste algo de tus entrevistas?	*And did you learn something from your interviews?*
Pero aprendí algo mucho más importante también.	*But I learned something much more important too.*
¡Abriste la cerca!	*You opened the fence!*
Trabajé mucho.	*I worked a lot.*

Irregular Preterite

¿Cuál fue la mejor entrevista?	*Which was the best interview?*
No, ¡porque me dijo qué hiciste tú la primera vez que estuviste en la granja!	*No, because he told me what you did the first time that you were at the farm!*
Hice todo lo posible.	*I did everything possible.*

GIVING INSTRUCTIONS TO SOMEONE

Dime.	*Tell me.*
¡Mira, Miguel!	*Look, Miguel!*
Cómprale una bolsa o un artículo de cuero.	*Buy her a handbag or leather goods.*
¡Ven!	*Come on!*
Hazme un favor.	*Do me a favor.*

Juego

1. ¿Qué pasa ahora?
2. ¿Qué pasó antes?
3. ¿Qué va a pasar?

a. *¡El caballo se va a escapar del corral!*

b. *La llama está jugando con Rocío.*

c. *El ganadero buscó su merienda.*

En tu propia voz

ESCRITURA

¡Busco trabajo!

A local newspaper is offering paid internships for Spanish students for the summer. Write a formal letter of application in which you emphasize your academic skills.

Function: Apply for employment
Context: Writing to a potential employer
Content: Your qualifications
Text type: Formal letter of application

PARA ESCRIBIR • STRATEGY: WRITING

Support a general statement with informative details Attract your reader's attention with a strong general statement about your academic skills. Then add details that support your statement.

Modelo del estudiante

5 de mayo de 2002

La Prensa
2255 Pacific Avenue
Los Ángeles, CA 90631

Estimado editor:

Me gustaría trabajar para La Prensa este verano. Soy un estudiante muy trabajador y serio. Saco buenas notas en mis clases en M.L. King High School, especialmente en inglés, historia y español. Me gusta estudiar otras culturas y escribir para todas mis clases. El mes pasado recibí un premio de nuestro Departamento de Historia por mi estudio sobre los otavaleños de Ecuador.

Después de mis clases, siempre voy a la biblioteca y hago mi tarea allí. En mi tiempo libre, juego al balconcesto y escribo poesía. Pienso ser escritor o periodista en el futuro. Quiero aprender más de estas profesiones y ahora busco trabajo y experiencia en su periódico. Muchas gracias por su tiempo.

Atentamente,

Bryan Walter

The writer makes a **strong general statement** about himself as a serious, skilled student.

Next, the writer adds **evidence** of his academic interests and achievements. He emphasizes writing and Spanish in his letter.

Here he includes **additional information** that he manages his time well.

At the end, the writer adds related **details** about his interest in the writing professions.

Writing Center
CLASSZONE.COM

Estrategias para escribir

Antes de escribir...

An effective letter requesting employment calls attention to your skills as a student and as a worker. Brainstorm ideas for the following categories: academic skills, interests, work-related experiences, and why you want the internship. Record them on a chart. Write a general statement about your skills. Add supporting evidence. Use the formal openings and closings given in the model.

habilidades académicas	estudio todos los días aprendo rápidamente hablo, leo y escribo en español
intereses	soy buena fotógrafa conferencias para artistas
trabajo, experiencias	periódico de la escuela Photo Finish voluntaria en la liga de fútbol
por qué quiero el trabajo	aprender a trabajar como fotógrafa aprender más del trabajo para un periódico

Revisiones

Share your draft with a partner. Then ask:

- *What makes my general statement impressive?*
- *How well do the details support my general statement?*
- *How appropriate is the information about my skills?*

La versión final

Before you write the final draft, ask yourself these questions:

- *Did I use the preterite correctly?*

Try this: Underline every preterite verb. Identify each as regular or irregular. Refer to pp. 451 and 453 to check the correct endings.

- *Are adverbs formed correctly?*

Try this: Circle all adverbs ending in **-mente.** Be sure the root word is correct and that **-mente** is appropriately placed.

Note the markings used to make a letter small and to capitalize.

Estimado editor:

Busco trabajo en el departamento de fotografía de su periódico. soy creativa, inteligente y muy trabajadora. También soy buena fotógrafa. Trabajo cuidadosamente y aprendo rápidomente. El año pasado fui a una conferencia para artistas y recibió un premio por una de mis fotos.

Trabajé como Fotógrafa en el periódico de mi escuela...

EDITORIAL MARKS

A = **lowercase** a = **capitalize**

RECURSOS

1 Unidad 1 Etapa 1 p. 37
¿Quién es?

1. el policía…
2. el maestro… Hernán Campos
3. las estudiantes…
4. el doctor… Raúl Guzmán
5. las maestras… Beatriz Simón y Laura Valdez
6. el estudiante…
7. la doctora…
8. los maestros… Patricio Díaz y Esteban Castillo

modelo

Estudiante A: *¿Quién es el policía?*
Estudiante B: *Es…*

Estudiante A The people in the neighborhood are being introduced at a town meeting, but it is hard to hear. Find out from your partner who they are.

Estudiante B The people in the neighborhood are being introduced at a town meeting, but it is hard to hear. Find out from your partner who they are.

modelo

Estudiante A: *¿Quién es el policía?*
Estudiante B: *Es el señor Ruiz.*

1. el policía... el señor Ruiz
2. el maestro…
3. las estudiantes… Carolina y Olivia
4. el doctor…
5. las maestras…
6. el estudiante… Felipe
7. la doctora… Ana Colón
8. los maestros…

2 Unidad 1 Etapa 1 p. 41
¿Le gusta…?

modelo

Estudiante A: *¿Le gusta nadar?*
Estudiante B: …

Estudiante A Daniela only likes to do the activities pictured. Find out from your partner if Gustavo likes to do the same.

Estudiante B Gustavo only likes to do the activities pictured. Find out from your partner if Daniela likes to do the same.

modelo

Estudiante B: *¿Le gusta correr?*
Estudiante A: …

3 Unidad 1 Etapa 2 p. 60
¿Cómo es?

Estudiante A Describe the person to your partner. Include what you think his personality might be like. Then draw the person your partner describes to you.

Estudiante B Draw the person your partner describes to you. Then describe your picture to your partner. Include what you think her personality might be like.

4 Unidad 1 Etapa 2 p. 63
¿De qué color son?

Estudiante A Ask about the colors of Esteban's clothes. Then describe the colors of Chela's clothing for your partner. Are they wearing anything the same color?

modelo

Estudiante A: *¿De qué color son los zapatos?*

Estudiante B: *Lleva zapatos...*

Estudiante B Describe the colors of Esteban's clothing for your partner. Then ask about the colors of Chela's clothes. Are they wearing anything the same color?

modelo

Estudiante A: *¿De qué color son los zapatos?*

Estudiante B: *Lleva zapatos negros.*

5 Unidad 1, Etapa 3 p. 79
¿Cuántos años tiene?

Estudiante A Complete the chart with the ages of members of the Zavala family.

modelo

Estudiante A: *¿Cuántos años tiene Josefa?*

Estudiante B: *Tiene….*

Nombre	Edad
1. Josefa	
2. Víctor	65
3. Victoria	38
4. José	
5. Lupita	
6. Eva	4

Estudiante B Complete the chart with the ages of members of the Zavala family.

modelo

Estudiante A: *¿Cuántos años tiene Josefa?*

Estudiante B: *Tiene cincuenta y nueve años.*

Nombre	Edad
1. Josefa	59
2. Víctor	
3. Victoria	
4. José	33
5. Lupita	15
6. Eva	

6 Unidad 1, Etapa 3 p. 85
La familia Zavala

Estudiante A Your partner is looking at the Zavala family tree. Find out the names of various family members.

modelo

Estudiante A: *¿Quién es la hermana de José?*

Estudiante B: …

1. hermana / José
2. tío / Eva
3. abuelo / Pepe
4. hermano / Lupita
5. madre / Victoria
6. hijo / Víctor
7. prima / Eva
8. padre / Lupita
9. tía / Pepe
10. hija / Paquita

Estudiante B Your partner wants to know the names of members of the Zavala family. Answer his or her questions according to the family tree.

modelo

Estudiante A: *¿Quién es la hermana de José?*

Estudiante B: *Victoria es la hermana de José.*

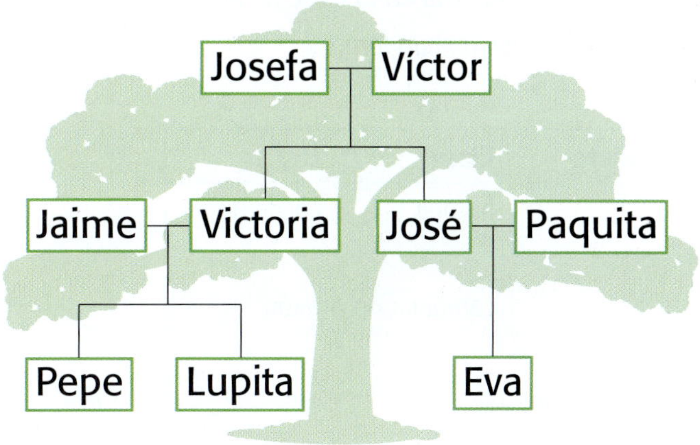

7 Unidad 2 Etapa 1 p. 110
¿Qué clase tiene?

Estudiante A Find out about the following students' classes by completing the chart with your partner.

modelo

Estudiante A: *¿Qué clase tiene Rosa?*
Estudiante B: *Tiene...*
Estudiante A: *¿Qué usa en la clase de...?*
Estudiante B: *Usa...*

Nombre	Clase	Usa...
Rosa		
César	inglés	pluma
Jesús		
Gilberto	matemáticas	calculadora
yo	¿?	¿?
Estudiante B	¿?	¿?

Estudiante B Find out about the following students' classes by completing the chart with your partner.

modelo

Estudiante A: *¿Qué clase tiene Rosa?*
Estudiante B: *Tiene historia.*
Estudiante A: *¿Qué usa en la clase de historia?*
Estudiante B: *Usa un cuaderno.*

Nombre	Clase	Usa...
Rosa	historia	cuaderno
César		
Jesús	computación	ratón
Gilberto		
Estudiante A	¿?	¿?
yo	¿?	¿?

8 Unidad 2 Etapa 1 p. 115
¿Siempre o nunca?

Estudiante A Ask your partner if Gabriela has to do the following activities in her class. Can you guess what class it is?

modelo

Estudiante A: *¿Gabriela tiene que estudiar?*
Estudiante B: *Gabriela tiene que estudiar...*

1. ¿Gabriela tiene que estudiar?
2. ¿leer?
3. ¿llevar uniforme?
4. ¿cantar?
5. ¿correr?
6. ¿mirar videos?
7. ¿escuchar al profesor?

Estudiante B Answer your partner's questions about Gabriela's class.

modelo

Estudiante A: *¿Gabriela tiene que estudiar?*
Estudiante B: *Gabriela tiene que estudiar de vez en cuando.*

Gabriela: la clase de educación física	
siempre	llevar uniforme
todos los días	correr
mucho	escuchar al profesor
a veces	mirar videos
de vez en cuando	estudiar
rara vez	leer
nunca	cantar

9 Unidad 2 Etapa 2 p. 133
¿A qué hora?

Estudiante A Ask what time your partner will do the following activities. Draw clocks to indicate the times. Then tell your partner what time you will do them.

modelo

Estudiante A: *¿A qué hora vas al doctor?*

Estudiante B: *Voy al doctor a las... ¿Y tú?*

Estudiante A: *Voy al doctor a las nueve y cuarto de la mañana.*

Por la mañana

1. 9:15 - ir al doctor
2. 10:50 - tomar una prueba
3. 12:00 - comprar papel

Por la tarde

4. 1:20 - tomar almuerzo
5. 2:45 - ir a casa
6. 4:30 - visitar a amigos
7. 5:10 - terminar la tarea
8. 7:45 - descansar

Estudiante B Tell your partner what time you will do the following activities. Then draw clocks to indicate what time your partner will do them.

modelo

Estudiante A: *¿A qué hora vas al doctor?*

Estudiante B: *Voy al doctor a las nueve menos cuarto de la mañana. ¿Y tú?*

Estudiante A: *Voy al doctor a las...*

Por la mañana

8:45 - ir al doctor
12:00 - tomar almuerzo

Por la tarde

1:05 - tomar una prueba
2:15 - comprar papel
3:50 - ir a casa
4:20 - terminar la tarea
6:30 - visitar a amigos
9:00 - descansar

10 Unidad 2 Etapa 2 p. 137
¿Doble visión?

Estudiante A You and your partner have similar drawings. Ask each other questions to find at least five differences between the two drawings.

Estudiante B You and your partner have similar drawings. Ask each other questions to find at least five differences between the two drawings.

11 Unidad 2 Etapa 3 p. 155
¿Qué va a hacer?

Estudiante A Find out about Marcos. Ask if he is going to do the following activities.

modelo

Estudiante A: *¿Marcos va a pasear?*

Estudiante B: ...

1. pasear
2. leer una novela
3. ir al supermercado
4. pintar
5. ver la televisión
6. cuidar el pájaro

Estudiante B Answer your partner's questions about Marcos according to your drawing.

modelo

Estudiante A: *¿Marcos va a pasear?*

Estudiante B: *Sí, Marcos va a pasear.*

12 Unidad 2 Etapa 3 p. 159
¿En qué orden?

Estudiante A Susana likes to organize her activities, but she left her other calendar at school. Work with your partner to determine the order of her evening activities.

modelo

Estudiante A: *¿Qué hace primero?*

Estudiante B: *Primero, ella... ¿Qué hace después de...?*

Estudiante A: *Entonces, ella hace ejercicio.*

6:00	
6:30	hacer ejercicio
7:00	
7:30	ir a la biblioteca
8:00	
8:30	escribir un poema
9:00	

Estudiante B Susana likes to organize her activities, but she left her other calendar at home. Work with your partner to determine the order of her evening activities.

modelo

Estudiante A: *¿Qué hace primero?*

Estudiante B: *Primero, ella lee el periódico. ¿Qué hace después de leer el periódico?*

Estudiante A: *Entonces, ella...*

6:00	leer el periódico
6:30	
7:00	escuchar música
7:30	
8:00	comer una merienda
8:30	
9:00	ver la televisión

13 Unidad 3 Etapa 1 p. 185
Muchas emociones

Estudiante A You and your partner are talking about friends. You know what each person has done and your partner knows how each is feeling. Exchange information.

modelo

Josefina: ayudar a su padre

Estudiante A: *¿Cómo está Josefina?*

Estudiante B: *Está… ¿Qué acaba de hacer?*

Estudiante A: *Acaba de ayudar a su padre.*

1. Milagros: sacar una mala nota
2. Carlos: visitar a su abuelo enfermo
3. Ricardo: tomar un examen
4. Martina: mirar un video

Estudiante B You and your partner are talking about friends. You know how each person is feeling and your partner knows what each has just done. Exchange information.

modelo

Josefina

Estudiante A: *¿Cómo está Josefina?*

Estudiante B: *Está tranquila. ¿Qué acaba de hacer?*

Estudiante A: *Acaba de…*

1. Milagros

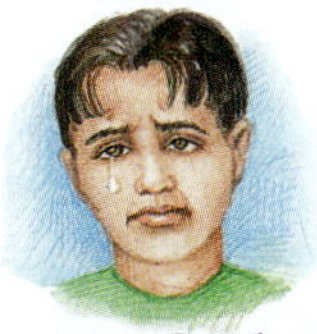

2. Carlos

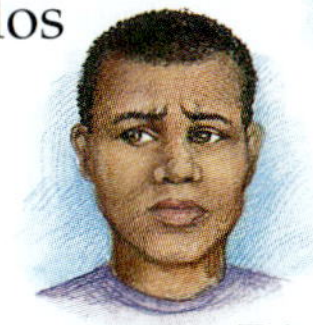

3. Ricardo

4. Martina

14 Unidad 3 Etapa 1 p. 189
Por teléfono

Estudiante A Practice making phone calls. Begin a conversation and then choose logical responses from the list. Your partner will begin the second conversation.

Conversación 1
Soy… ¿Cómo estás?
¿Te gustaría ir al cine por la noche?
Está bien. Hasta luego.
¡Qué lástima!
Buenos días. ¿Puedo hablar con…?

Conversación 2
Muy bien. Adiós.
¿Cuál es tu teléfono?
No está aquí. Regresa más tarde.
¡Claro que sí!

Estudiante B Your partner has just called you on the phone. Choose from the responses to carry on a logical conversation. Then begin a second conversation.

Conversación 1
Gracias, pero no puedo.
¡Muy bien! Voy a patinar por la tarde.
Nos vemos.
Tal vez otro día.
Soy… ¿Quién habla?

Conversación 2
Quiero dejar un mensaje para ella.
253-5652
Buenas tardes. ¿Puedo hablar con Carolina?
Dile que me llame, por favor.
Gracias. Adiós.

15 Unidad 3 Etapa 2 p. 208
Los deportes

Estudiante A By looking at Óscar's equipment, you can see which sports he plays. With your partner, determine how many sports he and Aída have in common.

modelo

Estudiante A: *Óscar juega al baloncesto. ¿Y Aída?*

Estudiante B: . . .

Óscar

Estudiante B By looking at Aída's equipment, you can see which sports she plays. With your partner, determine how many sports she and Óscar have in common.

modelo

Estudiante A: *Oscar juega al baloncesto. ¿Y Aída?*

Estudiante B: *No, no juega al baloncesto, pero patina.*

Aída

16 Unidad 3 Etapa 2 p. 211
En la escuela

Estudiante A Ask your partner to compare school experiences.

modelo

el (la) maestro(a) de historia / el (la) maestro(a) de español

Estudiante A: *¿Cómo son la maestra de historia y el maestro de español?*

Estudiante B: *La maestra de historia es más simpática que el maestro de español.*

o: *El maestro de español es más simpático que la maestra de historia.*

1. la clase de español / la clase de inglés
2. tu maestro(a) de educación física / tu maestro(a) de matemáticas
3. las tareas / las pruebas
4. la oficina / la biblioteca
5. la cafetería / el gimnasio
6. la clase de historia / la clase de arte

Estudiante B Answer your partner's questions about school, using the following expressions.

modelo

más simpático(a)

Estudiante A: *¿Cómo son la maestra de historia y el maestro de español?*

Estudiante B: *La maestra de historia es más simpática que el maestro de español.*

o: *El maestro de español es más simpático que la maestra de historia.*

1. tan fácil como
2. mayor
3. peor
4. menos interesante
5. menos grande
6. más divertida

17 Unidad 3 Etapa 3 p. 230
Los dibujos

Estudiante A Fernando feels differently at 7:30, 1:00, 6:00, and 9:00. Ask about Fernando.

modelo

Estudiante A: *¿Cómo está Fernando a las siete y media?*

Estudiante B: ...

1. 7:30
2. 9:00
3. 6:00
4. 1:00

Estudiante B Fernando feels differently at 7:30, 1:00, 6:00, and 9:00. Answer your partner's questions about Fernando, using **tener** expressions.

18 Unidad 3 Etapa 3 p. 233
¿Lo tiene?

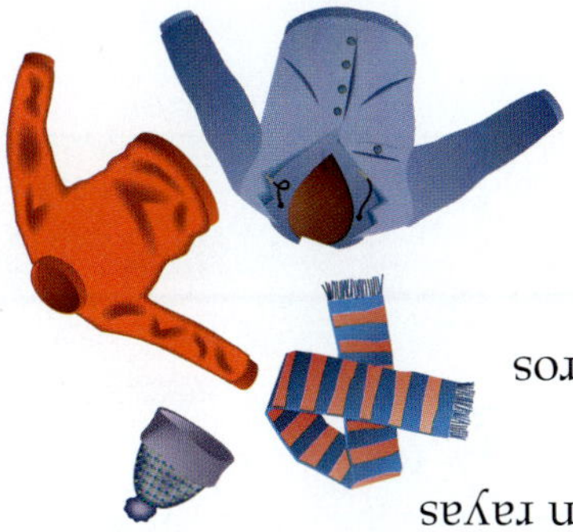

Estudiante A Catalina is going to the beach. Find out if she has the following items with her. Then tell which items Antonio has for his trip to the mountains.

modelo

los patines

Estudiante A: *¿Tiene Catalina los patines?*

Estudiante B: ...

1. las gafas de sol
2. el traje de baño con rayas
3. la merienda
4. los shorts de cuadros
5. el bronceador
6. una revista

Estudiante B Catalina is going to the beach. Answer your partner's questions about Catalina. Then find out if Antonio has the following items for his trip to the mountains.

modelo

los patines

Estudiante A: *¿Tiene Catalina los patines?*

Estudiante B: *No, no los tiene.*

7. el gorro
8. la chaqueta
9. el impermeable
10. la bufanda con rayas
11. las gafas de sol
12. el suéter

19 Unidad 4 Etapa 1 p. 259
¿Qué es?

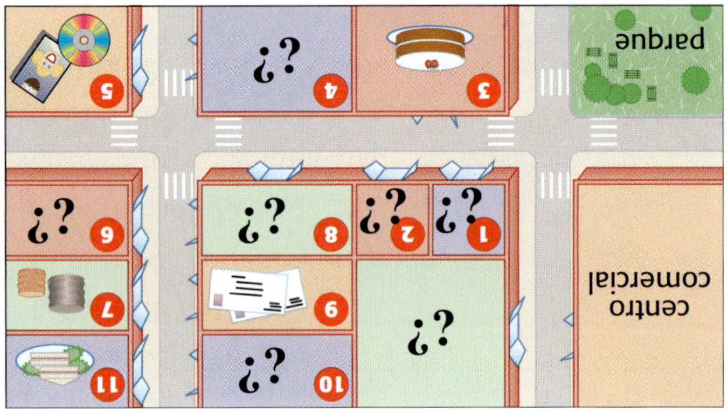

Estudiante A Tú no conoces el centro muy bien. Habla con tu amigo(a) para identificar todos los lugares. *(Hint: Identify the places.)*

modelo

Estudiante A: *¿Qué está enfrente del centro comercial?*

Estudiante B: *. . . está enfrente del centro comercial.*

Estudiante B Tú no conoces el centro muy bien. Habla con tu amigo(a) para identificar todos los lugares. *(Hint: Identify the places.)*

modelo

Estudiante A: *¿Qué está enfrente del centro comercial?*

Estudiante B: *La estación de autobuses está enfrente del centro comercial.*

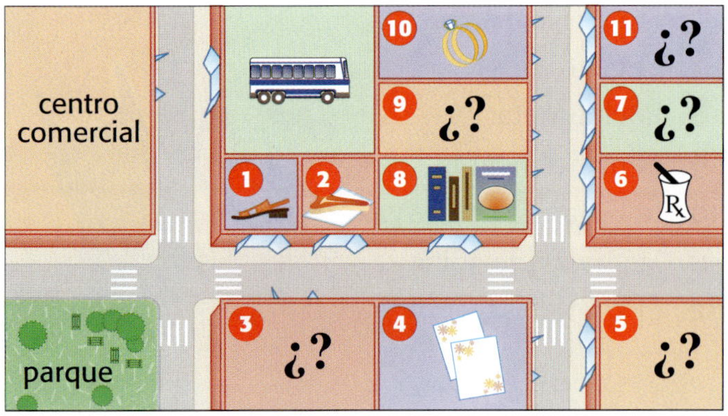

20 Unidad 4 Etapa 1 p. 263
¿Es posible?

Estudiante A Dile a tu amigo(a) qué hacer. Si tiene lo necesario, va a dramatizarla. Si no lo tiene, va a decirte que no es posible. Cambien de papel. *(Hint: Tell your partner what to do. If possible, your partner will act it out.)*

modelo

tocar el piano

Estudiante A: *Toca el piano.*

Estudiante B: *No es posible.*

1. sacar una foto
2. jugar al baloncesto
3. comer pizza
4. andar en bicicleta
5. beber un refresco
6. escribir tu nombre en un papel

Estudiante B Tu amigo(a) te va a decir qué hacer. Si tienes el objeto necesario, dramatiza la actividad. Si no lo tienes, dile que no es posible. Cambien de papel. *(Hint: Your partner will say what to do. If possible, act it out. If not, say so.)*

modelo

tocar el piano

Estudiante A: *Toca el piano.*

Estudiante B: *No es posible.*

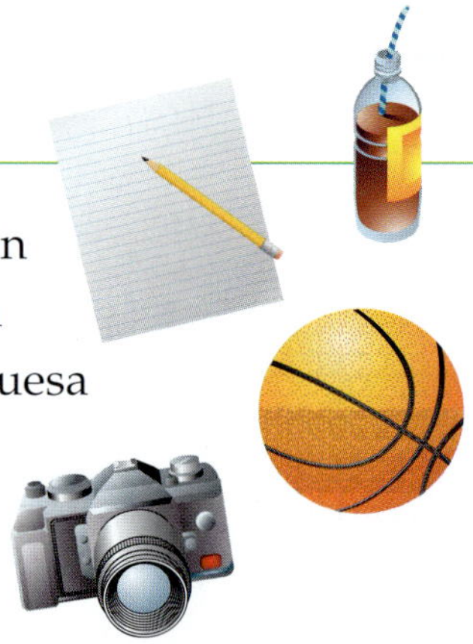

7. escribir en el pizarrón
8. usar la computadora
9. comer una hamburguesa
10. tocar la guitarra
11. correr en tu lugar
12. leer un libro

21 Unidad 4 Etapa 2 p. 280
¿Puede hacerlo bien?

Estudiante A Tu amigo(a) tiene las notas de Emilia. Pregúntale si puede hacer las siguientes actividades bien. *(Hint: Ask if Emilia does these well.)*

modelo

Estudiante A: *¿Puede hacer ejercicio bien?*

Estudiante B: *...*

1. hacer ejercicio
2. hacer un proyecto sobre los pájaros
3. trabajar con números
4. hablar español
5. comprender los mapas

Estudiante B Mira las notas de Emilia y contesta las preguntas de tu amigo(a). *(Hint: Tell if Emilia does these well.)*

modelo

Estudiante A: *¿Puede hacer ejercicio bien?*

Estudiante B: *Sí, puede hacer ejercicio bien.*

Colegio Alta Vista

Emilia Villarreal				
	1	2	3	
Español	A			
Matemáticas	B			
Ciencias	D			
Estudios sociales	C–			
Educación física	A+			

22 Unidad 4 Etapa 2 p. 285
Los regalos

Estudiante A Chavela hace una tabla de los regalos que da para la Navidad. Con tu amigo(a), completa la tabla. *(Hint: Complete the chart.)*

modelo

Estudiante A: *¿Qué le da a su madre?*

Estudiante B: *Le da... a su madre. ¿Cuánto cuesta(n)...?*

Estudiante A: *Cuesta(n) treinta dólares.*

mi madre	$30	
mis hermanos		carteras
mi padre	$25	
mis abuelos		olla
mi prima		casete
mi amiga	$15	

Estudiante B Chavela hace una tabla de los regalos que da para la Navidad. Con tu amigo(a), completa la tabla. *(Hint: Complete the chart.)*

modelo

Estudiante A: *¿Qué le da a su madre?*

Estudiante B: *Le da unos aretes a su madre. ¿Cuánto cuestan los aretes?*

Estudiante A: *Cuesta(n)...*

mi madre		aretes
mis hermanos	$20	
mi padre		cinturón
mis abuelos	$18	
mi prima	$9	
mi amiga		pulsera

23 Unidad 4 Etapa 3 p. 301
¿Riquísimo o no?

Estudiante A Vas a un restaurante con Memo y tu amigo(a). ¿A ellos les gustan estas comidas y bebidas? *(**Hint:** Do Memo and your partner like these?)*

modelo

Estudiante A: *¿Te gusta el bistec? ¿A Memo le gusta?*

Estudiante B: ...

1. el bistec
2. la salsa
3. el flan
4. la limonada
5. los frijoles

	Memo	Mi amigo(a)
las enchiladas	sí	¿?
el té	no	¿?
los postres	sí	¿?
el arroz	sí	¿?
la ensalada	no	¿?

Estudiante B Vas a un restaurante con Memo y tu amigo(a). ¿A ellos les gustan estas comidas y bebidas? *(**Hint:** Do Memo and your partner like these?)*

modelo

Estudiante A: *¿Te gusta el bistec? ¿A Memo le gusta?*

Estudiante B: *A mí me gusta el bistec. A Memo no le gusta.*

6. las enchiladas
7. el té
8. los postres
9. el arroz
10. la ensalada

	Memo	Mi amigo(a)
el bistec	no	¿?
la salsa	sí	¿?
el flan	sí	¿?
la limonada	no	¿?
los frijoles	sí	¿?

24 Unidad 4 Etapa 3 p. 307
¿Qué sirven?

Estudiante A Roberto pide las siguientes comidas. ¿Las sirven en el Café Veracruz? *(**Hint:** Say what Roberto is ordering.)*

modelo

papas fritas

Estudiante A: *Pide papas fritas.*

Estudiante B: ...

1. ensalada
2. flan
3. sopa
4. pollo
5. pan
6. bistec
7. hamburguesa
8. pastel
9. enchiladas
10. queso
11. pan dulce
12. arroz

Estudiante B Dile a tu amigo(a) si sirven las comidas que pide Roberto en el Café Veracruz. *(**Hint:** Tell your partner if these are served.)*

modelo

papas fritas

Estudiante A: *Pide papas fritas.*

Estudiante B: *Sí, sirven papas fritas.*

25 Unidad 5, Etapa 1 p. 333
¿Qué hago?

Estudiante A No recuerdas qué hacer hoy y tu amigo(a) tiene tu calendario. Adivina las cuatro actividades de la lista. *(Hint: Guess the four activities.)*

modelo

hacer la cama

Estudiante A: *¿Hago la cama hoy?*

Estudiante B: *Sí, haz la cama.*

o: *No, no está en tu calendario.*

1. poner la mesa
2. tocar el piano
3. ir al mercado
4. salir a las 7:30
5. escribir una carta
6. hacer la tarea

Estudiante B Tu amigo(a) no recuerda qué hacer hoy y tú tienes su calendario. Cuando te pregunta, dile qué hacer según su calendario. *(Hint: Tell your partner what to do.)*

modelo

hacer la cama

Estudiante A: *¿Hago la cama hoy?*

Estudiante B: *Sí, haz la cama.*

o: *No, no está en tu calendario.*

8 abril

poner la mesa
ir al mercado
salir a las 7:30
hacer la tarea

26 Unidad 5 Etapa 1 p. 337
Problemas y soluciones

Estudiante A Tú le dices varios problemas a tu amigo(a) y te dice una solución. Cambien de papel. *(Hint: Tell your partner your problems.)*

no ponerse shorts
no despertarse tan tarde
lavarse los dientes con otra pasta de dientes
peinarse

modelo

No tengo secador de pelo.

Estudiante A: *No tengo secador de pelo.*

Estudiante B: ...

1. Siempre estoy muy cansado(a).
2. Tengo mucho calor.
3. Quiero ver un programa a las diez.
4. No llevo nada en los pies.

Estudiante B Tu amigo(a) te dice sus problemas. Dile una solución con las expresiones de la lista. Cambien de papel. *(Hint: Suggest solutions to your partner.)*

ponerse los zapatos
bañarse en agua fresca
no acostarse tan tarde
secarse el pelo con una toalla
no dormirse antes de las diez

modelo

Estudiante A: *No tengo secador de pelo.*

Estudiante B: *Sécate el pelo con una toalla.*

5. Siempre llego tarde a la escuela.
6. No me gusta la pasta de dientes.
7. No me gusta mi pelo hoy.
8. Tengo frío.

27 Unidad 5 Etapa 2 p. 354
¿Dónde?

Estudiante A Diana y su familia preparan una fiesta. Pregúntale a tu amigo(a) dónde están haciendo los siguientes quehaceres. *(**Hint:** Ask where they do each chore.)*

modelo

ordenar las flores

Estudiante A: *¿Dónde están ordenando las flores?*

Estudiante B: *Están ordenándolas en...*

1. barrer el suelo
2. pasar la aspiradora
3. planchar la ropa
4. quitar la mesa

Estudiante B Diana y su familia preparan una fiesta. Dile a tu amigo(a) dónde están haciendo los siguientes quehaceres. *(**Hint:** Tell where they do each chore.)*

modelo

ordenar las flores

Estudiante A: *¿Dónde están ordenando las flores?*

Estudiante B: *Están ordenándolas en la cocina.*

28 Unidad 5 Etapa 2 p. 359
¿Cómo?

Estudiante A ¿Cómo debe hacer Pedro las siguientes actividades? *(**Hint:** How should Pedro do these?)*

modelo

quitar el polvo

Estudiante A: *¿Cómo debe quitar el polvo?*

Estudiante B: *Debe quitarlo...*

1. pasar la aspiradora
2. sacar la basura
3. barrer el suelo
4. hacer la tarea
5. hacer la cama
6. manejar

Estudiante B ¿Cómo debe hacer Pedro las siguientes actividades? *(**Hint:** How should Pedro do these?)*

modelo

quitar el polvo: cuidadoso

Estudiante A: *¿Cómo debe quitar el polvo?*

Estudiante B: *Debe quitarlo cuidadosamente.*

a. sacar la basura: rápido
b. hacer la tarea: paciente
c. manejar: tranquilo
d. pasar la aspiradora: lento
e. hacer la cama: fácil
f. barrer el suelo: frecuente

29 Unidad 5 Etapa 3 p. 375
¿Quién es?

Estudiante A Pregúntale a tu amigo(a) sobre tres nuevas estudiantes. *(Hint: Ask about three students.)*

modelo

más alta

Estudiante A: *¿Quién es la más alta?*

Estudiante B: *...es la más alta.*

1. ser menor
2. tener pelo más largo
3. estar más contenta
4. ser menos alta
5. tener pelo más corto
6. ser mayor
7. estar más cansada

Estudiante B Contesta las preguntas de tu amigo(a) sobre las tres nuevas estudiantes. *(Hint: Answer questions about three students.)*

modelo

Estudiante A: *¿Quién es la más alta?*

Estudiante B: *Olivia es la más alta.*

30 Unidad 5 Etapa 3 p. 381
En el supermercado

Estudiante A Pregúntale a tu amigo(a) qué compraron las siguientes personas. Cambien de papel. *(Hint: Ask what they bought.)*

modelo

el señor Matute / 5,19 €

Estudiante A: *¿Qué compró el señor Matute por cinco euros diecinueve?*

Estudiante B: *Compró...*

1. ustedes / 7,35 €
2. la señora García / 1,89 €
3. tú / 1 €
4. Alejandra y Cristóbal / 8,55 €

2/ 5,79 € | 4/ 8,29 € | 2 kilos/ 1,50 € | 2/ 3,45 €

Estudiante B Dile a tu amigo(a) qué compraron. Cambien de papel. *(Hint: Say what they bought.)*

modelo

Estudiante A: *¿Qué compró el señor Matute por cinco euros diecinueve?*

Estudiante B: *Compró medio kilo de salchichas.*

5. la señora Martínez / 8,29 €
6. tú / 3,45 €
7. tu amigo / 1,50 €
8. el señor Aguilera / 5,79 €

2 litros/ 1,89 € | 4/ 7,35 € | 1 kilo/ 8,55 € | 12/ 1 € | 1/2 kilo/ 5,19 €

31 Unidad 6 Etapa 1 p. 407
Una noche larga

Estudiante A ¿Qué leyeron u oyeron estas personas en sus camas? Completa la tabla con tu amigo(a). *(Hint: Complete the chart.)*

modelo

Estudiante A: *¿Ángela oyó o leyó algo?*

Estudiante B: *Ángela...*

Ángela	
María y Elena	una novela
Quique y Alex	
Gloria	
Alfredo y Paco	los aviones
Tavo	una revista

Estudiante B ¿Qué leyeron u oyeron estas personas en sus camas? Completa la tabla con tu amigo(a). *(Hint: Complete the chart.)*

modelo

Estudiante A: *¿Ángela oyó o leyó algo?*

Estudiante B: *Ángela oyó los pájaros.*

Ángela	los pájaros
María y Elena	
Quique y Alex	el periódico
Gloria	el tren
Alfredo y Paco	
Tavo	

32 Unidad 6 Etapa 1 p. 411
Vamos a...

Estudiante A Le sugieres a tu amigo(a) a hacer algo. Tu amigo(a) te dice la última vez que lo hizo. Cambien de papel. *(Hint: Suggest you do an activity.)*

la semana pasada
anteayer
anoche
el... pasado
ayer

modelo

estudiar

Estudiante A: *Vamos a estudiar.*

Estudiante B: *Estudié ayer.*

1. jugar al baloncesto
2. ver la televisión
3. ¿?
4. ¿?
5. leer revistas
6. ir a una fiesta
7. ¿?
8. ¿?

Estudiante B Tu amigo(a) te sugiere hacer algo. Dile la última vez que lo hiciste. Cambien de papel. *(Hint: Say the last time you did an activity after you hear the suggestion.)*

la semana pasada
anteayer
anoche
el... pasado
ayer

modelo

Estudiante A: *Vamos a estudiar.*

Estudiante B: *Estudié ayer.*

1. ¿?
2. ¿?
3. ir al cine
4. correr
5. ¿?
6. ¿?
7. comer helado
8. escuchar música

33 Unidad 6 Etapa 2 p. 429
¿Dónde están?

**Estudiante A: ** *Hay un corral en el centro…*

modelo

Estudiante A Describe la granja a tu amigo(a). Él (Ella) la va a dibujar. Cambien de papel. *(Hint: Describe the farm.)*

Estudiante B Tu amigo(a) te describe una granja. Dibuja lo que oyes. Cambien de papel. *(Hint: Draw the farm described.)*

modelo

Estudiante A: *Hay un corral en el centro…*

34 Unidad 6 Etapa 2 p. 433
La carrera

Estudiante B: *La primera es número…*

Estudiante A: *¿Quién es la primera?*

modelo

Estudiante A Hay una carrera y no puedes ver bien. Trabaja con tu amigo(a) para identificar a todos los participantes. *(Hint: Identify all the racers.)*

Estudiante B Hay una carrera y no puedes ver bien. Trabaja con tu amigo(a) para identificar a todos los participantes. *(Hint: Identify all the racers.)*

modelo

Estudiante A: *¿Quién es la primera?*

Estudiante B: *La primera es número cincuenta.*

35 Unidad 6 Etapa 3 p. 451
¿Lo hago?

Estudiante A No recuerdas qué hacer hoy y tu amigo(a) tiene tu calendario. Pregúntale qué haces hoy. *(Hint: Ask what you'll do today.)*

modelo

barrer el suelo

Estudiante A: *¿Barro el suelo hoy?*

Estudiante B: *Sí, barre el suelo hoy.* **o:** *Hoy no.*

1. almorzar con Angélica
2. estudiar en la biblioteca
3. sacar la basura
4. mandar una carta
5. ir al cine
6. estar en casa a las 8:30

Estudiante B Tu amigo(a) no recuerda qué hacer hoy y tú tienes su calendario. Cuando te pregunta, dile qué hacer según su calendario. *(Hint: Tell your partner what to do according to the calendar.)*

modelo

barrer el suelo

Estudiante A: *¿Barro el suelo hoy?*

Estudiante B: *Sí, barre el suelo hoy.* **o:** *Hoy no.*

26 junio

almorzar con Angélica
sacar la basura
ir al cine
estar en casa a las 8:30

36 Unidad 6 Etapa 3 p. 455
Parte de la historia

Estudiante A Viste algo en la televisión, pero solamente sabes parte de la historia. Con tu amigo(a), cuenta lo que pasó según los dibujos. Tu amigo(a) empieza. *(Hint: Take turns telling what happened.)*

modelo

Estudiante B: *Un hombre se levantó a las seis de la mañana.*

Estudiante B Viste algo en la televisión, pero solamente sabes parte de la historia. Con tu amigo(a), cuenta lo que pasó según los dibujos. Tú empiezas. *(Hint: Take turns telling what happened.)*

modelo

Estudiante B: *Un hombre se levantó a las seis de la mañana.*

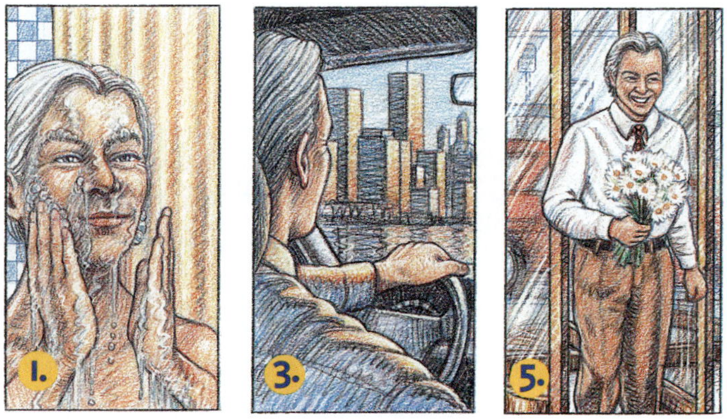

Juegos—respuestas

UNIDAD 1

Etapa 1 **En uso,** p. 47: A Marisol no le gusta hacer las actividades con la letra **c.**

Etapa 2 **En uso,** p. 69: b

Etapa 3 **En acción,** p. 83: El hermano de Marco tiene un año.; **En uso,** p. 93: 1. El abuelo tiene 61 años. 2. Carlos tiene 37 años. 3. Antonio tiene 2 años.

UNIDAD 2

Etapa 1 **En uso,** p. 121: 1. matemáticas, 2. computación, 3. inglés, 4. música

Etapa 2 **En uso,** p. 143: Marco va al auditorio. Maricarmen va a la biblioteca. Josefina va a la oficina.

Etapa 3 **En acción,** p. 152: El perro tiene sed.; **En uso,** p. 167: Adriana camina con el perro. José toca la guitarra. Jorge cuida a sus hermanos.

UNIDAD 3

Etapa 1 **En uso,** p. 195: 1. Miguel va a un concierto. 2. Mariela va al cine. 3. Martina y Martín van de compras (a la tienda).

Etapa 2 **En uso,** p. 217: 1. Ángela: levantar pesas, 2. Marco: surfing, 3. Juanito: fútbol

Etapa 3 **En acción,** p. 232: b; **En uso,** p. 241: c. Chile

UNIDAD 4

Etapa 1 **En uso,** p. 269: Adriana va al aeropuerto. Andrés va a la farmacia. Arturo va al banco.

Etapa 2 **En acción,** p. 282: Lola quiere darle la lila a Lidia.; **En uso,** p. 291: Compras un plato barato por pocos pesos.

Etapa 3 **En uso,** p. 315: Pablo le sirve sopa a Marco, ensalada a Martina y azúcar a Marisol.

UNIDAD 5

Etapa 1 **En acción,** p. 332: Necesita peinarse.; **En uso,** p. 343: 1. un despertador, 2. un secador de pelo, 3. un peine, 4. un espejo

Etapa 2 **En uso,** p. 365: 1. Sofía está en el comedor. 2. Felipe está en la sala. 3. Cristina está en la cocina.

Etapa 3 **En uso,** p. 389: 1. helado: el congelador, 2. platos sucios: el lavaplatos, 3. leche: el frigorífico, 4. carne de res: la estufa

UNIDAD 6

Etapa 1 **En uso,** p. 417: 1. El papá de Adriana es contador. 2. El padre de Susana es fotógrafo. 3. El Sr. Rodríguez es bombero.

Etapa 2 **En uso,** p. 439: El cerdo es el primero, la llama es la segunda y la vaca es la tercera.

Etapa 3 **En acción,** p. 452: a; **En uso,** p. 463:
1. b. La llama está jugando con Rocío.
2. c. El ganadero buscó su merienda.
3. a. ¡El caballo se va a escapar del corral!

Vocabulario adicional

Here are lists of additional vocabulary to supplement the words you know. They include musical instruments, classes, animals, professions, sports, and foods. If you do not find a word here, it may be listed as passive vocabulary in the glossaries.

Los instrumentos

el acordeón	*accordion*
la armónica	*harmonica*
el arpa (fem.)	*harp*
el bajo	*bass*
el bajón	*bassoon*
el banjo	*banjo*
la batería	*drum set*
el clarinete	*clarinet*
el corno francés	*French horn*
el corno inglés	*English horn*
la flauta	*flute*
la flauta dulce	*recorder*
el flautín	*piccolo*
la mandolina	*mandolin*
el oboe	*oboe*
el órgano	*organ*
la pandereta	*tambourine*
el saxofón	*saxophone*
el sintetizador	*synthesizer*
el tambor	*drum*
el trombón	*trombone*
la trompeta	*trumpet*
la tuba	*tuba*
la viola	*viola*
el violín	*violin*
el violonchelo	*cello*
el xilófono	*xylophone*

Más animales

la abeja	*bee*
el águila (fem.)	*eagle*
el alce	*moose*
la araña	*spider*
la ardilla	*squirrel*
la ballena	*whale*
el buey	*ox*
el búho	*owl*
el burro	*donkey*
la cabra	*goat*
el cangrejo	*crab*
el chapulín	*grasshopper*
el cisne	*swan*
el conejillo de Indias	*guinea pig*
el conejo	*rabbit*
el coyote	*coyote*
el delfín	*dolphin*
el elefante	*elephant*
el ganso	*goose*
el gerbo	*gerbil*
el grillo	*cricket*
el hámster	*hamster*
la hormiga	*ant*
el hurón	*ferret*
el jaguar	*jaguar*
la jirafa	*giraffe*
la lagartija	*small lizard*
el león	*lion*
el leopardo	*leopard*
el lobo	*wolf*
el loro	*parrot*
el mono	*monkey*
el mapache	*raccoon*
la mariposa	*butterfly*
la mosca	*fly*
el mosquito	*mosquito*
el (la) oso(a)	*bear*
la oveja	*sheep*
la paloma	*pigeon, dove*
la pantera	*panther*
el pato	*duck*
el pavo	*turkey*
el pavo real	*peacock*
el pingüino	*penguin*
la rana	*frog*
la rata	*rat*
el ratón	*mouse*
el sapo	*toad*
la serpiente	*snake*
el tiburón	*shark*
el tigre	*tiger*
la tortuga	*turtle*
el venado	*deer*
el zorro	*fox*

Más profesiones

el (la) abogado(a)	*lawyer*
el actor	*actor*
la actriz	*actress*
el (la) agente de bolsa	*stockbroker*
el (la) agente de viajes	*travel agent*
el (la) alcalde	*mayor*
el (la) artista	*artist*
el (la) asistente social	*social worker*
el (la) atleta	*athlete*
el (la) auxiliar de vuelo	*flight attendant*
el (la) cantante	*singer*
el (la) carnicero(a)	*butcher*
el (la) carpintero(a)	*carpenter*
el (la) científico(a)	*scientist*
el (la) dentista	*dentist*
el (la) director(a)	*principal, director*
el (la) empleado(a) de banco	*bank clerk*
el (la) enfermero(a)	*nurse*
el (la) farmacéutico(a)	*pharmacist*
el (la) funcionario(a)	*civil servant*
el (la) guía	*guide*
el (la) ingeniero(a)	*engineer*
el (la) jardinero(a)	*gardener*
el (la) joyero(a)	*jeweler*
el (la) mecánico(a)	*mechanic*
el (la) militar	*soldier*
el (la) modelo	*model*
el (la) músico(a)	*musician*
el (la) panadero(a)	*baker*
el (la) peluquero(a)	*hairstylist*
el (la) pescador(a)	*fisher*
el (la) piloto(a)	*pilot*
el (la) plomero(a)	*plumber*
el (la) profesor(a)	*teacher, professor*
el (la) sastre	*tailor*
el (la) vendedor(a)	*salesperson*
el (la) veterinario(a)	*veterinarian*
el (la) zapatero(a)	*shoemaker*

Las clases

el alemán	*German*
el álgebra (fem.)	*algebra*
la biología	*biology*
el cálculo	*calculus*
la composición	*writing*
la contabilidad	*accounting*
la física	*physics*
el francés	*French*
la geografía	*geography*
la geología	*geology*
la geometría	*geometry*
el italiano	*Italian*
el japonés	*Japanese*
el latín	*Latin*
la química	*chemistry*
el ruso	*Russian*
la salud	*health*
la trigonometría	*trigonometry*

Los deportes

el árbitro	*referee, umpire*
el arquero	*goalie*
el (la) bateador(a)	*batter*
el boxeo	*boxing*
el (la) campeón(ona)	*champion*
el campeonato	*championship*
la carrera	*race*
el cesto	*basket*
el (la) entrenador(a)	*trainer, coach*
el esquí	*ski*
la gimnasia	*gymnastics*
el golf	*golf*
los juegos olímpicos	*Olympics*
el (la) lanzador(a)	*pitcher*
el marcador	*scoreboard*
el palo	*stick, club*
el (la) parador(a)	*catcher*
la pista	*racetrack*
la red	*net*
la tabla hawaiana	*surfboard*
el trofeo	*trophy*
el uniforme	*uniform*

Las frutas y las verduras

el aguacate	*avocado*
la alcachofa	*artichoke*
el apio	*celery*
el arándano	*blueberry*
la banana	*banana*
la berenjena	*eggplant*
el bróculi	*broccoli*
el calabacín	*zucchini*
la calabaza	*squash*
la cereza	*cherry*
la ciruela	*plum*
el coco	*coconut*
la col	*cabbage*
la coliflor	*cauliflower*
el dátil	*date*
el espárrago	*asparagus*
la espinaca	*spinach*
la frambuesa	*raspberry*
la fresa	*strawberry*
la guayaba	*guava*
el kiwi	*kiwi*
el lima	*lime*
el limón	*lemon*
el mango	*mango*
la manzana	*apple*
el melocotón	*peach*
el melón	*melon*
la mora	*blackberry*
la naranja	*orange*
la papaya	*papaya*
el pepino	*cucumber*
la pera	*pear*
el plátano	*banana, plantain*
la sandía	*watermelon*
la toronja	*grapefruit*

Gramática—resumen

Grammar Terms

Adjective (pp. 59–60): a word that describes a noun

Adverb (pp. 111, 357): a word that describes a verb, an adjective, or another adverb

Article (pp. 56–57): a word that identifies the class of a noun (masculine or feminine, singular or plural); English articles are *a, an,* or *the*

Command (p. 260): a verb form used to tell someone to do something

Comparative (p. 208): a phrase that compares two things

Conjugation (pp. 109, 376): a verb form that uses the stem of an infinitive and adds endings that reflect subject and tense

Direct Object (p. 230): the noun, pronoun, or phrase that receives the action of the main verb in a sentence

Gender (p. 59): a property that divides adjectives, nouns, pronouns, and articles into masculine and feminine groups

Indirect Object (p. 281): a noun, pronoun, or phrase that tells to whom/what or for whom/what an action is done

Infinitive (p. 39): the basic form of a verb; it names the action without giving tense, person, or number

Interrogative (p. 135): a word that asks a question

Noun (p. 56): a word that names a thing, person, animal, place, feeling, or situation

Number (p. 60): a property that divides adjectives, nouns, pronouns, articles, and verbs into singular and plural groups

Preposition (p. 80): a word that shows the relationship between its object and another word in the sentence

Pronoun (p. 35): a word that can be used in place of a noun

Reflexive Verb (p. 330): a verb for which the subject and the direct object are the same participant

Subject (p. 35): the noun, pronoun, or phrase in a sentence that performs the action and is the focus of attention

Superlative (p. 374): a phrase that describes which item has the most or least of a quality

Tense (pp. 109, 376): when the action of a verb takes place

Nouns, Articles, and Pronouns

Nouns

Nouns identify things, people, animals, places, feelings, or situations. Spanish nouns are either masculine or feminine. They are also either **singular** or **plural.** **Masculine nouns** usually end in **-o** and **feminine nouns** usually end in **-a.**

To make a noun **plural**, add **-s** to a word ending in a vowel and **-es** to a word ending in a consonant.

Singular Nouns	
Masculine	**Feminine**
amigo	amiga
chico	chica
hombre	mujer
suéter	blusa
zapato	falda

Plural Nouns	
Masculine	**Feminine**
amigo**s**	amiga**s**
chico**s**	chica**s**
hombre**s**	mujer**es**
suéter**es**	blusa**s**
zapato**s**	falda**s**

Articles

Articles identify the class of a noun: masculine or feminine, singular or plural. **Definite articles** are the equivalent of the English word *the*. **Indefinite articles** are the equivalent of *a*, *an*, or *some*.

Definite Articles		
	Masculine	**Feminine**
Singular	**el** amigo	**la** amiga
Plural	**los** amigos	**las** amigas

Indefinite Articles		
	Masculine	**Feminine**
Singular	**un** amigo	**una** amiga
Plural	**unos** amigos	**unas** amigas

Pronouns

A **pronoun** takes the place of a noun. The pronoun used is determined by its function or purpose in the sentence.

Subject Pronouns	
yo	nosotros(as)
tú	vosotros(as)
usted	ustedes
él, ella	ellos(as)

Pronouns Used After Prepositions	
de **mí**	de **nosotros(as)**
de **ti**	de **vosotros(as)**
de **usted**	de **ustedes**
de **él, ella**	de **ellos(as)**

Direct Object Pronouns	
me	nos
te	os
lo, la	los, las

Indirect Object Pronouns	
me	nos
te	os
le	les

Reflexive Pronouns	
me	nos
te	os
se	se

Demonstrative Pronouns	
éste(a), esto	éstos(as)
ése(a), eso	ésos(as)
aquél(la), aquello	aquéllos(as)

Adjectives

Adjectives describe nouns. In Spanish, adjectives must match the **number** and **gender** of the nouns they describe. When an adjective describes a group with both genders, the masculine form is used. To make an adjective plural, apply the same rules that are used for making a noun plural. Most adjectives are placed after the noun.

Adjectives		
	Masculine	**Feminine**
Singular	el chico **guapo** el chico **paciente** el chico **fenomenal** el chico **trabajador**	la chica **guapa** la chica **paciente** la chica **fenomenal** la chica **trabajadora**
Plural	los chicos guapo**s** los chicos paciente**s** los chicos fenomenal**es** los chicos trabajador**es**	las chicas guapa**s** las chicas paciente**s** las chicas fenomenal**es** las chicas trabajadora**s**

Adjectives cont.

Sometimes adjectives are placed before the noun and **shortened**. **Grande** is shortened before any singular noun. Several others are shortened before a masculine singular noun.

Shortened Forms			
alguno	**algún** chico	primero	**primer** chico
bueno	**buen** chico	tercero	**tercer** chico
malo	**mal** chico		
ninguno	**ningún** chico	grande	**gran** chico(a)

Possessive adjectives identify to whom something belongs. They agree in gender and number with the noun possessed, not with the person who possesses it.

Possessive Adjectives	Masculine		Feminine	
Singular	**mi** amigo	**nuestro** amigo	**mi** amiga	**nuestra** amiga
	tu amigo	**vuestro** amigo	**tu** amiga	**vuestra** amiga
	su amigo	**su** amigo	**su** amiga	**su** amiga
Plural	**mis** amigos	**nuestros** amigos	**mis** amigas	**nuestras** amigas
	tus amigos	**vuestros** amigos	**tus** amigas	**vuestras** amigas
	sus amigos	**sus** amigos	**sus** amigas	**sus** amigas

Demonstrative adjectives point out which noun is being referred to. Their English equivalents are *this*, *that*, *these*, and *those*.

Demonstrative Adjectives	Masculine	Feminine
Singular	**este** amigo	**esta** amiga
	ese amigo	**esa** amiga
	aquel amigo	**aquella** amiga
Plural	**estos** amigos	**estas** amigas
	esos amigos	**esas** amigas
	aquellos amigos	**aquellas** amigas

Interrogatives

Interrogative words are used to ask questions.

Interrogatives		
¿Adónde?	¿Cuándo?	¿Por qué?
¿Cómo?	¿Cuánto(a)? ¿Cuántos(as)?	¿Qué?
¿Cuál(es)?	¿Dónde?	¿Quién(es)?

Comparatives and Superlatives

Comparatives

Comparatives are used when comparing two different things.

Comparatives		
más (+) **más** interesante **que...** Me gusta correr **más que** nadar.	menos (−) **menos** interesante **que...** Me gusta nadar **menos que** correr.	tan(to) (=) **tan** interesante **como...** Me gusta leer **tanto como** escribir.

There are a few irregular comparatives. When talking about the age of people, use **mayor** and **menor**.

Age	Quality
mayor menor	mejor peor

When talking about numbers, **de** is used instead of **que**.

más (menos) de cien...

Superlatives

Superlatives are used to distinguish one item from a group. They describe which item has the most or least of a quality.

The ending **-ísimo(a)** can be added to an adjective to form a superlative.

Superlatives		
	Masculine	**Feminine**
Singular	**el** chico **más** alto **el** chico **menos** alto	**la** chica **más** alta **la** chica **menos** alta
Plural	**los** chicos **más** altos **los** chicos **menos** altos	**las** chicas **más** altas **las** chicas **menos** altas
Singular	mole buen**ísimo**	pasta buen**ísima**
Plural	frijoles buen**ísimos**	enchiladas buen**ísimas**

Affirmative and Negative Words

Affirmative words are used to talk about something or someone, or to say that an event also or always happens. **Negative** words are used to refer to no one or nothing, or to say that events do not happen.

Affirmative	Negative
algo	nada
alguien	nadie
algún (alguna)	ningún (ninguna)
alguno(a)	ninguno(a)
siempre	nunca
también	tampoco

Adverbs

Adverbs modify a verb, an adjective, or another adverb. Many adverbs in Spanish are made by changing an existing adjective.

Adjective	→	Adverb
reciente	→	recientе**mente**
frecuente	→	frecuente**mente**
fácil	→	fácil**mente**
normal	→	normal**mente**
especial	→	especial**mente**
feliz	→	feliz**mente**
cuidadoso(a)	→	cuidadosa**mente**
rápido(a)	→	rápida**mente**
lento(a)	→	lenta**mente**
tranquilo(a)	→	tranquila**mente**

Verbs: Present Tense

Regular Verbs

Regular verbs ending in **-ar**, **-er**, or **-ir** always have regular endings in the present.

-ar Verbs		-er Verbs		-ir Verbs	
habl**o**	habl**amos**	com**o**	com**emos**	viv**o**	viv**imos**
habl**as**	habl**áis**	com**es**	com**éis**	viv**es**	viv**ís**
habl**a**	habl**an**	com**e**	com**en**	viv**e**	viv**en**

Verbs with Irregular yo Forms

Some verbs have regular forms in the present except for their **yo** forms.

Infinitive	→	Yo form
conocer	→	conozco
dar	→	doy
hacer	→	hago
ofrecer	→	ofrezco
poner	→	pongo
saber	→	sé
salir	→	salgo
traer	→	traigo
ver	→	veo

Stem-Changing Verbs

u → ue	
juego	jugamos
juegas	jugáis
juega	**jue**gan

Jugar is the only verb with a **u** → **ue** stem change.

e → ie	
c**ie**rro	cerramos
c**ie**rras	cerráis
c**ie**rra	c**ie**rran

Other **e** → **ie** verbs: **empezar, entender, merendar, nevar, pensar, perder, preferir, querer.** Reflexive: **despertarse.**

o → ue	
v**ue**lvo	volvemos
v**ue**lves	volvéis
v**ue**lve	v**ue**lven

Other **o** → **ue** verbs: **almorzar, contar, costar, devolver, dormir, encontrar, llover, mover, poder, recordar.** Reflexive: **acostarse.**

e → i	
p**i**do	pedimos
p**i**des	pedís
p**i**de	p**i**den

Other **e** → **i** verbs: **repetir, seguir, servir.**

Irregular Verbs

decir	
digo	decimos
dices	decís
dice	dicen

esquiar	
esquío	esquiamos
esquías	esquiáis
esquía	esquían

estar	
estoy	estamos
estás	estáis
está	están

ir	
voy	vamos
vas	vais
va	van

oír	
oigo	oímos
oyes	oís
oye	oyen

ser	
soy	somos
eres	sois
es	son

tener	
tengo	tenemos
tienes	tenéis
tiene	tienen

venir	
vengo	venimos
vienes	venís
viene	vienen

Verbs: Present Participles

Present participles are used with a form of **estar** to talk about something that is in the process of happening.

Regular Participles		
-ar Verbs	**-er Verbs**	**-ir Verbs**
habl**ando**	com**iendo**	compart**iendo**
toc**ando**	hac**iendo**	sal**iendo**
us**ando**	perd**iendo**	viv**iendo**

y Spelling Change		
creer	→	cre**y**endo
leer	→	le**y**endo
oír	→	o**y**endo
traer	→	tra**y**endo

Stem Changes		
decir	→	diciendo
dormir	→	durmiendo
pedir	→	pidiendo
servir	→	sirviendo
venir	→	viniendo

GRAMÁTICA—RESUMEN

Verbs: tú Commands

Affirmative tú Commands

Affirmative tú commands are used to tell a friend or family member to do something. Regular **tú** commands are the same as the third person singular form of the present tense.

Regular Commands		
-ar Verbs	**-er Verbs**	**-ir Verbs**
habla piensa almuerza	come entiende vuelve	vive pide sirve

Irregular Commands		
Infinitive	→	**Tú Command**
decir	→	di
hacer	→	haz
ir	→	ve
poner	→	pon
salir	→	sal
ser	→	sé
tener	→	ten
venir	→	ven

Negative tú Commands

Negative tú commands are used to tell a friend or family member **not** to do something.

Regular Commands		
-ar Verbs	**-er Verbs**	**-ir Verbs**
no habl**es** no mir**es** no entr**es**	no com**as** no hag**as** no vuelv**as**	no viv**as** no oig**as** no veng**as**

Commands with Spelling Changes		
-car Verbs	**-gar Verbs**	**-zar Verbs**
no bus**qu**es no practi**qu**es no to**qu**es	no jue**gu**es no lle**gu**es no pa**gu**es	no almuer**c**es no cru**c**es no empie**c**es

Irregular Commands		
Infinitive	→	**Tú Command**
dar	→	no des
estar	→	no estés
ir	→	no vayas
ser	→	no seas

Verbs: Preterite Tense

Regular Verbs

Regular preterite verbs ending in **-ar**, **-er**, or **-ir** have regular endings.

-ar Verbs		-er Verbs		-ir Verbs	
bail**é**	bail**amos**	corr**í**	corr**imos**	abr**í**	abr**imos**
bail**aste**	bail**asteis**	corr**iste**	corr**isteis**	abr**iste**	abr**isteis**
bail**ó**	bail**aron**	corr**ió**	corr**ieron**	abr**ió**	abr**ieron**

Verbs with Spelling Changes

-car Verbs	
c → qu	
practi**qu**é	practicamos
practicaste	practicasteis
practicó	practicaron

-gar Verbs	
g → gu	
pa**gu**é	pagamos
pagaste	pagasteis
pagó	pagaron

-zar Verbs	
z → c	
cru**c**é	cruzamos
cruzaste	cruzasteis
cruzó	cruzaron

creer	
i → y	
creí	creímos
creíste	creísteis
cre**y**ó	cre**y**eron

leer	
i → y	
leí	leímos
leíste	leísteis
le**y**ó	le**y**eron

oír	
i → y	
oí	oímos
oíste	oísteis
o**y**ó	o**y**eron

Irregular Verbs

dar	
di	dimos
diste	disteis
dio	dieron

decir	
dije	dijimos
dijiste	dijisteis
dijo	dijeron

estar	
estuve	estuvimos
estuviste	estuvisteis
estuvo	estuvieron

hacer	
hice	hicimos
hiciste	hicisteis
hizo	hicieron

ir	
fui	fuimos
fuiste	fuisteis
fue	fueron

ser	
fui	fuimos
fuiste	fuisteis
fue	fueron

tener	
tuve	tuvimos
tuviste	tuvisteis
tuvo	tuvieron

venir	
vine	vinimos
viniste	vinisteis
vino	vinieron

GLOSARIO
español-inglés

This Spanish-English glossary contains all of the active vocabulary words that appear in the text as well as passive vocabulary from readings, culture sections, and extra vocabulary lists. Most inactive cognates have been omitted. The active words are accompanied by the number of the unit and **etapa** in which they are presented. For example, **a pie** can be found in **4.1** (*Unidad* **4**, *Etapa* **1**). **EP** refers to the *Etapa preliminar.* Stem-changing verbs are indicated by the change inside the parentheses—**poder (ue)**, as are verbs that are irregular only in the **yo** form.

A

a to, at
- **A la(s)...** At.... o'clock. **2.2**
- **a la derecha (de)** to the right (of) **4.1**
- **a la izquierda (de)** to the left (of) **4.1**
- **a pie** on foot **4.1**
- **¿A qué hora es...?** (At) What time is...? **2.2**
- **a veces** sometimes **2.1**

abajo down **6.2**
abierto(a) open **5.2**
el abrigo coat **3.3**
abril April **1.3**
abrir to open **2.3**
la abuela grandmother **1.3**
el abuelo grandfather **1.3**
los abuelos grandparents **1.3**
aburrido(a) boring **1.2**
acá here **4.1**
acabar de... to have just... **3.1**
el aceite oil **5.3**
las aceitunas olives **5.2**
acostarse (ue) to go to bed **5.1**
actualmente nowadays
Adiós. Good-bye. **EP**
adónde (to) where **2.2**
el aeropuerto airport **4.1**
afeitarse to shave oneself **5.1**
agosto August **1.3**
el agua (fem.) water **2.2**
ahora now **1.3**
- **¡Ahora mismo!** Right now! **2.1**

al to the **2.2**
- **al aire libre** outdoors **3.2**
- **al lado (de)** beside, next to **4.1**

alegre happy **3.1**
el (la) alfarero(a) potter
algo something **4.3**
alguien someone **4.3**
- **conocer a alguien** to know, to be familiar with someone **2.3**

alguno(a) some **4.3**
allá there **4.1**
allí there **4.1**
almorzar (ue) to eat lunch **4.2**
el almuerzo lunch **2.2**
alquilar un video to rent a video **3.1**
alto(a) tall **1.2**
amarillo(a) yellow **1.2**
el (la) amigo(a) friend **1.1**
anaranjado(a) orange **1.2**
ancho(a) wide **6.1**
andar
- **andar en bicicleta** to ride a bike **2.3**
- **andar en patineta** to skateboard **3.2**

el anillo ring **4.2**
el animal animal **2.3**
anoche last night **5.3**
anteayer day before yesterday **5.3**
antes (de) before **2.3**
antiguo(a) old, ancient **6.1**
el año year **1.3**
- **el año pasado** last year **5.3**
- **¿Cuántos años tiene...?** How old is...? **1.3**
- **Tiene... años.** He/She is... years old. **1.3**

apagar la luz to turn off the light **5.3**
el apartamento apartment **1.1**
aparte separate
- **Es aparte.** Separate checks. **4.3**

el apellido last name, surname **EP**
el apoyo support
aprender to learn **2.3**
aquel(la) that (over there) **6.2**
aquél(la) that one (over there) **6.2**
aquello that (over there) **6.2**
aquí here **4.1**
el árbol tree **3.3**
el arete earring **4.2**
el armario closet **5.2**
el (la) arquitecto(a) architect **6.1**
la arquitectura architecture **6.1**
arriba up **6.2**
el arroz rice **4.3**
el arte art **2.1**
la artesanía handicraft **4.2**
el (la) artesano(a) artisan **6.2**
los artículos de cuero leather goods **4.2**
asado(a) roasted
el auditorio auditorium **2.2**
el autobús bus **4.1**
la avenida avenue **4.1**
el avión airplane **4.1**

ESPAÑOL-INGLÉS

ayer yesterday **5.3**
ayudar (a) to help **2.1**
  ¿Me ayuda a pedir?
    Could you help me order? **4.3**
el azúcar sugar **4.3**
azul blue **1.2**

B

bailar to dance **1.1**
bajo(a) short (height) **1.2**
el baloncesto basketball **3.2**
el banco bank **4.1**
bañarse to take a bath **5.1**
el baño bathroom **5.2**
barato(a) cheap, inexpensive **4.2**
el barco ship **4.1**
barrer el suelo
  to sweep the floor **5.2**
el barrio district
el barro clay
el bate bat **3.2**
beber to drink **2.3**
  ¿Quieres beber…?
    Do you want to drink…? **2.2**
  Quiero beber…
    I want to drink… **2.2**
la bebida beverage, drink **4.3**
el béisbol baseball **3.2**
la biblioteca library **2.2**
bien well **1.1**
  (No muy) Bien, ¿y tú/usted?
    (Not very) Well, and you? **1.1**
bienvenido(a) welcome **1.1**
el bistec steak **4.3**
blanco(a) white **1.2**
la blusa blouse **1.2**
la boca mouth **5.1**
la bola ball **3.2**
la bolsa bag **1.2;** handbag **4.2**
el bombero firefighter **6.1**
bonito(a) pretty **1.2**
el borrador eraser **2.1**
el bosque forest **3.3**
las botas boots **4.2**
la botella bottle **5.3**
el brazo arm **5.1**
el bronceador suntan lotion **3.3**
bueno(a) good **1.2**
  Buenas noches.
    Good evening. **EP**
  Buenas tardes.
    Good afternoon. **EP**
  Buenos días. Good morning. **EP**
la bufanda scarf **3.3**
buscar to look for, to search **2.1**

C

el caballo horse **6.2**
la cabeza head **5.1**
  lavarse la cabeza
    to wash one's hair **5.1**
cada each, every **2.3**
el café café **4.1;** coffee **4.3**
la cafetería cafeteria,
  coffee shop **2.2**
los calamares squid **5.2**
el calcetín sock **1.2**
la calculadora calculator **2.1**
la calidad quality **4.2**
caliente hot, warm **4.3**
¡Cállate! Be quiet! **5.3**
la calle street **4.1**
calor
  Hace calor. It is hot. **3.3**
  tener calor to be hot **3.3**
la cama bed **5.1**
  hacer la cama
    to make the bed **5.1**
la cámara camera **6.1**
los camarones shrimp
cambiar to change, to exchange **4.2**
el cambio change,
  money exchange **4.2**
caminar con el perro
  to walk the dog **2.3**
el camino road **4.1**
la camisa shirt **1.2**
la camiseta T-shirt **1.2**
el campo field **3.2;** countryside,
  country **6.2**
la cancha court **3.2**
cansado(a) tired **3.1**
cantar to sing **1.1**
la cara face **5.1**
la carne meat **4.3**
la carne de res beef **5.3**
la carnicería butcher's shop **4.1**
caro(a) expensive **4.2**
  ¡Es muy caro(a)!
    It's very expensive! **4.2**
la carretera highway
el carro car **4.1**
la cartera wallet **4.2**
el (la) cartero(a) mail carrier **6.1**
la casa house **1.1**
el casco helmet **3.2**
el casete cassette **4.2**
castaño(a) brown (hair) **1.2**
catorce fourteen **1.3**
la cebolla onion **5.3**
la cena supper, dinner **2.3**
cenar to have dinner, supper **2.3**
el centro center, downtown **4.1**
  el centro comercial
    shopping center **4.1**
el cepillo (de dientes)
  brush (toothbrush) **5.1**
la cerámica ceramics **4.2**
la cerca fence **6.2**
cerca (de) near (to) **4.1**
el cerdo pig **6.2**
el cereal cereal **5.3**
cero zero **EP**
cerrado(a) closed **5.2**
cerrar (ie) to close **3.2**
el champú shampoo **5.1**
la chaqueta jacket **1.2**
chévere awesome
  ¡Qué chévere!
    How awesome! **1.3**
la chica girl **1.1**
los chicharrones pork rinds **2.3**
el chico boy **1.1**
la chiringa kite
el chorizo sausage **5.2**
cien one hundred **1.3**
las ciencias science **2.1**
cinco five **EP**
cincuenta fifty **1.3**
el cinturón belt **4.2**
la cita appointment **2.2**
la ciudad city **1.3**
¡Claro que sí! Of course! **3.1**
la clase class, classroom **2.1**
la cocina kitchen **5.2**
cocinar to cook **5.3**
el (la) cocinero(a) chef
el colegio school
el collar necklace **4.2**

el color color **1.2**
¿De qué color...?
What color...? **1.2**
el comedor dining room **5.2**
comer to eat **1.1**
darle(s) de comer to feed **6.2**
¿Quieres comer...?
Do you want to eat...? **2.2**
Quiero comer...
I want to eat... **2.2**
cómico(a) funny, comical **1.2**
la comida food, a meal **2.3**
como like, as
cómo how **2.2**
¿Cómo es?
What is he/she like? **1.2**
¿Cómo está usted?
How are you? (formal) **1.1**
¿Cómo estás?
How are you? (familiar) **1.1**
¡Cómo no! Of course! **4.1**
¿Cómo se llama?
What is his/her name? **EP**
¿Cómo te llamas?
What is your name? **EP**
Perdona(e), ¿cómo llego a...?
Pardon, how do I get to...? **4.1**
la compañía company **6.1**
compartir to share **2.3**
comprar to buy **2.2**
comprender to understand **2.3**
la computación
computer science **2.1**
la computadora computer **2.1**
la comunidad community **1.1**
con with **1.3**
con rayas striped **3.3**
Con razón. That's why. **2.1**
el concierto concert **3.1**
el concurso contest **1.1**
el congelador freezer **5.3**
conmigo with me **3.1**
conocer (conozco) to know, to be familiar with **2.3**
conocer a alguien to know, to be familiar with someone **2.3**
el (la) contador(a) accountant **6.1**
la contaminación del aire
air pollution **6.1**
contar (ue) to count, to (re)tell **4.2**
el contenido contents
contento(a) content, pleased **3.1**
contestar to answer **2.1**
contigo with you **3.1**
el corazón heart **2.3**
corto(a) short (length) **1.2**
el corral corral, pen **6.2**
el correo post office **4.1**
correr to run **1.1**
la cosa thing **4.1**
costar (ue) to cost **4.2**
¿Cuánto cuesta(n)...?
How much is (are)...? **4.2**
la costumbre custom
creer to think, to believe **3.3**
Creo que sí/no. I think so. / I don't think so. **3.3**
la crema cream **5.3**
cruzar to cross **4.1**
el cuaderno notebook **2.1**
la cuadra city block **4.1**
cuál(es) which (ones), what **2.2**
¿Cuál es la fecha?
What is the date? **1.3**
¿Cuál es tu teléfono? What is your phone number? **EP**
cuando when, whenever **3.1**
cuándo when **2.2**
cuánto how much **4.2**
¿A cuánto está(n)...?
How much is (are)...? **5.3**
¿Cuánto cuesta(n)...?
How much is (are)...? **4.2**
¿Cuánto es?
How much is it? **4.3**
¿Cuánto le doy de propina?
How much do I tip? **4.3**
cuántos(as) how many
¿Cuántos años tiene...?
How old is...? **1.3**
cuarenta forty **1.3**
cuarto(a) quarter **5.3;** fourth **6.2**
cuatro four **EP**
cuatrocientos(as) four hundred **5.3**
la cuchara spoon **4.3**
el cuchillo knife **4.3**
la cuenta bill, check **4.3**
La cuenta, por favor.
The check, please. **4.3**
la cuerda string
el cuero leather
los artículos de cuero
leather goods **4.2**
el cuerpo body **5.1**
cuidadosamente carefully **5.2**
cuidadoso(a) careful **5.2**
cuidar (a) to take care of **2.3**
el cumpleaños birthday **1.3**

D

dar (doy) to give **4.2**
darle(s) de comer to feed **6.2**
de of, from **1.1**
de cuadros plaid, checked **3.3**
de la mañana
in the morning **2.2**
de la noche at night **2.2**
de la tarde in the afternoon **2.2**
De nada. You're welcome. **1.1**
de vez en cuando
once in a while **2.1**
debajo (de) underneath, under **6.2**
deber should, ought to **5.2**
decidir to decide **6.1**
décimo(a) tenth **6.2**
decir to say, to tell **4.1**
dejar to leave (behind)
dejar un mensaje
to leave a message **3.1**
Deje un mensaje después del tono. Leave a message after the tone. **3.1**
Le dejo... en...
I'll give... to you for... **4.2**
Quiero dejar un mensaje para... I want to leave a message for... **3.1**
del from the **3.1**
delante (de) in front (of) **4.1**
delgado(a) thin **1.2**
delicioso(a) delicious **4.3**
demasiado(a) too much **4.2**
dentro (de) inside (of) **6.2**
deportes: practicar deportes
to play sports **3.1**
deprimido(a) depressed **3.1**
la derecha right
a la derecha (de)
to the right (of) **4.1**
derecho straight ahead **4.1**
el desarrollo development
desayunar to have breakfast **4.3**
el desayuno breakfast **4.3**
descansar to rest **2.2**
desde from **4.1**
el desfile parade

ESPAÑOL-INGLÉS

el desierto desert **3.3**
el despertador alarm clock **5.1**
despertarse (ie) to wake up **5.1**
después (de) after, afterward **2.3**
detrás (de) behind **4.1**
devolver (ue) to return (item) **4.2**
el día day **EP**
Buenos días. Good morning. **EP**
¿Qué día es hoy? What day is today? **EP**
todos los días every day **2.1**
el diccionario dictionary **2.1**
diciembre December **1.3**
diecinueve nineteen **1.3**
dieciocho eighteen **1.3**
dieciséis sixteen **1.3**
diecisiete seventeen **1.3**
el diente tooth **5.1**
lavarse los dientes to brush one's teeth **5.1**
diez ten **EP**
difícil difficult, hard **2.1**
el dinero money **4.2**
la dirección address, direction **4.1**
el disco compacto compact disc **4.2**
divertido(a) enjoyable, fun **1.2**
doblar to turn **4.1**
doce twelve **1.3**
la docena dozen **5.3**
el (la) doctor(a) doctor **1.1**
el dólar dollar **4.2**
domingo Sunday **EP**
dónde where **2.2**
¿De dónde eres? Where are you from? **EP**
¿De dónde es? Where is he/she from? **EP**
dormir (ue) to sleep **4.2**
dormirse (ue) to fall asleep **5.1**
dos two **EP**
doscientos(as) two hundred **5.3**
ducharse to take a shower **5.1**
dulce sweet **4.3**
durante during **2.2**
duro(a) hard, tough **5.1**

E

la edad age **1.3**
el edificio building **6.1**
el (la) editor(a) editor **6.1**
la educación física physical education **2.1**
el efectivo cash **4.2**
él he **1.1**
ella she **1.1**
ellos(as) they **1.1**
emocionado(a) excited **3.1**
empezar (ie) to begin **3.2**
Encantado(a). Delighted/Pleased to meet you. **EP**
la enchilada enchilada **4.3**
en in **1.1**
en vez de instead of
encima (de) on top (of) **6.2**
encontrar (ue) to find, to meet **4.2**
el encuentro meeting
la encuesta survey
enero January **1.3**
enfermo(a) sick **3.1**
enfrente (de) facing **4.1**
enojado(a) angry **3.1**
enorme huge, enormous **6.1**
la ensalada salad **4.3**
enseñar to teach **2.1**
entender (ie) to understand **3.2**
entonces then, so **2.3**
entrar (a, en) to enter **2.1**
entre between **4.1**
la entrevista interview **6.1**
el equipo team **3.2**
escribir to write **1.1**
el (la) escritor(a) writer **6.1**
el escritorio desk **2.1**
la escritura writing
escuchar to listen (to) **2.1**
la escuela school **2.1**
ese(a) that **6.2**
ése(a) that one **6.2**
eso that **6.2**
el español Spanish **2.1**
especial special **5.2**
especialmente (e)specially, **5.2**
el espejo mirror **5.1**
esperar to wait for, to expect **2.1**
la esposa wife
el esposo husband
esquiar to ski **3.2**
la esquina corner **4.1**
la estación de autobuses bus station **4.1**
las estaciones seasons **3.3**
el estadio stadium **3.2**
estar to be **2.2**
¿Está incluido(a)…? Is… included? **4.3**
estar de acuerdo to agree **6.1**
este(a) this **6.2**
éste(a) this one **6.2**
esto this **6.2**
el estómago stomach **5.1**
estrecho(a) narrow **6.1**
la estrella star **5.3**
el (la) estudiante student **1.1**
estudiar to study **2.1**
los estudios sociales social studies **2.1**
la estufa stove **5.3**
la etapa step
el examen test **2.1**
el éxito success

F

fácil easy **2.1**
fácilmente easily **5.2**
la falda skirt **1.2**
la familia family **1.1**
la farmacia pharmacy **4.1**
favorito(a) favorite **3.2**
febrero February **1.3**
la fecha date **1.3**
¿Cuál es la fecha? What is the date? **1.3**
felicidades congratulations **1.3**
feliz happy **1.3**
felizmente happily **5.2**
feo(a) ugly **1.2**
fíjate take a look
la fiesta party **5.2**
el fin de semana weekend
el flan caramel custard dessert **4.3**
la flor flower **3.3**
el folleto brochure
formal formal **6.1**
fotos: sacar fotos to take pictures **3.3**
el (la) fotógrafo(a) photographer **6.1**
frecuente frequent **5.2**
frecuentemente often, frequently **5.2**
el frigorífico refrigerator **5.3**
los frijoles beans
frío
Hace frío. It is cold. **3.3**
tener frío to be cold **3.3**

la frontera border
la fruta fruit **2.2**
fuera (de) outside (of) **6.2**
fuerte strong **1.2**
el fútbol soccer **3.2**
el fútbol americano football **3.2**

G

las gafas de sol sunglasses **3.3**
la galleta cookie, cracker **5.3**
la gallina hen **6.2**
el gallo rooster **6.2**
las gambas shrimp
el (la) ganadero(a) rancher, farmer **6.2**
el (la) ganador(a) winner **6.1**
ganar to win **3.2**
el (la) gato(a) cat **1.2**
la gente people **2.3**
el (la) gerente manager **6.1**
el gimnasio gymnasium **2.2**
el gobierno government
el gol goal **3.2**
gordo(a) fat **1.2**
la gorra baseball cap **3.2**
el gorro cap **3.3**
la grabadora tape recorder **6.1**
Gracias. Thank you. **1.1**
  Gracias, pero no puedo. Thanks, but I can't. **3.1**
el grado degree **3.3**
el gramo gram **5.3**
grande big, large; great **1.2**
la granja farm **6.2**
gris gray
el guante glove **3.2**
guapo(a) good-looking **1.2**
la guía telefónica phone book **3.1**
los guisantes green peas
gustar to like
  Le gusta... He/She likes... **1.1**
  Me gusta... I like... **1.1**
  Me gustaría... I'd like... **3.1**
  Te gusta... You like... **1.1**
  ¿Te gustaría...? Would you like...? **3.1**
el gusto pleasure
  El gusto es mío. The pleasure is mine. **EP**
  Mucho gusto. Nice to meet you. **EP**

H

la habitación bedroom **5.2**
hablar to talk, to speak **2.1**
  ¿Puedo hablar con...? May I speak with...? **3.1**
hacer (hago) to make, to do **2.3**
  Hace buen (mal) tiempo. It is nice (bad) outside. **3.3**
  Hace calor. It is hot. **3.3**
  Hace fresco. It is cool. **3.3**
  Hace frío. It is cold. **3.3**
  Hace sol. It is sunny. **3.3**
  Hace viento. It is windy. **3.3**
  hacer ejercicio to exercise **2.3**
  hacer la cama to make the bed **5.1**
  hacer volar una chiringa to fly a kite
  ¿Qué tiempo hace? What is the weather like? **3.3**
la hamburguesa hamburger **2.2**
la harina flour **5.3**
hasta until, as far as **4.1**
  Hasta luego. See you later. **EP**
  Hasta mañana. See you tomorrow. **EP**
hay there is, there are **1.3**
  hay que one has to, must **2.1**
  Hay sol. It's sunny. **3.3**
  Hay viento. It's windy. **3.3**
hazlo do it
el helado ice cream **5.3**
la hermana sister **1.3**
la hermanastra stepsister
el hermanastro stepbrother
el hermano brother **1.3**
los hermanos brother(s) and sister(s) **1.3**
la hija daughter **1.3**
el hijo son **1.3**
los hijos son(s) and daughter(s), children **1.3**
la historia history **2.1**
el hockey hockey **3.2**
Hola. Hello. **EP**
el hombre man **1.1**
el hombre de negocios businessman **6.1**
el horario schedule **2.2**
el horno oven **5.3**
el hotel hotel **4.1**
hoy today **EP**
  Hoy es... Today is... **EP**
  ¿Qué día es hoy? What day is today? **EP**
el huevo egg **5.3**

I

la iglesia church **4.1**
Igualmente. Same here. **EP**
el impermeable raincoat **3.3**
la impresora printer **2.1**
informal informal **6.1**
el inglés English **2.1**
inteligente intelligent **1.2**
interesante interesting **1.2**
el invierno winter **3.3**
la invitación invitation **5.2**
invitar to invite
  Te invito. I'll treat you. I invite you. **3.1**
ir to go **2.2**
  ir a... to be going to... **2.3**
  ir al cine to go to a movie theater **3.1**
  ir al supermercado to go to the supermarket **2.3**
  ir de compras to go shopping **3.1**
  Vamos a... Let's... **6.1**
irse to leave, to go away **5.1**
la izquierda left
  a la izquierda (de) to the left (of) **4.1**

J

el jabón soap **5.1**
el jamón ham **5.2**
el jardín garden **5.2**
la jarra pitcher **4.2**
los jeans jeans **1.2**
el (la) jefe(a) boss **6.1**
joven young **1.3**
las joyas jewelry **4.2**
la joyería jewelry store **4.1**
el juego game
jueves Thursday **EP**

el (la) jugador(a) player
jugar (ue) to play **3.2**
el juguete toy
julio July **1.3**
junio June **1.3**
juntos together **4.2**

K

el kilo kilogram **5.3**

L

el lago lake **3.3**
la lámpara lamp **5.2**
la lana wool **6.2**
el lápiz pencil **2.1**
largo(a) long **1.2**
la lata can **5.3**
el lavaplatos dishwasher **5.3**
lavar los platos
to wash the dishes **5.1**
lavarse to wash oneself **5.1**
lavarse la cabeza
to wash one's hair **5.1**
lavarse los dientes
to brush one's teeth **5.1**
la lección lesson **2.1**
la leche milk **5.3**
la lechuga lettuce **4.3**
la lectura reading
leer to read **1.1**
lejos (de) far (from) **4.1**
¿Queda lejos? Is it far? **4.1**
la lengua language **4.3**
lentamente slowly **5.2**
lento(a) slow **5.2**
levantar pesas
to lift weights **3.2**
levantarse to get up **5.1**
la librería bookstore **4.1**
el libro book **2.1**
la limonada lemonade **4.3**
limpiar el cuarto
to clean the room **5.1**
limpio(a) clean **5.1**
listo(a) ready **4.3**
la literatura literature **2.1**
el litro liter **5.3**
la llama llama **6.2**
la llamada call **3.1**
llamar to call **3.1**
Dile/Dígale que me llame.
Tell him or her to call me. **3.1**
la llave key **5.2**
llegar to arrive **2.1**
llegar a ser to become
llevar to wear, to carry **2.1**;
to take along **3.3**
llover (ue) to rain **3.3**
la lluvia rain **3.3**
Lo siento... I'm sorry... **4.1**
loco(a) crazy **3.2**
luego later **2.3**
Hasta luego. See you later. **EP**
el lugar place **1.1**
lujoso(a) luxurious **6.1**
lunes Monday **EP**

M

la madrastra stepmother
la madre mother **1.3**
el (la) maestro(a) teacher **1.1**
el maíz corn
malo(a) bad **1.2**
mandar una carta
to send a letter **2.3**
manejar to drive **4.1**
la mano hand **5.1**
la manta blanket **5.1**
la mantequilla butter **5.3**
mañana tomorrow **EP**
Hasta mañana.
See you tomorrow. **EP**
Mañana es... Tomorrow is... **EP**
la mañana morning **2.2**
de la mañana
in the morning **2.2**
por la mañana
during the morning **2.2**
el mapa map **4.1**
maquillarse to put on makeup **5.1**
la máquina contestadora
answering machine **3.1**
el mar sea **3.3**
marcar to dial **3.1**
marrón brown **1.2**
martes Tuesday **EP**
marzo March **1.3**
más more **1.3**
más de more than **3.2**
más... que more... than **3.2**
las matemáticas mathematics **2.1**
la materia subject **2.1**
mayo May **1.3**
mayor older **1.3**
Me llamo... My name is... **EP**
la media hermana half-sister
la medianoche midnight **2.2**
medio(a) half **5.3**
el medio hermano half-brother
el mediodía noon **2.2**
mejor better **3.2**
menor younger **1.3**
menos to, before **2.2**; less **3.2**
menos de less than **3.2**
menos... que less... than **3.2**
el menú menu **4.3**
el mercado market **4.2**
merendar (ie) to have a snack **3.2**
la merienda snack **2.2**
el mes month **1.3**
el mes pasado last month **5.3**
la mesa table **5.2**
poner (pongo) la mesa
to set the table **4.3**
quitar la mesa
to clear the table **5.1**
el (la) mesero(a) waiter(ress) **4.3**
el metro subway **4.1**
la mezcla mixture
mi my **1.3**
el microondas microwave **5.3**
miércoles Wednesday **EP**
mil one thousand **5.3**
un millón one million **5.3**
mirar to watch, to look at **2.1**
mismo(a) same **2.1**
la mochila backpack **2.1**
moderno(a) modern **6.1**
el momento moment
Un momento. One moment. **3.1**
la montaña mountain **3.3**
morado(a) purple **1.2**
moreno(a) dark hair and skin **1.2**
la moto(cicleta) motorcycle **4.1**
mover (ue) los muebles
to move the furniture **5.2**
la muchacha girl **1.1**
el muchacho boy **1.1**
mucho often **2.1**
mucho(a) much, many **1.1**

los muebles furniture **5.2**
la mujer woman **1.1**
la mujer de negocios businesswoman **6.1**
el mundo world **1.1**
el museo museum **2.3**
la música music **2.1**
muy very **1.3**

N

nada nothing **4.3**
nadar to swim **1.1**
nadie no one **4.3**
la nariz nose **5.1**
necesitar to need **2.1**
negro(a) black **1.2**
nervioso(a) nervous **3.1**
nevar (ie) to snow **3.3**
ni nor
la nieta granddaughter
el nieto grandson
la nieve snow **3.3**
ninguno(a) none, not any **4.3**
el niño boy
la niña girl
no no **EP**; not **1.1**
  ¡No digas eso! Don't say that! **1.2**
  ¡No te preocupes! Don't worry! **3.1**
la noche night, evening
  Buenas noches. Good evening. **EP**
  de la noche at night **2.2**
  por la noche during the evening **2.2**
el nombre name, first name **EP**
normal normal **5.2**
normalmente normally **5.2**
nosotros(as) we **1.1**
novecientos(as) nine hundred **5.3**
la novela novel **2.3**
noveno(a) ninth **6.2**
noventa ninety **1.3**
noviembre November **1.3**
nublado cloudy
  Está nublado. It is cloudy. **3.3**
nuestro(a) our **1.3**
nueve nine **EP**
nuevo(a) new **1.2**
nunca never **2.1**

O

o or **1.1**
la obra work
  la obra maestra masterpiece
ochenta eighty **1.3**
ocho eight **EP**
ochocientos(as) eight hundred **5.3**
octavo(a) eighth **6.2**
octubre October **1.3**
ocupado(a) busy **3.1**
la oficina office **2.2**
ofrecer (ofrezco) to offer **6.1**
  Le puedo ofrecer... I can offer you... **4.2**
oír to hear **2.3**
el ojo eye **1.2**
la ola wave
la olla pot **4.2**
olvidar to forget **5.2**
once eleven **1.3**
el (la) operador(a) operator **6.1**
ordenar to arrange **5.2**
ordinario(a) ordinary **6.1**
la oreja ear **5.1**
el oro gold **4.2**
el otoño fall **3.3**
otro(a) other, another **1.2**

P

paciente patient **1.2**
el padrastro stepfather
el padre father **1.3**
los padres parents **1.3**
pagar to pay **4.2**
el país country **1.1**
el paisaje landscape
el pájaro bird **2.3**
el pan bread **4.3**
el pan dulce sweet roll **4.3**
la panadería bread bakery **4.1**
la pantalla screen **2.1**
los pantalones pants **1.2**
  los pantalones cortos shorts
la papa potato
  las papas fritas french fries **2.2**
el papel paper **2.1**
la papelería stationery store **4.1**
el paquete package **5.3**
para for, in order to **4.2**
el paraguas umbrella **3.3**
la pared wall **5.2**
el parque park **2.3**
el partido game **3.2**
pasar to happen, to pass (by) **2.1**
  pasar la aspiradora to vacuum **5.2**
  pasar un rato con los amigos to spend time with friends **2.3**
pasear to go for a walk **2.3**
el paseo walk
la pasta pasta **5.3**
la pasta de dientes toothpaste **5.1**
el pastel cake **4.3**
la pastelería pastry shop **4.1**
el (la) pastor(a) shepherd(ess) **6.2**
la patata potato **5.3**
patinar to skate **1.1**
los patines skates **3.2**
la patineta skateboard **3.2**
  andar en patineta to skateboard **3.2**
el pedazo piece **5.3**
pedir (i) to ask for, to order **4.3**
  ¿Me ayuda a pedir? Could you help me order? **4.3**
peinarse to comb one's hair **5.1**
el peine comb **5.1**
la película movie **3.1**
el peligro danger
peligroso(a) dangerous **3.2**
pelirrojo(a) redhead **1.2**
el pelo hair **1.2**
la pelota baseball **3.2**
pensar (ie) to think, to plan **3.2**
peor worse **3.2**
pequeño(a) small **1.2**
perder (ie) to lose **3.2**
Perdona(e)... Pardon...
  Perdona(e), ¿cómo llego a...? Pardon, how do I get to...? **4.1**
perezoso(a) lazy **1.2**
perfecto(a) perfect **4.2**
el periódico newspaper **2.3**
el (la) periodista journalist **6.1**
pero but **1.1**
el (la) perro(a) dog **1.2**
  caminar con el perro to walk the dog **2.3**
el pescado fish **5.3**
el pez fish **2.3**

picante spicy **4.3**
el pie foot **5.1**
a pie on foot **4.1**
la pierna leg **5.1**
la pimienta pepper **5.3**
pintar to paint **2.3**
la piña pineapple
la piscina swimming pool **3.2**
el pizarrón chalkboard **2.1**
placer: Es un placer. It's a pleasure. **EP**
planchar to iron **5.2**
la planta plant **3.3**
la plata silver **4.2**
el plato plate **4.2**
la playa beach **3.3**
la plaza town square **4.1**
la pluma pen **2.1**
poco a little **2.1**
poder (ue) to be able, can **4.2**
Gracias, pero no puedo. Thanks, but I can't. **3.1**
Le puedo ofrecer... I can offer you... **4.2**
¿Puedes (Puede usted) decirme dónde queda...? Could you tell me where... is? **4.1**
¿Puedo hablar con...? May I speak with...? **3.1**
el poema poem **2.3**
la poesía poetry **2.3**
el (la) policía police officer **1.1**
el pollo chicken **4.3**
poner (pongo) to put **4.3**
poner la mesa to set the table **4.3**
ponerse (me pongo) to put on **5.1**
ponerse la ropa to get dressed **5.1**
por for, by, around **4.1**
por favor please **2.2**
por fin finally **2.3**
por la mañana during the morning **2.2**
por la noche during the evening **2.2**
por la tarde during the afternoon **2.2**
por qué why **2.2**
porque because **3.1**
el postre dessert **4.3**
practicar deportes to play sports **3.1**
el precio price **4.2**
preferir (ie) to prefer **3.2**
preocupado(a) worried **3.1**
preparar to prepare **2.1**
presentar to introduce
Te/Le presento a... Let me introduce you to... **1.1**
la primavera spring **3.3**
primero first **2.3**
el primero first of the month **1.3**
primero(a) first **6.2**
el (la) primo(a) cousin **1.3**
el problema problem **2.3**
la profesión profession **6.1**
el programa program
pronto soon **2.1**
propio(a) own
la propina tip **4.3**
¿Cuánto le doy de propina? How much do I tip? **4.3**
la prueba quiz **2.1**
el pueblo town, village **4.3**
el puerco pork **5.3**
la puerta door **5.2**
pues well **1.2**
la pulsera bracelet **4.2**

Q

que that
qué what **2.2**
¿A qué hora es...? (At) What time is...? **2.2**
¡Qué (divertido)! How (fun)! **1.2**
¿Qué día es hoy? What day is today? **EP**
¿Qué hora es? What time is it? **2.2**
¡Qué lástima! What a shame! **3.1**
¿Qué lleva? What is he/she wearing? **1.2**
¿Qué tal? How is it going? **1.1**
¿Qué tiempo hace? What is the weather like? **3.3**
quedar (en) to be (in a specific place), to agree on **4.1**
¿Puedes (Puede usted) decirme dónde queda...? Could you tell me where... is? **4.1**
¿Queda lejos? Is it far? **4.1**
los quehaceres chores **5.1**
querer (ie) to want **3.2**
¿Quieres beber...? Do you want to drink...? **2.2**
¿Quieres comer...? Do you want to eat...? **2.2**
Quiero beber... I want to drink... **2.2**
Quiero comer... I want to eat... **2.2**
Quiero dejar un mensaje para... I want to leave a message for... **3.1**
el queso cheese **4.3**
quién(es) who **2.2**
¿De quién es...? Whose is...? **1.3**
¿Quién es? Who is it? **1.3**
¿Quiénes son? Who are they? **1.3**
quince fifteen **1.3**
quinientos(as) five hundred **5.3**
quinto(a) fifth **6.2**
Quisiera... I would like... **4.3**
quitar
quitar el polvo to dust **5.2**
quitar la mesa to clear the table **5.1**

R

el radio radio **4.2**
el radiocasete radio-tape player **4.2**
rápidamente quickly **5.2**
rápido(a) fast, quick **5.2**
la raqueta racket **3.2**
rara vez rarely **2.1**
el ratón mouse **2.1**
la razón reason **2.1**
Con razón. That's why. **2.1**
tener razón to be right **3.3**
el (la) recepcionista receptionist **6.1**
el receso break **2.2**
la receta recipe
recibir to receive **2.3**
reciente recent **5.2**
recientemente lately, recently **5.2**
recordar (ue) to remember **4.2**
el recuerdo souvenir
el recurso resource
el refrán saying
el refresco soft drink **2.2**
el regalo gift **4.2**
regatear to bargain **4.2**

regresar to return
Regresa más tarde. He/She will return later. **3.1**
Regular. So-so. **1.1**
el reloj clock, watch **2.2**
el repaso review
el restaurante restaurant **4.3**
el resumen summary
el retrato portrait
la revista magazine **2.3**
rico(a) tasty **4.3**; rich
el río river **3.3**
riquísimo(a) very tasty **4.3**
el ritmo rhythm
rojo(a) red **1.2**
la ropa clothing **1.2**
ponerse la ropa to get dressed **5.1**
rosado(a) pink **1.2**
rubio(a) blond **1.2**

S

sábado Saturday **EP**
saber (sé) to know **3.2**
el sabor flavor
sabroso(a) tasty **5.3**
sacar
sacar fotos to take pictures **3.3**
sacar la basura to take out the trash **5.2**
sacar una buena nota to get a good grade **2.1**
la sal salt **5.3**
la sala living room **5.2**
la salchicha sausage **5.3**
salir (salgo) to go out, to leave **4.1**
la salsa salsa **4.3**
la sartén frying pan
Se llama... His/Her name is... **EP**
el secador de pelo hair dryer **5.1**
secarse to dry oneself **5.1**
el (la) secretario(a) secretary **6.1**
segundo(a) second **6.2**
seis six **EP**
seiscientos(as) six hundred **5.3**
la selva jungle
la semana week **EP**
la semana pasada last week **5.3**
el semestre semester **2.2**
sencillo(a) simple, plain **6.1**
el señor Mr. **1.1**
la señora Mrs. **1.1**
la señorita Miss **1.1**
septiembre September **1.3**
séptimo(a) seventh **6.2**
ser to be **1.1**
Es la.../Son las... It is... o'clock. **2.2**
ser de... to be from... **1.1**
serio(a) serious **1.2**
servir (i) to serve **4.3**
sesenta sixty **1.3**
setecientos(as) seven hundred **5.3**
setenta seventy **1.3**
sexto(a) sixth **6.2**
los shorts shorts **3.3**
si if **5.2**
sí yes **EP**
Sí, me encantaría. Yes, I would love to. **3.1**
siempre always **2.1**
siete seven **EP**
el siglo century
la silla chair **5.2**
el sillón armchair **5.2**
simpático(a) nice **1.2**
sin without **4.3**
sobre on, about
sobre hielo on ice **3.2**
el sofá sofa, couch **5.2**
el sol sun **3.3**
las gafas de sol sunglasses **3.3**
Hace sol. It is sunny. **3.3**
Hay sol. It's sunny. **3.3**
tomar el sol to sunbathe **3.3**
sólo only **1.3**
solo(a) alone **3.1**
el sombrero hat **1.2**
el sonido sound
la sopa soup **4.3**
sorprender to surprise **5.2**
la sorpresa surprise **5.2**
su your, his, her, its, their **1.3**
sucio(a) dirty **5.1**
el suelo floor **5.2**
barrer el suelo to sweep the floor **5.2**
el suéter sweater **1.2**
el surfing surfing **3.2**

T

Tal vez otro día. Maybe another day. **3.1**
el taller workshop **6.2**
también also, too **1.1**
también se dice you can also say
tampoco neither, either **4.3**
tan... como as... as **3.2**
tanto como as much as **3.2**
las tapas appetizers **5.2**
tarde late **2.1**
la tarde afternoon **2.2**
Buenas tardes. Good afternoon. **EP**
de la tarde in the afternoon **2.2**
por la tarde during the afternoon **2.2**
la tarea homework **2.1**
la tarjeta de crédito credit card **4.2**
el taxi taxi, cab **4.1**
el (la) taxista taxi driver **6.1**
la taza cup **4.3**
el té tea **4.3**
el teatro theater **2.3**
la tecla key (of an instrument)
el teclado keyboard **2.1**
el teléfono telephone **3.1**
¿Cuál es tu teléfono? What is your phone number? **EP**
el televisor television set **5.2**
la temperatura temperature **3.3**
temprano early **3.1**
el tenedor fork **4.3**
tener to have **1.3**
¿Cuántos años tiene...? How old is...? **1.3**
tener calor to be hot **3.3**
tener cuidado to be careful **3.3**
tener frío to be cold **3.3**
tener ganas de... to feel like... **3.3**
tener hambre to be hungry **2.3**
tener miedo to be afraid **3.3**
tener prisa to be in a hurry **3.3**
tener que to have to **2.1**
tener razón to be right **3.3**
tener sed to be thirsty **2.3**
tener sueño to be sleepy **3.3**
tener suerte to be lucky **3.3**
Tiene... años. He/She is... years old. **1.3**

el tenis tennis **3.2**
tercero(a) third **6.2**
terminar to finish **2.2**
Terrible. Terrible./Awful. **1.1**
la tía aunt **1.3**
el tiempo time **3.1**; weather **3.3**
  Hace buen tiempo.
    It is nice outside. **3.3**
  Hace mal tiempo.
    It is bad outside. **3.3**
  ¿Qué tiempo hace?
    What is the weather like? **3.3**
  el tiempo libre free time **3.1**
la tienda store **2.3**
  la tienda de deportes sporting goods store **3.2**
  la tienda de música y videos music and video store **4.1**
la tierra land
las tijeras scissors **6.2**
el tío uncle **1.3**
los tíos uncle(s) and aunt(s) **1.3**
la tiza chalk **2.1**
la toalla towel **5.1**
tocar to play (an instrument)
  tocar el piano
    to play the piano **2.3**
  tocar la guitarra
    to play the guitar **2.3**
todavía still, yet **4.3**
todo(a) all **1.3**
  todos los días every day **2.1**
tomar to take, to eat or drink **2.2**
  tomar el sol to sunbathe **3.3**
el tomate tomato **5.3**
la tormenta storm **3.3**
el toro bull **6.2**
la torta sandwich (sub) **2.2**
la tortilla española potato omelet **5.2**
trabajador(a) hard-working **1.2**
trabajar to work **1.1**
el trabalenguas tongue twister
tradicional traditional **6.1**
traer (traigo) to bring **4.3**
  ¿Me trae...?
    Could you bring me...? **4.3**
el tráfico traffic **6.1**
el traje de baño bathing suit **3.3**
tranquilamente calmly **5.2**
tranquilo(a) calm **3.1**
trece thirteen **1.3**
treinta thirty **1.3**
el tren train **4.1**
tres three **EP**
trescientos(as) three hundred **5.3**
triste sad **3.1**
tu your (familiar) **1.3**
tú you (familiar singular) **1.1**

U

último(a) last **6.2**
la unidad unit
uno one **EP**
usar to use **2.1**
el uso use
usted you (formal singular) **1.1**
ustedes you (plural) **1.1**
la uva grape

V

la vaca cow **6.2**
el vaso glass
  el vaso de glass of **2.2**
el (la) vecino(a) neighbor
vegetariano(a) vegetarian **4.3**
veinte twenty **1.3**
veintiuno twenty-one **1.3**
vender to sell **2.3**
venir to come **3.1**
la ventana window **5.2**
ver (veo) to see **2.3**
  ¿Me deja ver...? May I see...? **4.2**
  Nos vemos. See you later. **EP**
  ver la televisión
    to watch television **2.3**
el verano summer **3.3**
la verdad truth **2.2**
  Es verdad. It's true. **1.2**
verde green **1.2**
la verdura vegetable **5.3**
el vestido dress **1.2**
viajar to travel **4.1**
el viaje trip **4.1**
la vida life **2.3**
el video video **4.2**
  alquilar un video
    to rent a video **3.1**
la videograbadora VCR **4.2**
el videojuego video game **4.2**
viejo(a) old **1.3**
el viento wind **3.3**
  Hace viento. It is windy. **3.3**
  Hay viento. It's windy. **3.3**
viernes Friday **EP**
visitar to visit **2.2**
vivir to live **2.3**
  Vive en... He/She lives in... **1.1**
  Vivo en... I live in... **1.1**
vivo(a) alive
el voleibol volleyball **3.2**
volver (ue) to return, to come back **4.2**
vosotros(as) you (familiar plural) **1.1**
la voz voice
vuestro(a) your (familiar plural) **1.3**

Y

y and **1.1**
  y cuarto quarter past **2.2**
  y media half past **2.2**
ya already, now
ya no no longer **3.1**
yo I **1.1**
el yogur yogurt **5.3**

Z

la zanahoria carrot **5.3**
la zapatería shoe store **4.1**
el zapato shoe **1.2**
el zumo juice **5.3**

GLOSARIO
inglés-español

This English–Spanish glossary contains all of the active words that appear as well as passive ones from readings, culture sections, and extra vocabulary lists. Active words are indicated by the unit and **etapa** number when they appear.

A

about sobre
accountant el (la) contador(a) **6.1**
address la dirección **4.1**
to be afraid tener miedo **3.3**
after después (de) **2.3**
afternoon la tarde **2.2**
  during the afternoon por la tarde **2.2**
  Good afternoon Buenas tardes. **EP**
  in the afternoon de la tarde **2.2**
afterward después **2.3**
age la edad **1.3**
to agree (on) quedar (en) **4.1**, estar de acuerdo **6.1**
air pollution la contaminación del aire **6.1**
airplane el avión **4.1**
airport el aeropuerto **4.1**
alarm clock el despertador **5.1**
all todo(a) **1.3**
alone solo(a) **3.1**
already ya
also también **1.1**
always siempre **2.1**
ancient antiguo(a) **6.1**
and y **1.1**
angry enojado(a) **3.1**
animal el animal **2.3**
another otro(a) **1.2**
to answer contestar **2.1**
answering machine la máquina contestadora **3.1**
apartment el apartamento **1.1**
appetizers las tapas **5.2**
appointment la cita **2.2**
April abril **1.3**
architect el (la) arquitecto(a) **6.1**
architecture la arquitectura **6.1**
arm el brazo **5.1**
armchair el sillón **5.2**
around por **4.1**
to arrange ordenar **5.2**
to arrive llegar **2.1**
art el arte **2.1**
artisan el (la) artesano(a) **6.2**
as como
  as... as tan... como **3.2**
  as far as hasta **4.1**
  as much as tanto como **3.2**
to ask for pedir (i) **4.3**
at a
  At... o'clock. A la(s)... **2.2**
auditorium el auditorio **2.2**
August agosto **1.3**
aunt la tía **1.3**
avenue la avenida **4.1**
awesome: How awesome! ¡Qué chévere! **1.3**
awful terrible **1.1**

B

backpack la mochila **2.1**
bad malo(a) **1.2**
  It is bad outside. Hace mal tiempo. **3.3**
bag la bolsa **1.2**
bakery (bread) panadería **4.1**, **(pastry)** pastelería **4.1**
ball la bola **3.2**
bank el banco **4.1**
to bargain regatear **4.2**
baseball (sport) el béisbol **3.2**; **(ball)** la pelota **3.2**
baseball cap la gorra **3.2**
basketball el baloncesto **3.2**
bat el bate **3.2**
bathing suit el traje de baño **3.3**
bathroom el baño **5.2**
to be ser **1.1**; estar **2.2**
  to be (in a specific place) quedar (en) **4.1**
  to be able poder (ue) **4.2**
  to be afraid tener miedo **3.3**
  to be careful tener cuidado **3.3**
  to be cold tener frío **3.3**
  to be familiar with conocer **2.3**
  to be from... ser de... **1.1**
  to be going to... ir a... **2.3**
  to be hot tener calor **3.3**
  to be hungry tener hambre **2.3**
  to be in a hurry tener prisa **3.3**
  to be lucky tener suerte **3.3**
  to be right tener razón **3.3**
  to be sleepy tener sueño **3.3**
  to be thirsty tener sed **2.3**
beach la playa **3.3**
beans los frijoles
because porque **3.1**
to become llegar a ser
bed la cama **5.1**
  to go to bed acostarse (ue) **5.1**
  to make the bed hacer la cama **5.1**
bedroom la habitación **5.2**
beef la carne de res **5.3**
before antes (de) **2.3**
to begin empezar (ie) **3.2**
behind detrás (de) **4.1**
to believe creer **3.3**
belt el cinturón **4.2**

beside al lado (de) **4.1**
better mejor **3.2**
between entre **4.1**
beverage la bebida **4.3**
big grande **1.2**
bike la bicicleta
to ride a bike andar en bicicleta **2.3**
bill la cuenta **4.3**
bird el pájaro **2.3**
birthday el cumpleaños **1.3**
black negro(a) **1.2**
blanket la manta **5.1**
blond rubio(a) **1.2**
blouse la blusa **1.2**
blue azul **1.2**
body el cuerpo **5.1**
book el libro **2.1**
bookstore la librería **4.1**
boots las botas **4.2**
border la frontera
boring aburrido(a) **1.2**
boss el (la) jefe(a) **6.1**
bottle la botella **5.3**
boy el chico **1.1**, el muchacho **1.1**, el niño
bracelet la pulsera **4.2**
bread el pan **4.3**
break el receso **2.2**
breakfast el desayuno **4.3**
to bring traer **4.3**
Could you bring me...? ¿Me trae...? **4.3**
brochure el folleto
brother el hermano **1.3**
brown marrón **1.2**
brown (hair) castaño(a) **1.2**
brush el cepillo **5.1**
to brush one's teeth lavarse los dientes **5.1**
building el edificio **6.1**
bull el toro **6.2**
bus el autobús **4.1**
bus station la estación de autobuses **4.1**
businessman el hombre de negocios **6.1**
businesswoman la mujer de negocios **6.1**
busy ocupado(a) **3.1**
but pero **1.1**
butcher's shop la carnicería **4.1**
butter la mantequilla **5.3**
to buy comprar **2.2**
by por **4.1**

C

cab el taxi **4.1**
café el café **4.1**
cafeteria la cafetería **2.2**
cake el pastel **4.3**
calculator la calculadora **2.1**
call la llamada **3.1**
to call llamar **3.1**
calm tranquilo(a) **3.1**
calmly tranquilamente **5.2**
camera la cámara **6.1**
can la lata **5.3**
can (to be able) poder (ue) **4.2**
I can offer you... Le puedo ofrecer... **4.2**
Thanks, but I can't. Gracias, pero no puedo. **3.1**
cap (knit) el gorro **3.3**, **(baseball)** la gorra **3.2**
car el carro **4.1**
careful cuidadoso(a) **5.2**
to be careful tener cuidado **3.3**
carefully cuidadosamente **5.2**
carrot la zanahoria **5.3**
to carry llevar **2.1**
cash el efectivo **4.2**
cassette el casete **4.2**
cat el (la) gato(a) **1.2**
center el centro **4.1**
century el siglo
ceramics la cerámica **4.2**
cereal el cereal **5.3**
chair la silla **5.2**
chalk la tiza **2.1**
chalkboard el pizarrón **2.1**
change el cambio **4.2**
to change cambiar **4.2**
cheap barato(a) **4.2**
check la cuenta **4.3**
Separate checks. Es aparte. **4.3**
The check, please. La cuenta, por favor. **4.3**
checked de cuadros **3.3**
cheese el queso **4.3**
chef el (la) cocinero(a)
chicken el pollo **4.3**
chores los quehaceres **5.1**
church la iglesia **4.1**
city la ciudad **1.3**
city block la cuadra **4.1**
class la clase **2.1**
classroom la clase **2.1**
clay el barro
to clean the room limpiar el cuarto **5.1**
clock el reloj **2.2**
to close cerrar (ie) **3.2**
closed cerrado(a) **5.2**
closet el armario **5.2**
clothing la ropa **1.2**
cloudy nublado
It is cloudy. Está nublado. **3.3**
coat el abrigo **3.3**
coffee el café **4.3**
coffee shop la cafetería **2.2**
cold
to be cold tener frío **3.3**
It is cold. Hace frío. **3.3**
color el color
What color...? ¿De qué color...? **1.2**
comb el peine **5.1**
to comb one's hair peinarse **5.1**
to come venir **3.1**
to come back volver(ue) **4.2**
comical cómico(a) **1.2**
community la comunidad **1.1**
compact disc el disco compacto **4.2**
company la compañía **6.1**
computer la computadora **2.1**
computer science la computación **2.1**
concert el concierto **3.1**
congratulations felicidades **1.3**
content contento(a) **3.1**
contest el concurso **1.1**
to cook cocinar **5.3**
cookie la galleta **5.3**
cool: It is cool. Hace fresco. **3.3**
corn el maíz
corner la esquina **4.1**
corral el corral **6.2**
to cost costar (ue) **4.2**
couch el sofá **5.2**
to count contar (ue) **4.2**
country el país **1.1;** el campo **6.2**
countryside el campo **6.2**
court la cancha **3.2**
cousin el (la) primo(a) **1.3**

INGLÉS–ESPAÑOL

cow la vaca **6.2**
cracker la galleta **5.3**
crazy loco(a) **3.2**
cream la crema **5.3**
credit card la tarjeta de crédito **4.2**
to cross cruzar **4.1**
cup la taza **4.3**
custom la costumbre

D

to dance bailar **1.1**
danger el peligro
dangerous peligroso(a) **3.2**
dark hair and skin moreno(a) **1.2**
date la fecha **1.3**
  What is the date?
    ¿Cuál es la fecha? **1.3**
daughter la hija **1.3**
day el día **EP**
  the day before yesterday
    anteayer **5.3**
  What day is today?
    ¿Qué día es hoy? **EP**
December diciembre **1.3**
to decide decidir **6.1**
degree el grado **3.3**
delicious delicioso(a) **4.3**
depressed deprimido(a) **3.1**
desert el desierto **3.3**
desk el escritorio **2.1**
dessert el postre **4.3**
development el desarrollo
to dial marcar **3.1**
dictionary el diccionario **2.1**
difficult difícil **2.1**
dining room el comedor **5.2**
dinner la cena **2.3**
direction la dirección **4.1**
dirty sucio(a) **5.1**
dishwasher el lavaplatos **5.3**
district el barrio
to do hacer **2.3**
doctor el (la) doctor(a) **1.1**
dog el (la) perro(a) **1.2**
  to walk the dog
    caminar con el perro **2.3**
dollar el dólar **4.2**
door la puerta **5.2**
down abajo **6.2**
downtown el centro **4.1**
dozen la docena **5.3**
dress el vestido **1.2**
drink la bebida **4.3**
to drink tomar **2.2;** beber **2.3**
  Do you want to drink...?
    ¿Quieres beber...? **2.2**
  I want to drink...
    Quiero beber... **2.2**
to drive manejar **4.1**
drugstore la farmacia **4.1**
to dry oneself secarse **5.1**
during durante **2.2**
to dust quitar el polvo **5.2**

E

each cada **2.3**
ear la oreja **5.1**
early temprano **3.1**
earring el arete **4.2**
easily fácilmente **5.2**
easy fácil **2.1**
to eat comer **1.1,** tomar **2.2**
  Do you want to eat...?
    ¿Quieres comer...? **2.2**
  to eat a snack merendar (ie) **3.2**
  to eat breakfast desayunar **4.3**
  to eat dinner cenar **2.3**
  to eat lunch almorzar (ue) **4.2**
  I want to eat...
    Quiero comer... **2.2**
editor el (la) editor(a) **6.1**
egg el huevo **5.3**
eight ocho **EP**
eight hundred ochocientos(as) **5.3**
eighteen dieciocho **1.3**
eighth octavo(a) **6.2**
eighty ochenta **1.3**
eleven once **1.3**
enchilada la enchilada **4.3**
English el inglés **2.1**
enjoyable divertido(a) **1.2**
enormous enorme **6.1**
to enter entrar (a, en) **2.1**
eraser el borrador **2.1**
especially especialmente **5.2**
evening la noche
  during the evening
    por la noche **2.2**
  Good evening.
    Buenas noches. **EP**
every cada **2.3**
  every day todos los días **2.1**
to exchange cambiar **4.2**
excited emocionado(a) **3.1**
to exercise hacer ejercicio **2.3**
to expect esperar **2.1**
expensive caro(a) **4.2**
  It's very expensive!
    ¡Es muy caro(a)! **4.2**
eye el ojo **1.2**

F

face la cara **5.1**
facing enfrente (de) **4.1**
fall el otoño **3.3**
to fall asleep dormirse (ue) **5.1**
family la familia **1.1**
far (from) lejos (de) **4.1**
  Is it far? ¿Queda lejos? **4.1**
farm la granja **6.2**
farmer el (la) ganadero(a) **6.2**
fast rápido(a) **5.2**
fat gordo(a) **1.2**
father el padre **1.3**
favorite favorito(a) **3.2**
February febrero **1.3**
to feed darle(s) de comer **6.2**
to feel like... tener ganas de... **3.3**
fence la cerca **6.2**
field el campo **3.2**
fifteen quince **1.3**
fifth quinto(a) **6.2**
fifty cincuenta **1.3**
finally por fin **2.3**
to find encontrar (ue) **4.2**
to finish terminar **2.2**
firefighter el bombero **6.1**
first primero **2.3;** primero(a) **6.2**
first name el nombre **EP**
fish el pez **2.3;** el pescado **5.3**
five cinco **EP**
five hundred quinientos(as) **5.3**
flavor el sabor
floor el suelo **5.2**
flour la harina **5.3**
flower la flor **3.3**
to fly a kite
  hacer volar una chiringa
food la comida **2.3**

INGLÉS–ESPAÑOL

foot el pie **5.1**
on foot a pie **4.1**
football el fútbol americano **3.2**
for por **4.1;** para **4.2**
forest el bosque **3.3**
to forget olvidar **5.2**
fork el tenedor **4.3**
formal formal **6.1**
forty cuarenta **1.3**
four cuatro **EP**
four hundred cuatrocientos(as) **5.3**
fourteen catorce **1.3**
fourth cuarto(a) **6.2**
free time el tiempo libre **3.1**
freezer el congelador **5.3**
french fries las papas fritas **2.2**
frequent frecuente **5.2**
frequently frecuentemente **5.2**
fresh fresco(a)
Friday viernes **EP**
friend el (la) amigo(a) **1.1**
to spend time with friends pasar un rato con los amigos **2.3**
from de **1.1;** desde **4.1**
fruit la fruta **2.2**
frying pan la sartén
fun divertido(a) **1.2**
funny cómico(a) **1.2**
furniture los muebles **5.2**

G

game el partido **3.2**
garden el jardín **5.2**
garlic el ajo
to get dressed ponerse la ropa **5.1**
to get up levantarse **5.1**
gift el regalo **4.2**
girl la chica **1.1,** la muchacha **1.1,** la niña
to give dar **4.2**
I'll give... to you for... Le dejo... en... **4.2**
glass el vaso **2.2**
glove el guante **3.2**
to go ir **2.2**
to go away irse **5.1**
to go for a walk pasear **2.3**
to go out salir **4.1**
to go to bed acostarse (ue) **5.1**
goal el gol **3.2**
gold el oro **4.2**
good bueno(a) **1.2**
Good afternoon. Buenas tardes. **EP**
Good evening. Buenas noches. **EP**
Good morning. Buenos días. **EP**
Good-bye. Adiós. **EP**
good-looking guapo(a) **1.2**
government el gobierno
grade la nota
to get a good grade sacar una buena nota **2.1**
gram el gramo **5.3**
grandchildren los nietos
granddaughter la nieta
grandfather el abuelo **1.3**
grandmother la abuela **1.3**
grandparents los abuelos **1.3**
grandson el nieto
grape la uva
gray gris
great grande **1.2**
green verde **1.2**
guitar la guitarra **2.3**
gymnasium el gimnasio **2.2**

H

hair el pelo **1.2**
hair dryer el secador de pelo **5.1**
half medio(a) **5.3**
half past y media **2.2**
half-brother el medio hermano
half-sister la media hermana
ham el jamón **5.2**
hamburger la hamburguesa **2.2**
hand la mano **5.1**
handbag la bolsa **4.2**
handicraft la artesanía **4.2**
to happen pasar **2.1**
happily felizmente **5.2**
happy feliz **1.3,** alegre **3.1,** contento(a) **3.1**
hard difícil **2.1;** duro(a) **5.1**
hard-working trabajador(a) **1.2**
hat el sombrero **1.2**
to have tener **1.3**
to have just... acabar de... **3.1**
to have to tener que **2.1**
one has to hay que **2.1**
he él **1.1**
head la cabeza **5.1**
health la salud
to hear oír **2.3**
heart el corazón **2.3**
Hello. Hola. **EP**
helmet el casco **3.2**
to help ayudar (a) **2.1**
Could you help me order? ¿Me ayuda a pedir? **4.3**
hen la gallina **6.2**
her su **1.3**
here acá/aquí **4.1**
highway la carretera
his su **1.3**
history la historia **2.1**
hockey el hockey **3.2**
homework la tarea **2.1**
horse el caballo **6.2**
hot caliente **4.3**
to be hot tener calor **3.3**
It is hot. Hace calor. **3.3**
hotel el hotel **4.1**
house la casa **1.1**
how cómo **2.2**
How (fun)! ¡Qué (divertido)! **1.2**
How are you? ***(familiar)*** ¿Cómo estás? **1.1** ***(formal)*** ¿Cómo está usted? **1.1**
How is it going? ¿Qué tal? **1.1**
How old is...? ¿Cuántos años tiene...? **1.3**
Pardon, how do I get to...? Perdona(e), ¿cómo llego a...? **4.1**
how much cuánto
How much do I tip? ¿Cuánto le doy de propina? **4.3**
How much is (are)...? ¿Cuánto cuesta(n)...? **4.2;** ¿A cuánto está(n)...? **5.3**
How much is it? ¿Cuánto es? **4.3**
huge enorme **6.1**
to be hungry tener hambre **2.3**
to be in a hurry tener prisa **3.3**
husband el esposo

I

I yo **1.1**
ice el hielo
  on ice sobre hielo **3.2**
ice cream el helado **5.3**
if si **5.2**
in en **1.1**
  in front (of) delante (de) **4.1**
  in order to para **4.2**
included incluido(a)
  Is... included?
    ¿Está incluido(a)...? **4.3**
inexpensive barato(a) **4.2**
informal informal **6.1**
inside (of) dentro (de) **6.2**
instead of en vez de
intelligent inteligente **1.2**
interesting interesante **1.2**
interview la entrevista **6.1**
introduce: Let me introduce you *(familiar/formal)* **to...**
  Te/Le presento a... **1.1**
invitation la invitación **5.2**
to invite invitar
  I invite you. Te invito. **3.1**
to iron planchar **5.2**
its su **1.3**

J

jacket la chaqueta **1.2**
January enero **1.3**
jeans los jeans **1.2**
jewelry las joyas **4.2**
jewelry store la joyería **4.1**
journalist el (la) periodista **6.1**
juice el zumo **5.3,** el jugo
July julio **1.3**
June junio **1.3**
jungle la selva

K

key la llave **5.2;** la tecla
keyboard el teclado **2.1**
kilogram el kilo **5.3**
kitchen la cocina **5.2**
kite la chiringa
  to fly a kite
    hacer volar una chiringa
knife el cuchillo **4.3**
to know (a fact) saber **3.2**
  to know someone
    conocer a alguien **2.3**

L

lake el lago **3.3**
lamp la lámpara **5.2**
land la tierra
landscape el paisaje
language la lengua **4.3**
large grande **1.2**
last último(a) **6.2**
  last month el mes pasado **5.3**
  last name el apellido **EP**
  last night anoche **5.3**
  last week la semana pasada **5.3**
  last year el año pasado **5.3**
late tarde **2.1**
lately recientemente **5.2**
later luego **2.3**
  See you later. Hasta luego. **EP**, Nos vemos. **EP**
lazy perezoso(a) **1.2**
to learn aprender **2.3**
leather goods
  los artículos de cuero **4.2**
to leave salir **4.1,** irse **5.1; (behind)** dejar **3.1**
  I want to leave a message for...
    Quiero dejar un mensaje para... **3.1**
  to leave a message
    dejar un mensaje **3.1**
  Leave a message after the tone.
    Deje un mensaje después del tono. **3.1**
left la izquierda
  to the left (of)
    a la izquierda (de) **4.1**
leg la pierna **5.1**
lemonade la limonada **4.3**
less menos
  less than menos de **3.2**
  less... than menos... que **3.2**
lesson la lección **2.1**
Let's... Vamos a... **6.1**
letter la carta
  to send a letter
    mandar una carta **2.3**
lettuce la lechuga **4.3**
library la biblioteca **2.2**
life la vida **2.3**
to lift weights levantar pesas **3.2**
like (as) como
to like gustar
  He/She likes... Le gusta... **1.1**
  I like... Me gusta... **1.1**
  I would like...
    Me gustaría... **3.1**
  Would you like...?
    ¿Te gustaría...? **3.1**
  You like... Te gusta... **1.1**
to listen (to) escuchar **2.1**
liter el litro **5.3**
literature la literatura **2.1**
a little poco **2.1**
to live vivir **2.3**
living room la sala **5.2**
llama la llama **6.2**
long largo(a) **1.2**
to look at mirar **2.1**
to look for buscar **2.1**
to lose perder (ie) **3.2**
to be lucky tener suerte **3.3**
lunch el almuerzo **2.2**
  to eat lunch almorzar (ue) **4.2**
luxurious lujoso(a) **6.1**

M

magazine la revista **2.3**
mail carrier el (la) cartero(a) **6.1**
to make hacer **2.3**
  to make the bed
    hacer la cama **5.1**
man el hombre **1.1**
manager el (la) gerente **6.1**
many mucho(a) **1.1**
map el mapa **4.1**
March marzo **1.3**
market el mercado **4.2**
masterpiece la obra maestra
mathematics las matemáticas **2.1**
May mayo **1.3**

INGLÉS–ESPAÑOL

maybe tal vez
Maybe another day. Tal vez otro día. **3.1**
meal la comida **2.3**
meat la carne **4.3**
to meet encontrar (ue) **4.2**
meeting el encuentro
menu el menú **4.3**
message el mensaje
I want to leave a message for... Quiero dejar un mensaje para... **3.1**
to leave a message dejar un mensaje **3.1**
Leave a message after the tone. Deje un mensaje después del tono. **3.1**
microwave el microondas **5.3**
midnight la medianoche **2.2**
milk la leche **5.3**
million un millón **5.3**
mirror el espejo **5.1**
Miss la señorita **1.1**
mixture la mezcla
modern moderno(a) **6.1**
moment el momento
One moment. Un momento. **3.1**
Monday lunes **EP**
money el dinero **4.2**
money exchange el cambio **4.2**
month el mes **1.3**
more más **1.3**
more than más de **3.2**
more... than más... que **3.2**
morning la mañana **2.2**
during the morning por la mañana **2.2**
Good morning. Buenos días. **EP**
in the morning de la mañana **2.2**
mother la madre **1.3**
motorcycle la moto(cicleta) **4.1**
mountain la montaña **3.3**
mouse el ratón **2.1**
mouth la boca **5.1**
to move (the furniture) mover (ue) (los muebles) **5.2**
movie la película **3.1**
to go to a movie theater ir al cine **3.1**
Mr. el señor **1.1**
Mrs. la señora **1.1**
much mucho(a) **1.1**
as much as tanto como **3.2**
museum el museo **2.3**
music la música **2.1**
music and video store la tienda de música y videos **4.1**
must: one must hay que **2.1**
my mi **1.3**

N

name el nombre **EP**
His/Her name is... Se llama... **EP**
My name is... Me llamo... **EP**
What is his/her name? ¿Cómo se llama? **EP**
What is your name? ¿Cómo te llamas? **EP**
narrow estrecho(a) **6.1**
near (to) cerca (de) **4.1**
necklace el collar **4.2**
to need necesitar **2.1**
neighbor el (la) vecino(a)
neither tampoco **4.3**
nervous nervioso(a) **3.1**
never nunca **2.1**
new nuevo(a) **1.2**
newspaper el periódico **2.3**
next to al lado de **4.1**
nice simpático(a) **1.2**
It is nice outside. Hace buen tiempo. **3.3**
Nice to meet you. Mucho gusto. **EP**
night la noche **2.2**
at night de la noche **2.2**
nine nueve **EP**
nine hundred novecientos(as) **5.3**
nineteen diecinueve **1.3**
ninety noventa **1.3**
ninth noveno(a) **6.2**
no no **EP**
no longer ya no **3.1**
no one nadie **4.3**
none ninguno(a) **4.3**
noon el mediodía **2.2**
nor ni
normal normal **5.2**
normally normalmente **5.2**
nose la nariz **5.1**
not no **1.1**
notebook el cuaderno **2.1**
nothing nada **4.3**
novel la novela **2.3**
November noviembre **1.3**
now ahora **1.3**
Right now! ¡Ahora mismo! **2.1**
nowadays actualmente
number el número
What is your phone number? ¿Cuál es tu teléfono? **EP**

O

October octubre **1.3**
of de
Of course! ¡Claro que sí! **3.1,** ¡Cómo no! **4.1**
to offer ofrecer **6.1**
I can offer you... Le puedo ofrecer... **4.2**
office la oficina **2.2**
often mucho **2.1,** frecuentemente **5.2**
oil el aceite **5.3**
old viejo(a) **1.3;** antiguo(a) **6.1**
How old is...? ¿Cuántos años tiene...? **1.3**
older mayor **1.3**
olives las aceitunas **5.2**
on en **1.1,** sobre
on ice sobre hielo **3.2**
on top (of) encima (de) **6.2**
once in a while de vez en cuando **2.1**
one uno **EP**
one hundred cien **1.3**
onion la cebolla **5.3**
only sólo **1.3**
open abierto(a) **5.2**
to open abrir **2.3**
operator el (la) operador(a) **6.1**
or o **1.1**
orange anaranjado(a) **1.2**
to order pedir (i) **4.3**
Could you help me order? ¿Me ayuda a pedir? **4.3**
ordinary ordinario(a) **6.1**
other otro(a) **1.2**
ought to deber **5.2**
our nuestro(a) **1.3**
outdoors al aire libre **3.2**
outside (of) fuera (de) **6.2**
oven el horno **5.3**

P

package el paquete **5.3**
to paint pintar **2.3**
pants los pantalones **1.2**
paper el papel **2.1**
parade el desfile
Pardon, how do I get to...? Perdona(e), ¿cómo llego a...? **4.1**
parents los padres **1.3**
park el parque **2.3**
party la fiesta **5.2**
to pass (by) pasar **2.1**
pasta la pasta **5.3**
pastry shop la pastelería **4.1**
patient paciente **1.2**
to pay pagar **4.2**
peas los guisantes
pen (enclosure) el corral **6.2, (instrument)** la pluma **2.1**
pencil el lápiz **2.1**
people la gente **2.3**
pepper la pimienta **5.3**
perfect perfecto(a) **4.2**
period la época
pharmacy la farmacia **4.1**
phone book la guía telefónica **3.1**
photographer el (la) fotógrafo(a) **6.1**
physical education la educación física **2.1**
piano el piano **2.3**
piece el pedazo **5.3**
picture la foto
  to take pictures sacar fotos **3.3**
pig el cerdo **6.2**
pineapple la piña
pink rosado(a) **1.2**
pitcher la jarra **4.2**
place el lugar **1.1**
plaid de cuadros **3.3**
plain sencillo(a) **6.1**
to plan pensar (ie) + *infinitive* **3.2**
plant la planta **3.3**
plate el plato **4.2**
to play tocar **2.3;** practicar **3.1,** jugar (ue) **3.2**
  to play sports practicar deportes **3.1**
  to play (the guitar, piano) tocar (la guitarra, el piano) **2.3**
player el (la) jugador(a)
please por favor **2.2**
pleased contento(a) **3.1**
  Pleased to meet you. Encantado(a). **EP**
pleasure
  It's a pleasure. Es un placer. **EP**
  The pleasure is mine. El gusto es mío. **EP**
poem el poema **2.3**
poetry la poesía **2.3**
police officer el (la) policía **1.1**
pork el puerco **5.3**
pork rinds los chicharrones **2.3**
portrait el retrato
post office el correo **4.1**
pot la olla **4.2**
potato la patata **5.3,** la papa
potter el (la) alfarero(a)
to practice practicar **3.1**
to prefer preferir (ie) **3.2**
to prepare preparar **2.1**
pretty bonito(a) **1.2**
price el precio **4.2**
printer la impresora **2.1**
problem el problema **2.3**
profession la profesión **6.1**
program el programa
purple morado(a) **1.2**
to put poner **4.3**
to put on (clothes) ponerse **5.1**
to put on makeup maquillarse **5.1**

Q

quality la calidad **4.2**
quarter cuarto(a) **5.3**
  quarter past y cuarto **2.2**
quick rápido(a) **5.2**
quickly rápidamente **5.2**
quiet: Be quiet! ¡Cállate! **5.3**
quiz la prueba **2.1**

R

race la carrera; la raza
racket la raqueta **3.2**
radio el radio **4.2**
radio-tape player el radiocasete **4.2**
rain la lluvia **3.3**
to rain llover (ue) **3.3**
raincoat el impermeable **3.3**
rancher el (la) ganadero(a) **6.2**
rarely rara vez **2.1**
to read leer **1.1**
ready listo(a) **4.3**
reason la razón **2.1**
to receive recibir **2.3**
recent reciente **5.2**
recently recientemente **5.2**
receptionist el (la) recepcionista **6.1**
recipe la receta
red rojo(a) **1.2**
redhead pelirrojo(a) **1.2**
refrigerator el frigorífico **5.3**
to remember recordar (ue) **4.2**
to rent a video alquilar un video **3.1**
to rest descansar **2.2**
restaurant el restaurante **4.3**
to retell contar (ue) **4.2**
to return regresar **3.1,** volver (ue) **4.2; (an item)** devolver (ue) **4.2**
  He/She will return later. Regresa más tarde. **3.1**
rhythm el ritmo
rice el arroz **4.3**
right
  to be right tener razón **3.3**
  to the right (of) a la derecha (de) **4.1**
ring el anillo **4.2**
river el río **3.3**
road el camino **4.1**
roasted asado(a)
room el cuarto **5.1**
rooster el gallo **6.2**
rule la regla
to run correr **1.1**

S

sad triste **3.1**
salad la ensalada **4.3**
salsa la salsa **4.3**
salt la sal **5.3**
same mismo(a) **2.1**
sandwich (sub) la torta **2.2**
Saturday sábado **EP**
sausage el chorizo **5.2,** la salchicha **5.3**
to say decir **4.1**
  Don't say that! ¡No digas eso! **1.2**
scarf bufanda **3.3**
schedule el horario **2.2**
school la escuela **2.1,** el colegio
science las ciencias **2.1**
scissors las tijeras **6.2**
screen la pantalla **2.1**
sea el mar **3.3**
to search buscar **2.1**
seasons las estaciones **3.3**
second segundo(a) **6.2**
secretary el (la) secretario(a) **6.1**
to see ver **2.3**
  May I see...? ¿Me deja ver...? **4.2**
to sell vender **2.3**
semester el semestre **2.2**
to send a letter mandar una carta **2.3**
September septiembre **1.3**
serious serio(a) **1.2**
to serve servir (i) **4.3**
to set the table poner la mesa **4.3**
seven siete **EP**
seven hundred setecientos(as) **5.3**
seventeen diecisiete **1.3**
seventh séptimo(a) **6.2**
seventy setenta **1.3**
shame: What a shame! ¡Qué lástima! **3.1**
shampoo el champú **5.1**
to share compartir **2.3**
to shave afeitarse **5.1**
she ella **1.1**
shepherd(ess) el (la) pastor(a) **6.2**
ship el barco **4.1**
shirt la camisa **1.2**
shoe el zapato **1.2**
  shoe store la zapatería **4.1**
shopping
  to go shopping ir de compras **3.1**
  shopping center el centro comercial **4.1**
short (height) bajo(a) **1.2; (length)** corto(a) **1.2**
shorts los shorts **3.3,** los pantalones cortos
should deber **5.2**
shrimp los camarones, las gambas
sick enfermo(a) **3.1**
silver la plata **4.2**
simple sencillo(a) **6.1**
to sing cantar **1.1**
sister la hermana **1.3**
six seis **EP**
six hundred seiscientos(as) **5.3**
sixteen dieciséis **1.3**
sixth sexto(a) **6.2**
sixty sesenta **1.3**
to skate patinar **1.1**
skateboard la patineta **3.2**
to skateboard andar en patineta **3.2**
skates los patines **3.2**
to ski esquiar **3.2**
skirt la falda **1.2**
to sleep dormir (ue) **4.2**
to be sleepy tener sueño **3.3**
slow lento(a) **5.2**
slowly lentamente **5.2**
small pequeño(a) **1.2**
snack la merienda **2.2**
  to have a snack merendar (ie) **3.2**
snow la nieve **3.3**
to snow nevar (ie) **3.3**
so entonces **2.3**
So-so. Regular. **1.1**
soap el jabón **5.1**
soccer el fútbol **3.2**
social studies los estudios sociales **2.1**
sock el calcetín **1.2**
sofa el sofá **5.2**
soft drink el refresco **2.2**
some alguno(a) **4.3**
someone alguien **4.3**
  to know, to be familiar with someone conocer a alguien **2.3**
something algo **4.3**
sometimes a veces **2.1**
son el hijo **1.3**
soon pronto **2.1**
sorry: I'm sorry... Lo siento... **4.1**
sound el sonido
soup la sopa **4.3**
souvenir el recuerdo
Spanish el español **2.1**
to speak hablar **2.1**
  May I speak with...? ¿Puedo hablar con...? **3.1**
special especial **5.2**
specially especialmente **5.2**
spicy picante **4.3**
spoon la cuchara **4.3**
sport el deporte
  to play sports practicar deportes **3.1**
sporting goods store la tienda de deportes **3.2**
spring la primavera **3.3**
squid los calamares **5.2**
stadium el estadio **3.2**
star la estrella **5.3**
stationery store la papelería **4.1**
steak el bistec **4.3**
stepbrother el hermanastro
stepfather el padrastro
stepmother la madrastra
stepsister la hermanastra
still todavía **4.3**
stomach el estómago **5.1**
store la tienda **2.3**
storm la tormenta **3.3**
stove la estufa **5.3**
straight ahead derecho **4.1**
street la calle **4.1**
string la cuerda
striped con rayas **3.3**
strong fuerte **1.2**
student el (la) estudiante **1.1**
to study estudiar **2.1**
subject la materia **2.1**
subway el metro **4.1**
success el éxito
sugar el azúcar **4.3**
summer el verano **3.3**
sun el sol **3.3**
to sunbathe tomar el sol **3.3**
Sunday domingo **EP**
sunglasses las gafas de sol **3.3**

sunny: It is sunny.
Hace sol. **3.3,** Hay sol. **3.3**
suntan lotion el bronceador **3.3**
supermarket el supermercado
to go to the supermarket
ir al supermercado **2.3**
supper la cena **2.3**
to have supper cenar **2.3**
surfing el surfing **3.2**
surname el apellido **EP**
surprise la sorpresa **5.2**
to surprise sorprender **5.2**
survey la encuesta
sweater el suéter **1.2**
to sweep the floor
barrer el suelo **5.2**
sweet dulce **4.3**
sweet roll el pan dulce **4.3**
to swim nadar **1.1**
swimming pool la piscina **3.2**

T

T-shirt la camiseta **1.2**
table la mesa **5.2**
to clear the table
quitar la mesa **5.1**
to set the table poner la mesa **4.3**
to take tomar **2.2**
to take a bath bañarse **5.1**
to take a shower ducharse **5.1**
to take along llevar **3.3**
to take care of cuidar (a) **2.3**
to take out the trash
sacar la basura **5.2**
to take pictures sacar fotos **3.3**
to talk hablar **2.1**
tall alto(a) **1.2**
tape recorder la grabadora **6.1**
tasty rico(a) **4.3,** sabroso(a) **5.3**
taxi el taxi **4.1**
taxi driver el (la) taxista **6.1**
tea el té **4.3**
to teach enseñar **2.1**
teacher el (la) maestro(a) **1.1**
team el equipo **3.2**
telephone el teléfono **3.1**
television la televisión
to watch television
ver la televisión **2.3**
television set el televisor **5.2**
to tell decir **4.1,** contar (ue) **4.2**
Tell *(familiar/formal)* **him or her to call me.** Dile/Dígale que me llame. **3.1**
temperature la temperatura **3.3**
ten diez **EP**
tennis el tenis **3.2**
tenth décimo(a) **6.2**
terrible terrible **1.1**
test el examen **2.1**
textile el tejido
Thank you. Gracias. **1.1**
that que; ese(a), eso **6.2**
that (over there)
aquel(la) **6.2;** aquello **6.2**
that one ése(a) **6.2**
that one (over there)
aquél(la) **6.2**
theater el teatro **2.3**
their su **1.3**
then entonces **2.3**
there allá/allí **4.1**
there is, there are hay **1.3**
they ellos(as) **1.1**
thin delgado(a) **1.2**
thing la cosa **4.1**
to think pensar (ie) **3.2;** creer **3.3**
I think so. / I don't think so.
Creo que sí/no. **3.3**
third tercero(a) **6.2**
thirsty: to be thirsty tener sed **2.3**
thirteen trece **1.3**
thirty treinta **1.3**
this este(a) **6.2;** esto **6.2**
this one éste(a) **6.2**
thousand mil **5.3**
three tres **EP**
three hundred trescientos(as) **5.3**
Thursday jueves **EP**
time el tiempo
free time el tiempo libre **3.1**
(At) What time is…?
¿A qué hora es…? **2.2**
What time is it?
¿Qué hora es? **2.2**
tip la propina **4.3**
How much do I tip? ¿Cuánto le doy de propina? **4.3**
tired cansado(a) **3.1**
to a
to the left (of)
a la izquierda (de) **4.1**
to the right (of)
a la derecha (de) **4.1**
today hoy **EP**
Today is… Hoy es… **EP**
What day is today?
¿Qué día es hoy? **EP**
together juntos **4.2**
tomato el tomate **5.3**
tomorrow mañana **EP**
See you tomorrow.
Hasta mañana. **EP**
Tomorrow is… Mañana es… **EP**
too también **1.1**
too much demasiado(a) **4.2**
tooth el diente **5.1**
toothbrush
el cepillo de dientes **5.1**
toothpaste la pasta de dientes **5.1**
tough duro(a) **5.1**
towel la toalla **5.1**
town el pueblo **4.3**
town square la plaza **4.1**
toy el juguete
traditional tradicional **6.1**
traffic el tráfico **6.1**
train el tren **4.1**
trash la basura **5.2**
to travel viajar **4.1**
to treat: I'll treat you. Te invito. **3.1**
tree el árbol **3.3**
trip el viaje **4.1**
true: It's true. Es verdad. **1.2**
truth la verdad **2.2**
Tuesday martes **EP**
to turn doblar **4.1**
to turn off the light
apagar la luz **5.3**
twelve doce **1.3**
twenty veinte **1.3**
twenty-one veintiuno **1.3**
two dos **EP**
two hundred doscientos(as) **5.3**

U

ugly feo(a) **1.2**
umbrella el paraguas **3.3**
uncle el tío **1.3**

under debajo (de) **6.2**
to understand comprender **2.3,** entender (ie) **3.2**
until hasta **4.1**
up arriba **6.2**
to use usar **2.1**

V

to vacuum pasar la aspiradora **5.2**
vacuum cleaner la aspiradora **5.2**
VCR la videograbadora **4.2**
vegetable la verdura **5.3**
vegetarian vegetariano(a) **4.3**
very muy **1.3**
video el video **4.2**
 to rent a video alquilar un video **3.1**
 video game el videojuego **4.2**
village el pueblo **4.3**
to visit visitar **2.2**
volleyball el voleibol **3.2**

W

to wait for esperar **2.1**
waiter el mesero **4.3**
waitress la mesera **4.3**
to wake up despertarse (ie) **5.1**
walk el paseo
to walk caminar
 to walk the dog caminar con el perro **2.3**
wall la pared **5.2**
wallet la cartera **4.2**
to want querer (ie) **3.2**
warm caliente **4.3**
to wash lavar
 to wash one's hair lavarse la cabeza **5.1**
 to wash oneself lavarse **5.1**
 to wash the dishes lavar los platos **5.1**
watch el reloj **2.2**
to watch mirar **2.1**
 to watch television ver la televisión **2.3**
water el agua *(fem.)* **2.2**
wave la ola
we nosotros(as) **1.1**
to wear llevar **2.1**
 What is he/she wearing? ¿Qué lleva? **1.2**
weather el tiempo **3.3**
 What is the weather like? ¿Qué tiempo hace? **3.3**
Wednesday miércoles **EP**
week la semana **EP**
weekend el fin de semana
weights: to lift weights levantar pesas **3.2**
welcome bienvenido(a) **1.1**
 You're welcome. De nada. **1.1**
well bien **1.1;** pues **1.2**
 (Not very) Well, and you *(familiar/formal)***?** (No muy) Bien, ¿y tú/usted? **1.1**
what cuál(es) **2.2;** qué **2.2**
 What a shame! ¡Qué lástima! **3.1**
 What day is today? ¿Qué día es hoy? **EP**
 What is he/she like? ¿Cómo es? **1.2**
 What is your phone number? ¿Cuál es tu teléfono? **EP**
when cuándo **2.2;** cuando **3.1**
where dónde **2.2; (to) where** adónde **2.2**
 Could you tell me where... is? ¿Puedes (Puede usted) decirme dónde queda...? **4.1**
 Where are you from? ¿De dónde eres? **EP**
 Where is he/she from? ¿De dónde es? **EP**
which (ones) cuál(es) **2.2**
white blanco(a) **1.2**
who quién(es) **2.2**
 Who are they? ¿Quiénes son? **1.3**
 Who is it? ¿Quién es? **1.3**
Whose is...? ¿De quién es...? **1.3**
why por qué **2.2**
 That's why. Con razón. **2.1**
wide ancho(a) **6.1**
wife la esposa
to win ganar **3.2**
wind el viento **3.3**
window la ventana **5.2**
windy: It is windy. Hace viento. **3.3,** Hay viento. **3.3**
winner el (la) ganador(a) **6.1**
winter el invierno **3.3**
with con **1.3**
 with me conmigo **3.1**
 with you contigo **3.1**
without sin **4.3**
woman la mujer **1.1**
wool la lana **6.2**
work la obra
to work trabajar **1.1**
workshop el taller **6.2**
world el mundo **1.1**
worried preocupado(a) **3.1**
to worry: Don't worry! ¡No te preocupes! **3.1**
worse peor **3.2**
to write escribir **1.1**
writer el (la) escritor(a) **6.1**

Y

year el año **1.3**
 He/She is... years old. Tiene... años. **1.3**
yellow amarillo(a) **1.2**
yes sí **EP**
 Yes, I would love to. Sí, me encantaría. **3.1**
yesterday ayer **5.3**
yet todavía **4.3**
yogurt el yogur **5.3**
you tú *(familiar singular)* **1.1,** usted *(formal singular)* **1.1,** ustedes *(plural)* **1.1,** vosotros(as) *(familiar plural)* **1.1**
young joven **1.3**
younger menor **1.3**
your su *(formal)* **1.3,** tu *(familiar)* **1.3,** vuestro(a) *(plural familiar)* **1.3**

Z

zero cero **EP**

INGLÉS–ESPAÑOL

Índice

ÍNDICE

Créditos

Photography

2 Nancy Sheehan (br); **3** Nancy Sheehan; **4** Nancy Sheehan (tl); Peter Menzel (br); **5** Nancy Sheehan (t, c); **6** Peter Menzel (b); **7** Robert Frerck/Odyssey/Chicago (b); **8** School Division, Houghton Mifflin Company (tl); Nancy Sheehan (tr); **12** Guía telefónica 1998, ICE Telecommunications, Costa Rica; School Division, Houghton Mifflin Company (c); **20** Nancy Sheehan; **23** SuperStock (tl); Ken O'Donahue (c); Larry Busacca/Retna Ltd. (br); **28** Michael Newman/PhotoEdit (tr); **33** Michael Newman/PhotoEdit (bl); **36** Michael Newman/PhotoEdit (cr); Patricia A. Eynon (br); **38** Dennie Cody; **39** Alain Benainous/Liaison International (cr); **42** Jim Whitmer; **45** Alain Banainous/Liaison International (br); Patricia A. Eynon (cl); **55** Richard Hutchings/Photo Researchers, Inc. (br); **58** Bob Daemmrich Photography (c); Courtesy *The Miami Herald* (cr); **60** Suzanne Murphy-Larronde (tr); **64** KXTN Radio Station/San Antonio (bl); Bob Daemmrich Photography (cr); Courtesy *¡Qué onda! Magazine* (bl); **65** Sygma (t); Courtesy, *¡Qué onda! Magazine* (cr); Jak Kilby/Retna (b); **68** Courtesy *¡Qué onda! Magazine*; **72** Ken O'Donahue (background); **78** Barney/inStock (b); **80** MichaelNewman/PhotoEdit (br); **81** Paul Barton/The Stock Market (tl); Jose L. Pelaez/The Stock Market (tr); Tim Theriault (mid cr); Rob Lewine/The Stock Market (cr); Blaine Harrington III/The Stock Market (br); **86** Patricia A. Eynon (r); Beryl Goldberg (l); **87** Robert Frerck/Odyssey Productions/Chicago (tl); Beryl Goldberg (r); **88** School Division, Houghton Mifflin Company (t); **89** School Division, Houghton Mifflin Company (t); **91** Patricia A. Eynon; **92** Bob Daemmrich Photography (r); **96** "The Flower Seller" (1942), Diego Rivera. Oil on masonite. © 2003 Banco de Mexico and Instituto Nacional de Bellas Artes y Literatura/Christie's Images/The Bridgeman Art Library (br); **97** Courtesy, Ballet Folklórico (tr); UPI/Corbis (br); School Division, Houghton Mifflin Company (bc); **98** David Sanger (tr); **99** David Ryan/Lonely Planet Images (tl); **113** David Ryan/Lonely Planet Images (b); **117** School Division, Houghton Mifflin Company; **132** School Division, Houghton Mifflin Company; **138** School Division, Houghton Mifflin Company (cr); **141** School Division, Houghton Mifflin Company; **150** Robert Frerck/Odyssey Productions (br); **160** John Boykin/PhotoEdit (r); **161** J. P. Courau/DDB Stock Photo (tr); Susan Kaye (cr); Doug Bryant/DDB Stock Photo (b); **162** Ed Dawson (c); North Wind Picture Archives (b); **163** Ed Dawson (tr); Sean Sprague (c); David Sanger Photography (cr); Beryl Goldberg (bl); **166** Chris Sharp/New England Stock Photo (br); **170** UPI/Bettmann/Corbis (t); **171** Robert Frerck/Odyssey Productions (tl, br); United States Postal Service (cl); Farrell Grehan/Photo Researchers, Inc. (tr); Ken O'Donohue (bl); **172** Raymond A. Mendez/Animals Animals (tl); **173** Suzanne Murphy-Larronde (tl); Bob Daemurich (bl); **186** Reuters Newsmedia, Inc./Corbis; **190** Bob Daemmrich Photography (l); Ken O'Donahue (r); **191** Bob Daemmrich/Stock Boston (t); Robert Frerck/Odyssey Productions (cr); **194** Robert Frerck/Odyssey Productions; **195** School Division, Houghton Mifflin Company (bl); Steve Azzara/Getty Images (br); **198** Tony Freeman/PhotoEdit (t); David Simson/Stock Boston (cr); Chris Brown/Unicorn Stock Photography & Dick Young/Unicorn Stock Photography (montage br); **199** Dave Nagel/Getty Images (cr); Scott Liles/Unicorn Stock Photography (br); **203** Randy Wells/Getty Images (bl); School Division, Houghton Mifflin Company (cr); **207** Suzanne Murphy/DDB Stock Photography (b); **210** School Division, Houghton Mifflin Company (tl); Randy Wells/Getty Images (br); **212** Robert Frerck/Odyssey Productions; **213** John Todd/AP Wide World Photos (cr); Andrew Wallace/Reuters News Media (cl); **215** School Division, Houghton Mifflin Company (br); **216** Russell Gordon/Odyssey Productions (r); **217** Bob Daemmrich Photography (tr, br); David Simson/Stock Boston (cr); **220** Ken O'Donahue (background); K. Scott Harris (cr); Nik Wheeler (br); **226** K. Scott Harris; **234** Thomas R. Fletcher/Stock Boston (br); Raymond A. Mendez/Animals Animals; **235** Jaime Santiago/DDB Stock Photography (t); School Division, Houghton Mifflin Company (c); **236** Ken O'Donahue (background); **237** Ulrike Welsch (t); Brenda Matthiesen/Unicorn Stock Photography (cl); Thayer Syme/Getty Images (cr); **241** Bruno Maso/Photo Researchers, Inc.; **242** Puerto Rico Postcard Inc., St. Thomas, U.S. Virgin Islands; **244** School Division, Houghton Mifflin Company (t, br); **245** School Division, Houghton Mifflin Company (c); The Granger Collection (tl); Gayna Hoffman (bl); "Woman Reaching for the Moon" (1946), Rufino Tamayo. Oil on canvas. © 2003 The Cleveland Museum of Art, Gift of the Hanna Fund, 1947.69 (br); **246** School Division, Houghton Mifflin Company (tr); **247** Patricia A. Eynon (cl); **251** Dave G. Houser (tc); **254** Patricia A. Eynon (cr); Dave G. Houser (br); **257** Mark Richards/PhotoEdit (tcr); Ed Simpson/Getty Images (tr); Robert Fried (bl); Cameramann/The Image Works (bcl); **259** Patricia A. Eynon; **261** Pamela Harper/Harper Horticultural Slide Library; **264** Dave G. Houser (c); Tom Bean/DRK Photo; **265** Patricia A. Eynon (t); Rogers/Monkmeyer Press (c, b); **268** Galyn C. Hammond; **282** Robert Frerck/Odyssey Productions; **283** School Division, Houghton Mifflin Company; **285** School Division, Houghton Mifflin Company (tr); Tom Trace/Getty Images (tl); **289** School Division, Houghton Mifflin Company (tl, tc, bc); **295** Ken O'Donoghue (r); **299** Ken O'Donoghue (tl, cl, br); PhotoDisc (bl); **305** School Division, Houghton Mifflin Company (cr); Ken O'Donahue (br); **310** Joe Viesti/The Viesti Collection (bl); **313** Felicia Martinez/PhotoEdit; **314** James Schaffer/PhotoEdit (r); **319** Robert Frerck/Odyssey Productions (tc); A.G.E. FotoStock (br); Tor Eigeland (tl); The Granger Collection (bl); **321** "Maya With Doll" (1938), Pablo Picasso. Oil on canvas, 73 cm x 60 cm. © 2003 Picasso Museum, Paris/Estate of Pablo Picasso, Paris/Artists Rights Society (ARS), New York / Giraudon, Paris /SuperStock (tr); **330** Bair/Monkmeyer Press (bc); Spencer Grant/PhotoEdit (tr); **336** Courtesy Sony Music Entertainment (Spain); **338** "Self Portrait with Palette" (1906), Pablo Picasso. Private Collection. © 2003 Estate of Pablo Picasso, Paris/Artists Rights Society (ARS), New York (bl); **339** "Maya With Doll" (1938), Pablo Picasso. Oil on canvas, 73 cm x 60 cm. © 2003 Picasso Museum, Paris/Estate of Pablo Picasso, Paris/Artists Rights Society (ARS), New York / Giraudon, Paris /SuperStock (tl); "Portrait of Jaime Sabartes" (1901), Pablo Picasso. Oil on canvas, 32 1/4 x 26 in (82 x 66 cm). Pushkin State Museum of Fine Arts, Moscow. © 2003 Estate of Pablo Picasso/Artists Rights Society (ARS), New York/Giraudon/Art Resource/NY (c); Robert

Frerck/Odyssey Productions (r); **364** Tony Arruza/Getty Images (r); **379** School Division, Houghton Mifflin Company; **380** Tom Trace/Getty Images (tl); Ken O'Donohue (cl, b); **381** Kindra Clineff/Index Stock (tl); Photo Disc (cl, bl); Brand X Pictures (cr); Eric Roth/Index Stock (br); **392** Robert Winslow/The Viesti Collection (bl); **393** Inga Spence/DDB Stock Photo (tr); **407** Joseph F. Viesti/The Viesti Collection (t); **409** Dan McCoy/Rainbow (tl); Richard Pasley/Stock Boston (cr); School Division, Houghton Mifflin Company; **410** Richard Pasley/Stock Boston (cr); **415** Llewellyn/Image State; **416** Tony Freeman/PhotoEdit (r); **417** Michele and Tom Grimm (tr); Sidney/Monkmeyer Press (br); **421** Mary Altier (cr); Robert Frerck/Odyssey Productions (bl); **424** Dietrich C. Gehring/The Viesti Collection (br); **425** Bob Daemmrich/The Image Works (cr); Dorothy Littell Greco/Stock Boston (br); **427** Robert Frerck/Odyssey Productions; **434** S. Aitchison/DDB Stock Photo; **450** Wolfgang Kaehler (bl); **452** School Division, Houghton Mifflin Company; **454** Robert Frerck/Odyssey Productions; **456** Jeff Greenberg/PhotoEdit; **457** School Division, Houghton Mifflin Company (tl); Eric A. Wessman/The Viesti Collection (cr); Wolfgang Kaehler (b); **459** Jan Butchofsky-Houser (background); Robert Pettit/Dembinsky Photo Association (b); Inga Spence/DDB Stock Photo (tr); Robert Frerck/Odyssey Productions (cr); **461** Mary Altier; **R20** School Division, Houghton Mifflin Company

All other photography: Martha Granger/EDGE Productions

Illustration

Lisa Adams **209**

Fian Arroyo **85** (b), **159, 211, 233** (b), **315, 332, 337, 411, 433** (r); **439, 463, R2**

Susan M. Blubaugh **164, 167, 255** (t), **257, 277, 288, 380**

Roger Chandler, Activity icons

Chris Costello **442**

Naverne Covington **112, 152, 165, 183, 193, 287, 288**

Jim Deigen **363**

Mike Dietz **41, 189**

Elisee Goldstein **146**

Nenad Jakesevic **368**

Catherine Leary **47, 83, 93, 115, 137, 343, 365, 377, 455, R15, R17** (r)

Jared D. Lee **263, 269, 282, 307, 329** (r)

John Lytle **50**, **61** (r), **272**

Patrick O'Brien **340, 426, 458; R17** (r)

Steve Patricia **28**, **250**, **251, 427, 429**

Gail Piazza **15, 19, 229, 233** (t), **239, 328, R9** (l)

Matthew Pippin **102**, **176, 177, 198, 199, 398**

Rick Powell **67** (b), **90, 206, 333, 354, 433** (l); **R5, R18**

Donna Ruff **33, 69, 85** (t), **124**, **387, 436, 437**

School Division, Houghton Mifflin Company **56, 57, 61** (l), **67** (t), **80, 226, 255** (b), **298, 329** (l), **350, 375, 389, R1, R6, R7, R8, R9** (r); **R10**, **R12, R14**

Stacey Shuitt **324**, **342**

Don Stewart **118, 225, 227**

Wood Ronsadille Harlin, Inc. **346**, **420**

Rosario Valderamma **224**

Cris Reverdy, Caroline McCarty, Jackie Reeves for Yellow House Studio **10**

Farida Zaman **294**